"By compiling such an extensive and thorough collection of primary documents relating to both the Arab-Israeli and Palestinian-Israeli conflicts, Gregory Mahler has performed a great service for scholars and students. This updated edition, with some new recent documents in it, will be an invaluable resource for anyone teaching or learning about these long-running conflicts."

Dov Waxman, *Rosalinde and Arthur Gilbert Foundation Professor of Israel Studies and Director of the UCLA Y&S Nazarian Center for Israel Studies, University of California, Los Angeles*

"Mahler's volume offers readers key maps and well selected documents that are essential for understanding Israel's conflict with the Arabs. A lively introduction provides historical context and unpacks a number of important controversies regarding this complex and still-unresolved dispute. Well designed to complement historical textbooks."

Neil Caplan, *Affiliate Faculty Member, Department of History, Concordia University, Montreal*

"Gregory Mahler's third edition of *The Arab-Israeli Conflict: An Introduction and Documentary Reader* is a welcome updated edition of a collection of documents related to the history of the Arab-Israeli conflict from the rise of Zionism at the end of the 19th century until the signing of the Abraham Accords in 2020. These primary sources constitute an essential and useful tool for teachers and students interested in meticulously studying the evolution of the Arab-Israeli conflict. Carefully chosen to represent a balanced account, these documents reflect the complexity of the conflict and attest to its intractability."

Elie Podeh, *The Hebrew University of Jerusalem*

The Arab-Israeli Conflict

This textbook examines the diplomatic and historical setting within which the Arab-Israeli conflict has developed and gives students the opportunity to study the Middle East peace process through a presentation of primary documents that have been instrumental in the development of the conflict from the mid-1800s through the present. This third edition includes an updated and expanded introduction and a significant expansion of the number of documents. *The Arab-Israeli Conflict:*

- includes an extensive introductory chapter which presents the history of the conflict and covers events from the nineteenth century to the present day
- presents 120 of the most important and widely cited documents in the history of the Israeli-Palestinian conflict in an edited form to highlight key elements
- incorporates a number of pedagogical aids, including the (edited) original documents, maps, and boxed sections that offer greater explanation of detailed topics
- presents "both sides" of the argument, allowing students to understand both the Israeli and the Palestinian positions on the issues

This important textbook is an essential aid for courses on the Arab-Israeli conflict and the Middle East peace process and will be an invaluable reference tool for all students of political science, Middle East studies, and history.

Gregory S. Mahler is Research Professor of Politics and Academic Dean Emeritus at Earlham College (Richmond, Indiana). He received his B.A. from Oberlin College and his M.A. and Ph.D. from Duke University. He is the author or editor of over 30 books in the field of comparative politics, primarily focusing on political institutions and political behavior. His text *Comparative Politics* has been in print since 1983 and is currently in its sixth edition (2019). His text on *Politics and Government in Israel* will be appearing in its fourth edition in 2024.

The Arab-Israeli Conflict

An Introduction and Documentary Reader

Third Edition
Gregory S. Mahler

Routledge
Taylor & Francis Group

LONDON AND NEW YORK

Designed cover image: © Tuomas A. Lehtinen/Getty Images

Third edition published 2024
by Routledge
4 Park Square, Milton Park, Abingdon, Oxon, OX14 4RN

and by Routledge
605 Third Avenue, New York, NY 10158

Routledge is an imprint of the Taylor & Francis Group, an informa business

First edition published by Routledge 2010
Second edition published by Routledge 2019

British Library Cataloguing-in-Publication Data
A catalogue record for this book is available from the British Library

Library of Congress Cataloging-in-Publication Data
Names: Mahler, Gregory S., 1950– author.
Title: The Arab-Israeli conflict : an introduction and documentary reader / Gregory S. Mahler.
Description: Third edition. | Abingdon, Oxon ; New York, NY : Routledge, 2024. | Includes bibliographical references and index.
Identifiers: LCCN 2023006388 (print) | LCCN 2023006389 (ebook) | ISBN 9781032392356 (hbk) | ISBN 9781032392363 (pbk) | ISBN 9781003348948 (ebk)
Subjects: LCSH: Arab-Israeli conflict—Sources. | Middle East—Politics and government—1945—Sources.
Classification: LCC DS119.7 .M2245 2024 (print) | LCC DS119.7 (ebook) | DDC 956.04—dc23/eng/20230228
LC record available at https://lccn.loc.gov/2023006388
LC ebook record available at https://lccn.loc.gov/2023006389

ISBN: 978-1-032-39235-6 (hbk)
ISBN: 978-1-032-39236-3 (pbk)
ISBN: 978-1-003-34894-8 (ebk)

DOI: 10.4324/9781003348948

Typeset in Times New Roman
by Apex CoVantage, LLC

Every effort has been made to contact copyright-holders. Please advise the publisher of any errors or omissions, and these will be corrected in subsequent editions.

For Marjorie

Contents

Maps

Acknowledgments

The opportunity to do a new edition of an already-published book is very satisfying, because it suggests that there is demand for the book and that publishers are willing to respond to that demand. I want to thank James "Joe" Whiting, Acquisitions Editor for Middle Eastern, Islamic & Jewish Studies at Routledge/Taylor & Francis Group, for his support of this project. Euan Rice-Coates, also at Routledge, was very helpful in the production process, and I appreciate his good work.

I was assisted in the expansion of the number of documents included in this volume – from 82 in the second edition to 120 in this edition – by a number of professional colleagues who were willing to look at my previous list of documents and make suggestions about what I should consider adding to make the collection more comprehensive. Rashid Khalidi, Jerome Slater, Rachel Harris, Elie Podeh, Mark Tessler, Neil Caplan, and Dov Waxman all made suggestions about additions, and I very much appreciate their counsel.

The search for sources of documents can be challenging. While Google puts all kinds of material at our fingertips, if we are going to be confident about sources, then we need to know where authoritative copies of documents can be found. I was assisted in some particularly challenging searches for source locations by Mitchell Bard at the *Jewish Virtual Library* and by Dan Rosen in the Digital Diplomacy Division of the Ministry of Foreign Affairs, Jerusalem, and I am grateful for their help.

Part I

Introduction

Alden Mahler Levine and Gregory S. Mahler

And as for Ishmael, I have heard thee; behold, I have blessed him, and will make him fruitful, and will multiply him exceedingly; twelve princes shall he beget, and I will make him a great nation. But My covenant will I establish with Isaac, whom Sarah shall bear unto thee at this set time in the next year.

Bereshit (Genesis) 17:20–21, JPS translation

We covenanted with Abraham and Isma'il, that they should sanctify My House for those who compass it round, or use it as a retreat, or bow, or prostrate themselves (therein in prayer).

Holy Qur'an 2:125, Yusufali translation

Thus, in theory, begins the cycle of tension between Arabs and Jews.[1] It may have been Isaac or it may have been Ishmael who was the favorite child and heir of Abraham (or, of course, it may have been neither at all). The fact remains that two peoples point to this millennia-old story as their "origin myth." More importantly, two peoples point to the land bequeathed by the shepherd Abraham and call it their own.

Because this is not a religious text but an academic inquiry into a modern political situation, this story cannot be the basis of our analysis or argument. Neither is it particularly useful to itemize the subsequent regimes in the region. As fascinating as the Babylonian, Assyrian, Greek, Roman, Old Kingdom, Caliphate, and Ottoman – in no particular order! – governments may have been, they will serve us as little more than a backdrop. In short: the portion of the Middle East currently known as Israel or Palestine has, for a very long time, been the object of much contention. Sometimes one group held power and sometimes another, and sometimes power was shared or contested by more than

DOI: 10.4324/9781003348948-2

one group. Poised at the crossroads of three continents, Palestine has rarely known peace.

But the situation currently known as the Arab-Israeli conflict is a thoroughly modern and wholly political predicament. It is a story of international machinations, citizen rebellion, and (quite literally) the quest for world domination. And in its modern incarnation, the Arab-Israeli conflict has left a paper trail.

This text will allow the reader to analyze the Arab-Israeli conflict through the words of those who have lived it. From the publication of *Der Judenstaat* at the end of the nineteenth century to *The Abraham Accords* in the early years of the twenty-first century, these documents speak for the times and ideas they embodied. By placing them within their historical context, we hope to allow the reader to better understand the motivations of the authors.

See reading #1, "Theodor Herzl, The Jewish State (1896)"

In 1896, an Austrian journalist named Theodore Herzl wrote a volume that would prove to play a historically crucial role in world history, titled *The Jewish State*. Herzl did not invent the concept of Zionism, but his book formalized a growing belief among Jews of the world about the need for a Jewish state. Anti-Semitism was an intense and apparently ever-present problem. In the decades dominated by emerging nation-states and the philosophies of self-determination and ethnic identity, the notion that the Jews deserved a homeland – or a state[2] – appealed to many people. There was much debate about the precise nature of that state and whether it should be "a Jewish state and not merely a state of Jews."[3]

See reading #2, "Ahad Ha'Am, The Jewish State and the Jewish Problem (1897)"

See reading #3, "The Basle Program (August 30, 1897)"

Eventually the focus of the early Zionist movement did turn toward Palestine, at the time a part of the centuries-old Ottoman Empire, known as the "Sick Old Man of Europe" for its persistence even as it lost territory and its government's hold became increasingly tenuous. Palestine at the time was controlled by the Ottoman Empire – Turkey – and the Zionists tried to work through Turkey to develop a state for the Jews. It was not to be.

See reading #4, "Letter From Dr. Theodore Herzl to M. Youssuf Zia al-Khalidi (March 19, 1899)"

See reading #5 "The Uganda Proposal (August 26, 1903)"

The precise location of the hypothetical Jewish homeland was far from a given. Although many Jews felt a religious tie to the land that today is Israel, the movement for a homeland was itself predominantly secular. In fact, many religious Jews considered it an affront to God for man to construct a Jewish state rather than waiting for it to occur naturally when the Messiah arrived. Without a strong religious mooring, proposals for a location ranged from rural areas of Argentina to Uganda or the island of Madagascar.

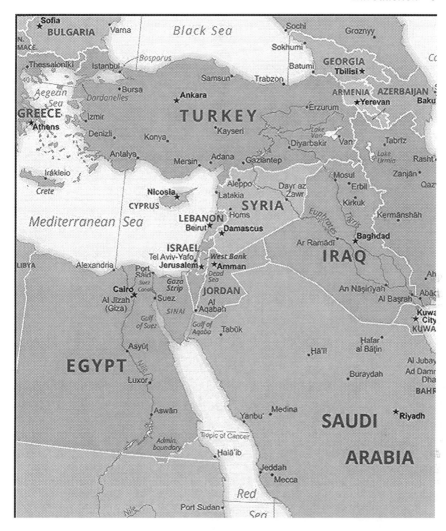

Map 1 Israel in the Middle East
Source: The World Factbook 2021. Washington, DC: Central Intelligence Agency, 2021, "World and Regional Maps; Political, Middle East."

The Ottomans had thrown their lot in with the losing side of the First World War and found themselves pitted against the United Kingdom, France, and Russia in that conflict. Moreover, Turkey faced the insurrection of its Arab citizens. The ruler of Mecca at the time, Sharif Hussein bin Ali, saw an opportunity for self-rule at long last. Corresponding with Sir Henry McMahon, British High Commissioner in Egypt, Hussein felt assured of Great Britain's support for

See reading #6, "The McMahon Letter (October 24, 1915)"

Arab independence after the War and threw his considerable influence behind the British objectives.

The Ottomans' days were numbered, and the Ottoman Empire crumbled in the First World War, leaving huge swaths of formerly Ottoman territory in a governmental

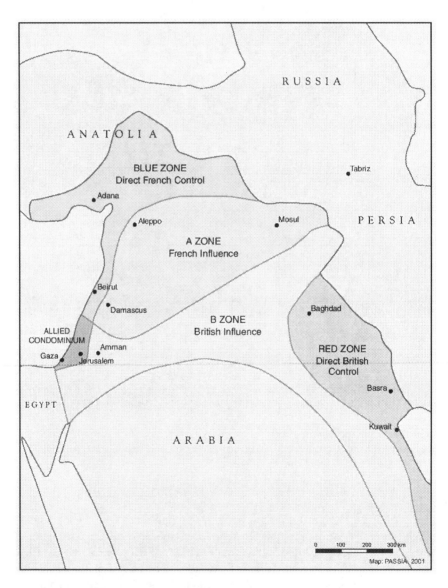

Map 2 The Sykes-Picot Agreement of 1916

Source: Abdul Hadi, Mahdi (ed.). The Palestine Question in Maps, 1878–2014, Jerusalem: Palestinian Academic Society for the Study of International Affairs (PASSIA), 2nd Updated and Revised Edition, August 2014. Map 4.

See reading #7, "The Sykes-Picot Agreement: May, 1916"

limbo. Into that vacuum stepped the newly dominant nations of Great Britain and France. Fiercely competitive throughout their modern histories, the former allies came prepared with the Sykes-Picot agreement, which had been secretly drawn up in negotiations between the two during the War. The agreement proposed to divide all former Ottoman lands into either French or British "spheres of influence." The area known as Palestine was awarded to the British.

See reading #8, "The Balfour Declaration (November 2, 1917)"

Over the next three decades, the question of who would permanently control Palestine was never fully settled. Both Arabs and Jews lobbied for influence and control over the land, and both felt they had been promised that control by the British government. The Balfour Declaration of 1917 implied a British goal of establishing "in Palestine of a national home for the Jewish people" – *in* but not exclusively *comprising*. The sons of Sherif Hussein pointed to the British promises to their father and demanded their fulfilment. And the British sought to control the valuable trade routes and resources of the Middle East for as long as possible.

See reading #9, "The Weizmann-Feisal Agreement (January 3, 1919)"

On January 3, 1919, Dr. Chaim Weizmann signed a political accord in the name of the Zionist Organization with the Emir Feisal, son of the Sherif of Mecca, within the framework of the Paris Peace Conference ending the First World War. In this agreement the Arabs promised to recognize the Balfour Declaration and said that they would permit Jewish immigration and settlement in Palestine. The agreement also included support for freedom of religion and worship in Palestine and promised that Muslim holy sites would remain under Muslim control. As part of the agreement, the Zionist Organization said that it would look into the economic possibilities of an Arab state.

Despite receiving a great deal of attention when it was announced, the Weizmann-Feisal agreement was repudiated by Arab leaders shortly after it was signed, and it was never implemented.

See reading #10, "Interview in Mr. Balfour's Apartment (June 24, 1919)"

Lord Balfour was the target of much pressure, from both Zionist leaders and Arab leaders, to steer the British policy on Palestine in their preferred direction. Zionist lobbyists, including top American diplomats, sought his understanding of Zionist goals to "assure the realization of the Zionist programme."

Even as the debate raged on, Jews flocked to Palestine from Europe and North Africa, fleeing political tensions and escalating anti-Semitism. This Jewish population shift and government instability in Palestine led to riots and general disturbance.

See reading #11, "The White Paper of 1922 (June 3, 1922)" (The "Churchill White Paper")

In the period from 1920 to 1922 tensions in Palestine increased between the native Arab and immigrant Jewish populations, and both sides were unhappy with the way that the British were handling the situation. In 1922 British Colonial Secretary Winston Churchill issued an official White Paper – a formal governmental policy statement – that put forward on behalf of the British Government a more restrictive interpretation of the Balfour Declaration. The White Paper concluded that Palestine as a whole would not become a Jewish "national home" and suggested limitations on Jewish immigration to Palestine through the introduction of the concept of "economic absorptive capacity" into regulations governing Jewish immigration.

See reading #12, "The Mandate for Palestine (July 24, 1922)"

The League of Nations issued its mandates for Mesopotamia, Syria, and Palestine in April of 1920. The details of the British mandate were approved by the Council of the League of Nations in July 1922 and came into force on September 29, 1922. In the Mandate, the League of Nations recognized the "historical connection of the Jewish people with Palestine" and the "grounds for reconstituting their national home in that country."

See reading #13, "The Passfield White Paper (October 20, 1930)"

Following the 1929 riots in Palestine, the British Colonial Secretary, Lord Passfield, wrote a formal statement of British policy intentions in Palestine, with the hope of clarifying the intentions of the British Mandate and the Balfour Declaration. The document, known as the "Passfield White Paper," called for a renewed attempt at establishing a Legislative Council in Palestine. The White Paper was more restrictive in its approach to the Zionist cause, and as a result the Zionist movement mounted a major campaign against the White Paper.

See reading #14, "British Prime Minister Ramsay MacDonald Letter to Chaim Weizmann (February 13, 1931)"

International Zionist reaction to the Passfield White Paper was overwhelmingly negative, and in a letter made public during February 1931, British Prime Minister Ramsay MacDonald promised Chaim Weizmann what amounted to the cancellation of the Passfield policy.

See reading #15, "The Palestine Royal Commission (Peel Commission): Report (July 24, 1937)"

In November of 1936 a royal commission of inquiry known as the Peel Commission (named after its chairman, William Robert Wellesley Peel, Earl of Peel) was sent on a fact-finding mission to Palestine by the British government in the hope that it might be able to recommend solutions to the tensions that were developing between the native Arab population and the immigrant Jewish population. It issued a report in July of 1937. The Peel Report found that many of the grievances of the Palestinians were reasonable and that the "disturbances" between the two populations were based

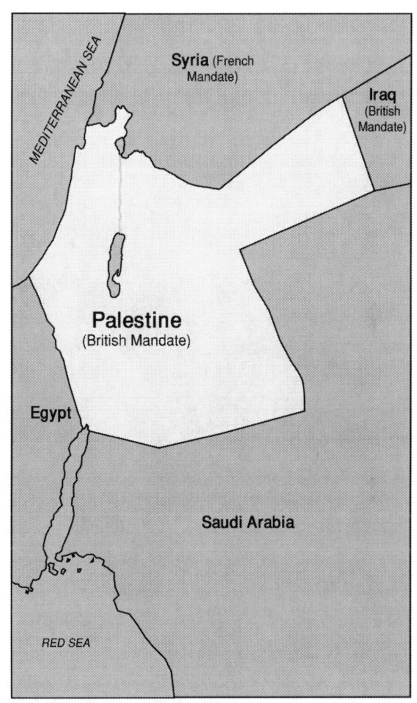

Area Allocated for Jewish National Home
San Remo Conference, 1920

Map 3 The British Mandate, 1920
Source: Government of Israel, Ministry of Foreign Affairs, About Israel, Israel in Maps, The British Mandate.

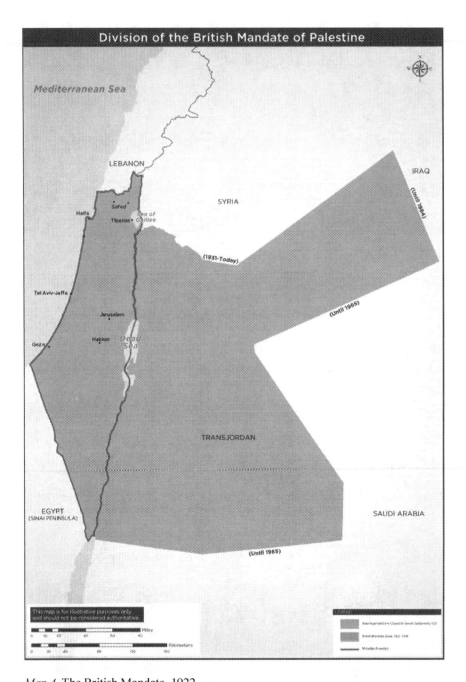

Map 4 The British Mandate, 1922
Source: Government of Israel, Ministry of Foreign Affairs, About Israel, Israel in Maps, The British Mandate.

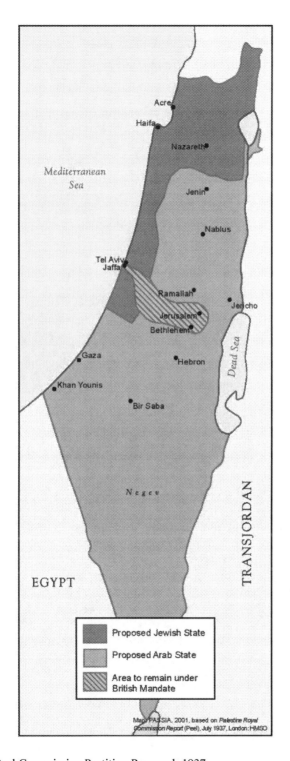

Map 5 The Peel Commission Partition Proposal, 1937

Source: Abdul Hadi, Mahdi (ed.). The Palestine Question in Maps, 1878–2014, Jerusalem: Palestinian Academic Society for the Study of International Affairs (PASSIA), 2nd Updated and Revised Edition, August 2014. Map 8.

on the issues of the Arab desire for national independence on one hand and a conflict between Arab nationalism and Zionist goals on the other. Ultimately the Peel Commission recommended partition of the Palestinian territory.

Although in 1937 the Twentieth Zionist Congress had rejected the boundaries proposed by the Peel Commission, it did agree in principle to the idea of partition of Palestine into a Jewish state and an Arab state (with the Arab state being made up of Jordan and part of Palestine). However, Palestinian Arab nationalists rejected any kind of partition.

See reading #16, "British Government: Policy Statement Against Partition (November 11, 1938)"

The British government sent a technical team in 1938, the Woodhead Commission, to make a detailed plan and to review the suggestions of the Peel Commission. The Woodhead Commission was in Palestine from April through August of 1938 and issued its report in November of that year. In its report it rejected the Peel plan and suggested other variations on the idea of partition. As a consequence of that report, the British Government took the position that it found the idea of partition impractical and suggested more work to reach Arab-Jewish agreement on a future of a united Palestine.

See reading #17, "British Government: The [MacDonald] White Paper (May 17, 1939)"

In the spring of 1939 a conference was held in London at St. James Palace to seek a solution to the problem of Palestine. It was not successful. As a result, in May of 1939, another British White Paper appeared, known as the MacDonald White Paper. This statement declared that the authors of the original mandate "could not have intended that Palestine should be converted into a Jewish state against the will of the Arab population of the country," and proposed the creation within ten years of a unitary Palestine state, to which it would eventually transfer political power. This was devastating to the Zionists and entirely consistent with the demands of the Arab population at the time. The White Paper also outlined a five-year plan for the immigration of 75,000 Jews (10,000 per year for five years, with a further allowance of 25,000 refugees) – and stated that after the five-year period no further Jewish immigration could take place without Arab consent. The next year, in a policy paper of March 1940, the British went on to severely restrict land sales.

The Zionist movement saw the MacDonald White Paper as "an act of betrayal," believing that it would condemn the Jewish population to a minority status in the country as well as ending any hopes of creating a Jewish state. It also argued that the White Paper was inconsistent with the Mandate that the British had received for Palestine.

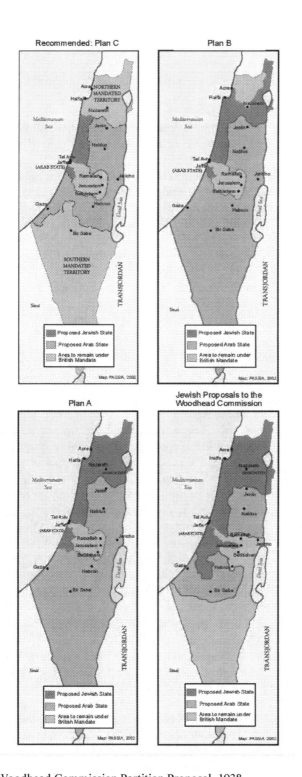

Map 6 The Woodhead Commission Partition Proposal, 1938

Source: Abdul Hadi, Mahdi (ed.). The Palestine Question in Maps, 1878–2014, Jerusalem: Palestinian Academic Society for the Study of International Affairs (PASSIA), 2nd Updated and Revised Edition, August 2014. Map 9.

The publication of the MacDonald White Paper was seen by the British government as a reasonable policy option for the British to pursue in the context of British policy prior to the outbreak of the Second World War. The British were worried about offending the Arab Middle East – not wanting Arab governments to side with the German rulers – and they were *not* worried about the possibility that the Zionists would start to support the Germans. The White Paper remained British policy until 1947 when the British announced their intention to leave the country and handed over the Palestine conflict to the United Nations.

See reading #18, "Zionist Reaction to the White Paper (1939)"

International Zionist organizations were not merely sitting by passively, however. In the United States the Biltmore Conference took place at New York City's Biltmore Hotel in early May 1942, with Zionist leaders from many different nations and over 500 delegates in attendance. The Biltmore Conference was a response to the British White Paper of 1939 and in a sense took international Zionist activism to a new level in terms of its support for the creation of a Jewish state in Palestine, something that major Zionist organizations were not prepared to do prior to the White Paper.

See reading #19, "The Biltmore Program: Towards a Jewish State (May 11, 1942)"

Arab response to the Zionist activism was not very flexible, and the Arab position continued to be that no Jewish state could be created in Palestine. In March of 1946 the document "Arab Office Report to Anglo-American Committee" was released, and it suggested that the Arab powers were prepared to accept a modest Zionist presence in Palestine but that presence would have to "satisfy certain conditions" and would have to have as its goal that "over time the exclusiveness of the Jews will be neutralized by the development of loyalty to the [Palestinian] state." This was not, of course, a satisfactory outcome for the Zionist activists, either the activists in Palestine or those in other areas of the world.

See reading #20, "Arab Office Report to Anglo-American Committee (March, 1946)"

The Anglo-American Committee ended up concluding that European nations needed to do more to meet the needs of the Jewish victims of the Nazis, that 100,000 certificates be issued right away for immigration into Palestine of Jews who had been the victims of Nazi and Fascist persecution, that Palestine be declared neither a Jewish nor an Arab state, that the United Nations extend the Mandate for Palestine, and that attention should be paid to both Arab and Jewish education in Palestine, among other points.

See reading #21, "Report of the Anglo-American Committee of Inquiry (April 20, 1946)"

It is probably unnecessary to explain why the Second World War was a defining historical moment for the Jews of the world. In the Holocaust, Jews faced the ultimate expression of the anti-Semitism they had known for so long. After the Holocaust, anti-Semitism was indisputably real. Moreover, after the Holocaust, many world leaders sympathized with the decimated Jewish population. Suddenly, a Jewish homeland seemed less like a dramatic overreaction and much more likely to happen.

In the light of the new global attitudes on the subject, and because few other options were available to them, survivors and other disaffected Jews flooded into the British holdings in Palestine. The fledgling United Nations attempted to equitably create an Israel and an Arab Palestine in United Nations General Assembly Resolution 181, but that proposal was unequivocally rejected by the Palestinian Arabs and representatives of other Arab states.

Sporadic but fierce violence erupted between Jews and Arabs, and tensions ran high. As they faced the diplomatic morass, the Jews in Palestine decided to take matters into their own hands. With the Partition of Palestine to be completed "by 1 August, 1948," Zionists were preparing to declare an independent state of Israel and were actively developing the international Zionist community for support, seeking to develop diplomatic support and raise funds that were clearly going to be needed for an anticipated war.

The preparation for warfare included some very detailed military planning. The army leaders began to work on a contingency plan to defend the planned Jewish state from invasion. The plan developed in several stages ("Stage 1," "Stage 2," "Stage 3," and "Stage 4"), and although it was primarily defensive in nature, the fourth stage of the plan also included planning for expulsion of the Palestinians by Israeli forces outside of the borders of the new state.

In May of 1948, the Zionist leadership declared to the international community the existence of the State of Israel.

The Arabs responded immediately – within hours. A force composed of Syrian, Egyptian, and Jordanian troops (and backed by those countries and Iraq, Lebanon, and Saudi Arabia as well) began an invasion to "drive Israel into the sea." It was nearly a year before the two sides reached an armistice, in April of 1949. The armistice reflected the *status quo* positions of each party, and as such, Israel was awarded significantly more territory than it had been given under the United Nation's earlier partition plan. The armistice did not allow for an independent Palestine but put the West Bank under the control of Jordan. Israel

---

See reading #22, "United Nations General Assembly: Resolution 181, The Partition of Palestine (November 29, 1947)"

See reading #23, "Golda Meir, Speech to the Illinois Council of Jewish Federations (January 2, 1948)"

See reading #24, "Plan Dalet: Preparing for the War of Independence (March 10, 1948)"

See reading #25, "Declaration of the Establishment of the State of Israel (May 14, 1948)"

See reading #26, "Creation of a Conciliation Commission, General Assembly Resolution 194 (III) (December 11, 1948)"

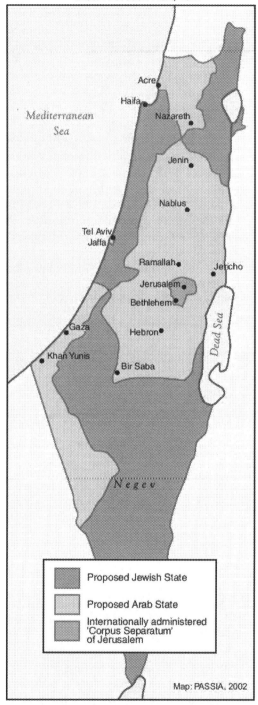

UNGA Partition Plan, 1947

Legend:
- Proposed Jewish State
- Proposed Arab State
- Internationally administered 'Corpus Separatum' of Jerusalem

Map: PASSIA, 2002

Map 7 The United Nations Partition Recommendation, 1947

Source: Abdul Hadi, Mahdi (ed.). The Palestine Question in Maps, 1878–2014, Jerusalem: Palestinian Academic Society for the Study of International Affairs (PASSIA), 2nd Updated and Revised Edition, August 2014. Map 15.

and Jordan shared Jerusalem, and Egypt controlled the area between it and Israel known as the Gaza Strip.

See reading #27, "Admission of Israel to the United Nations, General Assembly Resolution 273 (III) (May 11, 1949)"

Israel applied for membership in the United Nations in the fall of 1948 but did not receive a majority vote in the Security Council, which was required for membership, at that time. The next spring, in May of 1949, Israel tried again, and at that time it received a vote of 37 votes in favor of membership, 12 votes against, and 9 abstentions.

The status of Jerusalem continued to be a significant issue as part of the Middle East conflict. Resolution 303 in the General Assembly in 1949 reiterated the commitment of the United Nations to an internationalized Jerusalem, and the U.N. designated Jerusalem a *"corpus separatum"* – a separate body. In the original U.N. partition plan (Document 22, previously), Jerusalem was to have been administered under the United Nations as an international city. By the end of the war of independence, the city was *de facto* divided into an area controlled by Jordan in the east and an area controlled by Israel in the west.

See reading #28: General Assembly Resolution 303 (IV): Palestine: Question of an International Regime for the Jerusalem Area and the Protection of the Holy Places (December 9, 1949)"

An armistice, of course, is not a peace treaty, and the relations between Israel and its neighbors following the war did not resemble peace. The Arabs considered the existence of Israel absolutely unacceptable; the Arabic term "an-naqba" ("the catastrophe") is still used to refer to the creation of an Israeli state. Cross-border gunfire and conflicts, debate over land, and harassment of each other's citizens all contributed to an escalation of tensions between Israel and its neighbors.

WHAT'S THE PROBLEM?

Israelis and Palestinians each bring unique issues to the negotiating table, some of them very complex and some derived from events of the over 75 years since Israel became a state. In essence, however, the primary issues are the following.

- Palestinian refugees (including refugees currently living outside of territory controlled by Israel – both in Europe and North America – as well as refugees who have relocated to areas in the West Bank and Gaza) want their land back, or fiscal remuneration for their losses, in those cases in which family property

Armistice Lines, 1949

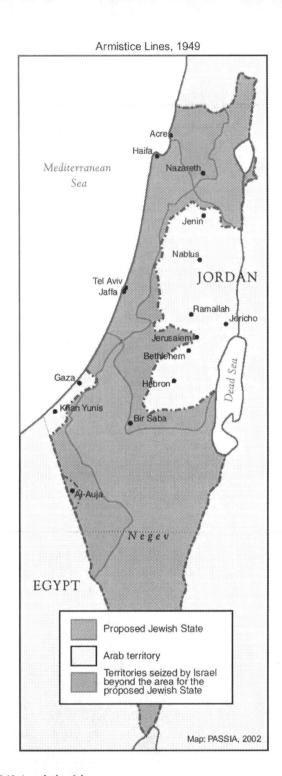

Map 8 The 1949 Armistice Lines

Source: Abdul Hadi, Mahdi (ed.). The Palestine Question in Maps, 1878–2014, Jerusalem: Palestinian Academic Society for the Study of International Affairs (PASSIA), 2nd Updated and Revised Edition, August 2014. Map 15.

was lost in either the 1948 fighting or the 1967 fighting. Many Palestinians in exile preserve titles, deeds, and even keys to their former homes, ready for the day when they are allowed to return. The Israelis say that the Palestinians left voluntarily, and therefore they have no legitimate claim either to return to their former property or receive compensation. Despite anecdotes to the contrary, Israel maintains that it does not and has never forced Arab families to leave their homes. Moreover, Israel simply could not repatriate all the Palestinian refugees – whose numbers have increased significantly over 75 years – and continue to exist as a Jewish state.

- Israel wants to be recognized by its neighbors and the world. From the very beginning years of modern Israel, most Arab states refused to even acknowledge the legitimacy of any Jewish state, although in recent years that has begun to change. Israel has been faced with constant, all-pervasive threats directed at its very existence, and Israeli culture and foreign policy are hugely affected by this pressure.

- Both Arabs and Israelis seek peace and security in their own homes. Because of occupation, insurgency, and terrorism, neither party can fully trust the other. Israel, essentially an occupying power, curtails Palestinians' livelihoods and opportunities. Palestinian suicide bombers kill Israeli civilians as they go about their lives. Lacking a government able to control these insurgents or to curtail these acts of violence, the Palestinians have little leverage in negotiations with the Israelis, who are often too wary of violent attacks to be willing to make concessions that might compromise security.

In July of 1950, the Knesset, Israel's Parliament, enacted the Law of Return. This law, combined with the Nationality Law of 1952, gave special citizenship rights to Jews living outside of Israel. The Law of Return declared that Israel is a home for all members of the Jewish people everywhere and that those individuals who are born Jews (having a Jewish mother or grandmother), those with Jewish ancestry (having a Jewish father or grandfather), and converts to Judaism

See reading #29, "State of Israel: Law of Return (July 5, 1950)"

(Orthodox, Reform, or Conservative denominations) have a right to Israeli citizenship.

In late 1956, Egypt formed a pact of mutual defense with Syria and Jordan. Egypt also closed the Suez Canal and the Strait of Tiran to Israeli shipping traffic and developed closer relations with the Soviet Union. This was not the first time that Egypt had closed the Suez Canal to Israeli shipping. Fearing the machinations of strong neighbors, Israel allied with France and Great Britain and participated in a brief armed conflict known as the Suez Campaign. When the conflict ended, Israel found itself controlling the Gaza Strip and portions of the Sinai Peninsula in Egypt. Here the United States stepped in to facilitate (or force) negotiations and was able to arrange for Israel to withdraw from these occupied territories in return for guaranteed, unfettered access to the Suez Canal and for free navigation and transport in the Gulf of Aqaba.[4] Once again, the immediate conflict had been resolved, but the underlying mistrust and antagonism between Israel and its neighbors continued to fester.

> See reading #30, "U.N. Security Council: Resolution 95, Concerning . . . the Passage of Ships Through the Suez Canal (September 1, 1951)"

> See reading #31: "Palestine National Authority: Palestine National Charter of 1964 (May 28, 1964)"

Meanwhile, the covenant of the Palestine Liberation Organization (PLO) was prepared in 1964 by Ahmed Shukairy, a lawyer born in Palestine who represented Saudi Arabia and later Syria in the United Nations. Shukairy later would become president of the PLO.

WHY DOES IT MATTER TO THE U.S.?

The nation of Israel – small in size – lies thousands of miles from the United States, and yet its welfare has long been a pressing concern to the American government. Foreign policy positions on Israel have often played significant roles in U.S. presidential elections, and the U.S. sends Israel billions of dollars per year in aid. Why is Israel such a concern?

- At the outset, the United States fully endorsed the creation of the state of Israel. This enthusiasm was partially fueled by a post-Holocaust sense that traumatized Jews were entitled to a homeland and partially by the U.S. role in the fledgling United Nations, which itself had endorsed the state.

- Israel is currently the only true democracy in the Middle East. As a nation preaching democracy as a governmental ideal, the United States is naturally inclined to support democracies like Israel. Moreover, its government makes Israel appear a safe, reliable ally against what have been referred to as "rogue" or "terrorist" states in the region, with whom the United States has more tenuous relations.
- As the Cold War developed, Israel rapidly became the United States' best ally in the region in the race for global influence with the Soviet Union. As Arab states moved closer to the U.S.S.R. for both fiscal and ideological reasons, the United States and Israel moved ever closer together.
- Although rumors persist to the contrary, there is no basis for the charge that a group of Zionist Jews is secretly running the U.S. government. Nonetheless, both Christian and Jewish lobbies in the United States do exert significant influence on the American political process in a pro-Israel direction – many Jews out of sympathy and a sense of identity with Israel and many Christians out of a religious conviction that the existence of a state of Israel is necessary to the arrival of the End Times.

WHO ARE TODAY'S REFUGEES?

One of the trickiest terms to define in the Arab-Israeli dialogue is "refugee." Before the rights and responsibilities of refugees can be determined, it is first necessary to figure out who they are. Definitions vary widely based upon who is doing the defining.

- According to the United Nations, a Palestinian refugee is a descendant (through the male line) of any person who had been residing in Palestine from 1946 to 1948 and who lost his home and livelihood as a consequence of the Israeli declaration of independence. Currently, over a million refugees (about one-third of those defined as such by the U.N.) live in

U.N. camps in Jordan, Lebanon, Syria, Gaza, and the West Bank. The U.N. does not recognize those who fled Palestine as a result of the 1967 conflict as refugees.

- *BADIL*, an organization dedicated to lobbying for Palestinian refugees, divides the refugees into five categories: those who left in 1948, those displaced in 1967, those who left at some subsequent time, and those currently residing in either Gaza or the West Bank, because they are not full citizens of a stable state. In 2003, *BADIL* estimated a total of over 7 million Palestinian refugees.

- Some pro-Israeli groups suggest that the definition of a Palestinian refugee is increasingly unfair to Israel. Even if a "refugee" is someone who was displaced from his or her home, they argue, the term is nearly never used elsewhere to apply to the descendants of those who fled, and they claim that expecting Israel to absorb over 10 million returnees is nonsensical.

Israeli settlements in northern Galilee often took fire from the Syrian front; border settlements further south were harassed by Egyptians and Jordanians. These attacks and the Israeli response strikes created an escalating, vicious cycle of grievances between Israel and its neighbors. Even worse, in early 1967, Egypt ordered the United Nations to withdraw its peacekeeping forces from the buffer zone between Israel and Egypt.

According to its procedural mandates, the United Nations could only maintain peacekeeping forces in the region when all parties involved in a conflict wanted their presence. The U.N. therefore had no choice but to withdraw from the Sinai. Israel, of course, viewed this development with great suspicion – a suspicion unfortunately bolstered by Egypt's closing (again) of the Straits of Tiran. This closure directly interfered with shipping to and from Israel and directly contradicted the terms of the 1956 ceasefire.

Once again, Israel turned to the United States for its help as a facilitator. In this instance, despite having stood as the guarantor of Israel's shipping rights in 1956, the United States declined to participate. Among other reasons, this

See reading #32, "Israeli Foreign Minister Abba Eban: Speech to the Security Council of the United Nations (June 6, 1967)"

was because U.S. President Lyndon Johnson was very occupied in 1967 with America's challenges in Southeast Asia – more specifically in Vietnam – and was not interested in American forces becoming involved in the Middle East. Faced with hostile escalations from both Egypt and Syria, and with no obvious diplomatic recourse, Israel attacked Egypt and Syria in early June of 1967. The Arab nations' ally, Jordan, also entered the fray. Israel gained control of the skies in the first two days of fighting and after that time controlled a significant strategic advantage in the fighting. In a mere six days, forces from all three Arab powers had been thoroughly routed. Thousands of Palestinians found themselves displaced and unable to return to their homes. Israel, meanwhile, found itself in control of the West Bank, the Gaza Strip, the Sinai, and Syria's Golan Heights.

This latter territory was extremely valuable for Israel. Possession of the entire northern region of Palestine allowed Israel to more effectively control its water resources. More immediately, the Golan Heights served an important security function. At the very northern tip of the Great Rift Valley (which continues to the south all the way to Kenya), the Golan Heights are quite literally above the Galilee. With very basic military technology, it was therefore extremely easy for militants in the Heights to shell and otherwise assault many Israeli settlements in the fertile Galilee area, and militants had been making good use of that geographic opportunity over the years. Now Israel could tightly control and monitor these lands with such dangerous access to Israeli citizens.

See reading #33, "The Allon Plan (June 18, 1967)"

After the 1967 war ended, Israel had to decide what to do with all of the territory it had conquered during the war. While many in Israel argued that the occupied territories could be exchanged for diplomatic peace with adversaries, many others argued that not all of the territory needed to be given back, and it could be used strategically. The Allon Plan, drafted by Israeli Foreign Minister Yigal Allon shortly after the war ended in June of 1967, suggested annexing most of the Jordan Valley to Israel, with the remaining parts of the West Bank becoming either autonomous Palestinian territory or returning to Jordan. The plan was rejected by Jordan's King Hussein.

See reading #34, "President Lyndon B. Johnson, Five Principles for Peace in the Middle East (June 19, 1967)"

The United States sought to control the effects of the 1967 war and promptly announced five principles that it would use to pursue peace and stability in the Middle East, including that nations had a right to exist in security and should

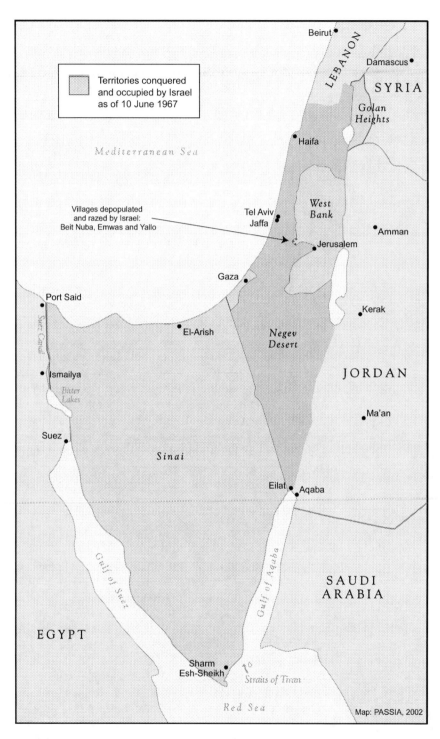

Map 9 Borders of Israel After the 1967 War

Source: Abdul Hadi, Mahdi (ed.). The Palestine Question in Maps, 1878–2014, Jerusalem: Palestinian Academic Society for the Study of International Affairs (PASSIA), 2nd Updated and Revised Edition, August 2014. Map 20.

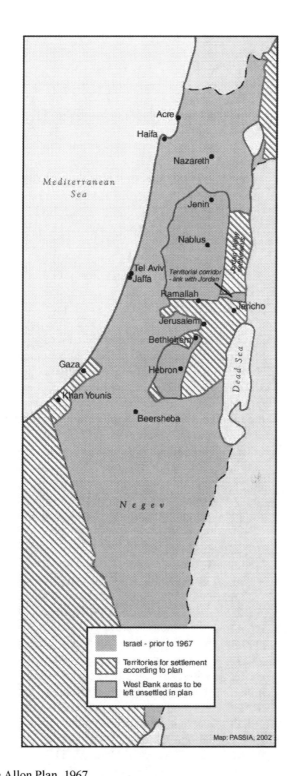

Map 10 The Allon Plan, 1967

Source: Abdul Hadi, Mahdi (ed.). The Palestine Question in Maps, 1878–2014, Jerusalem: Palestinian Academic Society for the Study of International Affairs (PASSIA), 2nd Updated and Revised Edition, August 2014. Map 21.

accept the rights of others to do so as well, that maritime rights needed to be respected, that external (to the Middle East) arms races posed a danger to the Middle East, and finally that the political independence and territorial integrity of all states in the area needed to be respected.

See reading #35, "Protection of Holy Places Law (June 27, 1967)"

One concern following the 1967 war had to do with Israeli treatment of religious minorities in the areas newly under its control. Shortly following the end of the war, on June 27, 1967, Prime Minister Levi Eshkol addressed the spiritual leaders of all communities and assured them of Israel's determination to protect the Holy Places. That day, the Knesset passed the Protection of Holy Places Law, 1967.

See reading #36, "The Khartoum Resolutions (September 1, 1967)"

In August of 1967 eight Arab heads of state attended an Arab summit conference in Khartoum to discuss pan-Arab responses to the outcome of the 1967 war. The outcome of that meeting served as the basis of most Arab foreign policy toward Israel through the 1970s. The resolution adopted at Khartoum called for a continued struggle against Israel, the creation of a fund to assist the economies of Egypt and Jordan, the lifting of an Arab oil boycott against the West, and a new agreement to end the war in Yemen. Perhaps the most famous dimension of the Khartoum conclusion was the "three nos" clause: no peace with Israel, no recognition of Israel, and no negotiations with Israel.

See reading #37, "U. N. Security Council: Resolution 242 (November 22, 1967)"

Israel's impressive defeat of its enemies in 1967 was not, of course, the end of the story. The postwar *status quo* satisfied none of Israel's neighbors, who had only succeeded in increasing Israel's territorial size and appearing weak in the public arena. Moreover, the Middle East had become involved in another global problem: the Cold War between the United States and the U.S.S.R. Israel had long been friendly to the interests of the United States, and Egypt found an eager sponsor in the Soviet Union. The United Nations sought to control the effect of the conflict through Resolution 242, which discussed Israeli withdrawal "from territories occupied" in the war and termination of all claims of belligerency and the right of states to live in peace within secure and recognized borders, as well as guaranteeing freedom of navigation on international waterways, a just settlement of the refugee problem, and guaranteeing territorial inviolability of every state in the area.

See reading #38, "The Palestinian National Charter (July 1–17, 1968)"

Palestinian nationalism continued to grow. In 1968 a Palestinian National Charter was published, a set of resolutions of the Palestine National Council. These resolutions were largely based upon documents dating back to January of

See reading #39, "The Seven Points of Fatah (January, 1969)"

1964, when at the Arab summit in Cairo a strategic decision was made to organize the Palestinian people. In February of 1969, at the Fifth Palestine National Congress, Fatah became the dominant faction of the PLO.

See reading #40 "Statement by U.S. Secretary of State William Rogers (December 9, 1969)"

The United States continued to try to effectively promote a peaceful solution to the Arab-Israeli conflict in the Nixon administration, but the positions of the adversaries as well as Cold War tensions between the United States and the Soviet Union prevented progress from being made, either multilaterally or through the United Nations. A multilateral initiative, including the United States, the Soviet Union, the United Kingdom, and France, was unable to make substantive progress at the time.

See reading #41, "King Hussein's Federation Plan (March 15, 1972)"

In March of 1972 King Hussein put forward a plan for a new United Arab Kingdom that would consist of the former West Bank and Gaza and "the Jordanian Region," with a federal capital in Amman and a Palestinian regional capital in Jerusalem. That proposal failed to receive substantial Palestinian support, and Israel's reaction was strongly negative, saying that the plan did not display an interest in negotiations and would not contribute to a peaceful outcome to the conflict in the Middle East.

By the fall of 1973 Israel was again seriously concerned about the developments on its borders and anticipated further Egyptian and Syrian hostilities. The United States, however, wary of military conflict between American and Soviet allies, strongly counselled Israel to avoid another preemptive strike on Egypt and Syria.

Emboldened by new relationships with the Soviet Union and heavily supplied with Soviet armaments, Egypt and Syria attacked Israel on October 6, 1973. This particular day was Yom Kippur, the Jewish Day of Atonement. The holiest day of the Jewish year, Yom Kippur mandates introspection, fasting, and a general withdrawal from secular society. As such, the Israel Defense Force – heavily dependent for manpower upon military reserves that require several days to reach full strength – was especially vulnerable to an attack and initially suffered significant loss of life and territory. Egyptian forces retook the Sinai; allied Syrian forces retook the Golan Heights.

The Israeli military found its footing, however, and eventually the military tides turned. At the end of two weeks, Israel had pushed Egypt back through the Sinai and across the Suez. Moreover, Israel had pushed back so far on Syrian forces that its troops were within 20 miles of Damascus.

See reading #42, "U. N. Security Council: Resolution 338 (October 22, 1973)"

See reading #43, "Palestine National Council: Resolutions at the 12th Session of the Palestine National Council (June 8, 1974)"

See reading #44, "Seventh Arab League Summit Conference (October 28, 1974)"

See reading #45, "Interim Agreement Between Israel and Egypt (September 1, 1975)"

See reading #46, "Memorandum of Agreement Between the Governments of Israel and the United States (September 1, 1975)"

See reading #47 "Statement to the Knesset by President Anwar el-Sadat (November 20, 1977)"

See reading #48 "Statement to the Knesset by Prime Minister Menachem Begin (November 20, 1977)"

The conflict, known by Israelis as the Yom Kippur War and by Arabs as the October War, came to a conclusion with Israel once again solidly the victor.

Originally the Palestine Liberation Organization called for the "total liberation of all occupied Palestine." At its Twelfth National Council in Cairo in 1974, however, it changed this goal, seeking instead to establish "a national authority in every part of Palestinian territory that is liberated."

Later that year, at the Seventh Arab League Summit Conference in Rabat, Morocco, the delegates passed a number of resolutions on Palestine. These resolutions affirmed the right of the Palestinian people to self-determination and urged Syria, Egypt, and Jordan to work with the Palestine Liberation Organization to help to ensure that outcome.

In 1975 an Egyptian-Israeli interim peace agreement was signed, providing for a separation of forces between the two parties, a U.N.-supervised buffer zone, Israeli and Egyptian electronic surveillance stations, and an additional station in the Sinai to be manned by American civilian technicians. The agreement was to be in force for at least three years, with annual extensions.

With that agreement, Israel would be giving up its control over the oil fields of the southern Sinai that it had occupied in 1967 and 1973, and in September of 1975 Israel and the United States signed an agreement that addressed both Israel's needs and the United States' willingness to provide replacements for the oil Israel would be giving up.

Despite having lost territory by the conclusion of the war, many Egyptians felt that their president, Anwar el-Sadat, had sent an important message to Israel and the world: that Egypt was a significant military force and not to be trifled with. Sadat was known among his fans as the "hero of the crossing,"[5] in honor of the taking of the Suez Canal.

Seeing himself as the emergent leader of the Arab world, Sadat did something that had been unthinkable only a few years earlier. In late 1977, he reached out to Israel and suggested his willingness to discuss an Israeli-Egyptian peace agreement, traveling to Israel and addressing a session of the Israeli Knesset. Later, in December of 1977, Sadat and Israeli Prime Minister Menachem Begin met again in Ismailia, Egypt.

The Ismailia talks were not particularly successful. There was a fundamental disagreement about the primary issue to be resolved; Egypt sought a resolution to the question of

Palestinian rights and refugee status before it would discuss a bilateral peace agreement between the two states, but Israel prioritized an open, public peace agreement between the two states that might set the tone for future developments in the region. Also, the Egyptian proposal called for a return to the 1967 east/west division of Jerusalem and offered guaranteed access to holy places for Israelis. Israel intended to maintain control of Jerusalem, with the exception of Muslim holy places, which could be controlled by some Arab authority.

Even if the two countries could have reached a peace agreement of sorts, they failed to agree about how that agreement would proceed. Israel preferred a schedule of phased withdrawal from the land it occupied, preceded by immediate and full Egyptian recognition of the state of Israel. Egypt offered exactly the opposite – a schedule of phases of diplomatic recognition, justified by the good-faith withdrawal of Israeli troops in the very short term. They differed, too, on the status of the West Bank and Gaza: Egypt wanted Israel to remove itself entirely from their internal affairs, but Israel offered only limited self-rule, with a final decision about state autonomy to be subject to later negotiations.

Finally, the Israeli and Egyptian delegations conflicted on the very touchy issue of settlements. While Israel held land formerly considered Palestinian, the land was not held in limbo. Thousands of Jews had poured into the fertile, abandoned areas and set up outposts that were rapidly flourishing. These "settlements," as they are most commonly called, served a primary Israeli purpose, precisely because they made negotiation more difficult. They created "facts on the ground," as Israeli Prime Minister Begin referred to them, facts that made it much more difficult for the Israeli government to even consider offering the return of those lands to Arab control. These settlements have continued to be a huge political and security issue for the state of Israel, and even in 1977 it was obvious to Sadat that their development needed to stop. Begin, however, considered the settlements perfectly legal and had no intention of curtailing them; in fact, he encouraged them.

Following the visit of Egyptian President Anwar Sadat to Jerusalem, the Palestine Liberation Movement met in Tripoli Libya and issued a reaction statement designed to bring together a group of states that would try to isolate Egypt and prevent peace with Israel. This became known

See reading #49, "Six-Point Program of the Palestine Liberation Organization (December 4, 1977)"

as the "refusal front." On December 4, 1977, they issued a statement that included rejection of both United Nations Security Council Resolution 242 and Resolution 338 and reaffirmed the commitment of the PLO to deny the right of Israel to exist.

See readings #50, 51 "The Camp David Accords (September 17, 1978)"

Eager to see a final peace agreement develop between Egypt and Israel, U.S. President Jimmy Carter stepped up American involvement in the issue. In the fall of 1978, he invited both Begin and Sadat to the presidential retreat at Camp David, where he set up each delegation in its own cabin. Shuttling between delegations with offers and suggestions, Carter facilitated the development of what became a final document of Egyptian-Israeli understanding. The final sticking point was the status of a luxury hotel that Israel had

See reading #52, "Peace Treaty Between Israel and Egypt (March 26, 1979)"

built in the formerly Egyptian city of Taba. After lengthy negotiations, Israel agreed to allow the status of Taba to be subjected to international arbitration,[6] and an overall agreement was reached. A final peace treaty was signed between the two nations in March of 1979.

Although Anwar el-Sadat had been careful to combine a broad Middle East peace agreement with a specific Egyptian-Israeli peace agreement (so that he could not be accused of "selling out" the Palestinians), he was not

See reading #53, "Arab League Summit Conference Communique, Baghdad (March 31, 1979)"

applauded in the rest of the Arab world for his agreement with Israel. Within a week of the peace treaty being signed, an Arab League summit conference convened in Baghdad and condemned Sadat's actions in ignoring Arab policy positions and his deviation from Arab ranks, colluding with the United States, standing with Zionist enemies, violating Arab nations' rights, and a variety of other offenses.

Sadat's regime became increasingly authoritarian, and in October of 1981, he was assassinated. His assassination presented an obvious problem to the Israeli government: would a new Egyptian government respect Sadat's renegade peace agreement with Israel? The new president, Hosni Mubarak, quickly reassured Israel that repudiating that agreement was not his intent, and it has in fact endured to this day.

It is important to understand one of the huge complexities of the Arab-Israeli conflict: a phenomenon that can be called "party agency." In general, Israel acts as a political unit. Although its military decisions are of course not subject to constant legislative overview, the general direction of Israeli policies about the military, settlements, and negotiation are determined by the political reality of the Israeli government. While this government has occasionally

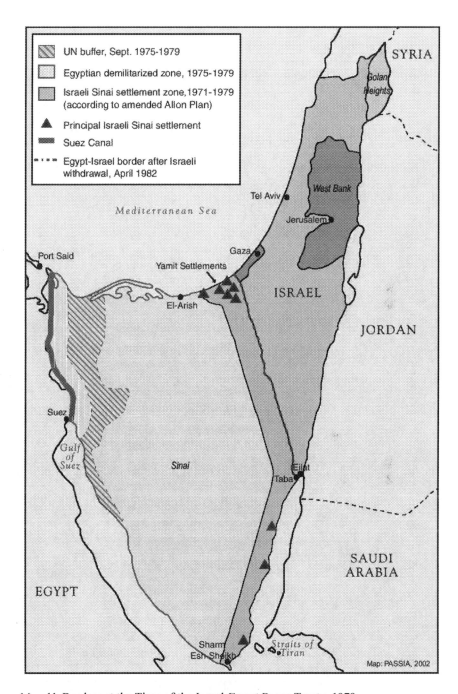

Map 11 Borders at the Time of the Israel-Egypt Peace Treaty, 1979

Source: Abdul Hadi, Mahdi (ed.). The Palestine Question in Maps, 1878–2014, Jerusalem: Jerusalem: Palestinian Academic Society for the Study of International Affairs (PASSIA), 2nd Updated and Revised Edition, August 2014. Map 25.

repositioned itself on a conservative-liberal spectrum, it is generally a visible movement, transparent to international understanding and analysis. The same cannot be said of the institutions representing (or claiming to represent) Arab and Palestinian interests. These institutions are many and varied and do not always share goals or approve of one another. It is therefore difficult for Israelis to know with whom they ought best to negotiate.

WHO SPEAKS FOR THE PALESTINIANS?

Far from having a united voice, the Palestinians have been represented by a number of different groups through the years – sometimes without particular concern for the Palestinians' approval. Some of the major players:

- The **Palestinian Liberation Organization** was founded in 1964 to liberate Palestine through military means. The PLO, under the leadership of Yasser Arafat, was recognized as the legitimate representative of the Palestinian people by the Arab League in 1974. Israel followed suit, but not until 1993, when the PLO accepted a two-state solution and declared its recognition of the state of Israel. Thereafter, the PLO has been the dominant force in the Palestinian National Authority.
- **Fatah**, also known as the Palestine National Liberation Movement, is one faction of the PLO. Fatah was founded by Yasser Arafat and brought to prominence under his influence. It has, in recent years, become the political, nonviolent voice in Palestine and was the undisputed primary political force until the 2006 elections. It has labored under accusations of inefficiency, corruption, and incoherency in recent years.
- **Hamas** is a Sunni Muslim group, founded by the pan-Arab Muslim Brotherhood movement. Hamas does not recognize the state of Israel and, in fact, calls for its destruction. It is considered a terrorist organization by many, including the United States, but is often hailed for its effective social services and true dedication to the quality of life of the Palestinian

people and Palestinian goals. Hamas is now the controlling party in the Gaza Strip.

- **Hezbollah** is a Shi'ite Muslim group heavily subsidized by Iran and primarily concerned with affairs in Lebanon. It is also considered a terrorist organization by the United States and many others. While it does not directly claim to speak for the Palestinians, Hezbollah has nonetheless become a key player in the Arab-Israeli conflict, calling for the destruction of Israel and encouraging or perpetrating cross-border attacks into Israel from Lebanon.

See reading #54,"Basic Law: Jerusalem, Capital of Israel (July 30, 1980)"

In July of 1980 the Knesset passed *Basic Law: Jerusalem, Capital of Israel.* The law took the position that Jerusalem's boundaries following the 1967 war would be the permanent boundaries of the city and was seen as an acceptance of a philosophical statement by Israel's right wing that territory conquered in 1967 might stay under Israeli control. The law generated much international criticism of Israel, and United Nations Security Resolution 478 in 1980 – adopted with 14 votes in favor, none against, and the United States abstaining – called for the Law to be rescinded.

While Israel saw political progress to its south with Egypt, the situation in the north was less tranquil. Ongoing cross-border attacks on Israeli cities near the border with Lebanon generated increasing Israeli concern. In the summer of 1981, Israel attacked Lebanon, pushing back the Palestinian Liberation Organization forces there and Syrian forces responsible for the cross-border attacks. The United States quickly stepped in to mediate a ceasefire, and the Israeli occupation lasted only about a month.

See reading #55, "Saudi Crown Prince Fadh ibn Abd al-Aziz: The Fahd Plan (August 7, 1981)"

In August of 1981, Saudi Crown Prince Fahd attempted to respond to several core issues of the Arab-Israeli conflict that had not yet been addressed with an eight-point peace proposal of his own. The starting point of his plan involved Israel's withdrawal from Arab territories occupied in 1967, including East Jerusalem, and the dismantling of Israel's settlements in those territories. It also included a key place for the Palestinian people's right to self-determination and compensation for Palestinian refugees not exercising the right of return. Fahd called for an independent Palestinian state with East Jerusalem as its capital. The plan was adopted in a modified form at the Arab summit in Fez, Morocco, on September 9, 1982, and remained the Arab position until the Madrid conference in 1991.

See reading #56, "The Golan Heights Law (December 14, 1981)"

In December of 1981 the Knesset passed the "Golan Heights Law," which extended Israeli law to the area of the Golan Heights, land captured by Israel from Syria in 1973. Many saw this law as an effort to pressure Syria into negotiating a peace agreement with Israel, although it did not end up producing that result. When the law was introduced in the Knesset, Prime Minister Begin stated that the time had come to implement the government's policy regarding the Golan Heights, citing Syria's implacable hostility to Israel.

See reading #57, "Prime Minister Begin: The Wars of No Alternative and Operation Peace for the Galilee (August 8, 1982)"

All was not resolved with Lebanon, however. Barely a year after its most recent withdrawal, after continued cross-border antagonism and conflict, Israel had once again had enough, and it invaded Lebanon in June of 1982. This time, its presence in Lebanon was to be much longer lasting. The PLO fled Lebanon for a more stable haven in Tunisia, while Israel occupied a significant area of southern Lebanon.

See reading #58, "The Reagan Plan: U.S. Policy for Peace in the Middle East (September 1, 1982)"

As the PLO was being relocated from Beirut, Lebanon, to Tunisia, U.S. President Ronald Reagan articulated an American appraisal of the situation in the Middle East. He suggested that the conflict in Lebanon was only part of the Middle East conflict and said that the Camp David framework was the only way to proceed. He lauded Israel for its successful completion of its withdrawal from Sinai and complimented both Israeli and Egyptian leaders for living up to the terms of the Camp David agreement. He again called for stability in the Middle East, Arab recognition of Israel, cessation of Israeli settlements on occupied Palestinian land, and the continuing of negotiations between Israel and Palestine.

The continued Israeli presence in Beirut led to one of the most controversial incidents in Israeli-Arab conflict: the massacres in the refugee camps of Sabra and Shatila on the morning of September 16, 1982. Although the forces behind the deaths of hundreds to thousands of Palestinians were Lebanese Christians, Israel was implicated in the disaster because the camps were in the territory occupied by Israel. Critics argued that the Israelis, as being nominally in charge of the territory, should have protected the victims of the slaughter from the Christian militias.

Later, both international and Israeli inquiries determined that Israel political and military leaders were indirectly

Map 12 Borders at the Time of the Golan Heights Law, 1981
Source: Government of Israel, Ministry of Foreign Affairs, About Israel, Israel in Maps, Golan Heights.

See reading #59, "Report of the [Kahan] Commis-sion of Inquiry Into the Events at the Refugee Camps in Beirut (February 8, 1983)"

See reading #60, "Agreement Between Israel and Lebanon (May 17, 1983)"

See reading #61 "Jordan-P.L.O. Agreement (Febru-ary 11, 1985)

See reading #62, "The Shultz Initiative (March 4, 1988)"

See reading #63, "King Hussein, Address to the Nation (July 31, 1988)"

responsible for the deaths in the refugee camps in June of 1982. At the time, international and domestic dismay was sufficient to cause the resignation of Israel's then-Defense Minister Ariel Sharon in 1983.

That same pressure, as well as mediation by the United States, helped lead to a 1983 agreement for Israel's with-drawal from most of southern Lebanon. In the summer of 1985, Israel withdrew from all but a small "security zone" on the Israel-Lebanon border.

Earlier that year the government of Jordan signed an agreement with the Palestinian Liberation Organization regarding the question of the future of Palestine. In that agreement Jordan committed to follow the positions of the Arab States and the United Nations regarding the Pal-estine question, calling for an end of Israeli occupation of Palestine and the withdrawal of Israel from the territories occupied in 1967 and the right of self-determination for the Palestinian people.

Once again, even as it appeared to resolve one set of issues with its neighbors, Israel found itself facing a new set of problems. In December of 1987, Palestinians in Gaza and the West Bank turned to demonstrations and protests, which quickly escalated into armed conflict with Israeli forces. Known by the term "intifada," the Arabic word for "uprising," this period of conflict and violence helped to bring the Palestinian situation back onto the international radar. Regardless of who started what, images of Palestin-ian children armed with rocks facing down powerful Israeli tanks in urban settings moved the international community, and Israel faced increasing pressure to find a solution for the Palestinian question.

In March of 1988, as part of President Ronald Reagan's continuing efforts in the Middle East, U.S. Secretary of State George Shultz called for a new round of peace negoti-ations based upon U.N. Resolutions 242 and 338, to be held between an Israeli delegation and a Jordanian-Palestinian delegation. The goal of the initiative was "a comprehen-sive peace providing for the security of all the states in the region and for the legitimate rights of the Palestinian peo-ple." Little came of the talks.

In July of 1988, King Hussein of Jordan officially relin-quished control of the West Bank to a hypothetical future Palestinian state. In practice, Jordan had not controlled the West Bank in 20 years; as a theoretical concession, how-ever, this action nonetheless had great symbolic impact.

See reading
#64, "Palestine
National Council:
Declaration of
Independence
(November 15,
1988)"

In November of 1988, the Palestine National Congress meeting in Algiers accepted a new policy outline from Yasser Arafat and called for the convening of an international peace conference for the Middle East. Arafat said that this should be done under the auspices of the United Nations Security Council and should be based upon Security Council Resolutions 242 and 338 and the assurance of the legitimate rights of the Palestinian people. The document proclaimed the independence of Palestine without defining its borders, with Jerusalem as its capital. The document also renounced terrorism but accepted the right of people to fight against foreign occupation and called for the continuation of the intifada. In December of that year, the Palestinian National Council formally accepted U.N. Resolution 181, including its partition plan creating an Israeli and a Palestinian state.

See reading #65,
"Israel's Peace
Initiative (May 14,
1989)"

See reading #66,
"U.S. Secretary
of State James
Baker's Five Point
Plan (October 10,
1989)"

In May of 1989, Israeli Prime Minister Yitzhak Shamir proposed a four-point peace plan allowing for Palestinian self-government. A few months later United States Secretary of State James Baker proposed a similar but slightly more expansive peace plan, which Israel rejected. Frustrated with its leaders' inability to move forward with the peace process, for the first time in its history, the Israeli Knesset voted to overturn a sitting government. Everything seemed optimistic for the future, positive development of Arab-Israeli relations.

In the summer of 1990, Iraqi President Saddam Hussein invaded tiny neighboring Kuwait. Hussein knew that the Arab world was unlikely to back his "reclamation" of Kuwait and had an idea to generate more support. Because "the enemy of my enemy is my friend," Hussein supposed that if Israel could be drawn into the conflict, he would be able to rely on political and financial support from the wealthy Gulf states. Accordingly, Iraq fired missiles at Jerusalem and Tel Aviv and suggested to the Palestinian National Council that a victorious Iraq would support the creation of a real, independent Palestinian state. Yasser Arafat willingly endorsed Iraq's sovereignty over Kuwait.

The results were not what Hussein had hoped, however. Complying with significant pressure from the United States, Israel did not respond to Iraq's opening salvo. Instead, Israel added its political (but not military) backing to the American invasion of Kuwait and southern Iraq, which pushed Saddam's forces back and out of the area. The Gulf states not only failed to support Iraq but actively joined in the

American opposition. Even worse, from the context of the Arab-Israeli situation, because of Arafat's support of Iraq, the Gulf states kicked thousands of Palestinian refugees out of their countries, exacerbating the refugee situation elsewhere and further straining the resources of the Palestinian community.

See reading #67, "Letter of Invitation to the Madrid Peace Conference (October 30, 1991)"

After the Gulf War, U.S. President George H.W. Bush refocused his administration's energies on the political situation in the Middle East. In October of 1991, the U.S. and Soviet governments sponsored a major conference in Madrid to facilitate conversation between Israel and Syria, Jordan, and Lebanon. Palestinians were included as part of a Jordanian delegation and not as a delegation of their own, but the Palestinian question was a pressing issue. Also on the table were questions of bilateral peace treaties between Israel and each of its neighbors, as well as issues of economic cooperation and development in the region as a whole.

Several rounds of talks followed. In the fourth round, in December of 1991, the Palestinians presented a demand for direct elections in a hypothetical Palestinian state. Unwilling to cede that much control so quickly, Israel rejected the demand, and talks ended. Subsequent rounds of talks allowed the parties to stumble through the process of negotiation about what a Palestinian state might look like, whether Israel would withdraw from all or some of the Golan Heights, and whether Israel would recognize Palestinian organizations like the PLO.

See reading #68, "Address to the Knesset by Prime Minister Rabin (July 13, 1992)"

The new government of Yitzhak Rabin sought to move forward on the peace issue. In a speech to the Knesset presenting his new government, Mr. Rabin indicated that a central goal of his administration would be to promote the making of peace, indicating his willingness to talk with the Palestinians and continue the Madrid process.

See reading #69, "Israel-P.L.O. Recognition (September 9, 1993)"

Finally, in August of 1993, the PLO revealed a breakthrough: Israel and Palestinian representatives had secretly reached something approximating an agreement. The two sides formally agreed to the Oslo Accords, named after the city where the secret negotiations had occurred. The Accords allowed for partial autonomy for a Palestinian Authority and greater autonomy in the Gaza Strip and in Jericho.

See reading #70, "Declaration of Principles on Interim Self-Government Arrangements ["Oslo Agreement"] (September 13, 1993)"

On September 13, 1993, Israeli Prime Minister Yitzhak Rabin and PLO Chairman Yasser Arafat met and watched Israeli Foreign Minister Shimon Peres and PLO Executive

See reading #71, "Israel-Jordan Common Agenda (September 14, 1993)"

Council Member Abou Abbas sign the *Oslo Agreement*, witnessed by President Bill Clinton, former presidents George H.W. Bush and Jimmy Carter, and many other dignitaries. The next day, Israel and Jordan agreed to an Israel-Jordan Common Agenda, marking the end of the state of war between the two nations and paving the way for talks leading to a formal peace treaty.

See reading #72, "Agreement on the Gaza Strip and the Jericho Area (May 4, 1994)"

Progress toward a normalization of relations continued to be made. In May of 1994 the Gaza-Jericho Agreement was signed. This brought about a withdrawal of Israeli forces and administration from specific areas of the West Bank and the Gaza Strip and also described the transfer of powers and responsibilities to the Palestine National Authority, with specific attention paid to security arrangements.

See reading #73, "The Washington Declaration (July 25, 1994)"

Jordan's King Hussein and Israeli Prime Minister Yitzhak Rabin signed the Washington Declaration at the White House on July 25, 1994. It formally ended the 46-year state of war between Jordan and Israel. The Declaration committed both Jordan and Israel to aim at the "achievement of a just, lasting and comprehensive peace between Arab states and the Palestinians, with Israel." It included agreements safeguarding Islamic control over the Muslim Holy Sites of Jerusalem. The Declaration also mandated practical steps such as the establishment of direct telephone links between Jordan and Israel, the opening of two new border crossings between the two

See reading #74, "Treaty of Peace Between the Hashemite Kingdom of Jordan and the State of Israel (October 26, 1994)"

countries, linking of the Jordanian and Israeli power grids, and police cooperation in combating crime. The signing of the Washington Declaration paved the way for Jordan and Israel to reach agreement on their Treaty of Peace, which was initialled at the border crossing between Eilat, Israel, and Aqaba, Jordan, on October 17, 1994, with United States President Bill Clinton witnessing the ceremony, and formally signed on October 26, 1994.

The year 1994 also saw three Middle East leaders – Israeli Prime Minister Yitzhak Rabin, Israeli Foreign Minister Shimon Peres, and Palestinian Authority Chairman Yasser Arafat – share the Nobel Prize for Peace. The three national leaders delivered Nobel Lectures on December 10, 1994, articulating their visions of peace and the future of the Middle East. While those speeches are not included in this volume, they can be found at the Nobel Prize Organization website: www.nobelprize.org/nobel_prizes/peace/laureates/1994/.

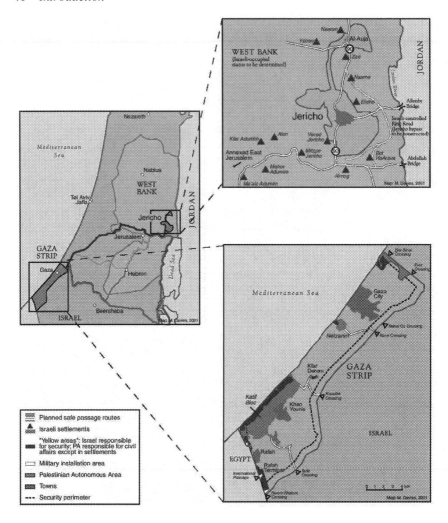

Map 13 Borders at the Time of the Gaza-Jericho Agreement, 1994

Source: Abdul Hadi, Mahdi (ed.). The Palestine Question in Maps, 1878–2014, Jerusalem: Palestinian Academic Society for the Study of International Affairs (PASSIA), 2nd Updated and Revised Edition, August 2014. Map 29.

SECRET LIAISONS

Although undeniably the best known, the negotiations leading to the Oslo Accords were not Israel's only secret negotiations with Arab leaders. For example, Israel's history with its neighbor to the east, the Hashemite Kingdom of Jordan, is peppered with tales of unofficial communications.

- In 1947, Golda Meir – who would become the first female prime minister of Israel – crossed the border into then-Transjordan disguised as a Muslim wife traveling with her husband. She and her "husband," a colleague, met with Jordan's King Abdullah I and pleaded with him to keep his country out of the upcoming military conflict with Israel.
- In the 1970s, Israelis met repeatedly with King Hussein of Jordan, often in his doctor's office in London.
- In March of 2004, King Abdullah flew in a helicopter to drop by Prime Minister Ariel Sharon's personal ranch. The two leaders lunched and discussed the wall/fence barrier being erected between Israeli and Palestinian lands.

See reading #75, "Israeli-Palestinian Interim Agreement on the West Bank and the Gaza Strip (September 28, 1995)"

See reading #76, "What Is Area C? Planning Policy in the West Bank" (1975)

See reading #77, "Speech by Prime Minister Yitzhak Rabin to the Knesset Supporting the Israeli-Palestinian Interim Agreement (October 5, 1995)"

See reading #78, [Beilin-Abu Mazen] Framework for the Conclusion of a Final Status Agreement Between Israel and the Palestine Liberation Organization (October 31, 1995)"

In September of 1995, Israel and Palestinian representatives signed an interim agreement derived from the Oslo negotiations. This "Interim Agreement on the West Bank and the Gaza Strip" called for the creation of an independent Palestinian Authority, as well as touching on issues of troop positions, Palestinian elections and self-governance, and prisoner exchanges. Those in favor of Arab-Israeli peace were pleased and expectant after this rapid progress.

The momentum did continue, and within a month the negotiators had completed a "Framework for the Conclusion of a Final Status Agreement" between Israel and the Palestine Liberation Organization. In the agreement both parties recognized and respected each other's sovereignty and territorial integrity, renounced the use of force, and committed themselves to a peaceful resolution of disputes. Israelis living in settlements in the Occupied Territories would be subject to Palestinian sovereignty and the Palestinian rule of law, and Jerusalem would be an open and undivided city. Palestinian refugees from 1947–1949 would be entitled to compensation and rehabilitation for their losses.

Then, on November 4, 1995, Prime Minister Yitzhak Rabin was assassinated by an Orthodox Jewish student displeased with the Oslo Accords and their subsequent developments. Rabin was succeeded by Shimon Peres, but Peres did not have the level of political support that Rabin had possessed. With the resulting political uncertainly in Israel following Rabin's assassination and

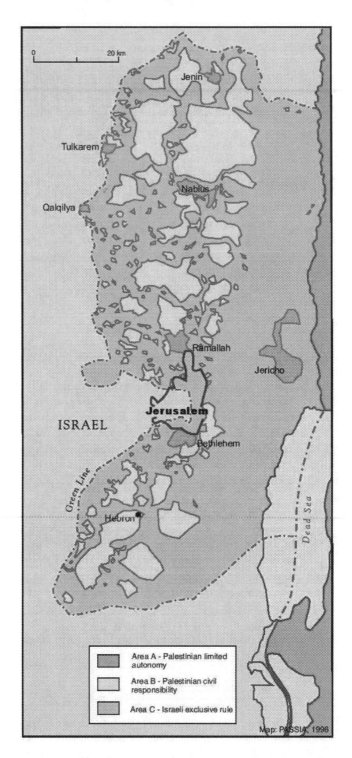

Map 14 Proposed Borders in the Israel-Palestine Interim Agreement, 1995

Source: Abdul Hadi, Mahdi (ed.). The Palestine Question in Maps, 1878–2014, Jerusalem: Palestinian Academic Society for the Study of International Affairs (PASSIA), 2nd Updated and Revised Edition, August 2014. Map 30.

See reading #79, "Speech by Prime Minister Rabin at a Peace Rally (November 4, 1995)"

Peres's accession to power, the momentum toward peace slowed considerably.

In April of 1996, after three weeks of fighting between Israeli and Lebanese Hezbollah forces, U.S. Secretary of State Warren Christopher was credited with brokering a peace between Israel and the Hezbollah guerrillas. Israel

See reading #80, "Israel-Lebanon Ceasefire Understanding (April 26, 1996)"

said it launched "Operation Grapes of Wrath" to halt Hezbollah rocket attacks on its northern settlements. Hezbollah contended that the barrage would stop when Israel left the southern Lebanon enclave it had occupied since 1982. The Israel-Lebanon Ceasefire Understanding led some observers to hope that Israel's northern border would remain calm in the future.

In June of 1996 the Labor party lost in the elections for the 14th Knesset, and Benjamin Netanyahu became prime minister. National security was a significant issue in the

See reading #81, "Hussein-Netanyahu Exchange of Letters (March 9/10, 1997)"

elections, and the government of Netanyahu took a different approach to the peace process. In the spring of 1997 King Hussein reached out to Prime Minister Netanyahu to complain about some of his government's policies regarding the Palestinians, policies that had been negotiated with agreements reached under the Rabin government. Netanyahu replied that he had been chosen by the Israeli public in June of 1996 as a result of a less-than-complete peace process and violence in Lebanon and suggested that Israel and Jordan had "faced worse crises in the past than the problem we are facing today."

See reading #82, "Secretary of State Madeleine Albright, The Israeli-Palestinian Peace Process (August 6, 1997)"

In the meantime, the United States continued to try to accelerate the peace process and finalize what had been begun by President Jimmy Carter with the Camp David agreements. Secretary of State Madeleine Albright was an active and visible player in negotiations, and President Clinton used her regularly to try to jump-start the peace process.

Over the next several years, international leaders of all stripes attempted to keep the Israeli-Arab peace process moving forward. The United States hosted a conference at the Wye River Conference Center in Maryland, where President Clinton and Secretary of State Madeleine Albright

See reading #83, "The Wye River Memorandum (October 23, 1998)"

met with Netanyahu and Palestinian President Yasser Arafat. The product of that meeting, known as the Wye River Memorandum, demonstrated that even a hard-line Israeli government could arrive at some form of agreement with its Palestinian neighbors.

In the spring of 1999, Labor Party leader Ehud Barak was elected prime minister of Israel. Despite his strong military

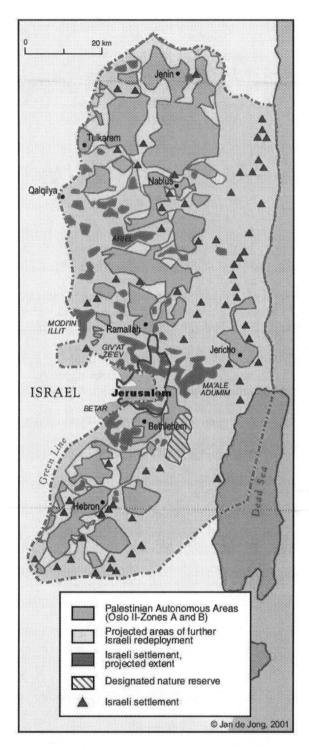

Map 15 Proposals From the Wye Negotiations, 1998

Source: Abdul Hadi, Mahdi (ed.). The Palestine Question in Maps, 1878–2014, Jerusalem: Palestinian Academic Society for the Study of International Affairs (PASSIA), 2nd Updated and Revised Edition, August 2014. Map 32.

See reading #84,
"Address in the
Knesset by Prime
Minister-Elect Ehud
Barak Upon the
Presentation of
His Government
(July 7, 1999)"

background, Barak championed peace and negotiation with Israel's Arab neighbors, and his election symbolized the ongoing hope in the Middle East that a solution was within reach. But Barak's administration was to be short lived.

On September 9, 2000, Ariel Sharon, now leader of the opposition Likud party, and approximately 1,000 members of the Israeli police force visited the Temple Mount in Jerusalem. The top of the Temple Mount is a huge compound enclosing the al-Aqsa Mosque and the Dome of the Rock, and the area is considered the third holiest site in Islam. It is also the site of the last Temple of the Jews in Biblical Israel, and the enclosing compound includes the Wailing Wall, making the site the holiest place in the world for Jews. Long under Jordanian protection, the area is a hotbed of contention and dispute.

During his visit, Sharon took the opportunity to proclaim Israel's sovereignty over the al-Aqsa Mosque and Temple Mount area. The next day, Palestinian protesters and Israeli police met and clashed in the first violent encounter of what would become known as the al-Aqsa Intifada. Whether Sharon's visit was an intentional attempt to contribute to his political aspirations may never be known, but subsequent international investigation did condemn Sharon for his inflammatory actions. The reactions were intense, and despite desperate negotiations, the cycle of Israeli and Palestinian violence spun out of control.

The international *zeitgeist*, of course, shifted dramatically in September of 2001 with the attacks on financial and military targets in the United States. It is important to note that the Palestinian insurgency is not, traditionally, associated with the religiously fundamental forces associated with Osama bin Laden and the 9/11 events – those moving out of Saudi Arabia and into areas like Pakistan, Afghanistan, and, in the last few years, Iraq. There has, however, been an uptick in religiously oriented political action in Palestinian communities, demonstrated most clearly in the 2006 election of a religiously motivated government in the Gaza Strip. But in 2001, it was fairly safe to say that those angrily rebelling in the streets of Gaza and the West Bank were not associated with the men flying the planes into the World Trade Center in New York City.

Nonetheless, the world did change, politically and philosophically. Buoyed by the insurgency in his own country and by the international sense of insecurity and instability,

Ariel Sharon was elected prime minister of Israel in 2001, promising more and better security. Within a year, the Sharon administration announced the expansion of the construction of a security wall between Israeli and Palestinian holdings to terminate the series of suicide attacks perpetrated by Palestinians in Israeli territory. Unfortunately, this barrier also divided many Palestinian families from each other, farmers from their land, children from their schools, and employees from their jobs.

WHAT'S IN A NAME?

The Arab-Israeli conflict has been plagued with persistent issues of nomenclature. Even a relatively small change of terminology can upset one side or the other. This fact is apparent in the ongoing struggle over what to call the Israeli/West Bank barrier.

- Israelis prefer to refer to the barrier as "a fence," implying a lack of permanence and a sense of permeability. Israel's flagship daily newspaper, *Ha'aretz*, has even gone so far as to refer to the sturdier sections as "concrete section[s] of separation fence."
- At their most generous, Palestinian sources prefer the term "wall." Some pro-Palestinian groups refer to the barrier as an "apartheid wall" and compare it to the Berlin Wall.
- Amnesty International, by way of an example only, carefully walks the line and chooses the term "fence/wall" wherever appropriate.
- This debate is complicated by the fact that the actual physical object of the discussion is not always the same. There are many miles of concrete wall, especially in the area near Jerusalem, typically 10 m (30 ft) high. In these areas the word "wall" is clearly correct, and the word "fence" would not be, since the object in question is solid, made of concrete, and 30 ft high. Far more of the border between Israeli territory and Palestinian territory is delimited by what elsewhere would be called a "fence": something made of wire, 10–12 ft high.

International opinion frowned on the construction of the barrier between Israel and its Palestinian neighbors. The United Nations General Assembly condemned it, and the International Court of Justice ruled that it was illegal according to international law. But the fence/wall spoke to Israeli frustration with ongoing terrorist attacks despite negotiations. Israel had also reached the limit of its tolerance for Palestinian President Yasser Arafat, who appeared to be failing to control the attacks coming from his territory – some even accused him of blatantly endorsing such attacks. Accordingly, the Israeli military temporarily placed Arafat under house arrest and for periods of time occupied portions of the West Bank, such as the Church of the Nativity in Bethlehem.

WHAT ABOUT THE DISSENTERS?

One of the fundamental problems in the process of Israeli-Arab negotiation is that the extant Palestinian government appears to be incapable of enforcing its own declarations of peace, even if it is truly willing to offer them. In other words, the government may negotiate as much as it likes, but it cannot deliver on a promise to Israeli leaders of safety and security. It only takes one dissenter dedicated to the cause to kill himself (or herself) and kill dozens of Israelis, too. And this applies to both sides of the conflict: in 1994, a disgruntled Israeli settler opened fire on morning prayers in a mosque and killed 29 Arab worshippers there. This problem of rejectionism – the refusal of some factions on both sides of the conflict to participate in the state-level peace process – is one of the most frustrating aspects of Israeli-Palestinian relations.

The Sharm el-Sheikh Memorandum on Implementation Timeline of Outstanding Commitments of Agreements Signed and the Resumption of Permanent Status Negotiations was a memorandum signed on September 4, 1999, by prime minister of Israel Ehud Barak and PLO Chairman Yasser Arafat at Sharm el-Sheikh in Egypt. The United States coordinated the process leading to the signing and was represented by Secretary of State Madeleine Albright. The memorandum was witnessed and co-signed by

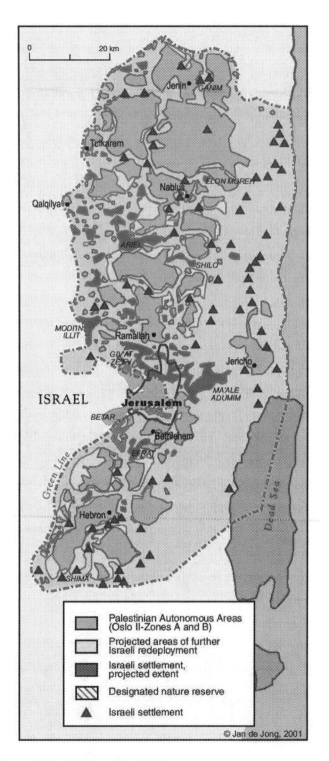

Map 16 Sharm el-Sheikh Proposals, 1999

Source: Abdul Hadi, Mahdi (ed.). The Palestine Question in Maps, 1878–2014, Jerusalem: Palestinian Academic Society for the Study of International Affairs (PASSIA), 2nd Updated and Revised Edition, August 2014. Map 33.

See reading #85, "Sharm el-Sheikh Memorandum and the Resumption of Permanent Status Negotiations (September 4, 1999)"

President Hosni Mubarak of Egypt and King Abdullah of Jordan. The purpose of the Memorandum was to implement the Interim Agreement on the West Bank and the Gaza Strip (known as "Oslo II") of September 1995 and to implement other agreements between the PLO and Israel since September 1993 that were not moving forward as quickly as parties might have liked.

See reading #86, "Protocol Concerning Safe Passage Between the West Bank and the Gaza Strip (October 5, 1999)"

The next month the Protocol Concerning Safe Passage was signed. This document was a result of the Wye River Memorandum and was intended to contribute to the normalization of life of the Palestinians living under occupation by making it easier to travel from the West Bank to Gaza – through Israel – and return. It was never implemented by Israel.

See reading #87, "Israel-Syria Draft Peace Agreement ["Clinton Plan"] (January 8, 2000)"

Momentum continued in the overall peace process. In January of 2000 a "working draft" of a Syria-Israel peace treaty was worked on Shepherdstown, West Virginia, by members of the Clinton administration, Syrian Foreign Minister Farouk al-Sharaa, and Israeli Prime Minister Ehud Barak. It was not a full-blown peace treaty but was more detailed than the Camp David-style framework from two decades earlier. The document showed a remarkable number of points that were not in dispute between the two parties and outlined the areas where work needed to be done, primarily focusing on the future border between the two countries. The conference ended without an agreement.

See reading #88, "Trilateral Statement on the Middle East Peace Summit at Camp David (July 25, 2000)"

See reading #89, "President William J. Clinton, Statement on the Middle East Peace Talks at Camp David (July 25, 2000)"

In July of 2000, U.S. President Bill Clinton invited Israeli Prime Minister Ehud Barak and Palestinian Authority Chairman Yasser Arafat to Camp David. Clinton hoped that in his final weeks in office he might be able to press the two leaders to reach a real and lasting agreement to move the parties forward toward a Middle East peace. The meetings were not successful. Although the final statement from the meeting made an effort to sound as though the meeting had been a success, leaders were disappointed.

See reading #90, "Taba Summit (January 21–27, 2001)"

Later that year, concerned parties worked on a meeting to be held at Taba, on the shore of the Gulf of Aqaba, to follow up on the Camp David meeting and to see if further progress could be made. These talks were reported by both sides to have come closer to reaching a final settlement than any previous talks, but Prime Minister Barak terminated the negotiations due to the upcoming Israeli elections. Barak lost those elections to Ariel Sharon, and the Sharon government was not interested in restarting the talks.

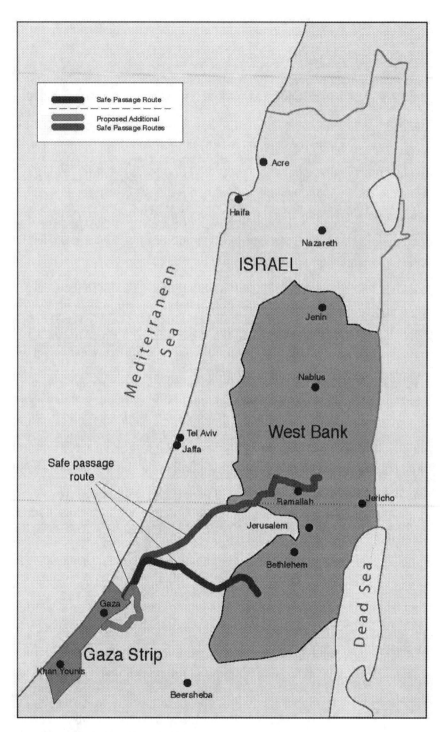

Map 17 Safe Passage Routes, 1999

Source: Abdul Hadi, Mahdi (ed.). The Palestine Question in Maps, 1878–2014, Jerusalem: Palestinian Academic Society for the Study of International Affairs (PASSIA), 2nd Updated and Revised Edition, August 2014. Map 34.

See reading #91, "Sharm El-Sheikh Fact-Finding Committee Final Report (April 30, 2001)"

On April 30, 2001, the Sharm el-Sheikh Fact-Finding Committee, chaired by former U.S. Senator George Mitchell, issued its final report on what could be done to break the cycle of violence that had developed between Israel and the Palestinians and how the Israeli-Palestinian negotiations might be reenergized, leading to a solution to the conflict. The report singled out Ariel Sharon's visit on September 28, 2000, to the Temple Mount area as significant in the start of the *al-Aqsa Intifada*, also known as the *Second Intifada*, and suggested that Israeli settlement building, Palestinian acts of terrorism, Israeli military responses to those acts, and injudicious public statements on both sides had all contributed to the cycle of violence in the Middle East.

See reading #92, "Israeli-Palestinian Ceasefire and Security Plan, Proposed by C.I.A. Director George Tenet (June 13, 2001)"

Another effort to break the increasing cycle of violence of the Second Intifada was led by Central Intelligence Agency Director George Tenet, who presented Israel and the Palestinian Authority (PA) with a cease-fire plan in June of 2001. The plan called on the PA to arrest terrorists and work to end violence directed at Israel and called on Israel to remove its military to pre-violence positions and scale back its responses to Palestinian attacks.

See reading #93, "U. N. Security Council Resolution 1397 (March 12, 2002)"

As the violence of the Second Intifada continued, even the United Nations got involved in trying to do something to slow the cycle. In March of 2002 the Security Council demanded an end to violence associated with the Second Intifada, calling for a two-state solution to the conflict. Before the adoption of the resolution the Secretary-General, Kofi Annan, called on Palestinians to end terrorism and suicide bombings and called on Israel to end its illegal occupation of Palestinian territory.

See reading #94, "The Arab Peace Initiative (March 28, 2002)"

The situation was not entirely bleak, however. At the end of March of 2002, Crown Prince Abdullah of Saudi Arabia proposed a new peace initiative at a conference in Beirut. This initiative called for a return to the 1967 borders of Israel and Palestine. In return, the Arab League promised to fully normalize relations with the State of Israel. This proposal was significant because it signified the willingness of the Saudi government to finally compromise. Although Israel rejected the substance of the proposal as a "nonstarter," this was the first time after nearly 40 years that Israel had had an offer of goodwill from one of its fiercest ideological opponents.

As Saudi Arabia and the Arab League moved toward normalization, or at least toward being willing to talk about normalization, the United States appeared to be moving away from its position as recurrent mediator. President George W. Bush did not share his predecessor's optimism that a solution to the Arab-Israeli quagmire was forthcoming; moreover, his attention was focused on the escalating situation in Iraq. In the summer of 2002, Bush gave a speech evidencing a hawkish frustration with Palestinians, calling the terrorist attacks "homicide bombings," in a somewhat redundant turn of phrase meant to emphasize their indefensibility.[7]

See reading #95, "President George W. Bush Speech (June 24, 2002)"

The next month a new proposal surfaced for an Israeli-Palestinian peace, the Nusseibeh-Ayalon Agreement, proposed by PLO Jerusalem representative Sari Nusseibeh and former Chief of Israel's Shin Bet (security services) Ami Ayalon. The Agreement was shorter than many of the preceding attempts at solutions and more direct: two states for two peoples, borders based on the June 4, 1967, lines, an open Jerusalem, a right for Palestinian refugees to return to the new State of Palestine, a demilitarized Palestine, and an end to the conflict.

See reading #96, "The Nusseibeh-Ayalon Agreement (July 27, 2002)"

Along with the United Nations, the European Union, and Russia, the United States proposed in 2003 what became known as the "Roadmap for Peace." The Roadmap reiterated the call for a two-state solution but designed the normalization process to be implemented based on the achievement of certain goals. That is, rather than imposing an external timeline on the peace process, the Roadmap called on Israel and the Palestinian Authority to meet certain benchmarks of goodwill and development, at which point the next phase of the plan would begin.

See reading #97, "Roadmap to a Solution of the Israeli-Palestinian Conflict (April 30, 2003)"

Chief among these benchmarks was the cessation of violence, including (and especially) suicide attacks by Palestinian insurgents. The enforcement and improvement of the Roadmap were not a priority of the Bush administration, unfortunately; President Bush did not even visit the Middle East as president until 2008, the last year of his eight-year term in office. The usefulness of the Roadmap has been questioned, as very few of its objectives have been met, although it still is referred to as an "active" agreement.

See reading # 98, "The Geneva Accord: A Model Israeli-Palestinian Peace Agreement (December 1, 2003)"

American attention soon turned almost exclusively to the new war in Iraq, which officially came to a head in 2003. On December 1, 2003, a "Model Israeli-Palestinian Peace Agreement" was launched by Yossi Beilin, a former Labor/Meretz Israeli cabinet member, and Yasser Abed Rabbo, a member of the P.L.O. Executive Committee, two long-time architects of Middle East peace initiatives. In a long and detailed document, they proposed details for a new permanent status agreement based upon U.N. Resolutions 242 and 338. Israeli Prime Minister Ariel Sharon did not support the initiative, and no further progress was made.

See reading #99, "Exchange of Letters Between Israeli Prime Minister Ariel Sharon and U.S. President George W. Bush (April 14, 2004)"

Although Prime Minister Sharon was the leader of the Likud party with a dubious record in Israeli-Palestinian peace initiatives (Sharon was an Israeli general in Lebanon in 1982 who was fired following the report of the Kahan Commission; see Reading 59), he recognized that there was no good future for Israel in the occupied Gaza territory. In 2004, Prime Minister Sharon announced that as a result of not having a partner with whom to negotiate – by which he meant that Israel could not trust negotiations with the Palestinians – Israel had decided to unilaterally withdraw entirely from Gaza, leaving it to govern itself, but surrounded and thoroughly locked down by its borders with Israel, with the goal of "reducing friction" with the Palestinian population. On April 14 he wrote to President George W. Bush describing his intentions. The Disengagement Plan from the Gaza Strip and Northern Samaria was announced that same week.

See reading #100, "The Disengagement Plan From the Gaza Strip and Northern Samaria (April 18, 2004)"

That same year, President Yasser Arafat died. Stepping into the leadership of the Palestinian Authority, new President Mahmoud Abbas promised to advance negotiations with Israel. Shortly thereafter, the militant groups still embroiled in the al-Aqsa Intifada agreed to a ceasefire with Israeli troops.

See reading #101, "The International Court of Justice Advisory Opinion Finds Israel's Construction of Wall 'Contrary to International Law' (July 9, 2004)"

In July of 2004, the International Court of Justice (I.C.J.) issued an advisory opinion dealing with the Israeli construction of a wall between Israeli territory and territories in the West Bank. The Court ruled that the construction of a wall was contrary to international law and said that Israel should cease further construction of a wall, dismantle what had already been built, and make reparations for all damage caused by the building of the wall. Israel rejected the I.C.J. ruling.

See reading #102, "Prime Minister Ariel Sharon's Address to the Knesset Prior to the Vote on the Disengagement Plan (October 25, 2004)

Sharon continued to press his unilateral Israeli disengagement from Gaza, and later in 2004 that move began. He offered an important explanation of his reasons for the move in a speech to the Knesset in October of 2004.

In 2006, Israel lashed out at Hezbollah on the Lebanese border after the kidnapping of several Israeli soldiers there. That conflict lasted barely a month but changed the political landscape significantly, as it was generally not considered a success for the Israeli forces. In fact, the Hezbollah

See reading #103, "U. N. Security Council: Resolution 1701 (August 11, 2006)"

insurgents in Lebanon gleefully claimed victory, and the missing soldiers were not returned. For the first time, it was fairly widely perceived that Israel had failed at a major military objective, rocking the government internally.

In the same year, Palestinians went to the polls and brought to life a dilemma beloved of political scientists: what happens when the winner of a democratic election is not fully a participant in the democratic process? Specifically, Palestinians elected an overwhelming majority government of Hamas members for their democratically chosen legislature. Long listed as a terrorist organization by the U.S. Department of State, the election of Hamas represented a move away from the peace process. Even the sitting government of the Palestinian Authority, long a Fatah stronghold, was horrified. The United States stopped all financial assistance to the Palestinian Authority, and politics in the West Bank and Gaza ground to a halt.

WHY HAMAS?[8]

In 2006, the Western world watched in surprise as Palestinians participated in a democratic election and a majority chose Hamas to represent them. Hamas denies the legitimacy of the state of Israel and has actively sought its destruction. Moreover, Western powers consider Hamas a violent terrorist organization. Why would a largely peaceful population of Palestinians choose Hamas to speak for them?

The answer, in a nutshell, is that Hamas is seen and understood differently by Palestinians than by Western observers. Palestinians looked at their previous government, run by Yasser Arafat's Fatah party, and saw corruption and inefficacy. They saw a frustrating lack of infrastructure, rampant graft, and an ongoing and apparently insolvable enmity with Israel. Like many populations chafing under an unpleasant status quo, Palestinians sought a political change.

By contrast, Hamas has been known among many Palestinians as a grassroots organization embracing reassuringly Muslim values. Hamas has successfully raised funds for hospitals, schools, and other infrastructure development in Palestine conducted completely outside government supervision. Perhaps most importantly,

> Hamas has served as a focus for identity politics in Palestine, returning pride and honor to Palestinians who feel humiliated by what has seemed to be decades of subjugation to everybody's will but their own.

Desperate to prevent the outbreak of civil war in the Palestinian Authority, Hamas and Fatah agreed to a Saudi proposal arranging a coalition government in Palestine. The two groups eyed each other warily until Hamas took over control of Gaza entirely in June of 2007. At that point, Fatah declared the unity government invalid and reclaimed unilateral control of the Palestinian Authority in the West Bank, and the United States resumed its financial assistance to the West Bank. Gaza remains under the control of Hamas – and without the benefit of international financial assistance – to this day.

In the final year of his eight years in office as President of the United States, George W. Bush sought to leave his mark on the Middle East peace process. On November 20, 1997, plans for an Annapolis Peace Conference were announced and nations were invited to come to Annapolis to discuss the peace process. The conference marked the first time both sides came to negotiations agreeing upon a two-state solution and was also noteworthy for the number of participants who appeared and the inclusion of many Arab nations that had not actively participated in the peace process before.

See reading #104, "Announcement of Annapolis Conference (November 20, 2007)"

The Annapolis Conference was held on November 27, 2007, at the United States Naval Academy in Annapolis, Maryland. The conference ended with the issuing of a joint statement from all parties. The objectives of the conference were an attempt to produce a substantive document on resolving the Israeli-Palestinian conflict along the lines of the earlier Roadmap For Peace (see Document # 97), with the eventual establishment of a Palestinian state. Although the goals were not met, the Conference was significant for the extraordinarily wide-ranging participation that it generated – countries that had never participated in the peace process attended the meeting. The final "Joint Understanding" that was issued left the door open for future progress.

See reading #105, "Joint Understanding on Negotiations (November 27, 2007)"

Ehud Olmert, who had succeeded Ariel Sharon as Israel's prime minister in January of 2006 when Sharon suffered a severe stroke, engaged in 36 negotiating sessions with Palestinian Authority President Mahmoud Abbas between 2006

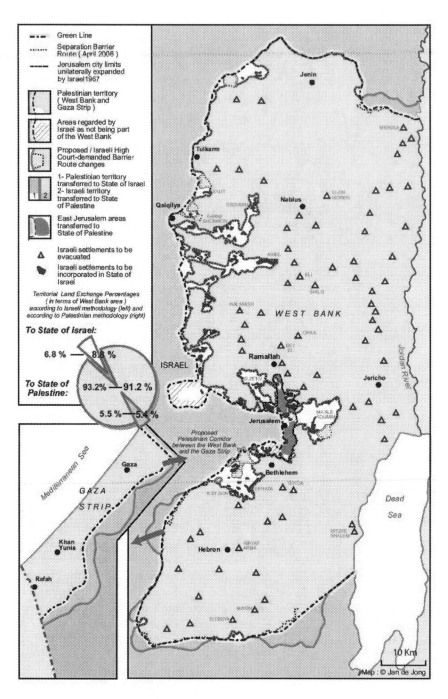

Map 18 The Olmert Maps, 2008

Source: Abdul Hadi, Mahdi (ed.). The Palestine Question in Maps, 1878–2014, Jerusalem: Palestinian Academic Society for the Study of International Affairs (PASSIA), 2nd Updated and Revised Edition, August 2014. Map 78.

See reading #106, "Confidential Summary of Israeli Prime Minister Olmert's 'Package' Offer to Palestine President Abu Mazen (August 31, 2008)"

and the end of September 2008, when Olmert resigned as prime minister. Olmert presented a comprehensive plan for peace to President Abbas at the end of August 2008, which went far beyond anything that had been offered by Israel to the Palestinians prior to that time, including ceding almost 94% of the West Bank for the establishment of a Palestinian state and agreeing to a land swap for the 6.4% of the West Bank that Israel would keep, a promise to evacuate many (but not all) Israeli settlements, maintain the contiguity of the Palestinian state and create a safe passage between the West Bank and Gaza, and many other important points. At the August meeting he showed Abbas a map which he considered a final offer, but Abbas rejected the deal.

While many wanted to continue to pursue progress toward peace, that did not appear to be high on the agenda for Hamas in Gaza, which continued to launch missiles at Israeli civilian targets in the south and center of Israel. In the final weeks of 2008, Israel launched a military initiative aimed at Hamas and its missiles. Because of the strategies of Hamas – specifically basing its missile-launching activity in densely populated civilian areas – the Israeli military action had significant consequences for the Gaza civilian population. Indeed, Israel received a great deal of criticism for disproportionate military response to Hamas's missiles. Many external actors tried to negotiate a ceasefire in the conflict, most notably including the United States and Egypt, and in January of 2009 Israeli Prime Minister Ehud Olmert announced a unilateral Israeli ceasefire when Hamas would not agree to a negotiated ceasefire.

See reading #107, "Israeli Prime Minister Ehud Olmert Declares Unilateral Ceasefire in Gaza (January 17, 2009)"

The external expectations of Israel were changing, as was the external setting within which Israel operated. In November of 2008 Barack Obama was elected as President of the United States, and many in Israel were concerned about whether he would be as strong a supporter of Israel as his predecessors. Indeed, in June of 2009 Obama delivered a much-anticipated speech at Cairo University in which he talked about a "new beginning" for American foreign policy in the Middle East and with the Muslim world. While his speech contained phrases extolling America's long-standing support of Israel and pledging future close relations, Obama's comments about America and the Muslim world concerned many in Israel and the United States as signalling a radical shift in American policy in the Middle East, and Obama never enjoyed the level of support in Israel that his predecessors had experienced.

See reading #108, "Remarks by President Barack Obama at Cairo University 'On a New Beginning' (June 4, 2009)"

See reading #109, "United Nations: Human Rights in Palestine and Other Occupied Arab Territories (September 25, 2009)"

In 2009 the United Nations Human Rights Council authorized a fact-finding mission on the Gaza conflict that took place between December 27, 2008, and January 18, 2009, specifically focused on whether international law was respected by both the Israeli side and the Hamas side and whether "disproportionate attacks in violation of customary international law" had been launched by Israel. Israel refused to cooperate with the inquiry and anticipated a very critical report to be issued; it was not disappointed. The report – known as the "Goldstone Report," named after its chair, Justice Richard Goldstone of South Africa – was highly critical of Israel and suggested that "crimes against humanity" may, indeed, have taken place.

See reading #110, "Secretary of State Hillary Rodham Clinton's Remarks to the American Task Force on Palestine (October 20, 2010)"

The Obama administration pressed Israel harder than was traditional for American administrations. Although it continued to express a "rock-solid and unwavering" commitment to Israel, it also pressed more vigorously than had been done in the past to a two-state solution to Israel-Palestine tensions. An example of that position was offered by Secretary of State Hillary Rodham Clinton in her "Remarks to the American Task Force on Palestine" in October of 2010.

See reading #111, "Understanding Regarding Ceasefire in Gaza Strip (November 21, 2012)"

Gaza continued to be a flash point in the tensions in the region, and in 2012 again open military action developed. Israel's "Operation Pillar of Defense" was focused on Hamas rockets that were being launched against civilian targets in Israel and also tunnels that were being dug by Hamas so that Hamas fighters could sneak into Israel and inflict damage on civilian communities.

Two years later the conflict flared up again, and "Operation Protective Edge" was launched by Israel against Gaza. Because of the Goldstone Report in 2009 and the international condemnation that it generated for the "disproportionate" Israeli response at the time, Israel was extremely

See reading #112, "The 2014 Gaza Conflict: Factual and Legal Aspects: Executive Summary (May, 2015)"

sensitive about documenting its actions in 2014, documenting what provoked the escalation in violence, its limited objectives, and that its military action was, indeed, "proportional." At the conclusion of the fighting, the Israeli Ministry of Foreign Affairs released a report on "Factual and Legal Aspects" of the 2014 Gaza conflict.

Although the rockets from Gaza continued to be concerning for the Israeli government, more worrying was a multinational initiative to negotiate with Iran about its nuclear capability. Israel has taken the position that it cannot tolerate the "existential" threat of one of its Middle Eastern neighbors developing a nuclear weapon capability; indeed, in June of 1981 a surprise Israeli air strike was carried out that destroyed an Iraqi nuclear reactor. Israel received a great deal of international criticism for its unilateral action at that time, although many suggested that Western European nations and the United States were privately happy with the outcome. Through 2014 and 2015 Israel became increasingly concerned about Western responses to Iran's developing nuclear program, and on more than one occasion Western analysts wondered whether Israel would act unilaterally against Iran in 2015 as it had acted against Iraq in 1981.

See reading #113, "Israeli Foreign Ministry: The Nuclear Deal With Iran: Questions and Answers (July 27, 2015)"

In 2015 a nuclear deal was reached between Iran and a number of Western powers, including the United States, Russia, France, Germany, and Britain. Israel was critical of Iran being permitted to develop *any* nuclear capability and suggested that "peaceful" energy development capacity in Iran could be secretly developed to be an existential threat against Israel. The Israeli government lobbied vigorously with the Western governments not to approve the agreement.

See reading #114, "Remarks by President Barack Obama on the Iran Nuclear Deal (August 5, 2015)"

While the Israeli Foreign Ministry was very critical of the agreement, Western leaders worked hard to explain why the deal was a good idea. Most notably, this group included U.S. President Barack Obama, who argued that both in terms of details and in terms of its long-term effects, the treaty should be supported. At the end of the day, the agreement was ratified, and it came into operation. It is worth noting that Iran has honored all dimensions of the agreement thus far.

The United States has not been the only actor from outside of the Middle East to work toward peace in the Middle East. Most recently we have seen several French initiatives to support peace negotiations. In June of 2016, the French Foreign Ministry sponsored a conference to work toward a resolution of the Israeli-Palestinian conflict, based upon Resolutions 242 and 338. The conference did not produce any breakthrough understandings but did indicate to those involved that the issue was not going away and that international actors were aware of the lack of progress toward peace being made. It also served as an opportunity for Western powers to again articulate their opposition to Israeli settlements in the West Bank and to continue to articulate their support for a two-state solution to the tensions there.

See reading #115, "Report of the Middle East Quartet (July 1, 2016)"

In its annual report in June of 2016, the Middle East Quartet – a group that first appeared in the Roadmap in 2003 consisting of the United States, Russia, Europe, and the United Nations – observed that current trends were threatening the viability of what was referred to as a "two-state solution" in the Palestine-Israeli conflict. Major threats continued to include security for Israel on one side and Israeli settlements in the West Bank on the other side. The Quartet indicated that it would continue to work toward a solution based upon Security Council Resolutions 242 (1967) and 338 (1973).

The French tried again in the early days of 2017 to start a new sense of momentum toward peace, but again nothing came of the meeting. Indeed, Israel refused to attend the Jan-

See reading #116, "Paris Conference Joint Communique (January 15, 2017)"

uary 2017 meeting on the grounds that nothing had changed and that there was no constructive partner with which to negotiate. The participants at the conference, including the French and the Palestinians, agreed to continue to do what they could to keep a sense of energy alive.

As the year 2017 came to an end, the question of progress toward peace in the Middle East was again on discussion agendas of world leaders when U.S. President Donald Trump did what no American president had done in the history of the State of Israel: declared American support for Jerusalem as Israel's capital and announced that the United States would begin the process of moving its embassy to Jerusalem from Tel Aviv. Trump had been widely counselled not to follow through with his campaign promise to recognize Jerusalem as Israel's capital and to move the U.S. Embassy from Tel Aviv to Jerusalem, but despite widespread criticism, he followed through with his intention. The decision sparked immediate protests in Jerusalem and throughout the Middle East.

See reading #117, "Trump Administration Recognition of Jerusalem as the Capital of Israel (December 6, 2017)"

Leaders from the Middle East and Europe – including leaders of all major American allies in Europe – criticized the announcement and said that the decision showed a lack of knowledge about security issues and would be harmful to the peace process. That did not sway Trump's decision, and in his statement he repeated his view that he was simply recognizing the obvious and that this was a step that would advance the peace process and work toward a lasting agreement in the region.

See reading #118, "Peace to Prosperity ["Trump Peace Plan"] Overview (January 28, 2020)"

President Trump's administrative team continued to press for progress on a Middle East peace plan, and on January 28, 2020, it released *Peace to Prosperity, A Vision to*

Improve the Lives of the Palestinian and Israeli People. The plan, which was very focused on business, outside investment, and economic development, also included support for Israeli settlement expansion and proposed creating a Palestinian state that many felt was not a viable state but rather a collection of disconnected Palestinian enclaves surrounded by Israel. The plan was accepted by Israel but was rejected by the Palestinians and the Arab League.

See reading #119, "Joint Statement of the United States, the State of Israel, and the United Arab Emirates (August 13, 2020)"

Later that year, Trump's final year in the White House, a major breakthrough came when the United States, Israel, and the United Arab Emirates announced in August that Israel and the UAE had "agreed to the full normalization of relations" and that a deal to be known as *The Abraham Accords* would be presented a month later. Israel and the UAE soon signed bilateral agreements relating to investment, tourism, direct flights, security, telecommunications, and other issues and agreed to open embassies and exchange ambassadors.

See reading #120, "The Abraham Accords Declaration (September 15, 2020)"

The Palestinians denounced the agreement, but the Arab League did not; the Arab League even denied the Palestinian Authority's request to hold an emergency meeting to discuss the new Accords.

* * *

In May of 2023, Israel will have celebrated the 75th anniversary of its independence. Mere miles away, hundreds of thousands of Palestinians and their sympathizers marked the 75th anniversary of the Naqba "catastrophe." Gaza continued to labor under the burden of closed borders, no income, and no infrastructure, while the Palestinian Authority dealt with its own issues of poor organization, corruption, and Israeli interference. Israeli citizens continued to live with the constant threat of random shelling from Arab territories and the ongoing threats of complete annihilation from bombastic leaders of neighboring countries.

This introductory chapter has barely touched upon the tensions within Israel itself, where secular citizens frequently butt heads with religious elements to create a contradictory, frustrating foreign policy. It is difficult to know how to end a survey examination of the history of Israel's relations with its neighbors. In a situation that changes as rapidly and as unpredictably as this one, any predictions or assessments of the future will inevitably sound dated and inappropriate before very long.

In the end, the Israeli-Arab conflict is the story of two peoples who are not so very different. It is an indisputable fact that both share roots in the dusty lands both consider holy. Until relatively recently, neither had governed themselves as a modern state. It is probably also true that each group has realized the futility of trying to outlast the other. Whether the acknowledgement of this futility will lead to a conclusion with which both can live is a matter only time can resolve.

Ye People of the Scripture! Why will ye argue about Abraham, when the Torah and the Gospel were not revealed till after him?
(Holy Qur'an, Pickthal translation, 003.065)

Notes

1. It is important to explain the terms used to refer to the various parties in this conflict. The term "Arab," which was originally a geography-based label referring to someone from Arabia, refers to an ethnic group of the Middle East. Arabs are largely Muslim, but many are Christian. A very small number of Arabs are, in fact, Jews. That said, the term "Jew" generally refers to a non-Arab person of Middle Eastern descent, who may be religious (Jewish) or secular. The term "Israeli" refers to a citizen of the state of Israel after 1948. It is worth noting that Israelis may be Arabs, although they are usually Jews. Many Israelis are not orthodox Jews, though the state itself is nominally a Jewish state.
2. This is an important distinction. A state, as the term is used here, is a political entity with political sovereignty – the ability to make public policy on its own. A homeland, on the other hand, is a geographical region within a state that does not have sovereignty or the ability to make public policy on its own without the permission or acquiescence of another state.
3. Ha'am, Ahad (1897), translated by Leon Simon, 1912, "The Jewish State and Jewish Problem," Jewish Virtual Library, Jewish Publication Society of America. Found online at www.jewish virtuallibrary.org/quot-the-jewish-state-and-jewish-problem-quot-ahad-ha-am.
4. The Israeli preference is to refer to this body of water as "The Gulf of Eilat." As general international consensus favors "Gulf of Aqaba," that is the term used here.
5. https://tinyurl.com/2zfmexzd.
6. In accordance with the outcome of that arbitration, Taba was returned to Egypt in 1989.
7. www.nationmaster.com/encyclopedia/Suicide-bombers.
8. www.counterpunch.org/gordon02072006.html.

Part II

From Herzl (1896) to Recognition as a State (1949)

1 Theodor Herzl, *The Jewish State* (1896)

I. Introduction

. . .

The world possesses slaves of extraordinary capacity for work, whose appearance has been fatal to the production of handmade goods: these slaves are the machines. . . . Only those who are ignorant of the conditions of Jews in many countries of Eastern Europe would venture to assert that Jews are either unfit or unwilling to perform manual labor.

But I do not wish to take up the cudgels for the Jews in this pamphlet. It would be useless. Everything rational and everything sentimental that can possibly be said in their defense has been said already . . .

This century has given the world a wonderful renaissance by means of its technical achievements; but at the same time its miraculous improvements have not been employed in the service of humanity. Distance has ceased to be an obstacle, yet we complain of insufficient space. Our great steamships carry us swiftly and surely over hitherto unvisited seas. Our railways carry us safely into a mountain-world hitherto tremblingly scaled on foot. Events occurring in countries undiscovered when Europe confined the Jews in Ghettos are known to us in the course of an hour. Hence the misery of the Jews is an anachronism – not because there was a period of enlightenment 100 years ago, for that enlightenment reached in reality only the choicest spirits.

I believe that electric light was not invented for the purpose of illuminating the drawing-rooms of a few snobs, but rather for the purpose of throwing light on some of the dark problems of humanity. One of these problems, and not the least of them, is the Jewish question. In solving it we are working not only for ourselves, but also for many other over-burdened and oppressed beings.

The Jewish question still exists. It would be foolish to deny it. It is a remnant of the Middle Ages, which civilized nations do not even yet seem able to shake off, try as they will. They certainly showed a generous desire to do so when they emancipated us. The Jewish question exists wherever Jews live in perceptible numbers. Where it does not exist, it is carried by Jews in the course of their migrations. We naturally move to those places where we are not persecuted, and there our presence produces persecution. This is the

DOI: 10.4324/9781003348948-4

case in every country, and will remain so, even in those highly civilized – for instance, France – until the Jewish question finds a solution on a political basis. The unfortunate Jews are now carrying the seeds of Anti-Semitism into England; they have already introduced it into America.

. . .

We are a people – one people.

We have honestly endeavored everywhere to merge ourselves in the social life of surrounding communities and to preserve the faith of our fathers. We are not permitted to do so. In vain are we loyal patriots, our loyalty in some places running to extremes; in vain do we make the same sacrifices of life and property as our fellow-citizens; in vain do we strive to increase the fame of our native land in science and art, or her wealth by trade and commerce. In countries where we have lived for centuries we are still cried down as strangers, and often by those whose ancestors were not yet domiciled in the land where Jews had already had experience of suffering. The majority may decide which are the strangers; for this, as indeed every point which arises in the relations between nations, is a question of might. I do not here surrender any portion of our prescriptive right, when I make this statement merely in my own name as an individual. In the world as it now is and for an indefinite period will probably remain, might precedes right. It is useless, therefore, for us to be loyal patriots, as were the Huguenots who were forced to emigrate. If we could only be left in peace . . .

But I think we shall not be left in peace.

. . .

For old prejudices against us still lie deep in the hearts of the people. He who would have proofs of this need only listen to the people where they speak with frankness and simplicity: proverb and fairy-tale are both Anti-Semitic. A nation is everywhere a great child, which can certainly be educated; but its education would, even in most favorable circumstances, occupy such a vast amount of time that we could, as already mentioned, remove our own difficulties by other means long before the process was accomplished.

Assimilation, by which I understood not only external conformity in dress, habits, customs, and language, but also identity of feeling and manner – assimilation of Jews could be effected only by intermarriage. But the need for mixed marriages would have to be felt by the majority; their mere recognition by law would certainly not suffice.

. . .

Those who really wished to see the Jews disappear through intermixture with other nations can only hope to see it come about in one way. The Jews must previously acquire economic power sufficiently great to overcome the old social prejudice against them. . . . A previous acquisition of power could be synonymous with that economic supremacy which Jews are already erroneously declared to possess. . . .

. . .

No human being is wealthy or powerful enough to transplant a nation from one habitation to another. An idea alone can achieve that and this idea of a State may have the requisite power to do so. The Jews have dreamt this kingly dream all through the long nights of their history. "Next year in Jerusalem" is our old phrase. It is now a question of showing that the dream can be converted into a living reality.

. . .

II. The Jewish Question

No one can deny the gravity of the situation of the Jews. Wherever they live in perceptible numbers, they are more or less persecuted. Their equality before the law, granted by statute, has become practically a dead letter. They are debarred from filling even moderately high positions, either in the army or in any public or private capacity. And attempts are made to thrust them out of business also: "Don't buy from Jews!"

. . .

I do not intend to arouse sympathetic emotions on our behalf. That would be foolish, futile, and undignified proceeding. I shall content myself with putting the following questions to the Jews: Is it not true that, in countries where we live in perceptible numbers, the position of Jewish lawyers, doctors, technicians, teachers, and employees of all descriptions becomes daily more intolerable? Is it not true, that the Jewish middle classes are seriously threatened? Is it not true, that the passions of the mob are incited against our wealthy people? Is it not true, that our poor endure greater sufferings than any other proletariat? I think that this external pressure makes itself felt everywhere. In our economically upper classes it causes discomfort, in our middle classes continual and grave anxieties, in our lower classes absolute despair.

Everything tends, in fact, to one and the same conclusion, which is clearly enunciated in that classic Berlin phrase: "Juden Raus" (Out with the Jews!).

I shall now put the Question in the briefest possible form: Are we to "get out" now, and where to?

Or, may we yet remain? And, how long?

Let us first settle the point of staying where we are . . . I say that we cannot hope for a change in the current of feeling. And why not? Even if we were as near to the hearts of princes as are their other subjects, they could not protect us. They would only feel popular hatred by showing us too much favor. By "too much," I really mean less than is claimed as a right by every ordinary citizen, or by every race. The nations in whose midst Jews live are all either covertly or openly Anti-Semitic.

The common people have not, and indeed cannot have, any historic comprehension. They do not know that the sins of the Middle Ages are now being visited on the nations of Europe. We are what the Ghetto made us. We have attained pre-eminence in finance, because medieval conditions drove us to it. . . . We are again being forced into finance, now it is the stock exchange, by being kept out of other branches of economic activity. Being on the stock exchange, we are consequently exposed afresh to contempt. . . . Educated Jews without means are now rapidly becoming Socialists. Hence we are certain to suffer very severely in the struggle between classes, because we stand in the most exposed position in the camps of both Socialists and capitalists.

. . .

We are one people – our enemies have made us one without our consent, as repeatedly happens in history. Distress binds us together, and, thus united, we suddenly discover our strength. Yes, we are strong enough to form a State, and, indeed, a model State. We possess all human and material resources necessary for the purpose.

This is therefore the appropriate place to give an account of what has been somewhat roughly termed our "human material." But it would not be appreciated till the broad lines of the plan, on which everything depends, has first been marked out.

THE PLAN

The whole plan is in its essence perfectly simple, as it must necessarily be if it is to come within the comprehension of all.

Let the sovereignty be granted us over a portion of the globe large enough to satisfy the rightful requirements of a nation; the rest we shall manage for ourselves.

The creation of a new State is neither ridiculous nor impossible. We have in our day witnessed the process in connection with nations which were not largely members of the middle class, but poorer, less educated, and consequently weaker than ourselves. The Governments of all countries scourged by Anti-Semitism will be keenly interested in assisting us to obtain the sovereignty we want.

The plan, simple in design, but complicated in execution, will be carried out by two agencies: The Society of Jews and the Jewish Company.

The Society of Jews will do the preparatory work in the domains of science and politics, which the Jewish Company will afterwards apply practically.

The Jewish Company will be the liquidating agent of the business interests of departing Jews and will organize commerce and trade in the new country.

We must not imagine the departure of the Jews to be a sudden one. It will be gradual, continuous, and will cover many decades. The poorest will go first to cultivate the soil. In accordance with a preconceived plan, they will construct roads, bridges, railways, and telegraph installations; regulate rivers; and build their own dwellings; their labor will create trade, trade will create markets, and markets will attract new settlers, for every man will go voluntarily, at his own expense and his own risk. The labor expended on the land will enhance its value, and the Jews will soon perceive that a new and permanent sphere of operation is opening here for that spirit of enterprise which has heretofore met only with hatred and obloquy.

If we wish to found a State today, we shall not do it in the way which would have been the only possible one a thousand years ago. It is foolish to revert to old stages of civilization, as many Zionists would like to do. Supposing, for example, we were obliged to clear a country of wild beasts, we should not set about the task in the fashion of Europeans of the fifth century. We should not take spear and lance and go out singly in pursuit of bears; we would organize a large and active hunting party, drive the animals together, and throw a melinite bomb into their midst.

. . .

The emigrants standing lowest in the economic scale will be slowly followed by those of a higher grade. Those who at this moment are living in despair will go first. They will be led by the mediocre intellects which we produce so superabundantly and which are persecuted everywhere.

This pamphlet will open a general discussion on the Jewish Question, but that does not mean that there will be any voting on it. Such a result would ruin the cause from the outset, and dissidents must remember that allegiance or opposition is entirely voluntary. He who will not come with us should remain behind.

Let all who are willing to join us, fall in behind our banner, and fight for our cause with voice and pen and deed.

. . .

Should the Powers declare themselves willing to admit our sovereignty over a neutral piece of land, then the Society will enter into negotiations for the possession of this land. Here two territories come under consideration, Palestine and Argentine. In both countries important experiments in colonization have been made, though on the mistaken principle of a gradual infiltration of Jews. An infiltration is bound to end badly. It continues till the inevitable moment when the native population feels itself threatened and forces the Government to stop a further influx of Jews. Immigration is consequently futile unless we have the sovereign right to continue such immigration.

. . .

PALESTINE OR ARGENTINE?

Shall we choose Palestine or Argentine? We shall take what is given us, and what is selected by Jewish public opinion. The Society will determine both these points.

Argentine is one of the most fertile countries in the world, extends over a vast area, has a sparse population and a mild climate. The Argentine Republic would derive considerable profit from the cession of a portion of its territory to us. . . .

Palestine is our ever-memorable historic home. The very name of Palestine would attract our people with a force of marvelous potency. If His Majesty the Sultan were to give us Palestine, we could in return undertake to regulate the whole finances of Turkey. We should there form a portion of a rampart of Europe against Asia, an outpost of civilization as opposed to barbarism. We should as a neutral State remain in contact with all Europe, which would have to guarantee our existence. The sanctuaries of Christendom would be safe-guarded by assigning to them an extra-territorial status such as is well-known to the law of nations. . . .

. . .

III. The Jewish Company

OUTLINES

The Jewish Company is partly modeled on the lines of a great land-acquisition company. It might be called a Jewish Chartered Company, though it cannot exercise sovereign power and has other than purely colonial tasks.

The Jewish Company will be founded as a joint stock company subject to English jurisdiction, framed according to English laws, and under the protec-tion of England. Its principal center will be London. . . .

The Jewish Company is an organization with a transitional character. It is strictly a business undertaking and must be carefully distinguished from the Society of Jews.

The Jewish Company will first of all convert into cash all vested inter-ests left by departing Jews. The method adopted will prevent the occurrences of crises, secure every man's property, and facilitate that inner migration of Christian citizens which has already been indicated.

. . .

IV. Local Groups

OUR TRANSMIGRATION

Previous chapters explained only how the emigration scheme might be car-ried out without creating any economic disturbance. . . . There are old cus-toms, old memories that attach us to our homes. We have cradles, we have graves, and we alone know how Jewish hearts cling to the graves. Our cradles we shall carry with us – they bold our future, rosy and smiling. Our beloved graves we must abandon – and I think this abandonment will cost us more than any other sacrifice. But it must be so.

Economic distress, political pressure, and social obloquy have already driven us from our homes and from our graves. We Jews are even now con-stantly shifting from place to place, a strong current actually carrying us westward over the sea to the United States, where our presence is also not desired. And where will our presence be desired, so long as we are a homeless nation?

But we shall give a home to our people. And we shall give it, not by dragging them ruthlessly out of their sustaining soil, but rather by transplanting them carefully to a better ground. Just as we wish to create new political and economic relations, so we shall preserve as sacred all of the past that is dear to our people's hearts.

Hence a few suggestions must suffice, as this part of my scheme will most probably be condemned as visionary. Yet even this is possible and real, though it now appears to be something vague and aimless. Organization will make of it something rational.

. . .

V. Society of Jews and Jewish State

. . .

We know and see for ourselves that States still continue to be created. Colonies secede from the mother country. . . . It is true that the Jewish State is conceived as a peculiarly modern structure on unspecified territory. But a State is formed, not by pieces of land, but rather by a number of men united under sovereign rule. The people is the subjective, land the objective foundation of a State, and the subjective basis is the more important of the two. One sovereignty, for example, which has no objective basis at all, is perhaps the most respected one in the world. I refer to the sovereignty of the Pope.

. . .

The Society will have scientific and political tasks, for the founding of a Jewish State, as I conceive it, presupposes the application of scientific methods. We cannot journey out of Egypt today in the primitive fashion of ancient times. We shall previously obtain an accurate account of our number and strength. . . .

. . .

Externally, the Society will attempt, as I explained before in the general part, to be acknowledged as a State-forming power. The free assent of many Jews will confer on it the requisite authority in its relations with Governments.

Internally, that is to say, in its relation with the Jewish people, the Society will create all the first indispensable institutions; it will be the nucleus out of which the public institutions of the Jewish State will later on be developed.

Our first object is, as I said before, supremacy, assured to us by international law, over a portion of the globe sufficiently large to satisfy our just requirements.

What is the next step?

THE OCCUPATION OF THE LAND

. . . this modern Jewish migration must proceed in accordance with scientific principles.

Not more than 40 years ago gold-digging was carried on in an extraordinarily primitive fashion. What adventurous days were those in California! A report brought desperados together from every quarter of the earth; they stole pieces of land, robbed each other of gold, and finally gambled it away, as robbers do.

But today! What is gold-digging like in the Transvaal today? Adventurous vagabonds are not there; sedate geologists and engineers alone are on the spot to regulate its gold industry, and to employ ingenious machinery in separating the ore from surrounding rock. Little is left to chance now.

Thus we must investigate and take possession of the new Jewish country by means of every modern expedient.

As soon as we have secured the land, we shall send over a ship, having on board the representatives of the Society, of the Company, and of the local groups, who will enter into possession at once.

These men will have three tasks to perform: (1) an accurate, scientific investigation of all natural resources of the country; (2) the organization of a strictly centralized administration; (3) the distribution of land. These tasks intersect one another and will all be carried out in conformity with the now familiar object in view.

One thing remains to be explained – namely, how the occupation of land according to local groups is to take place.

In America the occupation of newly opened territory is set about in naive fashion. The settlers assemble on the frontier, and at the appointed time make a simultaneous and violent rush for their portions.

We shall not proceed thus to the new land of the Jews. The lots in provinces and towns will be sold by auction, and paid for, not in money, but in work. The general plan will have settled on streets, bridges, waterworks, etc., necessary for traffic. These will be united into provinces. Within these provinces sites for towns will be similarly sold by auction. The local groups will pledge themselves to carry the business property through and will cover the cost by means of self-imposed assessments. The Society will be in a position to judge whether the local groups are not venturing on sacrifices too great for their means. The large communities will receive large sites for their activity. Great sacrifices will thus be rewarded by the establishment of universities, technical schools, academies, research institutes, etc., and these Government institutes, which do not have to be concentrated in the capital, will be distributed over the country.

. . .

CONSTITUTION

One of the great commissions which the Society will have to appoint will be the council of State jurists. These must formulate the best, that is, the best modern constitution possible. I believe that a good constitution should be of moderately elastic nature. In another work I have explained in detail what forms of government I hold to be the best. I think a democratic monarchy and an aristocratic republic are the finest forms of a State, because in them the form of State and the principle of government are opposed to each other, and thus preserve a true balance of power. . . .

Politics must take shape in the upper strata and work downwards. But no member of the Jewish State will be oppressed, every man will be able and will wish to rise in it. Thus a great upward tendency will pass through our people; every individual by trying to raise himself, raising also the whole body of citizens. The ascent will take a normal form, useful to the State and serviceable to the National Idea. . . .

LANGUAGE

It might be suggested that our want of a common current language would present difficulties. We cannot converse with one another in Hebrew. Who amongst us has a sufficient acquaintance with Hebrew to ask for a railway ticket in that language! Such a thing cannot be done. Yet the difficulty is very easily circumvented. Every man can preserve the language in which his thoughts are at home. Switzerland affords a conclusive proof of the possibility of a federation of tongues. We shall remain in the new country what we now are here, and we shall never cease to cherish with sadness the memory of the native land out of which we have been driven.

We shall give up using those miserable stunted jargons, those Ghetto languages which we still employ, for these were the stealthy tongues of prisoners. Our national teachers will give due attention to this matter; and the language which proves itself to be of greatest utility for general intercourse will be adopted without compulsion as our national tongue. Our community of race is peculiar and unique, for we are bound together only by the faith of our fathers.

THEOCRACY

Shall we end by having a theocracy? No, indeed. Faith unites us, knowledge gives us freedom. . . . We shall keep our priests within the confines of their temples in the same way as we shall keep our professional army within the confines of their barracks. . . .

Every man will be as free and undisturbed in his faith or his disbelief as he is in his nationality. And if it should occur that men of other creeds and different nationalities come to live amongst us, we should accord them honorable protection and equality before the law. We have learnt toleration in Europe. This is not sarcastically said; for the Anti-Semitism of today could only in a very few places be taken for old religious intolerance. It is for the most part a movement among civilized nations by which they try to chase away the spectres of their own past.

. . .

THE FLAG

We have no flag, and we need one. If we desire to lead many men, we must raise a symbol above their heads.

I would suggest a white flag, with seven golden stars. The white field symbolizes our pure new life; the stars are the seven golden hours of our working-day. For we shall march into the Promised Land carrying the badge of honor.

. . .

VI. Conclusion

OUTLINES

How much has been left unexplained, how many defects, how many harmful superficialities, and how many useless repetitions in this pamphlet, which I have thought over so long and so often revised!

But a fair-minded reader, who has sufficient understanding to grasp the spirit of my words, will not be repelled by these defects. He will rather be roused thereby to cooperate with his intelligence and energy in a work which is not one man's task alone, and to improve it.

Have I not explained obvious things and overlooked important objections?

I have tried to meet certain objections; but I know that many more will be made, based on high grounds and low. To the first class of objections belongs the remark that the Jews are not the only people in the world who are in a condition of distress. Here I would reply that we may as well begin by removing a little of this misery, even if it should at first be no more than our own.

. . . Universal brotherhood is not even a beautiful dream. Antagonism is essential to man's greatest efforts. But the Jews, once settled in their own State, would probably have no more enemies. As for those who remain behind, since prosperity enfeebles and causes them to diminish, they would soon disappear altogether. I think the Jews will always have sufficient enemies, such as every nation has. But once fixed in their own land, it will no longer be possible for them to scatter all over the world. The diaspora cannot be reborn, unless the civilization of the whole earth should collapse; and such a consummation could be feared by none but foolish men. . . .

Here it is, fellow Jews! Neither fable nor deception! Every man may test its reality for himself, for every man will carry over with him a portion of the Promised Land – one in his head, another in his arms, another in his acquired possessions.

Now, all this may appear to be an interminably long affair. Even in the most favorable circumstances, many years might elapse before the commencement of the foundation of the State. In the meantime, Jews in a thousand different places would suffer insults, mortifications, abuse, blows, depredation, and death. No; if we only begin to carry out the plans, Anti-Semitism would stop at once and for ever. For it is the conclusion of peace.

The news of the formation of our Jewish Company will be carried in a single day to the remotest ends of the earth by the lightning speed of our telegraph wires. . . .

Prayers will be offered up for the success of our work in temples and in churches also; for it will bring relief from an old burden, which all have suffered.

But we must first bring enlightenment to men's minds. The idea must make its way into the most distant, miserable holes where our people dwell. They will awaken from gloomy brooding, for into their lives will come a new significance. Every man need think only of himself, and the movement will assume vast proportions.

And what glory awaits those who fight unselfishly for the cause!

Therefore I believe that a wondrous generation of Jews will spring into existence. The Maccabeans will rise again.

Let me repeat once more my opening words: The Jews who wish for a State will have it. We shall live at last as free men on our own soil and die peacefully in our own homes.

The world will be freed by our liberty, enriched by our wealth, magnified by our greatness.

And whatever we attempt there to accomplish for our own welfare will react powerfully and beneficially for the good of humanity.

2 Ahad Ha'am, The Jewish State and the Jewish Problem (1897)

Some months have passed since the Zionist Congress, but its echoes are still heard in daily life and in the press. In daily life the echoes take the form of meetings small and big, local and central. . . . There has been a revolution in their world, and to emphasise it they give a new name to the cause: it is no longer "Love of Zion" (*Chibbath Zion*), but "Zionism" (*Zioniyuth*). Nay, the more careful among them, determined to leave no loop-hole for error, even keep the European form of the name ("Zionismus") – thus announcing to all and sundry that they are not talking about anything so antiquated as *Chibbath Zion*, but about a new, up-to-date movement, which comes, like its name, from the West, where people do not use Hebrew.

In the press all these meetings, with their addresses, motions and resolutions, appear over again in the guise of articles – articles written in a vein of enthusiasm and triumph. . . . And the Congress itself still produces a literature of its own. Pamphlets specially devoted to its praises appear in several languages. . . . It searches the press of every nation and every land, and wherever it finds a favourable mention of the Congress, even in some insignificant journal published in the language of one of the smaller European nationalities, it immediately gives a summary of the article, with much jubilation. Only one small nation's language has thus far not been honoured with such attention, though its journals too have lavished praise on the Congress: I mean Hebrew.

In short, the universal note is one of rejoicing; and it is therefore small wonder that in the midst of this general harmony my little Note on the Congress sounded discordant and aroused the most violent displeasure in many quarters. . . . Consequently I have now to perform the hard and ungrateful task of writing a commentary on myself, and expressing my views on the matter in hand with greater explicitness.

Nordau's address on the general condition of the Jews was a sort of introduction to the business of the Congress. . . . In Eastern countries their trouble is material: they have a constant struggle to satisfy the most elementary physical needs, to win a crust of bread and a breath of air – things which are denied them because they are Jews. In the West, in lands of emancipation, their material condition is not particularly bad, but the moral trouble is serious. They want to take full advantage of their rights, and cannot; they long

DOI: 10.4324/9781003348948-5

to become attached to the people of the country, and to take part in its social life, and they are kept at arm's length; they strive after love and brotherhood, and are met by looks of hatred and contempt on all sides; conscious that they are not inferior to their neighbours in any kind of ability or virtue, they have it continually thrown in their teeth that they are an inferior type, and are not fit to rise to the same level as the Aryans. And more to the same effect.

Well – what then?

Nordau himself did not touch on this question: it was outside the scope of his address. But the whole Congress was the answer. Beginning as it did with Nordau's address, the Congress meant this: that in order to escape from all these troubles it is necessary to establish a Jewish State.

Let us imagine, then, that the consent of Turkey and the other Powers has already been obtained, and the State is established . . . with the full sanction of international law, as the more extreme members of the Congress desire. Does this bring, or bring near, the end of the material trouble? No doubt, every poor Jew will be at perfect liberty to go to his State and to seek his living there, without any artificial hindrances in the shape of restrictive laws or anything of that kind. But liberty to *seek* a livelihood is not enough: he must be able to *find* what he seeks. . . . The single country is no longer an economic unit: the whole world is one great market, in which every State has to struggle hard for its place. . . . But if the Jews are to flock to their State in large numbers, all at once, we may prophesy with perfect certainty that home competition in every branch of production . . . will prevent any one branch from developing as it should. And then the Jews will turn and leave their State, flying from the most deadly of all enemies – an enemy not to be kept off even by the magic word *völkerrechtlich*: from hunger.

. . . But if the Jewish State sets out to save all those Jews who are in the grip of the material problems, or most of them, by turning them into agriculturists in Palestine, then it must first find the necessary capital. At Basle, no doubt, one heard naïve and confident references to a "National Fund" of ten million pounds sterling. . . . ten million pounds are a mere nothing compared with the sum necessary for the emigration of the Jews and their settlement in Palestine on an agricultural basis. Even if all the rich Jews suddenly became ardent "Zionists," and every one of them gave half his wealth to the cause, the whole would still not make up the thousands of millions that would be needed for the purpose.

. . .

Truth is bitter, but with all its bitterness it is better than illusion. We must confess to ourselves that the "ingathering of the exiles" is unattainable by natural means. We may, by natural means, establish a Jewish State one day, and the Jews may increase and multiply in it until the country will hold no more: but even then the greater part of the people will remain scattered in strange lands. "To gather our scattered ones from the four corners of the earth" (in the words of the Prayer Book) is impossible. Only religion, with its belief in a miraculous redemption, can promise that consummation.

. . .

The material problem, then, will not be ended by the foundation of a Jewish State, nor, generally speaking, does it lie in our power to end it (though it could be eased more or less even now by various means, such as the encouragement of agriculture and handicrafts among Jews in all countries); and whether we found a State or not, this particular problem will always turn at bottom on the economic condition of each country and the degree of civilisation attained by each people.

Thus we are driven to the conclusion that the only true basis of Zionism is to be found in the other problem, the moral one.

But the moral problem appears in two forms, one in the West and one in the East; and this fact explains the fundamental difference between Western "Zionism" and Eastern *Chibbath Zion*. Nordau dealt only with the Western problem, apparently knowing nothing about the Eastern; and the Congress as a whole concentrated on the first, and paid little attention to the second.

The Western Jew, after leaving the Ghetto and seeking to attach himself to the people of the country in which he lives, is unhappy because his hope of an open-armed welcome is disappointed. . . . Communal life and communal problems no longer satisfy him. He has already grown accustomed to a broader social and political life; and on the intellectual side Jewish cultural work has no attraction, because Jewish culture has played no part in his education from childhood, and is a closed book to him. So in his trouble he turns to the land of his ancestors, and pictures to himself how good it would be if a Jewish State were re-established there – a State arranged and organised exactly after the pattern of other States. Then he could live a full, complete life among his own people, and find at home all that he now sees outside, dangled before his eyes, but out of reach. . . . So he devotes himself to the ideal with all the ardour of which he is capable. . . .

This is the basis of Western Zionism and the secret of its attraction. But Eastern *Chibbath Zion* has a different origin and development. Originally, like "Zionism," it was political; but being a result of material evils, it could not rest satisfied with an "activity" consisting only of outbursts of feeling and fine phrases. These things may satisfy the heart, but not the stomach. So *Chibbath Zion* began at once to express itself in concrete activities – in the establishment of colonies in Palestine. . . .

The Eastern form of the moral trouble is absolutely different from the Western. In the West it is the problem of the Jews, in the East the problem of Judaism. The one weighs on the individual, the other on the nation. The one is felt by Jews who have had a European education, the other by Jews whose education has been Jewish. The one is a product of anti-Semitism, and is dependent on anti-Semitism for its existence; the other is a natural product of a real link with a culture of thousands of years, which will retain its hold even if the troubles of the Jews all over the world come to an end, together with anti-Semitism, . . .

It is not only Jews who have come out of the Ghetto: Judaism has come out, too. For Jews the exodus is confined to certain countries, and is due to toleration; but Judaism has come out (or is coming out) of its own accord wherever it has come into contact with modern culture. . . . When it leaves the Ghetto walls it is in danger of losing its essential being or – at best – its national unity: it is in danger of being split up into as many kinds of Judaism, each with a different character and life, as there are countries of the Jewish dispersion.

And now Judaism finds that it can no longer tolerate the *galuth* form which it had to take on, in obedience to its will-to-live, when it was exiled from its own country, and that if it loses that form its life is in danger. So it seeks to return to its historic centre, in order to live there a life of natural development, to bring its powers into play in every department of human culture . . . and thus to contribute to the common stock of humanity, in the future as in the past, a great national culture, the fruit of the unhampered activity of a people living according to its own spirit. For this purpose Judaism needs at present but little. . . . This Jewish settlement, which will be a gradual growth, will become in course of time the centre of the nation, wherein its spirit will find pure expression and develop in all its aspects up to the highest degree of perfection of which it is capable. Then from this centre the spirit of Judaism will go forth to the great circumference, to all the communities of the Diaspora, and will breathe new life into them and preserve their unity; and when our national culture in Palestine has attained that level, we may be confident that it will produce men in the country who will be able, on a favourable opportunity, to establish a State which will be a *Jewish* State, and not merely a State of Jews.

. . .

The secret of our people's persistence is . . . that at a very early period the Prophets taught it to respect only spiritual power, and not to worship material power. For this reason the clash with enemies stronger than itself never brought the Jewish nation . . . to the point of self-effacement. So long as we are faithful to this principle, our existence has a secure basis: for in spiritual power we are not inferior to other nations, and we have no reason to efface ourselves. . . .

In a word: *Chibbath Zion*, no less than "Zionism," wants a Jewish State and believes in the possibility of the establishment of a Jewish State in the future. But while "Zionism" looks to the Jewish State to provide a remedy for poverty, complete tranquillity and national glory, *Chibbath Zion* knows that our State will not give us all these things until "universal Righteousness is enthroned and holds sway over nations and States". . . . "Zionism," therefore, begins its work with political propaganda; *Chibbath Zion* begins with national culture, because only through the national culture and for its sake can a Jewish State be established in such a way as to correspond with the will and the needs of the Jewish people.

Dr. Herzl, it is true, said in the speech mentioned above that "Zionism" demands the return to Judaism before the return to the Jewish State. But these nice-sounding words are so much at variance with his deeds that we are forced to the unpleasant conclusion that they are nothing but a well-turned phrase.

. . .

If it were really the aim of "Zionism" to bring the people back to Judaism – to make it not merely a nation in the political sense, but a nation living according to its own spirit – then the Congress would not have postponed questions of national culture – of language and literature, of education and the diffusion of Jewish knowledge – to the very last moment, after the end of all the debates. . . . When all those present were tired out, and welcomed the setting sun on the last day as a sign of the approaching end, a short time was allowed for a discourse by one of the members on all those important questions, which are in reality the most vital and essential questions. . . .

But there is no need to ascertain the attitude of the Congress by inference, because it was stated quite explicitly in one of the official speeches – a speech which appeared on the agenda as "An Exposition of the basis of Zionism," and was submitted to Dr. Herzl before it was read to the Congress. In this speech we were told plainly that the Western Jews were nearer than those of the East to the goal of Zionism, because they had already done half the work: they had annihilated the Jewish culture of the Ghetto, and were thus emancipated from the yoke of the past. This speech, too, was received with prolonged applause, and the Congress passed a motion ordering it to be published as a pamphlet for distribution among Jews.

. . .

The whole Congress, too, was designed rather as a demonstration to the world than as a means of making it clear to ourselves what we want and what we can do. . . . In those countries where Jews are preoccupied with material troubles, and are not likely on the whole to get enthusiastic about a political ideal for the distant future, a special emissary went about, before the Congress, spreading favourable reports, from which it might be concluded that both the consent of Turkey and the necessary millions were nearly within our reach, and that nothing was lacking except a national representative body to negotiate with all parties on behalf of the Jewish people. . . . This Commission skillfully contrived a programme capable of a dozen interpretations, to suit all tastes; and this programme was put before Congress with a request that it should be accepted as it stood, without any discussion. But one delegate refused to submit, and his action led to a long debate on a single word. This debate showed, to the consternation of many people, that there were several kind of "Zionists," and the cloak of unanimity was in danger of being publicly rent asunder; but the leaders quickly and skilfully patched up the rent, before it had got very far. Dr. Herzl, in his new pamphlet, uses this to prove what great importance Zionists attached to this single word (*völkerrechtlich*). But in truth similar "dangerous" debates might have been raised on many other words. . . .

Yet, after all, I confess that Western "Zionism" is very good and useful for those Western Jews who have long since almost forgotten Judaism, and have no link with their people except a vague sentiment which they themselves do not understand. The establishment of a Jewish State by their agency is at present but a distant vision; but the idea of a State induces them meanwhile to devote their energies to the service of their people, lifts them out of the mire of assimilation, and strengthens their Jewish national consciousness. Possibly, when they find out that it will be a long time before we have police-men and watchmen of our own, many of them may leave us altogether; but even then our loss through this movement will not be greater than our gain, because undoubtedly there will be among them men of larger heart, who, in course of time, will be moved to get to the bottom of the matter and to understand their people and its spirit: and these men will arrive of themselves at that genuine *Chibbath Zion* which is in harmony with our national spirit. But in the East, the home of refuge of Judaism and the birthplace of Jewish *Chibbath Zion*, this "political" tendency can bring us only harm. Its attractive force is at the same time a force repellent to the moral ideal which has till now been the inspiration of Eastern Jewry. . . .

It was under the stress of that feeling that I wrote my Note on the Congress, a few days after its conclusion. The impression was all very fresh in my mind, and my grief was acute; and I let slip some hard expressions, which I now regret, because it is not my habit to use such expressions. But as regards the actual question at issue I have nothing to withdraw. What has happened since then has not convinced me that I was wrong: on the contrary, it has strength-ened my conviction that though I wrote in anger, I did not write in error.

3   The Basle Program, Resolutions of the First Zionist Congress (August 30, 1897)

Zionism seeks to establish a home for the Jewish people in Palestine secured under public law. The Congress contemplates the following means to the attainment of this end:

1. The promotion by appropriate means of the settlement in Palestine of Jewish farmers, artisans, and manufacturers.
2. The organization and uniting of the whole of Jewry by means of appropriate institutions, both local and international, in accordance with the laws of each country.
3. The strengthening and fostering of Jewish national sentiment and national consciousness. Preparatory steps toward obtaining the consent of governments, where necessary, in order to reach the goals of Zionism.

The handwritten copy of the program also states:

4. Preparatory steps toward obtaining the consent of governments, where necessary, in order to reach the goals of Zionism.

DOI: 10.4324/9781003348948-6

4   Letter From Dr. Theodore Herzl to M. Youssuf Zia al-Khalidi (March 19, 1899)[1]

Wien-Wahring
Carl Ludwigstrasse 50
19 March, 1899

Excellency,

I owe to Mr. Zadok Kahn's kindness the pleasure of having read the letter which you addressed to him. Let me tell you first of all that the feelings of friendship which you express for the Jewish people inspire in me the deepest appreciation. The Jews have been, and, and will be the best friends of Turkey since the day when Sultan Selim opened his Empire to the persecuted Jews of Spain.

And this friendship consists not only of words – it is ready to be transferred into acts and to aid the Moslems.

The Zionist idea, of which I am the humble servant, has no hostile tendency toward the Ottoman Government, but quite to the contrary this movement is concerned with opening up new resources for the Ottoman Empire. In allowing immigration to a number of Jews bringing their intelligence, their financial acumen and their means of enterprise to the country, no one can doubt that the well-being of the entire country would be the happy result. It is necessary to understand this, and make it known to everybody.

As Your Excellency said very well in your letter to the Grand Rabbi, the Jews have no belligerent Power behind them, neither are they themselves of a warlike nature. They are a completely peaceful element, and very content if they are left in peace. Therefore, there is absolutely nothing to fear from their immigration.

The question of the Holy Places?

But no one thinks of ever touching those. As I have said and written many times: These places have lost forever the faculty of belonging exclusively to one faith, to one race or to one people. The Holy Places are and will remain holy for all the world, for the Moslems as for the Christians as for the Jews.

DOI: 10.4324/9781003348948-7

The universal peace which all men of good will ardently hope for will have its symbol in a brotherly union in the Holy Places.

You see another difficulty, Excellency, in the existence of the non-Jewish population in Palestine. But who would think of sending them away? It is their well-being, their individual wealth which we will increase by bringing in our own. Do you think that an Arab who owns land or a house in Palestine worth three or four thousand francs will be very angry to see the price of his land rise in a short time, to see it rise five and ten times in value perhaps in a few months? Moreover, that will necessarily happen with the arrival of the Jews. That is what the indigenous population must realize, that they will gain excellent brothers as the Sultan will gain faithful and good subjects who will make this province flourish – this province which is their historic homeland.

When one looks at the situation in this light, which is the *true* one, one must be the friend of Zionism when one is the friend of Turkey.

I hope, Excellency, that these few explanations will suffice to give you a little more sympathy for our movement.

. . . I have had submitted to His Majesty the sultan some general propositions, and I am pleased to believe that the extreme clearness of his mind will make him accept in principle the idea of which one can afterwards discuss the details of execution. If he will not accept it, we will search and, believe me, we will find elsewhere what we need.

But then Turkey will have lost its last chance to regulate its finances and to recover its economic vigour.

It is a sincere friend of the Turks who tells you these things today. Remember that!

And accept, Excellency, the assurance of my very high consideration.

(signed)
Dr. Theodore Herzl

Note

1. Y. Z. Khalidi, Member for Jerusalem of the Ottoman Parliament, 2877, Palestinian scholar and Mayor of Jerusalem in 1899. Herzl's letter, which was written in French, was received by Y. Z. Khalidi while on a visit to Constantinople.

5   The Uganda Proposal (August 26, 1903)

Sir Clement Hill, Chief of Protectorate Dept to Mr. L. J. Greenberg, August 26, 1903

Sir:

Mr. Chamberlain communicated to the Marquess of Lansdowne the letter which you addressed to him on the 13th ultimo containing the form of an agreement which Dr. Herzl proposes should be entered into between His Majesty's Government and the Jewish Colonial Trust Ltd. for the establishment of a Jewish settlement in East Africa.

His Lordship has also had under his consideration the remarks made by you on 6th Just. on the occasion of your interview in this office with Sir E. Barrington and Mr. Hurst.

I am now directed by His Lordship to say that he has studied the question with the interest which His Majesty's Government must always take in any well-considered scheme for the amelioration of the position of the Jewish Race. The time at his disposal has been too short to enable him to go fully into the details of the plan or to discuss it with His Majesty's Commissioner for the East Africa Protectorate, and he regrets that he is therefore unable to pronounce any definite opinion in the matter.

He understands that the Trust desire to send some gentlemen to the East Africa Protectorate, who may ascertain personally whether there are any vacant lands suitable for the purposes in question, and, if this is so he will be happy to give them every facility to enable them to discuss with His Majesty's Commissioner the possibility of meeting the view which may be expressed at the forthcoming Zionist Congress in regard to the conditions upon which a settlement might be possible.

If a site can be found which the Trust and His Majesty's Commissioner consider suitable and which commends itself to His Majesty's Government, Lord Lansdowne will be prepared to entertain favourably proposals for the establishment of a Jewish colony or settlement on conditions which will enable the members to observe their National customs. For this purpose he would be

DOI: 10.4324/9781003348948-8

prepared to discuss (if a suitable site had been found and subject to the views of the advisers of the Secretary of State in East Africa) the details of a scheme comprising as its main features: the grant of a considerable area of land, the appointment of a Jewish Official as chief of the local administration, and permission to the Colony to have a free hand in regard to municipal legislation and as to the management of religious and purely domestic matters, such as Local Autonomy being conditional upon the right of His Majesty's Government to exercise a general control.

There is no need at present to consider the details of the terms upon which the land would be granted, whether by sale or lease, but His Lordship assumes that no portion of the administrative expenses of the settlement would fall on His Majesty's Government, and the latter would reserve power to reoccupy the land if the settlement should not prove a success.

I am, Sir,

Your most obedient

Humble servant

(signed)

Clement Hill

6   Sir Henry McMahon

The McMahon Letter
(October 24, 1915)

I have received your letter of the 29th Shawal, 1333, with much pleasure, and your expression of friendliness and sincerity have given me the greatest satisfaction.

I regret that you should have received from my last letter the impression that I regarded the question of limits and boundaries with coldness and hesitation; such was not the case, but it appeared to me that the time had not yet come when that question could be discussed in a conclusive manner.

I have realised, however, from your last letter that you regard this question as one of vital and urgent importance. I have, therefore, lost no time in informing the Government of Great Britain of the contents of your letter, and it is with great pleasure that I communicate to you on their behalf the following statement, which I am confident you will receive with satisfaction.

The two districts of Mersina and Alexandretta and portions of Syria lying to the west of the districts of Damascus, Homs, Hama, and Aleppo cannot be said to be purely Arab, and should be excluded from the limits demanded.

With the above modification, and without prejudice to our existing treaties with Arab chiefs, we accept those limits.

As for those regions lying within those frontiers wherein Great Britain is free to act without detriment to the interests of her ally, France, I am empowered in the name of the Government of Great Britain to give the following assurances and make the following assurances and make the following reply to your letter:

1. Subject to the above modifications, Great Britain is prepared to recognise and support the independence of the Arabs in all the regions within the limits demanded by the Sherif of Mecca.
2. Great Britain will guarantee the Holy Places against all external aggression and will recognise their inviolability.

DOI: 10.4324/9781003348948-9

3. When the situation admits, Great Britain will give to the Arabs her advice and will assist them to establish what may appear to be the most suitable forms of government those various territories.
4. On the other hand, it is understood that the Arabs have decided to seek the advice and guidance of Great Britain only, and that such European advisers and officials as may be required for the formation of a sound form of administration will be British.
5. With regard to the *vilayets* of Bagdad and Basra, the Arabs will recognise that the established position and interests of Great Britain necessitate special administrative arrangements in order to secure these territories from foreign aggression to promote the welfare of the local populations and to safeguard our mutual economic interests.

I am convinced that this declaration will assure you beyond all possible doubt of the sympathy of Great Britain towards the aspirations of her friends the Arabs and will result in a firm and lasting alliance, the immediate results of which will be the expulsion of the Turks from the Arab countries and the freeing of the Arab peoples from the Turkish yoke, which for so many years has pressed heavily upon them.

I have confined myself in this letter to the more vital and important questions, and if there are any other matters dealt with in your letters which I have omitted to mention, we may discuss them at some convenient date in the future.

It was with very great relief and satisfaction that I heard of the safe arrival of the Holy Carpet and the accompanying offerings which, thanks to the clearness of your directions and the excellence of your arrangements, were landed without trouble or mishap in spite of the dangers and difficulties occasioned by the present sad war. May God soon bring a lasting peace and freedom of all peoples.

I am sending this letter by the hand of your trusted and excellent messenger, Sheikh Mohammed ibn Arif ibn Uraifan, and he will inform you of the various matters of interest, but of less vital importance, which I have not mentioned in this letter.

(Compliments).

(Signed): A. Henry McMahon

7 The Sykes-Picot Agreement (May, 1916)

It is accordingly understood between the French and British governments:

That France and Great Britain are prepared to recognize and protect an independent Arab state or a confederation of Arab states (a) and (b) marked on the annexed map, under the suzerainty of an Arab chief. That in area (a) France, and in area (b) Great Britain, shall have priority of right of enterprise and local loans. That in area (a) France, and in area (b) Great Britain, shall alone supply advisers or foreign functionaries at the request of the Arab state or confederation of Arab states.

That in the blue area France, and in the red area Great Britain, shall be allowed to establish such direct or indirect administration or control as they desire and as they may think fit to arrange with the Arab state or confederation of Arab states.

That in the brown area there shall be established an international administration, the form of which is to be decided upon after consultation with Russia, and subsequently in consultation with the other allies, and the representatives of the sheriff of Mecca.

That Great Britain be accorded (1) the ports of Haifa and Acre, (2) guarantee of a given supply of water from the Tigris and Euphrates in area (a) for area (b). His Majesty's government, on their part, undertake that they will at no time enter into negotiations for the cession of Cyprus to any third power without the previous consent of the French government.

That Alexandretta shall be a free port as regards the trade of the British Empire, . . .

That Haifa shall be a free port as regards the trade of France, her dominions and protectorates, and there shall be no discrimination in port charges or facilities as regards French shipping and French goods. . . .

. . .

That Great Britain has the right to build, administer, and be sole owner of a railway connecting Haifa with area (b), and shall have a perpetual right to transport troops along such a line at all times. It is to be understood by both governments that this railway is to facilitate the connection of Baghdad with Haifa by rail, . . .

. . .

DOI: 10.4324/9781003348948-10

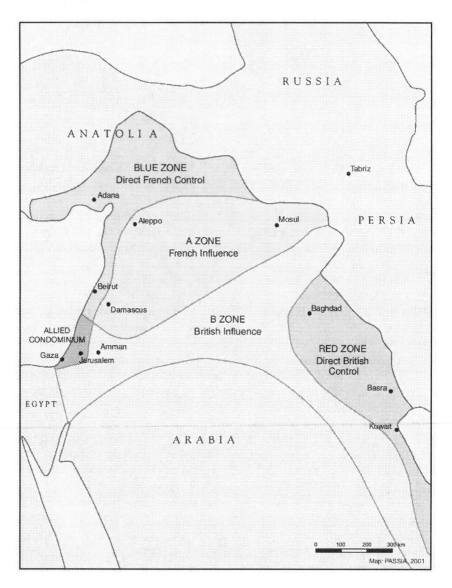

Map 2 The Sykes-Picot Agreement of 1916

Source: Permission granted by the Palestinian Academic Society for the Study of International Affairs to reprint their map of the Sykes-Picot Agreement in this book. The original can be found at: www.passia.org/maps/view/4.

There shall be no interior customs barriers between any of the above-mentioned areas. The customs duties leviable on goods destined for the interior shall be collected at the port of entry and handed over to the administration of the area of destination.

It shall be agreed that the French government will at no time enter into any negotiations for the cession of their rights and will not cede such rights in the blue area to any third power, . . .

The British and French government, as the protectors of the Arab state, shall agree that they will not themselves acquire and will not consent to a third power acquiring territorial possessions in the Arabian peninsula, nor consent to a third power installing a naval base either on the east coast, or on the islands, of the red sea. This, however, shall not prevent such adjustment of the Aden frontier as may be necessary in consequence of recent Turkish aggression.

The negotiations with the Arabs as to the boundaries of the Arab states shall be continued through the same channel as heretofore on behalf of the two powers.

It is agreed that measures to control the importation of arms into the Arab territories will be considered by the two governments.

I have further the honor to state that, in order to make the agreement complete, His Majesty's government are proposing to the Russian government to exchange notes analogous to those exchanged by the latter and your excellency's government on the 26th April last. . . .

His Majesty's government further consider that the Japanese government should be informed of the arrangements now concluded.

8 The Balfour Declaration (November 2, 1917)

Foreign Office
November 2nd, 1917

Dear Lord Rothschild,

I have much pleasure in conveying to you, on behalf of His Majesty's Government, the following declaration of sympathy with Jewish Zionist aspirations which has been submitted to, and approved by, the Cabinet.

"His Majesty's Government view with favour the establishment in Palestine of a national home for the Jewish people and will use their best endeavours to facilitate the achievement of this object, it being clearly understood that nothing shall be done which may prejudice the civil and religious rights of existing non-Jewish communities in Palestine, or the rights and political status enjoyed by Jews in any other country."

I should be grateful if you would bring this declaration to the knowledge of the Zionist Federation.

Yours sincerely,

Arthur James Balfour

DOI: 10.4324/9781003348948-11

9 The Weizmann-Feisal Agreement (January 3, 1919)

Agreement Between Emir Feisal Ibn al-Hussein al-Hashemi and the President of the World Zionist Organization, Dr. Chaim Weizmann (January 3, 1919)

His Royal Highness the Emir Feisal, representing and acting on behalf of the Arab Kingdom of Hedjaz, and Dr. Chaim Weizmann, representing and acting on behalf of the Zionist Organization, mindful of the racial kinship and ancient bonds existing between the Arabs and the Jewish people, and realizing that the surest means of working out the consummation of their natural aspirations is through the closest possible collaboration in the development of the Arab State and Palestine . . . have agreed upon the following:

ARTICLE I

The Arab State and Palestine in all their relations and undertakings shall be controlled by the most cordial goodwill and understanding, and to this end Arab and Jewish duly accredited agents shall be established and maintained in the respective territories.

ARTICLE II

Immediately following the completion of the deliberations of the Peace Conference, the definite boundaries between the Arab State and Palestine shall be determined by a Commission to be agreed upon by the parties hereto.

ARTICLE III

In the establishment of the Constitution and Administration of Palestine, all such measures shall be adopted as will afford the fullest guarantees for carrying into effect the British Government's Declaration of the 2nd of November, 1917.

DOI: 10.4324/9781003348948-12

ARTICLE IV

All necessary measures shall be taken to encourage and stimulate immigration of Jews into Palestine on a large scale, and as quickly as possible to settle Jewish immigrants upon the land through closer settlement and intensive cultivation of the soil. In taking such measures the Arab peasant and tenant farmers shall be protected in their rights and shall be assisted in forwarding their economic development.

ARTICLE V

No regulation or law shall be made prohibiting or interfering in any way with the free exercise of religion; and further, the free exercise and enjoyment of religious profession and worship, without discrimination or preference, shall forever be allowed. No religious test shall ever be required for the exercise of civil or political rights.

ARTICLE VI

The Mohammedan Holy Places shall be under Mohammedan control.

ARTICLE VII

The Zionist Organization proposes to send to Palestine a Commission of experts to make a survey of the economic possibilities of the country and to report upon the best means for its development. The Zionist Organization will place the aforementioned Commission at the disposal of the Arab State for the purpose of a survey of the economic possibilities of the Arab State and to report upon the best means for its development. The Zionist Organization will use its best efforts to assist the Arab State in providing the means for developing the natural resources and economic possibilities thereof.

ARTICLE VIII

The parties hereto agree to act in complete accord and harmony on all matters embraced herein before the Peace Congress.

ARTICLE IX

Any matters of dispute which may arise between the contracting parties shall be referred to the British Government for arbitration.

Given under our hand at London, England, the third day of January, 1919.

Chaim Weizmann and Feisal Ibn-Hussein

Reservation by the Emir Feisal

If the Arabs are established as I have asked in my manifesto of 4 January, addressed to the British Secretary of State for Foreign Affairs, I will carry out what is written in this agreement. If changes are made, I cannot be answerable for failing to carry out this agreement.

10 Interview in Mr. Balfour's Apartment, 23 Rue Nitot, Paris (June 24, 1919)[1]

Present: Mr. Balfour, Mr. Justice Brandeis, Lord Eustace Percy and Mr. Frankfurter

Mr. Balfour expressed great satisfaction that Justice Brandeis came to Europe. He said the Jewish problem (of which the Palestinian question is only a fragment, but an essential part) is to his mind as perplexing a question as any that confronts the statesmanship of Europe. He is exceedingly distressed by it and harassed by its difficulties. Mr. Balfour rehearsed summarily the pressure on Jews in Eastern Europe and said that the problem was, of course, complicated by the extraordinary phenomenon that Jews now are not only participating in revolutionary movements but are actually, to a large degree, leaders in such movements. He stated that a well informed person told him only the other day that Lenin also on his mother's side was a Jew.

Justice Brandeis stated that he had every reason to believe that this is not so and that Lenin on both sides is an upper class Russian. He continued to say that after all this is a minor matter, that all that Mr. Balfour said was quite so. He believes every Jew is potentially an intellectual and an idealist and the problem is one of direction of those qualities. He narrated his own approach to Zionism, that he came to it wholly as an American, for his whole life had been free from Jewish contacts or traditions. As an American he was confronted with the disposition of the vast number of Jews, particularly Russian Jews, that were pouring into the United States year by year. It was then that by chance a pamphlet on Zionism came his way and led him to the study of the Jewish problem and to the conviction that Zionism was the answer. The very same men, with the same qualities are now enlisted in revolutionary movements would find (and in the United States *do* find) constructive channels for expression and make positive contributions to civilization.

Mr. Balfour interrupted to express his agreement, adding: "Of course, these are the reasons that make you and me such ardent Zionists".

The Justice continued that for the realization of the Zionist programme three conditions were essential: –

DOI: 10.4324/9781003348948-13

First that Palestine should be the Jewish homeland and not merely that there be a Jewish homeland in Palestine. That, he assumed, is the commitment of the Balfour Declaration and will, of course, be confirmed by the Peace Conference.

Secondly, there must be economic elbow room for a Jewish Palestine; self sufficiency for a healthy social life. That meant adequate boundaries, not merely a small garden within Palestine. On the North that meant the control of the waters and he assumed that Great Britain was urging the northern boundary necessary for the control of the waters. That was a question substantially between England and France and, of course, must be determined by the Peace Conference. The southern and eastern boundaries, he assumed, raised internal British questions.

Mr. Balfour assented that that was so as to the southern boundary but questioned as to the eastern boundary.

The Justice added that, of course, the interests of the Hedjaz were involved, but after all, the disposition of questions between the Arabs and the Zionists was, in effect, an internal British problem. He urged on the east the Trans-Jordan line for there the land is largely unoccupied and settlement could be made without conflict with the Arabs much more easily than in the more settled portions of the North.

Mr. Balfour pointed out that in the East there is the Hedjaz railroad which can rightly be called a Mohammedan railroad.

The Justice replied that there is land right up to the railroad and Mr. Balfour stated that he thought that Feisul would agree to having an eastern boundary of Palestine go up to the Hedjaz railroad.

Thirdly, the Justice urged that the future Jewish Palestine must have control of the land and the natural resources which are at the heart of a sound economic life. It was essential that the values which are being and will be created because of the cessation of Turkish rule and due to British occupation and Jewish settlement should go to the State and not into private hands.

Mr. Balfour expressed entire agreement with the three conditions which the Justice laid down. He then proceeded to point out the difficulties which confronted England. He narrated at length the Syrian situation and the appointment of the Inter-Allied Commission which finally terminated in the present American Commission. Feisul was a comrade in arms with the British; he undoubtedly was of military help and by sheer force of events the British and the Arabs find themselves together in Syria. Feisul interpreted British action and British words as, in effect, a promise either of Arab independence or of Arab rule under British protection. On the other hand, are the old interests of France in Syria and the Prime Minister has given (and in Mr. Balfour's opinion, rightly given) definite word that under no circumstances will Great

Britain remain in Syria. It would involve a quarrel with France which would not be healed. But Feisul prefers Great Britain to France, (at least, so he says), and all advices indicate that French rule in Syria will meet with the greatest opposition and even bloodshed on the part of the populace.

The situation is further complicated by an agreement made early in November [1918] by the British and French, and brought to the President's attention, telling the people of the East that their wishes would be consulted in the disposition of their future. One day in the Council of Four, when the Syrian matter was under dispute, the President suggested the dispatch of a Commission to find out what the people really wanted. It began with Syria, but the field of enquiry was extended over the whole East. Mr. Balfour wrote a memorandum to the Prime Minister, and he believed it went to the President, pointing out that Palestine should be excluded from the terms of reference because the Powers had committed themselves to the Zionist programme, which inevitably excluded numerical self-determination. Palestine presented a unique situation. We are dealing not with the wishes of an existing community but are consciously seeking to re-constitute a new community and definitely building for a numerical majority in the future. He has great difficulty in seeing how the President can possibly reconcile his adherence to Zionism with any doctrine of self-determination and he asked the Justice how he thinks the President will do it. The Justice replied that Mr. Balfour had already indicated the solution and pointed out that the whole conception of Zionism as a Jewish homeland was a definite building up for the future as the means of dealing with a world problem and not merely with the disposition of an existing community. Mr. Balfour stated he supposed that would be the President's line. He continued to point out the great difficulties that are now besetting Great Britain in the East, namely the ferment in the whole Eastern world, the Mohammedan restlessness, the new Arabic imperialism and the relations with the French. Then there is also the Sykes-Picot Agreement; that is dead, but its ruins still encumber the earth. He was anxious that the Justice should know these difficulties for they all bear upon the Palestinian situation. He expressed the greatest satisfaction that the Justice was going to the East to study the problem at first hand.

The Justice hoped that while he was away at least nothing would be done which would embarrass the fulfilment of the three conditions which he laid down as essential to the realization of the Zionist programme.

Mr. Balfour then stated that he understood Justice Brandeis' request that no decision be taken as to the boundaries and the extent of control over land in any way counter to his views until his return in about four or five weeks. He thought it was perfectly safe to give him the assurance that no decision will be taken on those matters during that time to embarrass the aims which the Justice had indicated.

Mr. Balfour stated that he would be either in Paris or in London when the Justice returned and he hoped that he will report to him at once upon his return on the questions as they appear to him from a study on the spot.

No statesman could have been more sympathetic than Mr. Balfour was with the underlying philosophy and aims of Zionism as they were stated by Mr. Justice Brandeis, nor more eager that the necessary conditions should be secured at the hands of the Peace Conference and of Great Britain to assure the realization of the Zionist programme.

[signed]

F. F.

SOURCE: *From Haven to Conquest*, pp. 195–200. Reprinted with permission.

Note

1. Felix Frankfurter, professor of law at Harvard Law School, later associate justice, U.S. Supreme Court, 1939–1962, and President Wilson's consultant at the Paris Peace Conference in 1919. Lord Eustace Percy, British diplomat, later Conservative Member of Parliament, 1921–1937. Louis Brandeis was chairman of provisional commission for general Zionist affairs, U.S., 1914–1916, and associate justice, U.S. Supreme Court, 1916–1939. Arthur James Balfour was prime minister of Britain, 1902–1905, and foreign secretary, 1916–1919. The interview was recorded in a memorandum by Mr. Frankfurter.

11 The White Paper of 1922 (June 3, 1922) (The "Churchill White Paper")

The Secretary of State for the Colonies has given renewed consideration to the existing political situation in Palestine, with a very earnest desire to arrive at a settlement of the outstanding questions which have given rise to uncertainty and unrest among certain sections of the population. After consultation with the High Commissioner for Palestine [Sir Herbert Samuel] the following statement has been drawn up. It summarizes the essential parts of the correspondence that has already taken place between the Secretary of State and a delegation from the Moslem Christian Society of Palestine, which has been for some time in England, and it states the further conclusions which have since been reached.

The tension which has prevailed from time to time in Palestine is mainly due to apprehensions, which are entertained both by sections of the Arab and by sections of the Jewish population. These apprehensions, so far as the Arabs are concerned, are partly based upon exaggerated interpretations of the meaning of the Balfour Declaration favouring the establishment of a Jewish National Home in Palestine, made on behalf of His Majesty's Government on 2nd November, 1917.

Unauthorized statements have been made to the effect that the purpose in view is to create a wholly Jewish Palestine. Phrases have been used such as that Palestine is to become "as Jewish as England is English." His Majesty's Government regard any such expectation as impracticable and have no such aim in view. Nor have they at any time contemplated, as appears to be feared by the Arab delegation, the disappearance or the subordination of the Arabic population, language, or culture in Palestine. They would draw attention to the fact that the terms of the Declaration referred to do not contemplate that Palestine as a whole should be converted into a Jewish National Home, but that such a Home should be founded "in Palestine." In this connection it has been observed with satisfaction that at a meeting of the Zionist Congress, the supreme governing body of the Zionist Organization, held at Carlsbad in September, 1921, a resolution was passed expressing as the official statement of Zionist aims

> the determination of the Jewish people to live with the Arab people on terms of unity and mutual respect, and together with them to make the

DOI: 10.4324/9781003348948-14

common home into a flourishing community, the upbuilding of which may assure to each of its peoples an undisturbed national development.

It is also necessary to point out that the Zionist Commission in Palestine, now termed the Palestine Zionist Executive, has not desired to possess, and does not possess, any share in the general administration of the country. . . . That special position relates to the measures to be taken in Palestine affecting the Jewish population and contemplates that the organization may assist in the general development of the country, but does not entitle it to share in any degree in its government.

Further, it is contemplated that the status of all citizens of Palestine in the eyes of the law shall be Palestinian, and it has never been intended that they, or any section of them, should possess any other juridical status. So far as the Jewish population of Palestine are concerned it appears that some among them are apprehensive that His Majesty's Government may depart from the policy embodied in the Declaration of 1917. It is necessary, therefore, once more to affirm that these fears are unfounded, and that that Declaration, re-affirmed by the Conference of the Principle Allied Powers at San Remo and again in the Treaty of Sèvres, is not susceptible of change.

During the last two or three generations the Jews have recreated in Palestine a community, now numbering 80,000, of whom about one fourth are farmers or workers upon the land. This community has its own political organs; an elected assembly for the direction of its domestic concerns; elected councils in the towns; and an organization for the control of its schools. It has its elected Chief Rabbinate and Rabbinical Council for the direction of its religious affairs. Its business is conducted in Hebrew as a vernacular language, and a Hebrew Press serves its needs. It has its distinctive intellectual life and displays considerable economic activity. This community, then, with its town and country population, its political, religious, and social organizations, its own language, its own customs, its own life, has in fact "national" characteristics. When it is asked what is meant by the development of the Jewish National Home in Palestine, it may be answered that it is not the imposition of a Jewish nationality upon the inhabitants of Palestine as a whole, but the further development of the existing Jewish community, with the assistance of Jews in other parts of the world, in order that it may become a centre in which the Jewish people as a whole may take, on grounds of religion and race, an interest and a pride. But in order that this community should have the best prospect of free development and provide a full opportunity for the Jewish people to display its capacities, it is essential that it should know that it is in Palestine as of right and not on sufferance. . . .

This, then, is the interpretation which His Majesty's Government place upon the Declaration of 1917, and, so understood, the Secretary of State is of opinion that it does not contain or imply anything which need cause either alarm to the Arab population of Palestine or disappointment to the Jews.

For the fulfilment of this policy it is necessary that the Jewish community in Palestine should be able to increase its numbers by immigration. This
immigration cannot be so great in volume as to exceed whatever may be
the economic capacity of the country at the time to absorb new arrivals. It
is essential to ensure that the immigrants should not be a burden upon the
people of Palestine as a whole, and that they should not deprive any section
of the present population of their employment. Hitherto the immigration has
fulfilled these conditions. The number of immigrants since the British occupation has been about 25,000.

It is necessary also to ensure that persons who are politically undesirable
be excluded from Palestine, and every precaution has been and will be taken
by the Administration to that end.

It is intended that a special committee should be established in Palestine,
consisting entirely of members of the new Legislative Council elected by the
people, to confer with the administration upon matters relating to the regulation of immigration. Should any difference of opinion arise between this
committee and the Administration, the matter will be referred to His Majesty's Government, who will give it special consideration. In addition, under
Article 81 of the draft Palestine Order in Council, any religious community
or considerable section of the population of Palestine will have a general right
to appeal, through the High Commissioner and the Secretary of State, to the
League of Nations on any matter on which they may consider that the terms
of the Mandate are not being fulfilled by the Government of Palestine.

With reference to the Constitution which it is now intended to establish
in Palestine, the draft of which has already been published, it is desirable to
make certain points clear. In the first place, it is not the case, as has been represented by the Arab Delegation, that during the war His Majesty's Government gave an undertaking that an independent national government should be
at once established in Palestine. This representation mainly rests upon a letter
dated the 24th October, 1915, from Sir Henry McMahon, then His Majesty's
High Commissioner in Egypt, to the Sherif of Mecca, now King Hussein
of the Kingdom of the Hejaz. That letter is quoted as conveying the promise to the Sherif of Mecca to recognise and support the independence of the
Arabs within the territories proposed by him. But this promise was given subject to a reservation made in the same letter, which excluded from its scope,
among other territories, the portions of Syria lying to the west of the District
of Damascus. This reservation has always been regarded by His Majesty's
Government as covering the vilayet of Beirut and the independent Sanjak of
Jerusalem. The whole of Palestine west of the Jordan was thus excluded from
Sir Henry McMahon's pledge.

Nevertheless, it is the intention of His Majesty's government to foster the
establishment of a full measure of self-government in Palestine. But they are
of the opinion that, in the special circumstances of that country, this should
be accomplished by gradual stages. . . . The first step was taken when, on
the institution of a Civil Administration, the nominated Advisory Council,

which now exists, was established. It was stated at the time by the High Commissioner that this was the first step in the development of self-governing institutions, and it is now proposed to take a second step by the establishment of a Legislative Council containing a large proportion of members elected on a wide franchise. . . . The legislative Council would then consist of the High Commissioner as President and 12 elected and 10 official members. The Secretary of State is of the opinion that before a further measure of self-government is extended to Palestine and the Assembly placed in control over the Executive, it would be wise to allow some time to elapse. During this period the institutions of the country will have become well established; its financial credit will be based on firm foundations, and the Palestinian officials will have been enabled to gain experience of sound methods of government. After a few years the situation will be again reviewed, and if the experience of the working of the constitution now to be established so warranted, a larger share of authority would then be extended to the elected representatives of the people.

. . .

The Secretary of State believes that a policy upon these lines, coupled with the maintenance of the fullest religious liberty in Palestine and with scrupulous regard for the rights of each community with reference to its Holy Places, cannot but commend itself to the various sections of the population, and that upon this basis may be built up that a spirit of cooperation upon which the future progress and prosperity of the Holy Land must largely depend.

12 The Mandate for Palestine (July 24, 1922)

The Council of the League of Nations

Whereas the Principal Allied Powers have agreed, for the purpose of giving effect to the provisions of Article 22 of the Covenant of the League of Nations, to entrust to a Mandatory selected by the said Powers the administration of the territory of Palestine, which formerly belonged to the Turkish Empire, within such boundaries as may be fixed by them; and

Whereas the Principal Allied Powers have also agreed that the Mandatory should be responsible for putting into effect the declaration originally made on November 2nd, 1917, by the Government of His Britannic Majesty, and adopted by the said Powers, in favour of the establishment in Palestine of a national home for the Jewish people, it being clearly understood that nothing should be done which might prejudice the civil and religious rights of existing non-Jewish communities in Palestine, or the rights and political status enjoyed by Jews in any other country; and

Whereas recognition has thereby been given to the historical connection of the Jewish people with Palestine and to the grounds for reconstituting their national home in that country; and

Whereas the Principal Allied Powers have selected His Britannic Majesty as the Mandatory for Palestine; and

. . .

Whereas His Britannic Majesty has accepted the mandate in respect of Palestine and undertaken to exercise it on behalf of the League of Nations in conformity with the following provisions; and

Whereas by the aforementioned Article 22 (paragraph 8), it is provided that the degree of authority, control or administration to be exercised by the Mandatory, not having been previously agreed upon by the Members of the League, shall be explicitly defined by the Council of the League of Nations;

DOI: 10.4324/9781003348948-15

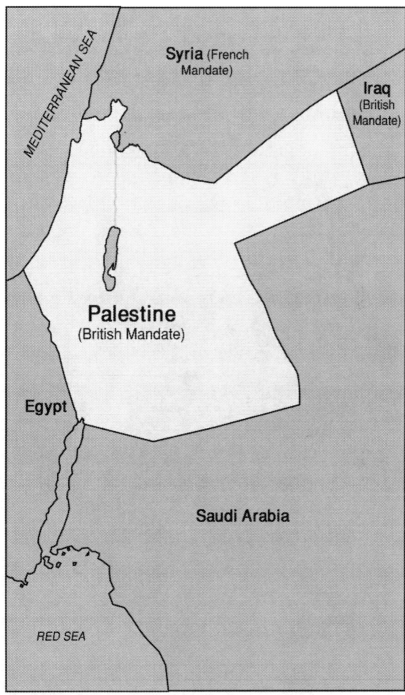

Area Allocated for Jewish National Home
San Remo Conference, 1920

Map 3 The British Mandate, 1920

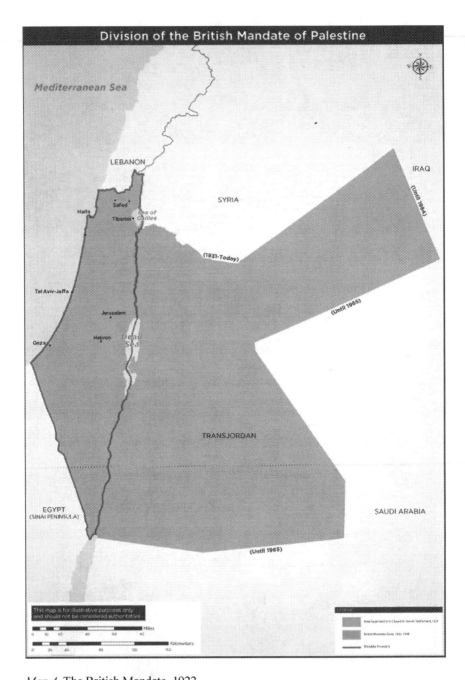

Map 4 The British Mandate, 1922

Source: Published by the Government of Israel, Ministry of Foreign Affairs. The originals can be found at: www.gov.il/en/Departments/General/the-british-mandate.

Confirming the said mandate, defines its terms as follows:

ARTICLE 1

The Mandatory shall have full powers of legislation and of administration, save as they may be limited by the terms of this mandate.

ARTICLE 2

The Mandatory shall be responsible for placing the country under such political, administrative, and economic conditions as will secure the establishment of the Jewish national home, as laid down in the preamble, and the development of self-governing institutions, and also for safeguarding the civil and religious rights of all the inhabitants of Palestine, irrespective of race and religion.

ARTICLE 3

The Mandatory shall, so far as circumstances permit, encourage local autonomy.

ARTICLE 4

An appropriate Jewish agency shall be recognised as a public body for the purpose of advising and co-operating with the Administration of Palestine in such economic, social, and other matters as may affect the establishment of the Jewish national home and the interests of the Jewish population in Palestine, and, subject always to the control of the Administration, to assist and take part in the development of the country.

The Zionist organisation, so long as its organisation and constitution are in the opinion of the Mandatory appropriate, shall be recognised as such agency. It shall take steps in consultation with His Britannic Majesty's Government to secure the cooperation of all Jews who are willing to assist in the establishment of the Jewish national home.

ARTICLE 5

The Mandatory shall be responsible for seeing that no Palestine territory shall be ceded or leased to, or in any way placed under the control of, the Government of any foreign Power.

ARTICLE 6

The Administration of Palestine, while ensuring that the rights and position of other sections of the population are not prejudiced, shall facilitate Jewish immigration under suitable conditions and shall encourage, in co-operation with the Jewish agency . . . close settlement by Jews, on the land, including State lands and waste lands not required for public purposes.

ARTICLE 7

The Administration of Palestine shall be responsible for enacting a nationality law. There shall be included in this law provisions framed so as to facilitate the acquisition of Palestinian citizenship by Jews who take up their permanent residence in Palestine.

ARTICLE 8

. . .

ARTICLE 9

The Mandatory shall be responsible for seeing that the judicial system established in Palestine shall assure to foreigners, as when as to natives, a complete guarantee of their rights.

Respect for the personal status of the various peoples and communities and for their religious interests shall be fully guaranteed. In particular, the control and administration of Waqfs shall be exercised in accordance with religious law and the dispositions of the founders.

ARTICLE 10

Pending the making of special extradition agreements relating to Palestine, the extradition treaties in force between the Mandatory and other foreign Powers shall apply to Palestine.

ARTICLE 11

The Administration of Palestine shall take all necessary measures to safeguard the interests of the community in connection with the development of the country, and, subject to any international obligations accepted by the Mandatory, shall have full power to provide for public ownership or control of any of the natural resources of the country or of the public works, services, and utilities established or to be established therein. . . .

The Administration may arrange with the Jewish agency mentioned in Article 4 to construct or operate, upon fair and equitable terms, any public works, services, and utilities, and to develop any of the natural resources of the country, insofar as these matters are not directly undertaken by the Administration. . . .

ARTICLE 12

The Mandatory shall be entrusted with the control of the foreign relations of Palestine. . . . He shall also be entitled to afford diplomatic and consular protection to citizens of Palestine when outside its territorial limits.

ARTICLE 13

All responsibility in connection with the Holy Places and religious buildings or sites in Palestine, including that of preserving existing rights and of securing free access to the Holy Places, religious buildings and sites and the free exercise of worship, while ensuring the requirements of public order and decorum, is assumed by the Mandatory, who shall be responsible solely to the League of Nations, in all matters connected herewith . . . provided also that nothing in this mandate shall be construed as conferring upon the Mandatory authority to interfere with the fabric or the management of purely Moslem sacred shrines, the immunities of which are guaranteed.

ARTICLE 14

A special Commission shall be appointed by the Mandatory to study, define, and determine the rights and claims in connection with the Holy Places and the rights and claims relating to the different religious communities in Palestine. . . .

ARTICLE 15

The Mandatory shall see that complete freedom of conscience and the free exercise of all forms of worship, subject only to the maintenance of public order and morals, are ensured to all. No discrimination of any kind shall be made between the inhabitants of Palestine on the ground of race, religion, or language. No person shall be excluded from Palestine on the sole ground of his religious belief.

The right of each community to maintain its own schools for the education of its own members in its own language, while conforming to such educational requirements of a general nature as the Administration may impose, shall not be denied or impaired.

ARTICLE 16

The Mandatory shall be responsible for exercising such supervision over religious or eleemosynary bodies of all faiths in Palestine as may be required for the maintenance of public order and good government. Subject to such supervision, no measures shall be taken in Palestine to obstruct or interfere with the enterprise of such bodies or to discriminate against any representative or member of them on the ground of his religion or nationality.

ARTICLE 17

The Administration of Palestine may organise on a voluntary basis the forces necessary for the preservation of peace and order, . . . but shall not use them for purposes other than those above specified save with the consent of the Mandatory. Except for such purposes, no military, naval, or air forces shall be raised or maintained by the Administration of Palestine.

Nothing in this article shall preclude the Administration of Palestine from contributing to the cost of the maintenance of the forces of the Mandatory in Palestine.

The Mandatory shall be entitled at all times to use the roads, railways, and ports of Palestine for the movement of armed forces and the carriage of fuel and supplies.

ARTICLE 18

The Mandatory shall see that there is no discrimination in Palestine against the nationals of any State Member of the League of Nations (including companies incorporated under its laws). . . .

. . . the Administration of Palestine may, on the advice of the Mandatory, impose such taxes and customs duties as it may consider necessary, and take such steps as it may think best to promote the development of the natural resources of the country and to safeguard the interests of the population. . . .

ARTICLE 19

The Mandatory shall adhere on behalf of the Administration of Palestine to any general international conventions already existing, or which may be concluded hereafter with the approval of the League of Nations . . .

ARTICLE 20

The Mandatory shall co-operate on behalf of the Administration of Palestine, so far as religious, social, and other conditions may permit, in the execution of any common policy adopted by the League of Nations for preventing and combating disease, including diseases of plants and animals.

ARTICLE 21

The Mandatory shall secure the enactment within 12 months from this date and shall ensure the execution of a Law of Antiquities . . .

ARTICLE 22

English, Arabic, and Hebrew shall be the official languages of Palestine. Any statement or inscription in Arabic on stamps or money in Palestine shall be repeated in Hebrew, and any statement or inscription in Hebrew shall be repeated in Arabic.

ARTICLE 23

The Administration of Palestine shall recognise the holy days of the respective communities in Palestine as legal days of rest for the members of such communities.

ARTICLE 24

The Mandatory shall make to the Council of the League of Nations an annual report to the satisfaction of the Council as to the measures taken during the year to carry out the provisions of the mandate. Copies of all laws and regulations promulgated or issued during the year shall be communicated with the report.

ARTICLE 25

In the territories lying between the Jordan and the eastern boundary of Palestine as ultimately determined, the Mandatory shall be entitled, with the consent of the Council of the League of Nations, to postpone or withhold application of such provisions of this mandate as he may consider inapplicable to the existing local conditions . . .

ARTICLE 26

The Mandatory agrees that, if any dispute whatever should arise between the Mandatory and another Member of the League of Nations relating to the interpretation or the application of the provisions of the mandate, such dispute, if it cannot be settled by negotiation, shall be submitted to the Permanent Court of International Justice provided for by Article 14 of the Covenant of the League of Nations.

ARTICLE 27

The consent of the Council of the League of Nations is required for any modification of the terms of this mandate.

ARTICLE 28

In the event of the termination of the mandate hereby conferred upon the Mandatory, the Council of the League of Nations shall make such arrangements as may be deemed necessary for safeguarding in perpetuity, under guarantee of the League, the rights secured by Articles 13 and 14, and shall use its influence for securing, under the guarantee of the League, that the Government of Palestine will fully honour the financial obligations legitimately incurred by the Administration of Palestine during the period of the mandate, including the rights of public servants to pensions or gratuities.

The present instrument shall be deposited in original in the archives of the League of Nations and certified copies shall be forwarded by the Secretary-General of the League of Nations to all Members of the League.

Done at London the 24th day of July 1922.

13 The Passfield White Paper
(October 20, 1930)

Palestine

Statement of Policy by His Majesty's Government in the United Kingdom

1. The Report of the Special Commission, under the Chairmanship of Sir Walter Shaw, which was published in April, gave rise to acute controversy, . . .
2. In a country such as Palestine, where the interests and aims of two sections of the community are at present diverse and in some respects conflicting, it is too much to expect that any declaration of policy will fully satisfy the aspirations of either party. . . . It will be the endeavour of His Majesty's Government, . . . to convince both Arabs and Jews of their firm intention to promote the essential interests of both races to the utmost of their power, and to work consistently for the development, in Palestine, of a prosperous community, living in peace under an impartial and progressive Administration. . . .

    It is unnecessary here to dwell upon the unhappy events of the past year and the deplorable conditions which have resulted from them. . . . It cannot be too strongly emphasised that on the establishment of better relations between Arabs and Jews depend the future peace and prosperity of the country which is dear to both races. This is the object which His Majesty's Government have constantly in view, . . .
3. Many of the misunderstandings which have unhappily arisen on both sides appear to be the result of a failure to appreciate the nature of the duty imposed upon His Majesty's Government by the terms of the Mandate. . . . in the words of the Prime Minister's statement in the House of Commons on the 3rd April last, "a double undertaking is involved, to the Jewish people on the one hand and to the non-Jewish population of Palestine on the other."

    . . .

    The Prime Minister, in the statement above referred to, announced, in words which could not have been made more plain, that it is the intention of His Majesty's Government to continue to administer Palestine in

DOI: 10.4324/9781003348948-16

accordance with the terms of the Mandate, as approved by the Council of the League of Nations. "That" said Mr. Ramsay MacDonald, "is an international obligation from which there can be no question of receding." . . . It must be realised, once and for all, that it is useless for Jewish leaders on the one hand to press His Majesty's Government to conform their policy in regard, for example, to immigration and land, to the aspirations of the more uncompromising sections of Zionist opinion. That would be to ignore the equally important duty of the Mandatory Power towards the non-Jewish inhabitants of Palestine. On the other hand, it is equally useless for Arab leaders to maintain their demands for a form of Constitution, which would render it impossible for His Majesty's Government to carry out, in the fullest sense, the double undertaking already referred to . . .

It becomes, therefore, essential that at the outset His Majesty's Government should make it clear that they will not be moved, by any pressure or threats, from the path laid down in the Mandate, and from the pursuit of a policy which aims at promoting the interests of the inhabitants of Palestine, both Arabs and Jews, in a manner which shall be consistent with the obligations which the Mandate imposes.

4. This is not the first time that His Majesty's Government have endeavoured to make clear the nature of their policy in Palestine. In 1922 a full statement was published and was communicated both to the Palestine Arab Delegation, then in London, and to the Zionist Organisation. This statement met with no acceptance on the part of the Arab Delegation, but the Executive of the Zionist Organisation passed a Resolution assuring His Majesty's Government that the activities of the Organisation would be conducted in conformity with the policy therein set forth. Moreover, in the letter conveying the text of this Resolution to His Majesty's Government, Dr. Weizmann wrote: –

"The Zionist Organisation has, at all time, been sincerely desirous of proceeding in harmonious co-operation with all sections of the people of Palestine. It has repeatedly made it clear, both in word and deed, that nothing is further from its purpose than to prejudice in the smallest degree the civil or religious rights, or the material interests of the non-Jewish population." . . .

5. Apart from proposals for the establishment of a Constitution in Palestine which will be dealt with in later paragraphs, there are three important points dealt with in this statement which must now be recalled: –

(a) The meaning attached by His Majesty's Government to the expression "the Jewish National Home," which is contained in the Mandate.
  On this point, the following passage may be quoted from the 1922 Statement:-
  "During the last two or three generations the Jews have recreated in Palestine a community, now numbering 80,000, of whom

about one-fourth are farmers or workers upon the land. . . . This community, then, with its town and country population, its political, religious and social organisation, its own language, its own customs, its own life, has in fact 'national' characteristics. When it is asked what is meant by the development of the Jewish National Home in Palestine, it may be answered that it is not the imposition of a Jewish nationality upon the inhabitants of Palestine as a whole, but the further development of the existing Jewish community, with the assistance of Jews in other parts of the world, in order that it may become a centre in which the Jewish people as a whole may take, on grounds of religion and race, an interest and a pride. But in order that this community should have the best prospect of free development and provide a full opportunity for the Jewish people to display its capacities, it is essential that it should know that it is in Palestine as of right and not on sufferance. That is the reason why it is necessary that the existence of a Jewish National Home in Palestine should be internationally guaranteed, and that it should be formally recognised to rest upon ancient historic connection." This, then, is the interpretation which His Majesty's Government place upon the Declaration of 1917, and, so understood, the Secretary of State is of opinion that it does not contain or imply anything which need cause either alarm to the Arab population of Palestine or disappointment to the Jews.

(b) The principles which should govern immigration.

On this point the statement of policy continues as follows: – "For the fulfilment of this policy it is necessary that the Jewish community in Palestine should be able to increase its numbers by immigration. This immigration cannot be so great in volume as to exceed whatever may be the economic capacity of the country at the time to absorb new arrivals. It is essential to ensure that the immigrants should not be a burden upon the people of Palestine as a whole, and that they should not deprive any section of the present population of their employment. Hitherto the immigration has fulfilled these conditions. The number of immigrants since the British occupation has been about 25,000.

"It is necessary also to ensure that persons who are politically undesirable are excluded from Palestine and every precaution has been and will be taken by the Administration to that end."

It will be observed that the principles enunciated above render it essential that in estimating the absorptive capacity of Palestine at any time account should be taken of Arab as well as Jewish unemployment in determining the rate at which immigration should be permitted. It is the intention of His Majesty's Government to take steps to ensure a more exact application of these principles in the future.

    (c) The position of the Jewish Agency.

In the passage quoted below, an attempt was made to indicate the limitations, implicit in the Mandate, necessarily imposed upon the scope of the Jewish Agency provided for in Article 4 of the Mandate: –

"It is also necessary to point out that the Zionist Commission in Palestine, . . . does not possess, any share in the general administration of the country. Nor does the special position assigned to the Zionist Organisation in Article IV of the draft Mandate for Palestine imply any such functions. That special position relates to the measures affecting the Jewish population, and contemplates that the Organisation may assist in the general development of the country, but does not entitle it to share in any degree in its Government."

6.   His Majesty's Government desire to reaffirm generally the policy outlined in the 1922 Statement, and, in particular, the three passages quoted above. . . . In particular, it is recognised as of the greatest importance that the efforts of the High Commissioner towards some closer and more harmonious form of co-operation and means of consultation between the Palestine Administration and the Jewish Agency should be further developed, always consistently, however, with the principle which must be regarded as basic, that the special position of the Agency, in affording advice and co-operation, does not entitle the Agency, as such, to share in the government of the country. . . .

7.   At this point it becomes desirable to remove any ground of misunderstanding that may exist as to the passages in the Mandate bearing upon the safeguarding of the rights of the non-Jewish community in Palestine. The passages in the Mandate specially bearing on this point will be found in –

Article 2. "The Mandatory shall be responsible for placing the country under such political administrative and economic conditions as will secure the establishment of the Jewish National Home, as laid down in the preamble, and the development of self-governing institutions, and also for safeguarding the civil and religious rights of all the inhabitants of Palestine, irrespective of race and religion."

Article 6. "The Administration of Palestine, while ensuring that the rights and position of other sections of the population are not prejudiced, shall facilitate Jewish immigration under suitable conditions, and shall encourage, in co-operation with the Jewish agency referred to in Article 4, close settlement by Jews on the land, including State lands and waste lands not required for public purposes."

Article 9. "The Mandatory shall be responsible for seeing that the judicial system established in Palestine shall assure to foreigners, as well as to natives, a complete guarantee of their rights . . ."

Article 18. "All responsibility in connection with the Holy Places and religious buildings or sites in Palestine, . . . , is assumed by the Mandatory, who shall be responsible solely to the League of Nations in all matters connected herewith, . . . and provided also that nothing in this Mandate shall be construed as conferring upon the Mandatory authority to interfere with the fabric or the management of purely Moslem sacred shrines, the immunities of which are guaranteed."

Article 15. "The Mandatory shall see that complete freedom of conscience and the free exercise of all forms of worship, subject only to the maintenance of public order and morals, are ensured to all. No discrimination of any kind shall be made between the inhabitants of Palestine on the ground of race, religion or language. No person shall be excluded from Palestine on the sole ground of his religious belief.

"The right of each community to maintain its own schools for the education of its own members in its own language, while conforming to such educational requirements of a general nature as the Administration may impose, shall not be denied or impaired."

On the other hand, special reference to the Jewish National Home and to Jewish interests are contained in Article 4: –

Article 4. "An appropriate Jewish agency shall be recognised as a public body for the purpose of advising and cooperating with the Administration of Palestine . . . and, . . . to assist and take part in the development of the country. The Zionist organisation, so long as its organisation and constitution are in the opinion of the Mandatory appropriate, shall be recognised as such agency. It shall take steps in consultation with His Britannic Majesty's Government to secure the cooperation of all Jews who are willing to assist in the establishment of the Jewish National Home."

Article 6. (Already quoted above.)

. . .

8. . . . it will be observed that Article 2 makes the Mandatory responsible for safeguarding the civil and religious rights of all the inhabitants of Palestine, irrespective of race or religion; and . . . that the obligation contained in Article 6 to facilitate Jewish immigration and to encourage close settlement by Jews on the land, is qualified by the requirement to ensure that the rights and position of other sections of the population are not prejudiced. Moreover, by Article 11 "the Administration of Palestine is required to take all necessary measures to safeguard the interests of the community in connection with the development of the country." It is clear from the wording of this Article that the population of Palestine as a whole, . . . is to be the object of the Government's care, and it may be noted that the provision for arranging with the Jewish Agency for the construction or operation of public works, services and utilities, is only permissive and not obligatory, and could not be allowed to conflict with the general interests of the community. These points are emphasised because claims have been made on behalf of the Jewish Agency to a position in regard to the general administration of the country, which His Majesty's Government cannot but regard as going far beyond the clear intention of the Mandate. . . .

"From all these statements two assertions emerge, which should be emphasised: –

(1) that the obligations laid down by the Mandate in regard to the two sections of the population are of equal weight;
(2) that the two obligations imposed on the Mandatory are in no sense irreconcilable.

"The Mandates Commission has no objection to raise to these two assertions, which, in its view, accurately express what it conceives to be the essence of the Mandate for Palestine and ensure its future."

. . .

9. The preceding paragraphs contain an exposition of the general principles which have to be taken into account as governing policy in Palestine and the limiting conditions under which it must be carried out. The practical problems with which His Majesty's Government are faced in Palestine must now be considered in detail.

These may be regarded as falling roughly under three heads: –

(1) Security,
(2) Constitutional development,
(3) Economic and Social development.

They will be dealt with in that order.

(1) Security

10. It is a primary duty of the Administration to ensure peace, order and good government in Palestine. In an earlier paragraph His Majesty's Government have intimated that they will not be moved from their duty by any pressure or threats.

. . .

(2) Constitutional Development

11. Reference has already been made to the demands of Arab leaders for a form of constitution which would be incompatible with the mandatory obligations of His Majesty's Government. It is, however, the considered opinion of His Majesty's Government that the time has now come when the important question of the establishment of a measure of self-government in Palestine must, in the interests of the community as a whole, be taken in hand without further delay.

. . .

In October 1920 there was set up in Palestine an Advisory Council composed in equal parts of official and nominated unofficial members.

Of the ten unofficial members, four were Moslems, three were Christians and three were Jews.

On the 1st September, 1922, the Palestine Order in Council was issued, setting up a Government in Palestine under the Foreign Jurisdiction Act. Part 3 of the Order in Council directed the establishment of a Legislative Council to be composed of the High Commissioner as President, with ten other official members, and 12 elected non-official members. . . .

The attempt failed owing to the refusal of the Arab population as a whole to co-operate . . .

The High Commissioner thereupon suspended the establishment of the proposed Legislative Council, and continued to act in consultation with an Advisory Council as before.

Two further opportunities were given to representative Arab leaders in Palestine to co-operate with the Administration in the government of the country, first, by the reconstitution of a nominated Advisory Council, but with membership conforming to that proposed for the Legislative Council, and, secondly, by a proposal for the formation of an Arab Agency. . . .

Neither of these opportunities was accepted and, accordingly, in December 1923, an Advisory Council was set up consisting only of official members. This position still continues; the only change being that the Advisory Council has been enlarged by the addition of more official members as the Administration developed.

. . .

12. His Majesty's Government have now carefully considered of this question in the light of the present stage of progress and development and with special regard to their obligation to place the country under such political, administrative and economic conditions as will secure the development of self-governing institutions. They have decided that the time has arrived for a further step in the direction of the grant to the people of Palestine, of a measure of self-government compatible with the terms of the Mandate.

His Majesty's Government accordingly intend to set up a Legislative Council generally on the lines indicated in the statement of British policy in Palestine issued by Mr. Churchill in June 1922, which is reproduced as Appendix 5 to the Report of the Commission on the Palestine disturbances of August 1929. His Majesty's Government trust that on this occasion they will secure the co-operation of all sections of the population of Palestine. . . .

18. As stated above, the new Legislative Council will be on the lines indicated in the statement of policy issued in 1922. . . .

(3) Economic and Social Development

14. Under this head the practical problems to be considered are mainly concerned with, questions relating to land, immigration and unemployment. . . .

15. As a result of these extensive and elaborate investigations, certain conclusions have emerged and certain facts have been established which will now be set out briefly: –

    (1) Land

    It can now be definitely stated that at the present time and with the present methods of Arab cultivation there remains no margin of land available for agricultural settlement by new immigrants, with the exception of such undeveloped land as the various Jewish agencies hold in reserve.

    There has been much criticism in the past in regard to the relatively small extent of State land which has been made available for Jewish settlement. It is, however, an error to imagine that the Palestine Government is in possession of large areas of vacant land which could be made available for Jewish settlement. . . . The Government claims considerable areas which are, in fact, occupied and cultivated by Arabs. Even were the title of the Government to these areas admitted, and it is in many cases disputed, it would not be possible to make these areas available for Jewish settlement, in view of their actual occupation by Arab cultivators and of the importance of making available additional land on which to place the Arab cultivators who are now landless.

    . . .

16. It now appears, in the light of the best available estimates, that the area of cultivable land in Palestine (excluding the Beer-Sheba region) is 6,544,000 dunams. This area is considerably less than had hitherto been estimated, previous official estimates being in the neighbourhood of 10 to 11 million dunams.

    . . .

17. . . .

    The sole agencies which have pursued a consistent policy of land development have been the Jewish Colonisation organisations, public and private.

    The Jewish settlers have had every advantage that capital, science and organisation could give them. To these and to the energy of the settlers themselves their remarkable progress is due. On the other hand, the Arab population, while lacking the advantages enjoyed by the Jewish settlers, has, by the excess of births over deaths, increased with great rapidity, while the land available for its sustenance has decreased by about a million dunams. This area has passed into Jewish hands.

18. Reference has been made to the energy evinced and the remarkable progress made in Jewish land settlement. It would be unjust to accept the contention, which has been advanced in the course of the controversy regarding relations between Jews and Arabs in Palestine, that the effect of Jewish settlement upon the Arab population has in all cases been detrimental to the interests of the Arabs. . . .

In so far as the past policy of the P.J.C.A. is concerned, there can be no doubt that the Arab has profited largely by the installation of the Colonies, and relations between the colonists and their Arab neighbours have in the past been excellent. . . .

19. Moreover, the effect of Jewish colonisation on the existing population is very intimately affected by the conditions on which the various Jewish bodies hold, utilise and lease their land. It is provided by the Constitution of the Enlarged Jewish Agency, signed at Zurich on the 14th August, 1929 (Article 3 (d) and (e)), that the land acquired shall be held as the "inalienable property of the Jewish people," and that in "all the works or undertakings carried out or furthered by the Agency, it shall be deemed to be a matter of principle that Jewish labour shall be employed." Moreover, by Article 23 of the draft lease, which it is proposed to execute in respect of all holdings granted by the Jewish National Fund, the lessee undertakes to execute all works connected with the cultivation of the holdings only with Jewish labour. Stringent conditions are imposed to ensure the observance of this undertaking.

An undertaking binding settlers in the Colonies of the Maritime Plain to hire Jewish workmen only, whenever they may be obliged to hire help, is inserted in the Agreement for the repayment of advances made by the Palestine Foundation Fund. Similar provision is contained in the Agreement for the Emek Colonies.

These stringent provisions are difficult to reconcile with the declaration at the Zionist Congress of 1921 of "the desire of the Jewish people to live with the Arab people in relations of friendship and mutual respect, and, together, with the Arab people, to develop the homeland common to both into a prosperous community which would ensure the growth of the peoples."

20. The Jewish leaders have been perfectly frank in their justification of this policy. The Executive of the General Federation of Jewish Labour . . . has contended that such restrictions are necessary to secure the largest possible amount of Jewish immigration and to safeguard the standard of life of the Jewish labourer from the danger of falling to the lower standard of the Arab . . .

21. . . .

22. As a result of recent investigations, His Majesty's Government are satisfied that, in order to attain these objects, a more methodical agricultural development is called for with the object of ensuring a better use of the land.

23. . . .

24. . . .

25. The finances of Palestine have been severely strained by the necessity of providing for large increases in its security forces. These increases have been deemed essential in the light of the events of the autumn of 1929,

and it is not possible to forecast the time that must elapse before it will be thought safe to reduce expenditure on this account. . . .

. . .

26. The whole system under which immigration into Palestine is controlled by the Administration has recently been most carefully examined, and in the month of May it was considered necessary by His Majesty's Government, whilst leaving undisturbed Jewish immigration in its various other forms, to suspend the further issue of certificates for the admission of immigrants. . . . This examination has revealed certain weaknesses in the existing system. It has been shown that under it there have been many cases of persons being admitted, who, if all the facts had been known, should not have received visas. No effective Government control exists in regard to the selection of immigrants from abroad, with the result that there are no adequate safeguards against irregularities in connection with the issue of immigration certificates, and also against the immigration of undesirables. A further unsatisfactory feature is that a large number of travellers, who enter Palestine with permission to remain for a limited time, stay on without sanction. It is calculated that the number of such cases during the last three years amounted to 7,800. Another serious feature is the number of persons who evade the frontier control.

. . .

In view of its responsibilities under the Mandate, it is essential that the Palestine Government, as the agent of the Mandatory Power, should be the deciding authority in all matters of policy relating to immigration . . .

27. As regards the relation of immigration to unemployment, great difficulties at present exist owing to the absence of efficient machinery for estimating the degree of unemployment existing at any time. This is especially true as regards the Arab section of the community . . . there is at present a serious degree of Arab unemployment, and that Jewish unemployment likewise exists to an extent which constitutes a definitely unsatisfactory feature. . . . The economic capacity of the country to absorb new immigrants must therefore be judged with reference to the position of Palestine as a whole in regard to unemployment, . . .

28. Article 6 of the Mandate directs that the rights and position of the other sections of the population shall not be prejudiced by Jewish immigration. Clearly, if immigration of Jews results in preventing the Arab population from obtaining the work necessary for its maintenance, or if Jewish unemployment unfavourably affects the general labour position, it is the duty of the Mandatory Power under the Mandate to reduce, or, if necessary, to suspend, such immigration until the unemployed portion of the "other sections" is in a position to obtain work. . . .

Any hasty decision in regard to more unrestricted Jewish immigration is to be strongly deprecated, not only from the point of view of the interests of the Palestine population as a whole, but even from the special point of view of the Jewish community. So long as widespread suspicion exists, and it does exist, amongst the Arab population, that the economic depression, under which they undoubtedly suffer at present, is largely due to excessive Jewish immigration, and so long as some grounds exist upon which this suspicion may be plausibly represented to be well founded, there can be little hope of any improvement in the mutual relations of the two races. But it is upon such improvement that the future peace and prosperity of Palestine must largely depend . . .

29. As has been shown in the foregoing paragraphs, the three problems of development, immigration and unemployment are closely inter-related, and upon the evolution of a policy which will take full account of these three factors must depend the future of Palestine. It is only in a peaceful and prosperous Palestine that the ideals of the Jewish National Home can in any sense be realised, and it is only by cordial co-operation between the Jews, the Arabs and the Government that prosperity can be secured. . . . Palestine has reached a critical moment in its development. In the past it may be said that the Government has left economic and social forces to operate with the minimum of interference or control, but it has become increasingly clear that such a policy can no longer continue. It is only the closest co-operation between the Government and the leaders of the Arab and Jewish communities that can prevent Palestine from drifting into a situation which would imperil, on the one hand, the devoted work of those who have sought to build up the Jewish National Home, and, on the other, the interests of the majority of the population who at present possess few resources of their own with which to sustain the struggle for existence. What is required is that both races should consent to live together and to respect each other's needs and claims. To the Arabs His Majesty's Government would appeal for a recognition of the facts of the situation, and for a sustained effort at co-operation in obtaining that prosperity for the country as a whole by which all will benefit. From the Jewish leaders, His Majesty's Government ask a recognition of the necessity for making some concessions on their side in regard to the independent and separatist ideals which have been developed in some quarters in connection with the Jewish National Home, and for accepting it as an active factor in the orientation of their policy that the general development of the country shall be carried out in such a way that the interests of the Arabs and Jews may each receive adequate consideration, with the object of developing prosperity throughout the country under conditions which will give no grounds for charges of partiality upon the one side or upon the other, but will permit of the Arab and Jewish communities developing in harmony and contentment.

14 British Prime Minister Ramsay MacDonald Letter to Chaim Weizmann (February 13, 1931)

13 February 1931

Dear Dr. Weizmann,

In order to remove certain misconceptions and misunderstandings which have arisen as to the policy of His Majesty's Government with regard to Palestine, as set forth in the White Paper of October, 1930, and which were the subject of a debate in the House of Commons on November 17, and also to meet certain criticisms put forward by the Jewish Agency, I have pleasure in forwarding you the following statement of our position, which will fall to be read as the authoritative interpretation of the White Paper on the matters with which this letter deals.

It has been said that the policy of His Majesty's Government involves a serious departure from the obligations of the mandate as hitherto understood; that it misconceives the mandatory obligations; and that it foreshadows a policy which is inconsistent with the obligations of the mandatory to the Jewish people.

His Majesty's Government did not regard it as necessary to quote *in extenso* the declarations of policy which have been previously made, but attention is drawn to the fact that, not only does the White Paper of 1930 refer to and endorse the White Paper of 1922, which has been accepted by the Jewish Agency, but it recognizes that the undertaking of the mandate is an undertaking to the Jewish people and not only to the Jewish population of Palestine. The White Paper places in the foreground of its statement my speech in the House of Commons on the 3rd of April, 1930, in which I announced, in words that could not have been made more plain, that it was the intention of His Majesty's Government to continue to administer Palestine in accordance with the terms of the mandate as approved by the Council of the League of Nations. That position has been reaffirmed and again made plain by my speech in the House of Commons on the 17th of November. In my speech on the 3rd of April, I used the following language:

His Majesty's Government will continue to administer Palestine in accordance with the terms of the mandate as approved by the Council of the League

DOI: 10.4324/9781003348948-17

of Nations. This is an international obligation from which there can be no question of receding.

Under the terms of the mandate his Majesty's Government are responsible for promoting the establishment of a national home for the Jewish people, it being clearly understood that nothing shall be done which might prejudice the civil and religious rights of existing non-Jewish communities in Palestine or the rights and political status enjoyed by Jews in any other country.

A double undertaking is involved, to the Jewish people on the one hand and to the non-Jewish population of Palestine on the other; and it is the firm resolve of His Majesty's Government to give effect, in equal measure, to both parts of the declaration and to do equal justice to all sections of the population of Palestine. That is the duty from which they will not shrink and to discharge of which they will apply all the resources at their command.

That declaration is in conformity not only with the articles but also with the preamble of the mandate, which is hereby explicitly reaffirmed.

. . .

A good deal of criticism has been directed to the White Paper upon the assertion that it contains injurious allegations against the Jewish people and Jewish labor organizations. Any such intention on the part of His Majesty's Government is expressly disavowed. It is recognized that the Jewish Agency have all along given willing cooperation in carrying out the policy of the mandate and that the constructive work done by the Jewish people in Palestine has had beneficial effects on the development and well-being of the country as a whole. His Majesty's Government also recognizes the value of the services of labor and trades union organizations in Palestine, to which they desire to give every encouragement.

A question has arisen as to the meaning to be attached to the words "safeguarding the civil and religious rights of all inhabitants of Palestine irrespective of race and religion" occurring in Article II, and the words "ensuring that the rights and position of other sections of the population are not prejudiced" occurring in Article VI of the mandate. . . . These words indicate that in respect of civil and religious rights the mandatory is not to discriminate between persons on the ground of religion or race, and this protective provision applies equally to Jews, Arabs, and all sections of the population.

The words "rights and position of other sections of the population," occurring in Article VI, plainly refer to the non-Jewish community. These rights and position are not to be prejudiced; that is, are not to be impaired or made worse. The effect of the policy of immigration and settlement on the economic position of the non-Jewish community cannot be excluded from consideration. But the words are not to be read as implying that existing economic conditions in Palestine should be crystallized. On the contrary, the obligation to facilitate Jewish immigration and to encourage close settlement by Jews on the land remains a positive obligation of the mandate and it can be fulfilled without prejudice to the rights and position of other sections of the population of Palestine.

We may proceed to the contention that the mandate has been interpreted in a manner highly prejudicial to Jewish interests in the vital matters of land settlement and immigration. It has been said that the policy of the White Paper would place an embargo on immigration and would suspend, if not indeed terminate, the close settlement of the Jews on the land, which is a primary purpose of the mandate. In support of this contention, particular stress has been laid upon the passage referring to State lands in the White Paper, which says that "it would not be possible to make available for Jewish settlement in view of their actual occupation by Arab cultivation and of the importance of making available suitable land on which to place the Arab cultivators who are now landless."

The language of this passage needs to be read in the light of the policy as a whole. It is desirable to make it clear that the landless Arabs, to whom it was intended to refer in the passage quoted, were such Arabs as can be shown to have been displaced from the lands which they occupied in consequence of the land passing into Jewish hands, and who have not obtained other holdings on which they establish themselves, or other equally satisfactory occupation. The number of such displaced Arabs must be a matter for careful inquiry. It is to landless Arabs within this category that His Majesty's Government feels itself under an obligation to facilitate their settlement upon the land. The recognition of this obligation in no way detracts from the larger purposes of development which His Majesty's Government regards as the most effectual means of furthering the establishment of a national home for the Jews . . .

Further, the statement of policy of His Majesty's Government did not imply a prohibition of acquisition of additional lands by Jews. It contains no such prohibition, nor is any such intended. . . .

But the intention of His Majesty's Government appears to have been represented as being that "no further immigration of Jews is to be permitted as long as it might prevent any Arab from obtaining employment." His Majesty's Government never proposed to pursue such a policy. They were concerned to state that, in the regulation of Jewish immigration, the following principles should apply: *viz.*, that "it is essential to ensure that the immigrants should not be burden on the people of Palestine as a whole, and that they should not deprive any section of the present population of their employment" *(White Paper 1922)*.

In one aspect, His Majesty's Government have to be mindful of their obligations to facilitate Jewish immigration under suitable conditions and to encourage close settlement by Jews on the land; in the other aspect, they have to be equally mindful of their duty to ensure that no prejudice results to the rights and position of the non-Jewish community. It is because of this apparent conflict of obligation that His Majesty's Government have felt bound to emphasize the necessity of the proper application of the absorptive principle.

That principle is vital to any scheme of development, the primary purpose of which must be the settlement both of Jews and of displaced Arabs on the land. It is for that reason that His Majesty's Government have insisted, and are compelled to insist, that government immigration regulations must be properly applied. The considerations relevant to the limits of absorptive capacity are purely economic considerations.

His Majesty's Government did not prescribe and do not contemplate any stoppage or prohibition of Jewish immigration in any of its categories. . . .

Immigrants with prospects of employment other than employment of a purely ephemeral character will not be excluded on the sole ground that the employment cannot be guaranteed to be of unlimited duration.

In determining the extent to which immigration at any time may be permitted, it is necessary also to have regard to the declared policy of the Jewish Agency to the effect that "in all the works or undertakings carried out or furthered by the Agency it shall be deemed to be a matter of principle that Jewish labor shall be employed." His Majesty's Government do not in any way challenge the right of the Agency to formulate or approve and endorse this policy. The principle of preferential, and indeed exclusive, employment of Jewish labor by Jewish organizations is a principle which the Jewish Agency are entitled to affirm. But it must be pointed out that if in consequence of this policy Arab labor is displaced or existing unemployment becomes aggravated, that is a factor in the situation to which the mandatory is bound to have regard.

His Majesty's Government desire to say, finally, as they have repeatedly and unequivocally affirmed, that the obligations imposed upon the mandatory by its acceptance of the mandate are solemn international obligations from which there is not now, nor has there been at any time, an intention to depart. To the tasks imposed by the mandate, His Majesty's Government have set their hand, and they will not withdraw it. But if their efforts are to be successful, there is need for cooperation, confidence, readiness on all sides to appreciate the difficulties and complexities of the problem, and, above all, there must be a full and unqualified recognition that no solution can be satisfactory or permanent which is not based upon justice, both to the Jewish people and to the non-Jewish communities of Palestine.

Ramsay MacDonald

15 The Palestine Royal Commission (Peel Commission)

Report (July 24, 1937)

C.495.M.336.1937.VI.
Geneva, November 30th, 1937.

LEAGUE OF NATIONS

MANDATES

PALESTINE

REPORT
of the
PALESTINE ROYAL COMMISSION

presented by the Secretary of State for the Colonies
to the United Kingdom Parliament
by Command of His Britannic Majesty
(July 1937)
Distributed at the request of the United Kingdom Government.

. . .

PALESTINE
Royal Commission

SUMMARY OF REPORT

SUMMARY OF THE REPORT OF THE PALESTINE ROYAL
COMMISSION.

The Members of the Palestine Royal Commission were:

Rt. Hon. EARL PEEL, G.C.S.I., G.B.E. (Chairman).
Rt. Hon. Sir HORACE RUMBOLD, Bart., G.C.B., G.C.M.G., M.V.O.
(Vice-Chairman).
Sir LAURIE HAMMOND, K.C.S.I., C.B.E.

DOI: 10.4324/9781003348948-18

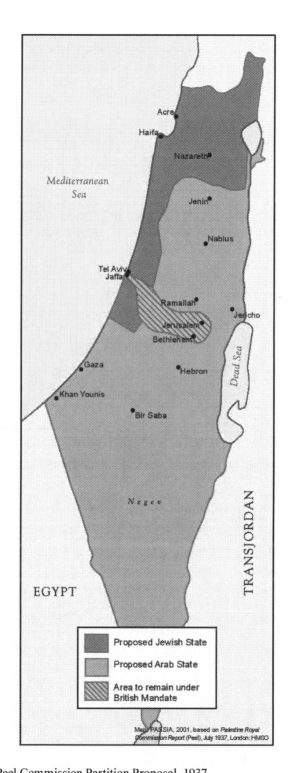

Map 5 The Peel Commission Partition Proposal, 1937

Source: Permission granted by the Palestinian Academic Society for the Study of International Affairs to reprint their map of the Peel Commission proposal in this book. The original can be found at: www.passia.org/maps/view/8.

Sir MORRIS CARTER, C.B.E.
Sir HAROLD MORRIS, M.B.E., K.C.
Professor REGINALD COUPLAND, C.I.E.

Mr. J. M. MARTIN was Secretary.

The Commission was appointed in August, 1936, with the following terms of reference:

> To ascertain the underlying causes of the disturbances which broke out in Palestine in the middle of April; to enquire into the manner in which the Mandate for Palestine is being implemented in relation to the obligations of the Mandatory towards the Arabs and the Jews respectively; and to ascertain whether, upon a proper construction of the terms of the Mandate, either the Arabs or the Jews have any legitimate grievances on account of the way in which the Mandate has been or is being implemented; and if the Commission is satisfied that any such grievances are well-founded, to make recommendation for their removal and for the prevention of their recurrence.

The following is a summary of the Commission's Report:

Summary

Part I: The Problem

CHAPTER I. – THE HISTORICAL BACKGROUND

A brief account of ancient Jewish times in Palestine, of the Arab conquest and occupation, of the dispersion of the Jews and the development of the Jewish Problem, and the growth and meaning of Zionism.

CHAPTER II. – THE WAR AND THE MANDATE

In order to obtain Arab support in the War, the British Government promised the Sherif of Mecca in 1915 that, in the event of an Allied victory, the greater part of the Arab provinces of the Turkish Empire would become independent. The Arabs understood that Palestine would be included in the sphere of independence.

In order to obtain the support of World Jewry, the British Government in 1917 issued the Balfour Declaration. The Jews understood that, if the experiment of establishing a Jewish National Home succeeded and a sufficient number of Jews went to Palestine, the National Home might develop in course of time into a Jewish State.

At the end of the War, the Mandate System was accepted by the Allied and Associated Powers as the vehicle for the execution of the policy of the Balfour Declaration, and, after a period of delay, the Mandate for Palestine was approved by the League of Nations and the United States. . . .

CHAPTER III. – PALESTINE FROM 1920 TO 1936

During the first years of the Civil Administration, which was set up in 1920, a beginning was made on the one hand with the provision of public services, which mainly affected the Arab majority of the population, and on the other hand with the establishment of the Jewish National Home. There were outbreaks of disorder in 1920 and 1921, but in 1925 it was thought that the prospects of ultimate harmony between the Arabs and the Jews seemed so favourable that the forces for maintaining order were substantially reduced.

These hopes proved unfounded because, although Palestine as a whole became more prosperous, the causes of the outbreaks of 1920 and 1921, namely, the demand of the Arabs for national independence and their antagonism to the National Home, remained unmodified and were indeed accentuated by the "external factors," namely, the pressure of the Jews of Europe on Palestine and the development of Arab nationalism in neighbouring countries.

These same causes brought about the outbreaks of 1929 and 1933. By 1936 the external factors had been intensified by –

(1) the sufferings of the Jews in Germany and Poland, resulting in a great increase of Jewish immigration into Palestine; and
(2) the prospect of Syria and the Lebanon soon obtaining the same independence as Iraq and Saudi Arabia. Egypt was also on the eve of independence.

CHAPTER IV. – THE DISTURBANCES OF 1936

These disturbances (which are briefly summarized) were similar in character to the four previous outbreaks, although more serious and prolonged. As in 1933, it was not only the Jews who were attacked, but the Palestine Government. A new feature was the part played by the Rulers of the neighbouring Arab States in bringing about the end of the strike.

The underlying causes of the disturbances of 1936 were –

(1) the desire of the Arabs for national independence;
(2) their hatred and fear of the establishment of the Jewish National Home.

These two causes were the same as those of all the previous outbreaks and have always been inextricably linked together. Of several subsidiary factors, the more important were

(1) the advance of Arab nationalism outside Palestine;
(2) the increased immigration of Jews since 1933;
(3) the opportunity enjoyed by the Jews for influencing public opinion in Britain;
(4) Arab distrust in the sincerity of the British Government;
(5) Arab alarm at the continued Jewish purchase of land;
(6) the general uncertainty as to the ultimate intentions of the Mandatory Power.

CHAPTER V. – THE PRESENT SITUATION

The Jewish National Home is no longer an experiment. The growth of its population has been accompanied by political, social, and economic developments along the lines laid down at the outset. . . . The temper of the Home is strongly nationalist. There can be no question of fusion or assimilation between Jewish and Arab cultures. The National Home cannot be half-national.

Crown Colony government is not suitable for such a highly educated, democratic community as the National Home and fosters an unhealthy irresponsibility.

The National Home is bent on forcing the pace of its development, not only because of the desire of the Jews to escape from Europe, but because of anxiety as to the future in Palestine.

. . .

Arab nationalism is as intense a force as Jewish. The Arab leaders' demand for national self-government and the shutting down of the Jewish National Home has remained unchanged since 1929 . . .

The only solution of the problem put forward by the Arab Higher Committee was the immediate establishment of an independent Arab Government, which would deal with the 400,000 Jews now in Palestine as it thought fit. To that it is replied that belief in British good faith would not be strengthened anywhere in the world if the National Home were now surrendered to Arab rule.

The Jewish Agency and the *Va'ad Leumi* asserted that the problem would be solved if the Mandate were firmly applied in full accordance with Jewish claims: thus, there should be no new restriction on immigration nor anything to prevent the Jewish population becoming in course of time a majority in Palestine. . . .

Part II: The Operation of the Mandate

The Commission exhaustively considered what might be done in one field after another in execution of the Mandate to improve the prospects of peace. . . .

CHAPTER VI. – ADMINISTRATION . . .

CHAPTER VII. – PUBLIC SECURITY . . .

CHAPTER VIII. – FINANCIAL AND FISCAL QUESTIONS . . .

CHAPTER IX. – THE LAND . . .

CHAPTER X. – IMMIGRATION . . .

CHAPTER XI. – TRANS-JORDAN . . .

CHAPTER XII. – HEALTH . . .

CHAPTER XIII. – PUBLIC WORKS AND SERVICES . . .

CHAPTER XIV. – THE CHRISTIANS

The religious stake of the Christians in the Holy Places is just as great as that of the Jews or Moslems. The Christians of the world cannot be indifferent to the justice and well-being of their co-religionists in the Holy Land. . . .

In political matters the Christian Arabs have thrown in their lot with their Moslem brethren.

CHAPTER XV. – NATIONALITY LAW AND ACQUISITION OF PALESTINIAN CITIZENSHIP . . .

CHAPTER XVI. – EDUCATION . . .

CHAPTER XVII. – LOCAL GOVERNMENT . . .

CHAPTER XVIII. – SELF-GOVERNING INSTITUTIONS . . .

CHAPTER XIX. – CONCLUSION AND RECOMMENDATIONS

The Commission recapitulate the conclusions set out in this part of the Report and summarize the Arab and Jewish grievances and their own recommendations for the removal of such as are legitimate. They add, however, that these are not the recommendations which their terms of reference require. They will not, that is to say, remove the grievances nor prevent their recurrence. They are the best palliatives the Commission can devise for the disease from which Palestine is suffering, but they are only palliatives. They cannot cure the trouble. The disease is so deep-rooted that in the Commissioners' firm conviction the only hope of a cure lies in a surgical operation.

Part III: The Possibility of a Lasting Settlement

CHAPTER XX. – THE FORCE OF CIRCUMSTANCES

The problem of Palestine is briefly restated.

Under the stress of the World War the British Government made promises to Arabs and Jews in order to obtain their support. On the strength of those promises both parties formed certain expectations.

The application to Palestine of the Mandate System in general and of the specific Mandate in particular implies the belief that the obligations thus undertaken towards the Arabs and the Jews respectively would prove in course of time to be mutually compatible owing to the conciliatory effect on the Palestinian Arabs of the material prosperity which Jewish immigration would bring in Palestine as a whole. That belief has not been justified, and there seems to be no hope of its being justified in the future.

. . .

The existing circumstances are summarized as follows.

An irrepressible conflict has arisen between two national communities within the narrow bounds of one small country. There is no common ground between them. Their national aspirations are incompatible. The Arabs desire to revive the traditions of the Arab golden age. The Jews desire to show what they can achieve when restored to the land in which the Jewish nation was born. Neither of the two national ideals permits of combination in the service of a single State.

The conflict has grown steadily more bitter since 1920 and the process will continue. Conditions inside Palestine, especially the systems of education, are strengthening the national sentiment of the two peoples. . . . "Who in the end will govern Palestine?" it is asked. . . . On the one hand in less than three years' time Syria and the Lebanon will attain their national sovereignty, and the claim of the Palestinian Arabs to share in the freedom of all Asiatic Arabia will thus be fortified. On the other hand, the hardships and anxieties of the Jews in Europe are not likely to grow less, and the appeal to the good faith and humanity of the British people will lose none of its force.

Meanwhile, the Government of Palestine, which is at present an unsuitable form for governing educated Arabs and democratic Jews, cannot develop into a system of self-government as it has elsewhere, because there is no such system which could ensure justice both to the Arabs and to the Jews. Government therefore remains unrepresentative and unable to dispel the conflicting grievances of the two dissatisfied and irresponsible communities it governs.

In these circumstances peace can only be maintained in Palestine under the Mandate by repression. . . . The moral objections to repression are self-evident. Nor need the undesirable reactions of it on opinion outside Palestine be emphasized. Moreover, repression will not solve the problem. It will exacerbate the quarrel. It will not help towards the establishment of a single self-governing Palestine. It is not easy to pursue the dark path of repression without seeing daylight at the end of it.

The British people will not flinch from the task of continuing to govern Palestine under the Mandate if they are in honour bound to do so, but they would be justified in asking if there is no other way in which their duty can be done.

Nor would Britain wish to repudiate her obligations. The trouble is that they have proved irreconcilable, and this conflict is the more unfortunate because each of the obligations taken separately accords with British sentiment and British interest. The development of self-government in the Arab world on the one hand is in accordance with British principles, and British public opinion is wholly sympathetic with Arab aspirations towards a new age of unity and prosperity in the Arab world. British interest similarly has always been bound up with the peace of the Middle East, and British statesmanship can show an almost unbroken record of friendship with the Arabs. There is a strong British tradition, on the other hand, of friendship with the Jewish people, and it is in the British interest to retain as far as may be the confidence of the Jewish people.

The continuance of the present system means the gradual alienation of two peoples who are traditionally the friends of Britain.

The problem cannot be solved by giving either the Arabs or the Jews all they want. The answer to the question which of them in the end will govern Palestine must be "Neither." No fair-minded statesman can think it right either that 400,000 Jews, whose entry into Palestine has been facilitated by the British Government and approved by the League of Nations, should be handed over to Arab rule, or that, if the Jews should become a majority, a million Arabs should be handed over to their rule. But while neither race can fairly rule all Palestine, each race might justly rule part of it.

The idea of Partition has doubtless been thought of before as a solution of the problem, but it has probably been discarded as being impracticable. . . . Partition offers a chance of ultimate peace. No other plan does.

CHAPTER XXI. – CANTONISATION

The political division of Palestine could be effected in a less thorough manner than by Partition. It could be divided like Federal States into provinces and cantons, which would be self-governing in such matters as immigration and land sales as well as social services. The Mandatory Government would remain as a central or federal government controlling such matters as foreign relations, defence, customs, and the like.

Cantonisation is attractive at first sight because it seems to solve the three major problems of land, immigration, and self-government, but there are obvious weaknesses in it. First, the working of federal systems depends on sufficient community of interest or tradition to maintain harmony between the Central Government and the cantons. In Palestine both Arabs and Jews would regard the Central Government as an alien and interfering body. Secondly, the financial relations between the Central Government and the cantons would revive the existing quarrel between Arabs and Jews as to the distribution of a surplus of federal revenue or as to the contributions of the cantons towards a federal deficit. Unrestricted Jewish immigration into the Jewish canton might lead to a demand for the expansion of federal services at the expense of the Arab canton. Thirdly, the costly task of maintaining law and order would still rest mainly on the Central Government. Fourthly, Cantonisation, like Partition, cannot avoid leaving a minority of each race in the area controlled by the other. The solution of this problem requires such bold measures as can only be contemplated if there is a prospect of final peace. Partition opens up such a prospect. Cantonisation does not. Lastly, Cantonisation does not settle the question of national self-government. Neither the Arabs nor the Jews would feel their political aspirations were satisfied with purely cantonal self-government.

Cantonisation, in sum, presents most, if not all, of the difficulties presented by Partition without Partition's one supreme advantage – the possibilities it offers of eventual peace.

CHAPTER XXII. – A PLAN OF PARTITION

While the Commission would not be expected to embark on the further protracted inquiry which would be needed for working out a scheme of Partition in full detail, it would be idle to put forward the principle of Partition and not to give it any concrete shape. Clearly it must be shown that an actual plan can be devised which meets the main requirements of the case.

1. A TREATY SYSTEM

The Mandate for Palestine should terminate and be replaced by a Treaty System in accordance with the precedent set in Iraq and Syria.

A new Mandate for the Holy Places should be instituted to fulfil the purposes defined in Section 2 below.

Treaties of alliance should be negotiated by the Mandatory with the Government of Trans-Jordan and representatives of the Arabs of Palestine on the one hand and with the Zionist Organisation on the other. These Treaties would declare that, within as short a period as may be convenient, two sovereign independent States would be established – the one an Arab State consisting of Trans-Jordan united with that part of Palestine which lies to the east and south of a frontier such as we suggest in Section 3 below; the other a Jewish State consisting of that part of Palestine which lies to the north and west of that frontier.

The Mandatory would undertake to support any requests for admission to the League of Nations which the Governments of the Arab and the Jewish States might make.

. . .

2. THE HOLY PLACES

The Partition of Palestine is subject to the overriding necessity of keeping the sanctity of Jerusalem and Bethlehem inviolate and of ensuring free and safe access to them for all the world. That, in the fullest sense of the mandatory phrase, is "a sacred trust of civilization" – a trust on behalf not merely of the peoples of Palestine but of multitudes in other lands to whom those places, one or both, are Holy Places.

. . .

3. THE FRONTIER

The natural principle for the Partition of Palestine is to separate the areas in which the Jews have acquired land and settled from those which are wholly or mainly occupied by Arabs. This offers a fair and practicable basis for Partition, provided that in accordance with the spirit of British obligations, (1) a reasonable allowance is made within the boundaries of the Jewish State for the growth of population and colonization, and (2) reasonable compensation is given to the Arab State for the loss of land and revenue.

. . .

4. INTER-STATE SUBVENTION

The Jews contribute more *per capita* to the revenues of Palestine than the Arabs, and the Government has thereby been enabled to maintain public services for the Arabs at a higher level than would otherwise have been possible. Partition would mean, on the one hand, that the Arab Area would no longer profit from the taxable capacity of the Jewish Area. On the other hand, (1) the Jews would acquire a new right of sovereignty in the Jewish Area; (2) that Area, as we have defined it, would be larger than the existing area of Jewish land and settlement; (3) the Jews would be freed from their present liability for helping to promote the welfare of Arabs outside that Area. It is suggested, therefore, that the Jewish State should pay a subvention to the Arab State when Partition comes into effect. There have been recent precedents for equitable financial arrangements of this kind in those connected with the separation of Sind from Bombay and of Burma from the Indian Empire, and in accordance with those precedents a Finance Commission should be appointed to consider and report as to what the amount of the subvention should be . . .

5. BRITISH SUBVENTION . . .

6. TARIFFS AND PORTS . . .

7. NATIONALITY . . .

8. CIVIL SERVICES . . .

9. INDUSTRIAL CONCESSIONS . . .

10. EXCHANGE OF LAND AND POPULATION . . .

The Treaties should provide that, if Arab owners of land in the Jewish State or Jewish owners of land in the Arab State should wish to sell their land and any plantations or crops thereon, the Government of the State concerned should be responsible for the purchase of such land, plantations, and crops at a price to be fixed, if requires, by the Mandatory Administration.

. . .

CHAPTER X. – CONCLUSION

Considering the attitude which both the Arab and the Jewish representatives adopted in giving evidence, the Commission think it improbable that either party will be satisfied at first sight with the proposals submitted for the adjustment of their rival claims. For Partition means that neither will get all it wants. It means that the Arabs must acquiesce in the exclusion from their sovereignty of a piece of territory, long occupied and once ruled by them. It means that the Jews must be content with less than the Land of Israel they once ruled and have hoped to rule again. But it seems possible that on reflection both parties will come to realize that the drawbacks of Partition are outweighed by its advantages. For, if it offers neither party all it wants, it offers each what it wants most, namely freedom and security.

The advantages to the Arabs of Partition on the lines we have proposed may be summarized as follows:

(i) They obtain their national independence and can co-operate on an equal footing with the Arabs of the neighbouring countries in the cause of Arab unity and progress.

(ii) They are finally delivered from the fear of being swamped by the Jews and from the possibility of ultimate subjection to Jewish rule.

(iii) In particular, the final limitation of the Jewish National Home within a fixed frontier and the enactment of a new Mandate for the protection of the Holy Places, solemnly guaranteed by the League of Nations, removes all anxiety lest the Holy Places should ever come under Jewish control.

(iv) As a set-off to the loss of territory the Arabs regard as theirs, the Arab State will receive a subvention from the Jewish State. It will also, in view of the backwardness of Trans-Jordan, obtain a grant of £2,000,000 from the British Treasury; and, if an agreement can be reached as to the exchange of land and population, a further grant will be made for the conversion, as far as may prove possible, of uncultivable land in the Arab State into productive land from which the cultivators and the State alike will profit.

The advantages of Partition to the Jews may be summarized as follows:

(i) Partition secures the establishment of the Jewish National Home and relieves it from the possibility of its being subjected in the future to Arab rule.

(ii) Partition enables the Jews in the fullest sense to call their National Home their own; for it converts it into a Jewish State. Its citizens will be able to admit as many Jews into it as they themselves believe can be absorbed. They will attain the primary objective of Zionism – a Jewish nation, planted in Palestine, giving its nationals the same status in the world as other nations give theirs. They will cease at last to live a minority life.

To both Arabs and Jews, Partition offers a prospect – and there is none in any other policy – of obtaining the inestimable boon of peace. It is surely worth some sacrifice on both sides if the quarrel which the Mandate started could he ended with its termination. It is not a natural or old-standing feud. The Arabs throughout their history have not only been free from anti-Jewish sentiment but have also shown that the spirit of compromise is deeply rooted in their life. Considering what the possibility of finding a refuge in Palestine means to many thousands of suffering Jews, is the loss occasioned by Partition, great as it would be, more than Arab generosity can bear? In this, as in so much else connected with Palestine, it is not only the peoples of that country who have to be considered. The Jewish Problem is not the least of the many problems which are disturbing international relations at this critical time and obstructing the path to peace and prosperity. If the Arabs at some sacrifice could help to solve that problem, they would earn the gratitude not of the Jews alone but of all the Western World.

There was a time when Arab statesmen were willing to concede little Palestine to the Jews, provided that the rest of Arab Asia were free. That condition was not fulfilled then, but it is on the eve of fulfilment now. In less than three years' time all the wide Arab area outside Palestine between the Mediterranean and the Indian Ocean will be independent, and, if Partition is adopted, the greater part of Palestine will be independent too.

As to the British people, they are bound to honour to the utmost of their power the obligations they undertook in the exigencies of war towards the Arabs and the Jews. When those obligations were incorporated in the Mandate, they did not fully realize the difficulties of the task it laid on them. They have tried to overcome them, not always with success. The difficulties have steadily become greater till now they seem almost insuperable. Partition offers a possibility of finding a way through them, a possibility of obtaining a final solution of the problem which does justice to the rights and aspirations of both the Arabs and the Jews and discharges the obligations undertaken towards them 20 years ago to the fullest extent that is practicable in the circumstances of the present time.

16 British Government

Policy Statement Against Partition (November 11, 1938)

PALESTINE

Statement by

His Majesty's Government

in the United Kingdom

. . .

November, 1938

1. The Royal Commission, presided over by the late Earl Peel, published its report in July, 1937, and proposed a solution of the Palestine problem by means of a scheme of partition under which independent Arab and Jewish States would be established while other areas would be retained under mandatory administration. . . . His Majesty's Government in the United Kingdom announced their general agreement with the arguments and conclusions of the Royal Commission and expressed the view that a scheme of partition on the general lines recommended by the Commission represented the best and most hopeful solution of the deadlock.

2. . . . This proposal was subsequently discussed in Parliament and at meetings of the Permanent Mandates Commission and the Council and Assembly of the League of Nations, when His Majesty's Government received authority to explore the practical application of the principle of partition. A despatch of 23rd December, 1937, from the Secretary of State for the Colonies to the High Commissioner for Palestine, announced the intention of His Majesty's Government to undertake the further investigations required for the drawing up of a more precise and detailed scheme. It was pointed out that the final decision could not be taken in merely general terms and that the further enquiry would provide the necessary material on which to judge, when the best possible partition scheme had been formulated, its equity and practicability. The despatch also defined the functions and terms of reference of the technical Commission who were

DOI: 10.4324/9781003348948-19

appointed to visit Palestine for the purpose of submitting in due course to His Majesty's Government proposals for such a detailed scheme.

3. His Majesty's Government have now received the report of the Palestine Partition Commission, who have carried out their investigations with great thoroughness and efficiency. . . . Their report is now published, together with a summary of their conclusions. It will be noted that the four members of the Commission advise unanimously against the adoption of the scheme of partition outlined by the Royal Commission. . . . The report points out that under either plan, while the budget of the Jewish State is likely to show a substantial surplus, the budgets of the Arab State (including Trans-Jordan) and of the Mandated Territories are likely to show substantial deficits. The Commission reject as impracticable the Royal Commission's recommendation for a direct subvention from the Jewish State to the Arab State. They think that, on economic grounds, a customs union between the States and the Mandated Territories is essential and they examine the possibility of finding the solution for the financial and economic problems of partition by means of a scheme based upon such a union. . . . Their conclusion is that, on a strict interpretation of their terms of reference, they have no alternative but to report that they are unable to recommend boundaries for the proposed areas which will afford a reasonable prospect of the eventual establishment of self-supporting Arab and Jewish States.

4. His Majesty's Government, after careful study of the Partition Commission's report, have reached the conclusion that this further examination has shown that the political, administrative, and financial difficulties involved in the proposal to create independent Arab and Jewish States inside Palestine are so great that this solution of the problem is impracticable.

5. His Majesty's Government will therefore continue their responsibility for the government of the whole of Palestine. They are now faced with the problem of finding alternative means of meeting the needs of the difficult situation described by the Royal Commission which will be consistent with their obligations to the Arabs and the Jews. His Majesty's Government believe that it is possible to find these alternative means. They have already given much thought to the problem in the light of the reports of the Royal Commission and of the Partition Commission. It is clear that the surest foundation for peace and progress in Palestine would be an understanding between the Arabs and the Jews, and His Majesty's Government are prepared in the first instance to make a determined effort to promote such an understanding. With this end in view, they propose immediately to invite representatives of the Palestinian Arabs and of neighbouring States, on the one hand, and of the Jewish Agency, on the other, to confer with them as soon as possible in London regarding future policy, including the question of immigration into Palestine. As regards the representation of the Palestinian Arabs, His Majesty's Government

must reserve the right to refuse to receive those leaders whom they regard as responsible for the campaign of assassination and violence.

6. His Majesty's Government hope that these discussions in London may help to promote agreement as to future policy regarding Palestine. They attach great importance, however, to a decision being reached at an early date. Therefore, if the London discussions should not produce agreement within a reasonable period of time, they will take their own decision in the light of their examination of the problem and of the discussions in London, and announce the policy which they propose to pursue.

7. In considering and settling their policy, His Majesty's Government will keep constantly in mind the international character of the Mandate with which they have been entrusted and their obligations in that respect.

17 British Government

The [MacDonald] White Paper (May 17, 1939)

PALESTINE

Statement of Policy

Presented by the Secretary of State for the Colonies to Parliament

by Command of His Majesty
May, 1939
Cmd. 6019.

Statement of Policy

In the Statement on Palestine, issued on 9th November, 1938, [Cmd. 5893] His Majesty's Government announced their intention to invite representatives of the Arabs of Palestine, of certain neighbouring countries, and of the Jewish Agency to confer with them in London regarding future policy. . . . In the light of the discussions as well as of the situation in Palestine and of the Reports of the Royal Commission [Cmd. 5479] and the Partition Commission [Cmd. 5854], certain proposals were formulated by His Majesty's Government and were laid before the Arab and Jewish delegations as the basis of an agreed settlement. Neither the Arab nor the Jewish delegations felt able to accept these proposals, and the conferences therefore did not result in an agreement. Accordingly, His Majesty's Government are free to formulate their own policy, and after careful consideration they have decided to adhere generally to the proposals which were finally submitted to, and discussed with, the Arab and Jewish delegations.

2. The Mandate for Palestine, the terms of which were confirmed by the Council of the League of Nations in 1922, has governed the policy of successive British Governments for nearly 20 years. It embodies the Balfour Declaration and imposes on the Mandatory four main obligations. These obligations are set out in Articles 2, 6, and 13 of the Mandate. There is no dispute regarding the interpretation of one of these obligations, that touching

DOI: 10.4324/9781003348948-20

the protection of and access to the Holy Places and religious buildings or sites. The other three main obligations are generally as follows:

(i) To place the country under such political, administrative, and economic conditions as will secure the establishment in Palestine of a national home for the Jewish people, to facilitate Jewish immigration under suitable conditions, and to encourage, in co-operation with the Jewish Agency, close settlement by Jews on the land.

(ii) To safeguard the civil and religious rights of all the inhabitants of Palestine irrespective of race and religion, and, whilst facilitating Jewish immigration and settlement, to ensure that the rights and position of other sections of the population are not prejudiced.

(iii) To place the country under such political, administrative, and economic conditions as will secure the development of self-governing institutions.

3. The Royal Commission and previous Commissions of Enquiry have drawn attention to the ambiguity of certain expressions in the Mandate, such as the expression "a national home for the Jewish people," and they have found in this ambiguity and the resulting uncertainty as to the objectives of policy a fundamental cause of unrest and hostility between Arabs and Jews. His Majesty's Government are convinced that in the interests of the peace and well-being of the whole people of Palestine a clear definition of policy and objectives is essential. The proposal of partition recommended by the Royal Commission would have afforded such clarity, but the establishment of self-supporting independent Arab and Jewish States within Palestine has been found to be impracticable. It has therefore been necessary for His Majesty's Government to devise an alternative policy which will, consistently with their obligations to Arabs and Jews, meet the needs of the situation in Palestine. Their views and proposals are set forth below under the three heads, (I) The Constitution, (II) Immigration, and (III) Land.

I. The Constitution

4. It has been urged that the expression "a national home for the Jewish people" offered a prospect that Palestine might in due course become a Jewish State or Commonwealth. His Majesty's Government do not wish to contest the view, which was expressed by the Royal Commission, that the Zionist leaders at the time of the issue of the Balfour Declaration recognised that an ultimate Jewish State was not precluded by the terms of the Declaration. But, with the Royal Commission, His Majesty's Government believe that the framers of the Mandate in which the Balfour Declaration was embodied could not have intended that Palestine should be converted into a Jewish State against the will of the Arab population of the country. That Palestine was not to be converted into a Jewish State might be held to be implied in

the passage from the Command Paper of 1922 [Cmd. 1700] which reads as follows:

> Unauthorised statements have been made to the effect that the purpose in view is to create a wholly Jewish Palestine. Phrases have been used such as that 'Palestine is to become as Jewish as England is English'. His Majesty's Government regard any such expectation as impracticable and have no such aim in view. Nor have they at any time contemplated . . . the disappearance or the subordination of the Arabic population, language or culture in Palestine. They would draw attention to the fact that the terms of the (Balfour) Declaration referred to do not contemplate that Palestine as a whole should be converted into a Jewish National Home, but that such a Home should be founded *in Palestine*.

But this statement has not removed doubts, and His Majesty's Government therefore now declare unequivocally that it is not part of their policy that Palestine should become a Jewish State. They would indeed regard it as contrary to their obligations to the Arabs under the Mandate, as well as to the assurances which have been given to the Arab people in the past, that the Arab population of Palestine should be made the subjects of a Jewish State against their will.

5. The nature of the Jewish National Home in Palestine was further described in the Command Paper of 1922 as follows:

> During the last two or three generations the Jews have recreated in Palestine a community, now numbering 80,000, of whom about one-fourth are farmers or workers upon the land. This community has its own political organs; an elected assembly for the direction of its domestic concerns; elected councils in the towns; and an organisation for the control of its schools. It has its elected Chief Rabbinate and Rabbinical Council for the direction of its religious affairs. Its business is conducted in Hebrew as a vernacular language, and a Hebrew press serves its needs. It has its distinctive intellectual life and displays considerable economic activity. This community, then, with its town and country population, its political, religious and social organisations, its own language, its own customs, its own life, has in fact 'national' characteristics. When it is asked what is meant by the development of the Jewish National Home in Palestine, it may be answered that it is not the imposition of a Jewish nationality upon the inhabitants of Palestine as a whole, but the further development of the existing Jewish community, with the assistance of Jews in other parts of the world, in order that it may become a centre in which the Jewish people as a whole may take, on grounds of religion and race, an interest and a pride. . . . it is essential that it should know that it is in Palestine as of right and not on sufferance. That is the reason why it is necessary that the

existence of a Jewish National Home in Palestine should be internationally guaranteed, and that it should be formally recognised to rest upon ancient historic connection.

6. His Majesty's Government adhere to this interpretation of the Declaration of 1917 and regard it as an authoritative and comprehensive description of the character of the Jewish National Home in Palestine. . . . Evidence that His Majesty's Government have been carrying out their obligation in this respect is to be found in the facts that, since the statement of 1922 was published, more than 300,000 Jews have immigrated to Palestine, and that the population of the National Home has risen to some 450,000, or approaching a third of the entire population of the country. . . .

7. In the recent discussions the Arab delegations have repeated the contention that Palestine was included within the area in which Sir Henry McMahon, on behalf of the British Government, in October, 1915, undertook to recognise and support Arab independence. The validity of this claim. . . . was thoroughly and carefully investigated by British and Arab representatives during the recent conferences in London. Their Report, which has been published, [Cmd. 5974] states that both the Arab and the British representatives endeavoured to understand the point of view of the other party but that they were unable to reach agreement upon an interpretation of the correspondence. . . . His Majesty's Government regret the misunderstandings which have arisen as regards some of the phrases used. For their part they can only adhere, for the reasons given by their representatives in the Report, to the view that the whole of Palestine west of Jordan was excluded from Sir Henry McMahon's pledge, and they therefore cannot agree that the McMahon correspondence forms a just basis for the claim that Palestine should be converted into an Arab State.

8. His Majesty's Government are charged as the Mandatory authority "to secure the development of self-governing institutions" in Palestine. Apart from this specific obligation, they would regard it as contrary to the whole spirit of the Mandate system that the population of Palestine should remain forever under Mandatory tutelage. It is proper that the people of the country should as early as possible enjoy the rights of self-government which are exercised by the people of neighbouring countries. His Majesty's Government are unable at present to foresee the exact constitutional forms which government in Palestine will eventually take, but their objective is self-government, and they desire to see established ultimately an independent Palestine State. It should be a State in which the two in Palestine, Arabs and Jews, share authority in government in such a way that the essential interests of each are secured.

9. The establishment of an independent State and the complete relinquishment of Mandatory control in Palestine would require such relations between the Arabs and the Jews as would make good government possible. Moreover, the growth of self-governing institutions in Palestine, as in

other countries, must be an evolutionary process. A transitional period will be required before independence is achieved, throughout which ultimate responsibility for the Government of the country will be retained by His Majesty's Government as the Mandatory authority, while the people of the country are taking an increasing share in the Government, and understanding and co-operation amongst them are growing. It will be the constant endeavour of His Majesty's Government to promote good relations between the Arabs and the Jews.

10. In the light of these considerations His Majesty's Government make the following declaration of their intentions regarding the future government of Palestine:

(1) The objective of His Majesty's Government is the establishment within 10 years of an independent Palestine State in such treaty relations with the United Kingdom as will provide satisfactorily for the commercial and strategic requirements of both countries in the future. This proposal for the establishment of the independent State would involve consultation with the Council of the League of Nations with a view to the termination of the Mandate.

(2) The independent State should be one in which Arabs and Jews share in government in such a way as to ensure that the essential interests of each community are safeguarded.

(3) The establishment of the independent State will be preceded by a transitional period throughout which His Majesty's Government will retain responsibility for the government of the country. . . . Both sections of the population will have an opportunity to participate in the machinery of government, and the process will be carried on whether or not they both avail themselves of it.

(4) As soon as peace and order have been sufficiently restored in Palestine steps will be taken to carry out this policy of giving the people of Palestine an increasing part in the government of their country, the objective being to place Palestinians in charge of all the Departments of Government, with the assistance of British advisers and subject to the control of the High Commissioner. With this object in view His Majesty's Government will be prepared immediately to arrange that Palestinians shall be placed in charge of certain Departments, with British advisers. . . . Arab and Jewish representatives will be invited to serve as heads of Departments approximately in proportion to their respective populations. The number of Palestinians in charge of Departments will be increased as circumstances permit until all heads of Departments are Palestinians, exercising the administrative and advisory functions which are at present performed by British officials. When that stage is reached consideration will be given to the question of converting the Executive Council into a Council of Ministers with a consequential change in the status and functions of the Palestinian heads of Departments.

(5) His Majesty's Government make no proposals at this stage regarding the establishment of an elective legislature. Nevertheless, they would regard this as an appropriate constitutional development, and, should public opinion in Palestine hereafter show itself in favour of such a development, they will be prepared, provided that local conditions permit, to establish the necessary machinery.

(6) At the end of five years from the restoration of peace and order, an appropriate body representative of the people of Palestine and of His Majesty's Government will be set up to review the working of the constitutional arrangements during the transitional period and to consider and make recommendations regarding the constitution of the independent Palestine State.

(7) His Majesty's Government will require to be satisfied that in the treaty contemplated by sub-paragraph (1) or in the constitution contemplated by sub-paragraph (6) adequate provision has been made for:

(a) the security of, and freedom of access to, the Holy Places, and the protection of the interests and property of the various religious bodies.

(b) the protection of the different communities in Palestine in accordance with the obligations of His Majesty's Government to both Arabs and Jews and for the special position in Palestine of the Jewish National Home.

(c) such requirements to meet the strategic situation as may be regarded as necessary by His Majesty's Government in the light of the circumstances then existing.

His Majesty's Government will also require to be satisfied that the interests of certain foreign countries in Palestine, for the preservation of which they are at present responsible, are adequately safeguarded.

(8) His Majesty's Government will do everything in their power to create conditions which will enable the independent Palestine State to come into being within 10 years. If, at the end of 10 years, it appears to His Majesty's Government that, contrary to their hope, circumstances require the postponement of the establishment of the independent State, they will consult with representatives of the people of Palestine, the Council of the League of Nations, and the neighbouring Arab States before deciding on such a postponement. If His Majesty's Government come to the conclusion that postponement is unavoidable, they will invite the co-operation of these parties in framing plans for the future with a view to achieving the desired objective at the earliest possible date.

    . . .

II. Immigration

12. Under Article 6 of the Mandate, the Administration of Palestine, "while ensuring that the rights and position of other sections of the population are not

prejudiced," is required to "facilitate Jewish immigration under suitable conditions." Beyond this, the extent to which Jewish immigration into Palestine is to be permitted is nowhere defined in the Mandate. But in the Command Paper of 1922 it was laid down that for the fulfilment of the policy of establishing a Jewish National Home

> it is necessary that the Jewish community in Palestine should be able to increase its numbers by immigration. This immigration cannot be so great in volume as to exceed whatever may be the economic capacity of the country at the time to absorb new arrivals. It is essential to ensure that the immigrants should not be a burden upon the people of Palestine as a whole, and that they should not deprive any section of the present population of their employment.

In practice, from that date onwards until recent times, the economic absorptive capacity of the country has been treated as the sole limiting factor, and in the letter which Mr. Ramsay MacDonald, as Prime Minister, sent to Dr. Weizmann in February 1931 [Hansard, Vol. 248, 13/2/31, Cols. 751–757] it was laid down as a matter of policy that economic absorptive capacity was the sole criterion. . . . But His Majesty's Government do not read either the Statement of Policy of 1922 or the letter of 1931 as implying that the Mandate requires them, for all time and in all circumstances, to facilitate the immigration of Jews into Palestine subject only to consideration of the country's economic absorptive capacity. Nor do they find anything in the Mandate or in subsequent Statements of Policy to support the view that the establishment of a Jewish National Home in Palestine cannot be effected unless immigration is allowed to continue indefinitely.

If immigration has an adverse effect on the economic position in the country, it should clearly be restricted; and equally, if it has a seriously damaging effect on the political position in the country, that is a factor that should not be ignored. . . . The methods employed by Arab terrorists against fellow-Arabs and Jews alike must receive unqualified condemnation. But it cannot be denied that fear of indefinite Jewish immigration is widespread amongst the Arab population and that this fear has made possible disturbances which have given a serious setback to economic progress, depleted the Palestine exchequer, rendered life and property insecure, and produced a bitterness between the Arab and Jewish populations which is deplorable between citizens of the same country.

If in these circumstances immigration is continued up to the economic absorptive capacity of the country, regardless of all other considerations, a fatal enmity between the two peoples will be perpetuated, and the situation in Palestine may become a permanent source of friction amongst all peoples in the Near and Middle East. His Majesty's Government cannot take the view that either their obligations under the Mandate, or considerations of common sense and justice, require that they should ignore these circumstances in framing immigration policy.

13. In the view of the Royal Commission, the association of the policy of the Balfour Declaration with the Mandate system implied the belief that Arab hostility to the former would sooner or later be overcome. It has been the hope of British Governments ever since the Balfour Declaration was issued that in time the Arab population, recognizing the advantages to be derived from Jewish settlement and development in Palestine, would become reconciled to the further growth of the Jewish National Home. This hope has not been fulfilled. The alternatives before His Majesty's Government are either (i) to seek to expand the Jewish National Home indefinitely by immigration, against the strongly expressed will of the Arab people of the country; or (ii) to permit further expansion of the Jewish National Home by immigration only if the Arabs are prepared to acquiesce in it. The former policy means rule by force. . . . Moreover, the relations between the Arabs and the Jews in Palestine must be based sooner or later on mutual tolerance and goodwill; the peace, security, and progress of the Jewish National Home itself require this. Therefore, His Majesty's Government, after earnest consideration, and taking into account the extent to which the growth of the Jewish National Home has been facilitated over the last 20 years, have decided that the time has come to adopt in principle the second of the alternatives referred to above.

14. It has been urged that all further Jewish immigration into Palestine should be stopped forthwith. His Majesty's Government cannot accept such a proposal. It would damage the whole of the financial and economic system of Palestine and thus affect adversely the interests of Arabs and Jews alike. Moreover, in the view of His Majesty's Government, abruptly to stop further immigration would be unjust to the Jewish National Home. But, above all, His Majesty's Government are conscious of the present unhappy plight of large numbers of Jews who seek a refuge from certain European countries, and they believe that Palestine can and should make a further contribution to the solution of this pressing world problem. In all these circumstances, they believe that they will be acting consistently with their Mandatory obligations to both Arabs and Jews, and in the manner best calculated to serve the interests of the whole people of Palestine, by adopting the following proposals regarding immigration:

(1) Jewish immigration during the next five years will be at a rate which, if economic absorptive capacity permits, will bring the Jewish population up to approximately one-third of the total population of the country. Taking into account the expected natural increase of the Arab and Jewish populations, and the number of illegal Jewish immigrants now in the country, this would allow of the admission, as from the beginning of April this year, of some 75,000 immigrants over the next five years. These immigrants would, subject to the criterion of economic absorptive capacity, be admitted as follows:

(a) For each of the next five years, a quota of 10,000 Jewish immigrants will be allowed, on the understanding that a shortage in any one year may be added to the quotas for subsequent years, within the five-year period, if economic absorptive capacity permits.

(b) In addition, as a contribution towards the solution of the Jewish refugee problem, 25,000 refugees will be admitted as soon as the High Commissioner is satisfied that adequate provision for their maintenance is ensured, special consideration being given to refugee children and dependents.

(2) The existing machinery for ascertaining economic absorptive capacity will be retained, and the High Commissioner will have the ultimate responsibility for deciding the limits of economic capacity. Before each periodic decision is taken, Jewish and Arab representatives will be consulted.

(3) After the period of five years, no further Jewish immigration will be permitted unless the Arabs of Palestine are prepared to acquiesce in it.

(4) His Majesty's Government are determined to check illegal immigration, and further preventive measure are being adopted. The numbers of any Jewish illegal immigrants who, despite these measures, may succeed in coming into the country and cannot be deported will be deducted from the yearly quotas.

15. His Majesty's Government are satisfied that, when the immigration over five years which is now contemplated has taken place, they will not be justified in facilitating, nor will they be under any obligation to facilitate, the further development of the Jewish National Home by immigration regardless of the wishes of the Arab population.

III. Land

. . .

18. In framing these proposals His Majesty's Government have sincerely endeavoured to act in strict accordance with their obligations under the Mandate to both the Arabs and the Jews. . . . His Majesty's Government cannot hope to satisfy the partisans of one party or the other in such controversy as the Mandate has aroused. Their purpose is to be just as between the two peoples in Palestine whose destinies in that country have been affected by the great events of recent years, and who, since they live side by side, must learn to practise mutual tolerance, goodwill, and co-operation. In looking to the future, His Majesty's Government are not blind to the fact that some events of the past make the task of creating these relations difficult; but they are encouraged by the knowledge that at many times and in many places in Palestine during recent years the Arab and Jewish inhabitants have lived

in friendship together. Each community has much to contribute to the welfare of their common land, and each must earnestly desire peace in which to assist in increasing the well-being of the whole people of the country. The responsibility which falls on them, no less than upon His Majesty's Government, to co-operate together to ensure peace is all the more solemn because their country is revered by many millions of Moslems, Jews, and Christians throughout the world who pray for peace in Palestine and for the happiness of her people.

18 Zionist Reaction to the White Paper (1939)

1. The new policy for Palestine laid down by the Mandatory in the White Paper now issued denies to the Jewish people the right to rebuild their national home in their ancestral country. It transfers the authority over Palestine to the present Arab. . . . It decrees the stoppage of Jewish immigration as soon as the Jews form a third of the total population. It puts up a territorial ghetto for Jews in their own homeland.

2. The Jewish people regard this policy as a breach of faith and a surrender to Arab terrorism. It delivers Britain's friends into the hands of those who are biting her and must lead to a complete breach between Jews and Arabs which will banish every prospect of peace in Palestine. It is a policy in which the Jewish people will not acquiesce. The new regime now announced will be devoid of any moral basis and contrary to international law. Such a regime can only he established and maintained by force.

3. The Royal Commission invoked by the White Paper indicated the perils of such a policy, saying it was convinced that an Arab Government would mean the frustration of all their (Jews') efforts and ideals and would convert the national home into one more cramped and dangerous ghetto. It seems only too probable that the Jews would fight rather than submit to Arab rule. And repressing a Jewish rebellion against British policy would be as unpleasant a task as the repression of the Arab rebellion has been. The Government has disregarded this warning.

4. The Jewish people have no quarrel with the Arab people. Jewish work in Palestine has not had an adverse effect upon the life and progress of the Arab people. The Arabs are not landless or homeless as are the Jews. They are not in need of emigration. Jewish colonization has benefited Palestine and all its inhabitants. Insofar as the Balfour Declaration contributed to British victory in the Great War, it contributed also, as was pointed out by the Royal Commission, to the liberation of the Arab peoples. The Jewish people has shown its will to peace even during the years of disturbances. It has not given way to temptation and has not retaliated to Arab violence. But neither have the Jews submitted to terror nor will

DOI: 10.4324/9781003348948-21

they submit to it even after the Mandatory has decided to reward the terrorists by surrendering the Jewish National Home.

5.   It is in the darkest hour of Jewish history that the British Government proposes to deprive the Jews of their last hope and to close the road hack to their Homeland. It is a cruel blow, doubly cruel because it comes from the government of a great nation which has extended a helping hand to the Jews, and whose position must rest on foundations of moral authority and international good faith. This blow will not subdue the Jewish people. The historic bond between the people and the land of Israel cannot be broken. The Jews will never accept the closing to them of the gates of Palestine nor let their national home be converted into a ghetto. The Jewish pioneers who, during the past three generations, have shown their strength in the unbuilding of a derelict country, will from now on display the same strength in defending Jewish immigration, the Jewish home, and Jewish freedom.

19 The Biltmore Program

Towards a Jewish State
(May 11, 1942)

Declaration adopted by the Extraordinary Zionist Conference at the Biltmore Hotel of New York City, May 11, 1942.

1. American Zionists assembled in this Extraordinary Conference reaffirm their unequivocal devotion to the cause of democratic freedom and international justice to which the people of the United States, allied with the other United Nations, have dedicated themselves, and give expression to their faith in the ultimate victory of humanity and justice over lawlessness and brute force.
2. This Conference offers a message of hope and encouragement to their fellow Jews in the Ghettos and concentration camps of Hitler-dominated Europe and prays that their hour of liberation may not be far distant.
3. The Conference sends its warmest greetings to the Jewish Agency Executive in Jerusalem, to the *Va'ad Leumi*, and to the whole Yishuv in Palestine. . . .
4. In our generation, and in particular in the course of the past 20 years, the Jewish people have awakened and transformed their ancient homeland; from 50,000 at the end of the last war, their numbers have increased to more than 500,000. . . . Their pioneering achievements in agriculture and in industry, embodying new patterns of cooperative endeavour, have written a notable page in the history of colonization.
5. In the new values thus created, their Arab neighbours in Palestine have shared. The Jewish people in its own work of national redemption welcomes the economic, agricultural, and national development of the Arab peoples and states. The Conference reaffirms the stand previously adopted at Congresses of the World Zionist Organization, expressing the readiness and the desire of the Jewish people for full cooperation with their Arab neighbours.
6. The Conference calls for the fulfillment of the original purpose of the Balfour Declaration and the Mandate which, recognizing the historical connection of the Jewish people with Palestine was to afford them the opportunity, as stated by President Wilson, to found there a Jewish Commonwealth.

DOI: 10.4324/9781003348948-22

The Conference affirms its unalterable rejection of the White Paper of May 1939 and denies its moral or legal validity. The White Paper seeks to limit, and in fact to nullify Jewish rights to immigration and settlement in Palestine, and, as stated by Mr. Winston Churchill in the House of Commons in May 1939, constitutes "a breach and repudiation of the Balfour Declaration." The policy of the White Paper is cruel and indefensible in its denial of sanctuary to Jews fleeing from Nazi persecution; and at a time when Palestine has become a focal point in the war front of the United Nations, and Palestine Jewry must provide all available manpower for farm and factory and camp, it is in direct conflict with the interests of the allied war effort.

7. In the struggle against the forces of aggression and tyranny, of which Jews were the earliest victims, and which now menace the Jewish National Home, recognition must be given to the right of the Jews of Palestine to play their full part in the war effort and in the defence of their country, through a Jewish military force fighting under its own flag and under the high command of the United Nations.

8. The Conference declares that the new world order that will follow victory cannot be established on foundations of peace, justice, and equality, unless the problem of Jewish homelessness is finally solved.

The Conference urges that the gates of Palestine be opened; that the Jewish Agency be vested with control of immigration into Palestine and with the necessary authority for upbuilding the country, including the development of its unoccupied and uncultivated lands; and that Palestine be established as a Jewish Commonwealth integrated in the structure of the new democratic world.

Then and only then will the age old wrong to the Jewish people be righted.

20 Arab Office Report to Anglo-American Committee (March 1946)

. . .

(8) In the Arab view, any solution for the problem created by Zionist aspirations must satisfy certain conditions:

   (i) It must recognize the right of the indigenous inhabitants of Palestine to continue in occupation of the country and to preserve its traditional character.

   (ii) It must recognize that questions like immigration which affect the whole nature and destiny of the country should be decided in accordance with democratic principles by the will of the population.

   (iii) It must accept the principle that the only way by which the will of the population can be expressed is through the establishment of responsible representative government. (The Arabs find something inconsistent in the attitude of Zionists who demand the establishment of a free democratic commonwealth in Palestine and then hasten to add that this should not take place until the Jews are in a majority.)

   (iv) This representative Government should be based upon the principle of absolute equality of all citizens irrespective of race and religion.

   (v) . . .

   (vi) The settlement should recognize the fact that by geography and history Palestine is inescapably part of the Arab world; that the only alternative to its being part of the Arab world and accepting the implication of its position is complete isolation, which would be disastrous from every point of view; and that whether they like it or not the Jews in Palestine are dependent upon the goodwill of the Arabs.

   (vii) The settlement should be such as to make possible a satisfactory definition within the framework of U.N.O. the relations between Palestine and the Western powers who possess interests in the country.

DOI: 10.4324/9781003348948-23

(viii) The settlement should take into account that Zionism is essentially a political movement aiming at the creation of a Jewish state and should therefore avoid making any concessions which might encourage Zionists in the hope that their aim can be achieved in any circumstances.

(ix) In accordance with these principles, the Arabs urge the establishment in Palestine of a democratic government representative of all sections of the population on a level of absolute equality; the termination of the Mandate once the Government has been established; and the entry of Palestine into the United Nations Organization as a full member of the working community.

(9) Pending the establishment of a representative Government, all further Jewish immigration should be stopped, in pursuance of the principle that a decision on so important a matter should only be taken with the consent of the inhabitants of the country and that until representative institutions are established there is no way of determining consent. . . . Once a Palestinian state has come into existence, if any section of the population favours a policy of further immigration it will be able to press its case in accordance with normal democratic procedure; but in this as in other matters the minority must abide by the decision of the majority.

Similarly, all further transfer of land from Arabs to Jews should be prohibited prior to the creation of self-governing institutions. . . . Here again, once self-government exists, matters concerning land will be decided in the normal democratic manner.

(10) The Arabs are irrevocably opposed to political Zionism, but in no way hostile to the Jews as such nor to their Jewish fellow citizens of Palestine. Those Jews who have already entered Palestine, and who have obtained or shall obtain Palestinian citizenship by due legal process, will be full citizens of the Palestinian state, enjoying full civil and political rights and a fair share in government and administration. . . . They will be given the opportunity of belonging to and helping to mould the full community of the Palestinian state, joined to the Arabs by links of interest and goodwill, not the goodwill of the strong to the powerless, but of one citizen to another.

It is to be hoped that in course of time the exclusiveness of the Jews will be neutralized by the development of loyalty to the state and the emergence of new groupings which cut across communal divisions. This however will take time and during the transitional period the Arabs recognize the need for giving special consideration to the particular position and the needs of the Jews. No attempt would be made to interfere with their communal organization, their personal status, or their religious observances. Their schools and cultural institutions would be left to operate unchecked except for that general control which all governments exercise over education. In the districts in which they are most closely settled they would possess municipal autonomy and Hebrew would be an official language of administration, justice, and education.

(11) The Palestinian State would be an Arab state, not (as should be clear from the preceding paragraph) in any narrow racial sense, nor in the sense that non-Arabs should be placed in a position or inferiority, but because the form and policy of its government would be based on a recognition of two facts: first that the majority of the citizens are Arabs, and secondly that Palestine is part of the Arab world and has no future except through close cooperation with the other Arab states. . . . The Cairo Pact of March 1945 provided for the representation of Palestine on the Council of the Arab League even before its independence should be a reality; once it was really self-governing it would participate fully in all the work of the League, in the cultural and economic no less than the political sphere. This would be of benefit to the Jewish not less than the Arab citizens of Palestine since it would ensure those good relations with the Arab world without which their economic development would be impossible.

(12) The state would apply as soon as possible for admission into U.N.O. and would of course be prepared to bear its full share of the burdens of establishing a world security system. . . .

The state would recognize also the world's interest in the maintenance of a satisfactory regime for the Moslem, Christian, and Jewish Holy Places. In the Arab view however the need for such a regime does not involve foreign interference in or control of Palestine; no opportunity should be given to Great Powers to use the Holy Places as instruments of policy. The Holy Places can be most satisfactorily and appropriately guarded by a Government representative of the inhabitants, who include adherents of all three faiths and have every interest in preserving the holy character of their country.

Nor in the Arab view would any sort or foreign interference or control be justified by the need to protect the Christian minorities. The Christians are Arabs, who belong fully to the national community and share fully in its struggle. They would have all the rights and duties of citizens of a Palestinian state and would continue to have their own communal organizations and institutions. They themselves would ask for no more, having learnt from the example of other Middle Eastern countries the dangers of an illusory foreign "protection" of minorities.

(13) In economic and social matters, the Government of Palestine would follow a progressive policy with the aim of raising the standard of living and increasing the welfare of all sections off the population, and using the country's natural resources in the way most beneficial to all. Its first task naturally would be to improve the condition or the Arab peasants and thus to bridge the economic and social gulf which at present divides the two communities. . . .

(14) The Arabs believe that no other proposals would satisfy the conditions of a just and lasting settlement. In their view there are insuperable objections of principle or of practice to all other suggested solutions of the problem.

(15) The idea or partition and the establishment of a Jewish state in a part of Palestine is inadmissible for the same reasons of principle as the idea of establishing a Jewish state in the whole country. If it is unjust to the Arabs to impose a Jewish state on the whole of Palestine, it is equally unjust to impose it in any part of the country. Moreover, as the Woodhead Commission showed, there are grave practical difficulties in the way of partition; commerce would be strangled, communications dislocated, and the public finances upset. It would also be impossible to devise frontiers which did not leave a large Arab minority in the Jewish state. . . . Moreover, partition would not satisfy the Zionists. It cannot be too often repeated that Zionism is a political movement aimed at the domination at least of the whole of Palestine; to give it a foothold in part of Palestine would be to encourage it to press for more and to provide it with a base for its activities. Because of this, because of the pressure of population and in order to escape from its isolation it would inevitably be thrown into enmity with the surrounding Arab states and this enmity would disturb the stability of the whole Middle East.

(16) Another proposal is for the establishment of a bi-national state; based upon political parity, in Palestine and its incorporation into a Syrian or Arab Federation. The Arabs would reject this as denying the majority its normal position and rights. There are also serious practical objections to the idea of a bi-national state which cannot exist unless there is a strong sense of unity and common interest overriding the differences between the two parties. Moreover, the point made in regard to the previous suggestion may be repeated here: this scheme would in no way satisfy the Zionists. It would simply encourage them to hope for more and improve their chances of obtaining it.

21 Report of the Anglo-American Committee of Inquiry (April 20, 1946)

Preface

We were appointed by the Governments of the United States and of the United Kingdom, as a joint body of American and British membership, with the following Terms of Reference:

1. To examine political, economic and social conditions in Palestine as they bear upon the problem of Jewish immigration and settlement therein and the well-being of the peoples now living therein.
2. To examine the position of the Jews in those countries in Europe where they have been the victims of Nazi and Fascist persecution, and the practical measures taken or contemplated to be taken in those countries to enable them to live free from discrimination and oppression. . . .
3. To hear the views of competent witnesses and to consult representative Arabs and Jews on the problems of Palestine as such problems are affected by conditions subject to examination under paragraphs 1 and 2 above and by other relevant facts and circumstances, and to make recommendations to His Majesty's Government and the Government of the United States for *ad interim* handling of these problems as well as for their permanent solution.
4. To make such other recommendations to His Majesty's Government and the Government of the United States . . . to meet the immediate needs arising from conditions subject to examination under paragraph 2 above, by remedial action in the European countries in question or by the provision of facilities for emigration to and settlement in countries outside Europe. . . .

We assembled in Washington on Friday, 4th January, 1946, and began our public sessions on the following Monday. We sailed from the United States on 18th January and resumed our public sessions in London on 25th January. We left for Europe on 4th and 5th February, and, working in subcommittees, proceeded to our investigations in Germany, Poland, Czechoslovakia, Austria, Italy and Greece. On 28th February we flew to Cairo and, after sessions

DOI: 10.4324/9781003348948-24

there, reached Jerusalem on 6th March. In Palestine, our sessions were interspersed with personal visits to different parts of the country, during which we sought to acquaint ourselves at first hand with its various characteristics and the ways of life of its inhabitants. Subcommittees visited the capitals of Syria, Lebanon, Iraq, Saudi-Arabia and Trans-Jordan to hear the views of the Arab Governments and representatives of bodies concerned with the subjects before us. We left Palestine on 28th March and have concluded our deliberations in Switzerland. The detailed itinerary is shown in Appendix I.

We now submit the following Report.

Chapter I
Recommendations and Comments
The European Problem

Recommendation No. 1. We have to report that such information as we received about countries other than Palestine gave no hope of substantial assistance in finding homes for Jews wishing or impelled to leave Europe.

But Palestine alone cannot meet the emigration needs of the Jewish victims of Nazi and Fascist persecution; the whole world shares responsibility for them and indeed for the resettlement of all "displaced persons".

We therefore recommend that our Governments together, and in association with other countries, should endeavor immediately to find new homes for all such "displaced persons", irrespective of creed or nationality, whose ties with their former communities have been irreparably broken.

. . .

COMMENT

In recommending that our Governments, in association with other countries, should endeavor to find new homes for "displaced persons", we do not suggest that any country should be asked to make a permanent change in its immigration policy. The conditions, which we have seen in Europe, are unprecedented, and so unlikely to arise again that we are convinced that special provision could and should be made in existing immigration laws to meet this unique and peculiarly distressing situation. . . .

Our investigations have led us to believe that a considerable number of Jews will continue to live in most European countries. . . . Every effort should be made to enable the Jews to rebuild their shattered communities, while permitting those Jews, who wish to do so, to emigrate. . . . A real obstacle, however, to individual restitution is that the attempt to give effect to this legislation is frequently a cause of active anti-Semitism. We suggest that, for the reconstruction of the Jewish communities, restitution of their corporate property, either through reparations payments or through other means, is of the first importance.

Nazi occupation has left behind it a legacy of anti-Semitism. This cannot be combated by legislation alone. The only really effective antidotes are the enforcement by each Government of guaranteed civil liberties and equal rights, a program of education in the positive principles of democracy, the sanction of a strong world public opinion combined with economic recovery and stability.

Refugee Immigration Into Palestine

Recommendation No. 2. We recommend (a) that 100,000 certificates be authorized immediately for the admission into Palestine of Jews who have been the victims of Nazi and Fascist persecution; (b) that these certificates be awarded as far as possible in 1946 and that actual immigration be pushed forward as rapidly as conditions will permit.

COMMENT

The number of Jewish survivors of Nazi and Fascist persecution with whom we have to deal far exceeds 100,000; indeed there are more than that number in Germany, Austria and Italy alone. Although nearly a year has passed since their liberation, the majority of those in Germany and Austria are still living in assembly centers, the so-called "camps," island communities in the midst of those at whose hands they suffered so much.

In their interests and in the interests of Europe, the centers should be closed and their camp life ended. . . .

We-know of no country to which the great majority can go in the immediate future other than Palestine. Furthermore that is where almost all of them want to go. There they are sure that they will receive a welcome denied them elsewhere. . . .

We recommend the authorization and issue of 100,000 certificates for these reasons and because we feel that their immediate issue will have a most salutary effect upon the whole situation.

. . .

It should be made clear that no advantage in the obtaining of a certificate is to be gained by migrating from one country to another, or by entering Palestine illegally.

Receiving so large a number will be a heavy burden on Palestine. We feel sure that the authorities will shoulder it and that they will have the full cooperation of the Jewish Agency.

. . .

Those who have opposed the admission of these unfortunate people into Palestine should know that we have fully considered all that they have put before us. We hope that they will look upon the situation again, that they will appreciate the considerations which have led us to our conclusion, and that above all, if they cannot see their way to help, at least they will not make the position of these sufferers more difficult.

Principles of Government: No Arab, No Jewish State

Recommendation No. 3. In order to dispose, once and for all, of the exclusive claims of Jews and Arabs to Palestine, we regard it as essential that a clear statement of the following principles should be made:

I. That Jew shall not dominate Arab and Arab shall not dominate Jew in Palestine. II. That Palestine shall be neither a Jewish state nor an Arab state. III. That the form of government ultimately to be established, shall, under international guarantees, fully protect and preserve the interests in the Holy Land of Christendom and of the Moslem and Jewish faiths.

Thus Palestine must ultimately become a state which guards the rights and interests of Moslems, Jews and Christians alike; and accords to the inhabitants, as a whole, the fullest measure of self-government, consistent with the three paramount principles set forth above.

COMMENT

Throughout the long and bloody struggle of Jew and Arab for dominance in Palestine, each crying fiercely: "This land is mine" – except for the brief reference in the Report of the Royal Commission (hereinafter referred to as the Peel Report) and the little evidence, written and oral, that we received on this point – the great interest of the Christian World in Palestine has been completely overlooked, glossed over or brushed aside.

We, therefore, emphatically declare that Palestine is a Holy Land, sacred to Christian, to Jew and to Moslem alike; and because it is a Holy Land, Palestine is not, and can never become, a land which any race or religion can justly claim as its very own.

. . .

The Jews have a historic connection with the country. The Jewish National Home, though embodying a minority of the population, is today a reality established under international guarantee. It has a right to continued existence, protection and development.

Yet Palestine is not, and never can be, a purely Jewish land. It lies at the crossroads of the Arab world. Its Arab population, descended from long-time inhabitants of the area, rightly look upon Palestine as their homeland.

It is therefore neither just nor practicable that Palestine should become either an Arab State, in which an Arab majority would control the destiny of a Jewish minority, or a Jewish State, in which a Jewish majority would control that of an Arab minority. In neither case would minority guarantees afford adequate protection for the subordinated group.

. . .

Palestine, then, must be established as a country in which the legitimate national aspirations of both Jews and Arabs can be reconciled, without either side fearing the ascendancy of the other. . . . To ensure genuine self-government for both the Arab and the Jewish communities, this struggle must be made purposeless by the constitution itself.

Mandate and United Nations Trusteeship

Recommendation No. 4. We have reached the conclusion that the hostility between Jews and Arabs and, in particular, the determination of each to achieve domination, if necessary by violence make it almost certain that, now and for some time to come, any attempt to establish either an independent Palestinian State or independent Palestinian States would result in civil strife such as might threaten the peace of the world.

We therefore recommend that, until this hostility disappears, the Government of Palestine be continued as at present under mandate pending the execution of a trusteeship agreement under the United Nations.

COMMENT

We recognize that in view of the powerful forces both Arab and Jewish, operating from outside Palestine, the task of Great Britain, as Mandatory, has not been easy. The Peel Commission declared in 1937 that the Mandate was unworkable, and the Permanent Mandates Commission of the League of Nations thereupon pointed out that it became almost unworkable once it was publicly declared to be so by such a body. Two years later the British Government, having come to the conclusion that the alternative of partition proposed by the Peel Commission was also unworkable, announced their intention of taking steps to terminate the Mandate by the establishment of an independent Palestine State. . . .

Equality of Standards

Recommendation No. 5. Looking towards a form of ultimate self-government, consistent with the three principles laid down in Recommendation No. 3, we recommend that the mandatory or trustee should proclaim the principle that Arab economic, educational and political advancement in Palestine is of equal importance with that of the Jews . . .

COMMENT

Our examination of conditions in Palestine led us to the conclusion that one of the chief causes of friction is the great disparity between the Jewish and Arab standards of living. . . . Only by a deliberate and carefully planned policy on the part of the Mandatory can the Arab standard of living be raised to that of the Jews. In stressing the need for such a policy we would particularly call attention to the discrepancies between the social services, including hospitals, available in Palestine for Jews and Arabs.

. . .

We suggest that consideration be given to the advisability of encouraging the formation by the Arabs of an Arab community on the lines of the Jewish community which now largely controls and finances Jewish social services. The Arabs will have to rely, to far greater extent than the Jews, on financial aid from the Government. But the Jews of Palestine should accept the necessity that taxation, raised from both Jews and Arabs, will have to be spent very largely on the Arabs on order to bridge the gap which now exists between the standard of living of the two peoples.

Future Immigration Policy

Recommendation No. 6. We recommend that, pending the early reference to the United Nations and the execution of a trusteeship agreement, the mandatory should administer Palestine according to the mandate which declares with regard to immigration that "The administration of Palestine, while ensuring that the rights and position of other sections of the population are not prejudiced, shall facilitate Jewish immigration under suitable conditions".

COMMENT

We have recommended the admission of 100,000 immigrants, victims of Nazi persecution, as soon as possible. We now deal with the position after the admission of that number. . . . Until a Trusteeship Agreement is executed it is our clear opinion that Palestine should be administered in accordance with the terms of the Mandate quoted above.

. . .

The possibility of the country sustaining a largely increased population at a decent standard of living depends on its economic future, which in turn depends largely on whether or not plans referred to in Recommendation No. 8 can be brought to fruition.

The Peel Commission stated that political as well as economic considerations have to be taken into account in regard to immigration, and recommended a "political high level" of 12,000 a year. We cannot recommend the fixing of a minimum or of a maximum for annual immigration in the future. There are too many uncertain factors.

. . . it must, we think, be conceded that it should be the right of the Government of Palestine to decide, having regard to the well-being of all the people of Palestine, the number of immigrants to be admitted within any given period.

In Palestine there is the Jewish National Home, created in consequence of the Balfour Declaration. Some may think that Declaration was wrong and should not have been made; some that it was a conception on a grand scale and that effect can be given to one of the most daring and significant colonization plans in history. Controversy as to which view is right is fruitless. The National Home is there. Its roots are deep in the soil of Palestine. It cannot be argued out of existence; neither can the achievements of the Jewish pioneers.

. . .

The well-being of all the people of Palestine, be they Jews, Arabs, or neither, must be the governing consideration. We reject the view that there shall be no further Jewish immigration into Palestine without Arab acquiescence, a view which would result in the Arab dominating the Jew. We also reject the insistent Jewish demand that forced Jewish immigration must proceed apace in order to produce as quickly as possible a Jewish majority and a Jewish State. The well-being of the Jews must not be subordinated to that of the Arabs; nor that of the Arabs to the Jews. . . .

Palestine is a land sacred to three faiths and must not become the land of any one of them to the exclusion of the others, and Jewish immigration for the development of the National Home must not become a policy of discrimination against other immigrants. Any person, therefore, who desires and is qualified under applicable laws to enter Palestine must not be refused admission or subjected to discrimination on the ground that he is not a Jew. All provisions respecting immigration must be drawn, executed and applied with that principle always firmly in mind.

Further, while we recognize that any Jew who enters Palestine in accordance with its laws is there of right, we expressly disapprove of the position taken in some Jewish quarters that Palestine has in some way been ceded or granted as their State to the Jews of the world, that every Jew everywhere is, merely because he is a Jew, a citizen of Palestine and therefore can enter Palestine as of right without regard to conditions imposed by the Government upon entry, and that therefore there can be no illegal immigration of Jews into Palestine. We declare and affirm that any immigrant Jew who enters Palestine contrary to its laws is an illegal immigrant.

Land Policy

Recommendation No. 7. (a) We recommend that the Land Transfers Regulations of 1940 be rescinded and replaced by regulations based on a policy of freedom in the sale, lease or use of land, irrespective of race, community or creed, and providing adequate protection for the interests of small owners and tenant cultivators; (b) . . . (c) We recommend that the Government should exercise such close supervision over the Holy Places and localities such as the Sea of Galilee and its vicinity as will protect them from desecration and from uses which offend the conscience of religious people, and that such laws as are required for this purpose be enacted forthwith.

COMMENT

. . . We are opposed to any legislation or restrictions discriminating against Jew or Arab. We recognize the need for protecting the Arab small owner and tenant, for providing against a large landless Arab population, for maintaining, indeed for raising, the Arab standard of living. This necessity was also recognized in the Peel Report (Chapter IX, paragraph 10) which endorsed the following principles of earlier reports: that (i) unless there is a marked change in the methods of cultivation the land in Palestine is unable to support a large increase in population, and (ii) there is already congestion on the land in the hill districts. Those principles are as true, if not truer, today.

We do not believe that the necessary protection for the Arab can be provided only by confining the Jew to particular portions of Palestine. Such a policy, suggested by the Peel Commission, is consistent with their proposed solution, partition, but scarcely with that put forward by us.

. . .

As we have said we are opposed to such discrimination. We appreciate that one of the reasons for such provisions was to secure employment for Jewish immigrants on the land. We do not think that object justifies the retention of such stipulations which are harmful to cooperation and understanding between Arab and Jew.

. . .

In the small, thickly populated country of Palestine, with its rapidly increasing population, it is in the interest of Jews and Arabs alike that all land should be developed and put to the fullest possible use. The settlement of title to land should proceed as quickly as possible and the development of State lands, not required for public purposes and capable of use, should be facilitated.

The Holy Land of Palestine contains within its borders and throughout its territories places sacred to the followers of three great religions. The "Lido" with its dancing and swing music on the shore of the Sea of Galilee offends the sensibilities of many Christian people. Reports came to our notice of other projects the completion of which would be equally objectionable. We therefore feel it right by our recommendation to emphasize the necessity for close supervision and to recommend the strengthening of the law should that be required.

Economic Development

Recommendation No. 8. Various plans for large-scale agricultural and industrial development in Palestine have been presented for our consideration; . . .

We are not in a position to assess the soundness of these specific plans; but we cannot state too strongly that, however technically feasible they may be, they will fail unless there is peace in Palestine. Moreover their full success requires the willing cooperation of adjacent Arab states, since they are not merely Palestinian projects. . . .

COMMENT

The building of the Jewish economy has enjoyed the advantage of abundant capital, provided on such terms as to make economic return a secondary consideration. The Arabs have had no such advantage. In principle, we do not think it wise or appropriate that plans, such as the project for a Jordan Valley Authority, should, if judged technically sound, be undertaken by any private organization, . . .

. . .

We doubt whether Palestine can expand its economy to the full, having regard to its limited natural resources, without a full and free interchange of goods and services with neighboring countries. In some respects, indeed, as in certain projects involving water supply, their active collaboration is indispensable to full development on an economic basis.

The removal of Article 18 of the Mandate would clear the way to those comprehensive tariff and trade agreements, not conflicting with any international obligations that might be accepted by the Mandatory or Trustee, which could ultimately lead to something like a customs union-an objective already in mind as between the surrounding countries of the Arab League.

Education

Recommendation No. 9. We recommend that, in the interests of the conciliation of the two peoples and of general improvement of the Arab standard of living, the educational system of both Jews and Arabs be reformed, including the introduction of compulsory education within a reasonable time.

COMMENT

In Chapter XVI of the Peel Report, the bad features of the educational system of Palestine and the great disparity between the money spent on Arab and Jewish education were pointed out. The Report also emphasized that both Jewish and Arab education in Palestine were nationalistic in character. Particular attention was called to nationalist propaganda in Arab schools.

Our investigations disclosed that today the Jewish schools – also controlled and largely financed by the Jewish community – are imbued with a fiery spirit of nationalism. They have become most effective agencies for inculcating a spirit of aggressive Hebrew nationalism. We would urge most strongly that adequate control must be exercised by the Government over the education of both Jews and Arabs, in order to do away with the present excited emphasis on racialism and the perversion of education for propaganda purposes. . . .

We believe further that a large share of responsibility for Arab education might well be assumed by an Arab community, similar to the Jewish community already established in Palestine. But if the Arab and Jewish communities are to set themselves the goal of compulsory education, a much higher proportion of the annual Palestinian budget must be devoted to education than heretofore, most of which will be spent on Arab education. This will only be possible if the proportion of the budget now devoted to security can be substantially reduced.

We would also stress the urgent necessity of increasing the facilities for secondary, technical and university education available to Arabs. The disparity between the standard of living of the two peoples, to which we have already drawn attention, is very largely due to the fact that the Jewish professional and middle class so largely outnumbers that of the Arabs. This difference can only be removed by a very substantial increase in the facilities for higher education available to Arabs.

The Need for Peace in Palestine

Recommendation No. 10. We recommend that, if this Report is adopted, it should be made clear beyond all doubt to both Jews and Arabs that any attempt from either side, by threats of violence, by terrorism, or by the organization or use of illegal armies to prevent its execution, will be resolutely suppressed.

Furthermore, we express the view that the Jewish Agency should at once resume active cooperation with the Mandatory in the suppression of terrorism and of illegal immigration, and in the maintenance of that law and order throughout Palestine which is essential for the good of all, including the new immigrants.

SOURCE: The report was addressed to the US President, dated "Lausanne, Switzerland, April 20, 1946" and signed by the six American committee members: Joseph C. Hutchison (American Chairman), Frank Aydelotte, Frank W. Buxton, Bartley C. Crum, James G. McDonald and William Phillips. Reproduced here are the Preface and Chapter 1 only. The full Report (10 chapters and 7 appendices) is available at http://avalon.law.yale.edu/sub ject_menus/angtoc.asp.

22 United Nations General Assembly

Resolution 181, The Partition of Palestine (November 29, 1947)

The General Assembly,

Having met in special session at the request of the mandatory Power to constitute and instruct a Special Committee to prepare for the consideration of the question of the future Government of Palestine at the second regular session;

Having constituted a Special Committee and instructed it to investigate all questions and issues relevant to the problem of Palestine, and to prepare proposals for the solution of the problem, and

. . .

Considers that the present situation in Palestine is one which is likely to impair the general welfare and friendly relations among nations;

Takes note of the declaration by the mandatory Power that it plans to complete its evacuation of Palestine by 1 August 1948;

Recommends to the United Kingdom, as the mandatory Power for Palestine, and to all other Members of the United Nations, the adoption and implementation, with regard to the future Government of Palestine, of the Plan of Partition with Economic Union set out below;

Requests that

a. The Security Council take the necessary measures as provided for in the plan for its implementation.
b. The Security Council consider, if circumstances during the transitional period require such consideration, whether the situation in Palestine constitutes a threat to the peace. If it decides that such a threat exists, and in order to maintain international peace and security, the Security Council should supplement the authorization of the General Assembly by taking measures, under Articles 39 and 41 of the Charter, to empower the United Nations Commission, as provided in this resolution, to exercise in Palestine the functions which are assigned to it by this resolution.

DOI: 10.4324/9781003348948-25

UNGA Partition Plan, 1947

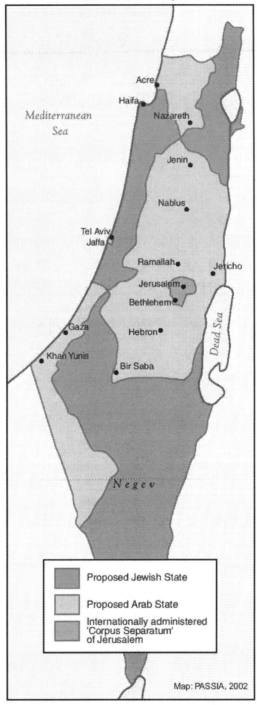

Map 7 The United Nations Partition Recommendation, 1947

Source: Permission granted by the Palestinian Academic Society for the Study of International Affairs to reprint their map of the United Nations partition lines in this book. The original can be found at: www.passia.org/maps/view/15.

c.   The Security Council determine as a threat to the peace, breach of the peace, or act of aggression, in accordance with Article 39 of the Charter, any attempt to alter by force the settlement envisaged by this resolution;
d.   The Trusteeship Council be informed of the responsibilities envisaged for it in this plan;

Calls upon the inhabitants of Palestine to take such steps as may be necessary on their part to put this plan into effect;

Appeals to all Governments and all peoples to refrain from taking any action which might hamper or delay the carrying out of these recommendations, and

Authorizes the Secretary-General to reimburse travel and subsistence expenses of the members of the Commission referred to in Part I, Section B, Paragraph I below, on such basis and in such form as he may determine most appropriate in the circumstances, and to provide the Commission with the necessary staff to assist in carrying out the functions assigned to the Commission by the General Assembly . . .

PLAN OF PARTITION WITH ECONOMIC UNION

Part I. – Future Constitution and Government of Palestine

A. TERMINATION OF MANDATE, PARTITION, AND INDEPENDENCE

1.   The *Mandate for Palestine* shall terminate as soon as possible but in any case not later than 1 August 1948.
2.   The armed forces of the mandatory Power shall be progressively withdrawn from Palestine, the withdrawal to be completed as soon as possible but in any case not later than 1 August 1948.

     The mandatory Power shall advise the Commission, as far in advance as possible, of its intention to terminate the mandate and to evacuate each area. The mandatory Power shall use its best endeavours to ensure that an area situated in the territory of the Jewish State, including a seaport and hinterland adequate to provide facilities for a substantial immigration, shall be evacuated at the earliest possible date and in any event not later than 1 February 1948.
3.   Independent Arab and Jewish States and the Special International Regime for the City of Jerusalem, set forth in Part III of this Plan, shall come into existence in Palestine two months after the evacuation of the armed forces of the mandatory Power has been completed but in any case not later than 1 October 1948. The boundaries of the Arab State, the Jewish State, and the City of Jerusalem shall be as described in Parts II and III below.

4. The period between the adoption by the General Assembly of its recommendation on the question of Palestine and the establishment of the independence of the Arab and Jewish States shall be a transitional period.

B. STEPS PREPARATORY TO INDEPENDENCE

1. A Commission shall be set up consisting of one representative of each of five Member States. The Members represented on the Commission shall be elected by the General Assembly on as broad a basis, geographically and otherwise, as possible.
2. The administration of Palestine shall, as the mandatory Power withdraws its armed forces, be progressively turned over to the Commission . . .
3. On its arrival in Palestine the Commission shall proceed to carry out measures for the establishment of the frontiers of the Arab and Jewish States and the City of Jerusalem in accordance with the general lines of the recommendations of the General Assembly on the partition of Palestine . . .
4. The Commission, after consultation with the democratic parties and other public organizations of the Arab and Jewish States, shall select and establish in each State as rapidly as possible a Provisional Council of Government . . .
5. . . .
6. . . .
7. The Commission shall instruct the Provisional Councils of Government of both the Arab and Jewish States, after their formation, to proceed to the establishment of administrative organs of government, central and local.
8. The Provisional Council of Government of each State shall, within the shortest time possible, recruit an armed militia from the residents of that State, sufficient in number to maintain internal order and to prevent frontier clashes . . .
9. The Provisional Council of Government of each State shall, not later than two months after the withdrawal of the armed forces of the mandatory Power, hold elections to the Constituent Assembly which shall be conducted on democratic lines. . . . Arabs and Jews residing in the City of Jerusalem who have signed a notice of intention to become citizens, the Arabs of the Arab State and the Jews of the Jewish State, shall be entitled to vote in the Arab and Jewish States respectively.

Women may vote and be elected to the Constituent Assemblies.

During the transitional period no Jew shall be permitted to establish residence in the area of the proposed Arab State, and no Arab shall be permitted to establish residence in the area of the proposed Jewish State, except by special leave of the Commission.

10. The Constituent Assembly of each State shall draft a democratic constitution for its State and choose a provisional government to succeed the Provisional Council of Government appointed by the Commission. . . .

C. DECLARATION

A declaration shall be made to the United Nations by the Provisional Government of each proposed State before independence. It shall contain, *inter alia*, the following clauses:

General Provision

. . .

Chapter I: Holy Places, Religious Buildings and Sites

1. Existing rights in respect of Holy Places and religious buildings or sites shall not be denied or impaired.
2. Insofar as Holy Places are concerned, the liberty of access, visit, and transit shall be guaranteed, in conformity with existing rights, to all residents and citizen of the other State and of the City of Jerusalem, as well as to aliens, without distinction as to nationality, subject to requirements of national security, public order, and decorum.

    Similarly, freedom of worship shall be guaranteed in conformity with existing rights, subject to the maintenance of public order and decorum.
3. Holy Places and religious buildings or sites shall be preserved. No act shall be permitted which may in any way impair their sacred character. If at any time it appears to the Government that any particular Holy Place, religious building or site is in need of urgent repair, the Government may call upon the community or communities concerned to carry out such repair. The Government may carry it out itself at the expense of the community or community concerned if no action is taken within a reasonable time.
4. No taxation shall be levied in respect of any Holy Place, religious building or site which was exempt from taxation on the date of the creation of the State. No change in the incidence of such taxation shall be made which would either discriminate between the owners or occupiers of Holy Places, religious buildings or sites, or would place such owners or occupiers in a position less favourable in relation to the general incidence of taxation than existed at the time of the adoption of the Assembly's recommendations.
5. The Governor of the City of Jerusalem shall have the right to determine whether the provisions of the Constitution of the State in relation to Holy Places, religious buildings and sites within the borders of the State and

the religious rights appertaining thereto are being properly applied and respected, and to make decisions on the basis of existing rights in cases of disputes which may arise between the different religious communities or the rites of a religious community with respect to such places, buildings, and sites. . . .

Chapter 2: Religious and Minority Rights

1. Freedom of conscience and the free exercise of all forms of worship, subject only to the maintenance of public order and morals, shall be ensured to all.
2. No discrimination of any kind shall be made between the inhabitants on the ground of race, religion, language, or sex.
3. All persons within the jurisdiction of the State shall be entitled to equal protection of the laws.
4. The family law and personal status of the various minorities and their religious interests, including endowments, shall be respected.
5. Except as may be required for the maintenance of public order and good government, no measure shall be taken to obstruct or interfere with the enterprise of religious or charitable bodies of all faiths or to discriminate against any representative or member of these bodies on the ground of his religion or nationality.
6. The State shall ensure adequate primary and secondary education for the Arab and Jewish minority, respectively, in its own language and its cultural traditions.

   The right of each community to maintain its own schools for the education of its own members in its own language, while conforming to such educational requirements of a general nature as the State may impose, shall not be denied or impaired. Foreign educational establishments shall continue their activity on the basis of their existing rights.
7. No restriction shall be imposed on the free use by any citizen of the State of any language in private intercourse, in commerce, in religion, in the Press, or in publications of any kind, or at public meetings.
8. No expropriation of land owned by an Arab in the Jewish State (by a Jew in the Arab State) shall be allowed except for public purposes. In all cases of expropriation, full compensation as fixed by the Supreme Court shall be said previous to dispossession.

Chapter 3: Citizenship, International Conventions, and Financial Obligations

1. Citizenship

Palestinian citizens residing in Palestine outside the City of Jerusalem, as well as Arabs and Jews who, not holding Palestinian citizenship, reside in

Palestine outside the City of Jerusalem shall, upon the recognition of independence, become citizens of the State in which they are resident and enjoy full civil and political rights. . . .

Arabs residing in the area of the proposed Jewish State and Jews residing in the area of the proposed Arab State who have signed a notice of intention to opt for citizenship of the other State shall be eligible to vote in the elections to the Constituent Assembly of that State, but not in the elections to the Constituent Assembly of the State in which they reside.

2. International Conventions

a. The State shall be bound by all the international agreements and conventions, both general and special, to which Palestine has become a party. Subject to any right of denunciation provided for therein, such agreements and conventions shall be respected by the State throughout the period for which they were concluded.
b. Any dispute about the applicability and continued validity of international conventions or treaties signed or adhered to by the mandatory Power on behalf of Palestine shall be referred to the International Court of Justice in accordance with the provisions of the Statute of the Court.

3. Financial Obligations

. . .

PART III. – CITY OF JERUSALEM

A. SPECIAL REGIME

The City of Jerusalem shall be established as a *corpus separatum* under a special international regime and shall be administered by the United Nations. The Trusteeship Council shall be designated to discharge the responsibilities of the Administering Authority on behalf of the United Nations.

B. BOUNDARIES OF THE CITY . . .

C. STATUTE OF THE CITY . . .

D. DURATION OF THE SPECIAL REGIME . . .

Adopted at the 128th plenary meeting:
In favour: 33
Australia, Belgium, Bolivia, Brazil, Byelorussian S.S.R., Canada, Costa Rica, Czechoslovakia, Denmark, Dominican Republic, Ecuador, France, Guatemala, Haiti, Iceland, Liberia, Luxemburg, Netherlands, New Zealand, Nicaragua, Norway, Panama, Paraguay, Peru, Philippines, Poland, Sweden, Ukrainian S.S.R., Union of South Africa, U.S.A., U.S.S.R., Uruguay, Venezuela.

Against: 13

Afghanistan, Cuba, Egypt, Greece, India, Iran, Iraq, Lebanon, Pakistan, Saudi Arabia, Syria, Turkey, Yemen.

Abstained: 10

Argentina, Chile, China, Colombia, El Salvador, Ethiopia, Honduras, Mexico, United Kingdom, Yugoslavia.

23 Golda Meir, Speech to the Illinois Council of Jewish Federations (January 2, 1948)

I have had the privilege of representing Palestine Jewry in this country and in other countries when the problems that we faced were those of building more kibbutzim, of bringing in more Jews in spite of political obstacles and Arab riots.

We always had faith that in the end we would win, that everything we were doing in the country led to the independence of the Jewish people and to a Jewish state.

Long before we had dared pronounce that word, we knew what was in store for us.

Today we have reached a point when the nations of the world have given us their decision – the establishment of a Jewish state in a part of Palestine. Now in Palestine we are fighting to make this resolution of the United Nations a reality, not because we wanted to fight. If we had the choice, we would have chosen peace to build in peace.

. . .

These young boys and girls, many in their teens, are bearing the burden of what is happening in the country with a spirit that no words can describe. You see these youngsters in open cars – not armoured cars – in convoys going from Tel Aviv to Jerusalem, knowing that every time they start out from Tel Aviv or from Jerusalem there are probably Arabs behind the orange groves or the hills, waiting to ambush the convoy. . . . .

We must ask the Jews the world over to see us as the front line.

All we ask of Jews the world over, and mainly of the Jews in the United States, is to give us the possibility of going on with the struggle.

When trouble started, we asked young people from the age of seventeen to twenty-five who were not members of Haganah, to volunteer. Up to the day that I left home on Thursday morning, when the registration of this age group was still going on, over 20,000 young men and women had signed up. As of now we have about 9,000 people mobilized in the various parts of the country. We must triple this number within the next few days.

We have to maintain these men. No government sends its soldiers to the front and expects them to take along from their homes the most elementary requirements – blankets, bedding, clothing.

DOI: 10.4324/9781003348948-26

. . .

I want to say to you, friends, that the Jewish community in Palestine is going to fight to the very end. If we have arms to fight with, we will fight with those, and if not, we will fight with stones in our hands.

I want you to believe me when I say that I came on this special mission to the United States today not to save 700,000 Jews. During the last few years the Jewish people lost 6,000,000 Jews, and it would be audacity on our part to worry the Jewish people throughout the world because a few hundred thousand more Jews were in danger. That is not the issue.

The issue is that if these 700,000 Jews in Palestine can remain alive, then the Jewish people as such is alive and Jewish independence is assured. If these 700,000 people are killed off, then for many centuries, we are through with this dream of a Jewish people and a Jewish homeland.

My friends, we are at war. There is no Jew in Palestine who does not believe that finally we will be victorious. That is the spirit of the country. We have known Arab riots since 1921 and '29 and '36. We know what happened to the Jews of Europe during this last war. And every Jew in the country also knows that within a few months a Jewish state in Palestine will be established.

. . .

Much must be prepared now so that we can hold out. There are unlimited opportunities, but are we going to get the necessary means? Considering myself not as a guest, but as one of you, I say that the question before each one is simply whether the Yishuv, and the youngsters that are in the front line, will have to fail because money that should have reached Palestine today will reach it in a month or two months from now?

. . .

I have come to the United States, and I hope you will understand me if I say that it is not an easy matter for any of us to leave home at present – to my sorrow I am not in the front line. I am not with my daughter in the Negev or with other sons and daughters in the trenches. But I have a job to do.

I have come here to try to impress Jews in the United States with the fact that within a very short period, a couple of weeks, we must have in cash between twenty-five and thirty million dollars. In the next two or three weeks we can establish ourselves. . . .

I said before that the Yishuv will give, is giving of its means. But please remember that even while shooting is going on, we must carry on so that our economy remains intact. Our factories must go on. Our settlements must not be broken up.

We know that this battle is being waged for those not yet in the country.

There are 30,000 Jews detained right next door to Palestine in Cyprus. I believe that within a very short period, within the next two or three months at most, these 30,000 will be with us, among them thousands of infants and young children. We must now think of preparing means of absorbing them. We know that within the very near future, hundreds of thousands more will be coming in. We must see that our economy is intact.

. . .

When you go to Tel Aviv now, you will find the city full of life; only the shooting that you hear on the outskirts of Tel Aviv and Jaffa reminds one that the situation in the country is not normal. But it would be a crime on my part not to describe the situation to you exactly as it is.

. . .

We have no government. But we have millions of Jews in the Diaspora, and exactly as we have faith in our youngsters in Palestine I have faith in Jews in the United States; I believe that they will realize the peril of our situation and will do what they have to do.

. . .

I know that many of you would be as anxious as our people to be on the very front line. I do not doubt that there are many young people among the Jewish community in the United States who would do exactly what our young people are doing in Palestine.

We are not a better breed; we are not the best Jews of the Jewish people. It so happened that we are there and you are here. I am certain that if you were in Palestine and we were in the United States, you would be doing what we are doing there, and you would ask us here to do what you will have to do.

I want to close with paraphrasing one of the greatest speeches that was made during the Second World War – the words of Churchill.

I am not exaggerating when I say that the Yishuv in Palestine will fight in the Negev and will fight in Galilee and will fight on the outskirts of Jerusalem until the very end. You cannot decide whether we should fight or not. We will. The Jewish community in Palestine will raise no white flag for the Mufti. That decision is taken. Nobody can change it. You can only decide one thing: whether we shall be victorious in this fight or whether the Mufti will be victorious. That decision American Jews can make. It has to be made quickly within hours, within days.

And I beg of you – don't be too late. Don't be bitterly sorry three months from now for what you failed to do today. The time is now.

I have spoken to you without a grain of exaggeration. I have not tried to paint the picture in false colours. It consists of spirit and certainty of our victory on the one hand, and dire necessity for carrying on the battle on the other.

I want to thank you again for having given me the opportunity at a conference that I am certain has a full agenda to say these few words to you. I leave the platform without any doubt in my mind or my heart that the decision that will be taken by American Jewry will be the same as that which was taken by the Jewish community in Palestine, so that within a few months from now we will all be able to participate not only in the joy of resolving to establish a Jewish state, but in the joy of laying the cornerstone of the Jewish state.

Speech from www.tamilnation.org/ideology/golda.htm.

24 Plan Dalet

Preparing for the War of Independence (March 10, 1948)

1. Introduction

(a) The objective of this plan is to gain control of the areas of the Hebrew state and defend its borders. It also aims at gaining control of the areas of Jewish settlement and concentration which are located outside the borders [of the Hebrew state] against regular, semi-regular, and small forces operating from bases outside or inside the state.

(b) This plan is based on three previous plans:

    1.   Plan B, September 1945.
    2.   The May 1946 Plan.[1]
    3.   Yehoshua Plan, 1948.[2]

(c) Since these plans were designed to deal with the situation inside the country (the first two plans deal with the first phase of incidents, while the third plan deals with the possibility of invasion by regular armies from the neighboring countries), the aim of Plan D is to fill the gaps in the previous three plans and to make them more suitable for the situation expected to obtain at the end of British rule in the country.

2. Basic Assumptions

This plan is based on the following basic assumptions:

(A) THE ENEMY

1.   Expected composition of forces:

- The semi-regular forces of the Liberation Army affiliated with the Arab League, which operate from already occupied bases or bases to be occupied in the future.
- The regular forces of neighboring countries, which will launch an invasion across the borders, or will operate from bases inside the country (the Arab Legion).[3]

DOI: 10.4324/9781003348948-27

- Small local forces which operate, or will operate, from bases inside the country and within the borders of the Hebrew state.

All three forces will be activated at the same time in accordance with a joint operational plan, and will sometimes engage in tactical coordination.

2. Actual operations expected from the enemy.

   - Isolation and, if possible, occupation of the eastern Galilee, western Galilee, and the Negev.
   - Infiltration into the heart of the area of Sharon[4] . . .
   - Isolation of the three major cities (especially Tel Aviv).[5]
   - Disruption of food supply lines and other vital services such as water, electricity, etc.

3. Expected tactical methods:

   - Attacks by the regular and semi-regular forces on settlements, . . .
   - Air strikes against centers within our cities (especially Tel Aviv)
   - Harassment operations carried out by small forces . . .

(B) THE AUTHORITIES

This plan rests on the general assumption that during its implementation, the forces of the [British] authorities will not be present in the country.

In the event that British forces continue to control certain bases and areas, the plan must be modified to deal with this situation in these areas. . . .

(C) INTERNATIONAL FORCES

This plan rests on the assumption that there will be no international forces stationed in the country which are capable of effective action,

(D) OPERATIONAL OBJECTIVES

1. Self-defense against invasion by regular or semi-regular forces. This will be achieved by the following:

   - A fixed defensive system to preserve our settlements, vital economic projects, and property, . . .
   - Launching pre-planned counter-attacks . . . whether within the borders of the country [Palestine] or in neighboring countries.

2. Ensuring freedom of military and economic activity within the borders of the [Hebrew] state and in Jewish settlements outside its borders by occupying and controlling important high-ground positions on a number of transportation arteries.

3. Preventing the enemy from using frontline positions within his territory which can easily be used for launching attacks. This will be effected by occupying and controlling them.
4. Applying economic pressure on the enemy by besieging some of his cities in order to force him to abandon some of his activities in certain areas of the country.
5. Restricting the capability of the enemy by carrying out limited operations: occupation and control of certain of his bases in rural and urban areas within the borders of the state.
6. Controlling government services and property within the borders of the state and ensuring the supply of essential public services in an effective manner.

3. Assignment of Duties

In view of the operational objectives outlined above, the various armed services are assigned the following duties:

(1) Strengthening the fixed defensive system designed to defend the zones, and coordinating its deployment on the regional level. . . .
(2) Consolidation of the defensive apparatus.
(3) Deployment in major cities.
(4) Control of the main transportation arteries country-wide.
(5) Encirclement of enemy cities.
(6) Occupation and control of frontline enemy positions.
(7) Counterattacks inside and outside the borders of the country.

(A) THE FIXED DEFENSIVE SYSTEM

1. The fixed defensive system in rural areas depends on two main factors: using protected areas. . . , on the one hand, and blocking main transportation routes used by the enemy, on the other hand.
2. The security arrangements pertaining to the zones in rural areas, . . . must be modified in terms of planning and reinforcement to suit the tactical measures expected to be employed by semi-regular or regular enemy forces. . . .
3. In addition, if we take into consideration the tactical measures expected to be employed by the enemy, efforts must be made to make a transition from a positional defense to a regional defense, so that the unit of defense is the region and not the zone.
4. In order to achieve this objective, the following steps must be taken:

    a) Transformation of the regional staff from an administrative staff to a general staff (selection of a location, setting up a communications network, etc.)

b) Formation of a regional mobile reserve, to be recruited from the forces appointed to the zones, . . .

c) Adaptation and incorporation of the plans concerning fortification and opening fire in the zones to those of the region, as far as possible, taking into consideration geographical circumstances and types of weapons used. . . .

5. Settlements which because of their geographical location cannot be included in a fixed regional defense plan must be organized into local defense zones. Accordingly, they must be equipped to block transport roads used by the enemy . . .

6. Blocking the main enemy transportation routes.

a) The main enemy transportation routes which link his lands to the lands of the state, such as roads, bridges, main passes, important crossroads, paths, etc. must be blocked by means of: acts of sabotage, explosions, series of barricades, mine fields, as well as by controlling the elevations near roads and taking up positions there.

b) A system of barricades must be set up in addition to the fixed defensive system. . . .

(B) CONSOLIDATION OF DEFENSE SYSTEMS AND FORTIFICATIONS

The following operations must be carried out if the fixed defensive system is to be effective and if the rear of this system is to be protected:

1. Occupation of police stations.[6]
2. Control of government installations and provision of services in each and every region.
3. Protection of secondary transportation arteries.
4. Mounting operations against enemy population centers located inside or near our defensive system in order to prevent them from being used as bases by an active armed force. These operations can be divided into the following categories:

Destruction of villages (setting fire to, blowing up, and planting mines in the debris), especially those population centers which are difficult to control continuously.

Mounting search and control operations according to the following guidelines: encirclement of the village and conducting a search[7] inside it. In the event of resistance, the armed force must be destroyed and the population must be expelled outside the borders of the state.

The villages which are emptied in the manner described above must be included in the fixed defensive system and must be fortified as necessary.

In the absence of resistance, garrison troops will enter the village and take up positions in it. . . . In every region, a [Jewish] person will be appointed to be responsible for arranging the political and administrative affairs of all [Arab] villages and population centers which are occupied within that region.

(C) DEPLOYMENT IN MAJOR CITIES

Positions will be taken in the large cities according to the following principles:

1. Occupation and control of government facilities and property (post offices, telephone exchanges, railroad stations, police stations, harbors, etc.)
2. Protection of all vital public services and installations.
3. Occupation and control of all isolated Arab neighborhoods located between our municipal center and the Arab municipal center, . . . In case of resistance, the population will be expelled to the area of the Arab municipal center.
4. Encirclement of the central Arab municipal area and its isolation from external transportation routes, as well as the termination of its vital services (water, electricity, fuel, etc.), as far as possible.

(D) CONTROL OF MAIN TRANSPORTATION ARTERIES ON THE REGIONAL LEVEL

1. Occupation and control of locations which overlook main regional transportation arteries, such as police stations, water pumps, etc. . . .
2. Occupation and control of Arab villages which constitute a serious obstruction on any of the main transportation arteries. . . .

(E) ENEMY CITIES WILL BE BESIEGED ACCORDING TO THE FOLLOWING GUIDELINES

1. By isolating them from transportation arteries by laying mines, blowing up bridges, and a system of fixed ambushes.
2. If necessary, by occupying high points which overlook transportation arteries leading to enemy cities, and the fortification of our units in these positions.
3. By disrupting vital services, such as electricity, water, and fuel, or by using economic resources available to us. or by sabotage.
4. By launching a naval operation against the cities that can receive supplies by sea, in order to destroy the vessels carrying the provisions, as well as by carrying out acts of sabotage against harbor facilities.

(F) OCCUPATION AND CONTROL OF FRONTLINE ENEMY POSITIONS

Generally, the aim of this plan is not an operation of occupation outside the borders of the Hebrew state. However, concerning enemy bases lying directly close to the borders . . . , these must be temporarily occupied and searched for hostiles according to the above guidelines, and they must then be incorporated into our defensive system until operations cease.

Bases located in enemy territory which are intended to be temporarily occupied and controlled will be listed among the operational targets for the various brigades.

(G) COUNTERATTACKS INSIDE AND OUTSIDE THE BORDERS OF THE STATE

Counterattacks will be used as ancillary measures for the fixed defensive system in order to abort the organized attacks launched by semi-regular and regular enemy forces, whether from bases inside the country or from outside the borders.

Counterattacks will be launched according to the following guidelines:

1. Diversionary attacks; i.e., while the enemy is launching an attack against one of our areas, [our forces will launch] a counterattack deep inside another area controlled by the enemy with the aim of diverting his forces in the direction of the counterattack.
2. Striking at transportation and supply routes deep inside enemy territory, especially against a regular enemy force which is invading from across the border.
3. Attacking enemy bases in his rear, both inside the country [Palestine] and across its borders.
4. Counterattacks will generally proceed as follows: a force the size of a battalion, on average, will carry out a deep infiltration and will launch concentrated attacks against population centers and enemy bases with the aim of destroying them along with the enemy force positioned there; . . .
5. A detailed list of counterattacks will be included in the [list of][8] operational targets of the Strategic Mobile Force [PALMACH].

4. Duties of the Armed Services

(a) Allocation of Duties in the Fixed Defensive System
1. The following duties are the responsibility of the Garrison Force [KHIM],[9] defense of the zones and of isolated and fortified posts and formation of the regional reserves.
2. Within the framework of the fixed defensive system, the Field Force [KHISH],[10] are responsible for the following duties:

Operations to block enemy transportation routes. . . .

. . . consolidating the fixed defensive system, as outlined in section 3 (b).

3. In special and exceptional circumstances, Field Force units may be positioned in the regions or zones, or in isolated and fortified positions, in order to reinforce zonal or regional defense. . . .

4. In addition to the duties detailed above, the Field Force's responsibilities within the fixed defensive system generally consist in mounting local counterattacks involving units no smaller than company (larger units should be used if possible) against enemy units. . . . These counterattacks will usually be launched from fixed operational bases which will be specified for the Field Force in the context of the duties for which it is responsible in the region as a whole. . . .

5. The chain of command in the cases mentioned above will be in accordance with Addendum 1 to the Order concerning Regional Infrastructure, November 1947.

6. . . . the commander of the Field Force battalion concerned will appoint the commander in charge of the entire defensive system.

(b) 1. In addition to the duties assigned to the Field Force brigade in question concerning the consolidation of the fixed defensive system, the brigade will also carry out the following duties:

- Consolidation of positions in the cities.
- Control of main transportation arteries country-wide.
- Encirclement of enemy cities.
- Occupation and control of enemy frontline positions. . . .

In order to carry out any or all of these duties, the supreme command can assign units of the Strategic Mobile Force [PALMACH],[11] which constitute the country-wide reserves, to the Field Force.

2. During the implementation of joint missions with the Field Force, units of the Strategic Mobile Force [PALMACH] will fall under the command of the Field Force brigade that controls the area in which these units are operating.

3. After completion of the mission, the units of the Strategic Mobile Force [PALMACH] will rejoin the country-wide reserves.

4. Efforts must be made to ensure that the period during which units of the country-wide reserves are assigned to the Field Force is as short as possible.

(c) 1. The Strategic Mobile Force [PALMACH] is responsible for carrying out counterattacks inside and outside the borders of the country.

2. The supreme command may reduce the number of duties assigned to one or another of the Field Force brigades as it sees fit . . . and allocate them directly to the Strategic Mobile Force [PALMACH] instead.

(d) The various departments and services of the general staff are required to complete the above planning orders in their various areas of responsibility and to present the plans to the Field Force brigades.

Notes

1. This is Plan Gimmel or Plan C.
2. This is an early version of Plan D, so called after Yehoshua Globerman, a Haganah commander killed in early December 1947. Plan D itself was finalized on 10 March 1948.
3. This was a British-commanded and financed army of King 'Abdallah's Transjordan, units of which served in Palestine under British army orders until the end of the mandate on 15 May 1948.
4. Sharon is the coastal plain between Haifa and Tel Aviv, Emek Hefer being its central section (in Arabic Wadi al-Hawarith).
5. The two others are Jerusalem and Haifa.
6. These "police stations" were in fact fortresses, 50 of which were built by the British throughout Palestine after the Arab rebellion of 1936–39 in order to control the Arab population.
7. In the original translation, the word "srika" was translated as "combing." The reference is to a search for hostile forces.
8. This list is not in the Hebrew original of this document.
9. [KHIM] is short for Khayl Matzav, the second line troops. By fall 1947, they numbered about 32,000. See Khalidi, *From Haven to Conquest*, 862. [Israeli sources give much lower numbers – A.I.]
10. KHISH is short for Khayl Sadeh, the front line troops. By 1 May 1948, they numbered about 30,000. See Khalidi, *From Haven to Conquest*, 861. [Israeli sources give much lower numbers – A.I.]
11. PALMACH is short for Plugot Machats, crushing battalions. By spring 1948, this force was made up of three brigades (Yiftach, Harel, and HaNegev) numbering just above 8,000 men. See Walid Khalidi, *From Haven to Conquest* (Washington: Institute for Palestine Studies, 1987), 861. [The Palmach was originally formed with the intention of repelling an invasion from Vichy-controlled Syria – A.I.]

25 Declaration of the Establishment of the State of Israel (May 14, 1948)

Text:

ERETZ-ISRAEL [(Hebrew) – the Land of Israel, Palestine] was the birthplace of the Jewish people. Here their spiritual, religious, and political identity was shaped. Here they first attained to statehood, created cultural values of national and universal significance, and gave to the world the eternal Book of Books.

After being forcibly exiled from their land, the people kept faith with it throughout their Dispersion and never ceased to pray and hope for their return to it and for the restoration in it of their political freedom.

Impelled by this historic and traditional attachment, Jews strove in every successive generation to re-establish themselves in their ancient homeland. In recent decades they returned in their masses. Pioneers, *ma'pilim* [(Hebrew) – immigrants coming to Eretz-Israel in defiance of restrictive legislation], and defenders, they made deserts bloom, revived the Hebrew language, built villages and towns, and created a thriving community controlling its own economy and culture, loving peace but knowing how to defend itself, bringing the blessings of progress to all the country's inhabitants, and aspiring towards independent nationhood.

In the year 5657 (1897), at the summons of the spiritual father of the Jewish State, Theodore Herzl, the First Zionist Congress convened and proclaimed the right of the Jewish people to national rebirth in its own country.

This right was recognized in the Balfour Declaration of the 2nd November, 1917, and re-affirmed in the Mandate of the League of Nations which, in particular, gave international sanction to the historic connection between the Jewish people and Eretz-Israel and to the right of the Jewish people to rebuild its National Home.

The catastrophe which recently befell the Jewish people – the massacre of millions of Jews in Europe – was another clear demonstration of the urgency of solving the problem of its homelessness by re-establishing in Eretz-Israel the Jewish State, which would open the gates of the homeland wide to every Jew and confer upon the Jewish people the status of a fully privileged member of the comity of nations.

Survivors of the Nazi holocaust in Europe, as well as Jews from other parts of the world, continued to migrate to Eretz-Israel, undaunted by difficulties,

DOI: 10.4324/9781003348948-28

restrictions, and dangers, and never ceased to assert their right to a life of dignity, freedom, and honest toil in their national homeland.

In the Second World War, the Jewish community of this country contributed its full share to the struggle of the freedom- and peace-loving nations against the forces of Nazi wickedness and, by the blood of its soldiers and its war effort, gained the right to be reckoned among the peoples who founded the United Nations.

On the 29th November, 1947, the United Nations General Assembly passed a resolution calling for the establishment of a Jewish State in Eretz-Israel; the General Assembly required the inhabitants of Eretz-Israel to take such steps as were necessary on their part for the implementation of that resolution. This recognition by the United Nations of the right of the Jewish people to establish their State is irrevocable.

This right is the natural right of the Jewish people to be masters of their own fate, like all other nations, in their own sovereign State.

ACCORDINGLY we, members of the People's Council, representatives of the Jewish community of Eretz-Israel and of the Zionist movement, are here assembled on the day of the termination of the British Mandate over Eretz-Israel and, by virtue of our natural and historic right and on the strength of the resolution of the United Nations General Assembly, hereby declare the establishment of a Jewish State in Eretz-Israel, to be known as the State of Israel.

WE DECLARE that, with effect from the moment of the termination of the Mandate being tonight, the eve of Sabbath, the 6th Iyar, 5708 (15th May, 1948), until the establishment of the elected, regular authorities of the State in accordance with the Constitution which shall be adopted by the Elected Constituent Assembly not later than the 1st October 1948, the People's Council shall act as a Provisional Council of State, and its executive organ, the People's Administration, shall be the Provisional Government of the Jewish State, to be called "Israel".

THE STATE OF ISRAEL will be open for Jewish immigration and for the Ingathering of the Exiles; it will foster the development of the country for the benefit of all its inhabitants; it will be based on freedom, justice, and peace as envisaged by the prophets of Israel; it will ensure complete equality of social and political rights to all its inhabitants irrespective of religion, race, or sex; it will guarantee freedom of religion, conscience, language, education, and culture; it will safeguard the Holy Places of all religions; and it will be faithful to the principles of the Charter of the United Nations.

THE STATE OF ISRAEL is prepared to cooperate with the agencies and representatives of the United Nations in implementing the resolution of the General Assembly of the 29th November, 1947, and will take steps to bring about the economic union of the whole of Eretz-Israel.

WE APPEAL to the United Nations to assist the Jewish people in the building-up of its State and to receive the State of Israel into the comity of nations.

WE APPEAL – in the very midst of the onslaught launched against us now for months – to the Arab inhabitants of the State of Israel to preserve peace and participate in the upbuilding of the State on the basis of full and equal citizenship and due representation in all its provisional and permanent institutions.

WE EXTEND our hand to all neighbouring states and their peoples in an offer of peace and good neighbourliness, and appeal to them to establish bonds of cooperation and mutual help with the sovereign Jewish people settled in its own land. The State of Israel is prepared to do its share in a common effort for the advancement of the entire Middle East.

WE APPEAL to the Jewish people throughout the Diaspora to rally round the Jews of Eretz-Israel in the tasks of immigration and upbuilding and to stand by them in the great struggle for the realization of the age-old dream – the redemption of Israel.

Placing our trust in the "Rock of Israel," we affix our signatures to this proclamation at this session of the Provisional Council of State, on the soil of the homeland, in the city of Tel-Aviv, on this sabbath eve, the 5th day of Iyar, 5708 (14th May, 1948).

David Ben-Gurion

Daniel Auster	*Rachel Cohen*	*David Zvi Pinkas*
Mordekhai Bentov	*Rabbi Kalman Kahana*	*Aharon Zisling*
Yitzchak Ben Zvi	*Saadia Kobashi*	*Moshe Kolodny*
Eliyahu Berligne	*Rabbi Yitzchak Meir Levin*	*Eliezer Kaplan*
Fritz Bernstein	*Meir David Loewenstein*	*Abraham Katznelson*
Rabbi Wolf Gold	*Zvi Luria*	*Felix Rosenblueth*
Meir Grabovsky	*Golda Myerson*	*David Remez*
Yitzchak Gruenbaum	*Nachum Nir*	*Berl Repetur*
Dr. Abraham Granovsky	*Zvi Segal*	*Mordekhai Shattner*
Eliyahu Dobkin	*Rabbi Yehuda Leib*	*Ben Zion Sternberg*
Meir Wilner-Kovner	*Hacohen Fishman*	*Bekhor Shitreet*
Zerach Wahrhaftig		*Moshe Shapira*
Herzl Vardi		*Moshe Shertok*

Published in the *Official Gazette*, No. 1 of the 5th, Iyar, 5708 (14th May, 1948).

26 Creation of a Conciliation Commission, General Assembly Resolution 194 (III) (December 11, 1948)

The General Assembly,
Having considered further the situation in Palestine,

1. Expresses its deep appreciation of the progress achieved through the good offices of the late United Nations Mediator in promoting a peaceful adjustment of the future situation of Palestine, for which cause he sacrificed his life . . .
2. Establishes a Conciliation Commission consisting of three States Members of the United Nations . . .
3. Decides that a Committee of the Assembly, consisting of China, France, the Union of Soviet Socialist Republics, the United Kingdom, and the United States of America, shall present, before the end of the first part of the present session of the General Assembly, for the approval of the Assembly, a proposal concerning the names of the three States which will constitute the Conciliation Commission;
4. Requests the Commission to begin its functions at once . . .
5. Calls upon the Governments and authorities concerned to extend the scope of the negotiations provided for in the Security Council's resolution of 16 November 1948 and to seek agreement by negotiations conducted either with the Conciliation Commission or directly with a view to the final settlement of all questions outstanding between them;
6. Instructs the Conciliation Commission to take steps to assist the Government and authorities concerned to achieve a final settlement of all questions outstanding between them;
7. Resolves that the Holy Places – including Nazareth – religious buildings and sites in Palestine should be protected and free access to them assured . . . ;
8. Resolves that, in view of its association with three world religions, the Jerusalem area . . . should be accorded special and separate treatment from the rest of Palestine and should be placed under effective United Nations control;

Requests the Security Council to take further steps to ensure the demilitarization of Jerusalem at the earliest possible date;

DOI: 10.4324/9781003348948-29

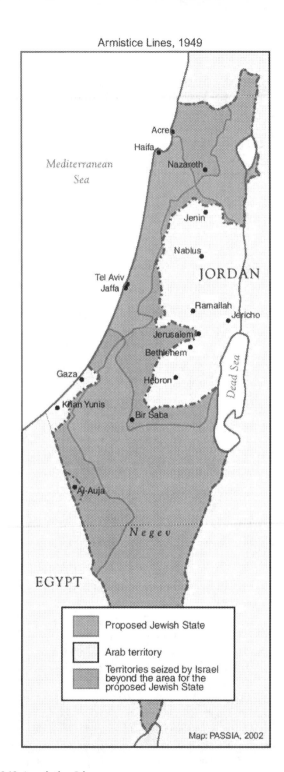

Armistice Lines, 1949

Proposed Jewish State

Arab territory

Territories seized by Israel
beyond the area for the
proposed Jewish State

Map: PASSIA, 2002

Map 8 The 1949 Armistice Lines
Source: Permission granted by the Palestinian Academic Society for the Study of International
Affairs to reprint their map of 1949 armistice lines in this book. The original can be found at:
www.passia.org/maps/view/15.

. . .

The Conciliation Commission is authorized to appoint a United Nations representative who shall cooperate with the local authorities with respect to the interim administration of the Jerusalem area;

9. Resolves that, pending agreement on more detailed arrangements among the Governments and authorities concerned, the freest possible access to Jerusalem by road, rail, or air should be accorded to all inhabitants of Palestine;

. . .

10. Instructs the Conciliation Commission to seek arrangements among the Governments and authorities concerned, which will facilitate the economic development of the area, including arrangements for access to ports and airfields and the use of transportation and communication facilities;

11. Resolves that the refugees wishing to return to their homes and live at peace with their neighbours should be permitted to do so at the earliest practicable date, and that compensation should be paid for the property of those choosing not to return and for loss of or damage to property which, under principles of international law or in equity, should be made good by the Governments or authorities responsible;

Instructs the Conciliation Commission to facilitate the repatriation, resettlement, and economic and social rehabilitation of the refugees and the payment of compensation, and to maintain close relations with the Director of the United Nations Relief for Palestine Refugees and, through him, with the appropriate organs and agencies of the United Nations;

12. . . .

13. Instructs the Conciliation Commission to render progress reports periodically to the Secretary-General for transmission to the Security Council and to the Members of the United Nations;

14. Calls upon all Governments and authorities concerned to cooperate with the Conciliation Commission and to take all possible steps to assist in the implementation of the present resolution;

15. Requests the Secretary-General to provide the necessary staff and facilities and to make appropriate arrangements to provide the necessary funds required in carrying out the terms of the present resolution.

27 Admission of Israel to the United Nations, General Assembly Resolution 273 (III) (May 11, 1949)

Having received the report of the Security Council on the application of Israel for membership in the United Nations,

Noting that, in the judgment of the Security Council, Israel is a peace-loving State and is able and willing to carry out the obligations contained in the Charter,

Noting that the Security Council has recommended to the General Assembly that it admit Israel to membership in the United Nations,

Noting furthermore the declaration by the State of Israel that it "unreservedly accepts the obligations of the United Nations Charter and undertakes to honour them from the day when it becomes a Member of the United Nations,"

Recalling its resolutions of 29 November 1947 and 11 December 1948 and taking note of the declarations and explanations made by the representatives of the Government of Israel before the *Ad Hoc* Political Committee in respect of the implementation of the said resolutions,

The General Assembly

Acting in discharge of its functions under Article 4 of the Charter and rule 125 of its rules of procedure,

1. Decides that Israel is a peace-loving State which accepts the obligations contained in the Charter and is able and willing to carry out those obligations;
2. Decides to admit Israel to membership in the United Nations.

DOI: 10.4324/9781003348948-30

Part III

From Recognition (1949) Through the Start of a Peace Process (1978)

28 U.N. General Assembly: Resolution 303 (IV)

Palestine: Question of an International Regime for the Jerusalem Area and the Protection of the Holy Places (December 9, 1949)

The General Assembly,

Having regard to its resolutions 181 (II)[1] of 29 November 1947 and 194 (III)[2] of 11 December 1948,

Having studied the reports of the United Nations Conciliation Commission for Palestine set up under the latter resolution,

I. *Decides*

In relation to Jerusalem,

Believing that the principles underlying its previous resolutions concerning this matter, and in particular its resolution of 29 November 1947, represent a just and equitable settlement of the question,

1. To restate, therefore, its intention that Jerusalem should be placed under a permanent international regime, which should envisage appropriate guarantees for the protection of the Holy Places, both within and outside Jerusalem, and . . . the City of Jerusalem shall be established as a *corpus separatum* under a special international regime and shall be administered by the United Nations; (2) the Trusteeship Council shall be designated to discharge the responsibilities of the Administering Authority . . . ; and (3) the City of Jerusalem shall include the present municipality of Jerusalem plus the surrounding villages and towns, . . .

2. To request for this purpose that the Trusteeship Council at its next session, whether special or regular, complete the preparation of the Statute of Jerusalem,[3] omitting the now inapplicable provisions, such as articles 32 and 39, and, without prejudice to the fundamental principles of the international regime for Jerusalem set forth in General Assembly resolution 181 (II) introducing therein amendments in the direction of its greater democratization, approve the Statue, and proceed immediately with its implementation. The Trusteeship Council shall not allow any actions taken by any interested Government or Governments to divert it from adopting and implementing the Statute of Jerusalem;

DOI: 10.4324/9781003348948-32

II. *Calls upon* the States concerned to make formal undertakings, at an early date and in the light of their obligations as Members of the United Nations, that they will approach these matters with good will and be guided by the terms of the present resolution.

Notes

1. See *Official Records of the second session of the General Assembly*, Resolutions, page 131.
2. See *Official Records of the third session of the General Assembly, Part I*, Resolutions, page 21.
3. See *Official Records of the second session of the Trusteeship Council*, Third Part, Annex, page 4.

29 State of Israel

Law of Return (July 5, 1950)

Law of Return 5710–1950

Right of aliyah*	1. Every Jew has the right to come to this country as an oleh*.
Oleh's visa	2. (a) Aliyah shall be by oleh's visa. (b) An oleh's visa shall be granted to every Jew who has expressed his desire to settle in Israel, unless the Minister of Immigration is satisfied that the applicant (1) is engaged in an activity directed against the Jewish people; or (2) is likely to endanger public health or the security of the State.
Oleh's certificate	3. (a) A Jew who has come to Israel and subsequent to his arrival has expressed his desire to settle in Israel may, while still in Israel, receive an oleh's certificate. (b) The restrictions specified in section 2(b) shall apply also to the grant of an oleh's certificate, but a person shall not be regarded as endangering public health on account of an illness contracted after his arrival in Israel.
Residents and persons born in this country	4. Every Jew who has immigrated into this country before the coming into force of this Law, and every Jew who was born in this country, whether before or after the coming into force of this Law, shall be deemed to be a person who has come to this country as an oleh under this Law.
Implementation and regulations	5. The Minister of Immigration is charged with the implementation of this Law and may make regulations as to any matter relating to such implementation and also as to the grant of oleh's visas and oleh's certificates to minors up to the age of 18 years.

DOI: 10.4324/9781003348948-33

DAVID BEN-GURION
Prime Minister

MOSHE SHAPIRA
Minister of Immigration

YOSEF SPRINZAK
Acting President of the State
Chairman of the Knesset

* Translator's Note: Aliyah means immigration of Jews, and oleh (plural: olim) means a Jew immigrating, into Israel.

30 U.N. Security Council

Resolution 95, Concerning . . . the Passage of Ships Through the Suez Canal (September 1, 1951)

The Security Council,

R*ecalling* that in its resolution 73 (1949) of 11 August 1949 relating to the conclusion of Armistice Agreements between Israel and the neighbouring Arab States it drew attention to the pledges in these Agreements "against any further acts of hostility between the parties"

Recalling further that in its resolution 89 (1950) of 17 November 1950 it reminded the States concerned that the Armistice Agreements to which they were parties contemplated "the return of permanent peace in Palestine," and, therefore, urged them and the other States in the area to take all such steps as would lead to the settlement of the issues between them,

. . .

Further noting that the Chief of Staff of the Truce Supervision Organization recalled the statement of the senior Egyptian delegate in Rhodes on 13 January 1949, to the effect that his delegation was "inspired with every spirit of co-operation, conciliation and a sincere desire to restore peace in Palestine," and that the Egyptian Government has not complied with the earnest plea of the Chief of Staff made to the Egyptian delegate on 12 June 1951, that it desist from the present practice of interfering with the passage through the Suez Canal of goods destined for Israel,

Considering that since the armistice regime, which has been in existence for nearly two and a half years, is of a permanent character, neither party can reasonably assert that it is actively a belligerent or requires to exercise the right of visit, search and seizure for any legitimate purpose of self-defence.

Finds that the maintenance of the practice mentioned in the fourth paragraph of the present resolution is inconsistent with the objectives of a peaceful settlement between the parties and the establishment of a permanent peace in Palestine set forth in the Armistice Agreement between Egypt and Israel;

Finds further that such practice is an abuse of the exercise of the right of visit, search and seizure;

. . .

And further noting that the restrictions on the passage of goods through the Suez Canal to Israel ports are denying to nations at no time connected with the conflict in Palestine valuable supplies required for their economic

DOI: 10.4324/9781003348948-34

reconstruction, and that these restrictions together with sanctions applied by Egypt to certain ships which have visited Israel ports represent unjustified interference with the rights of nations to navigate the seas and to trade freely with one another, including the Arab States and Israel,

Calls upon Egypt to terminate the restrictions on the passage of international commercial shipping and goods through the Suez Canal wherever bound and to cease all interference with such shipping beyond that essential to the safety of shipping in the Canal itself and to the observance of the international conventions in force.

Adopted at the 558th meeting by eight votes to none, with three abstentions (China, India, Union of Soviet Socialist Republics).

31 Palestine National Authority

Palestine National Charter of 1964
(May 28, 1964)

Introduction

We, the Palestinian Arab people, who waged fierce and continuous battles to safeguard its homeland, to defend its dignity and honor, and who offered all through the years continuous caravans of immortal martyrs, and who wrote the noblest pages of sacrifice, offering and giving.

We, the Palestinian Arab people, who faced the forces of evil, injustice and aggression, against whom the forces of international Zionism and colonialism conspire and worked to displace it, dispossess it from its homeland and property, abused what is holy in it and who in spite of all this refused to weaken or submit.

We, the Palestinian Arab people, who believe in its Arabism and in its right to regain its homeland, to realize its freedom and dignity, and who have determined to amass its forces and mobilize its efforts and capabilities in order to continue its struggle and to move forward on the path of holy war (al-jihad) until complete and final victory has been attained,

We, the Palestinian Arab people, based on our right of self-defense and the complete restoration of our lost homeland – a right that has been recognized by international covenants and common practices including the Charter of the United Nations – and in implementation of the principles of human rights, and comprehending the international political relations, with its various ramifications and dimensions, and considering the past experiences in all that pertains to the causes of the catastrophe, and the means to face it,

And embarking from the Palestinian Arab reality, and for the sake of the honor of the Palestinian individual and his right to free and dignified life,

And realizing the national grave responsibility placed upon our shoulders, for the sake of all this,

We, the Palestinian Arab people, dictate and declare this Palestinian National Charter and swear to realize it.

Article 1. Palestine is an Arab homeland bound by strong Arab national ties to the rest of the Arab Countries and which together form the great Arab homeland.

DOI: 10.4324/9781003348948-35

Article 2: Palestine, with its boundaries at the time of the British Mandate, is a indivisible territorial unit.

Article 3: The Palestinian Arab people has the legitimate right to its homeland and is an inseparable part of the Arab Nation. It shares the sufferings and aspirations of the Arab Nation and its struggle for freedom, sovereignty, progress and unity.

Article 4: The people of Palestine determine its destiny when it completes the liberation of its homeland in accordance with its own wishes and free will and choice.

Article 5: The Palestinian personality is a permanent and genuine characteristic that does not disappear. It is transferred from fathers to sons.

Article 6: The Palestinians are those Arab citizens who were living normally in Palestine up to 1947, whether they remained or were expelled. Every child who was born to a Palestinian Arab father after this date, whether in Palestine or outside, is a Palestinian.

Article 7: Jews of Palestinian origin are considered Palestinians if they are willing to live peacefully and loyally in Palestine.

Article 8: Bringing up Palestinian youth in an Arab and nationalist manner is a fundamental national duty. All means of guidance, education and enlightenment should be utilized to introduce the youth to its homeland in a deep spiritual way that will constantly and firmly bind them together.

Article 9: Ideological doctrines, whether political, social, or economic, shall not distract the people of Palestine from the primary duty of liberating their homeland. All Palestinian constitute one national front and work with all their feelings and material potentialities to free their homeland.

Article 10: Palestinians have three mottos: National Unity, National Mobilization, and Liberation. Once liberation is completed, the people of Palestine shall choose for its public life whatever political, economic, or social system they want.

Article 11: The Palestinian people firmly believe in Arab unity, and in order to play its role in realizing this goal, it must, at this stage of its struggle, preserve its Palestinian personality and all its constituents. It must strengthen the consciousness of its existence and stance and stand against any attempt or plan that may weaken or disintegrate its personality.

Article 12: Arab unity and the liberation of Palestine are two complementary goals; each prepares for the attainment of the other. Arab unity leads to the liberation of Palestine, and the liberation of Palestine leads to Arab unity. Working for both must go side by side.

Article 13: The destiny of the Arab Nation and even the essence of Arab existence are firmly tied to the destiny of the Palestine question. From this firm bond stems the effort and struggle of the Arab Nation to liberate Palestine. The people of Palestine assume a vanguard role in achieving this sacred national goal.

Article 14: The liberation of Palestine, from an Arab viewpoint, is a national duty. Its responsibilities fall upon the entire Arab nation, governments and peoples, the Palestinian peoples being in the forefront. For this purpose, the Arab nation must mobilize its military, spiritual and material potentialities; specifically, it must give to the Palestinian Arab people all possible support and backing and place at its disposal all opportunities and means to enable them to perform their role in liberating their homeland.

Article 15: The liberation of Palestine, from a spiritual viewpoint, prepares for the Holy Land an atmosphere of tranquillity and peace, in which all the Holy Places will be safeguarded, and the freedom to worship and to visit will be guaranteed for all, without any discrimination of race, color, language, or religion. For all this, the Palestinian people look forward to the support of all the spiritual forces in the world.

Article 16: The liberation of Palestine, from an international viewpoint, is a defensive act necessitated by the demands of self-defense as stated in the Charter of the United Nations. For that, the people of Palestine, desiring to befriend all nations which love freedom, justice, and peace, look forward to their support in restoring the legitimate situation to Palestine, establishing peace and security in its territory, and enabling its people to exercise national sovereignty and freedom.

Article 17: The partitioning of Palestine, which took place in 1947, and the establishment of Israel are illegal and null and void, regardless of the loss of time, because they were contrary to the will of the Palestinian people and its natural right to its homeland, and were in violation of the basic principles embodied in the Charter of the United Nations, foremost among which is the right to self-determination.

Article 18: The Balfour Declaration, the Palestine Mandate System, and all that has been based on them are considered null and void. The claims of historic and spiritual ties between Jews and Palestine are not in agreement with the facts of history or with the true basis of sound statehood. Judaism, because it is a divine religion, is not a nationality with independent existence. Furthermore, the Jews are not one people with an independent personality because they are citizens to their states.

Article 19: Zionism is a colonialist movement in its inception, aggressive and expansionist in its goal, racist in its configurations, and fascist in its means and aims. Israel, in its capacity as the spearhead of this destructive movement and as the pillar of colonialism, is a permanent source of tension and turmoil in the Middle East, in particular, and to the international community in general. Because of this, the people of Palestine are worthy of the support and sustenance of the community of nations.

Article 20: The causes of peace and security and the requirements of right and justice demand from all nations, in order to safeguard true relationships among peoples and to maintain the loyalty of citizens to their homeland, that they consider Zionism an illegal movement and outlaw its presence and activities.

Article 21: The Palestinian people believes in the principles of justice, freedom, sovereignty, self-determination, human dignity, and the right of peoples to practice these principles. It also supports all international efforts to bring about peace on the basis of justice and free international cooperation.

Article 22: The Palestinian people believe in peaceful co-existence on the basis of legal existence, for there can be no coexistence with aggression, nor can there be peace with occupation and colonialism.

Article 23: In realizing the goals and principles of this Convent, the Palestine Liberation Organization carries out its full role to liberate Palestine in accordance with the basic law of this Organization.

Article 24: This Organization does not exercise any territorial sovereignty over the West Bank in the Hashemite Kingdom of Jordan, on the Gaza Strip or in the Himmah Area. Its activities will be on the national popular level in the liberational, organizational, political and financial fields.

Article 25: This Organization is in charge of the movement of the Palestinian people in its struggle to liberate its homeland in all liberational, organizational, and financial matters, and in all other needs of the Palestine Question in the Arab and international spheres.

Article 26: The Liberation Organization cooperates with all Arab governments, each according to its ability, and does not interfere in the internal affairs of any Arab states.

Article 27: This Organization shall have its flag, oath and a national anthem. All this shall be resolved in accordance with special regulations.

Article 28: The basic law for the Palestine Liberation Organization is attached to this Charter. This law defines the manner of establishing the Organization, its organs, institutions, the specialties of each one of them, and all the needed duties thrust upon it in accordance with this Charter.

Article 29: This Charter cannot be amended except by two-thirds majority of the members of the National Council of the Palestine Liberation Organization in a special session called for this purpose.

32 Israeli Foreign Minister Abba Eban

Speech to the Security Council of the United Nations (June 6, 1967)

I thank you, Mr. President, for giving me this opportunity to address the Council. I have just come from Jerusalem to tell the Security Council that Israel, by its independent effort and sacrifice, has passed from serious danger to successful resistance.

Two days ago, Israel's condition caused much concern across the humane and friendly world. Israel had reached a sombre hour. Let me try to evoke the point at which our fortunes stood.

An army, greater than any force ever assembled in history in Sinai, had massed against Israel's southern frontier. Egypt had dismissed the United Nations forces which symbolized the international interest in the maintenance of peace in our region. Nasser had provocatively brought five infantry divisions and two armoured divisions up to our very gates; 80,000 men and 900 tanks were poised to move.

A special striking force, comprising an armoured division with at least 200 tanks, was concentrated against Eilat at the Negev's southern tip. Here was a clear design to cut the southern Negev off from the main body of our State. For Egypt had openly proclaimed that Eilat did not form part of Israel and had predicted that Israel itself would soon expire. The proclamation was empty; the prediction now lies in ruin. While the main brunt of the hostile threat was focused on the southern front, an alarming plan of encirclement was under way. With Egypt's initiative and guidance, Israel was already being strangled in its maritime approaches to the whole eastern half of the world. For 16 years, Israel had been illicitly denied passage in the Suez Canal, despite the Security Council's decision of 1 September 1951 [Resolution 95 (1951)]. And now the creative enterprise of 10 patient years which had opened an international route across the Strait of Tiran and the Gulf of Aqaba had been suddenly and arbitrarily choked. Israel was and is breathing only with a single lung.

Jordan had been intimidated, against its better interest, into joining a defence pact. It is not a defence pact at all: it is an aggressive pact, of which I saw the consequences with my own eyes yesterday in the shells falling upon institutions of health and culture in the City of Jerusalem. Every house and street in Jerusalem now came into the range of fire as a result of Jordan's adherence to this pact; so also did the crowded and pathetically

DOI: 10.4324/9781003348948-36

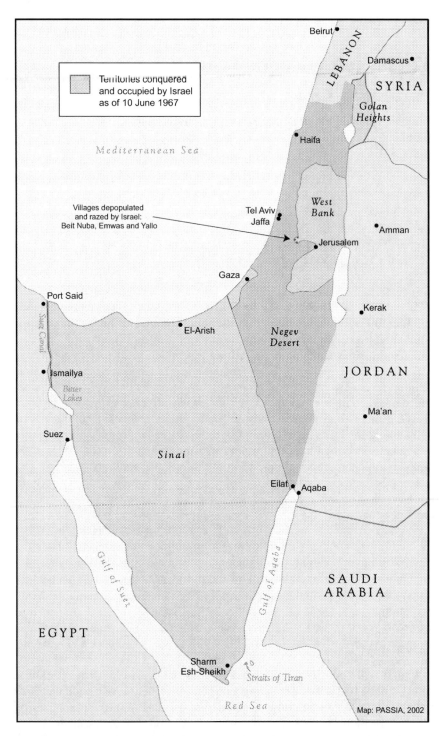

Map labels:
- Beirut
- LEBANON
- Damascus
- SYRIA
- Golan Heights
- Territories conquered and occupied by Israel as of 10 June 1967
- Mediterranean Sea
- Haifa
- West Bank
- Villages depopulated and razed by Israel: Beit Nuba, Emwas and Yallo
- Tel Aviv
- Jaffa
- Amman
- Jerusalem
- Gaza
- Port Said
- Kerak
- Suez Canal
- El-Arish
- Negev Desert
- JORDAN
- Ismailya
- Bitter Lakes
- Ma'an
- Suez
- Sinai
- Eilat
- Aqaba
- Gulf of Suez
- Gulf of Aqaba
- SAUDI ARABIA
- EGYPT
- Sharm Esh-Sheikh
- Straits of Tiran
- Red Sea
- Map: PASSIA, 2002

Map 9 Borders of Israel after the 1967 War.

Source: Permission granted by the Palestinian Academic Society for the Study of International Affairs to reprint their map of the 1967 borders of Israel in this book. The original can be found at: www.passia.org/maps/view/20.

narrow coastal strip in which so much of Israel's life and population is concentrated.

Iraqi troops reinforced Jordanian units in areas immediately facing vital and vulnerable Israel communication centres. Expeditionary forces from Algeria and Kuwait had reached Egyptian territory. Nearly all the Egyptian forces which had been attempting the conquest of the Yemen had been transferred to the coming assault upon Israel. Syrian units, including artillery, overlooked the Israel villages in the Jordan Valley. Terrorist troops came regularly into our territory to kill, plunder, and set off explosions; the most recent occasion was five days ago.

In short, there was peril for Israel wherever it looked. . . . There was an apocalyptic air of approaching peril. And Israel faced this danger alone.

. . .

Now there could be no doubt about what was intended for us. With my very ears I heard President Nasser's speech on 26 May. He said:

> *We intend to open a general assault against Israel. This will be total war. Our basic aim will be to destroy Israel.*

. . .

As time went on, there was no doubt that our margin of general security was becoming smaller and smaller. . . . In accordance with its inherent right of self-defence as formulated in Article 51 of the United Nations Charter, Israel responded defensively in full strength. Never in the history of nations has armed force been used in a more righteous or compelling cause.

Even when engaged with Egyptian forces, we still hoped to contain the conflict. Egypt was overtly bent on our destruction, but we still hoped that others would not join the aggression. Prime Minister Eshkol, who for weeks had carried the heavy burden of calculation and decision, published and conveyed a message to other neighbouring States proclaiming:

> *We shall not attack any country unless it opens war on us. Even now, when the mortars speak, we have not given up our quest for peace. We strive to repel all menace of terrorism and any danger of aggression to ensure our security and our legitimate rights.*

In accordance with this same policy of attempting to contain the conflict, yesterday I invited General Bull, the Chief of Staff of the Truce Supervision Organization, to inform the heads of the Jordanian State that Israel had no desire to expand the conflict beyond the unfortunate dimensions that it had already assumed and that if Israel were not attacked on the Jordan side, it would not attack and would act only in self-defence. It reached my ears that this message had been duly and faithfully conveyed and received. Nevertheless, Jordan decided to join the Egyptian posture against Israel and opened artillery attacks across the whole long frontier, including Jerusalem. Those attacks are still in progress.

To the appeal of Prime Minister Eshkol to avoid any further extension of the conflict, Syria answered at 12.25 yesterday morning by bombing Megiddo from the air and bombing Degania at 12.40 with artillery fire and kibbutz Ein Hammifrats and Kurdani with long-range guns. But Jordan embarked on a much more total assault by artillery and aircraft along the entire front, with special emphasis on Jerusalem, to whose dangerous and noble ordeal yesterday I come to bear personal witness.

There has been bombing of houses; there has been a hit on the great new National Museum of Art; there has been a hit on the University and on Shaare Zedek, the first hospital ever to have been established outside the ancient walls. . . . And in the Knesset building, whose construction had been movingly celebrated by the entire democratic world 10 months ago, the Israel Cabinet and Parliament met under heavy gunfire, whose echoes mingled at the end of our meeting with *Hatikvah*, the anthem of hope.

Thus, throughout the day and night of 5 June, the Jordan which we had expressly invited to abstain from needless slaughter became, to our surprise, and still remains, the most intense of all the belligerents; and death and injury, as so often in history, stalk Jerusalem's streets.

. . .

I should, however, be less than frank if I were to conceal the fact that the Government and people of Israel have been disconcerted by some aspects of the United Nations role in this conflict. The sudden withdrawal of the United Nations Emergency Force was not accompanied, as it should have been, by due international consultations on the consequences of that withdrawal. . . . After all, a new confrontation of forces suddenly arose. It suddenly had to be met and at Sharm el-Sheikh at the entrance to the Gulf of Aqaba, the Strait of Tiran, legality walked out and blockade walked in. The peace of the world trembled. And thus, the United Nations had somehow been put into a position of leaving Sinai safe for belligerency.

. . .

The United Nations Emergency Force rendered distinguished service. Nothing became it less than the manner of its departure. All gratitude and appreciation are owed to the individuals who sustained its action. And if in the course of the recent combats United Nations personnel have fallen dead or wounded – as they have – then I join my voice in an expression of the most sincere regret.

The problem of the future role of a United Nations presence in conflicts such as these is being much debated. But we must ask ourselves a question that has arisen as a result of this experience. People in our country and in many countries ask: What is the use of a United Nations presence if it is in effect an umbrella which is taken away as soon as it begins to rain? . . .

We have lived through three dramatic weeks. Those weeks, I think, have brought into clear view the main elements of tension and also the chief promise of relaxed tension in the future. The first link in the chain was the series of sabotage acts emanating from Syria. In October of 1966, the Security

Council was already seized of this problem, and a majority of its member States found it possible and necessary to draw attention to the Syrian Government's responsibility for altering that situation. . . .

But then there came a graver source of tension in mid-May, when abnormal troop concentrations were observed in the Sinai Peninsula. For the 10 years of relative stability beginning with March 1957 and ending with May 1967, the Sinai Desert had been free of Egyptian troops. In other words, a natural geographic barrier, a largely uninhabited space, separated the main forces of the two sides. It is true that in terms of sovereignty and law, any State has a right to put its armies in any part of its territory that it chooses. This, however, is not a legal question: it is a political and a security question.

. . .

We were puzzled in Israel by the relative lack of preoccupation on the part of friendly Governments and international agencies with this intense concentration which found its reflection in precautionary concentrations on our side. My Government proposed, I think at least two weeks ago, the concept of a parallel and reciprocal reduction of forces on both sides of the frontier. We elicited no response, and certainly no action.

To these grave sources of tension – the sabotage and terrorist movement, emanating mostly from Syria, and the heavy troop concentrations accompanied by dire, apocalyptic threats in Sinai – there was added in the third week of May the most electric shock of all, namely the closure of the international waterway consisting of the Strait of Tiran and the Gulf of Aqaba. It is not difficult, I think, to understand why this incident had a more drastic impact than any other. In 1957 the maritime nations, within the framework of the United Nations General Assembly, correctly enunciated the doctrine of free and innocent passage through the Strait.

Now, when that doctrine was proclaimed – and incidentally, not challenged by the Egyptian representative at that time – it was little more than an abstract principle for the maritime world. . . . But during the 10 years in which we and the other States of the maritime community have relied upon that doctrine and upon established usage, the principle has become a reality consecrated by hundreds of sailings under dozens of flags and the establishment of a whole complex of commerce and industry and communication. A new dimension has been added to the map of the world's communications, and on that dimension we have constructed Israel's bridge towards the friendly States of Asia and Africa, a network of relationships which is the chief pride of Israel in the second decade of its independence.

All this, then, had grown up as an effective usage under the United Nations flag. Does Mr. Nasser really think that he can come upon the scene in 10 minutes and cancel the established legal usage and interests of 10 years?

There was in this wanton act a quality of malice. For surely the closing of the Strait of Tiran gave no benefit whatever to Egypt except the perverse joy of inflicting injury on others. . . . And it was, in the literal sense, an act of arrogance, because there are other nations in Asia and East Africa that trade with the Port of Eilat, as they have every right to do, through the Strait of Tiran and across the Gulf of Aqaba. Other sovereign States from Japan to Ethiopia, from Thailand to Uganda, from Cambodia to Madagascar, have a sovereign right to decide for themselves whether they wish or do not wish to trade with Israel. These countries are not colonies of Cairo. They can trade with Israel or not trade with Israel as they wish, and President Nasser is not the policeman of other African and Asian States.

Here then was a wanton intervention in the sovereign rights of other States in the eastern half of the world to decide for themselves whether or not they wish to establish trade relations with either or both of the two ports at the head of the Gulf of Aqaba.

When we examine, then, the implications of this act, we have no cause to wonder that the international shock was great. There was another reason too for that shock. Blockades have traditionally been regarded, in the pre-Charter parlance, as acts of war. To blockade, after all, is to attempt strangulation; and sovereign States are entitled not to have their trade strangled. To understand how the State of Israel felt, one has merely to look around this table and imagine, for example, a foreign Power forcibly closing New York or Montreal, Boston or Marseille, Toulon or Copenhagen, Rio or Tokyo or Bombay harbour. How would your Governments react? What would you do? How long would you wait?

. . .

These then were the three main elements in the tension: the sabotage movement; the blockade of the port; and, perhaps more imminent than anything else, this vast and purposeful encirclement movement, against the background of an authorized presidential statement announcing that the objective of the encirclement was to bring about the destruction and the annihilation of a sovereign State.

These acts taken together – the blockade, the dismissal of the United Nations Emergency Force, and the heavy concentration in Sinai – effectively disrupted the *status quo* which had ensured a relative stability on the Egyptian-Israel frontier for 10 years. I do not use the words "relative stability" lightly, for in fact while those elements in the Egyptian-Israel relationship existed there was not one single incident of violence between Egypt and Israel for 10 years. . . . Surely, after what has happened we must have better assurance than before, for Israel and for the Middle East, of peaceful co-existence. The question is whether there is any reason to believe that such a new era may yet come to pass. If I am a little sanguine on this point, it is because of a conviction that men and nations do behave wisely once they have exhausted all other alternatives. Surely the other alternatives of war and belligerency have now been exhausted. And what has anybody gained from that? But in order that the new system of inter-State relationships may flourish in the Middle East, it is important that certain principles be applied above and beyond the cease-fire to which the Security Council has given its unanimous support.

. . .

And if, as everybody knows to be the fact, the universal conscience was in the last week or two most violently shaken at the prospect of danger to Israel, it was not only because there seemed to be a danger to a State, but also, I think, because the State was Israel, with all that this ancient name evokes, teaches, symbolizes, and inspires. How grotesque would be an international community which found room for 122 sovereign units and which did not acknowledge the sovereignty of that people which had given nationhood its deepest significance and its most enduring grace.

No wonder, then, that when danger threatened we could hear a roar of indignation sweep across the world, that men in progressive movements and members of the scientific and humanistic cultures joined together in sounding an alarm bell about an issue that vitally affected the human conscience. And no wonder, correspondingly, that a deep and universal sense of satisfaction and relief has accompanied the news of Israel's gallant and successful resistance.

But the central point remains the need to secure an authentic intellectual recognition by our neighbours of Israel's deep roots in the Middle Eastern reality. There is an intellectual tragedy in the failure of Arab leaders to come to grips, however reluctantly, with the depth and authenticity of Israel's roots in the life, the history, the spiritual experience, and the culture of the Middle East.

This, then, is the first axiom. A much more conscious and uninhibited acceptance of Israel's statehood is an axiom requiring no demonstration, for there will never be a Middle East without an independent and sovereign State of Israel in its midst.

The second principle must be that of the peaceful settlement of disputes. The Resolution thus adopted falls within the concept of the peaceful settlement of disputes. I have already said that much could be done if the Governments of the area would embark much more on direct contacts. They must find their way to each other. After all, when there is conflict between them they come together face to face. Why should they not come together face to face to solve the conflict? And perhaps on some occasions it would not be a bad idea to have the solution before, and therefore instead of, the conflict.

When the Council discusses what is to happen after the cease-fire, we hear many formulas: back to 1956, back to 1948 – I understand our neighbours would wish to turn the clock back to 1947. The fact is, however, that most clocks move forward and not backward, and this, I think, should be the case with the clock of Middle Eastern peace – not backward to belligerency, but forward to peace.

The point was well made this evening by the representative of Argentina, who said: the cease-fire should be followed immediately by the most intensive efforts to bring about a just and lasting peace in the Middle East. In a similar sense, the representative of Canada warned us against merely reproducing the old positions of conflict, without attempting to settle the underlying issues of Arab-Israel co-existence. After all, many things in recent days have been mixed up with each other. Few things are what they were. And in order to create harmonious combinations of relationships, it is inevitable that the States should come together in negotiation.

Another factor in the harmony that we would like to see in the Middle East relates to external Powers. From these, and especially from the greatest amongst them, the small States of the Middle East – and most of them are small – ask for a rigorous support, not for individual States, but for specific principles; not to be for one State against other States, but to be for peace against war, for free commerce against belligerency, for the pacific settlement of disputes against violent irredentist threats; in other words, to exercise an even-handed support for the integrity and independence of States and for the rights of States under the Charter of the United Nations and other sources of international law.

There are not two categories of States. The United Arab Republic, Iraq, Syria, Jordan, Lebanon – not one of these has a single ounce or milligram of statehood which does not adhere in equal measures to Israel itself.

   . . .

I raise these points of elementary logic. Of course, a Great Power can take refuge in its power from the exigencies of logic. All of us in our youth presumably recounted La Fontaine's fable, "*La raison du plus fort est toujours la meilleure.*" But here, after all, there is nobody who is more or less strong than others; we sit here around the table on the concept of sovereign equality. But I think we have an equal duty to bring substantive proof for any denunciation that we make, each of the other.

I would say in conclusion that these are, of course, still grave times. And yet they may perhaps have a fortunate issue. This could be the case if those who for some reason decided so violently, three weeks ago, to disrupt the *status quo* would ask themselves what the results and benefits have been. As he looks around him at the arena of battle, at the wreckage of planes and tanks, at the collapse of intoxicated hopes, might not an Egyptian ruler ponder whether anything was achieved by that disruption? What has it brought but strife, conflict with other powerful interests, and the stern criticism of progressive men throughout the world?

I think that Israel has in recent days proved its steadfastness and vigour. It is now willing to demonstrate its instinct for peace. Let us build a new system of relationships from the wreckage of the old. Let us discern across the darkness the vision of a better and a brighter dawn.

33 The Allon Plan
(June 18, 1967)

As the 1967 War drew to a close, Israel's 'unity government' and its military strategists were forced to formulate an approach to the control of their vast new conquests. Early on it was held that the Sinai and Golan Heights might be eventually returned in exchange for treaties with Egypt and Syria. . . .

But the demographic aspect of absorbing the indigenous Palestinian population into the Jewish State ruled out annexing these areas outright to Israel. In contrast, the conquest of Jerusalem was instantly deemed irreversible and, by 28 June, the Knesset had amended its laws and placed the entire city and expanded municipal area under Israeli sovereignty, later annexing the 70-km^2 area. Here the demographic problem was considered a price worth paying, though subsequent Israeli policy would aim at ridding Jerusalem of its Palestinian population. Thus, in the days following the Israeli occupation, frantic and often conflicting plans for the future of the occupied territories were drawn up in each of these areas: Jerusalem; the Golan; Sinai; the Gaza Strip; and the West Bank.

While no single plan was ever officially sanctioned, the Allon Plan, drawn up by Labor Minister Yigal Allon, was the scheme most acceptable to the military and was the first to be presented before the cabinet – in late July, barely six weeks after the cease-fire. . . . The Allon Plan initially focused on the occupied Palestinian territories (OPT). The plan evolved and expanded according to the divergent views and levels of influence of other cabinet figures, but was nonetheless to remain Israel's loose master plan for the OPT for nearly a decade . . .

The Allon Plan provided the initial boundaries and priorities for this settlement drive. Allon, . . . planned a broad corridor of paramilitary and civilian sites along the Jordan Valley, to run down the western shore of the Dead Sea . . . , reaching west to Hebron. This created a settled strip from the Israeli town of Arad (in the northeastern Negev), north to Beit Shean . . . in Israel's southern Galilee. The corridor between Israel's coastal plain and unilaterally annexed Jerusalem was broadened extensively, creating a wide settlement zone between Ramallah and Bethlehem.

Allon tentatively planned for Gaza's refugees – ca. 75% of the Gaza population – to be transferred to the two militarily administered cantons

DOI: 10.4324/9781003348948-37

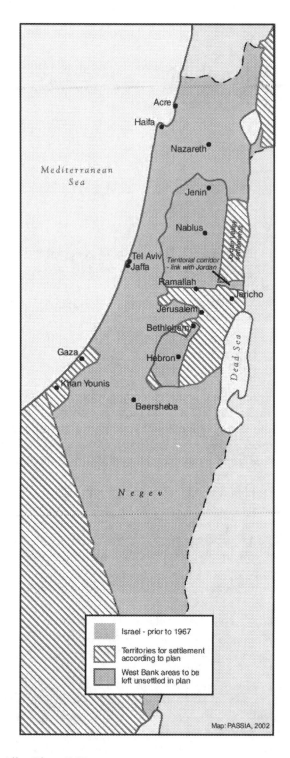

Map 10 The Allon Plan, 1967

Source: Permission granted by the Palestinian Academic Society for the Study of International Affairs to reprint their map of the Allon Plan and use their text in this book. The original can be found at: www.passia.org/maps/view/21.

created on the West Bank, followed by the annexation and settlement of the Gaza Strip, though this never eventuated. By remaining unofficial and vaguely worded, the Allon Plan bridged the gap between the government's need to appear moderate to the international community and its desire to maintain the option of 'stretching' settlement boundaries in the future. . . . Some months later, Allon amended his plan to include a corridor linking Ramallah with Jordan and a 'highway' connecting the north and south Palestinian cantons from Bethlehem to Ramallah . . .

In 1976, Prime Minister Rabin and Defense Minister Peres eventually made the decision to break with Allon's settlement 'lines' and pursue settlement deep in the northern canton (i.e., in the Ramallah, Salfit and Qalqilya areas). By then, the rise of . . . settlement bodies and extensive unauthorized settlement activity throughout the OPT had made strict adherence to the Allon Plan a political liability, if not an impossibility. The Allon Plan's erosion . . . was confirmed by Rabin, but its guiding principles were only finally cast off with the 1977 Likud victory. The Likud came to power having adopted a pro-settlement platform highly critical of the Allon Plan limitations and having pledged their support for the initiation of unfettered settlement programs throughout the OPT. Prime Minister Begin appointed Agriculture Minister Ariel Sharon head of 'Allon's' Settlement Committee.

34 President Lyndon B. Johnson, Five Principles for Peace in the Middle East (June 19, 1967)

Crisis in the Middle East

. . .

Now, finally, let me turn to the Middle East – and to the tumultuous events of the past months. Those events have proved the wisdom of five great principles of peace in the region.

The first and greatest principle is that every nation in the area has a fundamental right to live and to have this right respected by its neighbors.

For the people of the Middle East the path to hope does not lie in threats to end the life of any nation. Such threats have become a burden to the peace, not only of that region but a burden to the peace of the entire world.

In the same way, no nation would be true to the United Nations Charter or to its own true interests if it should permit military success to blind it to the fact that its neighbors have rights and its neighbors have interests of their own. Each nation, therefore, must accept the right of others to live.

This last month, I think, shows us another basic requirement for settlement. It is a human requirement: justice for the refugees.

A new conflict has brought new homelessness. The nations of the Middle East must at last address themselves to the plight of those who have been displaced by wars. . . . There will be no peace for any party in the Middle East unless this problem is attacked with new energy by all and, certainly, primarily by those who are immediately concerned.

A third lesson from this last month is that maritime rights must be respected. Our nation has long been committed to free maritime passage through international waterways; and we, along with other nations, were taking the necessary steps to implement this principle when hostilities exploded. If a single act of folly was more responsible for this explosion than any other, I think it was the arbitrary and dangerous announced decision that the Strait of Tiran would be closed. The right of innocent maritime passage must be preserved for all nations.

Fourth, this last conflict has demonstrated the danger of the Middle Eastern arms race of the last 12 years. . . . We believe that scarce resources could be used much better for technical and economic development. We have always

DOI: 10.4324/9781003348948-38

opposed this arms race, and our own military shipments to the area have consequently been severely limited.

Now the waste and futility of the arms race must be apparent to all the peoples of the world. . . . The United States of America, for its part, will use every resource of diplomacy and every counsel of reason and prudence to try to find a better course.

As a beginning, I should like to propose that the United Nations immediately call upon all of its members to report all shipments of all military arms into this area and to keep those shipments on file for all the peoples of the world to observe.

Fifth, the crisis underlines the importance of respect for political independence and territorial integrity of all the states of the area. . . . The nations of the region have had only fragile and violated truce lines for 20 years. What they now need are recognized boundaries and other arrangements that will give them security against terror, destruction, and war. Further, there just must be adequate recognition of the special interest of three great religions in the holy places of Jerusalem.

These five principles are not new, but we do think they are fundamental. Taken together, they point the way from uncertain armistice to durable peace. We believe there must be progress toward all of them if there is to be progress toward any.

Settlement Depends on Nations of the Area

There are some who have urged, as a single, simple solution, an immediate return to the situation as it was on June 4. As our distinguished and able Ambassador, Mr. Arthur Goldberg, has already said, this is not a prescription for peace but for renewed hostilities.

Certainly, troops must be withdrawn; but there must also be recognized rights of national life, progress in solving the refugee problem, freedom of innocent maritime passage, limitation of the arms race, and respect for political independence and territorial integrity.

But who will make this peace where all others have failed for 20 years or more?

Clearly the parties to the conflict must be the parties to the peace. . . . It is hard to see how it is possible for nations to live together in peace if they cannot learn to reason together.

But we must still ask. Who can help them? Some say it should be the United Nations; some call for the use of other parties. We have been first in our support of effective peacekeeping in the United Nations, and we also recognize the great values to come from mediation.

. . .

I issue an appeal to all to adopt no rigid view on these matters. I offer assurance to all that this Government of ours, the Government of the United States, will do its part for peace in every forum, at every level, at every hour.

Yet there is no escape from this fact: The main responsibility for the peace of the region depends upon its own peoples and its own leaders of that region. What will be truly decisive in the Middle East will be what is said and what is done by those who live in the Middle East.

. . . The world this morning is watching, watching for the peace of the world, because that is really what is at stake. It will look for patience and justice, it will look for humility and moral courage. It will look for signs of movement from prejudice and the emotional chaos of conflict to the gradual, slow shaping steps that lead to learning to live together and learning to help mold and shape peace in the area and in the world.

The Middle East is rich in history, rich in its people and in its resources. It has no need to live in permanent civil war. It has the power to build its own life as one of the prosperous regions of the world in which we live.

U.S. Will Help in Works of Peace

If the nations of the Middle East will turn toward the works of peace, they can count with confidence upon the friendship and the help of all the people of the United States of America.

. . .

Our country is committed – and we here reiterate that commitment today – to a peace that is based on five principles.

– first, the recognized right of national life;

– second, justice for the refugees;

– third, innocent maritime passage;

– fourth, limits on the wasteful and destructive arms race; and

– fifth, political independence and territorial integrity for all.

This is not a time for malice, but for magnanimity; not for propaganda, but for patience; not for vituperation, but for vision.

On the basis of peace we offer our help to the people of the Middle East. That land, known to every one of us since childhood as the birthplace of great religions and learning, can flourish once again in our time. We here in the United States shall do all in our power to help make it so.

35 Protection of Holy Places Law (June 27, 1967)

1. The Holy Places shall be protected from desecration and any other violation and from anything likely to violate the freedom of access of the members of the different religions to the places sacred to them or their feelings with regard to those places.

Offences

2. (a) Whosoever desecrates or otherwise violates a Holy Place shall be liable to imprisonment for a term of seven years.
   (b) Whosoever does anything likely to violate the freedom of access of the members of the different religions to the places sacred to them or their feelings . . . shall be liable to imprisonment for a term of five years.

Saving of laws

3. This Law shall add to, and not derogate from, any other law.

Implementation and regulations

4. The Minister of Religious Affairs is charged with the implementation of this Law, and he may, after consultation with, or upon the proposal of, representatives of the religions concerned and with the consent of the Minister of Justice make regulations as to any matter relating to such implementation.

Commencement

5. This Law shall come into force on the date of its adoption by the Knesset.

Levi Eshkol
Prime Minister

Yaakov S. Shapiro
Minister of Justice

Shneur Zalman Shazar

DOI: 10.4324/9781003348948-39

36 The Khartoum Resolutions (September 1, 1967)

1. The conference has affirmed the unity of Arab ranks, the unity of joint action, and the need for coordination and for the elimination of all differences. The Kings, Presidents, and representatives of the other Arab Heads of State at the conference have affirmed their countries' stand by and implementation of the Arab Solidarity Charter which was signed at the third Arab summit conference in Casablanca.

2. The conference has agreed on the need to consolidate all efforts to eliminate the effects of the aggression on the basis that the occupied lands are Arab lands. . . .

3. The Arab Heads of State have agreed to unite their political efforts at the international and diplomatic level to eliminate the effects of the aggression and to ensure the withdrawal of the aggressive Israeli forces from the Arab lands which have been occupied since the aggression of June 5. This will be done within the framework of the main principles by which the Arab States abide, namely, no peace with Israel, no recognition of Israel, no negotiations with it, and insistence on the rights of the Palestinian people in their own country.

4. The conference of Arab Ministers of Finance, Economy and Oil recommended that suspension of oil pumping be used as a weapon in the battle. However, after thoroughly studying the matter, the summit conference has come to the conclusion that the oil pumping can itself be used as a positive weapon, since oil is an Arab resource which can be used to strengthen the economy of the Arab States directly affected by the aggression, so that these States will be able to stand firm in the battle. The conference has, therefore, decided to resume the pumping of oil, since oil is a positive Arab resource that can be used in the service of Arab goals. It can contribute to the efforts to enable those Arab States which were exposed to the aggression and thereby lost economic resources to stand firm and eliminate the effects of the aggression. The oil-producing States have, in fact, participated in the efforts to enable the States affected by the aggression to stand firm in the face of any economic pressure.

5. The participants in the conference have approved the plan proposed by Kuwait to set up an Arab Economic and Social Development Fund on the

DOI: 10.4324/9781003348948-40

basis of the recommendation of the Baghdad conference of Arab Ministers of Finance, Economy and Oil.

6. The participants have agreed on the need to adopt the necessary measures to strengthen military preparation to face all eventualities.

7. The conference has decided to expedite the elimination of foreign bases in the Arab States.

37 U.N. Security Council

Resolution 242 (November 22, 1967)

The Security Council,

Expressing its continuing concern with the grave situation in the Middle East,

Emphasizing the inadmissibility of the acquisition of territory by war . . . ,

Emphasizing further that all Member States in their acceptance of the Charter of the United Nations have undertaken a commitment to act in accordance with Article 2 of the Charter,

1. Affirms that the fulfillment of Charter principles requires the establishment of a just and lasting peace in the Middle East which should include the application of both the following principles:

    *   Withdrawal of Israeli armed forces from territories occupied in the recent conflict;
    *   Termination of all claims or states of belligerency and respect for and acknowledgement of the sovereignty, territorial integrity, and political independence of every State in the area and their right to live in peace within secure and recognized boundaries free from threats or acts of force;

2. Affirms further the necessity:

    *   For guaranteeing freedom of navigation through international waterways in the area;
    *   For achieving a just settlement of the refugee problem;
    *   For guaranteeing the territorial inviolability and political independence of every State in the area, through measures including the establishment of demilitarized zones;

3. Requests the Secretary General to designate a Special Representative to proceed to the Middle East to . . . maintain contacts with the States concerned in order to promote agreement and assist efforts to achieve a peaceful and accepted settlement in accordance with the provisions and principles in this resolution;
4. Requests the Secretary-General to report to the Security Council on the progress of the efforts of the Special Representative as soon as possible.

DOI: 10.4324/9781003348948-41

38 The Palestinian National Charter

Resolutions of the Palestine National Council (July 1–17, 1968)

Article 1: Palestine is the homeland of the Arab Palestinian people; it is an indivisible part of the Arab homeland, and the Palestinian people are an integral part of the Arab nation.

Article 2: Palestine, with the boundaries it had during the British Mandate, is an indivisible territorial unit.

Article 3: The Palestinian Arab people possess the legal right to their homeland and have the right to determine their destiny after achieving the liberation of their country in accordance with their wishes and entirely of their own accord and will.

Article 4: The Palestinian identity is a genuine, essential, and inherent characteristic. . . . The Zionist occupation and the dispersal of the Palestinian Arab people, through the disasters which befell them, do not make them lose their Palestinian identity and their membership in the Palestinian community, nor do they negate them.

Article 5: The Palestinians are those Arab nationals who, until 1947, normally resided in Palestine regardless of whether they were evicted from it or have stayed there. Anyone born, after that date, of a Palestinian father – whether inside Palestine or outside it – is also a Palestinian.

Article 6: The Jews who had normally resided in Palestine until the beginning of the Zionist invasion will be considered Palestinians.

Article 7: That there is a Palestinian community and that it has material, spiritual, and historical connection with Palestine are indisputable facts. . . . All means of information and education must be adopted in order to acquaint the Palestinian with his country in the most profound manner, both spiritual and material, that is possible. He must be prepared for the armed struggle and ready to sacrifice his wealth and his life in order to win back his homeland and bring about its liberation.

Article 8: The phase in their history, through which the Palestinian people are now living, is that of national (watani) struggle for the liberation of Palestine . . .

Article 9: Armed struggle is the only way to liberate Palestine. . . . The Palestinian Arab people assert their absolute determination and firm resolution to continue their armed struggle and to work for an armed popular

DOI: 10.4324/9781003348948-42

revolution for the liberation of their country and their return to it. They also assert their right to normal life in Palestine and to exercise their right to self-determination and sovereignty over it.

Article 10: Commando action constitutes the nucleus of the Palestinian popular liberation war. This requires its escalation, comprehensiveness, and the mobilization of all the Palestinian popular and educational efforts and their organization and involvement in the armed Palestinian revolution. It also requires the achieving of unity for the national (watani) struggle among the different groupings of the Palestinian people, and between the Palestinian people and the Arab masses, so as to secure the continuation of the revolution, its escalation, and victory.

Article 11: The Palestinians will have three mottoes: national (wataniyya) unity, national (qawmiyya) mobilization, and liberation.

Article 12: The Palestinian people believe in Arab unity. In order to contribute their share toward the attainment of that objective, however, they must, at the present stage of their struggle, safeguard their Palestinian identity and develop their consciousness of that identity, and oppose any plan that may dissolve or impair it.

Article 13: Arab unity and the liberation of Palestine are two complementary objectives, the attainment of either of which facilitates the attainment of the other. Thus, Arab unity leads to the liberation of Palestine; the liberation of Palestine leads to Arab unity; and work toward the realization of one objective proceeds side by side with work toward the realization of the other.

Article 14: The destiny of the Arab nation . . . depend[s] upon the destiny of the Palestine cause. From this interdependence springs the Arab nation's pursuit of, and striving for, the liberation of Palestine. The people of Palestine play the role of the vanguard in the realization of this sacred (qawmi) goal.

Article 15: The liberation of Palestine, from an Arab viewpoint, is a national (qawmi) duty and it attempts to repel the Zionist and imperialist aggression against the Arab homeland, and aims at the elimination of Zionism in Palestine. Absolute responsibility for this falls upon the Arab nation – peoples and governments – with the Arab people of Palestine in the vanguard. . . .

Article 16: The liberation of Palestine, from a spiritual point of view, will provide the Holy Land with an atmosphere of safety and tranquility, which in turn will safeguard the country's religious sanctuaries and guarantee freedom of worship and of visit to all, without discrimination of race, color, language, or religion. Accordingly, the people of Palestine look to all spiritual forces in the world for support.

Article 17: The liberation of Palestine, from a human point of view, will restore to the Palestinian individual his dignity, pride, and freedom. Accordingly, the Palestinian Arab people look forward to the support of all those who believe in the dignity of man and his freedom in the world.

Article 18: The liberation of Palestine, from an international point of view, is a defensive action necessitated by the demands of self-defense.

Accordingly, the Palestinian people, desirous as they are of the friendship of all people, look to freedom-loving and peace-loving states for support in order to restore their legitimate rights in Palestine, to re-establish peace and security in the country, and to enable its people to exercise national sovereignty and freedom.

Article 19: The partition of Palestine in 1947 and the establishment of the state of Israel are entirely illegal, regardless of the passage of time, because they were contrary to the will of the Palestinian people and to their natural right in their homeland, and inconsistent with the principles embodied in the Charter of the United Nations, particularly the right to self-determination.

Article 20: The Balfour Declaration, the Mandate for Palestine, and everything that has been based upon them are deemed null and void. Claims of historical or religious ties of Jews with Palestine are incompatible with the facts of history and the true conception of what constitutes statehood. Judaism, being a religion, is not an independent nationality. Nor do Jews constitute a single nation with an identity of its own; they are citizens of the states to which they belong.

Article 21: The Arab Palestinian people, expressing themselves by the armed Palestinian revolution, reject all solutions which are substitutes for the total liberation of Palestine and reject all proposals aiming at the liquidation of the Palestinian problem, or its internationalization.

Article 22: Zionism is a political movement organically associated with international imperialism and antagonistic to all action for liberation and to progressive movements in the world. It is racist and fanatic in its nature, aggressive, expansionist, and colonial in its aims, and fascist in its methods. Israel is the instrument of the Zionist movement, and geographical base for world imperialism placed strategically in the midst of the Arab homeland to combat the hopes of the Arab nation for liberation, unity, and progress. . . . Since the liberation of Palestine will destroy the Zionist and imperialist presence and will contribute to the establishment of peace in the Middle East, the Palestinian people look for the support of all the progressive and peaceful forces and urge them all, irrespective of their affiliations and beliefs, to offer the Palestinian people all aid and support in their just struggle for the liberation of their homeland.

Article 23: The demand of security and peace, as well as the demand of right and justice, require all states to consider Zionism an illegitimate movement, to outlaw its existence, and to ban its operations, in order that friendly relations among peoples may be preserved, and the loyalty of citizens to their respective homelands safeguarded.

Article 24: The Palestinian people believe in the principles of justice, freedom, sovereignty, self-determination, human dignity, and in the right of all peoples to exercise them.

Article 25: For the realization of the goals of this Charter and its principles, the Palestine Liberation Organization will perform its role in the liberation of Palestine in accordance with the Constitution of this Organization.

Article 26: The Palestine Liberation Organization, representative of the Palestinian revolutionary forces, is responsible for the Palestinian Arab people's movement in its struggle – to retrieve its homeland, liberate and return to it and exercise the right to self-determination in it – in all military, political, and financial fields and also for whatever may be required by the Palestine case on the inter-Arab and international levels.

Article 27: The Palestine Liberation Organization shall cooperate with all Arab states, each according to its potentialities; and will adopt a neutral policy among them in the light of the requirements of the war of liberation; and on this basis it shall not interfere in the internal affairs of any Arab state.

Article 28: The Palestinian Arab people assert the genuineness and independence of their national (wataniyya) revolution and reject all forms of intervention, trusteeship, and subordination.

Article 29: The Palestinian people possess the fundamental and genuine legal right to liberate and retrieve their homeland. The Palestinian people determine their attitude toward all states and forces on the basis of the stands they adopt vis-à-vis to the Palestinian revolution to fulfill the aims of the Palestinian people.

Article 30: Fighters and carriers of arms in the war of liberation are the nucleus of the popular army which will be the protective force for the gains of the Palestinian Arab people.

Article 31: The Organization shall have a flag, an oath of allegiance, and an anthem. All this shall be decided upon in accordance with a special regulation.

Article 32: Regulations, which shall be known as the Constitution of the Palestinian Liberation Organization, shall be annexed to this Charter. It will lay down the manner in which the Organization, and its organs and institutions, shall be constituted; the respective competence of each; and the requirements of its obligation under the Charter.

Article 33: This Charter shall not be amended save by [vote of] a majority of two-thirds of the total membership of the National Congress of the Palestine Liberation Organization [taken] at a special session convened for that purpose.

39   The Seven Points of Fatah (January 1969)

1. Fatah, the Palestine National Liberation Movement, is the expression of the Palestinian people and of its will to free its land from Zionist colonisation in order to recover its national identity.
2. Fatah, the Palestine National Liberation Movement, is not struggling against the Jews as an ethnic and religious community. It is struggling against Israel as the expression of colonisation based on a theocratic, racist, and expansionist system and of Zionism and colonialism.
3. Fatah, the Palestine National Liberation Movement, rejects any solution that does not take account of the existence of the Palestinian people and its right to dispose of itself.
4. Fatah, the Palestine National Liberation Movement, categorically rejects the Security Council Resolution of 22 November 1967 and the Jarring Mission to which it gave rise.

    This resolution ignores the national rights of the Palestinian people, failing to mention its existence. . . . In any event, the acceptance of the resolution of 22 November 1967, or any pseudo-political solution, by whatsoever party, is in no way of binding upon the Palestinian people, which is determined to pursue mercilessly its struggle against foreign occupation and Zionist colonisation.
5. Fatah, the Palestine National Liberation Movement, solemnly proclaims that the final objective of its struggle is the restoration of the independent, democratic State of Palestine, all of whose citizens will enjoy equal rights irrespective of their religion.
6. Since Palestine forms part of the Arab fatherland, Fatah, the Palestine National Liberation Movement, will work for the State of Palestine to contribute actively towards the establishment of a progressive and united Arab society.
7. The struggle of the Palestinian People, like that of the Vietnamese people and other peoples of Asia, Africa, and Latin America, is part of the historic process of the liberation of the oppressed peoples from colonialism and imperialism.

DOI: 10.4324/9781003348948-43

40 Statement by U.S. Secretary of State William Rogers (December 9, 1969)

Following the third Arab-Israeli war in twenty years, there was an upsurge of hope that a lasting peace could be achieved. That hope has unfortunately not been realized. . . .

When this Administration took office, one of our first actions in foreign affairs was to examine carefully the entire situation in the Middle East. . . .

The United States decided it had a responsibility to play a direct role in seeking a solution.

Thus, we accepted a suggestion put forward both by the French Government and the Secretary-General of the United Nations. We agreed that the major Powers – the United States, the Soviet Union, the United Kingdom, and France – should cooperate to assist the Secretary-General's representative, Ambassador Jarring, in working out a settlement in accordance with the Resolution of the Security Council of the United Nations of November 1967. We also decided to consult directly with the Soviet Union, hoping to achieve as wide an area of agreement as possible between us.

These decisions were made in full recognition of the following important factors.

First, we knew that nations not directly involved could not make a durable peace for the peoples and Governments involved. Peace rests with the parties to the conflict. . . . an agreement among other Powers cannot be a substitute for agreement among the parties themselves.

Second, we knew that a durable peace must meet the legitimate concerns of both sides.

Third, we were clear that the only framework for a negotiated settlement was one in accordance with the entire text of the UN Security Council Resolution. That Resolution was agreed upon after long and arduous negotiations; it is carefully balanced; it provides the basis for a just and lasting peace – a final settlement – not merely an interlude between wars.

Fourth, we believed that a protracted period of war, no peace, recurrent violence and spreading chaos would serve the interests of no nation, in or out of the Middle East.

. . .

DOI: 10.4324/9781003348948-44

. . . We regret that the Soviets have delayed in responding to new formulations submitted to them on 28 October. However, we will continue to discuss these problems with the Soviet Union as long as there is any realistic hope that such discussion might further the cause of peace.

. . .

On the one hand, the Arab leaders fear that Israel is not in fact prepared to withdraw from Arab territory occupied in the 1967 war.

Now on the other hand, Israeli leaders fear that the Arab States are not in fact prepared to live in peace with Israel.

. . .

What can the United States do to help overcome these roadblocks?

Our policy is and will continue to be a balanced one.

We have friendly ties with both Arabs and Israelis. To call for Israeli withdrawal as envisaged in the UN Resolution without achieving an agreement on peace would be partisan towards the Arabs. To call on the Arabs to accept peace without Israeli withdrawal would be partisan towards Israel. Therefore, our policy is to encourage the Arabs to accept a permanent peace based on a binding agreement and to urge the Israelis to withdraw from occupied territory when their territorial integrity is assured as envisaged by the Security Council Resolution.

. . .

Let me outline our policy on various elements of the Security Council Resolution. The basic and related issues might be described as peace, security, withdrawal and territory. Peace between the parties: – the Resolution of the Security Council makes clear that the goal is the establishment of a state of peace between the parties instead of the state of belligerency which has characterized relations for over 20 years. . . .

But peace, of course, involves much more than this. It is also a matter of the attitudes and intentions of the parties. Are they ready to co-exist with one another? Can a live-and-let-live attitude replace suspicion, mistrust and hate? A peace agreement between the parties must be based on clear and stated intentions and a willingness to bring about basic changes in the attitudes and conditions which are characteristic of the Middle East today.

Security: a lasting peace must be sustained by a sense of security on both sides. To this end, as envisaged in the Security Council Resolution, there should be demilitarized zones and related security arrangements more reliable than those which existed in the area in the past. . . .

Withdrawal and territory: – the Security Council Resolution endorses the principle of the non-acquisition of territory by war and calls for withdrawal of Israeli armed forces from territories occupied in the 1967 war. We support this part of the Resolution, including withdrawal, just as we do its other elements.

The boundaries from which the 1967 war began were established in the 1949 Armistice Agreements and have defined the areas of national jurisdiction in the Middle East for 20 years. Those boundaries were armistice lines, not final political borders. The rights, claims and positions of the parties in an ultimate peaceful settlement were reserved by the Armistice Agreements.

. . .

We believe that while recognized political boundaries must be established, and agreed upon by the parties, any change in the pre-existing lines should not reflect the weight of conquest and should be confined to insubstantial alterations required for mutual security. . . . We support Israel's security and the security of the Arab States as well. We are for a lasting peace that requires security for both.

By emphasizing the key issues of peace, security, withdrawal and territory, I do not want to leave the impression that other issues are not equally important. Two in particular deserve special mention – the questions of refugees and of Jerusalem.

There can be no lasting peace without a just settlement of the problem of those Palestinians whom the wars of 1948 and 1967 made homeless. This human dimension of the Arab-Israeli conflict has been of special concern to the United States for over 20 years. During this period, the United States has contributed about 500 million dollars for the support and education of the Palestine refugees. We are prepared to contribute generously, along with others, to solve this problem. . . .

The problem posed by the refugees will become increasingly serious if their future is not resolved. There is a new consciousness among the young Palestinians who have grown up since 1948, which needs to be channelled away from bitterness and frustration towards hope and justice.

The question of the future status of Jerusalem, because it touches deep emotional, historical and religious well-springs, is particularly complicated. We have made clear repeatedly in the past two and a half years that we cannot accept unilateral actions by any party to decide the final status of the city. We believe its status can be determined only through the agreement of the parties concerned, which in practical terms means primarily the Governments of Israel and Jordan, taking into account the interests of other countries in the area and the international community. We do, however, support certain principles which we believe would provide an equitable framework for a Jerusalem settlement.

Specifically, we believe Jerusalem should be a unified city within which there would no longer be restrictions on the movement of persons and goods. There should be open access to the unified city for persons of all faiths and nationalities. Arrangements for the administration of the unified city should take into account the interests of all its inhabitants and of the Jewish, Islamic and Christian communities. And there should be roles for both Israel and Jordan in the civic, economic and religious life of the City.

It is our hope that agreement on the key issues of peace, security, withdrawal and territory will create a climate in which these questions of refugees and of Jerusalem, as well as other aspects of the conflict, can be resolved as part of the overall settlement.

. . .

I have already referred to our talks with the Soviet Union. In connection with those talks there have been allegations that we have been seeking to divide the Arab States by urging the UAR to make a separate peace. These allegations are false. It is a fact that we and the Soviets have been concentrating on the questions of a settlement between Israel and the United Arab Republic. We have been doing this in the full understanding on both our parts that, before there can be a settlement of the Arab-Israeli conflict, there must be agreement between the parties on other aspects of the settlement – not only those related to the United Arab Republic but also those related to Jordan and other States which accept the Security Council Resolution of November 1967.

We started with the Israeli-United Arab Republic aspect because of its inherent importance for future stability in the area and because one must start somewhere.

We are also ready to pursue the Jordanian aspects of a settlement – in fact the Four Powers in New York have begun such discussions. Let me make it perfectly clear that the US position is that implementation of the overall settlement would begin only after complete agreement had been reached on related aspects of the problem.

In our recent meetings with the Soviets, we have discussed some new formulas in an attempt to find common positions. They consist of three principal elements:

First, there should be a binding commitment by Israel and the United Arab Republic to peace with each other, with all the specific obligations of peace spelled out, including the obligation to prevent hostile acts originating from their respective territories.

Second, the detailed provisions of peace relating to security safeguards on the ground should be worked out between the parties, under Ambassador Jarring's auspices, utilizing the procedures followed in negotiating the Armistice Agreements under Ralph Bunche in 1949 at Rhodes. . . .

So far as a settlement between Israel and the United Arab Republic goes, these safeguards relate primarily to the area of Sharm el-Sheikh controlling access to the Gulf of Aqaba, the need for demilitarized zones as foreseen in the Security Council Resolution, and final arrangements in the Gaza Strip.

Third, in the context of peace and agreement on specific security safeguards, withdrawal of Israeli forces from Egyptian territory would be required.

Such an approach directly addresses the principal national concerns of both Israel and the UAR. It would require the UAR to agree to a binding and specific commitment to peace. It would require withdrawal of Israeli armed forces from UAR territory to the international border between Israel and Egypt which has been in existence for over half a century. It would also require the parties themselves to negotiate the practical security arrangements to safeguard the peace.

We believe that this approach is balanced and fair.

We remain interested in good relations with all States in the area. Whenever and wherever Arab States which have broken off diplomatic relations with the United States are prepared to restore them, we shall respond in the same spirit.

Meanwhile, we will not be deterred from continuing to pursue the paths of patient diplomacy in our search for peace in the Middle East. We will not shrink from advocating necessary compromises, even though they may and probably will be unpalatable to both sides. We remain prepared to work with others – in the area and throughout the world – so long as they sincerely seek the end we seek: a just and lasting peace.

41 King Hussein's Federation Plan (March 15, 1972)

[broadcast on Amman Radio]

I am pleased to meet you and to speak to you about the affairs of the current stage and their connection with the affairs and experiences of the past and the aspirations and hopes of the future. The establishment of the State of Jordan in 1921 was the most important stage of the Arab revolution following the exposure of the conspiracy against this revolution during the First World War. After the issue of the Balfour Declaration in 1917, the establishment of the State became even more significant because it spared the territory east of the Jordan river from that Declaration and consequently from the Zionist plans at that time.

When the Arab armies entered Palestine in 1948, the Jordanian army was the smallest in terms of men and equipment. Yet, this army was able to save from Palestine that area which extends from Jenin in the north to Hebron in the south and from the Jordan river in the east to a point not more than 15 kilometres from the coast in the west. It was also able to save the entire Holy City of Jerusalem and other areas outside the city walls – those areas north, south and east of the walls which later became known as Arab Jerusalem. That area which later became known as the West Bank was all that was left for the Arabs from Palestine, in addition to that narrow strip which later became known as the Gaza Strip.

After a short period of temporary administration in the West Bank, a group of leaders, notables and elders representing Palestinian Arabs who had emigrated from the occupied territories considered joining the East Bank, a patriotic and nationalist demand and a guarantee against Israeli dangers. They held two great historic meetings. . . . These meetings were attended by the representatives of all the people leaders, thinkers, youth, the aged, workers and farmers – and their organizations.

Those present adopted resolutions calling on the late King Abdullah Bin al-Husein to take immediate steps to unify and merge the two Banks in a single State under his leadership. The old king responded to the nation's call and ordered that constitutional and practical measures be taken to achieve that important patriotic and nationalist demand. The measures included holding

DOI: 10.4324/9781003348948-45

elections to select the legitimate representatives of the West Bank people in the Chamber of Deputies.

On 24 April 1950, the new Jordanian National Assembly – with its two chambers, deputies and senators – representing the two Banks held an historic meeting which marked the first real step in modern Arab history towards Arab unity, which the revolution has advocated since its inception. The meeting announced the unity and merger of the two Banks in a single independent Arab State, a parliamentary monarchy known as the Hashemite Kingdom of Jordan.

. . .

The primary fact that the unity of the two Banks represented day after day has been that the people in both Banks are one and not two peoples. This fact was manifested for the first time in the reunion of the sons of the East Bank with their emigrant brothers, the sons of the Palestine areas occupied in 1948. . . .

The unity of blood and destiny reached its greatest significance in 1967 when the sons of the two Banks stood together on the West Bank as they have been doing for twenty years and jointly sacrificed their blood on its pure soil. . . .

In the sea of suffering that the June catastrophe left behind, the objectives of the Jordanian State in the post-war era have been summarized as (1) valiant steadfastness in the face of the unabating and unending aggressions against the East Bank and (2) confident resolve to liberate the land, the people and the brothers in the West Bank. . . .

A New Catastrophe

But suddenly Jordan found itself face to face with a new catastrophe whose inevitable result, if it had been destined to come true, would have been the loss of the East Bank and the establishment of the situation needed to liqui-date the Palestine issue once and for all on the ruins of the East Bank. . . .

Naturally Jordan had to stand up and deal with the imminent catastrophe. This it did by taking a stand in which that unique mixture of its sons, the emigrants and the supporters, participated equally. The dissension was crushed on the solid rock of national unity. The dissension ceased to exist thanks to the enlighten-ment of the new man who had been born on that distant day in 1950 and grew up on the challenges which the ordeals have been posing for the past 20 years.

Throughout all this, since the June 1967 war and perhaps even before then, the Jordanian leaders have been thinking and planning for the future of the State. . . . The Palestine issue was viewed from all the aspects of the entire Arab-Zionist conflict. Palestine was the first objective of the Zionist plans. The people in Palestine were the first prey and victim of these plans. The next were the people of the two dear Banks.

. . .

Jordan understood the magnitude of the catastrophe which had befallen the Palestinian people. When the Zionist plot dispersed them, the sons of this people could not find in any country, Arab or non-Arab, the honourable and dignified life found by those who came to Jordan for shelter in 1948 and afterwards. Under the unity of the two Banks in Jordan, the real Palestinian regrouping, the vast majority of the people, came to live on the two banks of the immortal river. . . .

The Palestinian people existed for hundreds of years before 1948. The Palestinian people continued to exist after 1948. But the forces and currents behind the conditions which had started to prevail in the Arab world began overriding and ignoring these facts. . . . It was as if it was desired that the Palestinian should cut off his domestic and national links and place himself in a small bottle which could be easily smashed at any time. . . . If certain powers who are encouraging and strengthening these trends do not conceal their desire to rid themselves of the responsibilities for the Palestinian issue and people, the glitter of this situation, no matter now attractive to some, should not blind us to the danger that the Palestinian people may end up in a position in which they will once again be an easy and isolated prey to Israel and its insatiable ambitions. That is why this move is trying to portray the Jordanian regime as coveting booty and gain. That is why it is trying to penetrate the national unity to weaken it and cast doubt on it.

The Arab World

The first inevitable result of all the conditions prevailing in the Arab world – the dispersed ranks, scattered efforts, non-existent co-ordination, rivalry ill establishing axes and camps, abandonment of the essence of the issue and its prerequisite, paying lip service to the issue once and exploiting it several times, the abandonment of real work for liberation and the devotion of efforts to domination and achievement of power – has been the continued Israeli occupation of the West Bank of Jordan and other dear Arab territories. The second inevitable result has been a further intensification of the Palestinian people's suffering. . . .

Despite all this, Jordan has never for one day stopped advocating the unity of ranks. . . . Jordan has never hesitated to extend a true capable hand to all the brothers out of its belief in the unity of the cause and fate. Jordan has never spared any effort in working for the goal of liberation.

Though Arab conditions have obstructed Jordan and impeded its steps, contemplation of the future of the State has continued along its course. . . .

For this reason it has been decided to move the country into a new phase which basically centres on liberation. . . . Furthermore, it is based on absolute adherence to the legitimate rights of the Palestinian people and aims at leading the Palestinian people to the point which will enable them to regain and safeguard these rights.

This was the pledge we took – to give the people the right of self-determination. This is our reply to all those who chose to cast doubts on this pledge and to render it void of all meaning. . . .

We wish to declare here that planning for the new phase has come as a blessed result of a long series of uninterrupted discussions and continued consultations which we have had with people's representatives, personalities, leaders and thinkers of both Banks . . .

We are happy to declare that the bases of the proposed formula for the new phase are as follows:

(1) The Hashemite Kingdom of Jordan will become a United Arab Kingdom and will bear this name.

(2) The United Arab Kingdom will consist of two regions: (a) The Palestine region which will consist of the West Bank and any other Palestinian territories which are liberated and whose inhabitants desire to join it. (b) The Jordan region, which will consist of the East Bank.

(3) Amman will be the central capital of the kingdom as well as capital of the Jordan region.

(4) Jerusalem will be the capital of the Palestine region.

(5) The Head of State will be the king, who will assume the central executive authority with the help of a central cabinet. The central legislative authority will be vested in the king and an assembly to be known as the National Assembly. Members of this assembly will be elected by direct secret ballot. Both regions will be equally represented in this assembly.

(6) The central judicial authority will be vested in a central supreme court.

(7) The kingdom will have unified armed forces whose supreme commander is the king.

(8) The responsibilities of the central executive authority will be confined to affairs connected with the kingdom as an international entity to guarantee the kingdom's security, stability and prosperity.

(9) The executive authority in each region will be assumed by a governor-general from among its sons and a regional cabinet also from among its sons.

(10) Legislative authority in each region will be assumed by a council to be called the People's Council. It will be elected by a direct secret ballot. This council will elect the region's governor-general.

(11) The judicial authority in the region will be in the hands of the region's courts and nobody will have power over them.

(12) The executive authority in each region will assume responsibility for all the affairs of the region except such affairs as the Constitution defines as coming under the jurisdiction of the central executive authority.

Naturally, the implementation of this formula and its bases must be according to the constitutional principles in force. It will be referred to the (Jordanian)

National Assembly to adopt the necessary measures to prepare a new constitution.

The new phase which we look forward to will guarantee the reorganization of the Jordanian-Palestinian house in a manner which will provide it with more intrinsic power and ability to work to attain its ambition and aspirations . . .

This formula gathers and does not disperse, strengthens and does not weaken, unites and does not divide. It does not contain anything to change anything gained by any person during a unity of 20 years.

Every attempt to cast doubt on any of this or discredit it is treason against the unity of the kingdom, the cause, the people and the homeland. . . . For this reason this formula is the title for a new bright, shining and confident page in the history of this country in which each citizen has a part and responsibility. It is partly based on sound allegiance to his faithful country and sincere devotion to his nation.

The armed forces, which from the very beginning marched under the banner of the great Arab revolution and which included and will always include in its ranks the best sons of the people in both Banks, will always be prepared to welcome more sons of both Banks . . .

This Arab country is the country of the cause, just as it is from the Arabs and for all the Arabs. The record of its sacrifices for the nation and the cause is long and well-known. . . .

This Arab country belongs to all, Jordanians and Palestinians alike. When we say Palestinians we mean every Palestinian throughout the world, provided he is Palestinian by loyalty and affinity. When we call on every citizen to rise to play his part and carry out his responsibilities in the new stage, we call on every Palestinian brother outside Jordan to respond to the call of duty – unaffected by appearances and attempts to outdo others and free from weaknesses and deviations – to proceed with his relatives and brothers in a march whose basis is this formula and to be united in rank and clear in aim in order that all may participate in attaining the aim of liberation and establishing the cherished edifice and strong structure.

If God helps you, none can defeat you. For God is mighty and strong. Peace be with you.

42 U.N. Security Council

Resolution 338 (October 22, 1973)

The Security Council,

1. Calls upon all parties to present fighting to cease all firing and terminate all military activity immediately, no later than 12 hours after the moment of the adoption of this decision, in the positions after the moment of the adoption of this decision, in the positions they now occupy;
2. Calls upon all parties concerned to start immediately after the cease-fire the implementation of Security Council Resolution 242 (1967) in all of its parts;
3. Decides that, immediately and concurrently with the cease-fire, negotiations start between the parties concerned under appropriate auspices aimed at establishing a just and durable peace in the Middle East.

DOI: 10.4324/9781003348948-46

43 Palestine National Council

Resolutions at the 12th Session
of the Palestine National Council
(June 8, 1974)

Cairo, 8 June 1974

The Palestine National Council,

On the basis of the Palestine National Charter and the Political Program drawn up at the eleventh session, held from 6 to 12 January 1997; and from its belief that it is impossible for a permanent and just peace to be established in the area unless our Palestinian people recover all their national rights and, first and foremost, their rights to return and to self-determination on the whole of the soil of their homeland; . . .

1. To reaffirm the Palestine Liberation Organization's previous attitude to Resolution 242, which obliterates the national right of our people and deals with the cause of our people as a problem of refugees. The Council therefore refuses to have anything to do with this resolution at any level, Arab or international, including the Geneva Conference.
2. The Palestine Liberation Organization will employ all means, and first and foremost armed struggle, to liberate Palestinian territory and to establish the independent combatant national authority for the people over every part of Palestinian territory that is liberated. . . .
3. The Liberation Organization will struggle against any proposal for a Palestinian entity the price of which is recognition, peace, secure frontiers, renunciation of national rights, and the deprival of our people of their right to return and their right to self-determination on the soil of their homeland.
4. Any step taken towards liberation is a step towards the realization of the Liberation Organization's strategy of establishing the democratic Palestinian State specified in the resolutions of the previous Palestinian National Councils.
5. Struggle along with the Jordanian national forces to establish a Jordanian-Palestinian national front whose aim will be to set up in Jordan a democratic national authority in close contact with the Palestinian entity that is established through the struggle.

DOI: 10.4324/9781003348948-47

6. The Liberation Organization will struggle to establish unity in struggle between the two peoples and between all the forces of the Arab liberation movement that are in agreement on this program.

7. In the light of this program, the Liberation Organization will struggle to strengthen national unity and to raise it to the level where it will be able to perform its national duties and tasks.

8. Once it is established, the Palestinian national authority will strive to achieve a union of the confrontation countries, with the aim of completing the liberation of all Palestinian territory, and as a step along the road to comprehensive Arab unity.

9. The Liberation Organization will strive to strengthen its solidarity with the socialist countries, and with the forces of liberation and progress throughout the world, with the aim of frustrating all the schemes of Zionism, reaction and imperialism.

10. In light of this program, the leadership of the revolution will determine the tactics which will serve and make possible the realization of the objectives.

The Executive Committee of the Palestine Liberation Organization will make every effort to implement this program, and should a situation arise affecting the destiny and the future of the Palestinian people, the National Assembly will be convened in extraordinary session.

44 Seventh Arab League Summit Conference, Resolution on Palestine (October 28, 1974)

The Seventh Arab Summit Conference after exhaustive and detailed discussions conducted by their majesties, Excellencies, and Highnesses, the Kings, Presidents and Amirs on the Arab situation in general and the Palestine problem in particular, . . . resolves the following:

1. To affirm the right of the Palestinian people to self-determination and to return to their homeland;
2. To affirm the right of the Palestinian people to establish an independent national authority under the command of the Palestine Liberation Organization, the sole legitimate representative of the Palestinian people in any Palestinian territory that is liberated. This authority, once it is established, shall enjoy the support of the Arab states in all fields and at all levels;
3. To support the Palestine Liberation Organization in the exercise of its responsibility at the national and international levels within the framework of Arab commitment;
4. To call on the Hashemite Kingdom of Jordan, the Syrian Arab Republic, the Arab Republic of Egypt and the Palestine Liberation Organization to devise a formula for the regulation of relations between them in the light of these decisions so as to ensure their implementation;
5. That all the Arab states undertake to defend Palestinian national unity and not to interfere in the internal affairs of Palestinian action.

DOI: 10.4324/9781003348948-48

45 Interim Agreement Between Israel and Egypt (September 1, 1975)

The Government of the Arab Republic of Egypt and the Government of Israel have agreed that:

Article I

The conflict between them and in the Middle East shall not be resolved by military force but by peaceful means.

The Agreement concluded by the parties on 18 January 1974, within the framework of the Geneva Peace Conference, constituted a first step towards a just and durable peace according to the provisions of Security Council Resolution 338 of 22 October 1973.

They are determined to reach a final and just peace settlement by means of negotiations called for by Security Council Resolution 338, this Agreement being a significant step towards that end.

Article II

The parties hereby undertake not to resort to the threat or use of force or military blockade against each other.

Article III

The parties shall continue scrupulously to observe the cease-fire on land, sea, and air and to refrain from all military or para-military actions against each other. The parties also confirm that the obligations contained in the annex and, when concluded, the Protocol shall be an integral part of this Agreement.

Article IV

The military forces of the parties shall be deployed in accordance with [negotiated positions] . . .

DOI: 10.4324/9781003348948-49

Article V

The United Nations Emergency Force is essential and shall continue its functions and its mandate shall be extended annually.

Article VI

The parties hereby establish a joint commission for the duration of this Agreement. It will function under the aegis of the chief coordinator of the United Nations peace-keeping missions in the Middle East in order to consider any problem arising from this Agreement . . .

Article VII

Non-military cargoes destined for or coming from Israel shall be permitted through the Suez Canal.

Article VIII

This Agreement is regarded by the parties as a significant step toward a just and lasting peace. It is not a final peace agreement.

The parties shall continue their efforts to negotiate a final peace agreement within the framework of the Geneva peace conference in accordance with Security Council Resolution 338.

Article IX

This Agreement shall enter into force upon signature of the Protocol and remain in force until superseded by a new agreement.

Annex to the Egypt-Israel Agreement

Within five days after the signature of the Egypt-Israel Agreement, representatives of the two parties shall meet in the military working group of the Middle East peace conference at Geneva to begin preparation of a detailed Protocol for the implementation of the Agreement. . . .

1. DEFINITIONS OF LINES AND AREAS . . .

2. BUFFER ZONES

(A) Access to the buffer zones will be controlled by the United Nations Emergency Force, according to procedures to be worked out by the working group and the United Nations Emergency Force.

(B) Aircraft of either party will be permitted to fly freely up to the forward line of that party. Reconnaissance aircraft of either party may fly up to the middle line of the buffer zone . . .

(C) In the buffer zone . . . there will be established under Article IV of the Agreement an early warning system entrusted to United States civilian personnel as detailed in a separate proposal, which is a part of this Agreement.

(D) Authorized personnel shall have access to the buffer zone for transit to and from the early warning system; the manner in which this is carried out shall be worked out by the working group and the United Nations Emergency Force.

3. AREA SOUTH OF LINE E AND WEST OF LINE M . . .

4. AERIAL SURVEILLANCE

There shall be a continuation of aerial reconnaissance missions by the United States over the areas covered by the Agreement . . .

5. LIMITATION OF FORCES AND ARMAMENTS . . .

6. PROCESS OF IMPLEMENTATION

The detailed implementation and timing of the redeployment of forces, turnover of oil fields, and other arrangements called for by the Agreement, annex, and Protocol shall be determined by the working group, which will agree on the stages of this process, including the phased movement of Egyptian troops to line E and Israeli troops to line J. The first phase will be the transfer of the oil fields and installations to Egypt. This process will begin within two weeks from the signature of the Protocol with the introduction of the necessary technicians, and it will be completed no later than eight weeks after it begins. The details of the phasing will be worked out in the military working group . . .

PROPOSAL

In connection with the early warning system referred to in Article IV of the Agreement between Egypt and Israel concluded on this date and as an integral part of that Agreement (hereafter referred to as the basic Agreement), the United States proposes the following:

1. The early warning system to be established in accordance with Article IV in the area shown on the map attached to the basic agreement will be entrusted to the United States . . .

2. The United States civilian personnel shall perform the following duties in connection with the operation and maintenance of these stations.

(A) At the two surveillance stations described in paragraph 1 A. above, United States civilian personnel will verify the nature of the operations of the stations and all movement into and out of each station and will immediately report any detected divergency from its authorized role of visual and electronic surveillance to the parties to the basic Agreement and to the United Nations Emergency Force.

(B) At each watch station described in paragraph 1 B. above, the United States civilian personnel will immediately report to the parties to the basic Agreement and to the United Nations Emergency Force any movement of armed forces, other than the United Nations Emergency Force, into either Pass and any observed preparations for such movement.

(C) The total number of United States civilian personnel assigned to functions under this proposal shall not exceed 200. Only civilian personnel shall be assigned to functions under this proposal.

3. No arms shall be maintained at the stations and other facilities covered by this proposal, except for small arms required for their protection.

4. The United States personnel serving the early warning system shall be allowed to move freely within the area of the system.

5. The United States and its personnel shall be entitled to have such support facilities as are reasonably necessary to perform their functions provided for in the United Nations Emergency Force Agreement of 13 February 1957.

6. The United States personnel shall be immune from local criminal, civil, tax, and customs jurisdiction and may be accorded any other specific privileges and immunities provided for in the United Nations Emergency Force Agreement of 13 February 1957.

7. The United States affirms that it will continue to perform the functions described above for the duration of the basic Agreement.

8. Notwithstanding any other provision of this proposal, the United States may withdraw its personnel only if it concludes that their safety is jeopardized or that continuation of their role is no longer necessary. In the latter case the parties to the basic Agreement will be informed in advance in order to give them the opportunity to make alternative arrangements. If both parties to the basic Agreement request the United States to conclude its role under this proposal, the United States will consider such requests conclusive.

9. Technical problems including the location of the watch stations will be worked out through consultation with the United States.

46 Memorandum of Agreement Between the Governments of Israel and the United States (September 1, 1975)

The United States recognizes that the Egypt–Israel Agreement initialled on September 1, 1975, (hereinafter referred to as the Agreement), entailing the withdrawal from vital areas in Sinai, constitutes an act of great significance on Israel's part in the pursuit of final peace. That Agreement has full United States support.

United States-Israeli Assurances

1. The United States Government will make every effort to be fully responsive, within the limits of its resources and Congressional authorization and appropriation, on an on-going and long-term basis to Israel's military equipment and other defense requirements, to its energy requirements and to its economic needs. . . .

2. Israel's long-term military supply needs from the United States shall be the subject of periodic consultations between representatives of the United States and Israeli defense establishments, with agreement reached on specific items to be included in a separate United States-Israeli memorandum. . . .

3. Israel will make its own independent arrangements for oil supply to meet its requirements through normal procedures. In the event Israel is unable to secure its needs in this way, the United States Government, upon notification of this fact by the Government of Israel, will act as follows for five years, at the end of which period either side can terminate this arrangement on one-year's notice.

    (a) If the oil Israel needs to meet all its normal requirements for domestic consumption is unavailable for purchase . . . the United States Government will promptly make oil available for purchase by Israel to meet all of the aforementioned normal requirements of Israel. If Israel is unable to secure the necessary means to transport such oil to Israel, the United States Government will make every effort to help Israel secure the necessary means of transport.

    (b) If the oil Israel needs to meet all of its normal requirements for domestic consumption is unavailable for purchase in circumstances

DOI: 10.4324/9781003348948-50

where quantitative restrictions through embargo or otherwise also prevent the United States from procuring oil to meet its normal requirements, the United States Government will promptly make oil available for purchase by Israel in accordance with the International Energy Agency conservation and allocation formula as applied by the United States Government, in order to meet Israel's essential requirements. If Israel is unable to secure the necessary means to transport such oil to Israel, the United States Government will make every effort to help Israel secure the necessary means of transport.

Israeli and United States experts will meet annually or more frequently at the request of either party, to review Israel's continuing oil requirement.

4. . . .
5. The United States Government will not expect Israel to begin to implement the Agreement before Egypt fulfils its undertaking under the January 1974 Disengagement Agreement to permit passage of all Israeli cargoes to and from Israeli ports through the Suez Canal.
6. The United States Government agrees with Israel that the next agreement with Egypt should be a final peace agreement.
7. In case of an Egyptian violation of any of the provisions of the Agreement, the United States Government is prepared to consult with Israel as to the significance of the violation and possible remedial action by the United States Government.
8. The United States Government will vote against any Security Council resolution which in its judgment affects or alters adversely the Agreement.
9. The United States Government will not join in and will seek to prevent efforts by others to bring about consideration of proposals which it and Israel agree are detrimental to the interests of Israel.
10. In view of the long-standing United States commitment to the survival and security of Israel, the United States Government will view with particular gravity threats to Israel's security or sovereignty by a world power. . . .
11. The United States Government and the Government of Israel will, at the earliest possible time, and if possible, within two months after the signature of this document, conclude the contingency plan for a military supply operation to Israel in an emergency situation.
12. It is the United States Government's position that Egyptian commitments under the Egypt–Israel Agreement, its implementation, validity and duration are not conditional upon any act or developments between the other Arab states and Israel. The United States Government regards the Agreement as standing on its own.
13. The United States Government shares the Israeli position that under existing political circumstances negotiations with Jordan will be directed toward an overall peace settlement.

14. In accordance with the principle of freedom of navigation on the high seas and free and unimpeded passage through and over straits connecting international waters, the United States Government regards the Straits of Bab-el-Mandeb and the Strait of Gibraltar as international waterways. It will support Israel's right to free and unimpeded passage through such straits. Similarly, the United States Government recognizes Israel's right to freedom of flights over the Red Sea and such straits and will support diplomatically the exercise of that right.

15. In the event that the United Nations Emergency Force or any other United Nations organ is withdrawn without the prior agreement of both Parties to the Egypt–Israel Agreement and the United States before this Agreement is superseded by another agreement, it is the United States view that the Agreement shall remain binding in all its parts.

16. The United States and Israel agree that signature of the Protocol of the Egypt–Israel agreement and its full entry into effect shall not take place before approval by the United States Congress of the United States role in connection with the surveillance and observation functions described in the Agreement and its Annex. The United States has informed the Government of Israel that it has obtained the Government of Egypt agreement to the above. . . .

Memorandum of Agreement Between the Governments of Israel and the United States

THE GENEVA PEACE CONFERENCE

1. The Geneva Peace Conference will be reconvened at a time coordinated between the United States and Israel.

2. The United States will continue to adhere to its present policy with respect to the Palestine Liberation Organization, whereby it will not recognize or negotiate with the Palestine Liberation Organization so long as the Palestine Liberation Organization does not recognize Israel's right to exist and does not accept Security Council Resolutions 242 and 338. . . . Similarly, the United States will consult fully and seek to concert its position and strategy with Israel with regard to the participation of any other additional states. It is understood that the participation at a subsequent phase of the Conference of any possible additional state, group or organization will require the agreement of all the initial participants.

3. The United States will make every effort to ensure at the Conference that all the substantive negotiations will be on a bilateral basis.

4. The United States will oppose and, if necessary, vote against any initiative in the Security Council to alter adversely the terms of reference of the Geneva Peace Conference or to change Resolutions 242 and 338 in ways which are incompatible with their original purpose.

5. The United States will seek to ensure that the role of the cosponsors will be consistent with what was agreed in the Memorandum of Understanding between the United States Government and the Government of Israel of December 20, 1973.
6. The United States and Israel will concert action to assure that the Conference will be conducted in a manner consonant with the objectives of this document and with the declared purpose of the Conference, namely the advancement of a negotiated peace between Israel and each one of its neighbors.

47 Statement to the Knesset by President Anwar el-Sadat (November 20, 1977)

In the name of God, the Gracious and Merciful.

Mr. Speaker, Ladies and Gentlemen:

Peace and the mercy of God Almighty be upon you and may peace be for us all, God willing. . . .

I come to you today on solid ground, to shape a new life, to establish peace. We all, on this land, the land of God; we all, Muslims, Christians, and Jews, worship God and no one but God. God's teachings and commandments are love, sincerity, purity, and peace.

I do not blame all those who received my decision – when I announced it to the entire world before the Egyptian People's Assembly – with surprise and amazement. . . . I would go as far as to tell you that one of my aides at the Presidential Office contacted me at a late hour following my return home from the People's Assembly and sounded worried as he asked me: "Mr. President, what would be our reaction if Israel should actually extend an invitation to you?" I replied calmly, I will accept it immediately. I have declared that I will go to the end of the world; I will go to Israel, for I want to put before the People of Israel all the facts.

. . .

But, to be absolutely frank with you, I took this decision after long thinking, knowing that it constitutes a grave risk for, if God Almighty has made it my fate to assume the responsibility on behalf of the Egyptian People and to share in the fate-determining responsibility of the Arab Nation and the Palestinian People, the main duty dictated by this responsibility is to exhaust all and every means in a bid to save my Egyptian Arab People and the entire Arab Nation the horrors of new, shocking and destructive wars, the dimensions of which are foreseen by no other than God himself.

. . .

I have shouldered the prerequisites of the historical responsibility and, therefore, I declared – on 4 February 1971, to be precise – that I was willing to sign a peace agreement with Israel. This was the first declaration made by a responsible Arab official since the outbreak of the Arab-Israeli conflict.

Motivated by all these factors dictated by the responsibilities of leadership, I called, on 16 October 1973, before the Egyptian People's Assembly, for an

DOI: 10.4324/9781003348948-51

international conference to establish permanent peace based on justice. I was not in the position of he who was pleading for peace or asking for a ceasefire.

Motivated by all these factors dictated by duties of history and leadership, we signed the first disengagement agreement, followed by the second dis-engagement agreement in Sinai. Then we proceeded trying both open and closed doors in a bid to find a certain path leading to a durable and just peace. We opened our hearts to the peoples of the entire world to make them under-stand our motivations and objectives, and to leave them actually convinced of the fact that we are advocates of justice and peace-makers.

. . .

Ladies and Gentlemen, let us be frank with each other, . . . Let us be frank with each other today while the entire world, both East and West, follows these unparalleled moments which could prove to be a radical turning point in the history of this part of the world, if not in the history of the world as a whole. Let us be frank with each other as we answer this important question: how can we achieve permanent peace based on justice?

. . .

Before I proclaim my answer, I wish to assure you that, in my clear and frank answer, I am basing myself on a number of facts which no one can deny.

The first fact: no one can build his happiness at the expense of the misery of others.

The second fact: never have I spoken or will ever speak in two languages. Never have I adopted or will adopt two policies. I never deal with anyone except in one language, one policy, and with one face.

The third fact: direct confrontation and a straight line are the nearest and most successful methods to reach a clear objective.

The fourth fact: the call for permanent and just peace, based on respect for the United Nations resolutions, has now become the call of the whole world. It has become a clear expression of the will of the international com-munity, whether in official capitals, where policies are made and decisions taken, or at the level of world public opinion which influences policy-making and decision-taking.

The fifth fact: and this is probably the clearest and most prominent, is that the Arab Nation, in its drive for permanent peace based on justice, does not proceed from a position of weakness or hesitation, but it has the potential of power and stability which tells of a sincere will for peace. . . .

In the light of these facts which I meant to place before you the way I see them, I would also wish to warn you in all sincerity; I warn you against some thoughts that could cross your minds; frankness makes it incumbent upon me to tell you the following:

First: I have not come here for a separate agreement between Egypt and Israel. This is not part of the policy of Egypt. The problem is not that of Egypt and Israel. Any separate peace between Egypt and Israel, or between any Arab confrontation State and Israel, will not bring permanent peace based on justice in the entire region. Rather, even if peace between all the confrontation

States and Israel were achieved, in the absence of a just solution to the Palestinian problem, never will there be that durable and just peace upon which the entire world insists today.

Second: I have not come to you to seek a partial peace, namely to terminate the state of belligerency at this stage, and put off the entire problem to a subsequent stage. This is not the radical solution that would steer us to permanent peace.

Equally, I have not come to you for a third disengagement agreement in Sinai, or in the Golan and the West Bank. For this would mean that we are merely delaying the ignition of the fuse; it would mean that we are lacking the courage to confront peace, that we are too weak to shoulder the burdens and responsibilities of a durable peace based on justice.

. . .

Here, I would go back to the answer to the big question: how can we achieve a durable peace based on justice?

In my opinion, and I declare it to the whole world from this forum, the answer is neither difficult nor impossible, despite long years of feud, blood vengeance, spite and hatred, and breeding generations on concepts of total rift and deep-rooted animosity . . .

We used to reject you. We had our reasons and our claims, yes. We used to brand you as "so-called" Israel, yes. We were together in international conferences and organizations and our representatives did not, and still do not, exchange greetings, yes. This has happened and is still happening.

It is also true that we used to set, as a precondition for any negotiations with you, a mediator who would meet separately with each party. Through this procedure, the talks of the first and second disengagement agreements took place.

Our delegates met in the first Geneva Conference without exchanging a direct word. Yes, this has happened.

Yet, today I tell you, and declare it to the whole world, that we accept to live with you in permanent peace based on justice. . . . I have announced on more than one occasion that Israel has become a *fait accompli*, recognized by the world, and that the two superpowers have undertaken the responsibility of its security and the defence of its existence.

As we really and truly seek peace, we really and truly welcome you to live among us in peace and security.

. . .

What is peace for Israel? It means that Israel lives in the region with her Arab neighbours, in security and safety. To such logic, I say yes. It means that Israel lives within her borders, secure against any aggression. To such logic, I say yes. It means that Israel obtains all kinds of guarantees that ensure those two factors. To this demand, I say yes. More than that: we declare that we accept all the international guarantees you envisage and accept. We declare that we accept all the guarantees you want from the two superpowers or from either of them, or from the Big Five, or some of them.

Once again, I declare clearly and unequivocally that we agree to any guarantees you accept because, in return, we shall obtain the same guarantees.

In short, then, when we ask: what is peace for Israel, the answer would be: it is that Israel live within her borders with her Arab neighbours, in safety and security within the framework of all the guarantees she accepts and which are offered to the other party. But how can this be achieved? How can we reach this conclusion which would lead us to permanent peace based on justice?

There are facts that should be faced with all courage and clarity. There are Arab territories which Israel has occupied by armed force. We insist on complete withdrawal from these territories, including Arab Jerusalem.

I have come to Jerusalem, as the City of Peace, which will always remain as a living embodiment of coexistence among believers of the three religions. It is inadmissible that anyone should conceive the special status of the City of Jerusalem within the framework of annexation or expansionism, but it should be a free and open city for all believers.

Above all, the city should not be severed from those who have made it their abode for centuries. Instead of awakening the prejudices of the Crusaders, we should revive the spirit of Ornar ibn el-Khattab and Saladin, namely the spirit of tolerance and respect for rights. The holy shrines of Islam and Christianity are not only places of worship, but a living testimony of our uninterrupted presence here politically, spiritually, and intellectually. Let us make no mistake about the importance and reverence we Christians and Muslims attach to Jerusalem.

Let me tell you, without the slightest hesitation, that I did not come to you under this dome to make a request that your troops evacuate the occupied territories. Complete withdrawal from the Arab territories occupied in 1967 is a logical and undisputed fact. Nobody should plead for that. Any talk about permanent peace based on justice, and any move to ensure our coexistence in peace and security in this part of the world, would become meaningless, while you occupy Arab territories by force of arms. For there is no peace that could be in consonance with, or be built on, the occupation of the land of others. Otherwise, it would not be a serious peace. . . .

As for the Palestinians' cause, nobody could deny that it is the crux of the entire problem. Nobody in the world could accept, today, slogans propagated here in Israel, ignoring the existence of the Palestinian People and questioning their whereabouts. The cause of the Palestinian People and their legitimate rights are no longer ignored or denied today by anybody. Rather, nobody who has the ability of judgement can deny or ignore it.

. . .

I hail the Israeli voices that called for the recognition of the Palestinian People's rights to achieve and safeguard peace. Here I tell you, ladies and gentlemen, that it is no use to refrain from recognizing the Palestinian People and their rights to statehood and rights of return.

. . .

You have to face reality bravely, as I have done. There can never be any solution to a problem by evading it or turning a deaf ear to it. Peace cannot last if attempts are made to impose fantasy concepts on which the world has turned its back and announced its unanimous call for the respect of rights and facts. There is no need to enter a vicious circle as to Palestinian rights. It is useless to create obstacles. Otherwise the march of peace will be impeded or peace will be blown up.

. . .

Conceive with me a peace agreement in Geneva that we would herald to a world thirsty for peace, a peace agreement based on the following points:

First: ending the Israeli occupation of the Arab territories occupied in 1967.

Second: achievement of the fundamental rights of the Palestinian People and their right to self-determination, including their right to establish their own state.

Third: the right of all states in the area to live in peace within their boundaries, which will be secure and guaranteed through procedures to be agreed upon, which provide appropriate security to international boundaries, in addition to appropriate international guarantees.

Fourth: commitment of all states in the region to administer the relations among them in accordance with the objectives and principles of the United Nations Charter, particularly the principles concerning the non-resort to force and the solution of differences among them by peaceful means.

Fifth: ending the state of belligerency in the region.

Ladies and Gentlemen, peace is not the mere endorsement of written lines; rather, it is a rewriting of history. Peace is not a game of calling for peace to defend certain whims or hide certain ambitions. Peace is a giant struggle against all and every ambition and whim. Perhaps the examples taken from ancient and modern history teach us all that missiles, warships, and nuclear weapons cannot establish security. Rather, they destroy what peace and security build. . . .

Allow me to address my call from this rostrum to the People of Israel. I address myself with true and sincere words to every man, woman, and child in Israel.

From the Egyptian People who bless this sacred mission of peace, I convey to you the message of peace, the message of the Egyptian People who do not know fanaticism, and whose sons, Muslims, Christians, and Jews, live together in a spirit of cordiality, love, and tolerance. This is Egypt whose people have entrusted me with that sacred message, the message of security, safety, and peace. To every man, woman, and child in Israel, I say: encourage your leadership to struggle for peace. Let all endeavours be channeled towards building a huge edifice for peace, instead of strongholds and hideouts defended by destructive rockets. Introduce to the entire world the image of the new man in this area, so that he might set an example to the man of our age, the man of peace everywhere.

. . .

Ladies and Gentlemen, before I came to this place, with every beat of my heart and with every sentiment, I prayed to God Almighty, while performing the Curban Bairarn prayers, and while visiting the Holy Sepulchre, to give me strength and to confirm my belief that this visit may achieve the objectives I look forward to, for a happy present and a happier future.

I have chosen to set aside all precedents and traditions known by warring countries, in spite of the fact that occupation of the Arab territories is still there. Rather, the declaration of my readiness to proceed to Israel came as a great surprise that stirred many feelings and astounded many minds. Some opinions even doubted its intent. Despite that, the decision was inspired by all the clarity and purity of belief, and with all the true expression of my People's will and intentions.

. . .

It is not my battle alone, nor is it the battle of the leadership in Israel alone. It is the battle of all and every citizen in all our territories whose right it is to live in peace. It is the commitment of conscience and responsibility in the hearts of millions.

When I put forward this initiative, many asked what is it that I conceived as possible to achieve during this visit, and what my expectations were. And, as I answered the questioners, I announce before you that I have not thought of carrying out this initiative from the concept of what could be achieved during this visit, but I have come here to deliver a message. I have delivered the message, and may God be my witness.

I repeat with Zechariah, "Love right and justice."

I quote the following verses from the holy Koran:

We believe in God and in what has been revealed to us and what was revealed to Abraham, Ismail, Isaac, Jacob, and the tribes and in the books given to Moses, Jesus, and the prophets from their lord. We make no distinction between one and another among them and to God we submit.

48 Statement to the Knesset by Prime Minister Menachem Begin (November 20, 1977)

Mr. Speaker, Honourable President of the State of Israel, Honourable President of the Arab Republic of Egypt, Worthy and Learned Knesset Members:

We send our greetings to the President and to all adherents of the Islamic faith, in our own country and wherever they may be, on the occasion of the Feast of Sacrifice, Id el-Adha.

. . .

I greet the President of Egypt on the occasion of his visit to our country and his participation in this session of the Knesset. The duration of the flight from Cairo to Jerusalem is short but, until last night, the distance between them was infinite. President Sadat showed courage in crossing this distance. We Jews can appreciate courage, as exhibited by our guest, because it is with courage that we arose, and with it we shall continue to exist.

Mr. Speaker, this small People, the surviving remnant of the Jewish People which returned to our historic Homeland, always sought peace. And, when the dawn of our freedom rose on the 14th of May, 1948, the 4th of Iyar, 5708, David Ben-Gurion said, in the Declaration of Independence, the charter of our national independence:

> We extend our hand to all neighbouring states and their peoples in an offer of peace and good neighbourliness, and appeal to them to establish bonds of cooperation and mutual help with the sovereign Jewish People settled in its own Land.

. . .

But it is my duty – my duty Mr. Speaker, and not only my privilege – to assert today in truth that our hand, extended in peace, was rejected. And, one day after our independence was renewed, in accordance with our eternal and indisputable right, we were attacked on three fronts, and we stood virtually without arms – few against many, weak against strong. One day after the declaration of our independence, an attempt was made to strangle it with enmity, and to extinguish the last hope of the Jewish People in the generation of Holocaust and Resurrection.

. . .

DOI: 10.4324/9781003348948-52

I agree, Mr. President, that you have not come here and we did not invite you to our country in order, as has been suggested in recent days, to drive a wedge between the Arab Peoples, or, expressed more cleverly in accord with the ancient saying, "*divide et impera*." Israel has no desire to rule and does not wish to divide. We want peace with all our neighbours – with Egypt and with Jordan, with Syria and with Lebanon.

There is no need to differentiate between a peace treaty and the termination of the state of war. We neither propose this, nor do we seek it. On the contrary, the first article of a peace treaty determines the end of the state of war, forever. We wish to establish normal relations between us, as exist among all nations after all wars. We have learned from history, Mr. President, that war is avoidable. It is peace that is inevitable.

Many nations have waged war against one another, and sometimes they have made use of the foolish term "eternal enemy." There are no eternal enemies. After all wars comes the inevitable – peace. Therefore, in the context of a peace treaty, we seek to stipulate the establishment of diplomatic relations, as is customary among civilized nations.

Today, Jerusalem is bedecked with two flags – the Egyptian and the Israeli. Together, Mr. President, we have seen our little children waving both flags. Let us sign a peace treaty and establish such a situation forever, both in Jerusalem and in Cairo. I hope the day will come when Egyptian children will wave Israeli and Egyptian flags together, just as the Israeli children are waving both of these flags together in Jerusalem; when you, Mr. President, will be represented by a loyal Ambassador in Jerusalem, and we, by an Ambassador in Cairo and, should differences of opinion arise between us, we will clarify them, like civilized peoples, through our authorized emissaries.

. . .

With all due respect, I am prepared to endorse the words of His Highness, the King of Morocco, who said, publicly, that, if peace were to be established in the Middle East, the combination of Arab and Jewish genius can together convert the region into a paradise on earth.

. . .

Therefore, I renew my invitation to the President of Syria to follow in your footsteps, Mr. President, and to come to our country to begin negotiations on the establishment of peace between Israel and Syria and on the signing of a peace treaty between us. I am sorry to say, there is no justification for the mourning that has been decreed on the other side of our northern border. On the contrary, such visits, such contacts and discussions, can and should be a cause of happiness, a cause of elation for all peoples.

I invite King Hussein to come here and we shall discuss with him all the problems that exist between us. I also invite genuine spokesmen of the Palestinian Arabs to come and to hold talks with us on our common future, on guaranteeing human freedom, social justice, peace, and mutual respect.

And, if they should invite us to come to their capitals, we shall respond to their invitation. Should they invite us to begin negotiations in Damascus,

Amman, or Beirut, we shall go to those capitals in order to negotiate there. We do not wish to divide. We seek true peace with all our neighbours, to be expressed in peace treaties, the context of which shall be as I have already clarified.

Mr. Speaker, it is my duty today to tell our guests and all the nations who are watching us and listening to our words about the bond between our People and this Land. The President mentioned the Balfour Declaration. No, sir, we took no foreign land. We returned to our Homeland. The bond between our People and this Land is eternal. It was created at the dawn of human history. It was never severed. In this Land we established our civilization; here our prophets spoke those holy words you cited this very day; here the Kings of Judah and Israel prostrated themselves; here we became a nation; here we established our Kingdom and, when we were exiled from our country by the force that was exercised against us, even when we were far away, we did not forget this Land, not even for a single day. We prayed for it; we longed for it; we have believed in our return to it ever since the day these words were spoken:

> When the Lord brought back the captivity of Zion we were like those who dream. Then our mouth was filled with laughter and our tongue with joyful shouting.

. . .

This, our right, has been recognized. The Balfour Declaration was included in the Mandate which was recognized by the nations of the world, including the United States of America. And the preamble to that authoritative international document states:

> Whereas recognition has thereby been given to the historical connection of the Jewish People with Palestine (or, in Hebrew, 'Eretz Israel') and to the grounds for reconstituting their National Home in that country (that is, in 'Eretz Israel') . . .

In 1919, we also gained recognition of this right from the spokesman of the Arab People. The agreement of 3 January 1919, signed by Emir Feisal and Chaim Weizmann, states:

> Mindful of the racial kinship and ancient bonds existing between the Arabs and the Jewish People, and realizing that the surest means of working out the consummation of their national aspirations is through the closest possible collaboration in the development of the Arab State and of Palestine . . .

Afterwards, follow all the articles on cooperation between the Arab State and Eretz Israel. That is our right; its fulfilment – the truth.

What happened to us when our Homeland was taken from us? I accompanied you this morning, Mr. President, to Yad Vashem. With your own eyes you saw what the fate of our People was when this Homeland was taken from it. It is an incredible story. We both agreed, Mr. President, that whoever has not himself seen what is found in Yad Vashem cannot understand what befell this People when it was homeless, robbed of its own Homeland. And we both read a document dated 30 January 1939, in which the word *"vernichtung"* appears – "if war breaks out the Jewish race in Europe will be annihilated." Then, too, we were told to pay no heed to such words. The whole world heard. No one came to our rescue; not during the nine critical, fateful months following this announcement – the likes of which had never been heard since God created man and man created Satan – and not during those six years when millions of our people, among them a million and a half small Jewish children, were slaughtered in every possible way.

No one came to our rescue, not from the East and not from the West. And therefore we, this entire generation, the generation of Holocaust and Resurrection, swore an oath of allegiance: never again shall we endanger our People; never again will our wives and our children – whom it is our duty to defend, if need be even at the cost of our own lives – be put in the devastating range of enemy fire.

. . .

President Sadat knows, as he knew from us before he came to Jerusalem, that our position concerning permanent borders between us and our neighbours differs from his. However, I call upon the President of Egypt and upon all our neighbours: do not rule out negotiations on any subject whatsoever. I propose, in the name of the overwhelming majority of this Parliament, that everything will be negotiable. Anybody who says that, in the relationship between the Arab People – or the Arab Nations in the area – and the State of Israel there are subjects that should be excluded from negotiations, is assuming an awesome responsibility. Everything is negotiable. No side shall say the contrary. No side shall present prior conditions. We will conduct the negotiations with respect.

. . .

We shall conduct the negotiations as equals. There are no vanquished and there are no victors. All the Peoples of the region are equal, and all will relate to each other with respect. In this spirit of openness, of readiness of each to listen to the other – to facts, reasons, explanations – with every reasonable attempt at mutual persuasion – let us conduct the negotiations as I have asked and propose to open them, to conduct them, to continue them persistently until we succeed, in good time, in signing a peace treaty between us.

We are prepared, not only, to sit with representatives of Egypt and with representatives of Jordan, Syria, and Lebanon – if it so desires – at a Peace Conference in Geneva. We proposed that the Geneva Conference be renewed on the basis of Resolutions 242 and 338 of the Security Council. However, should problems arise between us prior to the convening of the Geneva

Conference, we will clarify them today and tomorrow and, if the President of Egypt will be interested in continuing to clarify them in Cairo – all the better; if on neutral ground – no opposition. Anywhere. Let us clarify – even before the Geneva Conference convenes – the problems that should be made clear before it meets, with open eyes and a readiness to listen to all suggestions.

Allow me to say a word about Jerusalem. Mr. President, today you prayed in a house of worship sacred to the Islamic faith, and from there you went to the Church of the Holy Sepulchre. You witnessed the fact, known to all who come from throughout the world, that, ever since this city was joined together, there is absolutely free access, without any interference or obstacle, for the members of all religions to their holy places. This positive phenomenon did not exist for 19 years. It has existed now for about 11 years, and we can assure the Moslem world and the Christian world – all the nations – that there will always be free access to the holy places of every faith. We shall defend this right of free access, for it is something in which we believe – in the equality of rights for every man and every citizen, and in respect for every faith.

Mr. Speaker, this is a special day for our Parliament, and it will undoubtedly be remembered for many years in the annals of our Nation, in the history of the Egyptian People, and perhaps, also, in the history of nations.

And on this day, with your permission, worthy and learned Members of the Knesset, I wish to offer a prayer that the God of our common ancestors will grant us the requisite wisdom of heart in order to overcome the difficulties and obstacles, the calumnies and slanders. With the help of God, may we arrive at the longed-for day for which all our people pray – the day of peace.

For indeed, as the Psalmist of Israel said, "Righteousness and peace have kissed," and, as the prophet Zecharia said, "Love truth and peace."

49 Six-Point Program of the Palestine Liberation Organization (December 4, 1977)

We, all factions of the PLO, announce the following:

FIRST: We call for the formation of a "Steadfastness and Confrontation Front" composed of Libya, Algeria, Iraq, Democratic Yemen, Syria, and the PLO to oppose all confrontationist solutions planned by imperialism, Zionism, and their Arab tools.

SECOND: We fully condemn any Arab party in the Tripoli Summit which rejects the formation of this Front, and we announce this.

THIRD: We reaffirm our rejection of Security Council resolutions 242 and 338.

FOURTH: We reaffirm our rejection of all international conferences based on these two resolutions, including the Geneva Conference.

FIFTH: To strive for the realization of the Palestinian people's rights to return and self-determination within the context of an independent Palestinian national state on any part of Palestinian land, without reconciliation, recognition or negotiations, as an interim aim of the Palestinian Revolution.

SIXTH: To apply the measures related to the political boycott of the Sadat regime.

. . .

The conference pledges to the Arab nation that it will continue the march of struggle, steadfastness, combat, and adherence to the objectives of the Arab struggle. The conference also expresses its deep faith and absolute confidence that the Arab nation, which has staged revolutions, overcome difficulties, and defeated plots during its long history of struggle . . . is today capable of replying with force to those who have harmed its dignity, squandered its rights, split its solidarity, and departed from the principles of its struggle. It is confident of its own capabilities in liberation, progress, and victory, thanks to God.

The conference records with satisfaction the national Palestinian unity within the framework of the PLO.

DOI: 10.4324/9781003348948-53

50 The Camp David Accords (September 17, 1978)

The Framework for Peace in the Middle East

Preamble

The search for peace in the Middle East must be guided by the following:

- The agreed basis for a peaceful settlement of the conflict between Israel and its neighbors is United Nations Security Council Resolution 242, in all its parts.
- After four wars during 30 years, despite intensive human efforts, the Middle East, which is the cradle of civilization and the birthplace of three great religions, does not enjoy the blessings of peace. . . .
- The historic initiative of President Sadat in visiting Jerusalem and the reception accorded to him by the parliament, government, and people of Israel, and the reciprocal visit of Prime Minister Begin to Ismailia, . . . have created an unprecedented opportunity for peace which must not be lost if this generation and future generations are to be spared the tragedies of war.
- The provisions of the Charter of the United Nations and the other accepted norms of international law and legitimacy now provide accepted standards for the conduct of relations among all states.
- To achieve a relationship of peace, in the spirit of Article 2 of the United Nations Charter, future negotiations between Israel and any neighbor prepared to negotiate peace and security with it are necessary for the purpose of carrying out all the provisions and principles of Resolutions 242 and 338.
- Peace requires respect for the sovereignty, territorial integrity, and political independence of every state in the area and their right to live in peace within secure and recognized boundaries free from threats or acts of force. Progress toward that goal can accelerate movement toward a new era of reconciliation in the Middle East marked by cooperation in promoting economic development, in maintaining stability, and in assuring security.
- Security is enhanced by a relationship of peace and by cooperation between nations which enjoy normal relations. In addition, . . . the parties

DOI: 10.4324/9781003348948-54

can, on the basis of reciprocity, agree to special security arrangements such as demilitarized zones, limited armaments areas, early warning stations, the presence of international forces, liaison, agreed measures for monitoring, and other arrangements that they agree are useful.

Framework

Taking these factors into account, the parties are determined to reach a just, comprehensive, and durable settlement of the Middle East conflict through the conclusion of peace treaties based on Security Council resolutions 242 and 338 in all their parts. . . . They recognize that for peace to endure, it must involve all those who have been most deeply affected by the conflict. They therefore agree that this framework, as appropriate, is intended by them to constitute a basis for peace not only between Egypt and Israel, but also between Israel and each of its other neighbors which is prepared to negotiate peace with Israel on this basis. With that objective in mind, they have agreed to proceed as follows:

A. West Bank and Gaza

1. Egypt, Israel, Jordan, and the representatives of the Palestinian people should participate in negotiations on the resolution of the Palestinian problem in all its aspects. To achieve that objective, negotiations relating to the West Bank and Gaza should proceed in three stages:

   (a) Egypt and Israel agree that, in order to ensure a peaceful and orderly transfer of authority, . . . there should be transitional arrangements for the West Bank and Gaza for a period not exceeding five years. In order to provide full autonomy to the inhabitants, under these arrangements the Israeli military government and its civilian administration will be withdrawn as soon as a self-governing authority has been freely elected by the inhabitants of these areas to replace the existing military government. To negotiate the details of a transitional arrangement, Jordan will be invited to join the negotiations on the basis of this framework. These new arrangements should give due consideration both to the principle of self-government by the inhabitants of these territories and to the legitimate security concerns of the parties involved.

   (b) Egypt, Israel, and Jordan will agree on the modalities for establishing elected self-governing authority in the West Bank and Gaza. The delegations of Egypt and Jordan may include Palestinians from the West Bank and Gaza. . . . A withdrawal of Israeli armed forces will take place and there will be a redeployment of the remaining Israeli forces into specified security locations.

The agreement will also include arrangements for assuring internal and external security and public order. A strong local police force will be established, which may include Jordanian citizens. In addition, Israeli and Jordanian forces will participate in joint patrols and in the manning of control posts to assure the security of the borders.

(c) When the self-governing authority (administrative council) in the West Bank and Gaza is established and inaugurated, the transitional period of five years will begin. As soon as possible, but not later than the third year after the beginning of the transitional period, negotiations will take place to determine the final status of the West Bank and Gaza and its relationship with its neighbors and to conclude a peace treaty between Israel and Jordan by the end of the transitional period. . . . The negotiations shall be based on all the provisions and principles of UN Security Council Resolution 242. The negotiations will resolve, among other matters, the location of the boundaries and the nature of the security arrangements. The solution from the negotiations must also recognize the legitimate right of the Palestinian peoples and their just requirements. In this way, the Palestinians will participate in the determination of their own future through:

(i) The negotiations among Egypt, Israel, Jordan, and the representatives of the inhabitants of the West Bank and Gaza to agree on the final status of the West Bank and Gaza and other outstanding issues by the end of the transitional period.

(ii) Submitting their agreements to a vote by the elected representatives of the inhabitants of the West Bank and Gaza.

(iii) Providing for the elected representatives of the inhabitants of the West Bank and Gaza to decide how they shall govern themselves consistent with the provisions of their agreement.

(iv) Participating as stated above in the work of the committee negotiating the peace treaty between Israel and Jordan.

(d) All necessary measures will be taken and provisions made to assure the security of Israel and its neighbors during the transitional period and beyond. To assist in providing such security, a strong local police force will be constituted by the self-governing authority. . . .

(e) During the transitional period, representatives of Egypt, Israel, Jordan, and the self-governing authority will constitute a continuing committee to decide by agreement on the modalities of admission of persons displaced from the West Bank and Gaza in 1967, together with necessary measures to prevent disruption and disorder. Other matters of common concern may also be dealt with by this committee.

(f) Egypt and Israel will work with each other and with other interested parties to establish agreed procedures for a prompt, just, and permanent implementation of the resolution of the refugee problem.

B. Egypt-Israel

1. Egypt-Israel undertake not to resort to the threat or the use of force to settle disputes. Any disputes shall be settled by peaceful means in accordance with the provisions of Article 33 of the U.N. Charter.

2. In order to achieve peace between them, the parties agree to negotiate in good faith with a goal of concluding within three months from the signing of the Framework a peace treaty between them while inviting the other parties to the conflict to proceed simultaneously to negotiate and conclude similar peace treaties with a view the achieving a comprehensive peace in the area. The Framework for the Conclusion of a Peace Treaty between Egypt and Israel will govern the peace negotiations between them. The parties will agree on the modalities and the timetable for the implementation of their obligations under the treaty.

C. Associated Principles

1. Egypt and Israel state that the principles and provisions described below should apply to peace treaties between Israel and each of its neighbors – Egypt, Jordan, Syria, and Lebanon.

2. Signatories shall establish among themselves relationships normal to states at peace with one another. To this end, they should undertake to abide by all the provisions of the U.N. Charter. Steps to be taken in this respect include:

   (a) full recognition;
   (b) abolishing economic boycotts;
   (c) guaranteeing that under their jurisdiction the citizens of the other parties shall enjoy the protection of the due process of law.

3. Signatories should explore possibilities for economic development in the context of final peace treaties, with the objective of contributing to the atmosphere of peace, cooperation, and friendship which is their common goal.

4. Claims commissions may be established for the mutual settlement of all financial claims.

5. The United States shall be invited to participate in the talks on matters related to the modalities of the implementation of the agreements

and working out the timetable for the carrying out of the obligations of the parties.

6.   The United Nations Security Council shall be requested to endorse the peace treaties and ensure that their provisions shall not be violated. The permanent members of the Security Council shall be requested to underwrite the peace treaties and ensure respect or the provisions. They shall be requested to conform their policies and actions with the undertaking contained in this Framework.

For the Government of Israel:
Menachem Begin

For the Government of
the Arab Republic of Egypt:
Muhammed Anwar al-Sadat

Witnessed by
Jimmy Carter,
President of the United States of America

51 The Camp David Accords (September 17, 1978)

The Framework for the Conclusion of a Peace Treaty Between Egypt and Israel

In order to achieve peace between them, Israel and Egypt agree to negotiate in good faith with a goal of concluding within three months of the signing of this framework a peace treaty between them:

It is agreed that:

- The site of the negotiations will be under a United Nations flag at a location or locations to be mutually agreed.
- All of the principles of U.N. Resolution 242 will apply in this resolution of the dispute between Israel and Egypt.
- Unless otherwise mutually agreed, terms of the peace treaty will be implemented between two and three years after the peace treaty is signed.

The following matters are agreed between the parties:

1. the full exercise of Egyptian sovereignty up to the internationally recognized border between Egypt and mandated Palestine;
2. the withdrawal of Israeli armed forces from the Sinai;
3. the use of airfields left by the Israelis . . . for civilian purposes only, including possible commercial use only by all nations;
4. the right of free passage by ships of Israel through the Gulf of Suez and the Suez Canal on the basis of the Constantinople Convention of 1888 applying to all nations; the Strait of Tiran and Gulf of Aqaba are international waterways to be open to all nations for unimpeded and nonsuspendable freedom of navigation and overflight;
5. the construction of a highway between the Sinai and Jordan near Eilat with guaranteed free and peaceful passage by Egypt and Jordan; and
6. the stationing of military forces listed below.

DOI: 10.4324/9781003348948-55

Stationing of Forces

No more than one division (mechanized or infantry) of Egyptian armed forces will be stationed within an area lying approximately 50 km. (30 miles) east of the Gulf of Suez and the Suez Canal.

. . .

Early warning stations may exist to insure compliance with the terms of the agreement.

After a peace treaty is signed, and after the interim withdrawal is complete, normal relations will be established between Egypt and Israel, including full recognition, including diplomatic, economic, and cultural relations; termination of economic boycotts and barriers to the free movement of goods and people; and mutual protection of citizens by the due process of law.

Interim Withdrawal

Between three months and nine months after the signing of the peace treaty, all Israeli forces will withdraw east of a line extending from a point east of El-Arish to Ras Muhammad, the exact location of this line to be determined by mutual agreement.

For the Government of
the Arab Republic of Egypt:
Muhammed Anwar al-Sadat

For the Government of Israel:
Menachem Begin

Witnessed by:
Jimmy Carter

Part IV

From Israeli-Egyptian Peace (1979) to Israeli-Jordanian Peace (1994)

52 Peace Treaty Between Israel and Egypt (March 26, 1979)

Text:

The Government of the Arab Republic of Egypt and the Government of the State of Israel;

Preamble

Convinced of the urgent necessity of the establishment of a just, comprehensive, and lasting peace in the Middle East in accordance with Security Council Resolutions 242 and 338;

Reaffirming their adherence to the "Framework for Peace in the Middle East Agreed at Camp David," dated September 17, 1978;

Noting that the aforementioned Framework as appropriate is intended to constitute a basis for peace not only between Egypt and Israel but also between Israel and each of its other Arab neighbors which is prepared to negotiate peace with it on this basis;

Desiring to bring to an end the state of war between them and to establish a peace in which every state in the area can live in security;

Convinced that the conclusion of a Treaty of Peace between Egypt and Israel is an important step in the search for comprehensive peace in the area and for the attainment of settlement of the Arab-Israeli conflict in all its aspects;

Inviting the other Arab parties to this dispute to join the peace process with Israel guided by and based on the principles of the aforementioned Framework;

. . .

Agree to the following provisions in the free exercise of their sovereignty, in order to implement the "Framework for the Conclusion of a Peace Treaty Between Egypt and Israel";

DOI: 10.4324/9781003348948-57

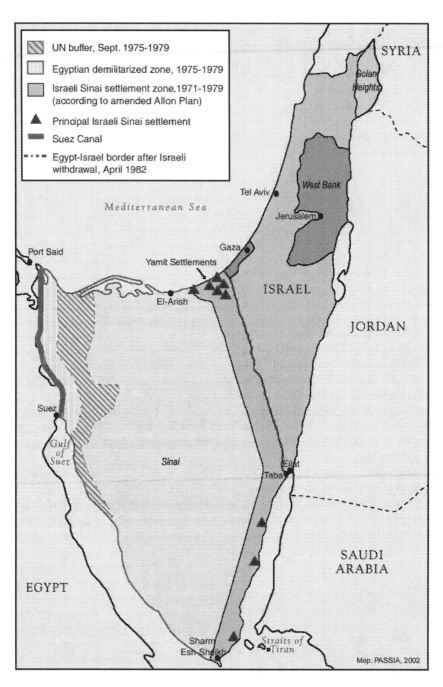

Map 11 Borders at the Time of the Israel-Egypt Peace Treaty, 1979

Source: Permission granted by the Palestinian Academic Society for the Study of International Affairs to reprint their map of the 1979 Israel-Egypt Peace Treaty in this book. The original can be found at: www.passia.org/maps/view/25.

Article I

1. The state of war between the Parties will be terminated and peace will be established between them upon the exchange of instruments of ratification of this Treaty.
2. Israel will withdraw all its armed forces and civilians from the Sinai behind the international boundary between Egypt and mandated Palestine, as provided in the annexed protocol . . . , and Egypt will resume the exercise of its full sovereignty over the Sinai.
3. Upon completion of the interim withdrawal . . . the parties will establish normal and friendly relations . . .

Article II

The permanent boundary between Egypt and Israel is the recognized international boundary between Egypt and the former mandated territory of Palestine, . . . without prejudice to the issue of the status of the Gaza Strip. The Parties recognize this boundary as inviolable. Each will respect the territorial integrity of the other, including their territorial waters and airspace.

Article III

1. The Parties will apply between them the provisions of the Charter of the United Nations and the principles of international law governing relations among states in times of peace. In particular:

    (a) They recognize and will respect each other's sovereignty, territorial integrity, and political independence;
    (b) They recognize and will respect each other's right to live in peace within their secure and recognized boundaries;
    (c) They will refrain from the threat or use of force, directly or indirectly, against each other and will settle all disputes between them by peaceful means.

2. Each Party undertakes to ensure that acts or threats of belligerency, hostility, or violence do not originate from and are not committed from within its territory, or by any forces subject to its control . . . , against the population, citizens, or property of the other Party. Each Party also undertakes to refrain from organizing, instigating, inciting, assisting, or participating in acts or threats of belligerency, hostility, subversion, or violence against the other Party, anywhere, and undertakes to ensure that perpetrators of such acts are brought to justice.
3. The Parties agree that the normal relationship established between them will include full recognition, diplomatic, economic and cultural relations, termination of economic boycotts and discriminatory barriers to the free movement of people and goods, and will guarantee the mutual enjoyment by citizens of the due process of law . . .

Article IV [Stationing of security arrangements] . . .
Article V [Israeli shipping through the Strait of Tiran and Gulf of Aqaba] . . .
Article VI [Obligations under this agreement] . . .
Article VII [Dispute resolution] . . .
Article VIII [Claims Commission] . . .
Article IX [Treaty effectiveness] . . .

Annex I: Protocol Concerning Israeli Withdrawal and Security Agreements

ARTICLE I: CONCEPT OF WITHDRAWAL

1. Israel will complete withdrawal of all its armed forces and civilians from the Sinai not later than three years from the date of exchange of instruments of ratification of this Treaty.
2. . . .
3. The withdrawal from the Sinai will be accomplished in two phases:

    (a) The interim withdrawal behind the line from east of El-Arish to Ras Mohammed . . . within nine months from the date of exchange of instruments of ratification of this Treaty.
    (b) The final withdrawal from the Sinai behind the international boundary not later than three years from the date of exchange of instruments of ratification of this Treaty.

4. A Joint Commission will be formed immediately after the exchange of instruments of ratification of this Treaty in order to supervise and coordinate movements and schedules during the withdrawal, and to adjust plans and timetables as necessary within the limits established by paragraph 3, above . . .

ARTICLE II: DETERMINATION OF FINAL LINES AND ZONES . . .

ARTICLE III: AERIAL MILITARY REGIME

1. Flights of combat aircraft and reconnaissance flights of Egypt and Israel shall take place only over [specific negotiated areas], respectively.
2. Only unarmed, non-combat aircraft of Egypt and Israel will be stationed in Zones A and D, respectively.
3. Only Egyptian unarmed transport aircraft will take off and land in Zone B and up to eight such aircraft may be maintained in Zone B. The Egyptian border unit . . . may be equipped with unarmed helicopters to perform their functions in Zone B.
4. The Egyptian civil police may be equipped with unarmed police helicopters to perform normal police functions in Zone C.

5. Only civilian airfields maybe built in the Zones.
6. Without prejudice to the provisions of this Treaty, only those military aerial activities specifically permitted by this Annex shall be allowed in the Zones and the airspace above their territorial waters.

ARTICLE IV: NAVAL REGIME

1. Egypt and Israel may base and operate naval vessels along the coasts of Zones A and D, respectively.
2. Egyptian coast guard boats, lightly armed, may be stationed and operate in the territorial waters of Zone B to assist the border units in performing their functions in this Zone.
3. Egyptian civil police equipped with light boats, lightly armed, shall perform normal police functions within the territorial waters of Zone C.
4. Nothing in this Annex shall be considered as derogating from the right of innocent passage of the naval vessels of either party.
5. Only civilian maritime ports and installations may be built in the Zones.
6. Without prejudice to the provisions of this Treaty, only those naval activities specifically permitted by this Annex shall be allowed in the Zones and in their territorial waters.

ARTICLE V: EARLY WARNING SYSTEMS

Egypt and Israel may establish and operate early warning systems only in Zones A and D respectively.

ARTICLE VI: UNITED NATIONS OPERATIONS . . .

ARTICLE VII: LIAISON SYSTEM

1. Upon dissolution of the Joint Commission, a liaison system between the Parties will be established. This liaison system is intended to provide an effective method to assess progress in the implementation of obligations under the present Annex and to resolve any problem that may arise in the course of implementation . . .

ARTICLE VIII: RESPECT FOR WAR MEMORIALS

Each Party undertakes to preserve in good condition the War Memorials erected in the memory of soldiers of the other Party, namely those erected by Egypt in Israel, and shall permit access to such monuments.

ARTICLE IX: INTERIM ARRANGEMENTS . . .

Appendix to Annex I: Organization of Movements in the Sinai . . .

Article I: Principles of Withdrawal . . .
Article II: Subphases of the Withdrawal to the Interim Withdrawal Line . . .
Article III: United Nations Forces . . .
Article IV: Joint Commission and Liaison . . .
Article V: Definition of the Interim Buffer Zone and Its Activities . . .
Article VI: Disposition of Installations and Military Barriers . . .
Article VII: Surveillance Activities . . .
Article VIII: Exercise of Egyptian Sovereignty

Egypt will resume the exercise of its full sovereignty over evacuated parts of the Sinai upon Israeli withdrawal as provided for in Article I of this Treaty.

Annex II: Map of Israel-Egypt International Boundary . . .
Annex III: Protocol Concerning Relations of the Parties

ARTICLE 1: DIPLOMATIC AND CONSULAR RELATIONS

The Parties agree to establish diplomatic and consular relations and to exchange ambassadors upon completion of the interim withdrawal.

ARTICLE 2: ECONOMIC AND TRADE RELATIONS

1.   The Parties agree to remove all discriminatory barriers to normal economic relations and to terminate economic boycotts of each other upon completion of the interim withdrawal.
2.   As soon as possible, and not later than six months after the completion of the interim withdrawal, the Parties will enter negotiations with a view to concluding an agreement on trade and commerce for the purpose of promoting beneficial economic relations.

ARTICLE 3: CULTURAL RELATIONS

1.   The Parties agree to establish normal cultural relations following completion of the interim withdrawal.
2.   They agree on the desirability of cultural exchanges in all fields, and shall, as soon as possible and not later than six months after completion of the interim withdrawal, enter into negotiations with a view to concluding a cultural agreement for this purpose.

ARTICLE 4: FREEDOM OF MOVEMENT

1. Upon completion of the interim withdrawal, each Party will permit the free movement of the nationals and vehicles of the other into and within its territory according to the general rules applicable to nationals and vehicles of other states. Neither Party will impose discriminatory restrictions on the free movement of persons and vehicles from its territory to the territory of the other.
2. Mutual unimpeded access to places of religious and historical significance will be provided on a non-discriminatory basis.

ARTICLE 5: COOPERATION FOR DEVELOPMENT AND GOOD NEIGHBORLY RELATIONS

1. The Parties recognize a mutuality of interest in good neighbourly relations and agree to consider means to promote such relations.
2. The Parties will cooperate in promoting peace, stability, and development in their region. Each agrees to consider proposals the other may wish to make to this end.
3. The Parties shall seek to foster mutual understanding and tolerance and will, accordingly, abstain from hostile propaganda against each other.

ARTICLE 6: TRANSPORTATION AND TELECOMMUNICATIONS . . .

ARTICLE 7: ENJOYMENT OF HUMAN RIGHTS

The Parties affirm their commitment to respect and observe human rights and fundamental freedoms for all, and they will promote these rights and freedoms in accordance with the United Nations Charter.

ARTICLE 8: TERRITORIAL SEAS

Without prejudice to the provisions of Article 5 of the Treaty of Peace, each Party recognizes the right of the vessels of the other Party to innocent passage through its territorial sea in accordance with the rules of international law.

. . .

Agreed Minutes

ARTICLE I

Egypt's resumption of the exercise of full sovereignty over the Sinai provided for in paragraph 2 of Article I shall occur with regard to each area upon Israel's withdrawal from the area.

ARTICLE IV

It is agreed between the parties that the review provided for in Article IV (4) will be undertaken when requested by either party, commencing within three months of such a request, but that any amendment can be made only by mutual agreement of both parties.

ARTICLE V

The second sentence of paragraph 2 of Article V shall not be construed as limiting the first sentence of that paragraph. The foregoing is not to be construed as contravening the second sentence of paragraph 2 of Article V, which reads as follows: "The Parties will respect each other's right to navigation and overflight for access to either country through the Strait of Tiran and the Gulf of Aqaba."

ARTICLE VI (2)

The provisions of Article VI shall not be construed in contradiction to the provisions of the framework for peace in the Middle East agreed at Camp David. The foregoing is not to be construed as contravening the provisions of Article VI (2) of the Treaty, which reads as follows: "The Parties undertake to fulfill in good faith their obligations under this Treaty, without regard to action of any other Party and independently of any instrument external to this Treaty."

ARTICLE VI (5)

It is agreed by the Parties that there is no assertion that this Treaty prevails over other Treaties or agreements or that other Treaties or agreements prevail over this Treaty. The foregoing is not to be construed as contravening the provisions of Article VI (5) of the Treaty, which reads as follows:

Subject to Article 103 of the United Nations Charter, in the event of a conflict between the obligations of the Parties under the present Treaty and any of their other obligations, the obligation under this Treaty will be binding and implemented.

ANNEX I

Article VI, Paragraph 8, of Annex I provides as follows:

"The Parties shall agree on the nations from which the United Nations forces and observers will be drawn. They will be drawn from nations other than those which are permanent members of the United Nations Security Council."

The Parties have agreed as follows:

"With respect to the provisions of paragraph 8, Article VI, of Annex 1, if no agreement is reached between the Parties, they will accept or support a U.S. proposal concerning the composition of the United Nations force and observers."

ANNEX III

The Treaty of Peace and Annex III thereto provide for establishing normal economic relations between the Parties. In accordance herewith, it is agreed that such relations will include normal commercial sales of oil by Egypt to Israel, and that Israel shall be fully entitled to make bids for Egyptian-origin oil not needed for Egyptian domestic oil consumption, and Egypt and its oil concessionaires will entertain bids made by Israel, on the same basis and terms as apply to other bidders for such oil.

For the Government of Israel
For the Government of the Arab Republic of Egypt

Witnessed by:
Jimmy Carter
President of the United States of America

53 Arab League Summit Conference Communique, Baghdad (March 31, 1979)

As the Government of the Arab Republic of Egypt has ignored the Arab summit conferences' resolutions, especially those of the sixth and seventh conferences held in Algiers and Rabat; as it has at the same time ignored the ninth Arab summit conference resolutions – especially the call made by the Arab kings, presidents and princes to avoid signing the peace treaty with the Zionist enemy – and signed the peace treaty on 26 March 1979;

It has thus deviated from the Arab ranks and has chosen, in collusion with the United States, to stand by the side of the Zionist enemy in one trench; has behaved unilaterally in the Arab-Zionist struggle affairs; has violated the Arab nations' rights; has exposed the nation's destiny, its struggle and aims to dangers and challenges; has relinquished its pan-Arab duty of liberating the occupied Arab territories, particularly Jerusalem, and of restoring the Palestinian Arab people's inalienable national rights, including their right to repatriation, self-determination and establishment of the independent Palestinian state on their national soil.

. . .

The Arab League Council, on the level of Arab foreign ministers, has decided the following:

1. A. To withdraw the ambassadors on the Arab states from Egypt immediately.
   B. To recommend the severance of political and diplomatic relations with the Egyptian Government. The Arab governments will adopt the necessary measures to apply this recommendation within a maximum period of one month from the date of issuance of this decision, in accordance with the constitutional measures in force in each country.
2. To consider the suspension of the Egyptian Government's membership in the Arab League as operative from the date of the Egyptian Government's signing of the peace treaty with the Zionist enemy. This means depriving it of all rights resulting from this membership.
3. To make the city of Tunis, capital of the Tunisian Republic, the temporary headquarters of the Arab League . . .

. . .

DOI: 10.4324/9781003348948-58

6. To continue to cooperate with the fraternal Egyptian people and with Egyptian individuals, with the exception of those who cooperate with the Zionist enemy directly or indirectly.
7. The member-states shall inform all foreign countries of their stand on the Egyptian-Israeli treaty and will ask these countries not to support this treaty as it constitutes an aggression against the rights of the Palestinian people and the Arab nation as well as a threat to world peace and security.
8. To condemn the policy that the United States is practising regarding its role in concluding the Camp David agreements and the Egyptian-Israeli treaty.

. . .

54 Basic Law

Jerusalem, Capital of Israel
(July 30, 1980)

1. Jerusalem, complete and united, is the capital of Israel.
2. Jerusalem is the seat of the President of the State, the Knesset, the Government, and the Supreme Court.
3. The Holy Places shall be protected from desecration and any other violation and from anything likely to violate the freedom of access of the members of the different religions to the places sacred to them or their feelings towards those places.
4. (a) The Government shall provide for the development and prosperity of Jerusalem and the well-being of its inhabitants by allocating special funds, including a special annual grant to the Municipality of Jerusalem (Capital City Grant) with the approval of the Finance Committee of the Knesset.
   (b) Jerusalem shall be given special priority in the activities of the authorities of the State so as to further its development in economic and other matters.
   (c) The Government shall set up a special body or special bodies for the implementation of this section.

MENAHEM BEGIN
Prime Minister

YITZCHAK NAVON
President of the State

Passed by the Knesset on the 17th Av, 5740 (July 30, 1980) and published in Sefer Ha-Chukkim No. 980 of the 23rd Av, 5740 (August 5, 1980), p. 186; the Bill and an Explanatory Note were published in Hatza'ot Chok No. 1464 of 5740, p. 287.

DOI: 10.4324/9781003348948-59

55 Saudi Crown Prince Fahd ibn Abd al-Aziz

The Fahd Plan (August 7, 1981)

The Fahd Plan consists of eight points, calling for:

1. Israeli withdrawal from all Arab territories taken in the Six Day War, including Arab (East) Jerusalem.
2. The dismantling of Israeli settlements in the territories captured in 1967.
3. The assurance of the freedom of worship for all religions in the holy sites.
4. The emphasis of the rights of the Palestinian nation, including compensation for those who do not wish to return.
5. A brief transition period for Gaza and the West Bank under the auspices of the United Nations.
6. The establishment of an independent Palestinian state with Jerusalem as its capital.
7. The right for all nations in the area to live in peace.
8. The UN or some of its members to guarantee the implementation of the above-mentioned principles.

DOI: 10.4324/9781003348948-60

56 The Golan Heights Law (December 14, 1981)

Text:

1. The Law, jurisdiction, and administration of the state shall apply to the Golan Heights, as described in the Appendix.
2. This Law shall become valid on the day of its passage in the Knesset.
3. The Minister of the Interior shall be charged with the implementation of this Law, and he is entitled, in consultation with the Minister of Justice, to enact regulations for its implementation and to formulate in regulations transitional provisions concerning the continued application of regulations, orders, administrative orders, rights, and duties which were in force on the Golan Heights prior to the application of this Law.

DOI: 10.4324/9781003348948-61

Map 12 Borders at the Time of the Golan Heights Law, 1981

Source: Published by the Government of Israel, Ministry of Foreign Affairs. The original maps can be found at: https://embassies.gov.il/MFA/AboutIsrael/Maps/Pages/Golan%20Heights.aspx.

57 Prime Minister Menachem Begin

The Wars of No Alternative and Operation Peace for the Galilee (August 8, 1982)

... A classic war of no alternative was the Second World War waged by the Allies. On August 23, 1939, Great Britain stood helpless. Although she still had an empire embracing an area of 40 million square kilometres, on which the sun never set, her prestige had sunk deep in the seven seas over which it still ruled, though no longer exclusively.

Britain and France disavowed the assurance given to Czechoslovakia and together forced that small and courageous nation to bend its knee before Hitler . . .

On August 23, 1939, the German Ribbentrop and the Soviet Molotov signed a treaty. Behind them stood the blood tyrant named Joseph Vissarionovich Stalin . . .

And so war broke out on September 1, 1939, when the Nazi German army crossed the Polish-German border.

Poland fought because she had no alternative. Within three days the Polish army was crushed and the Polish state ceased to exist.

In those days the Bolshevik propagandists told everyone who would listen that there was a supreme genius sitting in the Kremlin, but in international relations, he understood nothing. . . . On June 22, 1941, the German army attacked the Soviet army . . .

This was, then, a war of no alternative for Poland, a war without option for France, and a war without choice for Russia.

. . .

This is the terrible consequence of a war of no alternative. All mankind was placed on the edge of the abyss, when Nazi Germany was not far from total victory. In 1944, Germany was close to developing the atom bomb.

Was it possible to prevent the Second World War?

Today, thanks to research and the facts known to us, there is no longer any doubt about the answer: Yes, indeed, it was possible to prevent it.

On March 7, 1936, Hitler announced that he was abrogating the Treaty of Versailles. In order to implement his decision, he introduced two battalions of the German army into the demilitarized Rhineland. At that time, two French divisions would have sufficed to capture all the German soldiers who entered the Rhineland. As a result of that, Hitler would have fallen.

DOI: 10.4324/9781003348948-62

His prestige would have crumbled. At that time, he did not yet have an army worthy of the name, only gangs of SS, SA, and Gestapo. Two French divisions, with their tanks and with the air force at their disposal, would have blasted this entire German armed force to the four winds.

If this had happened, the Second World War would have been prevented, more than 30 million people would have remained alive, tens of millions of others would not have been wounded, and the tragedy of Hiroshima would have been averted. . . . The six million Jews slaughtered then would today be more than 12 million, and the whole of Eretz Yisrael would be in our hands.

The Second World War, which broke out on September 1, 1939, actually began on March 7, 1936. If only France, without Britain . . . had attacked the aggressor, there would have remained no trace of Nazi German power, and war which, in three years, changed the whole of human history, would have been prevented.

This, therefore, is the international example that explains what is a war without choice, or a war of one's choosing.

Let us turn from the international example to ourselves. Operation Peace for Galilee is not a military operation resulting from the lack of an alternative. The terrorists did not threaten the existence of the State of Israel; they "only" threatened the lives of Israel's citizens and members of the Jewish people. There are those who find fault with the second part of that sentence. If there was no danger to the existence of the state, why did you go to war?

I will explain why. We had three wars which we fought without alternative. The first was the War of Independence, which began on November 30, 1947, and lasted until January 1949. . . . This was a war without alternative, after the Arab armies invaded Eretz Israel. If not for our ability, none of us would have remained alive.

What happened in that war, which we went off to fight with no alternative?

Six thousand of our fighters were killed. We were then 650,000 Jews in Eretz Israel, and the number of fallen amounted to about 1% of the Jewish population. In proportion to our population today, about 1% would mean 30,000 killed and about 90,000 wounded. Could we live with such losses? Let us imagine 30,000 soldiers killed, the best of our youth, those who say, "Follow me!"

We carried on our lives then by a miracle, with a clear recognition of life's imperative: to win, to establish a state, a government, a parliament, a democracy, an army – a force to defend Israel and the entire Jewish people.

The second war of no alternative was the Yom Kippur War and the War of Attrition that preceded it. What was the situation on that Yom Kippur day . . . ? We had 177 tanks deployed on the Golan Heights against 1,400 Soviet Syrian tanks; and fewer than 500 of our soldiers manned positions along the Suez Canal against five divisions sent to the front by the Egyptians.

Is it any wonder that the first days of that war were hard to bear? I remember Aluf Avraham Yaffe came to us, to the Knesset Foreign Affairs and Defence

Committee, and said: "Oy, it's so hard! Our boys, 18- and 19-year-olds, are falling like flies and are defending our nation with their very bodies."

In the Golan Heights there was a moment when the O/C Northern Command – today our chief of staff – heard his deputy say, "This is it." What that meant was "We've lost; we have to come down off the Golan Heights." And the then OIC said, "Give me another five minutes."

Sometimes five minutes can decide a nation's fate. During those five minutes, several dozen tanks arrived, which changed the entire situation on the Golan Heights.

If this had not happened, if the Syrian enemy had come down from the heights to the valley, he would have reached Haifa – for there was not a single tank to obstruct his armoured column's route to Haifa. Yes, we would even have fought with knives – as one of our esteemed wives has said – with knives against tanks. Many more would have fallen, and in every settlement there would have been the kind of slaughter at which the Syrians are experts.

. . .

Our total casualties in that war of no alternative were 2,297 killed, 6,067 wounded. Together with the War of Attrition – which was also a war of no alternative – 2,659 killed, 7,251 wounded. The terrible total: almost 10,000 casualties.

Our other wars were not without an alternative. In November 1956 we had a choice. The reason for going to war then was the need to destroy the fedayeen, who did not represent a danger to the existence of the state.

However, the political leadership of the time thought it was necessary to do this. As one who served in the parliamentary opposition, I was summoned to David Ben-Gurion before the cabinet received information of the plan, and he found it necessary to give my colleagues and myself these details: We are going to meet the enemy before it absorbs the Soviet weapons which began to flow to it from Czechoslovakia in 1955.

. . .

In June 1967 we again had a choice. The Egyptian army concentrations in the Sinai approaches do not prove that Nasser was really about to attack us. We must be honest with ourselves. We decided to attack him.

This was a war of self-defence in the noblest sense of the term. The government of national unity then established decided unanimously: We will take the initiative and attack the enemy, drive him back, and thus assure the security of Israel and the future of the nation.

We did not do this for lack of an alternative. We could have gone on waiting. We could have sent the army home. Who knows if there would have been an attack against us? . . . There are several arguments to the contrary. While it is indeed true that the closing of the Straits of Tiran was an act of aggression, a *causus belli*, there is always room for a great deal of consideration as to whether it is necessary to make a *causus* into a *bellum*.

And so there were three wars with no alternative – the War of Independence, the War of Attrition, and the Yom Kippur War – and it is our misfortunate that our wars have been so. If in the two other wars, the wars of choice – the Sinai Campaign and the Six Day War – we had losses like those in the no alternative wars, we would have been left today with few of our best youth, without the strength to withstand the Arab world.

As for Operation Peace for Galilee, it does not really belong to the category of wars of no alternative. We could have gone on seeing our civilians injured in Metulla or Kiryat Shmona or Nahariya. We could have gone on counting those killed by explosive charges left in a Jerusalem supermarket or a Petah Tikva bus stop.

All the orders to carry out these acts of murder and sabotage came from Beirut. Should we have reconciled ourselves to the ceaseless killing of civilians, even after the agreement ending hostilities reached last summer, which the terrorists interpreted as an agreement permitting them to strike at us from every side, besides southern Lebanon? They tried to infiltrate gangs of murderers via Syria and Jordan, and by a miracle we captured them. We might also not have captured them. There was a gang of four terrorists which infiltrated from Jordan, whose members admitted they had been about to commandeer a bus (and we remember the bus on the coastal road).

. . .

There are slanderers who say that a full year of quiet has passed between us and the terrorists. Nonsense. There was not even one month of quiet. The newspapers and communications media, including *The New York Times* and *The Washington Post*, did not publish even one line about our capturing the gang of murderers that crossed the Jordan in order to commandeer a bus and murder its passengers.

True, such actions were not a threat to the existence of the state. But they did threaten the lives of civilians, whose number we cannot estimate, day after day, week after week, month after month.

During the past nine weeks, we have in effect destroyed the combat potential of 20,000 terrorists. We hold 9,000 in a prison camp. Between 2,000 and 3,000 were killed and between 7,000 and 9,000 have been captured and cut off in Beirut. . . . They will leave soon. We made a second condition: After the exit of most of the terrorists, an integrated multi-national force will enter. But if the minority refuse to leave, you – the U.S., Italy, and France – must promise us in writing that you, together with the Lebanese army, will force them, the terrorists, to leave Beirut and Lebanon. They have the possibility of forcing 2,000–2,500 terrorists who will remain after the majority leaves.

And one more condition: If you aren't willing to force them, then, please, leave Beirut and Lebanon, and the I.D.F. will solve the problem.

This is what I wrote the Secretary of State today, and I want you and all the citizens of Israel and the U.S. to know it.

The problem will be solved. We can already now look beyond the fighting. It will end, as we hope, shortly. And then, as I believe, recognize, and logically assume, we will have a protracted period of peace. There is no other country around us that is capable of attacking us.

We have destroyed the best tanks and planes the Syrians had. We have destroyed 24 of their ground-to-air missile batteries. After everything that happened, Syria did not go to war against us, not in Lebanon and not in the Golan Heights.

Jordan cannot attack us. We have learned that Jordan is sending telegrams to the Americans, warning that Israel is about to invade across the Jordan and capture Amman.

For our part, we will not initiate any attack against any Arab country. We have proved that we do not want wars. We made many painful sacrifices for a peace treaty with Egypt. That treaty stood the test of the fighting in Lebanon; in other words, it stood the test.

The demilitarized zone of 150 kilometres in Sinai exists and no Egyptian soldier has been placed there. From the experience of the 1930s, I have to say that if ever the other side violated the agreement about the demilitarized zone, Israel would be obliged to introduce, without delay, a force stronger than that violating the international commitment; not in order to wage war, but to achieve one of two results: restoration of the previous situation, i.e., resumed demilitarization, and the removal of both armies from the demilitarized zone; or attainment of strategic depth, in case the other side has taken the first step towards a war of aggression, as happened in Europe only three years after the abrogation of the demilitarized zone in the Rhineland.

Because the other Arab countries are completely incapable of attacking the State of Israel, there is reason to expect that we are facing a historic period of peace. It is obviously impossible to set a date.

It may well be that "The land shall be still for 40 years." Perhaps less, perhaps more. But from the facts before us, it is clear that, with the end of the fighting in Lebanon, we have ahead of us many years of establishing peace treaties and peaceful relations with the various Arab countries.

The conclusion – both on the basis of the relations between states and on the basis of our national experience – is that there is no divine mandate to go to war only if there is no alternative. There is no moral imperative that a nation must, or is entitled to, fight only when its back is to the sea, or to the abyss. Such a war may avert tragedy, if not a Holocaust, for any nation; but it causes it terrible loss of life.

Quite the opposite. A free, sovereign nation, which hates war and loves peace, and which is concerned about its security, must create the conditions under which war, if there is a need for it, will not be for lack of alternative. The conditions much be such – and their creation depends upon man's reason and his actions – that the price of victory will be few casualties, not many.

58 The Reagan Plan

U.S. Policy for Peace in the Middle East (September 1, 1982)

My fellow Americans:

Today has been a day that should make us proud. It marked the end of the successful evacuation of PLO from Beirut, Lebanon. This peaceful step could never have been taken without the good offices of the United States and especially the truly heroic work of a great American diplomat, Ambassador Philip Habib.

. . .

But the situation in Lebanon is only part of the overall problem of conflict in the Middle East. So, over the past 2 weeks, while events in Beirut dominated the front page, America was engaged in a quiet, behind-the-scenes effort to lay the groundwork for a broader peace in the region. . . .

It seemed to me that with the agreement in Lebanon we had an opportunity for a more far-reaching peace effort in the region, and I was determined to seize that moment. In the words of the scripture, the time had come to "follow after the things which make for peace." Tonight I want to report to you the steps we've taken and the prospects they can open up for a just and lasting peace in the Middle East.

. . .

When our administration assumed office in January of 1981, I decided that the general framework for our Middle East policy should follow the broad guidelines laid down by my predecessors. There were two basic issues we had to address. First, there was the strategic threat to the region posed by the Soviet Union and its surrogates, best demonstrated by the brutal war in Afghanistan, and, second, the peace process between Israel and its Arab neighbors.

With regard to the Soviet threat, we have strengthened our efforts to develop with our friends and allies a joint policy to deter the Soviets and their surrogates from further expansion in the region and, if necessary, to defend against it.

With respect to the Arab-Israeli conflict, we've embraced the Camp David framework as the only way to proceed. We have also recognized, however, solving the Arab-Israeli conflict in and of itself cannot assure peace throughout a region as vast and troubled as the Middle East.

DOI: 10.4324/9781003348948-63

Our first objective under the Camp David process was to ensure the successful fulfilment of the Egyptian-Israeli peace treaty. . . . Throughout this period of difficult and time-consuming negotiations, we never lost sight of the next step of Camp David – autonomy talks to pave the way for permitting the Palestinian people to exercise their legitimate rights. However, owing to the tragic assassination of President Sadat and other crises in the area, it was not until January 1982 that we were able to make a major effort to renew these talks.

. . . The successful completion of Israel's withdrawal from Sinai and the courage shown on this occasion by Prime Minister Begin and President Mubarak in living up to their agreements convinced me the time had come for a new American policy to try to bridge the remaining differences between Egypt and Israel on the autonomy process. So, in May I called for specific measures and a timetable for consultations with the Governments of Egypt and Israel on the next steps in the peace process. However, before this effort could be launched, the conflict in Lebanon preempted our efforts.

The autonomy talks were basically put on hold while we sought to untangle the parties in Lebanon and still the guns of war. The Lebanon war, tragic as it was, has left us with a new opportunity for Middle East peace. We must seize it now and bring peace to this troubled area so vital to world stability while there is still time . . .

The evacuation of the PLO from Beirut is now complete, and we can now help the Lebanese to rebuild their war-torn country. . . . As we help Lebanon rebuild, we must also move to resolve the root causes of conflict between Arabs and Israelis.

The war in Lebanon has demonstrated many things, but two consequences are key to the peace process. First, the military losses of the PLO have not diminished the yearning of the Palestinian people for a just solution of their claims; and, second, while Israel's military successes in Lebanon have demonstrated that its armed forces are second to none in the region, they alone cannot bring just and lasting peace to Israel and her neighbors.

The question now is how to reconcile Israel's legitimate security concerns with the legitimate rights of the Palestinians. And that answer can only come at the negotiating table. Each party must recognize that the outcome must be acceptable to all and that true peace will require compromises by all.

. . .

I call on Israel to make clear that the security for which she yearns can only be achieved through genuine peace, a peace requiring magnanimity, vision, and courage.

I call on the Palestinian people to recognize that their own political aspirations are inextricably bound to recognition of Israel's right to a secure future.

And I call on the Arab States to accept the reality of Israel – and the reality that peace and justice are to be gained only through hard, fair, direct negotiation.

. . .

The time has come for a new realism on the part of all the peoples of the Middle East. The State of Israel is an accomplished fact; it deserves unchallenged legitimacy within the community of nations. But Israel's legitimacy has thus far been recognized by too few countries and has been denied by every Arab State except Egypt. Israel exists; it has a right to exist in peace behind secure and defensible borders; and it has a right to demand of its neighbors that they recognize those facts.

I have personally followed and supported Israel's heroic struggle for survival, ever since the founding of the State of Israel 34 years ago. In the pre-1967 borders Israel was barely 10 miles wide at its narrowest point. The bulk of Israel's population lived within artillery range of hostile Arab armies. I am not about to ask Israel to live that way again.

The war in Lebanon has demonstrated another reality in the region. The departure of the Palestinians from Beirut dramatizes more than ever the homelessness of the Palestinian people. Palestinians feel strongly that their cause is more than a question of refugees. I agree. The Camp David agreement recognized that fact when it spoke of the legitimate rights of the Palestinian people and their just requirements.

. . .

These, then, are our general goals. What are the specific new American positions, and why are we taking them? In the Camp David talks thus far, both Israel and Egypt have felt free to express openly their views as to what the outcome should be. Understandably their views have differed on many points. . . . But it's become evident to me that some clearer sense of America's position on the key issues is necessary to encourage wider support for the peace process.

First, as outlined in the Camp David accords, there must be a period of time during which the Palestinian inhabitants of the West Bank and Gaza will have full autonomy over their own affairs. Due consideration must be given to the principle of self-government by the inhabitants of the territories and to the legitimate security concerns of the parties involved. The purpose of the 5-year period of transition which would begin after free elections for a self-governing Palestinian authority is to prove to the Palestinians that they can run their own affairs and that such Palestinian autonomy poses no threat to Israel's security.

The United States will not support the use of any additional land for the purpose of settlements during the transitional period. Indeed, the immediate adoption of a settlement freeze by Israel, more than any other action, could create the confidence needed for wider participation in these talks. . . .

I want to make the American position well understood. The purpose of this transitional period is the peaceful and orderly transfer of authority from Israel to the Palestinian inhabitants of the West Bank and Gaza. At the same time, such a transfer must not interfere with Israel's security requirements.

Beyond the transition period, as we look to the future of the West Bank and Gaza, it is clear to me that peace cannot be achieved by the formation of an independent Palestinian state in those territories, nor is it achievable on the basis of Israeli sovereignty or permanent control over the West Bank and Gaza. So, the United States will not support the establishment of an independent Palestinian state in the West Bank and Gaza, and we will not support annexation or permanent control by Israel.

There is, however, another way to peace. The final status of these lands must, of course, be reached through the give and take of negotiations. But it is the firm view of the United States that self-government by the Palestinians of the West Bank and Gaza in association with Jordan offers the best chance for a durable, just, and lasting peace. . . .

This exchange is enshrined in United Nations Security Council Resolution 242, which is, in turn, incorporated in all its parts in the Camp David agreements. U.N. Resolution 242 remains wholly valid as the foundation stone of America's Middle East peace effort. It is the United States position that, in return for peace, the withdrawal provision of Resolution 242 applies to all fronts, including the West Bank and Gaza. When the border is negotiated between Jordan and Israel, our view on the extent to which Israel should be asked to give up territory will be heavily affected by the extent of true peace and normalization, and the security arrangements offered in return.

Finally, we remain convinced that Jerusalem must remain undivided, but its final status should be decided through negotiation.

. . .

During the past few days, our Ambassadors in Israel, Egypt, Jordan, and Saudi Arabia have presented to their host governments the proposals, in full detail, that I have outlined here today. Now I'm convinced that these proposals can bring justice, bring security, and bring durability to an Arab-Israeli peace. The United States will stand by these principles with total dedication. They are fully consistent with Israel's security requirements and the aspirations of the Palestinians.

. . .

It has often been said – and, regrettably, too often been true – that the story of the search for peace and justice in the Middle East is a tragedy of opportunities missed. In the aftermath of the settlement in Lebanon, we now face an opportunity for a broader peace. This time we must not let it slip from our grasp. . . . For if we miss this chance to make a fresh start, we may look back on this moment from some later vantage point and realize how much that failure cost us all.

These, then, are the principles upon which American policy toward the Arab-Israeli conflict will be based. I have made a personal commitment to see that they endure and, God willing, that they will come to be seen by all reasonable, compassionate people as fair, achievable, and in the interests of all who wish to see peace in the Middle East.

Tonight, on the eve of what can be a dawning of new hope for the people of the troubled Middle East – and for all the world's people who dream of a just and peaceful future – I ask you, my fellow Americans, for your support and your prayers in this great undertaking.

Thank you, and God bless you.

59 Report of the [Kahan] Commission of Inquiry Into the Events at the Refugee Camps in Beirut (February 8, 1983)

Introduction

At a meeting of the Cabinet on 28 September 1982, the Government of Israel resolved to establish a commission of inquiry in accordance with the Commissions of Inquiry Law of 1968. The Cabinet charged the commission as follows:

"The matter which will be subjected to inquiry is: all the facts and factors connected with the atrocity carried out by a unit of the Lebanese Forces against the civilian population in the Shatilla and Sabra camps."

In the wake of this resolution, the President of the Supreme Court, by virtue of the authority vested in him under Section 4 of the aforementioned law, appointed a commission of inquiry comprised as follows:

Yitzhak Kahan, President of the Supreme Court, commission chairman; Aharon Barak, Justice of the Supreme Court; Yona Efrat, Major General (Res.).

. . .

A Description of the Events

THE PERIOD BEFORE THE EVENTS IN BEIRUT

. . .

The "Peace for the Galilee" war (henceforth the war) began on 6.6.82. On 12–14 June, I.D.F.[Israel Defence Forces] forces took over the suburbs of Beirut and linked up with the Christian forces who controlled East Beirut. On 25 June the encirclement of West Beirut was completed and I.D.F. forces were in control of the Beirut-Damascus road. . . .

In all the testimony we have heard, there has been unanimity regarding [the fact] that the battle ethics of the Phalangists, from the standpoint of their attitude to non-combatants, differ greatly from those of the I.D.F. It has already been noted above that in the course of the civil war in Lebanon, many massacres had been perpetrated by the various forces that had taken part in the fighting. . . . These reports reinforced the feeling among certain people – and

DOI: 10.4324/9781003348948-64

especially among experienced intelligence officers – that in the event that the Phalangists had an opportunity to massacre Palestinians, they would take advantage of it.

. . .

According to an inexact estimate, in mid-September 1982 there were about 56,000 people in the Sabra camp . . . but there is no assurance that this number reflects reality.

. . .

THE EVENTS FROM THE ENTRY OF THE PHALANGISTS INTO THE SABRA AND SHATILLA CAMPS UNTIL THEIR DEPARTURE

On Thursday, 16.9.82, at approximately 18:00 hours, members of the Phalangists entered the Shatilla camp from the west and south. . . .

At approximately 8:00 p.m., the Phalangists' liaison officer, G., said that the Phalangists who had entered the camps had sustained casualties, and the casualties were evacuated from the camps. . . .

An additional report relating to the actions of the Phalangists in the camps vis-à-vis the civilians there came from liaison officer G. of the Phalangists. When he entered the dining room in the forward command post building at approximately 8:00 p.m., that liaison officer told various people that about 300 persons had been killed by the Phalangists, among them also civilians. . . . Shortly thereafter, Phalangist officer G. returned to the dining room and amended his earlier report by reducing the number of casualties from 300 to 120.

. . .

With respect to the consequences of [Lebanese president] Bashir's assassination, the Chief of Staff said that in the situation which had been created, two things could happen. One was that the entire power structure of the Phalangists would collapse, though as yet this had not occurred. Regarding the second possibility, the Chief of Staff said as follows . . . :

> A second thing that will happen – and it makes no difference whether we are there or not – is an eruption of revenge which, I do not know, I can imagine how it will begin, but I do not know how it will end. it will be between all of them, and neither the Americans nor anyone else will be of any help. We can cut it down, but today they already killed Druze there. What difference does it make who or what? They have already killed them, and one dead Druze is enough so that tomorrow four Christian children will be killed; they will find them slaughtered, just like what happened a month ago; and that is how it will begin, if we are not there – it will be an eruption the likes of which has never been seen; I can already see in their eyes what they are waiting for.

. . .

The Departure of the Phalangists and the Reports of the Massacre

. . .

The furor that erupted in the wake of the massacre, and various accusations that were levelled, led those concerned to carry out debriefings and clarifications. A clarification of this kind was carried out on behalf of the General Staff . . . and in the office of the director of Military Intelligence. . . . A more detailed clarification was carried out in a Senior Command Meeting (SCM) with the participation of the Chief of Staff. . . . At that meeting, the Chief of Staff said, *inter alia*, that whereas prior to the I.D.F.'s entry into Lebanon atrocities had been perpetrated throughout that country, after the I.D.F.'s entry "the Phalangists did not commit any excesses officially and did nothing that could have indicated any danger from them," . . .

In his remarks the Chief of Staff also stressed the pressure from various elements for the Phalangists to take part in the combat operations. Major General Drori . . . said, *inter alia*, that he had originally wanted the I.D.F. or the Lebanese army to enter the camps, and that he did not concur in the considerations which had led to the decision regarding the entry of the Phalangists. . . . Brigadier General Yaron stressed that he had warned the Phalangists not to harm civilians, women, children, old people or anyone raising his hands . . . Brigadier General Yaron responded to the remarks of the participants by stating, *inter alia* . . . :

> The mistake, as I see it, the mistake is everyone's. The entire system showed insensitivity. I am speaking now of the military system. I am not speaking about the political system. The whole system manifested insensitivity . . .
>
> On this point everyone showed insensitivity, pure and simple. Nothing else. So you start asking me, what exactly did you feel in your gut on Friday . . . I did badly, I admit it. I did badly. I cannot, how is it possible that a divisional commander – and I think this applies to the Division Commander and up – how is it possible that a Division Commander is in the field and does not know that 300, 400, 500 or a thousand, I don't know how many, are being murdered here? If he's like that, let him go. How can such a thing be"? But why didn't he know? Why was he oblivious? That's why he didn't know and that's why he didn't stop it . . . but I take myself to task . . .
>
> I admit here, from this rostrum, we were all insensitive, that's all.

At the conclusion of his remarks, the Chief of Staff stressed that if the I.D.F. had provided the Phalangists with the tank and artillery support they had requested, far more people would have been killed (p. 121).

. . .

The Responsibility for the Massacre

In this section of the report, we shall deal with the issue of the responsibility for the massacre from two standpoints: first from the standpoint of direct responsibility − i.e., who actually perpetrated the massacre − and then we shall examine the problem of indirect responsibility, to the extent that this applies to Israel or those who acted on its behalf.

THE DIRECT RESPONSIBILITY

According to the above description of events, all the evidence indicates that the massacre was perpetrated by the Phalangists between the time they entered the camps on Thursday, 16.9.82, at 18:00 hours, and their departure from the camps on Saturday, 18.9.82, at approximately 8:00 a.m. The victims were found in those areas where the Phalangists were in military control during the aforementioned time period. . . . It can be stated with certainty that no organized military force entered the camps at the aforementioned time besides the Phalangist forces.

. . .

Here and there, hints, and even accusations, were thrown out to the effect that I.D.F. soldiers were in the camps at the time the massacre was perpetrated. We have no doubt that these notions are completely groundless and constitute a baseless libel. . . . Following the massacre, the Phalangist commanders denied, in various interviews in the media, that they had perpetrated the massacre. . . . That denial is patently incorrect.

Contentions and accusations were advanced that even if I.D.F. personnel had not shed the blood of the massacred, the entry of the Phalangists into the camps had been carried out with the prior knowledge that a massacre would be perpetrated there . . . ; and therefore all those who had enabled the entry of the Phalangists into the camps should be regarded as accomplices to the acts of slaughter and sharing in direct responsibility. These accusations too are unfounded. We have no doubt that no conspiracy or plot was entered into between anyone from the Israeli political echelon or from the military echelon in the I.D.F. and the Phalangists, with the aim of perpetrating atrocities in the camps. . . .

. . .

Our conclusion is therefore that the direct responsibility for the perpetration of the acts of slaughter rests on the Phalangist forces. No evidence was brought before us that Phalangist personnel received explicit orders from their command to perpetrate acts of slaughter, but it is evident that the forces who entered the area were steeped in hatred for the Palestinians, in the wake of the atrocities and severe injuries done to the Christians during the civil war in Lebanon by the Palestinians and those who fought alongside them; and these feelings of hatred were compounded by a longing for revenge in the wake of the assassination of the Phalangists' admired leader Bashir and the killing of several dozen Phalangists two days before their entry into the camps. The execution of acts of slaughter was approved for the Phalangists on the site by the remarks of the two commanders to whom questions were addressed over the radios, as was related above.

THE INDIRECT RESPONSIBILITY

. . .

We would like to note here that we will not enter at all into the question of indirect responsibility of other elements besides the State of Israel. . . . We do not view it as our function to discuss these issues, which perhaps should be clarified in another framework; we will only discuss the issue of Israel's indirect responsibility, knowing that if this responsibility is determined, it is not an exclusive responsibility laid on Israel alone.

Here it is appropriate to discuss the question whether blame may be attached regarding the atrocities done in the camps to those who decided on the entry into West Beirut and on including the Phalangists in actions linked to this entry.

. . .

The demand made in Israel to have the Phalangists take part in the fighting was a general and understandable one; and political, and to some extent military, reasons existed for such participation. . . . We do not find it justified to assert that the decision on this participation was unwarranted or that it should not have been made . . .

In our view, everyone who had anything to do with events in Lebanon should have felt apprehension about a massacre in the camps, if armed Phalangist forces were to be moved into them without the I.D.F. exercising concrete and effective supervision and scrutiny of them. All those concerned were well aware that combat morality among the various combatant groups in Lebanon differs from the norm in the I.D.F. that the combatants in Lebanon belittle the value of human life far beyond what is necessary and accepted in wars between civilized peoples, and that various atrocities against the non-combatant population had been widespread in Lebanon since 1975. . . .

. . .

We do not say that the decision to have the Phalangists enter the camps should under no circumstances have been made. . . . Serious considerations existed in favor of such a decision; and on this matter we shall repeat what has already been mentioned, that an understandable desire existed to prevent I.D. F. losses in hazardous combat in a built-up area, that it was justified to demand of the Phalangists to take part in combat which they regarded as a broad opening to assume power and for the restoration of Lebanese independence, and that the Phalangists were more expert than the I.D.F. in uncovering and identifying terrorists. . . .

To sum up this chapter, we assert that the atrocities in the refugee camps were perpetrated by members of the Phalangists, and that absolutely no direct responsibility devolves upon Israel or upon those who acted in its behalf. At the same time, it is clear from what we have said above that the decision on the entry of the Phalangists into the refugee camps was taken without consideration of the danger – which the makers and executors of the decision were obligated to foresee as probable – that the Phalangists would commit massacres and pogroms against the inhabitants of the camps, and without an examination of the means for preventing this danger. . . .

The Responsibility of the Political Echelon

. . .

In the report of the "Commission of Inquiry – the Yom Kippur War" (henceforth the Agranat Commission), the subject of "personal responsibility of the government echelon" was discussed in Clause 30 of the partial report. It is appropriate to cite what was stated there, since we believe that it reflects the essence of the correct approach, from a legal and public standpoint, to the problem of the personal responsibility of the political echelon. The partial report of the Agranat Commission states (Section 30):

> . . . Indeed, in Israel, as in England – whence it came to us – the principle prevails that a member of the Cabinet is responsible to the elected assembly for all the administrative actions of the apparatus within his ministry, even if he was not initially aware of them and was not a party to them. However, while it is clear that this principle obligates him to report to the members of the elected assembly on such actions, including errors and failures; to reply to parliamentary questions; to defend them or to report on what has been done to correct errors – even the English experience shows that the traditions have not determined anything regarding the question of which cases of this kind require him to resign from his ministerial office; this varies, according to circumstances, from one case to the next. The main reason for this is that the question of the possible resignation of a Cabinet member in cases of this kind is essentially a political question par excellence, and therefore we believe that we should not deal with it . . .

. . .

Personal Responsibility

. . .

THE PRIME MINISTER, MR. MENACHEM BEGIN

The notice sent to the Prime Minister, Mr. Menachem Begin, stated that he was liable to be harmed if the Commission were to determine "that the Prime Minister did not properly weigh the part to be played by the Lebanese Forces during and in the wake of the I.D.F.'s entry into West Beirut, and disregarded the danger of acts of revenge and bloodshed by these forces vis-à-vis the population in the refugee camps."

The Prime Minister's response to the notice stated that in the conversations between him and the Defense Minister in which the decision was taken to have I.D.F. units enter West Beirut, and in the conversations he had held with the Chief of Staff during the night between 14.9.82 and 15.9.82, nothing at all was said about a possible operation by the Lebanese Forces.

. . .

We may certainly wonder that the participation of the Phalangists in the entry to West Beirut and their being given the task of "mopping up" the camps seemed so unimportant that the Defense Minister did not inform the Prime Minister of it and did not get his assent for the decision; however, that question does not bear on the responsibility of the Prime Minister. What is clear is that the Prime Minister was not a party to the decision to have the Phalangists move into the camps, and that he received no report about that decision until the Cabinet session on the evening of 16.9.82.

We do not believe that we ought to be critical of the Prime Minister because he did not on his own initiative take an interest in the details of the operation of the entry into West Beirut, and did not discover, through his own questions, that the Phalangists were taking part in that operation of the entry into West Beirut. The tasks of the Prime Minister are many and diverse, and he was entitled to rely on the optimistic and calming report of the Defense Minister that the entire operation was proceeding without any hitches and in the most satisfactory manner.

. . .

THE MINISTER OF DEFENSE, MR. ARIEL SHARON

The notice sent to the Minister of Defense under Section 15(A) stated that the Minister of Defense might be harmed if the commission determined that he ignored or disregarded the danger of acts of revenge or bloodshed perpetrated by Lebanese forces against the population of the refugee camps in Beirut and did not order the adoption of the withdrawal of the Lebanese forces from the refugee camps as quickly as possible and the adoption of measures to protect the population in the camps when information reached him about the acts of killing or excesses that were perpetrated by the Lebanese forces.

In his testimony before us, and in statements he issued beforehand, the Minister of Defense also adopted the position that no one had imagined the Phalangists would carry out a massacre in the camps. . . . It is true that no clear warning was provided by military intelligence or the Mossad about what might happen if the Phalangist forces entered the camps, and we will relate to this matter when we discuss the responsibility of the director of Military Intelligence and the head of the Mossad. But in our view, even without such warning, it is impossible to justify the Minister of Defense's disregard of the danger of a massacre. . . .

. . . The sense of such a danger should have been in the consciousness of every knowledgeable person who was close to this subject, and certainly in the consciousness of the Defense Minister, who took an active part in everything relating to the war. His involvement in the war was deep, and the connection with the Phalangists was under his constant care. If in fact the Defense Minister, when he decided that the Phalangists would enter the camps without the I.D.F. taking part in the operation, did not think that that decision could bring about the very disaster that in fact occurred, the only possible explanation for this is that he disregarded any apprehensions about what was to be expected because the advantages – which we have already noted – to be gained from the Phalangists' entry into the camps distracted him from the proper consideration in this instance.

. . . In our view, the Minister of Defense made a grave mistake when he ignored the danger of acts of revenge and bloodshed by the Phalangists against the population in the refugee camps.

. . .

It is our view that responsibility is to be imputed to the Minister of Defense for having disregarded the danger of acts of vengeance and bloodshed by the Phalangists against the population of the refugee camps, and having failed to take this danger into account when he decided to have the Phalangists enter the camps. In addition, responsibility is to be imputed to the Minister of Defense for not ordering appropriate measures for preventing or reducing the danger of massacre as a condition for the Phalangists' entry into the camps. These blunders constitute the non-fulfillment of a duty with which the Defense Minister was charged.

. . .

THE FOREIGN MINISTER MR. YITZHAK SHAMIR

The Foreign Minister, Mr. Yitzhak Shamir, was sent a notice under Section 15(A) that he might be harmed if the commission determined that after he heard from Minister Zipori on 17.9.82 of the report regarding the Phalangists' actions in the refugee camps, he did not take the appropriate steps to clarify whether this information was based in fact and did not bring the information to the knowledge of the Prime Minister or the Minister of Defense.

. . . The Foreign Minister should at least have called the Defense Minister's attention to the information he had received and not contented himself with asking someone in his office whether any new information had come in from Beirut and with the expectation that those people coming to his office would know what was going on and would tell him if anything out of the ordinary had happened. In our view, the Foreign Minister erred in not taking any measures after the conversation with Minister Zipori in regard to what he had heard from Zipori about the Phalangist actions in the camps.

THE CHIEF OF STAFF, LIEUTENANT GENERAL RAFAEL EITAN

The notice sent to the Chief of Staff, Lieutenant General Rafael Eitan, according to Section 15(A), detailed a number of findings or conclusions that might be harmful to the Chief of Staff if the commission established them.

The first point in the notice has to do with the Chief of Staff disregarding the danger of acts of vengeance and bloodshed being perpetrated by the Phalangists, against the population of the refugee camps and his failure to take the appropriate measures to prevent this danger. In this matter, the Chief of Staff took a position similar to that of the Minister of Defense which was discussed above and which we have rejected. . . .

We are not prepared to accept these explanations. In our view, none of these reasons had the power to cancel out the serious concern that in going into the refugee camps, the Phalangist forces would perpetrate indiscriminate acts of killing. . . .

Past experience in no way justified the conclusion that the entry of the Phalangists into the camps posed no danger. . . . We have already said a number of times that the traumatic event of the murder of [Lebanese President] Bashir Jemayel and of a group of Phalangists was sufficient reason to whip up the Phalangists. . . . The Chief of Staff should have known and foreseen – by virtue of common knowledge, as well as the special information at his disposal – that there was a possibility of harm to the population in the camps at the hands of the Phalangists. Even if the experts did not fulfill their obligation, this does not absolve the Chief of Staff of responsibility . . .

If the Chief of Staff did not imagine at all that the entry of the Phalangists into the camps posed a danger to the civilian population, his thinking on this matter constitutes a disregard of important considerations that he should have taken into account. Moreover, . . . it is difficult to avoid the conclusion that the Chief of Staff ignored this danger out of an awareness that there were great advantages to sending the Phalangists into the camps, and perhaps also out of a hope that in the final analysis, the Phalangist excesses would not be on a large scale. . . .

. . .

We find that the Chief of Staff did not consider the danger of acts of vengeance and bloodshed being perpetrated against the population of the refugee camps in Beirut; he did not order the adoption of the appropriate steps to avoid this danger; and his failure to do so is tantamount to a breach of duty that was incumbent upon the Chief of Staff.

. . .

The outstanding impression that emerges from the Chief of Staff's testimony is that his refraining from raising the issue of the Phalangists' excesses against the population in the camps stemmed from a fear of offending their honor; . . .

In our opinion, after the Chief of Staff received the information from Major General Drori in a telephone conversation that the Phalangists had "overdone it" and Major General Drori had halted their operation, this information should have alerted him to the danger that acts of slaughter were being perpetrated in the camps and made him aware of his obligation to take appropriate steps to clarify the matter and prevent the continuation of such actions if the information proved to be of substance. . . . If, as a result of this clarification, he was not satisfied that excesses had not been committed in the camps, he should have ordered the immediate removal of the Phalangist forces from the camp, admonished the Phalangist commanders about the aberrant actions, and demanded that they issue immediate orders to their forces to refrain from any act that would cause harm to civilians while they were still in the camp. None of these things were done by the Chief of Staff. . . .

We determine that the Chief of Staff's inaction, described above, and his order to provide the Phalangist forces with tractors, or a tractor, constitute a breach of duty and dereliction of the duty incumbent upon the Chief of Staff.

DIRECTOR OF MILITARY INTELLIGENCE MAJOR GENERAL YEHOSHUA SAGUY

In the notice sent to the Director of Military Intelligence, Major General Yehoshua Saguy, non-fulfillment of duty was ascribed to him because he did not give sufficient attention to the decision regarding sending the Phalangists into the camps and did not warn after the murder of Bashir Jemayel of the danger of acts of revenge and bloodshed by these forces against the Palestinian population in West Beirut, and especially in the refugee camps.

. . .

We cannot believe that no information about the plan to send the Phalangists into the camps reached the Director of Military Intelligence until Friday morning, keeping in mind that he was present at a number of meetings in which this plan was mentioned and he had ample opportunities to ascertain the role given to the Phalangists. Even if we were to unreservedly accept Major Saguy's testimony in this matter, his statements would have been surprising. . . .

. . .

We believe that in these remarks Major General Saguy revealed the main reason why he "stepped aside" regarding the whole issue; and these remarks of his explain not only his inaction after receiving the report on Friday, but also his behavior at previous stages, as we have described. In our opinion, it was the duty of the director of Military Intelligence, as long as he occupies this post, to demonstrate alertness regarding the role of the Phalangists in the entry into Beirut after Bashir's assassination, to demand an appropriate clarification, and to explicitly and expressly warn all those concerned of the expected danger even prior to receipt of the report on Friday, and certainly after receipt of the report. The fear that his words would not receive sufficient attention and be rejected does not justify total inaction. This inaction constitutes breach of the duty incumbent on the director of Military Intelligence in this capacity.

HEAD OF THE INSTITUTE FOR INTELLIGENCE AND SPECIAL PROJECTS (MOSSAD)

The head of the Mossad was sent a notice under Section 15(A) of the law in which it is stated that he is liable to be harmed if the commission determines that he did not pay appropriate attention to the decision taken regarding the roles to be played by the Phalangists during the I.D.F.'s entry into West Beirut, and did not warn after the murder of Bashir Jemayel of the danger of bloodshed by these forces against the Palestinian population.

. . .

Apparently, the Mossad was not explicitly informed of the Phalangists' entry into the camps, and the head of the Mossad did not know of the decision which had been made on this matter. The testimony of the head of the Mossad should therefore be accepted, that only at the cabinet meeting of Thursday evening did he hear of the decision regarding the role of the Phalangists and of their entry into the camps, which by then had already taken place.

In the aforementioned circumstances it does not appear to us that the head of the Mossad was obligated, before knowing of the decision regarding the role of the Phalangists, to offer at his initiative an assessment regarding the situation which was liable to develop, if the Phalangists would be given the opportunity to take revenge on the Palestinians and attempt to carry out their plans for them in West Beirut. The head of the Mossad was present at the cabinet meeting until its conclusion. He heard what was said there, but did not himself give a situation assessment regarding the entry of the Phalangists into the camps, and did not express any reservation about this entry. . . .

The question is whether this inaction by the head of the Mossad constitutes breach of a duty incumbent upon the head of the Mossad.

The answer to this question is not easy. As mentioned above, the view of the Mossad, which had been expressed for a fairly long period prior to the I.D.F.'s entry into Lebanon, as well as afterwards, was that there should be greater cooperation with the Phalangists. The view prevalent in the Mossad, as expressed in various documents, was that the Phalangists are a trustworthy element which can be relied upon, and this despite the Phalangists' past regarding their attitude to the Palestinians and their statements on the way to solve the Palestinian problem once they reach power. . . . We do not believe that the head of the Mossad can be held responsible for the existence of such a "conception." He assumed the position of head of the Mossad only on 12.9.82 that is, two days before the murder of Bashir. He had previously been the deputy head of the Mossad and was acquainted with the Mossad's affairs; but the responsibility for the way in which the Mossad operated was not his. The entry of the Phalangists into the camps did not contradict the Mossad's situation assessment; and therefore it is difficult to expect that the head of the Mossad would have reservations about this decision when he heard about it at the Cabinet meeting on 16.9.82. In this matter as well, it should be taken into account that he had then been serving as head of the Mossad for only four days, and that this was the first Cabinet meeting in which he participated in this capacity.

It appears to us, that even in the situation described above, the head of the Mossad was obligated to express his opinion at the Cabinet meeting on the entry of the Phalangists and deal in this expression of opinion with the dangers involved in the Phalangists' operations – especially after he had heard Minister David Levy's remarks. In consideration of all the aforementioned circumstances, it is our opinion that this inaction of the head of the Mossad should not be considered serious.

G.O.C. NORTHERN COMMAND MAJOR GENERAL AMIR DRORI

In the notification sent to G.O.C. Northern Command Amir Drori, it was stated that he is liable to be harmed if the commission determines that he did not take appropriate or sufficient steps to prevent the continuation of the Phalangists' actions in the refugee camps when he received reports of acts of killing or acts which deviate from regular combat operations which were carried out in the camps.

. . .

Taking into consideration that it has not been proved that Major General Drori had [received] explicit reports about acts of killing and about their extent, it appears to us that he acted properly, wisely, and responsibly, with sufficient alertness at this stage. He heard from the Chief of Staff that the latter was to arrive in Beirut in the afternoon hours and could rely on the fact that this visit by the Chief of Staff, which was to take place within a few hours, would lead to positive results regarding the Phalangists' activity in the camps.

. . .

We determine that it was the duty of the G.O.C. to warn the Chief of Staff when the latter arrived in Beirut on 17.9.82 and during the rest of the Chief of Staff's stay in Beirut, that the population in the camps is endangered by the continued presence of the Phalangist forces in the camps, and that they should be removed from there immediately – or that at least steps be taken to ensure the safety of the population in the camps or to reduce the danger they face to the barest possible minimum. Major General Drori's refraining from any action regarding the danger facing the civilian population from the Phalangist forces, from the time the Chief of Staff arrived in Beirut and until Saturday, 18.9.82, constitutes, in our opinion, a breach of the duty which was incumbent on Major General Drori.

DIVISION COMMANDER BRIGADIER GENERAL AMOS YARON

The first issue specified in the notice sent to Brigadier General Amos Yaron under section 15(A) of the law is that Brigadier General Yaron did not properly evaluate and did not check reports that reached him concerning acts of killing and other irregular actions of the Phalangists in the camps, did not pass on that information to the G.O.C. and to the Chief of Staff immediately after it had been received on 16.9.82, and did not take the appropriate steps to stop the Phalangists' actions and to protect the population in the camps immediately upon receiving the reports.

. . .

A number of times, Brigadier General Yaron approached the Phalangist officers who were at the forward command post, including Elie Hobeika and repeated the admonition not to do harm to women and children; but other than this he did not take any initiative and only suggested that the Phalangists be ordered not to advance – and an order to this effect was issued by Major General Drori. . . . Brigadier General Yaron should have known that halting the advance did not ensure an end to the killing.

The notice sent to Brigadier General Yaron under Section 15(A) also speaks of the failure to provide any warning to the Chief of Staff when the latter reached Beirut on 17.9.82, as well as of Brigadier General Yaron's granting the Phalangists permission to send a new force into the camps without taking any steps that would bring a stop to the excesses. . . .

Brigadier General Yaron's inaction regarding the continuation of the Phalarigist operation in the camps was epitomized by the fact that he did not issue, any order to prevent them from replacing forces on Friday and did not impose any supervision on the movement of the Phalangist forces to and from the camps, despite the fact that the order halting the operation was not rescinded.

We have already cited Brigadier General Yaron's statement at the Senior Command Meeting in which he admitted with laudable candor that this was an instance of "insensitivity" on his part and on the part of others concerned. As we have already stated above, Brigadier General Yaron's desire was to save I.D.F. soldiers from having to carry out the operation in the camps, and this appears to be the main reason for his insensitivity to the dangers of the massacre in the camps. This concern of a commander for the welfare of his men would be praiseworthy in other circumstances; but considering the state of affairs in this particular instance, it was a thoroughly mistaken judgment on the part of Brigadier General Yaron, and a grave error was committed by a high-ranking officer of an I.D.F. force in this sector.

We determine that by virtue of his failings and his actions, detailed above, Brigadier General Yaron committed a breach of the duties incumbent upon him by virtue of his position.

. . .

Recommendations and Closing Remarks

RECOMMENDATIONS

With regard to the following recommendations concerning a group of men who hold senior positions in the Government and the Israel Defense Forces, we have taken into account [the fact] that each one of these men has to his credit [the performance of] many public or military services rendered with sacrifice and devotion on behalf of the State of Israel. If nevertheless we have reached the conclusion that it is incumbent upon us to recommend certain measures against some of these men, it is out of the recognition that the gravity of the matter and its implications for the underpinnings of public morality in the State of Israel call for such measures.

THE PRIME MINISTER, THE FOREIGN MINISTER, AND THE HEAD OF THE MOSSAD

We have heretofore established the facts and conclusions with regard to the responsibility of the Prime Minister, the Foreign Minister, and the head of the Mossad. In view of what we have determined with regard to the extent of the responsibility of each of them, we are of the opinion that it is sufficient to determine responsibility and there is no need for any further recommendations.

G.O.C. NORTHERN COMMAND MAJOR GENERAL AMIR DRORI

We have detailed above our conclusions with regard to the responsibility of G.O.C. Northern Command Major General Amir Drori. Major General Drori was charged with many difficult and complicated tasks during the week the I.D.F. entered West Beirut, missions which he had to accomplish after a long period of difficult warfare. He took certain measures for terminating the Phalangists' actions, and his guilt lies in that he did not continue with these actions. Taking into account these circumstances, it appears to us that it is sufficient to determine the responsibility of Major General Drori without recourse to any further recommendation.

THE MINISTER OF DEFENSE, MR. ARIEL SHARON

We have found . . . that the Minister of Defense bears personal responsibility. In our opinion, it is fitting that the Minister of Defense draw the appropriate personal conclusions arising out of the defects revealed with regard to the manner in which he discharged the duties of his office – and if necessary, that the Prime Minister consider whether he should exercise his authority under Section 21-A(a) of the Basic Law: the Government, according to which "the Prime Minister may, after informing the Cabinet of his intention to do so, remove a minister from office."

THE CHIEF OF STAFF, LT.-GEN. RAFAEL EITAN

We have arrived at grave conclusions with regard to the acts and omissions of the Chief of Staff, Lt-Gen. Rafael Eitan . . . we have resolved that it is sufficient to determine responsibility without making any further recommendation.

THE DIRECTOR OF MILITARY INTELLIGENCE, MAJOR GENERAL YEHOSHUA SAGUY

We have detailed the various extremely serious omissions of the Director of Military Intelligence, Major General Yehoshua Saguy, in discharging the duties of his office. We recommend that Major General Yehoshua Saguy not continue as Director of Military Intelligence.

DIVISION COMMANDER BRIGADIER GENERAL, AMOS YARON

We have detailed above the extent of the responsibility of Brigadier General Amos Yaron. . . . we recommend that Brigadier General Amos Yaron not serve in the capacity of a field commander in the Israel Defense Forces . . .

In the course of this inquiry, shortcomings in the functioning of [several] establishments have been revealed, . . . One must learn the appropriate lessons from these shortcomings, and we recommend that, in addition to internal control in this matter, an investigation into the shortcomings and the manner of correcting them be undertaken by an expert or experts, to be appointed by a Ministerial Defense Committee. . . .

CLOSING REMARKS

In the witnesses' testimony and in various documents, stress is laid on the difference between the usual battle ethics of the I.D.F. and the battle ethics of the bloody clashes and combat actions among the various ethnic groups, militias, and fighting forces in Lebanon. The difference is considerable. In the war the I.D.F. waged in Lebanon, many civilians were injured and much loss of life was caused, despite the effort the I.D.F. and its soldiers made not to harm civilians. . . . It is regrettable that the reaction by I.D.F. soldiers to such deeds was not always forceful enough to bring a halt to the despicable acts. It seems to us that the I.D.F. should continue to foster the [consciousness of] basic moral obligations which must be kept even in war conditions, without prejudicing the I.D.F.'s combat ability. The circumstances of combat require the combatants to be tough – which means to give priority to sticking to the objective and being willing to make sacrifices – in order to attain the objectives assigned to them, even under the most difficult conditions. But the end never justifies the means, and basic ethical and human values must be maintained in the use of arms.

Among the responses to the commission from the public, there were those who expressed dissatisfaction with the holding of an inquiry on a subject not directly related to Israel's responsibility. The argument was advanced that in previous instances of massacre in Lebanon, when the lives of many more people were taken than those of the victims who fell in Sabra and Shatilla, world opinion was not shocked and no inquiry commissions were established. We cannot justify this approach to the issue of holding an inquiry, and not only for the formal reason that it was not we who decided to hold the inquiry, but rather the Israeli Government resolved thereon. The main purpose of the inquiry was to bring to light all the important facts relating to the perpetration of the atrocities; it therefore has importance from the perspective of Israel's moral fortitude and its functioning as a democratic state that scrupulously maintains the fundamental principles of the civilized world.

. . .

This report was signed on 7 February 1983.

Yitzhak Kahan
Commission Chairman

Aharon Barak
Commission Member

Yona Efrat
Commission Member

60 Agreement Between Israel and Lebanon (May 17, 1983)

Agreement between the Government of the State of Israel and the Government of the Republic of Lebanon

The Government of the State of Israel and the Government of the Republic of Lebanon:

Bearing in mind the importance of maintaining and strengthening international peace based on freedom, equality, justice, and respect for fundamental human rights;

Reaffirming their faith in the aims and principles of the Charter of the United Nations and recognizing their right and obligation to live in peace with each other as well as with all states, within secure and recognized boundaries;

Having agreed to declare the termination of the state of war between them;

Desiring to ensure lasting security for both their States and to avoid threats and the use of force between them;

Desiring to establish their mutual relations in the manner provided for in this Agreement;

. . .

Having agreed to the following provisions:

Article I

1. The Parties agree and undertake to respect the sovereignty, political independence, and territorial integrity of each other. They consider the existing international boundary between Israel and Lebanon inviolable.
2. The Parties confirm that the state of war between Israel and Lebanon has been terminated and no longer exists.
3. Taking into account the provisions of paragraphs 1 and 2, Israel undertakes to withdraw all its armed forces from Lebanon in accordance with the Annex of the present Agreement.

DOI: 10.4324/9781003348948-65

Article 2

The Parties, being guided by the principles of the Charter of the United Nations and of international law, undertake to settle their disputes by peaceful means in such a manner as to promote international peace and security, and justice.

Article 3

In order to provide maximum security for Israel and Lebanon, the Parties agree to establish and implement security arrangements, . . .

Article 4

1. The territory of each Party will not be used as a base for hostile or terrorist activity against the other Party, its territory, or its people.
2. Each Party will prevent the existence or organization of irregular forces, armed bands, organizations, bases, offices, or infrastructure, the aims and purposes of which include incursions or any act of terrorism into the territory of the other Party, or any other activity aimed at threatening or endangering the security of the other Party and safety of its people. . . .
3. Without prejudice to the inherent right of self-defense in accordance with international law, each Party will refrain:

   a. from organizing, instigating, assisting, or participating in threats or acts of belligerency, subversion, or incitement or any aggression directed against the other Party, its population, or property, both within its territory and originating therefrom, or in the territory of the other Party.
   b. from using the territory of the other Party for conducting a military attack against the territory of a third state.
   c. from intervening in the internal or external affairs of the other Party . . .

Article 5

Consistent with the termination of the state of war and within the framework of their constitutional provisions, the Parties will abstain from any form of hostile propaganda against each other.

Article 6

Each Party will prevent entry into, deployment in, or passage through its territory, its air space and, subject to the right of innocent passage in accordance with international law, its territorial sea, by military forces, armament, or military equipment of any state hostile to the other Party.

Article 7

Except as provided in the present Agreement, nothing will preclude the deployment on Lebanese territory of international forces requested and accepted by the Government of Lebanon to assist in maintaining its authority. New contributors to such forces shall be selected from among states having diplomatic relations with both Parties to the present Agreement.

Article 8

1. a. Upon entry into force of the present Agreement, a Joint Liaison Committee will be established by the parties, in which the U.S. will be a participant, and will commence its functions ...

Article 9 ...

2. The Parties undertake not to apply existing obligations, enter into any obligations, or adopt laws or regulations in conflict with the present Agreement.

Article 10 ...

Article 11

1. Disputes between the Parties arising out of the interpretation or application of the present Agreement will be settled by negotiation in the Joint Liaison Committee. ...

Article 12

The present Agreement shall be communicated to the Secretariat of the United Nations for registration in conformity with the provisions of Article 102 of the Charter of the United Nations.

Done at Kiryat Shmona and Khaldeh this seventeenth day of May, 1983, in triplicate in four authentic texts in the Hebrew, Arabic, English, and French languages. In case of any divergence of interpretation, the English and French texts will be equally authoritative.

For the Government of the State of Israel
For the Government of Republic of Lebanon

Witnessed by:
For the Government of the United States of America

61 Jordan-P.L.O. Agreement (February 11, 1985)

(The Hussein-Arafat Accord)

Emanating from the spirit of the Fez summit resolutions, approved by Arab states, and from United Nations resolutions relating to the Palestine question,

In accordance with international legitimacy, and deriving from a common understanding on the establishment of a special relationship between the Jordanian and Palestinian peoples,

The Government of the Hashemite Kingdom of Jordan and the Palestine Liberation Organization have agreed to move together toward the achievement of a peaceful and just settlement of the Middle East crisis and the termination of Israeli occupation of the occupied Arab territories, including Jerusalem, on the basis of the following principles:

1. Total withdrawal from the territories occupied in 1967 for comprehensive peace as established in United Nations and Security Council resolutions.
2. Right of self-determination for the Palestinian people: Palestinians will exercise their inalienable right of self-determination when Jordanians and Palestinians will be able to do so within the context of the formation of the proposed confederated Arab states of Jordan and Palestine.
3. Resolution of the problem of Palestinian refugees in accordance with United Nations resolutions.
4. Resolution of the Palestine question in all its aspects.
5. And on this basis, peace negotiations will be conducted under the auspices of an international conference in which the five permanent members of the Security Council and all the parties to the conflict will participate, including the Palestine Liberation Organization, the sole legitimate representative of the Palestine people, within a joint delegation (joint Jordanian-Palestinian delegation).

DOI: 10.4324/9781003348948-66

62   The Shultz Initiative (March 4, 1988)

I set forth below the statement of understanding which I am convinced is necessary to achieve the prompt opening of negotiations on a comprehensive peace. This statement of understandings emerges from discussions held with you and other regional leaders. I look forward to the letter of reply of the Government of Israel in confirmation of this statement.

The agreed objective is a comprehensive peace providing for the security of all the states in the region and for the legitimate rights of the Palestinian people.

Negotiations will start on an early date certain between Israel and each of its neighbors which is willing to do so. These negotiations could begin May 1, 1988. Each of these negotiations will be based on the United Nations Security Council Resolutions 242 and 338, in all their parts. The parties to each bilateral negotiation will determine the procedure and agenda at their negotiation. All participants in the negotiations must state their willingness to negotiate with one another.

As concerns negotiations between the Israeli delegation and the Jordanian-Palestinian delegation, negotiations will begin on arrangements for a transitional period, with the objective of completing them within six months. Seven months after transitional negotiations begin, final status negotiations will begin, with the objective of completing them within one year. These negotiations will be based on all the provisions and principles of United Nations Security Council Resolution 242. Final status talks will start before the transitional period begins. The transitional period will begin three months after the conclusion of the transitional agreement and will last for three years. The United States will participate in both negotiations and will promote their rapid conclusion. In particular, the United States will submit a draft agreement for the parties' consideration at the outset of the negotiations on transitional arrangements.

Two weeks before the opening of negotiations, an international conference will be held. The Secretary General of United Nations will be asked to issue invitations to the parties involved in the Arab-Israeli conflict and the five

DOI: 10.4324/9781003348948-67

permanent members of the United Nations Council. All participants in the conference must accept United Nations Security Council Resolutions 242 and 338, and renounce violence and terrorism. The parties to each bilateral negotiation may refer reports on the status of their negotiations to the conference, in a manner to be agreed. The conference will not be able to impose solutions or veto agreements reached.

Palestinian representation will be within the Jordanian-Palestinian delegation. The Palestinian issue will be addressed in the negotiations between the Jordanian-Palestinian and Israeli delegations. Negotiations between the Israeli delegation and the Jordanian-Palestinian delegation will proceed independently of any other negotiations.

This statement of understandings in an integral whole. The United States understands that your acceptance is dependent on the implementation of each element in good faith.

Sincerely yours,
George P. Shultz

63 King Hussein, Address to the Nation (July 31, 1988)

(Translated from the original Arabic)

In the name of God, the Merciful, the Compassionate,

Peace be upon His Faithful Arab Messenger.

Brother Citizens,

I send you greetings and am pleased to address you in your cities and villages, in your camps and dwellings, in your institutions of learning, and in your places of work. . . . This is all the more important at this juncture, when we have initiated – after seeking God's help and after thorough and extensive study – a series of measures to enhance Palestinian national orientation and highlight Palestinian identity; our goal is the benefit of the Palestinian cause and the Arab Palestinian people.

Our decision, as you know, comes after 38 years of the unity of the two banks, and fourteen years after the Rabat Summit resolution designating the Palestine Liberation Organization (PLO) as the sole legitimate representative of the Palestinian people. It also comes six years after the Fez Summit resolution that agreed unanimously on the establishment of an independent Palestinian state in the occupied West Bank and the Gaza Strip as one of the bases and results of the peaceful settlement.

We are certain that our decision to initiate these measures does not come as a surprise to you. Many among you have anticipated it, and some of you have been calling for it for some time. As for its contents, it has been a topic of discussion and consideration for everyone since the Rabat Summit.

Nevertheless, some may wonder: Why now? Why today and not after the Rabat or Fez summits, for instance?

To answer this question, we need to recall certain facts that preceded the Rabat resolution. We also need to recall considerations that led to the debate over the slogan-objective which the PLO raised and worked to gain Arab and international support for. Namely, the establishment of an independent Palestinian state. This meant, in addition to the PLO's ambition to embody the

DOI: 10.4324/9781003348948-68

Palestinian identity on Palestinian national soil, the separation of the West Bank from the Hashemite Kingdom of Jordan.

I reviewed the facts preceding the Rabat resolution, as you recall, before the Arab leaders in the Algiers Extraordinary Summit last June. It may be important to recall that one of the main facts I emphasized was the text of the unity resolution of the two banks of April 1950. This resolution affirms the preservation of all Arab rights in Palestine and the defense of such rights by all legitimate means without prejudicing the final settlement of the just cause of the Palestinian people – within the scope of the people's aspirations and of Arab cooperation and international justice.

. . .

The relationship of the West Bank with the Hashemite Kingdom of Jordan in light of the PLO's call for the establishment of an independent Palestinian state, can be confined to two considerations: First, the principled consideration pertaining to the issue of Arab unity as a pan-Arab aim, which Arab peoples aspire to and want to achieve. Second, the political consideration pertaining to the extent of the Palestinian struggles from the continuation of the legal relationship to the Kingdom's two banks. Our answer to the question, "why now?", also derives from these two factors, and the background of the clear and constant Jordanian position on the Palestinian cause, as already outlined.

Regarding the principled consideration, Arab unity between any two or more countries is an option of any Arab people. This is what we believe. Accordingly, we responded to the wish of the Palestinian people's representatives for unity with Jordan in 1950. From this premise, we respect the wish of the PLO, the sole and legitimate representative of the Palestinian people, to secede from us as an independent Palestinian state. . . .

Regarding the political consideration, since the June 1967 aggression we have believed that our actions and efforts should be directed at liberating the land and the sanctities from Israeli occupation. . . . We did not imagine that maintaining the legal and administrative relationship between the two banks could constitute an obstacle to liberating the occupied Palestinian land. Hence, in the past and before we took measures, we did not find anything requiring such measures, especially since our support for the Palestinian people's right to self-determination was clear.

Lately, it has transpired that there is a general Palestinian and Arab orientation which believes in the need to highlight the Palestinian identity in full in all efforts and activities that are related to the Palestine question and its developments. It has also become clear that there is a general conviction that maintaining the legal and administrative links with the West Bank, and the ensuing Jordanian interaction with our Palestinian brothers under occupation through Jordanian institutions in the occupied territories, contradicts this orientation. It is also viewed that these links hamper the Palestinian struggle to gain international support for the Palestinian cause of a people struggling against foreign occupation.

. . .

At the Rabat Summit of 1974 we responded to the Arab leaders' appeal to us to continue our interaction with the Occupied West Bank through Jordanian institutions, to support the steadfastness of our brothers there. Today we respond to the wish of the Palestine Liberation Organization, the sole legitimate representative of the Palestinian People, and to the Arab orientation to affirm the Palestinian identity in all its aspects. We pray to God that this step be a substantive addition to the intensifying Palestinian struggle for freedom and independence.

Brother Citizens,

These are the reasons, the considerations, and the convictions that led us to respond favorably to the wish of the PLO, and to the general Arab direction consistent with it. . . .

At the same time, it has to be understood in all clarity, and without any ambiguity or equivocation, that our measures regarding the West Bank concern only the occupied Palestinian land and its people. They naturally do not relate in any way to the Jordanian citizens of Palestinian origin in the Hashemite Kingdom of Jordan. They all have the full rights of citizenship and all its obligations, the same as any other citizen irrespective of his origin. They are an integral part of the Jordanian state to which they belong, on whose soil they live, and in whose life and various activities they participate. Jordan is not Palestine and the independent Palestinian state will be established on the occupied Palestinian territory after its liberation, God willing. There the Palestinian identity will be embodied, and there the Palestinian struggle shall come to fruition, as confirmed by the glorious uprising of the Palestinian people under occupation.

. . .

Based on that, safeguarding national unity is a sacred duty that will not be compromised. Any attempt to undermine it, under any pretext, would only help the enemy carry out his policy of expansion at the expense of Palestine and Jordan alike. Consequently, true nationalism lies in bolstering and fortifying national unity. Moreover, the responsibility to safeguard it falls on every one of you, leaving no place in our midst for sedition or treachery. With God's help, we shall be as always, a united cohesive family, whose members are joined by bonds of brotherhood, affection, awareness, and common national objectives.

. . .

The constructive plurality which Jordan has lived since its foundation, and through which it has witnessed progress and prosperity in all aspects of life, emanates not only from our faith in the sanctity of national unity, but also in the importance of Jordan's pan-Arab role. Jordan presents itself as the living example of the merger of various Arab groups on its soil, within the framework of good citizenship, and one Jordanian people. This paradigm that we live on our soil gives us faith in the inevitability of attaining Arab unity, God willing . . .

Citizens,

Palestinian brothers in the occupied Palestinian lands,

To display any doubts that may arise out of our measures, we assure you that these measures do not mean the abandonment of our national duty, either towards the Arab-Israeli conflict, or towards the Palestinian cause. Nor do they mean a relinquishing our faith in Arab unity. As I have stated, these steps were taken only in response to the wish of the Palestine Liberation Organization, the sole legitimate representative of the Palestinian people, and the prevailing Arab conviction that such measures will contribute to the struggle of the Palestinian people and their glorious uprising. . . . I have to mention, that when we decided to cancel the Jordanian development plan in the occupied territories, we contacted, at the same time, various friendly governments and international institutions, which had expressed their wish to contribute to the plan, urging them to continue financing development projects in the occupied Palestinian lands, through the relevant Palestinian quarters.

Jordan, dear brothers, has not nor will it give up its support and assistance to the Palestinian people, until they achieve their national goals, God willing. No one outside Palestine has had, nor can have, an attachment to Palestine, or its cause, firmer than that of Jordan or of my family. Moreover, Jordan is a confrontation state, whose borders with Israel are longer than those of any other Arab state, longer even than the combined borders of the West Bank and Gaza with Israel.

In addition, Jordan will not give up its commitment to take part in the peace process. We have contributed to the peace process until it reached the stage of a consensus to convene an international peace conference on the Middle East. The purpose of the conference would be to achieve a just and comprehensive peace settlement to the Arab Israeli conflict, and the settlement of the Palestinian problem in all its aspects. We have defined our position in this regard, as everybody knows, through the six principles which we have already made public.

Jordan, dear brothers, is a principal party to the Arab-Israeli conflict, and to the peace process. It shoulders its national responsibilities on that basis.

I thank you and I repeat my heartfelt wishes to you, beseeching Almighty God to help us, guide us, enable us to please Him, and to grant our Palestinian brothers victory and success. He is the best of helpers.

May God's peace and blessings be upon you.

64 Palestine National Council

Declaration of Independence
(November 15, 1988)

In the name of God, the Compassionate, the Merciful

Palestine, the land of the three monotheistic faiths, is where the Palestinian Arab people was born, on which it grew, developed, and excelled. Thus the Palestinian Arab people ensured for itself an everlasting union between itself, its land, and its history.

. . .

Nourished by an unfolding series of civilizations and cultures, inspired by a heritage rich in variety and kind, the Palestinian Arab people added to its stature by consolidating a union between itself and its patrimonial Land. The call went out from Temple, Church, and Mosque that to praise the Creator, to celebrate compassion and peace was indeed the message of Palestine. And in generation after generation, the Palestinian Arab people gave of itself unsparingly. . . . For what has been the unbroken chain of our people's rebellions but the heroic embodiment of our will for national independence. And so the people was sustained in the struggle to stay and to prevail.

When in the course of modern times a new order of values was declared with norms and values fair for all, it was the Palestinian Arab people that had been excluded from the destiny of all other peoples by a hostile array of local and foreign powers. Yet again had unaided justice been revealed as insufficient to drive the world's history along its preferred course.

And it was the Palestinian people, . . . over which floated that falsehood that "Palestine was a land without people." This notion was foisted upon some in the world, whereas in Article 22 of the Covenant of the League of Nations (1919) and in the Treaty of Lausanne (1923), the community of nations had recognized that all the Arab territories, including Palestine, of the formerly Ottoman provinces, were to have granted to them their freedom as provisionally independent nations.

Despite the historical injustice inflicted on the Palestinian Arab people resulting in their dispersion and depriving them of their right to self-determination, following upon U.N. General Assembly Resolution 181 (1947), which partitioned Palestine into two states, one Arab, one Jewish, yet it is this Resolution that still provides those conditions of international legitimacy that ensure the right of the Palestinian Arab people to sovereignty.

DOI: 10.4324/9781003348948-69

By stages, the occupation of Palestine and parts of other Arab territories by Israeli forces, the willed dispossession and expulsion from their ancestral homes of the majority of Palestine's civilian inhabitants, was achieved by organized terror; those Palestinians who remained, as a vestige subjugated in its homeland, were persecuted and forced to endure the destruction of their national life.

Thus were principles of international legitimacy violated. Thus were the Charter of the United Nations and its Resolutions disfigured, for they had recognized the Palestinian Arab people's national rights, including the right of Return, the right to independence, the right to sovereignty over territory and homeland.

In Palestine and on its perimeters, in exile distant and near, the Palestinian Arab people never faltered and never abandoned its conviction in its rights of Return and independence. Occupation, massacres, and dispersion achieved no gain in the unabated Palestinian consciousness of self and political identity, as Palestinians went forward with their destiny, undeterred and unbowed. And from out of the long years of trial in ever-mounting struggle, the Palestinian political identity emerged further consolidated and confirmed. And the collective Palestinian national will forged for itself a political embodiment, the Palestine Liberation Organization, its sole, legitimate representative recognized by the world community as a whole, as well as by related regional and international institutions. Standing on the very rock of conviction in the Palestinian people's inalienable rights, and on the ground of Arab national consensus and of international legitimacy, the PLO led the campaigns of its great people, molded into unity and powerful resolve, one and indivisible in its triumphs, even as it suffered massacres and confinement within and without its home. And so Palestinian resistance was clarified and raised into the forefront of Arab and world awareness, as the struggle of the Palestinian Arab people achieved unique prominence among the world's liberation movements in the modern era.

. . .

Whereas the Palestinian people reaffirms most definitively its inalienable rights in the land of its patrimony:

> *Now by virtue of natural, historical, and legal rights, and the sacrifices of successive generations who gave of themselves in defense of the freedom and independence of their homeland;*
>
> *In pursuance of Resolutions adopted by Arab Summit Conferences and relying on the authority bestowed by international legitimacy as embodied in the Resolutions of the United Nations Organization since 1947;*
>
> *And in exercise by the Palestinian Arab people of its rights to self-determination, political independence, and sovereignty over its territory,*
>
> *The Palestine National Council, in the name of God, and in the name of the Palestinian Arab people, hereby proclaims the establishment of the State of Palestine on our Palestinian territory with its capital Jerusalem (Al-Quds Ash-Sharif).*

The State of Palestine is the state of Palestinians wherever they may be. The state is for them to enjoy in it their collective national and cultural identity, theirs to pursue in it a complete equality of rights. In it will be safeguarded their political and religious convictions and their human dignity by means of a parliamentary democratic system of governance, itself based on freedom of expression and the freedom to form parties. The rights of minorities will duly be respected by the majority, as minorities must abide by decisions of the majority. Governance will be based on principles of social justice, equality, and non-discrimination in public rights of men or women, on grounds of race, religion, color or sex, and the aegis of a constitution which ensures the rule of law and an independent judiciary. Thus shall these principles allow no departure from Palestine's age-old spiritual and civilizational heritage of tolerance and religious coexistence.

The State of Palestine is an Arab state, an integral and indivisible part of the Arab nation, at one with that nation in heritage and civilization, with it also in its aspiration for liberation, progress, democracy, and unity. The State of Palestine affirms its obligation to abide by the Charter of the League of Arab States, whereby the coordination of the Arab states with each other shall be strengthened. It calls upon Arab compatriots to consolidate and enhance the emergence in reality of our state, to mobilize potential, and to intensify efforts whose goal is to end Israeli occupation.

The State of Palestine proclaims its commitment to the principles and purposes of the United Nations, and to the Universal Declaration of Human Rights. It proclaims its commitment as well to the principles and policies of the Non-Aligned Movement.

It further announces itself to be a peace-loving State, in adherence to the principles of peaceful coexistence. It will join with all states and peoples in order to assure a permanent peace based upon justice and the respect of rights so that humanity's potential for well-being may be assured, an earnest competition for excellence may be maintained, and in which confidence in the future will eliminate fear for those who are just and for whom justice is the only recourse.

. . .

The State of Palestine herewith declares that it believes in the settlement of regional and international disputes by peaceful means, in accordance with the U.N. Charter and resolutions. With prejudice to its natural right to defend its territorial integrity and independence, it therefore rejects the threat or use of force, violence and terrorism against its territorial integrity or political independence, as it also rejects their use against territorial integrity of other states.

Therefore, on this day unlike all others, November 15, 1988, as we stand at the threshold of a new dawn, in all honor and modesty we humbly bow to the sacred spirits of our fallen ones, Palestinian and Arab, by the purity of whose sacrifice for the homeland our sky has been illuminated and our Land given life. Our hearts are lifted up and irradiated by the light emanating from the much blessed intifada, from those who have endured and have fought the fight of the camps, of dispersion, of exile, from those who have borne the standard for freedom, our children, our aged, our youth, our prisoners, detainees, and wounded, all those ties to our sacred soil are confirmed in camp, village, and town. We render special tribute to that brave Palestinian Woman, guardian of sustenance and Life, keeper of our people's perennial flame. To the souls of our sainted martyrs, the whole of our Palestinian Arab people that our struggle shall be continued until the occupation ends, and the foundation of our sovereignty and independence shall be fortified accordingly.

Therefore, we call upon our great people to rally to the banner of Palestine, to cherish and defend it, so that it may forever be the symbol of our freedom and dignity in that homeland, which is a homeland for the free, now and always.

In the name of God, the Compassionate, the Merciful:

"Say: 'O God, Master of the Kingdom,
Thou givest the Kingdom to whom Thou wilt,
and seizes the Kingdom from whom Thou wilt,
Thou exalted whom Thou wilt, and Thou
abasest whom Thou wilt; in Thy hand
is the good; Thou are powerful over everything.' "

65 Israel's Peace Initiative (May 14, 1989)

General

1. This document presents the principles of a political initiative of the Government of Israel which deals with the continuation of the peace process; the termination of the state of war with the Arab states; a solution for the Arab residents of Judea, Samaria, and the Gaza district; peace with Jordan; and a resolution of the problem of the refugee camps in Judea, Samaria, and the Gaza district.

2. The document includes:

   (a) The principles upon which the initiative is based.
   (b) Details of the processes for its implementation.
   (c) Reference to the subjects of the elections under consideration . . .

Basic Premises

3. The initiative is founded upon the assumption that there is a national consensus for it on the basis of the basic guidelines of the Government of Israel, including the following points:

   (a) Israel yearns for peace and the continuation of the political process by means of direct negotiations based on the principles of the Camp David Accords.
   (b) Israel opposes the establishment of an additional Palestinian state in the Gaza district and in the area between Israel and Jordan.
   (c) Israel will not conduct negotiations with the PLO.
   (d) There will be no change in the status of Judea, Samaria, and Gaza other than in accordance with the basic guidelines of the government.

Subjects to be Dealt With in the Peace Process

4. (a) Israel deems important that the peace between Israel and Egypt, based on the Camp David Accords, serve as a cornerstone for enlarging the

DOI: 10.4324/9781003348948-70

circle of peace in the region; Israel calls for a common endeavor for the strengthening of the peace and its extension; through continued consultation.

(b) Israel calls for the establishment of peaceful relations between it and those Arab states which still maintain a state of war with it. Israel seeks to promote a comprehensive settlement for the Arab-Israel conflict, including recognition, direct negotiation, ending the boycott, diplomatic relations, cessation of hostile activity in international institutions or forums, and regional and bilateral cooperation.

(c) Israel calls for an international endeavor to resolve the problem of the residents of the Arab refugee camps in Judea, Samaria, and the Gaza district in order to improve their living conditions and to rehabilitate them. Israel is prepared to be a partner in this endeavor.

(d) In order to advance the political negotiation process leading to peace, Israel proposes free and democratic elections among the Palestinian Arab inhabitants of Judea, Samaria, and the Gaza district in an atmosphere devoid of violence, threats, and terror. In these elections a representation will be chosen to conduct negotiations for a transitional period of self-rule. This period will constitute a test for coexistence and cooperation. At a later stage, negotiations will be conducted for a permanent solution during which all the proposed options for an agreed settlement will be examined, and peace between Israel and Jordan will be achieved.

(e) All the above-mentioned steps should be dealt with simultaneously.

(f) The details of what has been mentioned in (d) above will be given below.

The Principles Constituting the Initiative

STAGES

5. The initiative is based on two stages:

(a) Stage A – a transitional period for an interim agreement.
(b) Stage B – permanent solution.

6. The interlock between the stages is a timetable on which the Plan is built: the peace process delineated by the initiative is based on United Nations Resolutions 242 and 338, upon which the Camp David Accords are founded.

TIMETABLE

7. The transitional period will continue for five years.

8. As soon as possible, but not later than the third year after the beginning of the transitional period, negotiations for achieving a permanent solution will begin.

Parties Participating in the Negotiations in Both Stages

9. The parties participating in the negotiations for the first stage (the interim agreement) shall include Israel and the elected representation of the Palestinian Arab inhabitants of Judea, Samaria, and the Gaza district. Jordan and Egypt will be invited to participate in these negotiations if they so desire.

10. The parties participating in the negotiations for the second stage (permanent solution) shall include Israel and the elected representation of the Palestinian Arab inhabitants of Judea, Samaria, and the Gaza district, as well as Jordan; furthermore, Egypt may participate in these negotiations. In negotiations between Israel and Jordan, in which the elected representation of the Palestinian Arab inhabitants of Judea, Samaria, and the Gaza district will participate, a peace treaty between Israel and Jordan will be concluded.

Substance of Transitional Period

11. During the transitional period the Palestinian Arab inhabitants of Judea, Samaria, and the Gaza district will be accorded self-rule whereby they will conduct the affairs of daily life. Israel will continue to be responsible for security, foreign affairs, and all matters concerning Israeli citizens in Judea, Samaria, and the Gaza district. Topics involving the implementation of the plan for self-rule will be considered and decided within the framework of the negotiations for an interim agreement.

Substance of Permanent Solution

12. In the negotiations for a permanent solution every party shall be entitled to present for discussion all the subjects it may wish to raise.

13. The aim of the negotiations should be:

    (a) The achievement of a permanent solution acceptable to the negotiating parties.

    (b) The arrangements for peace and establishment of borders between Israel and Jordan.

Details of the Process for the Implementation of the Initiative

14. First and foremost, dialogue and basic agreement by the Palestinian Arab inhabitants of Judea, Samaria, and the Gaza district, as well as Egypt and Jordan if they wish to take part, in the negotiations, on the principles constituting the initiative.

15. (a) Immediately afterwards will follow the stage of preparations and implementation of the election process in which a representation of

the Palestinian Arab inhabitants of Judea, Samaria, and Gaza will be elected. This representation:

   (i)   Shall be a partner to the negotiations for the transitional period (interim agreement).

   (ii) Shall constitute the self-governing authority in the course of the transitional period.

   (iii) Shall be the central Palestinian component, subject to agreement after three years, in the negotiations for the permanent solution.

(b) In the period of preparation and implementation, there shall be a calming of the violence in Judea, Samaria, and the Gaza district.

16. As to the substance of the elections, it is recommended that a proposal for regional elections be adopted, the details of which shall be determined in further discussions.

17. Every Palestinian Arab residing in Judea, Samaria, and the Gaza district, who shall be elected by the inhabitants to represent them – after having submitted his candidacy in accordance with the detailed document which shall determine the subject of the elections – may be a legitimate participant in the negotiations with Israel.

18. The elections shall be free, democratic, and secret.

19. Immediately after the election of the Palestinian representation, negotiations shall be conducted with it on an interim agreement for a transitional period which shall continue for five years, as mentioned above. In these negotiations the parties shall determine all the subjects relating to the substance of self-rule and the arrangements necessary for its implementation.

20. As soon as possible, but not later than the third year after the establishment of self-rule, negotiations for a permanent solution shall begin. During the whole period of these negotiations until the signing of the agreement for a permanent solution, self-rule shall continue in effect as determined in the negotiations for an interim agreement.

Israeli Foreign Ministry

66 U.S. Secretary of State James Baker's Five-Point Plan (October 10, 1989)

1. The United States understands that because Egypt and Israel have been working hard on the peace process, there is agreement that an Israel delegation should conduct a dialogue with a Palestinian delegation in Cairo.
2. The United States understands that Egypt cannot substitute itself for the Palestinians and Egypt will consult with Palestinians on all aspects of that dialogue. Egypt will also consult with Israel and the United States.
3. The United States understands that Israel will attend the dialogue only after a satisfactory list of Palestinians has been worked out.
4. The United States understands that the Government of Israel will come to the dialogue on the basis of the Israeli Government's Initiative. The United States further understands that Palestinians will come to the dialogue prepared to discuss elections and the negotiating process in accordance with Israel's initiative. The United States understands, therefore, that Palestinians would be free to raise issues that relate to their opinions on how to make elections and the negotiating process succeed.
5. In order to facilitate this process, the United States proposes that the Foreign Ministers of Israel, Egypt, and the United States meet in Washington within two weeks.

DOI: 10.4324/9781003348948-71

67 Letter of Invitation to the Madrid Peace Conference (October 30, 1991), Jointly Issued by the United States and the Soviet Union

TEXT:

After extensive consultations with Arab states, Israel, and the Palestinians, the United States and the Soviet Union believe that an historic opportunity exists to advance the prospects for genuine peace throughout the region. The United States and the Soviet Union are prepared to assist the parties to achieve a just, lasting, and comprehensive peace settlement, through direct negotiations along two tracks, between Israel and the Arab states, and between Israel and the Palestinians, based on United Nations Security Council Resolutions 242 and 338. The objective of this process is real peace.

Toward that end, the president of the U.S. and the president of the USSR invite you to a peace conference, which their countries will co-sponsor, followed immediately by direct negotiations. The conference will be convened in Madrid on October 30, 1991.

President Bush and President Gorbachev request your acceptance of this invitation no later than 6 PM Washington time, October 23, 1991, in order to ensure proper organization and preparation of the conference.

Direct bilateral negotiations will begin four days after the opening of the conference. Those parties who wish to attend multilateral negotiations will convene two weeks after the opening of the conference to organize those negotiations. The co-sponsors believe that those negotiations should focus on region-wide issues of water, refugee issues, environment, economic development, and other subjects of mutual interest.

... Governments to be invited include Israel, Syria, Lebanon, and Jordan. Palestinians will be invited and attend as part of a joint Jordanian-Palestinian delegation. Egypt will be invited to the conference as a participant. The European Community will be a participant in the conference, alongside the United States and the Soviet Union and will be represented by its presidency. The Gulf Cooperation Council will be invited to send its secretary-general to the conference as an observer, and GCC member states will be invited to participate in organizing the negotiations on multilateral issues. The United Nations will be invited to send an observer, representing the secretary-general.

DOI: 10.4324/9781003348948-72

The conference will have no power to impose solutions on the parties or veto agreements reached by them. . . . The conference can reconvene only with the consent of all the parties.

With respect to negotiations between Israel and Palestinians who are part of the joint Jordanian-Palestinian delegation, negotiations will be conducted in phases, beginning with talks on interim self-government arrangements. These talks will be conducted with the objective of reaching agreement within one year. Once agreed, the interim self-government arrangements will last for a period of five years; beginning the third year of the period of interim self-government arrangements, negotiations will take place on permanent status. These permanent status negotiations, and the negotiations between Israel and the Arab states, will take place on the basis of Resolutions 242 and 338.

It is understood that the co-sponsors are committed to making this process succeed. It is their intention to convene the conference and negotiations with those parties who agree to attend.

The co-sponsors believe that this process offers the promise of ending decades of confrontation and conflict and the hope of a lasting peace. Thus, the co-sponsors hope that the parties will approach these negotiations in a spirit of good will and mutual respect. In this way, the peace process can begin to break down the mutual suspicions and mistrust that perpetuate the conflict and allow the parties to begin to resolve their differences. Indeed, only through such a process can real peace and reconciliation among the Arab states, Israel, and the Palestinians be achieved. And only through this process can the peoples of the Middle East attain the peace and security they richly deserve.

68 Address to the Knesset by Prime Minister Rabin Presenting His Government (July 13, 1992)

Your Excellency Mr. President, Speaker of the Knesset, Members of the Knesset:

The Government asking for the confidence of the 13th Knesset is keenly aware that the eyes of every one of Israel's citizens are focused on it with a prayer of great hope. Many people in Israel and in countries throughout the world look forward today to our embarking upon a new path, to fresh momentum, to turning a new page in the annals of the State of Israel. Attended by their best wishes and concern, we are today setting out on the long and difficult journey.

. . .

Members of the Knesset, on the first day of Tammuz 5752, July 2, 1992, the President of the State charged me with forming a Government for Israel, and on Friday, the 9th of Tammuz, July 10th, I informed him that I had succeeded in that task. Participating in the Government that is asking for the Knesset's confidence today are the Labor, Democratic Israel (Meretz), and Sephardi Torah Guardians (Shas) parties. Following clarifications of its policy towards the Arab population in Israel, the Government will also be supported by the Democratic Front for Peace and Equality and the Democratic Arab Party. The Government will keep its doors open to parties that are prepared to endorse its basic policies.

. . .

The new Government has accordingly made it a central goal to promote the making of peace and take vigorous steps that will lead to the end of the Arab Israeli conflict. We shall do so based on the recognition by the Arab countries, and the Palestinians, that Israel is a sovereign state with a right to live in peace and security. We believe wholeheartedly that peace is possible, that it is imperative, and that it will ensue. "I shall believe in the future," wrote the poet Shaul Tchernikovsky, "even if it is far off, the day will come when peace and blessings are borne from nation to nation" – and I want to believe that that day is not far off.

The Government will propose to the Arab states and the Palestinians the continuation of the peace talks based upon the framework forged at the Madrid Conference. As a first step toward a permanent solution we shall discuss the

DOI: 10.4324/9781003348948-73

institution of autonomy in Judea, Samaria, and the Gaza District. We do not intend to lose precious time. The Government's first directive to the negotiating teams will be to step up the talks and hold ongoing discussions between the sides. Within a short time we shall renew the talks in order to diminish the flame of enmity between the Palestinians and the State of Israel.

As a first step, to illustrate our sincerity and good will, I wish to invite the Jordanian-Palestinian delegation to an informal talk, here in Jerusalem, so that we can hear their views, make ours heard, and create an appropriate atmosphere for neighborly relations.

To you, the Palestinians in the territories, I wish to say from this rostrum: We have been fated to live together on the same patch of land, in the same country. We lead our lives with you, beside you and against you. You have failed in the war against us. One hundred years of your bloodshed and terror against us have brought you only suffering, humiliation, bereavement and pain. You have lost thousands of your sons and daughters, and you are losing ground all the time. For 44 years now, you have been living under a delusion. Your leaders have led you through lies and deceit. They have missed every opportunity, rejected all the proposals for a settlement, and have taken you from one tragedy to another.

And you, Palestinians in the territories, who live in the wretched poverty of Gaza and Khan Yunis, in the refugee camps of Hebron and Shechem; you who have never known a single day of freedom and joy in your lives – listen to us, if only this once. We offer you the fairest and most viable proposal from our standpoint today – autonomy – self-government – with all its advantages and limitations. You will not get everything you want. Perhaps neither will we. So once and for all, take your destiny in your hands. Don't lose this opportunity that may never return. Take our proposal seriously – to avoid further suffering and grief –, to end the shedding of tears and of blood.

The new Government urges the Palestinians in the territories to give peace a chance – and to cease all violent and terrorist activity for the duration of the negotiations on autonomy. We are well aware that the Palestinians are not all of a single mold, that there are exceptions and differences among them. But we urge the population, which has been suffering for years, and the perpetrators of the riots in the territories, to forswear stones and knives and await the results of the talks that may well bring peace to the Middle East. If you reject this proposal, we shall go on talking but treat the territories as though there were no dialogue going on between us. Instead of extending a friendly hand, we will employ every possible means to prevent terror and violence. The choice, in this case, is yours.

We have lost our finest sons and daughters in the struggle over this land and in the war against the Arab armies. My comrades in the Israel Defense Forces, and I myself, as a former military man who took part in Israel's wars, lovingly preserve the memory of the fallen and regard ourselves as sharing in the pain of the families whose sleepless nights, year in and year out, are one long Day of Remembrance to them. Only people who have lost those dearest to them can understand us. Our hearts also go out to the disabled, whose bodies bear the scars of war and terrorism.

Neither have we forgotten, on this distinguished occasion, the IDF soldiers who are prisoners of war or missing in action. We shall continue to make every effort to bring them home, and our thoughts are with their families today, as well.

Members of the Knesset, we shall continue to fight for our right to live here in peace and tranquility. No knife or stone, no fire-bomb or land-mine will stop us. The Government presented here today sees itself as responsible for the security of every one of Israel's citizens, Jews and Arabs, within the State of Israel, in Judea, in Samaria and in the Gaza District.

We shall strike hard, without flinching, at terrorists and those who abet them. There will be no compromises in the war against terror. The IDF and the other security forces will prove to the agents of bloodshed that our lives are not free for the taking. We shall act to contain the hostile activities as much as possible and maintain the personal security of the inhabitants of Israel and the territories, while both upholding the law and guarding the rights of the individual.

. . .

Members of the Knesset, the plan to apply self-government to the Palestinians in Judea, Samaria, and Gaza – the autonomy of the Camp David Accords – is an interim settlement for a period of five years. No later than three years after its institution, discussions will begin on the permanent solution. It is only natural that the holding of talks on the subject creates concern among those among us who have chosen to settle in Judea, Samaria and the Gaza District. I hereby inform you that the Government, by means of the IDF and the other security services, will be responsible for the security and welfare of the residents of Judea, Samaria and the Gaza District. However, at the same time, the Government will refrain from any steps and activities that would disrupt the proper conduct of the peace negotiations.

We see the need to stress that the Government will continue to enhance and strengthen Jewish settlement along the lines of confrontation, due to their importance for security, and in Greater Jerusalem.

This Government, like all of its predecessors, believes there is no disagreement in this House concerning Jerusalem as the eternal capital of Israel. United Jerusalem has been and will forever be the capital of the Jewish People, under Israeli sovereignty, a focus of the dreams and longings of every Jew. The Government is firm in its resolve that Jerusalem will not be open to negotiation. The coming years will also be marked by the extension of construction in Greater Jerusalem. All Jews, religious and secular, have vowed "If I forget, thee, O Jerusalem, may my right hand wither." This vow unites us all and certainly includes me as a native of Jerusalem.

The Government will safeguard freedom of worship for the followers of all religions and all communities in Jerusalem. It will rigorously maintain free access to the holy places for all sects and ensure the conduct of a normal and pleasant life for those who visit and reside in the city.

Members of the Knesset, the winds of peace have lately been blowing from Moscow to Washington, from Berlin to Beijing. The voluntary liquidation of weapons of mass destruction and the abrogation of military pacts have lessened the risk of war in the Middle East, as well. And yet this region, with Syria and Jordan, Iraq and Lebanon, is still fraught with danger. Thus, when it comes to security, we will concede nothing. From our standpoint, security takes preference even over peace. A number of countries in our region have recently stepped up their efforts to develop and produce nuclear weapons. According to published reports, Iraq was very close to attaining nuclear arms. Fortunately, its nuclear capability was discovered in time and, according to various testimonies, was damaged during and following the Gulf War. The possibility that nuclear weapons will be introduced into the Middle East in the coming years is a very grave and negative development from Israel's standpoint. The Government, from its very outset – and possibly in collaboration with other countries – will address itself to thwarting any possibility that one of Israel's enemies will possess nuclear weapons. Israel has long been prepared to face the threat of nuclear arms. At the same time, this situation requires us to give further thought to the urgent need to end the Arab-Israeli conflict and live in peace with our Arab partners.

Members of the Knesset, from this moment on the concept of a "peace process" is no longer relevant. From now on we shall not speak of a "process" but of making peace. In that peace-making we wish to call upon the aid of Egypt, whose late leader, President Anwar Sadat, exhibited such courage and was able to bequeath to his people – and to us – the first peace agreement. The Government will seek further ways of improving neighborly relations and strengthening ties with Egypt and its president, Hosni Mubarak.

I call upon the leaders of the Arab countries to follow the lead of Egypt and its president and take the step that will bring us – and them – peace. I invite the King of Jordan and the Presidents of Syria and Lebanon to this rostrum in Israel's Knesset, here in Jerusalem, for the purpose of talking peace. In the service of peace, I am prepared to travel to Amman, Damascus and Beirut today or tomorrow, for there is no greater victory than the victory of peace. Wars have their victors and their vanquished, but everyone is a victor in peace.

Sharing with us in the making of peace will also be the United States, whose friendship and special closeness we prize. We shall spare no effort to strengthen and improve the special relationship we have with the single superpower in the world. Of course we shall avail ourselves of its advice, but the decisions will be ours alone, those of Israel as a sovereign and independent state. We shall also take care to cultivate and strengthen our ties with the European Community. Even if we have not always seen eye to eye and have had our differences with the Europeans, we have no doubt that the road to peace will pass through Europe as well.

We shall strengthen every possible tie with Russia and the other states of the Commonwealth, with China and with every country that responds to our outstretched hand.

Mr. Speaker, Members of the Knesset, security is not only the tank, the plane, and the missile boat. Security is also, and perhaps above all, the person; the Israeli citizen. Security is a man's education; it is his home, his school, his street and neighborhood, the society that has fostered him. Security is also a man's hope. It is the peace of mind and livelihood of the immigrant from Leningrad, the roof over the head of the immigrant from Gondar in Ethiopia, the factory that employs a demobilized soldier, a young native son. It means merging into our way of life and culture; that, too, is security.

. . .

Members of the Knesset, it is proper to admit that for years we have erred in our treatment of Israel's Arab and Druze citizens. Today, almost 45 years after the establishment of the state, there are substantial gaps between the Jewish and Arab communities in a number of spheres. On behalf of the new Government, I see it as fitting to promise the Arab, Druze, and Bedouin population that we shall do everything possible to close those gaps. We shall try to make the great leap that will enhance the welfare of the minorities that have tied their fate to our own.

Members of the Knesset, Theodor Herzl once said: "All of men's achievements are rooted in dreams." We have dreamed and fought and created – despite all the difficulties, despite all the criticism – a safe haven for the Jewish People. This is the essence of Zionism, the dream of generations come true.

. . .

Mr. Speaker, Distinguished Members of the Knesset, this is our declaration of intent, this is our "identity card," these are the desires that we wish to turn into reality. Everything I have said on behalf of the Government and myself has been stated in good faith and in an eagerness to set out on a new path, to stimulate, to reawaken, to create and maintain here a state that every Jew, everywhere, will consider his home and the object of his dreams. Our entire policy can be summarized by a single verse from the Book of Books: "May the Lord give his people strength, may the Lord bless His people with peace."

69 Israel-P.L.O. Recognition

Exchange of Letters Between Prime
Minister Rabin and Chairman
Arafat (September 9, 1993)

1. Letter From Yasser Arafat to Prime Minister Rabin

September 9, 1993

Yitzhak Rabin
Prime Minister of Israel

Mr. Prime Minister,

The signing of the Declaration of Principles marks a new era in the history of the Middle East. In firm conviction thereof, I would like to confirm the following PLO commitments:

The PLO recognizes the right of the State of Israel to exist in peace and security.

The PLO accepts United Nations Security Council Resolutions 242 and 338.

The PLO commits itself to the Middle East peace process and to a peaceful resolution of the conflict between the two sides and declares that all outstanding issues relating to permanent status will be resolved through negotiations.

The PLO considers that the signing of the Declaration of Principles constitutes a historic event, inaugurating a new epoch of peaceful coexistence, free from violence and all other acts which endanger peace and stability. Accordingly, the PLO renounces the use of terrorism and other acts of violence and will assume responsibility over all PLO elements and personnel in order to assure their compliance, prevent violations, and discipline violators.

In view of the promise of a new era and the signing of the Declaration of Principles and based on Palestinian acceptance of Security Council Resolutions 242 and 338, the PLO affirms that those *articles of the Palestinian Covenant* which deny Israel's right to exist and the provisions of the Covenant which are inconsistent with the commitments of this letter are now inoperative and no longer valid. Consequently, the PLO undertakes to submit to the Palestinian National Council for formal approval the necessary changes in regard to the Palestinian Covenant.

DOI: 10.4324/9781003348948-74

Sincerely,

Yasser Arafat
Chairman
The Palestine Liberation Organization

2. Letter From Yasser Arafat to Norwegian Foreign Minister Holst

September 9, 1993

His Excellency
Johan Jorgen Holst
Foreign Minister of Norway

Dear Minister Holst,

I would like to confirm to you that, upon the signing of the Declaration of Principles, the PLO encourages and calls upon the Palestinian people in the West Bank and Gaza Strip to take part in the steps leading to the normalization of life, rejecting violence and terrorism, contributing to peace and stability, and participating actively in shaping reconstruction, economic development, and cooperation.

Sincerely,

Yasser Arafat
Chairman
The Palestine Liberation Organization

3. Letter From Yitzhak Rabin to Chairman Yasser Arafat

September 9, 1993

Yasser Arafat
Chairman
The Palestinian Liberation Organization

Mr. Chairman,

In response to your letter of September 9, 1993, I wish to confirm to you that, in light of the PLO commitments included in your letter, the Government of Israel has decided to recognize the PLO as the representative of the Palestinian people and commence negotiations with the PLO within the Middle East peace process.

Yitzhak Rabin
Prime Minister of Israel

70 Declaration of Principles on Interim Self-Government Arrangements ["Oslo Agreement"] (September 13, 1993)

The Government of the State of Israel and the P.L.O. team (in the Jordanian-Palestinian delegation to the Middle East Peace Conference) (the "Palestinian Delegation"), representing the Palestinian people, agree that it is time to put an end to decades of confrontation and conflict, recognize their mutual legitimate and political rights, and strive to live in peaceful coexistence and mutual dignity and security and achieve a just, lasting, and comprehensive peace settlement and historic reconciliation through the agreed political process. Accordingly, the two sides agree to the following principles:

Article I: Aim of the Negotiations

The aim of the Israeli-Palestinian negotiations within the current Middle East peace process is, among other things, to establish a Palestinian Interim Self-Government Authority, the elected Council (the "Council"), for the Palestinian people in the West Bank and the Gaza Strip, for a transitional period not exceeding five years, leading to a permanent settlement based on Security Council Resolutions 242 and 338.

It is understood that the interim arrangements are an integral part of the whole peace process and that the negotiations on the permanent status will lead to the implementation of Security Council Resolutions 242 and 338.

Article II: Framework for the Interim Period

The agreed framework for the interim period is set forth in this Declaration of Principles.

Article III: Elections

1. In order that the Palestinian people in the West Bank and Gaza Strip may govern themselves according to democratic principles, direct, free, and general political elections will be held for the Council under agreed supervision and international observation, while the Palestinian police will ensure public order.

DOI: 10.4324/9781003348948-75

2. An agreement will be concluded on the exact mode and conditions of the elections . . . , with the goal of holding the elections not later than nine months after the entry into force of this Declaration of Principles. . . .

Article IV: Jurisdiction

Jurisdiction of the Council will cover West Bank and Gaza Strip territory, except for issues that will be negotiated in the permanent status negotiations. The two sides view the West Bank and the Gaza Strip as a single territorial unit, whose integrity will be preserved during the interim period.

Article V: Transitional Period and Permanent Status Negotiations

1. The five-year transitional period will begin upon the withdrawal from the Gaza Strip and Jericho area.
2. Permanent status negotiations will commence as soon as possible, but not later than the beginning of the third year of the interim period, between the Government of Israel and the Palestinian people representatives.
3. It is understood that these negotiations shall cover remaining issues, including: Jerusalem, refugees, settlements, security arrangements, borders, relations and cooperation with other neighbors, and other issues of common interest.
4. The two parties agree that the outcome of the permanent status negotiations should not be prejudiced or preempted by agreements reached for the interim period.

Article VI: Preparatory Transfer of Powers and Responsibilities

1. Upon the entry into force of this Declaration of Principles and the withdrawal from the Gaza Strip and the Jericho area, a transfer of authority from the Israeli military government and its Civil Administration to the authorised Palestinians for this task, . . . , will commence. This transfer of authority will be of a preparatory nature until the inauguration of the Council.
2. Immediately after the entry into force of this Declaration of Principles and the withdrawal from the Gaza Strip and Jericho area, with the view to promoting economic development in the West Bank and Gaza Strip, authority will be transferred to the Palestinians on the following spheres: education and culture, health, social welfare, direct taxation, and tourism. The Palestinian side will commence in building the Palestinian police force. . . . Pending the inauguration of the Council, the two parties may negotiate the transfer of additional powers and responsibilities, as agreed upon.

Article VII: Interim Agreement

1. The Israeli and Palestinian delegations will negotiate an agreement on the interim period (the "Interim Agreement")
2. The Interim Agreement shall specify, among other things, the structure of the Council, the number of its members, and the transfer of powers and responsibilities from the Israeli military government and its Civil Administration to the Council. . . .

Article VIII: Public Order and Security

In order to guarantee public order and internal security for the Palestinians of the West Bank and the Gaza Strip, the Council will establish a strong police force, while Israel will continue to carry the responsibility for defending against external threats, as well as the responsibility for overall security of Israelis for the purpose of safeguarding their internal security and public order.

Article IX: Laws and Military Orders

1. The Council will be empowered to legislate, in accordance with the Interim Agreement, within all authorities transferred to it.
2. Both parties will review jointly laws and military orders presently in force in remaining spheres.

Article X: Joint Israeli-Palestinian Liaison Committee

In order to provide for a smooth implementation of this Declaration of Principles and any subsequent agreements pertaining to the interim period, upon the entry into force of this Declaration of Principles, a Joint Israeli-Palestinian Liaison Committee will be established in order to deal with issues requiring coordination, other issues of common interest, and disputes.

Article XI: Israeli-Palestinian Cooperation in Economic Fields

Recognizing the mutual benefit of cooperation in promoting the development of the West Bank, the Gaza Strip, and Israel, upon the entry into force of this Declaration of Principles, an Israeli-Palestinian Economic Cooperation Committee will be established.

Article XII: Liaison and Cooperation With Jordan and Egypt

The two parties will invite the Governments of Jordan and Egypt to participate in establishing further liaison and cooperation arrangements between the Government of Israel and the Palestinian representatives, on the one hand,

and the Governments of Jordan and Egypt, on the other hand, to promote cooperation between them. . . .

Article XIII: Redeployment of Israeli Forces

1. After the entry into force of this Declaration of Principles, and not later than the eve of elections for the Council, a redeployment of Israeli military forces in the West Bank and the Gaza Strip will take place . . .
2. In redeploying its military forces, Israel will be guided by the principle that its military forces should be redeployed outside populated areas.
3. Further redeployments to specified locations will be gradually implemented commensurate with the assumption of responsibility for public order and internal security by the Palestinian police force pursuant to Article VIII above.

Article XIV: Israeli Withdrawal From the Gaza Strip and Jericho Area

Israel will withdraw from the Gaza Strip and Jericho area . . .

Article XV: Resolution of Disputes

1. Disputes arising out of the application or interpretation of this Declaration of Principles, or any subsequent agreements pertaining to the interim period, shall be resolved by negotiations through the Joint Liaison Committee.

Article XVI: Israeli-Palestinian Cooperation Concerning Regional Programs

Both parties view the multilateral working groups as an appropriate instrument for promoting a "Marshall Plan," the regional programs, and other programs, including special programs for the West Bank and Gaza Strip, as indicated in the protocol attached as Annex IV.

Article XVII: Miscellaneous Provisions

1. This Declaration of Principles will enter into force one month after its signing.
2. All protocols annexed to this Declaration of Principles and Agreed Minutes pertaining thereto shall be regarded as an integral part hereof.

Done at Washington, D.C., this thirteenth day of September, 1993.

For the Government of Israel
For the P.L.O.

Witnessed By:
The United States of America
The Russian Federation

71 Israel-Jordan Common Agenda (September 14, 1993)

Washington, D.C.

A. Goal

The achievement of just, lasting, and comprehensive peace between the Arab States, the Palestinians, and Israel as per the Madrid invitation.

B. Components of Israel-Jordan Peace Negotiations

1. Searching for steps to arrive at a state of peace based on Security Council Resolutions 242 and 338 in all their aspects.
2. Security:

    a. Refraining from actions or activities by either side that may adversely affect the security of the other or may prejudge the final outcome of negotiations.
    b. Threats to security resulting from all kinds of terrorism.

        i. Mutual commitment not to threaten each other by any use of force and not to use weapons by one side against the other including conventional and non-conventional mass destruction weapons.
        ii. Mutual commitment, . . . , to work towards a Middle East free from weapons of mass destruction, conventional and non-conventional weapons; this goal is to be achieved in the context of a comprehensive, lasting, and stable peace characterized by the renunciation of the use of force, reconciliation, and openness. . . .

    c. Mutually agreed upon security arrangements and security confidence building measures.

3. Water:

    a. Securing the rightful water shares of the two sides.
    b. Searching for ways to alleviate water shortage.

DOI: 10.4324/9781003348948-76

4. Refugees and Displaced Persons:
    Achieving an agreed just solution to the bilateral aspects of the problem of refugees and displaced persons in accordance with international law.
5. Borders and Territorial Matters:
    Settlement of territorial matters and agreed definitive delimitation and demarcation of the international boundary between Israel and Jordan with reference to the boundary definition under the Mandate, without prejudice to the status of any territories that came under Israeli Military Government control in 1967. Both parties will respect and comply with the above international boundary.
6. Exploring the potentials of future bilateral cooperation, within a regional context where appropriate, in the following:

    a. Natural Resources:

        *   Water, energy, and environment
        *   Rift Valley development

    b. Human Resources:

        *   Demography
        *   Labor
        *   Health
        *   Education
        *   Drug Control

    c. Infrastructure:

        *   Transportation: land and air
        *   Communication

    d. Economic areas including tourism.

7. Phasing the discussion, agreement, and implementation of the items above including appropriate mechanisms for negotiations in specific fields.
8. Discussion on matters related to both tracks to be decided upon in common by the two tracks.

    It is anticipated that the above endeavor will ultimately, following the attainment of mutually satisfactory solutions to the elements of this agenda, culminate in a peace treaty.

72 Agreement on the Gaza Strip and the Jericho Area (May 4, 1994)

The Government of the State of Israel and the Palestine Liberation Organization (hereinafter "the PLO"), the representative of the Palestinian people;

Preamble

WITHIN the framework of the Middle East peace process initiated at Madrid in October 1991;

REAFFIRMING their determination to live in peaceful coexistence, mutual dignity, and security, while recognizing their mutual legitimate and political rights;

REAFFIRMING their desire to achieve a just, lasting, and comprehensive peace settlement through the agreed political process;

REAFFIRMING their adherence to the mutual recognition and commitments expressed in the letters dated September 9, 1993, signed by and exchanged between the Prime Minister of Israel and the Chairman of the PLO;

REAFFIRMING their understanding that the interim self-government arrangements, including the arrangements to apply in the Gaza Strip and the Jericho Area contained in this Agreement, are an integral part of the whole peace process and that the negotiations on the permanent status will lead to the implementation of Security Council Resolutions 242 and 338;

DESIROUS of putting into effect the Declaration of Principles on Interim Self-Government Arrangements signed at Washington, D.C. on September 13, 1993, and the Agreed Minutes thereto (hereinafter "the Declaration of Principles"), and in particular the Protocol on withdrawal of Israeli forces from the Gaza Strip and the Jericho Area;

HEREBY AGREE to the following arrangements regarding the Gaza Strip and the Jericho Area:

Article I: Definitions

For the purpose of this Agreement:

a.   the Gaza Strip and the Jericho Area are delineated . . . attached to this Agreement;

DOI: 10.4324/9781003348948-77

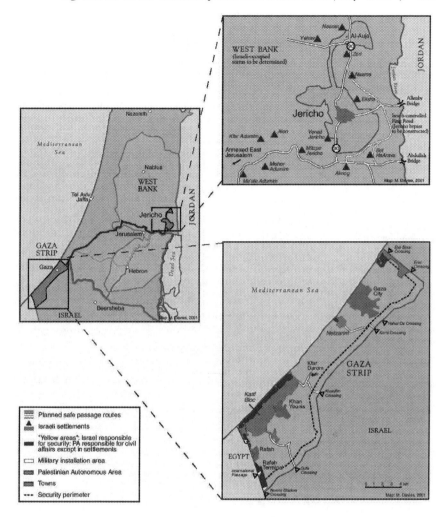

Map 13 Borders at the Time of the Gaza-Jericho Agreement, 1994
Source: Permission granted by the Palestinian Academic Society for the Study of International Affairs to reprint their map of the 1994 Gaza Strip agreement in this book. The original can be found at: www.passia.org/maps/view/29.

b. "the Settlements" means the Gush Katif and Erez settlement areas, as well as the other settlements in the Gaza Strip, as shown . . . ;
c. "the Military Installation Area" means the Israeli military installation area along the Egyptian border in the Gaza Strip, as shown . . . ; and
d. the term "Israelis" shall also include Israeli statutory agencies and corporations registered in Israel.

Article II: Scheduled Withdrawal of Israeli Military Forces

1. Israel shall implement an accelerated and scheduled withdrawal of Israeli military forces from the Gaza Strip and from the Jericho Area to begin immediately with the signing of this Agreement. Israel shall complete such withdrawal within three weeks from this date.
2. Subject to the arrangements included in the Protocol Concerning Withdrawal of Israeli Military Forces and Security Arrangements . . ., the Israeli withdrawal shall include evacuating all military bases and other fixed installations to be handed over to the Palestinian Police, to be established pursuant to Article IX below (hereinafter "the Palestinian Police").
3. In order to carry out Israel's responsibility for external security and for internal security and public order of Settlements and Israelis, Israel shall, concurrently with the withdrawal, redeploy its remaining military forces to the Settlements and the Military Installation Area, in accordance with the provisions of this Agreement. Subject to the provisions of this Agreement, this redeployment shall constitute full implementation of Article XIII of the Declaration of Principles with regard to the Gaza Strip and the Jericho Area only.
4. For the purposes of this Agreement, "Israeli military forces" may include Israel police and other Israeli security forces.
5. Israelis, including Israeli military forces, may continue to use roads freely within the Gaza Strip and the Jericho Area. Palestinians may use public roads crossing the Settlements freely, as provided for in Annex I.
6. The Palestinian Police shall be deployed and shall assume responsibility for public order and internal security of Palestinians in accordance with this Agreement . . .

Article III: Transfer of Authority

1. Israel shall transfer authority as specified in this Agreement from the Israeli military government and its Civil Administration to the Palestinian Authority, hereby established, in accordance with Article V of this Agreement, except for the authority that Israel shall continue to exercise as specified in this Agreement.
2. . . .
3. . . .
4. Upon the completion of the Israeli withdrawal and the transfer of powers and responsibilities . . . , the Civil Administration in the Gaza Strip and the Jericho Area will be dissolved and the Israeli military government will be withdrawn. The withdrawal of the military government shall not prevent it from continuing to exercise the powers and responsibilities specified in this Agreement.
5. . . .

6. The offices of the Palestinian Authority shall be located in the Gaza Strip and the Jericho Area pending the inauguration of the Council to be elected pursuant to the Declaration of Principles.

Article IV: Structure and Composition of the Palestinian Authority

1. The Palestinian Authority will consist of one body of 24 members which shall carry out and be responsible for all the legislative and executive powers and responsibilities transferred to it under this Agreement, in accordance with this Article, and shall be responsible for the exercise of judicial functions . . .
2. The Palestinian Authority shall administer the departments transferred to it and may establish, within its jurisdiction, other departments and subordinate administrative units as necessary for the fulfillment of its responsibilities. It shall determine its own internal procedures.
3. . . .
4. . . .

Article V: Jurisdiction

1. The authority of the Palestinian Authority encompasses all matters that fall within its territorial, functional, and personal jurisdiction, as follows:

   a. The territorial jurisdiction covers the Gaza Strip and the Jericho Area territory . . . , except for Settlements and the Military Installation Area.
   b. Territorial jurisdiction shall include land, subsoil, and territorial waters, in accordance with the provisions of this Agreement.
   c. The functional jurisdiction encompasses all powers and responsibilities as specified in this Agreement. This jurisdiction does not include foreign relations, internal security and public order of Settlements and the Military Installation Area and Israelis, and external security.
   d. . . .

2. The Palestinian Authority has, within its authority, legislative, executive, and judicial powers and responsibilities, as provided for in this Agreement.
3. a. . . .

   b. Israel has authority over the Settlements, the Military Installation Area, Israelis, external security, internal security and public order of Settlements, the Military Installation Area and Israelis, and those agreed powers and responsibilities specified in this Agreement.
   c. Israel shall exercise its authority through its military government, which, for that end, shall continue to have the necessary legislative, judicial, and executive powers and responsibilities, in accordance

with international law. This provision shall not derogate from Israel's applicable legislation over Israelis *in personam*.

4.   . . .
5.   . . .
6.   . . .

Article VI: Powers and Responsibilities of the Palestinian Authority

1. Subject to the provisions of this Agreement, the Palestinian Authority, within its jurisdiction:

    a. has legislative powers as set out in Article VII of this Agreement, as well as executive powers;
    b. will administer justice through an independent judiciary;
    c. will have, *inter alia*, power to formulate policies, supervise their implementation, employ staff, establish departments, authorities, and institutions, sue and be sued, and conclude contracts; and
    d. will have, *inter alia*, the power to keep and administer registers and records of the population, and issue certificates, licenses, and documents.

2.   . . .

Article VII: Legislative Powers of the Palestinian Authority . . .

Article VIII: Arrangements for Security and Public Order

1. In order to guarantee public order and internal security for the Palestinians of the Gaza Strip and the Jericho Area, the Palestinian Authority shall establish a strong police force . . . Israel shall continue to carry the responsibility for defense against external threats, including the responsibility for protecting the Egyptian border and the Jordanian line, and for defense against external threats from the sea and from the air, as well as the responsibility for overall security of Israelis and Settlements . . . , and will have all the powers to take the steps necessary to meet this responsibility . . .

Article IX: The Palestinian Directorate of Police Force . . .

Article X: Passages . . .

Article XI: Safe Passage Between the Gaza Strip and the Jericho Area . . .

Article XII: Relations Between Israel and the Palestinian Authority

1. Israel and the Palestinian Authority shall seek to foster mutual understanding and tolerance and shall accordingly abstain from incitement,

including hostile propaganda, against each other and, without derogating from the principle of freedom of expression, shall take legal measures to prevent such incitement by any organizations, groups, or individuals within their jurisdiction.

2. Without derogating from the other provisions of this Agreement, Israel and the Palestinian Authority shall cooperate in combatting criminal activity which may affect both sides, including offenses related to trafficking in illegal drugs and psychotropic substances, smuggling, and offenses against property, including offenses related to vehicles.

Article XIII: Economic Relations ...

Article XIV: Human Rights and the Rule of Law ...

Article XV: The Joint Israeli-Palestinian Liaison Committee ...

Article XVI: Liaison and Cooperation With Jordan and Egypt ...

Article XVII: Settlement of Differences and Disputes ...

Article XVIII: Prevention of Hostile Acts ...

Article XIX: Missing Persons ...

Article XX: Confidence Building Measures

With a view to creating a positive and supportive public atmosphere to accompany the implementation of this Agreement, and to establish a solid basis of mutual trust and good faith, both Parties agree to carry out confidence building measures as detailed herewith:

1. Upon the signing of this Agreement, Israel will release, or turn over, to the Palestinian Authority within a period of five weeks, about 5,000 Palestinian detainees and prisoners, residents of the West Bank and the Gaza Strip. Those released will be free to return to their homes anywhere in the West Bank or the Gaza Strip. Prisoners turned over to the Palestinian Authority shall be obliged to remain in the Gaza Strip or the Jericho Area for the remainder of their sentence.
2. After the signing of this Agreement, the two Parties shall continue to negotiate the release of additional Palestinian prisoners and detainees, building on agreed principles.
3. The implementation of the above measures will be subject to the fulfillment of the procedures determined by Israeli law for the release and transfer of detainees and prisoners.
4. With the assumption of Palestinian authority, the Palestinian side commits itself to solving the problem of those Palestinians who were in contact with the Israeli authorities. Until an agreed solution is found, the

Palestinian side undertakes not to prosecute these Palestinians or to harm them in any way.

5. Palestinians from abroad whose entry into the Gaza Strip and the Jericho Area is approved pursuant to this Agreement, and to whom the provisions of this Article are applicable, will not be prosecuted for offenses committed prior to September 13, 1993.

Article XXI: Temporary International Presence

1. The Parties agree to a temporary international or foreign presence in the Gaza Strip and the Jericho Area (hereinafter "the TIP"), in accordance with the provisions of this Article.
2. The TIP shall consist of 400 qualified personnel, including observers, instructors, and other experts, from five or six of the donor countries.
3. The two Parties shall request the donor countries to establish a special fund to provide finance for the TIP.
4. The TIP will function for a period of six months. The TIP may extend this period, or change the scope of its operation, with the agreement of the two Parties.
5. The TIP shall be stationed and operate within the following cities and villages: Gaza, Khan Yunis, Rafah, Deir El Ballah, Jabaliya, Absan, Beit Hanun, and Jericho.
6. Israel and the Palestinian Authority shall agree on a special Protocol to implement this Article, with the goal of concluding negotiations with the donor countries contributing personnel within two months.

Article XXII: Rights, Liabilities, and Obligations . . .

Article XXIII: Final Clauses . . .

73 The Washington Declaration (July 25, 1994)

A. After generations of hostility, bloodshed, and tears, and in the wake of years of pain and wars, His Majesty King Hussein and Prime Minister Yitzhak Rabin are determined to bring an end to bloodshed and sorrow. It is in this spirit that His Majesty King Hussein of the Hashemite Kingdom of Jordan and Prime Minister and Minister of Defense, Mr. Yitzhak Rabin of Israel, met in Washington today at the invitation of President William J. Clinton of the United States of America. This initiative of President William J. Clinton constitutes an historic landmark in the United States' untiring efforts in promoting peace and stability in the Middle East. The personal involvement of the President has made it possible to realize agreement on the content of this historic declaration. The signing of this declaration bears testimony to the President's vision and devotedness to the cause of peace.

B. In their meeting, His Majesty King Hussein and Prime Minister Yitzhak Rabin have jointly reaffirmed the five underlying principles of their understanding on an Agreed Common Agenda designed to reach the goal of a just, lasting, and comprehensive peace between the Arab States and the Palestinians, with Israel.

   1. Jordan and Israel aim at the achievement of just, lasting, and comprehensive peace between Israel and its neighbors and at the conclusion of a Treaty of Peace between both countries.

   2. The two countries will vigorously continue their negotiation to arrive at a state of peace, based on (UN) Security Council Resolutions 242 and 338 in all their aspects, and founded on freedom, equality, and justice.

   3. Israel respects the present special role of the Hashemite Kingdom of Jordan in the Muslim holy shrines in Jerusalem. When negotiations on the permanent status will take place, Israel will give high priority to the Jordanian historic role in these shrines. In addition, the two sides have agreed to act together to promote interfaith relations among the three monotheistic religions.

DOI: 10.4324/9781003348948-78

4.   The two countries recognize their right and obligation to live in peace with each other, as well as with all states, within secure and recognized boundaries. The two states affirmed their respect for and acknowledgment of the sovereignty, territorial integrity, and political independence of every state in the area.

5.   The two countries desire to develop good neighborly relations of cooperation between them to ensure lasting security and to avoid threats and the use of force between them.

C.   The long conflict between the two states is now coming to an end. In this spirit, the state of belligerency between Jordan and Israel has now been terminated.

D.   Following this declaration and in keeping with the Agreed Common Agenda, both countries will refrain from actions or activities by either side that may adversely affect the security of the other or may prejudice the final outcome of negotiations. Neither side will threaten the other by use of force, weapons, or any other means against each other, and both sides will thwart threats to security resulting from all kinds of terrorism.

E.   His Majesty King Hussein and Prime Minister Yitzhak Rabin took note of the progress made in the bilateral negotiations within the Jordan-Israel track last week on the steps decided to implement the sub-agendas on borders, territorial matters, security, water, energy, environment, and the Jordan Rift Valley.

In this framework, mindful of items of the Agreed Common Agenda (borders and territorial matters), they noted that the boundary sub-commission has reached agreement in July 1994 in fulfillment of part of the role entrusted to it in the sub-agenda. They also noted that the sub-commission for water, environment, and energy agreed to mutually recognize, as the role of their negotiations, the rightful allocations of the two sides in Jordan River and Yarmouk River waters and to fully respect and comply with the negotiated rightful allocations, in accordance with agreed acceptable principles with mutually acceptable quality.

Similarly, His Majesty King Hussein and Prime Minister Yitzhak Rabin expressed their deep satisfaction and pride in the work of the tri-lateral commission in its meeting held in Jordan on Wednesday, July 20, 1994, hosted by the Jordanian Prime Minister Abdel-Salam al-Majali, and attended by Secretary of State Warren Christopher and Foreign Minister Shimon Peres. They voiced their pleasure at the association and commitment of the United States in this endeavor.

F.   His Majesty King Hussein and Prime Minister Yitzhak Rabin believe that steps must be taken both to overcome psychological barriers and to break with the legacy of war. By working with optimism towards the dividends of peace for all the people in the region, Jordan and Israel are determined to shoulder their responsibilities towards the human dimension of peace-making. They recognize that imbalances and disparities are a root cause of extremism, which thrives on poverty and unemployment and the degradation of human dignity. In this spirit, His Majesty King Hussein and Prime Minister Yitzhak Rabin have today approved a series of steps to symbolize the new era now at hand:

1. Direct telephone links will be opened between Jordan and Israel.
2. The electricity grids of Jordan and Israel will be linked as part of a regional concept.
3. Two new border crossings will be opened between Jordan and Israel – one at the tip of Aqaba-Eilat and the other at a mutually agreed point in the north.
4. In principle, free access will be given to third country tourists traveling between Jordan and Israel.
5. Negotiations will be accelerated on opening an international air corridor between the two countries.
6. The police forces of Jordan and Israel will cooperate in combating crime with emphasis on smuggling and particularly drug smuggling. The United States will be invited to participate in this joint endeavor.
7. Negotiations on economic matters will continue in order to prepare for future bilateral cooperation including the abolition of all economic boycotts.

All these steps are being implemented within the framework of regional infrastructure development plans and in conjunction with the Jordan-Israel bilateral interests on boundaries, security, water, and related issues and without prejudice to the final outcome of the negotiations on the items included in the Agreed Common Agenda between Jordan and Israel.

G. His Majesty King Hussein and Prime Minister Yitzhak Rabin have agreed to meet periodically or whenever they feel necessary to review the progress of the negotiations and express their firm intention to shepherd and direct the process in its entirety.

H. His Majesty King Hussein and Prime Minister Yitzhak Rabin wish to express once again their profound thanks and appreciation to President William J. Clinton and his administration for their untiring efforts in furthering the cause of peace, justice, and prosperity for all the peoples of the region. They wish to thank the president personally for his warm welcome and hospitality. In recognition of their appreciation to the president, His Majesty King Hussein and Prime Minister Yitzhak Rabin have asked President William J. Clinton to sign this document as a witness and as a host to their meeting.

His Majesty King Hussein

Prime Minister Yitzhak Rabin

President William J. Clinton

74 Treaty of Peace Between the Hashemite Kingdom of Jordan and the State of Israel (October 26, 1994)

Preamble

The Government of the Hashemite Kingdom of Jordan and the Government of the State of Israel:

Bearing in mind the Washington Declaration, signed by them on 25th July, 1994, and which they are both committed to honor;

Aiming at the achievement of a just, lasting, and comprehensive peace in the Middle East based on Security Council resolutions 242 and 338 in all their aspects;

Bearing in mind the importance of maintaining and strengthening peace based on freedom, equality, justice, and respect for fundamental human rights, thereby overcoming psychological barriers and promoting human dignity;

Reaffirming their faith in the purposes and principles of the Charter of the United Nations and recognizing their right and obligation to live in peace with each other as well as with all states, within secure and recognized boundaries;

Desiring to develop friendly relations and co-operation between them in accordance with the principles of international law governing international relations in time of peace;

Desiring as well to ensure lasting security for both their States and in particular to avoid threats and the use of force between them;

Bearing in mind that in their Washington Declaration of 25th July, 1994, they declared the termination of the state of belligerency between them;

Deciding to establish peace between them in accordance with this Treaty of Peace;

Have agreed as follows:

Article 1 – **Establishment of Peace**

Peace is hereby established between the Hashemite Kingdom of Jordan and the State of Israel (the "Parties"), effective from the exchange of the instruments of ratification of this Treaty.

DOI: 10.4324/9781003348948-79

Article 2 – **General Principles**

The Parties will apply between them the provisions of the Charter of the United Nations and the principles of international law governing relations among states in time of peace.

In particular:

1. They recognize and will respect each other's sovereignty, territorial integrity, and political independence;
2. They recognize and will respect each other's right to live in peace within secure and recognized boundaries;
3. They will develop good neighborly relations of co-operation between them to ensure lasting security, will refrain from the threat or use of force against each other, and will settle all disputes between them by peaceful means;
4. They respect and recognize the sovereignty, territorial integrity, and political independence of every state in the region;
5. They respect and recognize the pivotal role of human development and dignity in regional and bilateral relationships;
6. They further believe that within their control, involuntary movements of persons in such a way as to adversely prejudice the security of either Party should not be permitted.

Article 3 – **International Boundary**

1. The international boundary between Jordan and Israel is delimited with reference to the boundary definition under the Mandate . . .
2. The boundary . . . is the permanent, secure, and recognized international boundary between Jordan and Israel, without prejudice to the status of any territories that came under Israeli military government control in 1967.
3. The Parties recognize the international boundary, as well as each other's territory, territorial waters, and airspace, as inviolable, and will respect and comply with them.
4. The demarcation of the boundary . . . will be concluded not later than nine months after the signing of the Treaty.
5. It is agreed that where the boundary follows a river, in the event of natural changes in the course of the flow of the river . . . the boundary shall follow the new course of the flow. In the event of any other changes, the boundary shall not be affected unless otherwise agreed.
6. Immediately upon the exchange of the instruments of ratification of this Treaty, each Party will deploy on its side of the international boundary . . .
7. The parties shall, upon the signature of the Treaty, enter into negotiations to conclude, within nine months, an agreement on the delimitation of their maritime boundary in the Gulf of Aqaba . . .

Article 4 – **Security**

1. Both Parties, acknowledging that mutual understanding and cooperation
    in security-related matters will form a significant part of their relations
    . . .
2. The obligations referred to in this Article are without prejudice to the
    inherent right of self-defense in accordance with the United Nations
    Charter.
3. . . .
4. Consistent with the area of peace and with the efforts to build regional
    security and to avoid and prevent aggression and violence, the Parties
    further agree to refrain from the following:

    A. Joining or in any way assisting, promoting, or co-operating with any
        coalition, organization, or alliance with a military or security char-
        acter with a third party, the objectives or activities of which include
        launching aggression or other acts of military hostility against the
        other Party, in contravention of the provisions of the present Treaty;
    B. Allowing the entry, stationing, and operating on their territory, or
        through it, of military forces, personnel, or material of a third party,
        in circumstances which may adversely prejudice the security of the
        other Party.

5. Both Parties will take necessary and effective measures and will
    co-operate in combating terrorism of all kinds. The Parties undertake:

    A. To take necessary and effective measures to prevent acts of terror-
        ism, subversion, or violence from being carried out from their ter-
        ritory or through it and to take necessary and effective measures to
        combat such activities and all their perpetrators;
    B. Without prejudice to the basic rights of freedom of expression and
        association, to take necessary and effective measures to prevent the
        entry, presence, and operation in their territory of any group or organ-
        ization, and their infrastructure which threatens the security of the
        other Party by the use of, or incitement to the use of, violent means;
    C. To co-operate in preventing and combating cross-boundary
        infiltrations.

6. . . .
7. The Parties undertake to work as a matter of priority, and as soon as pos-
    sible, in the context of the Multilateral Working Group on Arms Control
    and Regional Security, and jointly, towards the following:

    A. The creation in the Middle East of a region free from hostile alli-
        ances and coalitions;
    B. The creation of a Middle East free from weapons of mass destruc-
        tion, both conventional and non-conventional, in the context of a
        comprehensive, lasting, and stable peace, . . .

Article 5 – **Diplomatic and Other Bilateral Relations**

1. The Parties agree to establish full diplomatic and consular relations and to exchange resident ambassadors within one month of the exchange of the instruments of ratification of this Treaty.
2. The Parties agree that the normal relationship between them will further include economic and cultural relations.

Article 6 – **Water**

With the view to achieving a comprehensive and lasting settlement of all the water problems between them:

1. The Parties agree mutually to recognize the rightful allocations of both of them in Jordan River and Yarmouk River waters and Araba/Arava ground water in accordance with the agreed acceptable principles, quantities, and quality . . . , which shall be fully respected and complied with.
2. The parties, recognizing the necessity to find a practical, just, and agreed solution to their water problems and with the view that the subject of water can form the basis for the advancement of co-operation between them, . . .
3. The parties recognize that their water resources are not sufficient to meet their needs. More water should be supplied for their use through various methods, including projects of regional and international co-operation . . .

Article 7 – **Economic Relations**

1. Viewing economic development and prosperity as pillars of peace, security, and harmonious relations between states . . . , the parties, . . . affirm their mutual desire to promote economic co-operation between them, as well as within the framework of wider regional economic co-operation.
2. In order to accomplish this goal, the parties agree to the following:

   A. To remove all discriminatory barriers to normal economic relations, to terminate economic boycotts directed at the other Party, and to co-operate in terminating boycotts against either Party by third parties;
   B. Recognizing that the principle of free and unimpeded flow of goods and services should guide their relations, the parties will enter into negotiations with a view to concluding agreements on economic co-operation, . . .
   C. To co-operate bilaterally, as well as in multilateral forums, toward the promotion of their respective economies and of their neighborly economic relations with other regional parties.

Article 8 – **Refugees and Displaced Persons**

Recognizing the massive human problems caused to both Parties by the conflict in the Middle East, as well as the contribution made by them towards the alleviation of human suffering, the parties will seek to further alleviate those problems arising on a bilateral level . . .

Article 9 – **Places of Historical and Religious Significance and Interfaith Relations**

1. Each Party will provide freedom of access to places of religious and historical significance.
2. In this regard, in accordance with the Washington Declaration, Israel respects the present special role of the Hashemite Kingdom of Jordan in Muslim Holy shrines in Jerusalem. When negotiations on the permanent status will take place, Israel will give high priority to the Jordanian historic role in these shrines.
3. The Parties will act together to promote interfaith relations among the three monotheistic religions, with the aim of working towards religious understanding, moral commitment, freedom of religious worship, and tolerance and peace.

Article 10 – **Cultural and Scientific Exchanges**

The parties, wishing to remove biases developed through periods of conflict, recognize the desirability of cultural and scientific exchanges in all fields, and agree to establish normal cultural relations between them. . . .

Article 11 – **Mutual Understanding and Good Neighborly Relations**

1. The Parties will seek to foster mutual understanding and tolerance based on shared historic values, and accordingly undertake:

   A. To abstain from hostile or discriminatory propaganda against each other, and to take all possible legal and administrative measures to prevent the dissemination of such propaganda by any organization or individual present in the territory of either Party;
   B. As soon as possible, and not later than three months from the exchange of the instruments of ratification of this Treaty, to repeal all adverse or discriminatory references and expressions of hostility in their respective legislation;
   C. To refrain in all government publications from any such references or expressions;
   D. To ensure mutual enjoyment by each other's citizens of due process of law within their respective legal systems and before their courts.

2. . . .
3. A joint committee shall be formed to examine incidents where one Party claims there has been a violation of these Articles.

Article 12 – **Combating Crime and Drugs**

The Parties will co-operate in combating crime, with an emphasis on smuggling, and will take all necessary measures to combat and prevent such activities as the production of, as well as the trafficking in illicit drugs, and will bring to trial perpetrators of such acts. . . .

Article 13 – **Transportation and Roads**

Taking note of the progress already made in the area of transportation, the Parties recognize the mutuality of interest in good neighborly relations in the area of transportation and agree to the following means to promote relations between them in this sphere:

1. Each party will permit the free movement of nationals and vehicles of the other into and within its territory according to the general rules applicable to nationals and vehicles of other states. . . .
2. The Parties will open and maintain roads and border crossings between their countries and will consider further roads and rail links between them.
3. The Parties will continue their negotiations concerning mutual transportation agreements in the above and other areas, . . . to be concluded not later than six months from the exchange of the instruments of ratification of this Treaty.
4. The Parties agree to continue their negotiations for a highway to be constructed and maintained between Egypt, Jordan, and Israel near Eilat.

Article 14 – **Freedom of Navigation and Access to Ports**

1. Without prejudice to the provisions of paragraph 3, each party recognizes the right of the vessels of the other Party to innocent passage through its territorial waters in accordance with the rules of international law.
2. Each party will grant normal access to its ports for vessels and cargoes of the other, as well as vessels and cargoes destined for or coming from the other party. Such access will be granted on the same conditions as generally applicable to vessels and cargoes of other nations.
3. International waterways will be open to all nations for unimpeded and non-suspendable freedom of navigation and overflight. The parties will respect each other's right to navigation and overflight for access to either Party through the Straits of Tiran and the Gulf of Aqaba.

Article 15 – **Civil Aviation . . .**

Article 16 – **Post and Telecommunications . . .**

Article 17 – **Tourism . . .**

Article 18 – **Environment**

The Parties will co-operate in matters relating to the environment, a sphere to which they attach great importance, including conservation of nature and prevention of pollution, as set forth in Annex IV. . . .

Article 19 – **Energy . . .**

Article 20 – **Rift Valley Development**

The Parties attach great importance to the integrated development of the Jordan Rift Valley area . . .

Article 21 – **Health . . .**

Article 22 – **Agriculture . . .**

Article 23 – **Aqaba and Eilat**

The Parties agree to enter into negotiations, as soon as possible, and not later than one month from the exchange of the instruments of ratification of this Treaty, on arrangements that would enable the joint development of the towns of Aqaba and Eilat with regard to such matters, *inter alia*, as joint tourism development, joint customs posts, free trade zone, co-operation in aviation, prevention of pollution, maritime matters, police, customs, and health co-operation. . . .

Article 24 – **Claims . . .**

Article 25 – **Rights and Obligations . . .**

Article 26 – **Legislation . . .**

Article 27 – **Ratification and Annexes . . .**

Article 28 – **Interim Measures . . .**

Article 29 – **Settlement of Disputes . . .**

Article 30 – **Registration**

This Treaty shall be transmitted to the Secretary-General of the United Nations for registration in accordance with the previsions of Article 102 of the Charter of the United Nations.

Done at the Araba/Arava Crossing point this day Jumada Al-Ula 21st, 1415, Heshvan 21st, 5755, to which corresponds to 26th October, 1994, in the Arabic, Hebrew, and English languages, all texts being equally authentic. In case of divergence of interpretation, the English text shall prevail.

Abdul Salam Majali
Prime Minister
The Hashemite Kingdom of Jordan

Witnessed by:
William J. Clinton
President of the United States of America

Yitzhak Rabin
Prime Minister
The State of Israel

Part V

From Interim Agreements (1995) to the Present Time

75 Israeli-Palestinian Interim Agreement on the West Bank and the Gaza Strip (September 28, 1995)

The Government of the State of Israel and the Palestine Liberation Organization (hereinafter "the PLO"), the representative of the Palestinian people;

PREAMBLE

WITHIN the framework of the Middle East peace process initiated at Madrid in October 1991;

REAFFIRMING their determination to put an end to decades of confrontation and to live in peaceful coexistence, mutual dignity, and security, while recognizing their mutual legitimate and political rights;

REAFFIRMING their desire to achieve a just, lasting, and comprehensive peace settlement and historic reconciliation through the agreed political process;

RECOGNIZING that the peace process and the new era that it has created, as well as the new relationship established between the two Parties as described above, are irreversible, and the determination of the two Parties to maintain, sustain, and continue the peace process;

RECOGNIZING that the aim of the Israeli-Palestinian negotiations . . . is, among other things, to establish a Palestinian Interim Self-Government Authority, i.e. the elected Council (hereinafter "the Council" or "the Palestinian Council"), and the elected Ra'ees of the Executive Authority, for the Palestinian people in the West Bank and the Gaza Strip, for a transitional period not exceeding five years from the date of signing the Agreement on the Gaza Strip and the Jericho Area (hereinafter "the Gaza-Jericho Agreement") on May 4, 1994, leading to a permanent settlement based on Security Council Resolutions 242 and 338;

REAFFIRMING their understanding that the interim self-government arrangements contained in this Agreement are an integral part of the whole peace process, that the negotiations on the permanent status, that will start as soon as possible . . . , will lead to the implementation of Security Council Resolutions 242 and 338, and that the Interim Agreement shall settle all the issues of the interim period and that no such issues will be deferred to the agenda of the permanent status negotiations;

REAFFIRMING their adherence to the mutual recognition and commitments expressed in the letters dated September 9, 1993, signed by and

DOI: 10.4324/9781003348948-81

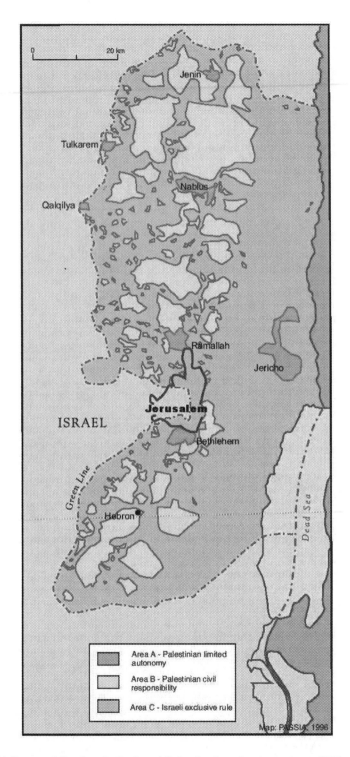

Map 14 Proposed Borders in the Israel-Palestine Interim Agreement, 1995.

Source: Permission granted by the Palestinian Academic Society for the Study of International Affairs to reprint their map of the 1995 Israel-Palestine Interim Agreement in this book. The original can be found at: www.passia.org/maps/view/30.

exchanged between the Prime Minister of Israel and the Chairman of the PLO;

DESIROUS of putting into effect the Declaration of Principles on Interim Self-Government Arrangements signed at Washington, D.C. on September 13, 1993, and the Agreed Minutes thereto (hereinafter "the DOP") . . . concerning the holding of direct, free, and general political elections for the Council and the Ra'ees of the Executive Authority in order that the Palestinian people in the West Bank, Jerusalem, and the Gaza Strip may democratically elect accountable representatives;

RECOGNIZING that these elections will constitute a significant interim preparatory step toward the realization of the legitimate rights of the Palestinian people and their just requirements and will provide a democratic basis for the establishment of Palestinian institutions;

REAFFIRMING their mutual commitment to act, in accordance with this Agreement, immediately, efficiently, and effectively against acts or threats of terrorism, violence, or incitement, whether committed by Palestinians or Israelis;

FOLLOWING the Gaza-Jericho Agreement; the Agreement on Preparatory Transfer of Powers and Responsibilities signed at Erez on August 29, 1994 (hereinafter "the Preparatory Transfer Agreement"); and the Protocol on Further Transfer of Powers and Responsibilities signed at Cairo on August 27, 1995 (hereinafter "the Further Transfer Protocol"); which three agreements will be superseded by this Agreement;

HEREBY AGREE as follows:

Chapter 1 – The Council

Article I: Transfer of Authority

1. Israel shall transfer powers and responsibilities as specified in this Agreement from the Israeli military government and its Civil Administration to the Council in accordance with this Agreement. Israel shall continue to exercise powers and responsibilities not so transferred.
2. Pending the inauguration of the Council, the powers and responsibilities transferred to the Council shall be exercised by the Palestinian Authority established in accordance with the Gaza-Jericho Agreement, which shall also have all the rights, liabilities, and obligations to be assumed by the Council in this regard. Accordingly, the term "Council" throughout this Agreement shall, pending the inauguration of the Council, be construed as meaning the Palestinian Authority.
3. . . .
4. . . .
5. After the inauguration of the Council, the Civil Administration in the West Bank will be dissolved, and the Israeli military government shall be withdrawn. The withdrawal of the military government shall not prevent it from exercising the powers and responsibilities not transferred to the Council.

6. . . .
7. The offices of the Council, and the offices of its Ra'ees and its Executive Authority and other committees, shall be located in areas under Palestinian territorial jurisdiction in the West Bank and the Gaza Strip.

Article II: Elections

1. In order that the Palestinian people of the West Bank and the Gaza Strip may govern themselves according to democratic principles, direct, free, and general political elections will be held for the Council and the Ra'ees of the Executive Authority of the Council . . .
2. These elections will constitute a significant interim preparatory step towards the realization of the legitimate rights of the Palestinian people and their just requirements and will provide a democratic basis for the establishment of Palestinian institutions.
3. . . .
4. . . .

Article III: Structure of the Palestinian Council

1. The Palestinian Council and the Ra'ees of the Executive Authority of the Council constitute the Palestinian Interim Self-Government Authority, which will be elected by the Palestinian people of the West Bank, Jerusalem, and the Gaza Strip for the transitional period agreed in Article I of the DOP.
2. The Council shall possess both legislative power and executive power. . . . The Council shall carry out and be responsible for all the legislative and executive powers and responsibilities transferred to it under this Agreement. The exercise of legislative powers shall be in accordance with Article XVIII of this Agreement (Legislative Powers of the Council).
3. The Council and the Ra'ees of the Executive Authority of the Council shall be directly and simultaneously elected by the Palestinian people of the West Bank, Jerusalem, and the Gaza Strip, in accordance with the provisions of this Agreement and the Election Law and Regulations, . . .
4. The Council and the Ra'ees of the Executive Authority of the Council shall be elected for a transitional period not exceeding five years from the signing of the Gaza-Jericho Agreement on May 4, 1994.
5. . . .
6. . . .
7. . . .
8. . . .
9. . . .

Article IV: Size of the Council

The Palestinian Council shall be composed of 82 representatives and the Ra'ees of the Executive Authority, who will be directly and simultaneously elected by the Palestinian people of the West Bank, Jerusalem, and the Gaza Strip.

Article V: The Executive Authority of the Council

1. The Council will have a committee that will exercise the executive authority of the Council, formed in accordance with paragraph 4 below (hereinafter "the Executive Authority").
2. The Executive Authority shall be bestowed with the executive authority of the Council and will exercise it on behalf of the Council. It shall determine its own internal procedures and decision-making processes.
3. . . .
4. . . .

Article VI: Other Committees of the Council . . .

Article VII: Open Government . . .

Article VIII: Judicial Review . . .

Article IX: Powers and Responsibilities of the Council . . .

Article X: Redeployment of Israeli Military Forces . . .

Article XI: Land

1. The two sides view the West Bank and the Gaza Strip as a single territorial unit, the integrity and status of which will be preserved during the interim period.
2. The two sides agree that West Bank and Gaza Strip territory, except for issues that will be negotiated in the permanent status negotiations, will come under the jurisdiction of the Palestinian Council in a phased manner, to be completed within 18 months from the date of the inauguration of the Council . . .

Article XII: Arrangements for Security and Public Order

1. In order to guarantee public order and internal security for the Palestinians of the West Bank and the Gaza Strip, the Council shall establish a strong police force as set out in Article XIV below. Israel shall continue

to carry the responsibility for defense against external threats, including the responsibility for protecting the Egyptian and Jordanian borders, and for defense against external threats from the sea and from the air, as well as the responsibility for overall security of Israelis and Settlements, for the purpose of safeguarding their internal security and public order, and will have all the powers to take the steps necessary to meet this responsibility. . . .

Article XIII: Security

1. The Council will, upon completion of the redeployment of Israeli military forces in each district, as set out in Appendix 1 to Annex I, assume the powers and responsibilities for internal security and public order in Area A in that district.
2. a. There will be a complete redeployment of Israeli military forces from Area B. Israel will transfer to the Council and the Council will assume responsibility for public order for Palestinians. Israel shall have the overriding responsibility for security for the purpose of protecting Israelis and confronting the threat of terrorism.

   b. In Area B the Palestinian Police shall assume the responsibility for public order for Palestinians and shall be deployed in order to accommodate the Palestinian needs and requirements . . .

Article XIV: The Palestinian Police . . .

Article XV: Prevention of Hostile Acts . . .

Article XVI: Confidence Building Measures

With a view to fostering a positive and supportive public atmosphere to accompany the implementation of this Agreement, to establish a solid basis of mutual trust and good faith, and in order to facilitate the anticipated cooperation and new relations between the two peoples, both Parties agree to carry out confidence building measures as detailed herewith:

1. Israel will release or turn over to the Palestinian side, Palestinian detainees and prisoners, residents of the West Bank and the Gaza Strip. The first stage of release of these prisoners and detainees will take place on the signing of this Agreement and the second stage will take place prior to the date of the elections. There will be a third stage of release of detainees and prisoners. Detainees and prisoners will be released from among categories detailed in Annex VII (Release of Palestinian Prisoners and Detainees). Those released will be free to return to their homes in the West Bank and the Gaza Strip.

2. Palestinians who have maintained contact with the Israeli authorities will not be subjected to acts of harassment, violence, retribution, or prosecution. Appropriate ongoing measures will be taken, in coordination with Israel, in order to ensure their protection. . . .

Chapter 3 – Legal Affairs

Article XVII: Jurisdiction . . .

Article XVIII: Legislative Powers of the Council . . .

Article XIX: Human Rights and the Rule of Law

Israel and the Council shall exercise their powers and responsibilities pursuant to this Agreement with due regard to internationally-accepted norms and principles of human rights and the rule of law.

Article XX: Rights, Liabilities and Obligations . . .

Article XXI: Settlement of Differences and Disputes . . .

Chapter 4 – Cooperation

Article XXII: Relations between Israel and the Council . . .

Article XXIII: Cooperation with Regard to Transfer of Powers and Responsibilities . . .

Article XXIV: Economic Relations . . .

Article XXV: Cooperation Programs . . .

Article XXVI: The Joint Israeli-Palestinian Liaison Committee . . .

Article XXVII: Liaison and Cooperation with Jordan and Egypt . . .

Article XXVIII: Missing Persons . . .

Article XXIX: Safe Passage between the West Bank and the Gaza Strip . . .

Article XXX: Passages . . .

Article XXXI: Final Clauses . . .

Done at Washington DC, this 28th day of September, 1995.

76 "What Is Area C? Planning Policy in the West Bank" (1995)

Israel's planning and building policy in the West Bank is aimed at preventing Palestinian development and dispossessing Palestinians of their land. This is masked by use of the same professional and legal terms applied to development in settlements and in Israel proper, such as "planning and building laws", "urban building plans (UBPs)", "planning proceedings" and "illegal construction". However, while the planning and building laws benefit Jewish communities by regulating development and balancing different needs, they serve the exact opposite purpose when applied to Palestinian communities in the West Bank. There, Israel exploits the law to prevent development, thwart planning and carry out demolitions. This is part of a broader political agenda to maximize the use of West Bank resources for Israeli needs, while minimizing the land reserves available to Palestinians.

Geared towards enabling Israel to use as much West Bank land as possible, Israel's planning policy prevents Palestinian development and dispossesses Palestinians of their land.

The 1995 Oslo II Accord divided the West Bank into three types of areas. Concentrations of Palestinian population in built-up areas, which were – and still are – home to most of the Palestinian population in the West Bank, were designated Areas A and B and officially handed over to Palestinian Authority control. They are dotted throughout the West Bank in 165 disconnected 'islands'. The remaining 61% of the West Bank were designated Area C – the land mass surrounding Areas A and B, where Israel retains full control over security and civil affairs, including planning, building, laying infrastructure and development. This artificial division, which was meant to remain in effect for five years only, does not reflect geographic reality or Palestinian space.

In the West Bank, the potential for urban, agricultural and economic development remains in Area C. Israel uses its control over the area to quash Palestinian planning and building. In about 60% of Area C – 36% of the West Bank – Israel has blocked Palestinian development by designating large swathes of land as state land, survey land, firing zones, nature reserves and national parks; by allocating land to settlements and their regional councils; or by

DOI: 10.4324/9781003348948-82

introducing prohibitions to the area now trapped between the Separation Barrier and the Green Line (the boundary between Israel's sovereign territory and the West Bank).

Even in the remaining 40% of Area C, Israel restricts Palestinian construction by seldom approving requests for building permits, whether for housing, for agricultural or public uses, or for laying infrastructure. . . . As of November 2017, the Civil Administration had drafted and approved plans for only 16 of the 180 communities which lie in their entirety in Area C. The plans cover a total of 17,673 dunams (1 dunam = 1,000 square meters), less than 1% of Area C, most of which are already built-up. . . . Since 2011, seeing that the Civil Administration did not draft plans as it is obliged to do, dozens of Palestinian communities – with the help of Palestinian and international organizations and in coordination with the PA – drafted their own plans. Some of the plans covered communities or villages located in full in Area C and others covered places only partly in Area C. As of September 2018, 102 plans had been submitted to the Civil Administration's planning bodies, but by the end of 2018, a mere five plans – covering an area of about 1,00 dunams (or about 0.03% of Area C) – had received approval.

The odds of a Palestinian receiving a building permit in Area C – even on privately owned land – are slim to none. Given the futility of the effort, many Palestinians forgo requesting a permit altogether. Without any possibility of receiving a permit and building legally, the needs of a growing population leave Palestinians no choice but to develop their communities and build homes without permits. This, in turn, forces them to live under the constant threat of seeing their homes and businesses demolished . . .

Without land for construction, local Palestinian authorities cannot supply public services that require new structures, such as medical clinics and schools, nor can they plan open spaces for recreation within communities. Realizing the economic potential of Area C – in branches such as agriculture, quarrying for minerals and stone for construction, industry, tourism and community development – is essential to the development of the entire West Bank, including creating jobs and reducing poverty. Area C is also vital for regional planning, including laying infrastructure and connecting Palestinian communities throughout the West Bank.

In contrast to the restrictive planning for Palestinian communities, Israeli settlements – all of which are located in Area C – are allocated vast tracts of land, drawn up detailed plans, connected to advanced infrastructure, and the authorities turn a blind eye to illegal construction in them. Detailed, modern plans have been drawn up for the settlements, including public areas, green zones and, often, spacious residential areas. They enjoy a massive amount of land, including farmland that can serve for future development.

Israel's policy in Area C is based on the assumption that the area is primarily meant to serve Israeli needs, and on the ambition to annex large parts of it to the sovereign territory of Israel. To that end, Israel works to strengthen its hold on Area C, to further exploit the area's resources and achieve a permanent situation in which Israeli settlements thrive and Palestinian presence is negligible. In doing so, Israel has de facto annexed Area C and created circumstances that will leverage its influence over the final status of the area.

77 Speech by Prime Minister Yitzhak Rabin to the Knesset Supporting the Israeli-Palestinian Interim Agreement (October 5, 1995)

. . .

We view the permanent solution in the framework of the State of Israel which will include most of the area of the Land of Israel as it was under the rule of the British Mandate, and alongside it a Palestinian entity which will be a home to most of the Palestinian residents living in the Gaza Strip and the West Bank.

We would like this to be an entity which is less than a state, and which will independently run the lives of the Palestinians under its authority. The borders of the State of Israel, during the permanent solution, will be beyond the lines which existed before the Six-Day War. We will not return to the June 4, 1967, lines.

And these are the main changes, not all of them, which we envision and want in the permanent solution:

- First and foremost, united Jerusalem, which will include both Ma'ale Adumim and Givat Ze'ev – as the capital of Israel, under Israeli sovereignty, while preserving the rights of the members of the others faiths, Christianity and Islam, to freedom of access and freedom of worship in their holy places, according to the customs of their faiths.
- The security border of the State of Israel will be located in the Jordan Valley, in the broadest meaning of that term.
- Changes which will include the addition of Gush Etzion, Efrat, Betar, and other communities, most of which are in the area east of what was the "Green Line," prior to the Six-Day War.
- The establishment of blocs of settlements in Judea and Samaria, like the one in Gush Katif . . .

. . .

The first stage of this redeployment of IDF forces will be carried out in three areas, in order to enable the Palestinians to hold elections for the Palestinian Council, and for its chairman, without the IDF being permanently present in Palestinian communities:

DOI: 10.4324/9781003348948-83

Area A, or the "brown" area, the redeployment of IDF forces will be carried out in three areas – will include the municipal areas of the six cities: Jenin, Nablus, Tulkarem, Kalkilyah, Ramallah, and Bethlehem. Responsibility for civilian security in this area will be transferred to the Palestinian Authority.

Area B, or the "yellow" area, includes almost all of the 450 towns and villages in which the Palestinians of the West Bank live. In this area, there will be a separation of responsibilities. The Palestinians will be responsible for managing their own lives, and Israel will have overall responsibility for the security of Israelis and the war against the terrorist threat. That is, IDF forces and the security services will be able to enter any place in Area B at any time.

The third area, Area C, or the "white" area, is everywhere that is not included in the areas that have been mentioned until now. In this area are the Jewish settlements, all IDF installations and the border areas with Jordan. This area will remain under IDF control.

Areas A and B constitute less than 30% of the area of the West Bank. Area C, which is under our control, constitutes more than 70% of the area of the West Bank . . .

I want to remind you: we committed ourselves, that is, we came to an agreement, and committed ourselves before the Knesset, not to uproot a single settlement in the framework of the interim agreement, and not to hinder building for natural growth . . .

An examination of the maps and of the paragraphs of the agreement regarding the additional stages of the redeployment shows that Israel retains complete freedom of action, in order to implement its security and political objectives relating to the permanent solution, and that the division of the areas gives the IDF and the security branches complete security control in Areas B and C, except for the urban areas.

A difficult problem arose in Hebron, and with both sides in agreement it was determined that, prior to the completion of the Halhoul bypass road, there would not be a complete redeployment in the city of Hebron, and this will take another half a year from the signing of the agreement, that is, until March 28, 1996. In our assessment, six months are required in order to build this bypass road. When the Halhoul bypass road and the Hebron bypass road (in the Beit Hagai-Har Manoah-Kiryat Arba section) are built, this will enable the movement of Israelis without their passing through those sections of Hebron which do not have a Jewish presence . . .

I should further emphasize that activity for providing security measures for the Israeli communities – fences, peripheral roads, lighting, gates – will continue on a wide scale. Bypass roads will be built, whose purpose will be to enable Israeli residents to move about without having to pass through Palestinian population centers in places which will be transferred to the responsibility of the Palestinian Authority. In any case, the IDF will not carry out a redeployment from the first seven cities, before the bypass roads are completed. In all, investment in the bypass roads will be about NIS 500 million [$166 million].

. . .

From the depths of our heart, we call upon all citizens of the State of Israel, certainly those who live in Judea, Samaria, and the Gaza Strip, as well as the Palestinian residents to give the establishment of peace a chance, to give the end of acts of hostility a chance, to give another life a chance, a new life. We appeal to Jews and Palestinians alike to act with restraint, to preserve human dignity, to behave in a fitting manner – and, to live in peace and security . . .

78 [Beilin-Abu Mazen] Framework for the Conclusion of a Final Status Agreement Between Israel and the Palestine Liberation Organization (October 31, 1995)

THE ATTAINMENT OF PEACE BETWEEN THE ISRAELI AND THE PALESTINIAN PEOPLES, RESOLVES THE CORE PROBLEM AT THE HEART OF THE ISRAELI-ARAB CONFLICT AND COMMENCES AN ERA OF COMPREHENSIVE PEACE CONTRIBUTING THEREBY TO THE STABILITY, SECURITY, AND PROSPERITY OF THE ENTIRE MIDDLE EAST.

The Government of the State of Israel and the Palestine Liberation Organization (hereafter "the P.L.O."), the representative of the Palestinian people;

WITHIN the framework of the Middle East peace process initiated at Madrid in October 1991;

AIMING at the achievement of a just, lasting and comprehensive peace in the Middle East based on the implementation of UN Security Council Resolutions 242 and 338 in all their aspects;

REAFFIRMING their adherence to the commitments expressed in the Declaration of Principles (hereinafter "the DOP") signed in Washington D.C. on September 13th 1993, the Cairo Agreement of May 4th 1994, and the Interim-Agreement of September 28th, 1995;

REAFFIRMING their determination to live in peaceful coexistence, mutual dignity and security;

DECLARING as null and void any agreement, declaration, document or statement which contradicts this Framework Agreement;

DESIROUS of reaching a full agreement on all outstanding final status issues as soon as possible, not later than May 5th 1999, as stipulated in the DOP;

HEREBY AGREE on the following Framework for a Final Status Agreement;

Article I: The Establishment of the Palestinian State and Its Relations With the State of Israel

1. As an integral part of this Framework Agreement and the full Final Status Agreement:

DOI: 10.4324/9781003348948-84

a.   The Government of Israel shall extend its recognition to the independent State of Palestine within agreed and secure borders with its capital al-Quds upon its coming into being not later than May 5th 1999.

b.   Simultaneously, the State of Palestine shall extend its recognition to the State of Israel within agreed and secure borders with its capital Yerushalayim.

c.   Both sides continue to look favorably at the possibility of establishing a Jordanian-Palestinian confederation, to be agreed upon by the State of Palestine and the Hashemite Kingdom of Jordan.

2.   The State of Israel and the State of Palestine (hereinafter: "the parties") will thereby extend mutual recognition of their right to live in peace and security within mutually agreed borders as defined in Article II of this agreement and in the Final Status Agreement. In particular, the Parties shall:

a.   Recognize and respect each other's sovereignty, territorial integrity and political and economic independence.

b.   Renounce the use of force, and the threat of force as an instrument of policy and commit themselves to a peaceful resolution of all disputes between them.

c.   Refrain from organizing, instigating, inciting, assisting or participating in acts of violence, subversion or terrorism against the other party.

d.   Take effective measures to ensure that acts of or threats of violence do not originate from or through their respective territories, including their airspace and territorial waters, and take appropriate measures against those who perpetrate such acts.

e.   Undertake not to join, assist, or cooperate with any military or security coalition, organization, or alliance hostile to either party.

f.   Exchange and ratify the instruments of peace between them as shall be defined in the full Final Status Agreement.

Article II: The Delineation of Secure and Recognized Borders

. . .

Article III: The Creation of Normal and Stable Inter-State Relations

1.   Upon the exchange of the instruments of ratification of the peace treaty, the Parties agree to establish full diplomatic and consular relations between them and to promote economic and cultural relations including the free movement of people, goods, capital and services across their borders.

. . .

Article IV: Schedule of Israeli Military Withdrawal
and Security Arrangements

1. In implementing UN Security Council Resolutions 242 and 338, the parties agree that the withdrawal of Israeli Military and Security Forces shall be carried out in three stages:
    . . .
2. Thereafter Israel shall maintain a minimal residual force within agreed military compounds and in specified locations. . . .
3. The Parties agree to the formation of an Israeli-Palestinian Coordinating Security Commission (hereinafter "the CSC") to oversee the implementation of Israel's military withdrawal, to establish the modalities governing its residual military presence, and to coordinate all other security matters . . .
4. Joint Israeli-Palestinian patrols will be held along the Jordan River as well as along both sides of the Israeli-Palestinian border, in order to deter, prevent and combat the infiltration or organization of cross-border terrorism and other forms of violent activities. . . .
5. The Parties agree that the State of Palestine shall be demilitarized. . . .
6. The Parties agree that the co-sponsors and other parties agreed upon, shall be invited to guarantee the arrangements for Israel's military withdrawal and other bilateral security agreements as stipulated in this Framework Agreement. . . .

Article V: Israeli Settlements

1. Subsequent to the establishment of the Independent State of Palestine and its recognition by the State of Israel as described in Articles I and III of this agreement:

    a. There will be no exclusive civilian residential areas for Israelis in the State of Palestine.
    b. Individual Israelis remaining within the borders of the Palestinian State shall be subject to Palestinian sovereignty and Palestinian rule of law.
    c. Individual Israelis who have their permanent domicile within the Palestinian State as of May 5th 1999, shall be offered Palestinian citizenship or choose to remain as alien residents, all without prejudice to their Israeli citizenship.
        . . .

Article VI: Jerusalem

1. Jerusalem shall remain an open and undivided city with free and unimpeded access for people of all faiths and nationalities.
2. The Parties further agree that a reform of the current Jerusalem Municipal System and its boundaries shall be introduced not later than May 5th

1999, and shall not be subject to further change by law or otherwise, unless by mutual consent, prior to the fulfillment of the provisions of paragraph 9 below. . . .

3. Within the "City of Jerusalem", neighborhoods inhabited by Palestinians will be defined as "Palestinian boroughs". . . . The number of Israeli boroughs and of Palestinian boroughs will reflect the present demographic balance of 2:1. . . .

4. The Parties agree to maintain one Municipality for the "City of Jerusalem" in the form of a Joint Higher Municipal Council, formed by representatives of the boroughs. . . .

5. . . .

6. The Parties further agree that the municipality of the "City of Jerusalem" shall:

   a. Delegate strong local powers to the sub-municipalities including the right to local taxation, local services, an independent education system, separate religious authorities, and housing planning and zoning, as detailed in Annex Three to the Final Status Agreement;

      . . .

   c. Provide for Israeli and Palestinian citizens resident within the jurisdiction of the City of Jerusalem Municipality and sub-municipalities to vote and seek election for all elected posts as shall be specified in the Jerusalem Municipal bylaws.

7. Within the "City of Jerusalem" both parties recognize the Western part of the city, to be "Yerushalayim" and the Arab Eastern part of the city, under Palestinian sovereignty, to be "al-Quds" (see attached Map/s).

8. Upon the exchange of the instruments of ratification of the peace treaty between them:

   a. The Government of the State of Palestine shall recognize Yerushalayim, as defined under Article VI, paragraph 7 and Annex Three to the Final Status Agreement, as the sovereign Capital of the State of Israel.

   b. The Government of the State of Israel shall recognize al-Quds, as defined under Article VI, paragraph 7 and Annex Three to the Final Status Agreement, as the sovereign Capital of the State of Palestine.

9. The ultimate sovereignty of the area outside Yerushalayim and al-Quds, but inside the present municipal boundaries of Jerusalem, shall be determined by the parties as soon as possible. . . . Without prejudice to the determination of the final status of this area:

   a. Palestinian citizenship shall be extended to Palestinian residence of this area.

   b. In certain matters Palestinian citizens residing in this area shall resort to Palestinian law . . .

   c. The Parties will enjoy free access to and use of the Qalandia Airport in this area. . . .

10. The Parties acknowledge Jerusalem's unique spiritual and religious role for all three great monotheistic religions. Wishing to promote interfaith relations and harmony among the three great religions, the Parties accordingly agree to guarantee freedom of worship and access to all Holy Sites for members of all faiths and religions without impediment or restriction.

11. ...

12. The Parties further agree that:

    ...

13. The State of Palestine shall be granted extra-territorial sovereignty over the Haram ash-Sharif under the administration of the al-Quds Waqaf. The present status quo regarding the right of access and prayer for all, will be secured.

14. The Church of the Holy Sepulchre shall be managed by the Palestinian sub-Municipality. The Joint Parity Committee, shall examine the possibility of assigning extra-territorial status to the Church of the Holy Sepulchre.

15. ...

Article VII: Palestinian Refugees

1. Whereas the Palestinian side considers that the right of the Palestinian refugees to return to their homes is enshrined in international law and natural justice, it recognizes that the prerequisites of the new era of peace and coexistence, as well as the realities that have been created on the ground since 1948, have rendered the implementation of this right impracticable. The Palestinian side, thus, declares its readiness to accept and implement policies and measures that will ensure, insofar as this is possible, the welfare and well-being of these refugees.

2. Whereas the Israeli side acknowledges the moral and material suffering caused to the Palestinian people as a result of the war of 1947–1949. It further acknowledges the Palestinian refugees' right of return to the Palestinian state and their right to compensation and rehabilitation for moral and material losses.

3. The parties agree on the establishment of an International Commission for Palestinian Refugees (hereinafter "the ICPR") for the final settlement of all aspects of the refugee issue as follows:

    a. The Parties extend invitations to donor countries to join them in the formation of the ICPR.

    b. The Parties welcome the intention of the Government of Sweden to lead the ICPR and to contribute financially to its activities.

    c. The Government of Israel shall establish a fund for its contribution, along with others, to the activities of the ICPR.

    d. The ICPR shall conduct all fundraising activities and coordinate donors' involvement in the program.

       ...

5. The State of Israel undertakes to participate actively in implementing the program for the resolution of the refugee problem. . . .
6. The Palestinian side undertakes to participate actively in implementing the program for the resolution of the refugee problem. The Palestinian side shall enact a program to encourage the rehabilitation and resettlement of Palestinian refugees presently resident in the West Bank and Gaza Strip, within these areas.
7. . . .

Article VIII: Israeli-Palestinian Standing Committee

1. The Parties shall establish an Israeli-Palestinian Standing Committee (hereafter: "IPSC"), which will commence activities upon the signing of this Framework Agreement.
2. This IPSC shall be authorized to deal with all matters related to the smooth transition between the Interim Agreement and Final Status Agreement . . .

Article IX: Water Resources

1. The Parties agree that they possess the same natural water resources essential for each nation's livelihood and survival.
2. . . .
4. The Parties further agree to the following:

   a. The development of existing and new water resources to increase availability and minimize wastage.
   b. The prevention of contamination of water resources.
   c. The transfer of information and joint research and the review of the potential for water enhancement.

5. The Parties agree to prepare as soon as possible, but not later than May 5, 1999, an agreed upon coordinated separate and joint water management plan for the joint aquifers that will guarantee optimal use and development of water resources for the benefit of the Israeli and Palestinian nations.
6. The Parties agree to seek to extend their joint co-operation to the Hashemite Kingdom of Jordan, in particular with regard to the waters of the Jordan River and the Dead Sea and to seek to promote wider regional understanding on the exploitation and management of water resources in the Middle East.

Article X: Time Frame and Implementation

A. *The Preparatory Period: May 5th 1996 to May 4th 1999*

   . . .

   The Preparatory Period shall end not later than May 4th 1999.

2.   During this period it is agreed that the following shall be implemented:

   a.   The Final Status Agreement with all Annexes will be prepared, based on the agreements and principles laid down in this Framework Agreement.

   . . .

   e.   The Government of Israel shall establish a program to encourage Israeli settlers to resettle within Israel's sovereign territory. Settlers wishing to take part in this program shall be compensated by the Israeli government before January 1st, 1999, according to guidelines to be announced within three months of the entry into force of this Framework Agreement.

   . . .

   k.   As soon as possible, but not later than May 4th 1999, the interim period shall come to an end and a full Final Status Agreement shall be signed and a Peace Treaty shall be initiated.

B.   *The Implementation Period: May 5th 1999 to May 4th 2000*

   1.   With the signing and entry into force of the Israeli-Palestinian Final Status Agreement, the implementation of the Final Status settlement will commence. The creation of the Independent State of Palestine within secure and recognized borders shall be promulgated by the PLO and its relevant agencies. Immediately thereafter, but not later than within two months, the Peace Treaty shall be signed.
   2.   The Government of the State of Israel shall extend immediate and full diplomatic recognition to the State of Palestine and to al-Quds as its capital, as described in Article VI and Annex Three to the Final Status Agreement.
   3.   The Government of the State of Palestine shall extend immediate and full diplomatic recognition to the State of Israel and to Yerushalayim as its capital, as described in Article VI and Annex Three to the Final Status Agreement.
   4.   . . .
   5.   Upon entry into force of the Israeli-Palestinian Final Status Agreement, the withdrawal of Israeli Military and Security Forces shall commence . . .
   6.   Within the "City of Jerusalem" elections for the two sub-municipalities will be held. . . .
   7.   . . .

C.   *The Post-Implementation Period: May 5th 2000 to May 4th 2007*

   1.   Israeli residual forces shall remain on Palestinian territory. The CSC shall continue to coordinate Israeli and Palestinian security needs.

2. Responsibility for the security of Israeli citizens residents in the State of Palestine, shall remain with the CSC.

D. *The Post-November 5th 2007 Period*

Remaining Israeli residual forces shall withdraw from the Palestinian State contingent on the attainment of peace treaties and security arrangements between Israel and the relevant Arab parties.

79 Speech by Prime Minister Rabin at a Peace Rally (November 4, 1995)

. . .

I was a soldier for 27 years. I fought as long as there was no prospect of peace. I believe that there is now a chance for peace, a great chance, which must be seized . . .

I have always believed most of the nation wants peace and is prepared to take risks for peace. And you here, who have come to take a stand for peace, as well as many others who are not here, are proof that the nation truly wants peace and rejects violence. Violence is undermining the foundations of Israeli democracy. It must be rejected and condemned, and it must be contained. It is not the way of the State of Israel. Democracy is our way . . .

Peace is not just a prayer. It is at first a prayer, but it is also the realistic aspiration of the Jewish people. But peace has its enemies, who are trying to harm us, to torpedo the peace.

We have found a partner in peace among the Palestinians as well – the PLO, which was an enemy and has now forsaken terrorism . . .

There is no painless way forward for Israel. But the way of peace is preferable to war . . .

This rally must send a message to the Israeli public, to the Jews of the world, to the multitudes in the Arab lands and in the world at large, that the nation of Israel wants peace, supports peace – and for this, I thank you.

DOI: 10.4324/9781003348948-85

80 Israel-Lebanon Ceasefire Understanding (April 26, 1996)

The United States understands that after discussions with the governments of Israel and Lebanon, and in consultation with Syria, Lebanon and Israel will ensure the following:

1. Armed groups in Lebanon will not carry out attacks by Katyusha rockets or by any kind of weapon into Israel.
2. Israel and those cooperating with it will not fire any kind of weapon at civilians or civilian targets in Lebanon.
3. Beyond this, the two parties commit to ensuring that under no circumstances will civilians be the target of attack and that civilian populated areas and industrial and electrical installations will not be used as launching grounds for attacks.
4. Without violating this understanding, nothing herein shall preclude any party from exercising the right of self-defense.

A Monitoring Group is established consisting of the United States, France, Syria, Lebanon, and Israel. Its task will be to monitor the application of the understanding stated above. Complaints will be submitted to the Monitoring Group.

In the event of a claimed violation of the understanding, the party submitting the complaint will do so within 24 hours. Procedures for dealing with the complaints will be set by the Monitoring Group.

The United States will also organize a Consultative Group, to consist of France, the European Union, Russia, and other interested parties, for the purpose of assisting in the reconstruction needs of Lebanon.

It is recognized that the understanding to bring the current crisis between Lebanon and Israel to an end cannot substitute for a permanent solution. The United States understands the importance of achieving a comprehensive peace in the region.

Toward this end, the United States proposes the resumption of negotiations between Syria and Israel and between Lebanon and Israel at a time to be agreed upon, with the objective of reaching comprehensive peace.

DOI: 10.4324/9781003348948-86

The United States understands that it is desirable that these negotiations be conducted in a climate of stability and tranquility.

This understanding will be announced simultaneously at 18:00 hours, April 26, 1996, in all countries concerned.

The time set for implementation is 04:00 hours, April 27, 1996.

81 Hussein-Netanyahu Exchange of Letters (March 9/10, 1997)

King Hussein to Israeli Prime Minister Benjamin Netanyahu, 9 March 1997

Prime Minister,

My distress is genuine and deep over the accumulating tragic actions which you have initiated at the head of the government of Israel, making peace – the worthiest objective of my life – appear more and more like a distant, elusive mirage. I could remain aloof if the very lives of all Arabs and Israelis and their future were not fast sliding toward an abyss of bloodshed and disaster, brought about by fear and despair. I frankly cannot accept your repeated excuse for having to act the way you do under great duress and pressure. I cannot believe that the people of Israel seek bloodshed and disaster and oppose peace. Nor can I believe that the most constitutionally powerful prime minister in Israeli history would act on other than his total convictions.

. . .

Mr Prime Minister, if it is your intention to manoeuvre our Palestinian brethren into inevitable violent resistance, then order your bulldozers into the proposed settlement site . . . , then order the young Israeli members of your powerful armed forces surrounding Palestinian towns to commit wanton murder and mayhem . . .

On the question of your withdrawal from territories you have committed Israel, before the U.S., Jordan, and the world, to complete the process by mid-1988, what good did it serve to offer such an insignificant first phase withdrawal? . . . Why are Palestinians still confirming that their agricultural products still rot while awaiting entry into Israel and export? Why the delay when it is known that unless work is authorized to commence on the Gaza port before the end of the month, the complete project would suffer a year's delay? Finally, the Gaza airport – . . . I had requested permission and intended to fly President Arafat myself, in Jordan's official State Tristar, to the Palestinian airport at Gaza . . .

DOI: 10.4324/9781003348948-87

I anticipated your positive response this time. . . . but, alas, it was not to be. . . . How can I work with you as a partner and true friend in this confused and confusing atmosphere when I sense an intent to destroy all I worked to build between our peoples and states. Stubbornness over real issues is one thing, but for its own sake, I wonder. In any event I have discovered that you have your own mindset and appear in no need for any advice from a friend.

I deeply regret having to write you this personal message but it is my sense of responsibility and concern which has prompted me for posterity to do so in the face of the unknown.

Prime Minister Benjamin Netanyahu to King Hussein, 10 March 1997

Your Majesty,

I read your letter with deep concern. The last thing I want is to cause you anguish and disappointment.

But your thorough knowledge of recent events must surely make you aware that the difficulties we face in the peace process did not begin with my government. Had there been a successful and vibrant peace process in May 1996, I would not have been elected by the Israeli public. I was chosen to lead Israel because of the bitter dissatisfaction of the Israeli people with the way the peace process was progressing.

. . .

Nor was the further redeployment (FRD) that we undertook at the end of last week insignificant. I know that there are those around Chairman Arafat who built up his expectations about its dimensions. But the fact is that the Oslo II interim agreement says nothing about the size of the FRD: It leaves this decision wholly to Israel's discretion. This may not be what Mr Arafat wants, but it is the reality of the agreement that he signed.

My predecessors Prime Minister Rabin and Foreign Minister Peres only turned over 2.8 per cent of the West Bank to area A status – to complete Palestinian control. After our FRD, 10.1 per cent of the West Bank will have this status. This is an increase by more than a factor of three. And this is only the first of three FRDs. . . .

What made the FRD particularly difficult for my government was the lack of Palestinian reciprocity. As you recall, the post-Hebron "Note for the Record" listed the obligations of both parties . . . Since Hebron, we explained to the Palestinian Authority that they had violated their obligation by releasing Hamas and Islamic Jihad hardcore terrorists – many of whom were involved in the 1996 bus bombings. The Palestinian Authority failed to respond to our presentations. We informed them that at least four of the twenty or so PA institutions in Jerusalem had unquestionably violated the Palestinian undertaking to restrict PA activities to areas under their jurisdiction. Again the PA failed to respond.

. . .

The Oslo process has not left us an easy legacy. It put off the greatest differences between Israel and the Palestinians to later stages. The process began with Gaza-Jericho, then turned to the cities of the West Bank, and finally the countryside surrounding the cities. Each stage represented a higher level of sensitivity and risk for Israel. . . . We cannot make the Jordanian-Israeli relationship hostage to the Palestinian-Israeli negotiating track. We cannot give every Palestinian-Israeli impasse the power to hurt our own relationship.

. . .

I believe my record speaks for itself. Despite tremendous resistance from some in my own constituency, I have chosen the path of the Oslo process. But I believe that once a decision to take this path is made, both sides must decide that the option of violence has ceased to exist.

Let me assure you that I have always appreciated the courage and resolve with which you have helped keep the peace process alive. I hold you in the highest esteem and I value our friendship and understanding. That is why I must confess I am baffled by the personal level of the attacks against me. . . . We cannot allow the periodic and inevitable disagreements in the peace process to cause such volatile fluctuations in the relations between nations. I can only conclude that you are not being fully apprised of the true picture of the situation in Israel as well as our overriding responsibility to ensure the survival and future of our country. The quest for peace belongs to both camps of the Israeli political spectrum.

Israel and Jordan faced worse crises in the past than the problem we are facing today. . . . Surely, we can achieve this end in a spirit of mutual respect and understanding and with the unrelenting hope and resolve to secure a better future for all the peoples of this region.

Sincerely yours

Benjamin Netanyahu

82 Secretary of State Madeleine Albright, "The Israeli-Palestinian Peace Process," (August 6, 1997)

Remarks and Q&A Session at the National Press Club
Washington, D.C., August 6, 1997
[https://1997-2001.state.gov/www/statements/970806.html]

Secretary Albright: ...

Members of the National Press Club, distinguished guests, colleagues and friends, good afternoon. It is gratifying that, with President Clinton's leadership, we have made progress during the six months I have served as Secretary of State in a number of areas of importance to the security, prosperity and values of the American people.

. . . Unfortunately, progress achieved between Israelis and Palestinians in the Middle East, an area vital to our interests, is now threatened. Today, I would like to discuss the reasons why progress towards peace in this region has stalled and offer some suggestions for restoring positive momentum.

The urgency of that goal was underlined one week ago, when bombs exploded in the Mahane Yehuda market in Jerusalem, killing 13 Israelis – one of whom was also an American citizen – and wounding 168. . . . Sadly and tragically, the Israeli people – almost fifty years into the history of their state – are still the targets of a murderous campaign of terror. No people should have to live this way.

. . .

It also says something hopeful about the future of the Middle East that, as we speak, 162 Arab, Israeli and Palestinian teenagers are in a summer camp in the woods of Maine – a camp sponsored by the Seeds of Peace program – and that this tragic bombing has brought those young people closer together in shock, sorrow and determination to end the cycle of violence in their region.

. . . We stand by Israel in its fight against terror. We maintain our unshakable commitment to Israeli security. And we join governments and peoples from every part of the globe who have condemned last week's savage attack.

Our convictions are clear. Terrorism is evil. It can never be justified. It is the instrument of cowards. It kills the innocent not by accident, but by design.

DOI: 10.4324/9781003348948-88

And its design in the Middle East is to murder the peace process by shredding security and destroying the hope for peace.

. . .

We have come too far in the process of Arab-Israeli peacemaking to allow the vultures of violence to shape the region's future. The stakes are too high; past sacrifices have been too great; and the peoples of the region have been burdened for too long by bloodshed and strife.

. . .

Nevertheless, in Madrid, Oslo, Washington, Cairo and in the Arava, we have seen historic enemies come together, speaking the language of peace. We have seen ties between Arabs and Israelis expand and a process of regional cooperation begin to tackle tough issues such as water, the environment and refugees. We have seen a series of economic summits bring Arab and Israeli business people together to lay the groundwork for increased trade, investment and prosperity.

. . . We must ask ourselves why this process has survived all the traumas and how it has endured despite bitterness, sorrow, suffering and anger.

The answer is that the vast majority of the people of the region – Israelis, Arabs and Palestinians – have come to believe that the status quo is unacceptable, that the costs of conflict are too high, and that the effort to achieve peace holds at least the promise of a better future. . . .

. . .

The question today is not whether the Israelis and Palestinians will reach a mutually acceptable agreement, but when. . . .

Unfortunately, in recent months, since the promising agreement over Hebron, progress has stalled. We now face a crisis of confidence that has put at risk past gains, re-kindled old animosities, and left Israelis and Palestinians alike fearful about what the future may bring.

In order to break the current deadlock, Israelis and Palestinians must return to basic principles. These principles do not focus on the substance of negotiations, which the parties must resolve between themselves at the bargaining table, but rather on the even more fundamental question of how the parties should approach negotiations in order to create the best possible environment for success.

What are these principles?

First, the *sine qua non* for progress is a mutual commitment to security and against violence. . . . There is no place in the peace process for violence or terror and there is no room for using security cooperation as leverage in a negotiation. . . .

In recent months, many Israelis have come to believe that the Palestinian Authority is not taking seriously its vow to combat terror; that Palestinian words are not followed by action; and that the words, themselves, are not consistent or clear. . . . They fear that violence is being given a green light, or a yellow light, or a blinking light – when what is called for in Oslo and what is essential for peace is an unceasing red.

We do not ask the impossible. . . .We cannot expect 100 percent success. But there must be 100 percent effort both with regard to unilateral Palestinian Authority measures against terror and in Israeli-Palestinian security cooperation. What does this mean? Specifically it means sharing information and coordinating law enforcement actions. It means an unrelenting effort to detect and deter potential terrorist acts.

. . .

On this issue, there can be no winks, no double standards, no double meanings and with respect to the imprisonment of terrorists – no revolving doors. Nor can the level of security cooperation ebb and flow with the ups and downs of negotiation. . . . Extremist violence is a grave threat to Palestinian society. Palestinians are sometimes the direct targets of this violence. And they are the ones who suffer economic and humanitarian hardships when Israel clamps down on access.

. . .

The second principle is that both sides agreed to settle their differences over the subjects of negotiation at the bargaining table, and not somewhere else. . . . In practice, this means forgoing unilateral acts which pre-judge or pre-determine issues reserved for permanent status negotiations.

Let me be clear. There is no moral equivalency between suicide bombers and bulldozers, between killing innocent people and building houses. It is simply not possible to address political issues seriously in a climate of intimidation and terror. . . .

Palestinians argue that Israel has taken some actions in recent months that pre-judge issues reserved for permanent status negotiations. These include settlement activity, construction at Har Homa and the confiscation of land. . . . It is fair to ask, how can you create a credible environment for negotiation when actions are being taken that seem to pre-determine the outcome?

. . .

The third rule of the road for the negotiating process is that both parties must demonstrate, in word and deed, their understanding of peace not as one option among many, but as the only option that will provide for the security and well-being of their people. . . . And it is the logic of this partnership that has made it possible to overcome past obstacles and setbacks, as demonstrated by the Hebron agreement earlier this year.

Both Israeli and Palestinian leaders have been consistent in stating their commitment to peace. . . . They must re-iterate their understanding that the future of their two peoples is not a zero-sum game in which one party will win and the other will lose; or in which one will get up from the bargaining table with an advantage over the other. If two people are in a boat heading for the rapids, they should not be arguing about how they got there; they should be rowing together in the direction of security and shore.

. . .

As Israelis and Palestinians move to re-energize their negotiations, it is imperative that the international community do its share to support this effort and to recognize that prosperity is a parent to peace. Every nation with an interest in the region – especially Israel – has a stake in the social and economic progress of the Palestinian Authority and should contribute appropriately to it.

And Arab states have a responsibility to build peace through a normalization of relations throughout their region. Dialogue, business contracts and personal contacts should take the place of boycotts and hostility. . . .

In this regard, I salute King Hussein of Jordan both for his direct contributions to the peace process, and for the effort he has made to persuade Arabs and Israelis alike of the economic and political benefits of peace.

For decades, the United States has been deeply engaged in the pursuit of a comprehensive Middle East peace. President Clinton – like his predecessors – has considered this to be a top priority and has worked hard to support the efforts of the parties to reach that goal. Over the years, U.S. policy towards the Arab-Israeli peace process has been based on key elements which have underlined our approach. These core elements remain valid today. Let me reaffirm them.

We seek a just and lasting peace achieved through direct negotiations, based on UN Security Council Resolutions 242 and 338, including the principle upon which every Arab-Israeli agreement has been built – land for peace. We believe that peace must be accompanied by real security for Israel and her Arab neighbors both from external threats and from terror.

. . .

We cannot, should not, and will not impose solutions. Nor can we create the political will required for Arabs and Israelis to make the tough decisions for peace. These are their decisions, not ours . . .

In the past several months, as the negotiations floundered, and Israeli-Palestinian recriminations intensified, we sought in several ways to put the process back on track. Working closely with President Mubarak of Egypt, our strategic partner in peace, we tried to define a basis on which the parties could re-engage. . . .

We focused on parallel steps each side could take to address the concerns of the other. We built on these contacts to renew discussions on the interim agreement issues and were developing ideas to overcome the differences that had prevented the permanent status talks from convening.

Indeed, on the eve of the July 30 attack in Jerusalem, the President and I felt it was time to send Dennis Ross to the region to convey U.S. ideas. . . .

We must also, however, prepare to do more. The Israeli-Palestinian crisis of confidence has cost the peace process six months. . . . The logic of Oslo, based on mutual recognition, is sound, but the incremental approach of the interim agreement needs to be married to an accelerated approach to permanent status.

To restore momentum, we have to increase confidence on both sides about where the negotiating process is leading and what the outcome of permanent status talks might be. . . . This will require accelerating permanent status negotiations.

Today, this step is urgent and important. Accordingly, provided there is some progress on security issues, I am prepared to travel to the Middle East at the end of this month. I will consult closely with the leaders of the region – and especially with Israeli and Palestinian leaders – to improve the climate for negotiations, and to discuss the procedural and substantive aspects of the permanent status issues.

. . .

Let there be no doubt, the United States will continue to do all it can to promote peace between Israelis and Palestinians throughout the Middle East. We will do so because progress towards peace serves our vital interests, helps protect our friends, reflects our values and because it is right.

. . .

As we approach the new century, there are no Cold War divisions fueling regional rivalry. And the way to peace – once obscure – has been laid out first at Madrid, then more clearly at Oslo, and in the agreements since. . . .

For Israelis, that is the promise of a bustling economy with Pacific Rim potential. It is assurance of a common front in the fight against terror, a steady growth in regional cooperation and the ability to raise children in security and peace.

For Palestinians, it is the promise of an end to decades of strife. It is the chance, as full participants in a growing regional economy, to use their energy and skills to create a future for themselves of steadily increasing prosperity, dignity and hope.

And for all the people of the region, it is the promise, as President Clinton has said, of building a land that is as bountiful and peaceful as it is holy, and of offering to Israelis and Palestinians alike the quiet miracle of a normal life.

The United States cannot choose this future for Israel or for the Palestinians. That is their choice and their challenge. We do not under-estimate the difficulties. We are cognizant of the dangers. But America was built on optimism and on the faith that the future can be made better than the past, not only within our own borders but within all the borders of the Earth. It is in that spirit, and with that faith, that we ask of ourselves and of our partners a renewed and determined effort to transform from hope to reality the elusive dream of a Middle East peace. Thank you very much.

83 The Wye River Memorandum (October 23, 1998)

The following are steps to facilitate implementation of the Interim Agreement on the West Bank and Gaza Strip of September 28, 1995 (the "Interim Agreement") and other related agreements including the Note for the Record of January 17, 1997 (hereinafter referred to as "the prior agreements") so that the Israeli and Palestinian sides can more effectively carry out their reciprocal responsibilities, including those relating to further redeployments and security respectively. These steps are to be carried out in a parallel phased approach in accordance with this Memorandum and the attached time line. They are subject to the relevant terms and conditions of the prior agreements and do not supersede their other requirements.

I. Further Redeployments ...

II. Security

In the provisions on security arrangements of the Interim Agreement, the Palestinian side agreed to take all measures necessary in order to prevent acts of terrorism, crime, and hostilities directed against the Israeli side, against individuals falling under the Israeli side's authority and against their property, just as the Israeli side agreed to take all measures necessary in order to prevent acts of terrorism, crime, and hostilities directed against the Palestinian side, against individuals falling under the Palestinian side's authority, and against their property. The two sides also agreed to take legal measures against offenders within their jurisdiction and to prevent incitement against each other by any organizations, groups, or individuals within their jurisdiction.

Both sides recognize that it is in their vital interests to combat terrorism and fight violence in accordance with Annex I of the Interim Agreement and the Note for the Record. They also recognize that the struggle against terror and violence must be comprehensive in that it deals with terrorists, the terror support structure, and the environment conducive to the support of terror. It must be continuous and constant over a long-term, in that there can be no pauses in the work against terrorists and their structure. It must be cooperative in that

DOI: 10.4324/9781003348948-89

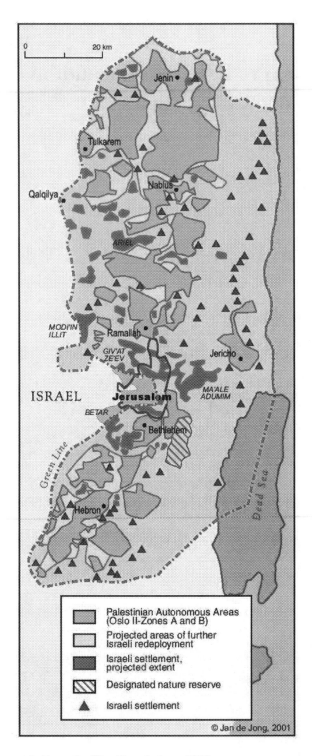

Map 15 Proposals From the Wye Negotiations, 1998

Source: Permission granted by the Palestinian Academic Society for the Study of International Affairs to reprint their map of the 1998 Wye River Memorandum in this book. The original can be found at: www.passia.org/maps/view/32.

no effort can be fully effective without Israeli-Palestinian cooperation and the continuous exchange of information, concepts, and actions. . . .

A. SECURITY ACTIONS

1. OUTLAWING AND COMBATING TERRORIST ORGANIZATIONS

The Palestinian side will make known its policy of zero tolerance for terror and violence against both sides. . . .

The Palestinian side will apprehend the specific individuals suspected of perpetrating acts of violence and terror for the purpose of further investigation, and prosecution and punishment of all persons involved in acts of violence and terror. . . .

2. PROHIBITING ILLEGAL WEAPONS

The Palestinian side will ensure an effective legal framework is in place to criminalize, in conformity with the prior agreements, any importation, manufacturing, or unlicensed sale, acquisition or possession of firearms, ammunition or weapons in areas under Palestinian jurisdiction. . . .

3. PREVENTING INCITEMENT

. . . the Palestinian side will issue a decree prohibiting all forms of incitement to violence or terror, and establishing mechanisms for acting systematically against all expressions or threats of violence or terror. This decree will be comparable to the existing Israeli legislation which deals with the same subject . . .

B. SECURITY COOPERATION

The two sides agree that their security cooperation will be based on a spirit of partnership and will include, among other things, the following steps:

1. BILATERAL COOPERATION

There will be full bilateral security cooperation between the two sides which will be continuous, intensive, and comprehensive.

2. FORENSIC COOPERATION

There will be an exchange of forensic expertise, training, and other assistance.

3. TRILATERAL COMMITTEE

In addition to the bilateral Israeli-Palestinian security cooperation, a high-ranking U.S.-Palestinian-Israeli committee will meet as required and not less than biweekly to assess current threats, deal with any impediments to effective security cooperation and coordination, and address the steps being taken to combat terror and terrorist organizations. The committee will also serve as a forum to address the issue of external support for terror . . .

C. OTHER ISSUES

1. PALESTINIAN POLICE FORCE

The Palestinian side will provide a list of its policemen to the Israeli side in conformity with the prior agreements.

Should the Palestinian side request technical assistance, the U.S. has indicated its willingness to help meet these needs in cooperation with other donors. . . .

2. PLO CHARTER

The Executive Committee of the Palestine Liberation Organization and the Palestinian Central Council will reaffirm the letter of 22 January 1998 from PLO Chairman Yasir Arafat to President Clinton concerning the nullification of the Palestinian National Charter provisions that are inconsistent with the letters exchanged between the PLO and the Government of Israel on 9/10 September 1993. . . .

3. LEGAL ASSISTANCE IN CRIMINAL MATTERS . . .

4. HUMAN RIGHTS AND THE RULE OF LAW

. . . the Palestinian Police will exercise powers and responsibilities to implement this Memorandum with due regard to internationally accepted norms of human rights and the rule of law, and will be guided by the need to protect the public, respect human dignity, and avoid harassment.

III. Interim Committees and Economic Issues

1. The Israeli and Palestinian sides reaffirm their commitment to enhancing their relationship and agree on the need actively to promote economic development in the West Bank and Gaza . . .
2. The Israeli and Palestinian sides have agreed on arrangements which will permit the timely opening of the Gaza Industrial Estate. They also have concluded a "Protocol Regarding the Establishment and Operation of the International Airport in the Gaza Strip During the Interim Period."
3. Both sides will renew negotiations on Safe Passage immediately. As regards the southern route, the sides will make best efforts to conclude

the agreement within a week of the entry into force of this Memorandum. Operation of the southern route will start as soon as possible thereafter. As regards the northern route, negotiations will continue with the goal of reaching agreement as soon as possible. Implementation will take place expeditiously thereafter.

4. The Israeli and Palestinian sides acknowledge the great importance of the Port of Gaza for the development of the Palestinian economy and the expansion of Palestinian trade. They commit themselves to proceeding without delay to conclude an agreement to allow the construction and operation of the port in accordance with the prior agreements. The Israeli-Palestinian Committee will reactivate its work immediately with a goal of concluding the protocol within 60 days, which will allow commencement of the construction of the port.

5. The two sides recognize that unresolved legal issues adversely affect the relationship between the two peoples. They therefore will accelerate efforts through the Legal Committee to address outstanding legal issues and to implement solutions to these issues in the shortest possible period. . . .

6. The Israeli and Palestinian sides also will launch a strategic economic dialogue to enhance their economic relationship . . .

7. The two sides agree on the importance of continued international donor assistance to facilitate implementation by both sides of agreements reached. They also recognize the need for enhanced donor support for economic development in the West Bank and Gaza. They agree to jointly approach the donor community to organize a Ministerial Conference before the end of 1998 to seek pledges for enhanced levels of assistance.

IV. Permanent Status Negotiations

The two sides will immediately resume permanent status negotiations on an accelerated basis and will make a determined effort to achieve the mutual goal of reaching an agreement by May 4, 1999. The negotiations will be continuous and without interruption. The U.S. has expressed its willingness to facilitate these negotiations.

V. Unilateral Actions

Recognizing the necessity to create a positive environment for the negotiations, neither side shall initiate or take any step that will change the status of the West Bank and the Gaza Strip in accordance with the Interim Agreement.
    . . .

This Memorandum will enter into force ten days from the date of signature.

Done at Washington, D.C. this 23d day of October 1998.

For the Government of the State of Israel:
Benjamin Netanyahu

For the PLO:
Yasir Arafat

Witnessed by:
William J. Clinton
The United States of America

----

84 Address in the Knesset by Prime Minister-Elect Ehud Barak Upon the Presentation of His Government (July 7, 1999)

Your Excellency President and Mrs. Weizman, Mr. Speaker, our friend Avraham Burg, please accept my heartfelt congratulations on your deserved election as Speaker of the Knesset.

. . .

Let me begin with a personal comment. I have been a soldier for practically all my adult life. I have known the pride of victory, but also the pain of failure. . . . I am not alone here today on this podium. Together with me are generations of IDF soldiers who withstood the most severe trials of fire in order to secure our liberty. Together with me are those who returned at dawn from the nighttime inferno, carrying on their shoulders the silent stretchers bearing their lifeless comrades.

. . .

I am proud to submit to the people and the House a new, broad-based, good, representative government, supported by the large majority of Knesset members and the citizens of the state. It was not in vain that I took advantage of the full time allotted by law to form the government. I did not take the easy way. The lessons of Jewish history and the depth of the social and political chasm in Israel today required me to choose the long and patient way in order to achieve the goal which I had set for myself: to form a government which will act during a time of difficult national decisions, through consent and balance between most sections of the people. I did not accept any disqualification of any side.

During the negotiations I seriously examined the possibility of expanding the basis of the coalition even further. This was not possible and in retrospect, this may have been best. In a democratic system, there is great importance to the role of a parliamentary opposition, and it is my intention to express my recognition of this by maintaining ongoing contacts with, providing information to, and holding consultations with the heads of those factions which are not members of the coalition. I expect substantive and constructive criticism from the opposition which will also enable consideration of its opinion in managing affairs of state.

Mr. Speaker, Members of the Knesset,

DOI: 10.4324/9781003348948-90

The basic guidelines of the government and the coalition agreements are before you. Everything is open and fully disclosed. Nothing is concealed, there are no secret agreements, no "under-the-table" understandings, and as you have seen, there are neither financial commitments nor favors to specific sectors or groups.

. . .

The Zionist idea which was proclaimed in Basel over 100 years ago has brought about a revolution in the life of the Jewish people and restored it to the stage of history as a sovereign, independent, strong, and prosperous people.

The ingathering of the exiles, the settlement of the land, the revival of the language, culture, and scientific and intellectual life, the creation of a splendid educational system and Torah institutions, the establishment of a strong national economy, an exemplary defense force and security services, sophisticated infrastructure systems and advanced health and welfare services, the creation of a democratic, free, and diverse society based on the supremacy of the rule of law – all of these are achievements which are utterly unparalleled in the history of nations. They were achieved despite the Holocaust, which wiped out a third of our people, and during an unrelenting struggle and a bloody war in which the best of our children and comrades gave their lives. It is because of them that we are here – determined and confident and aspiring to historic acceptance and an end to wars and enmity.

We embrace the bereaved families and the families of the MIAs and POWs, the disabled and wounded of the security establishment. May peace ease their suffering. We know that the victory of Zionism will not be complete until the achievement of genuine peace, full security, and relations of friendship, trust, and cooperation with all our neighbors. And therefore, the government's supreme goal will be to bring peace and security to Israel, while safeguarding the vital interests of the State of Israel. The great historic breakthrough to peace took place 20 years ago, through the vision and courage of two outstanding leaders: the late Menahem Begin and the late Anwar Sadat, may they rest in peace.

A further milestone was the Madrid Conference during the tenure of Prime Minister Yitzhak Shamir. Renewed and far-reaching impetus was imparted by Yitzhak Rabin, the courageous and unswerving leader, from whom I learned so much, and who was assassinated during the struggle for his path, the path of peace, and with him, by our friend Shimon Peres.

The government of Benjamin Netanyahu indeed opened with the Hebron agreement, but it was unable to implement the Wye accords which it had signed.

Now it is our duty to complete the mission and establish a comprehensive peace in the Middle East which has known so much war. It is our duty to ourselves and our children to take decisive measures to strengthen Israel by ending the Arab-Israeli conflict. This government is determined to make every effort, pursue every path, and do everything necessary for Israel's security, the achievement of peace, and the prevention of war.

We have an historic obligation to take advantage of the "window of opportunity" which has opened before us in order to bring long-term security and peace to Israel. We know that comprehensive and stable peace can be established only if it rests, simultaneously, on four pillars: Egypt, Jordan, and Syria and Lebanon, in some sense as a single bloc, and of course the Palestinians. As long as peace is not grounded on all these four pillars, it will remain incomplete and unstable. The Arab countries must know that only a strong and self-confident Israel can bring peace.

Here, today, I call upon all the leaders of the region to extend their hands to meet our outstretched hand, and toward a "peace of the brave," in a region which has known so much war, blood, and suffering. To our neighbors the Palestinians, I wish to say: The bitter conflict between us has brought great suffering to both our peoples. Now, there is no reason to settle accounts over historical mistakes. Perhaps things could have been otherwise, but we cannot change the past; we can only make the future better. I am not only cognizant of the sufferings of my people, but I also recognize the sufferings of the Palestinian people. My ambition and desire is to bring an end to violence and suffering, and to work with the elected Palestinian leadership, under Chairman Yasser Arafat, in partnership and respect, in order to jointly arrive at a fair and agreed settlement for co-existence in freedom, prosperity, and good neighborliness in this beloved land where the two peoples will always live.

To Syrian President Hafez Assad, I say that the new Israeli government is determined, as soon as possible, to advance the negotiations for the achievement of full, bilateral treaty of peace and security, on the basis of Security Council Resolutions 242 and 338.

We have been tough and bitter adversaries on the battlefield. The time has come to establish a secure and courageous peace which will ensure the futures of our peoples, our children, and our grandchildren.

It is my intention to bring an end to the IDF presence in Lebanon within one year, to deploy the IDF, through agreement, along the border, and to bring our boys home while also taking the necessary measures to guarantee the welfare and security of residents along the northern border, as well as the future of the Lebanese security and civilian assistance personnel who have worked alongside us, over all these years, for the sake of the residents of the region.

. . .

Mr. Speaker, distinguished Knesset,

These two missions – arriving at a permanent settlement with the Palestinians and achieving peace with Syria and Lebanon – are, in my eyes, equally vital and urgent. One neither outranks the other, nor has priority over it.

. . .

I know very well that difficult negotiations, replete with crises and ups-and-downs, await us before we reach our desired goal. I can only promise that, if the other side displays the same degree of determination and good will to reach an agreement as on our side, no force in the world will prevent us from achieving peace here.

In this context, I attach the greatest importance to the support of our partners to peace treaties: Egypt and Jordan. I believe that President Hosni Mubarak and King Abdullah can play a vital role in creating the dynamics and an atmosphere of trust so needed for progress toward peace. They can also advance education for peace among the children of Egypt and Jordan, the Palestinians and, in the future, also of Syria and Lebanon – education for peace, which is a condition for any long-term, stable peace. I am convinced that King Hassan of Morocco can also contribute to this, as can other countries who already, in the past, opened channels of communication with Israel, cooperating with the peace process in various spheres. My aspiration will be to firmly resume these contacts in order to create a favorable regional atmosphere that can assist the negotiations.

It goes without saying that the assistance of the United States is a fundamental condition for any progress toward resolving the conflict in the region. The friendship of America, under the leadership of President Clinton, its generosity, and the intensity of its support for the peace process in the Middle East constitute a vital component in the chance to achieve our goal. I will soon leave for the United States, at the invitation of President Clinton, a loyal friend of Israel, in order to discuss the gamut of issues facing us: first and foremost, the renewal of the peace process on all tracks, and the fortification of the strength and security of Israel.

. . .

In the coming days, I will bring before the Knesset a proposed to change the Basic Law: The Government, for an increase in the number of ministers, as required by the size of the coalition and the composition of the Knesset. In any form, this is the best government for the State of Israel at this time. We are the bearers of the torch which our predecessors have transferred to us, and we assume full responsibility for moving forward. Today, the government requests the confidence of the 15th Knesset in the knowledge that the eyes of all Israelis are focused thereon, in prayer and with great hope.

Today, millions of eyes in Israel, millions of eyes of Jews around the world, and millions of eyes around the whole world are focused on us, praying that we will know to lead the country, with determination and a sure hand toward a new path, momentum and a new page in the chronicles of the State of Israel. A new page of peace in an arena which, in recent generations, has known mostly pain, bereavement, and suffering.

Accompanied by the blessings and concern of everyone, we embark today on the long and arduous path. I would be most appreciative if you would express your confidence in the government today and wish it well and God speed.

85 Sharm el-Sheikh Memorandum and the Resumption of Permanent Status Negotiations (September 4, 1999)

The Government of the State of Israel ("GOI") and the Palestine Liberation Organization ("PLO") commit themselves to full and mutual implementation of the Interim Agreement and all other agreements concluded between them since September 1993 (hereinafter "the prior agreements"), and all outstanding commitments emanating from the prior agreements. Without derogating from the other requirements of the prior agreements, the two Sides have agreed as follows:

1. Permanent Status negotiations:
    1. In the context of the implementation of the prior agreements, the two Sides will resume the Permanent Status negotiations in an accelerated manner and will make a determined effort to achieve their mutual goal of reaching a Permanent Status Agreement based on the agreed agenda i.e. the specific issues reserved for Permanent Status negotiators and other issues of common interest.
    2. The two Sides reaffirm their understanding that the negotiations on the Permanent Status will lead to the implementation of Security Council Resolutions 242 and 338;
    3. The two Sides will make a determined effort to conclude a Framework Agreement on all Permanent Status issues in five months from the resumption of the Permanent Status negotiations;
    4. The two Sides will conclude a comprehensive agreement on all Permanent Status issues within one year from the resumption of the Permanent Status negotiations;
    5. . . .

2. Phase One and Phase Two of the Further Redeployments
    The Israeli Side undertakes the following with regard to Phase One and Phase Two of the Further Redeployments:

    1. On September 5, 1999, to transfer 7% from Area C to Area B;
    2. On November 15, 1999, to transfer 2% from Area B to Area A and 3% from Area C to Area B;

DOI: 10.4324/9781003348948-91

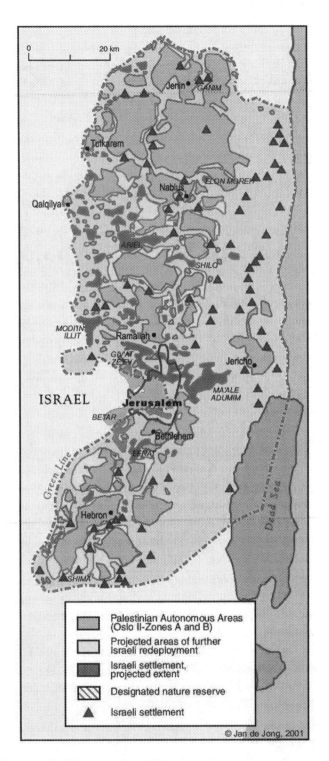

Map 16 Sharm el-Sheikh Proposals, 1999

Source: Permission granted by the Palestinian Academic Society for the Study of International Affairs to reprint their map of the 1999 Sharm el-Sheikh Memorandum in this book. The original can be found at: www.passia.org/maps/view/33.

3. On January 20, 2000, to transfer 1% from Area C to Area A, and 5.1% from Area B to Area A.

3. Release of Prisoners

    1. The two Sides shall establish a joint committee that shall follow-up on matters related to release of Palestinian prisoners.
    2. The Government of Israel shall release Palestinian and other prisoners who committed their offences prior to September 13, 1993, and were arrested prior to May 4, 1994 . . .
    3. The first stage of release of prisoners shall be carried out on September 5, 1999 and shall consist of 200 prisoners. The second stage of release of prisoners shall be carried out on October 8, 1999 and shall consist of 150 prisoners;
    4. . . .
    5. The Israeli side will aim to release Palestinian prisoners before next Ramadan.

4. Committees . . .
5. Safe Passage

    1. The operation of the Southern Route of the Safe Passage for the movement of persons, vehicles, and goods will start on October 1, 1999 . . . in accordance with the details of operation, which will be provided for in the Safe Passage Protocol that will be concluded by the two Sides not later than September 30, 1999;
    2. The two Sides will agree on the specific location of the crossing point of the Northern Route of the Safe Passage . . . not later than October 5, 1999;
    3. . . .
    4. . . .
    5. In between the operation of the Southern crossing point of the Safe Passage and the Northern crossing point of the Safe Passage, Israel will facilitate arrangements for the movement between the West Bank and the Gaza Strip, using non-Safe Passage routes other than the Southern Route of the Safe Passage;
    6. . . .

6. Gaza Sea Port

    The two Sides have agreed on the following principles to facilitate and enable the construction works of the Gaza Sea Port. . . .

    1. The Israeli Side agrees that the Palestinian Side shall commence construction works in and related to the Gaza Sea Port on October 1, 1999;
    2. The two Sides agree that the Gaza Sea Port will not be operated in any way before reaching a joint Sea Port protocol on all aspects of operating the Port, including security;

3. The Gaza Sea Port is a special case, like the Gaza Airport, being situated in an area under the responsibility of the Palestinian Side and serving as an international passage. Therefore, until the conclusion of a joint Sea Port Protocol, all activities and arrangements relating to the construction of the Port shall be in accordance with the provisions of the Interim Agreement, especially those relating to international passages, as adapted in the Gaza Airport Protocol;

4. . . .

5. In this context, the Israeli side will facilitate on an on-going basis the works related to the construction of the Gaza Sea Port, including the movement in and out of the Port of vessels, equipment, resources, and material required for the construction of the Port;

6. . . .

7. Hebron Issues

    1. The Shuhada Road in Hebron shall be opened for the movement of Palestinian vehicles in two phases . . .

    2. The wholesale market-Hasbahe will be opened not later than November 1, 1999, in accordance with arrangements which will be agreed upon by the two Sides;

    3. . . .

8. Security

    1. The two Sides will, in accordance with the prior agreements, act to ensure the immediate, efficient, and effective handling of any incident involving a threat or act of terrorism, violence, or incitement, whether committed by Palestinians or Israelis. To this end, they will cooperate in the exchange of information and coordinate policies and activities. Each side shall immediately and effectively respond to the occurrence or anticipated occurrence of an act of terrorism, violence, or incitement and shall take all necessary measures to prevent such an occurrence;

    2. Pursuant to the prior agreements, the Palestinian side undertakes to implement its responsibilities for security, security cooperation, on-going obligations, and other issues emanating from the prior agreements, including, in particular, the following obligations emanating from the Wye River Memorandum:

        1. continuation of the program for the collection of the illegal weapons, including reports;

        2. apprehension of suspects, including reports;

        3. forwarding of the list of Palestinian policemen to the Israeli Side not later than September 13, 1999;

        4. beginning of the review of the list by the Monitoring and Steering Committee not later than October 15, 1999.

9. The two Sides call upon the international donor community to enhance its commitment and financial support to the Palestinian economic development and the Israeli-Palestinian peace process.

10. . . .

11. Obligations pertaining to dates, which occur on holidays or Saturdays, shall be carried out on the first subsequent working day.

This memorandum will enter into force one week from the date of its signature.

Made and signed in Sharm el-Sheikh, this fourth day of September 1999.

For the Government of the State of Israel
For the PLO

Witnessed by
For the Arab Republic of Egypt
For the United States of America
For the Hashemite Kingdom of Jordan

86 Protocol Concerning Safe Passage Between the West Bank and the Gaza Strip (October 5, 1999)

1. Preamble

    A. Pursuant to the Wye River Memorandum of October 23, 1998 and the Sharm el-Sheikh Memorandum on Implementation Timeline of Outstanding Commitments of Agreements Signed and the Resumption of Permanent Status Negotiations of September 4, 1999; and

    In accordance with the Israeli-Palestinian Interim Agreement on the West Bank and the Gaza Strip, signed in Washington, D.C. on September 28, 1995 (hereinafter "the Agreement"); . . .

    both sides hereby agree to the following "Protocol Concerning Safe Passage between the West Bank and the Gaza Strip" (hereinafter the "Protocol").

    B. This Protocol establishes the modalities for the use of safe passage . . .

    C. This Protocol may be amended by a decision of both sides.

    D. This Protocol will come into force upon the signing thereof by both parties.

    E. This Preamble is an integral part of this Protocol.

2. General Provisions

    A. . . .

    B. 1. Israel will ensure safe passage for persons and transportation during daylight hours (from sunrise to sunset) or as otherwise agreed, but in any event not less than 10 hours a day.

    2. Travelers will be required to commence their journey as follows,

        1. one and a half hours for travellers using private vehicles and taxis;

        2. two hours for commercial traffic and buses, before sunset on the day of the journey.

    C. 1. Safe passage will be effected by means of privately owned road vehicles and public transportation, as detailed in paragraph 5 below.

    2. Safe passage shall be via the following designated crossing points:

        1. the Erez crossing point (for persons and vehicles only);

DOI: 10.4324/9781003348948-92

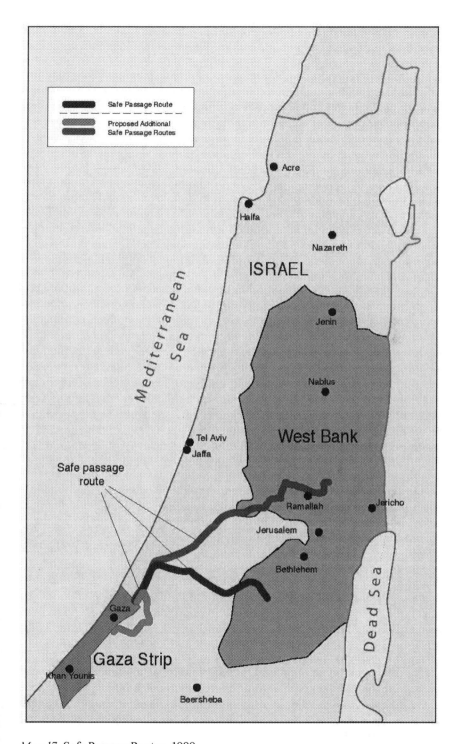

Map 17 Safe Passage Routes, 1999

Source: Permission granted by the Palestinian Academic Society for the Study of International Affairs to reprint their map of the 1999 Safe Passage routes in this book. The original can be found at: www.passia.org/maps/view/34.

      2. the Karni crossing point (Commercial) (for goods only);

      3. the Tarkumya crossing point (for persons, vehicles, and goods); and

      4. an additional crossing point around Mevo Horon.

D. 1. The safe passage arrangements will not be available on Yom Kippur, Israel's Memorial Day, and Israel's Independence Day.
2. Both sides may make special arrangements for other designated days, as agreed between them.

E. Israel shall signpost the safe passage routes clearly and shall take all necessary measures to ensure smooth movement while preserving safety and security on the route or routes in use on any specific day.

F. . . .

G. Israel may, for security or safety reasons, temporarily halt the operation of a safe passage route or modify the passage arrangements while ensuring that one of the routes is kept open for safe passage. Notice of such temporary closure or modification shall be given to the Palestinian side, through agreed channels, as far in advance as the circumstances will allow.

H. Israel may deny the use of its territory for safe passage by persons who have seriously or repeatedly violated the safe passage provisions detailed in this Protocol or in the Agreement. Israel will notify the Palestinian side, through agreed channels, of any decision to deny the use of its territory as a result of such violations. The notification shall include details of the violations giving rise to the denial. The individual in question shall have the right to request, through the Palestinian side, that Israel reconsider its decision.

I. . . .

J. Israel shall notify the Palestinian side of incidents involving persons using safe passage routes through the agreed channels.

K. It is understood that the safe passage shall be operated on a cost-reimbursement basis, in accordance with an agreement on the modalities to be reached in the Joint Economic Committee.

L. Israel shall be compensated for damages incurred by Israel, Israelis, or their property as a result of the use of safe passage, in accordance with an agreement on the modalities to be reached in the Joint Economic Committee.

3. Use of Safe Passage

A. Residents of the West Bank and the Gaza Strip wishing to make use of safe passage shall arrive with a safe passage card at the safe passage terminal at one of the crossing points specified at paragraph 2.C.2 above, where they will identify themselves by means of identification documents . . .

B. . . .

C. ...

D. A safe passage card shall be valid for one year for multiple two-way journeys on the safe passage routes. ...

E. Upon completion of the journey, the safe passage slips and safe passage stickers shall be returned to the Israeli authorities at the destination crossing point.

F. Residents of the West Bank and the Gaza Strip in possession of permits enabling them to enter Israel will be able to use these permits as safe passage cards, subject to the conditions of such permits and to the modalities set out in this Protocol.

G. ...

H. 1. Persons and vehicles using safe passage under these arrangements shall neither break their journey nor depart from the designated routes, and shall complete the passage within the designated time, unless a delay is caused by a medical emergency or a technical breakdown.

2. Notwithstanding paragraph 3.H.1 above, in the case of a medical emergency travellers may drive directly to the nearest hospital or first aid station. Such travellers will be required to report the incident to the relevant authorities at the destination crossing point as soon as circumstances allow.

3. ...

I. ...

J. Persons and vehicles shall not carry explosives, firearms, or other weapons or ammunition except for special cases that may be agreed by both sides. Transportation of dangerous substances shall be in accordance with the provisions of the Agreement.

4. Use of Safe Passage Routes by Visitors from Abroad ...

5. Use of Vehicles on Safe Passage Routes

A. 1. Residents of the West Bank and the Gaza Strip wishing to use their privately owned vehicles to travel along the safe passage shall apply for a vehicle safe passage permit through the Palestinian side. The Israeli side shall respond to such applications within five working days. ...

2. In addition to the above, the two sides may agree on specific categories or persons who may use a vehicle not owned by them ...

B. 1. On the day of the journey, the drivers will arrive at the safe passage terminal at the departure crossing point with their vehicle safe passage permits; safe passage cards or permits enabling them entry into Israel; identity cards; valid drivers' licenses; valid vehicle licenses; valid insurance policies; and, if applicable, the permit referred to in paragraph 5.A.2 above. After identification, and after the validity check of the vehicle safe passage permit, drivers will be issued with an individual safe passage slip and a safe passage sticker, to be displayed on the right-hand side of the front windshield of the vehicle.

   2.   ...
   3.   ...

C. Residents of the West Bank or the Gaza Strip in possession of valid permits enabling them to enter Israel with their vehicles will be able to use these permits as vehicle safe passage permits, subject to the conditions of such permits and to the modalities set out in this Protocol.

D. ...

E. ....

F. All vehicles used for the purpose of safe passage shall meet Israeli standards and applicable Israeli law.

G. ...

H. In special emergency related cases, to be handled through agreed channels, safe passage may be used by privately owned vehicles without having submitted an application in advance.

6. Use of Safe Passage by Persons Denied Entry into Israel

   A. Persons who are denied entry into Israel will use safe passage by means of shuttle buses which will be escorted by Israeli security forces vehicles, and which will operate from 7:00 AM to 2:00 PM on Mondays and Wednesdays of every week.

   B. Applications by persons denied entry into Israel to use the safe passage must be submitted to, and agreed upon, at least five working days prior to the planned journey.

   C. Cases of persons denied entry into Israel whose applications to use safe passage are not agreed upon shall he discussed in the agreed channels.

   D. ... 1. Persons denied entry into Israel who have used the safe passage will be able to return that same day to their original point of departure.

   E. ...

7. Passage of Palestinian Police

   A. ... uniformed and plainclothes Palestinian policemen required to use the safe passage so as to perform their duty in the West Bank and the Gaza Strip, or Palestinian policemen other than in instances covered by paragraph 7.E below, using privately owned vehicles, official vehicles, or other means of transportation, will be able to use the safe passage after the Palestinian police has submitted an application and after that application was approved ...

B.   ...
C.   When in safe passage, the weapons of the Palestinian policemen will be handed over to the Israeli police and placed in a closed trailer affixed to the Israel police vehicle ...
D.   ...
E.   ...

8. Use of Safe Passage for Commercial Traffic ...
9. Future Meetings for Improving Operation of the Safe Passage ...
10. Use of Safe Passage by the Ra'ees of the Executive Authority ...
11. Final Clauses ...

Done at Jerusalem, this 5th day of October, 1999.

87 Israel-Syria Draft Peace Agreement ("Clinton Plan"; January 8, 2000)

A Framework for Peace Between Israel and Syria

The draft peace treaty presented by the Clinton administration to Jerusalem and Damascus

(Shepherdstown, W. VA)

The Government of the State of Israel and the Government of the Syrian Arab Republic:

Aiming at the achievement of a just, lasting and comprehensive peace in the Middle East based on Security Council resolutions 242 and 338 and within the framework of the peace process initiated at Madrid on 31 October 1991;

Reaffirming their faith in the purposes and principles of the Charter of the United Nations and recognizing their right and obligation to live in peace with each other, as well as with all states, within secure and recognized boundaries;

Desiring to establish mutual respect and to develop honorable, friendly and good neighborly relations;

Resolved to establish permanent peace between them in accordance with this Treaty.

Have agreed as follows:

Article I – Establishment of Peace and Security Within Recognized Boundaries

1. The state of war between Israel and Syria (hereinafter "the Parties") is hereby terminated and peace is established between them. The Parties will maintain normal, peaceful relations as set out in Article III below.
2. The permanent secure and recognized international boundary between Israel and Syria is the boundary set forth in Article II below. The location of the boundary has been commonly agreed (Syrian position: and is based on the June 4, 1967 line) (Israeli position: taking into account security and other vital interests of the Parties as well as legal considerations of both sides). Israel will (S: withdraw) (I: relocate) all its armed forces (S: and civilians) behind this boundary in accordance with Annex – of this

DOI: 10.4324/9781003348948-93

Treaty. (S: Thereafter, each Party will exercise its full sovereignty on its side of the international boundary, including as agreed in this Treaty.)

3. To enhance the security of both Parties, agreed security measures will be implemented in accordance with Article IV below.
4. The time line at Annex – sets forth an agreed schedule for synchronized implementation of this and the other Articles of this Treaty.

Article II – International Boundary

1. The international boundary between Israel and Syria is as shown on the mapping materials and co-ordinates specified in Annex –. This boundary is the permanent, secure and recognized international boundary between Israel and Syria and supersedes any previous boundary or line of demarcation between them.
2. The Parties will respect the inviolability of this boundary and of each other's territory, territorial waters and airspace.
   . . .

Article III – Normal Peaceful Relations

1. The Parties will apply between them the provisions of the Charter of the United Nations and the principles of international law governing relations among states in time of peace. . . .
2. The Parties will establish full diplomatic and consular relations, including the exchange of resident ambassadors.
3. . . .
4. . . .

Notes:
   . . .

Article IV – Security

A. SECURITY ARRANGEMENTS

Recognizing the importance of security for both Parties as an important element of permanent peace and stability, the Parties will employ the following security arrangements to build mutual confidence in the implementation of this Treaty and to provide for the security needs of both Parties:
   . . .

B. OTHER SECURITY MEASURES

   . . .

1. Each Party undertakes to refrain from cooperating with any third party in a hostile alliance of a military character and will ensure that territory under its control is not used by any military forces of a third party (including their equipment and armaments) in circumstances that would adversely affect the security of the other Party.
2. Each Party undertakes to refrain from organizing, instigating, inciting, assisting or participating in any acts or threats of violence against the other Party, . . .
3. Both Parties recognize that international terrorism in all its forms threatens the security of all nations and therefore share a common interest in the enhancement of international cooperative efforts to deal with this problem.

C. COOPERATION AND LIAISON IN SECURITY MATTERS

The Parties will establish a direct liaison and coordination mechanism between them as described in Annex – to facilitate implementation of the security provisions in this Treaty. Its responsibilities will include: direct and real-time communication on security issues, minimization of friction along the international border, addressing any problems arising during the implementation process, helping to prevent errors or misinterpretations, and maintaining direct and continuous contacts with the monitoring, inspection and verification mechanism.

Article V – Water

1. The Parties recognize that full resolution of all water issues between them constitutes a fundamental element in ensuring a stable and lasting peace. (S: Based on relevant international principles and practices), the Parties have agreed to establish (I: arrangements that will ensure the continuation of Israel's current use in quantity and quality of all) (S: mutually agreeable arrangements with respect to water quantities and quality from) the surface and underground waters in the areas from which Israeli forces will (I: relocate) (S: withdraw) pursuant to Article I, as detailed in Annex –. (I: The arrangements should include all necessary measures to prevent contamination, pollution or depletion of the Kinneret/Tiberias and Upper Jordan River and their sources.)
2. . . .

Article VI – Rights and Obligations

1. This Treaty does not affect and shall not be interpreted as affecting in any way the rights and obligations of the Parties under the Charter of the United Nations.

   . . .

4. The Parties undertake not to enter into any obligation in conflict with this Treaty.
5. Subject to Article 103 of the United Nations Charter, in the event of a conflict between the obligations of the Parties under the present Treaty and any of their other obligations, the obligations under this Treaty will be binding and implemented.

Article VII – Legislation

The Parties undertake to enact any legislation necessary in order to implement the Treaty, and to repeal any legislation that is inconsistent with the Treaty.

Article VIII – Settlement of Disputes

Disputes between the Parties arising out of the interpretation or application of the present Treaty shall be settled by negotiation.

Article IX – Final Clauses

1. This treaty shall be ratified by both Parties in conformity with their respective constitutional procedures. It shall enter into force on the exchange of instruments of ratification and shall supersede all previous bilateral agreements between the Parties.
2. The Annexes and other attachments attached to this Treaty shall constitute integral parts thereof.
3. The Treaty shall be communicated to the Secretary General of the United Nations for registration in accordance with the provisions of Article 102 of the Charter of the United Nations.

DONE THIS DAY ------ IN -------- IN THE ENGLISH, HEBREW AND ARABIC LANGUAGES, ALL LANGUAGES BEING EQUALLY AUTHENTIC. IN CASE OF ANY DIVERGENCE OF INTERPRETATION, THE ENGLISH TEXT WILL BE AUTHORITATIVE

88 Trilateral Statement on the Middle East Peace Summit at Camp David (July 25, 2000)

President William J. Clinton
  Israeli Prime Minister Ehud Barak
  Palestinian Authority Chairman Yasser Arafat
  . . .

(1) The two sides agreed that the aim of their negotiations is to put an end to decades of conflict and achieve a just and lasting peace.
(2) The two sides commit themselves to continue their efforts to conclude an agreement on all permanent status issues as soon as possible.
(3) Both sides agree that negotiations based on UN Security Council Resolutions 242 and 338 are the only way to achieve such an agreement and they undertake to create an environment for negotiations free from pressure, intimidation, and threats of violence.
(4) The two sides understand the importance of avoiding unilateral actions that prejudge the outcome of negotiations and that their differences will be resolved only by good faith negotiations.
(5) Both sides agree that the United States remains a vital partner in the search for peace and will continue to consult closely with President Clinton and Secretary Albright in the period ahead.

DOI: 10.4324/9781003348948-94

89 President William J. Clinton, Statement on the Middle East Peace Talks at Camp David (July 25, 2000)

. . .

After 14 days of intensive negotiations between Israelis and Palestinians, I have concluded with regret that they will not be able to reach an agreement at this time. As I explained on the eve of the summit, success was far from guaranteed – given the historical, religious, political and emotional dimensions of the conflict.

Still, because the parties were not making progress on their own and the September deadline they set for themselves was fast approaching, I thought we had no choice. We can't afford to leave a single stone unturned in the search for a just, lasting and comprehensive peace.

. . .

While we did not get an agreement here, significant progress was made on the core issues. I want to express my appreciation to Prime Minister Barak, Chairman Arafat and their delegations for the efforts they undertook to reach an agreement.

Prime Minister Barak showed particular courage vision, and an understanding of the historical importance of this moment. Chairman Arafat made it clear that he, too, remains committed to the path of peace. The trilateral statement we issued affirms both leaders' commitment to avoid violence or unilateral actions which will make peace more difficult and to keep the peace process going until it reaches a successful conclusion.

. . .

Israelis and Palestinians are destined to live side by side, destined to have a common future. They have to decide what kind of future it will be. Though the differences that remain are deep, they have come a long way in the last seven years, and, notwithstanding the failure to reach an agreement, they made real headway in the last two weeks.

. . .

The children of Abraham, the descendants of Isaac and Ishmael can only be reconciled through courageous compromise. In the spirit of those who have already given their lives for peace and all Israelis, Palestinians, friends of peace in the Middle East and across the world, we long for peace and deserve a Holy Land that lives for the values of Judaism, Islam and Christianity.

DOI: 10.4324/9781003348948-95

Thank you.

Question: Was Jerusalem – Mr. President, was Jerusalem the main stumbling block? And where do you go from here?

The President: It was the most difficult problem. And I must tell you that we tried a lot of different approaches to it, and we have not yet found a solution. But the good news is that there is not a great deal of disagreement – and I want to emphasize this – it seemed to me, anyway, there was not a great deal of disagreement in many of these areas about what the facts on the ground would be after an agreement were made – that is, how people would live.

. . .

But obviously, the questions around Jerusalem go to the core identity of both the Palestinians and the Israelis. . . .

Question: There is a striking contrast between the way you described Prime Minister Barak's courageous and visionary approach to this, and Mr. Arafat seemed to be still committed to the path of peace. It sounds like that at the end of the day, Prime Minister Barak was ready to really step up to something that President Arafat wasn't yet ready to step up to.

The President: Let me be more explicit. I will say again: We made progress on all of the core issues. We made really significant progress on many of them. . . . But I think it is fair to say that at this moment in time, maybe because they had been preparing for it longer, maybe because they had thought through it more, that the Prime Minister moved forward more from his initial position than Chairman Arafat, on – particularly surrounding the questions of Jerusalem.

. . .

So I said what I said, and my remarks should stand for themselves, because not so much as a criticism of Chairman Arafat, because this is really hard and never been done before, but in praise of Barak. He came there knowing that he was going to have to take bold steps, and he did it. And I think you should look at it more as a positive toward him than as a condemnation of the Palestinian side.

This is agonizing for them – both of them. . . . But I do think – I stand by the statement as written. I think they both remain committed to peace, I think they will both find a way to get there if they don't let time run away with them so that external events rob them of their options. And that's why I decided to call the summit in the first place.

I got worried that – this is like going to the dentist without having your gums deadened, you know. . . . Now, I believe because of the work that was done within both teams and what they did with each other, we can still do it. Let me just make one other observation and then I'll answer your question.

. . .

Let me give you some good news. Of all the peace groups I ever worked with, these people know each other, they know the names of each other's children, they know how many grandchildren the grandparents have, they know their life stories, they have a genuine respect and understanding for each other. It is truly extraordinary and unique in my experience in almost eight years of dealing with it.

So I'm not trying to put a funny gloss on this; they couldn't get there. That's the truth. They couldn't get there. But this was the first time in an organized, disciplined way they had to work through, both for themselves and then with each other how they were going to come to grips with issues that go to the core of their identity.

   . . .

Now, I promised you, you could ask now.

Question: What is your assessment of whether Arafat's going to go through with the threat to declare statehood unilaterally? Did you get any sort of sense on whether he's going to go through with that? Did you have any–

The President: Well, let me say this. One of the reasons that I wanted to have this summit is that they're both under – will be under conflicting pressures as we go forward . . .

One of the reasons I called this summit is so that we could set in motion a process that would give the Palestinians the confidence that all of us – and most of all, the Israelis – really did want to make peace, so that it would offset the pressure that will be increasingly on Chairman Arafat as we approach the September 13th deadline.

Question: Are you implying that he should give up his claim to East Jerusalem – the Palestinians should?

The President: No, I didn't say that.

Question: Or any kind of a foothold?

The President: I didn't say that. I didn't say that. I didn't say that. And let me say, I presume, I am bound – I'm going to honor my promise not to leak about what they talked about, but I presume it will come out. No, I didn't say that. I said only this: I said – I will say again – the Palestinians changed their position; they moved forward. The Israelis moved more from the position they had. I said what I said; I will say again: I was not condemning Arafat, I was praising Barak. But I would be making a mistake not to praise Barak because I think he took a big risk. And I think it sparked, already, in Israel a real debate, which is moving Israeli public opinion toward the conditions that will make peace. . . .

But what we have to find here, if there is going to be an agreement – by definition, an agreement is one in which everybody is a little disappointed and nobody is defeated, in which neither side requires the other to say they have lost everything and they find a way to – a shared result.

And there's no place in the world like Jerusalem. There is no other place in the world like Jerusalem, which is basically at the core of the identity of all three monotheistic religions in the world, at the core of the identity of what it means to be a Palestinian, at the core of the identity of what it means to be an Israeli. . . .

Question: But did they make enough progress, sir, to now go back home, check with their people, and possibly come back during your administration – next month or in September – to come back to Camp David and try again?

The President: . . . I think if you asked me did they make enough progress to get this done? Yes. But they've got to go home and check; they've got to feel around. And what I want to say to you is, the reason I tried to keep them there so long – and I feel much better about this than I did when we almost lost it before – and you remember, and I got them and we all agreed to stay – I didn't feel that night like I feel today.

. . .

But, yes, I think it can happen–

Question: During your administration?

The President: Yes. Not because it's my administration, that's irrelevant. They're operating on their timetable, not mine. It has nothing to do with the fact that it's my administration. I think it can happen because they set for themselves a September 13th deadline. . . .

. . .

Question: But, Mr. President, the Prime Minister came here in quite a precarious position to begin with back home. And some of the things you call bold and courageous, his critics back home have called treason. . . .

The President: First of all, this is not a weak man. It's not for nothing that he's the most decorated soldier in the history of Israel. He didn't come over here to play safe with his political future; he came over here to do what he thought was right for the people of Israel, . . .

So I think the people of Israel should be very proud of him. He did nothing to compromise Israel's security, and he did everything he possibly could within the limits that he thought he had, . . . to reach a just peace. So I would hope the people of Israel will support him, and let this thing percolate, not overreact, and say keep trying.

I want the people on both sides to tell their leaders to keep trying – to keep trying. You know, that's the only real answer here is just to bear down and go on.

Question: Mr. President, couldn't you have gotten a partial agreement and left Jerusalem for later? Was that a possibility at all?

The President: That possibility was explored and rejected.

Question: Why?

The President: I can't talk about it. If they want to talk about it, that's their business; but I can't.

Question: Have you done all you can do, sir, or would you be making more proposals?

The President: Oh, I think – well, first of all, we all agreed to reassess here . . .

Last night, we quit at 3:00 a.m.; the night before, we went all night long. . . . So what I'm going to do is let them take a deep breath and then our side,

Madeleine and Sandy and all of our team and I – Dennis, we'll try to think what we think we ought to do, . . .

Keep in mind: When the Oslo Agreement was drafted, these things were put down as final status issues because the people that drafted them knew it would be hard. And they took a gamble. And their gamble was that if the Israelis and the Palestinians worked together over a seven-year period . . . that by the time we got to the end of the road, there would be enough knowledge and trust and understanding of each other's positions that these huge, epochal issues could be resolved.

Now, we started the process and we've got to finish. . . . The venue is not important; the mechanisms aren't important. But we know what the state of play is now and if we'll keep at it, I still think we can get it done.

Question: Can you describe what type of U.S. role was discussed in sealing the agreement financially and otherwise?

The President: Let me say, first of all, anything that would require our participation, other than financial, was not finalized. . . . But there was no decision made about that.

On the money, basically, you know, I think that the United States should be prepared to make a significant contribution to resolving the refugee problem. You've got refugees that have to be resettled, you've got some compensation which has to be given, and there are lots of issues in that refugee pot that cost money, and then there's the whole question of working out the economic future of the Palestinians and the whole question of working out what the security relationships will be and the security needs will be for Israel and in this new partnership that they will have – the Palestinians. How is that going to work and what should we do.

. . .

Thank you.

90 Taba Summit (January 21–27, 2001)

1. Territory

The two sides agree that in accordance with the U.N. Security Council Resolution 242, the June 4, 1967 lines would be the basis for the borders between Israel and the State of Palestine.

1.1 WEST BANK

For the first time both sides presented their own maps over the West Bank. The maps served as a basis for the discussion on territory and settlements . . .

Both sides accepted the principle of land swap, but the proportionality of the swap remained under discussion. Both sides agreed that Israeli and Palestinian sovereign areas will have respective sovereign contiguity . . .

1.2 GAZA STRIP

Neither side presented any maps over the Gaza Strip. It was implied that the Gaza Strip will be under total Palestinian sovereignty, but details have still to be worked out. All settlements will be evacuated . . .

2. Jerusalem

2.1 SOVEREIGNTY

Both sides accepted in principle the Clinton suggestion of having a Palestinian sovereignty over Arab neighborhoods and an Israeli sovereignty over Jewish neighborhoods. The Palestinian side affirmed that it was ready to discuss an Israeli request to have sovereignty over those Jewish settlements in East Jerusalem that were constructed after 1967, but not Jebal Abu Ghneim and Ras al-Amud. The Palestinian side rejected Israeli sovereignty over

DOI: 10.4324/9781003348948-96

settlements in the Jerusalem Metropolitan Area, namely Ma'ale Adumim and Givat Ze'ev.

2.2 CAPITAL FOR TWO STATES

The Israeli side accepted that the City of Jerusalem would be the capital of two states: Jerusalem, capital of Israel, and Al-Quds, capital of the State of Palestine. The Palestinian side expressed its only concern, namely that East Jerusalem is the capital of the State of Palestine.

2.3 HOLY SITES: WESTERN WALL

Both parties have accepted the principle of respective control over each side's respective holy sites (religious control and management). According to this principle, Israel's sovereignty over the Western Wall would be recognized although there remained a dispute regarding the delineation of the area covered by the Western Wall . . .

2.4 HARAM AL-SHARIF/TEMPLE MOUNT

Both sides agreed that the question of Haram al-Sharif/Temple Mount has not been resolved . . .

3. Refugees

. . . Both sides suggested, as a basis, that the parties should agree that a just settlement of the refugee problem in accordance with the U.N. Security Council Resolution 242 must lead to the implementation of U.N. General Assembly Resolution 194.

4. Security

4.1 EARLY WARNING STATIONS

The Israeli side requested to have three early warning stations on Palestinian territory. The Palestinian side was prepared to accept the continued operations of early warning stations but subject to certain conditions . . .

4.2 MILITARY CAPABILITY OF THE STATE OF PALESTINE

The Israeli side maintained that the State of Palestine would be non-militarized as per the Clinton proposals. The Palestinian side was prepared to accept limitation on its acquisition of arms and be defined as a State with limited arms.

4.3 TIMETABLE FOR WITHDRAWAL FROM THE WEST BANK AND JORDAN VALLEY

Based on the Clinton proposal, the Israeli side agreed to a withdrawal from the West Bank over a 36-month period with an additional 36 months for the Jordan Valley in conjunction with an international force . . .

The Palestinian side proposed an 18-month withdrawal under the supervision of international forces. As to the Jordan Valley, the Palestinian side was prepared to consider the withdrawal of Israeli armed forces for an additional 10-month period.

4.4 BORDERS AND INTERNATIONAL CROSSINGS

The Palestinian side was confident that Palestinian sovereignty over borders and international crossings would be recognized in the agreement. The two sides had, however, not yet resolved this issue including the question of monitoring and verification at Palestine's international borders (Israeli or international presence).

91 Sharm El-Sheikh Fact-Finding Committee Final Report (April 30, 2001)

The Honorable George W. Bush
President of the United States
The White House
Washington, DC 20500

Dear Mr. President,

We enclose herewith the report of the Sharm el-Sheikh Fact-Finding Committee.

We sought and received information and advice from a wide range of individuals, organizations, and governments. However, the conclusions and recommendations are ours alone.

We are grateful for the support that you and your administration have provided to the Committee.

Respectfully,

Suleyman Demirel

Thorbjoern Jagland

Warren B. Rudman

Javier Solana

George J Mitchell, Chairman

Summary of Recommendations

The Government of Israel (GOI) and the Palestinian Authority (PA) must act swiftly and decisively to halt the violence. Their immediate objectives then should be to rebuild confidence and resume negotiations.

During this mission our aim has been to fulfill the mandate agreed at Sharm el-Sheikh. . . . Our principal recommendation is that they recommit themselves to the Sharm el-Sheikh spirit and that they implement the decisions

DOI: 10.4324/9781003348948-97

made there in 1999 and 2000. We believe that the summit participants will support bold action by the parties to achieve these objectives.

The restoration of trust is essential, and the parties should take affirmative steps to this end. Given the high level of hostility and mistrust, the timing and sequence of these steps are obviously crucial. This can be decided only by the parties. We urge them to begin the process of decision immediately.

Accordingly, we recommend that steps be taken to:

End the Violence

- The GOI and the PA should reaffirm their commitment to existing agreements and undertakings and should immediately implement an unconditional cessation of violence.
- The GOI and PA should immediately resume security cooperation.

Rebuild Confidence

- The PA and GOI should work together to establish a meaningful "cooling off period" and implement additional confidence building measures, some of which were detailed in the October 2000 Sharm el-Sheikh Statement and some of which were offered by the U.S. on January 7, 2001 in Cairo (see Recommendations section for further description).
- The PA and GOI should resume their efforts to identify, condemn, and discourage incitement in all its forms.
- The PA should make clear through concrete action to Palestinians and Israelis alike that terrorism is reprehensible and unacceptable, and that the PA will make a 100% effort to prevent terrorist operations and to punish perpetrators. This effort should include immediate steps to apprehend and incarcerate terrorists operating within the PA's jurisdiction.
- The GOI should freeze all settlement activity, including the "natural growth" of existing settlements.
- The GOI should ensure that the IDF adopt and enforce policies and procedures encouraging non-lethal responses to unarmed demonstrators, with a view to minimizing casualties and friction between the two communities.
- The PA should prevent gunmen from using Palestinian populated areas to fire upon Israeli populated areas and IDF positions. This tactic places civilians on both sides at unnecessary risk.
- The GOI should lift closures, transfer to the PA all tax revenues owed, and permit Palestinians who had been employed in Israel to return to their jobs; and should ensure that security forces and settlers refrain from the destruction of homes and roads, as well as trees and other agricultural property in Palestinian areas. We acknowledge the GOI's position that actions of this nature have been taken for security reasons. Nevertheless, the economic effects will persist for years.

- The PA should renew cooperation with Israeli security agencies to ensure, to the maximum extent possible, that Palestinian workers employed within Israel are fully vetted and free of connections to organizations and individuals engaged in terrorism.
- The PA and GOI should consider a joint undertaking to preserve and protect holy places sacred to the traditions of Jews, Muslims, and Christians.
- The GOI and PA should jointly endorse and support the work of Palestinian and Israeli non-governmental organizations involved in cross-community initiatives linking the two peoples.

Resume Negotiations

In the spirit of the Sharm el-Sheikh agreements and understandings of 1999 and 2000, we recommend that the parties meet to reaffirm their commitment to signed agreements and mutual understandings, and take corresponding action. This should be the basis for resuming full and meaningful negotiations.

. . .

The parties are at a crossroads. If they do not return to the negotiating table, they face the prospect of fighting it out for years on end, with many of their citizens leaving for distant shores to live their lives and raise their children. We pray they make the right choice. That means stopping the violence now. Israelis and Palestinians have to live, work, and prosper together. History and geography have destined them to be neighbors. That cannot be changed. Only when their actions are guided by this awareness will they be able to develop the vision and reality of peace and shared prosperity.

Suleyman Demirel
9th President of the Republic of Turkey

Thorbjoern Jagland
Minister of Foreign Affairs of Norway

George J. Mitchell, Chairman
Former Member and Majority Leader of the United States Senate

Warren B. Rudman
Former Member of the United States Senate

Javier Solana
High Representative for the Common Foreign and Security Policy, European Union

92 Israeli-Palestinian Ceasefire and Security Plan, Proposed by C.I.A. Director George Tenet (June 13, 2001)

The security organizations of the Government of Israel (GOI) and of the Palestinian Authority (PA) reaffirm their commitment to the security agreements forged at Sharm el-Sheikh in October 2000, embedded in the Mitchell Report of April 2001.

The operational premise of the work plan is that the two sides are committed to a mutual, comprehensive cease-fire, applying to all violent activities, in accordance with the public declaration of both leaders. In addition, the joint security committee referenced in this work plan will resolve issues that may arise during the implementation of this work plan.

The security organizations of the GOI and PA agree to initiate the following specific, concrete, and realistic security steps immediately to reestablish security cooperation and the situation on the ground that existed prior to 28 September.

1. The GOI and the PA will immediately resume security cooperation.

    A senior-level meeting of Israeli, Palestinian, and U.S. security officials will be held immediately and will reconvene at least once a week, with mandatory participation by designated senior officials.

    Israeli-Palestinian District Coordination Offices (DCOs) will be reinvigorated. They will carry out their daily activities, to the maximum extent possible, according to the standards established prior to September 28, 2000. As soon as the security situation permits, barriers to effective cooperation – which include the erection of walls between the Israeli and Palestinian sides – will be eliminated and join Israeli-Palestinian patrols will be reinitiated.

    U.S.-supplied video conferencing systems will be provided to senior-level Israeli and Palestinian officials to facilitate frequent dialogue and security cooperation.

2. Both sides will take immediate measures to enforce strict adherence to the declared cease-fire and to stabilize the security environment.

    . . .

    Israel will not conduct attacks of any kind against the Palestinian Authority Ra'is facilities: the headquarters of Palestinian security,

DOI: 10.4324/9781003348948-98

intelligence, and police organization; or prisons in the West Bank and Gaza.

The PA will move immediately to apprehend, question, and incarcerate terrorists in the West Bank and Gaza and will provide the security committee the names of those arrested as soon as they are apprehended, as well as a readout of actions taken.

Israel will release all Palestinians arrested in security sweeps who have no association with terrorist activities.

In keeping with its unilateral cease-fire declaration, the PA will stop any Palestinian security officials from inciting, aiding, abetting, or conducting attacks against Israeli targets, including settlers.

In keeping with Israel's unilateral cease-fire declaration, Israeli forces will not conduct "proactive" security operations in areas under the control of the PA or attack innocent civilian targets.

The GOI will re-institute military police investigations into Palestinian deaths resulting from Israel Defense Forces actions in the West Bank and Gaza in incidents not involving terrorism.

3. Palestinian and Israeli security officials will use the security committee to provide each other, as well as designated U.S. officials, information on terrorist threats, including information on known or suspected terrorist operation in – or moving to – areas under the other's control.

    . . .

The PA will undertake preemptive operations against terrorists, terrorist safe houses, arms depots, and mortar factories. The PA will provide regular progress reports of these actions to the security committee.

Israeli authorities will take action against Israeli citizens inciting, carrying out, or planning to carry out violence against Palestinians, with progress reports on these activities provided to the security committee.

4. The PA and GOI will move aggressively to prevent individuals and groups from using areas under their respective control to carry out acts of violence. . . .

Palestinian and Israeli security officials will identify and agree to the practical measures needed to enforce "no demonstration zones" and "buffer zones" around flash points to reduce opportunities for confrontation. Both sides will adopt all necessary measures to prevent riots and to control demonstration, particularly in flash-point areas.

Palestinian and Israeli security officials will make a concerted effort to locate and confiscate illegal weapons, including mortars, rockets, and explosives, in areas under their respective control In addition, intensive efforts will be made to prevent smuggling and illegal production of weapons. Each side will inform the security committee of the status and success of these efforts.

The Israeli Defense Forces (IDF) will adopt additional non-lethal measures to deal with Palestinian crowds and demonstrators, and more generally, seek to minimize the danger to lives and property of Palestinian civilians in responding to violence.

5. The GOI and the PA, through the auspices of the senior-level security committee, will forge . . . an agreed-upon schedule to implement the complete redeployment of IDF forces to positions held before September 28, 2000.

   Demonstrable on-the-ground redeployment will be initiated within the first 48 hours of this one-week period and will continue while the schedule is being forged.

6. Within one week of the commencement of security committee meetings and resumption of security cooperation, a specific timeline will be developed for the lifting of internal closures as well as for the reopening of internal roads, the Allenby Bridge, Gaza Airport, the Port of Gaza, and border crossings. Security checkpoints will be minimized according to legitimate security requirements and following consultation between the two sides.

   Demonstrable on-the-ground actions on the lifting of the closures will be initiated within the first 48 hours of this one-week period and will continue while the timeline is being developed.

   The parties pledge that even if untoward events occur, security cooperation will continue through the joint security committee.

93 U.N. Security Council Resolution 1397 (March 12, 2002)

The Security Council,

Recalling all its previous relevant resolutions, in particular resolutions 242 (1967) and 338 (1973),

Affirming a vision of a region where two States, Israel and Palestine, live side by side within secure and recognized borders,

Expressing its grave concern at the continuation of the tragic and violent events that have taken place since September 2000, especially the recent attacks and the increased number of casualties,

Stressing the need for all concerned to ensure the safety of civilians,

Stressing also the need to respect the universally accepted norms of international humanitarian law,

Welcoming and encouraging the diplomatic efforts of special envoys from the United States of America, the Russian Federation, the European Union and the United Nations Special Coordinator and others to bring about a comprehensive, just and lasting peace in the Middle East,

Welcoming the contribution of Saudi Crown Prince Abdullah,

1. *Demands* immediate cessation of all acts of violence, including all acts of terror, provocation, incitement and destruction;
2. *Calls upon* the Israeli and Palestinian sides and their leaders to cooperate in the implementation of the Tenet work plan and Mitchell Report recommendations with the aim of resuming negotiations on a political settlement;
3. *Expresses* support for the efforts of the Secretary-General and others to assist the parties to halt the violence and to resume the peace process;
4. *Decides* to remain seized of the matter.

Adopted by the Security Council at its 4489th meeting by a vote of 14 in favour to none against with 1 abstention (Syria).

DOI: 10.4324/9781003348948-99

94 The Arab Peace Initiative (March 28, 2002)

The Council of the League of Arab States at the Summit Level, at its 14th Ordinary Session,

- Reaffirms the resolution taken in June 1996 at the Cairo extraordinary Arab summit that a just and comprehensive peace in the Middle East is the strategic option of the Arab countries, to be achieved in accordance with international legality, and which would require a comparable commitment on the part of the Israeli government.
- Having listened to the statement made by his royal highness Prince Abdullah Bin Abdullaziz, the crown prince of the Kingdom of Saudi Arabia, in which his highness presented his initiative, calling for full Israeli withdrawal from all the Arab territories occupied since June 1967, in implementation of Security Council Resolutions 242 and 338, reaffirmed by the Madrid Conference of 1991 and the land for peace principle, and Israel's acceptance of an independent Palestinian state, with East Jerusalem as its capital, in return for the establishment of normal relations in the context of a comprehensive peace with Israel.
- Emanating from the conviction of the Arab countries that a military solution to the conflict will not achieve peace or provide security for the parties, the council:

    1. Requests Israel to reconsider its policies and declare that a just peace is its strategic option as well.
    2. Further calls upon Israel to affirm:

        a. Full Israeli withdrawal from all the territories occupied since 1967, including the Syrian Golan Heights to the lines of June 4, 1967 as well as the remaining occupied Lebanese territories in the south of Lebanon.
        b. Achievement of a just solution to the Palestinian refugee problem to be agreed upon in accordance with U.N. General Assembly Resolution 194.
        c. The acceptance of the establishment of a Sovereign Independent Palestinian State on the Palestinian territories occupied since

DOI: 10.4324/9781003348948-100

the 4th of June 1967 in the West Bank and Gaza strip, with east Jerusalem as its capital.

3. Consequently, the Arab countries affirm the following:

   a. Consider the Arab-Israeli conflict ended, and enter into a peace agreement with Israel, and provide security for all the states of the region.

   b. Establish normal relations with Israel in the context of this comprehensive peace.

4. Assures the rejection of all forms of Palestinian patriation which conflict with the special circumstances of the Arab host countries.

5. Calls upon the government of Israel and all Israelis to accept this initiative in order to safeguard the prospects for peace and stop the further shedding of blood, enabling the Arab Countries and Israel to live in peace and good neighborliness and provide future generations with security, stability, and prosperity.

6. Invites the international community and all countries and organizations to support this initiative.

7. Requests the chairman of the summit to form a special committee composed of some of its concerned member states and the secretary general of the League of Arab States to pursue the necessary contacts to gain support for this initiative at all levels, particularly from the United Nations, the security council, the United States of America, the Russian Federation, the Muslim States, and the European Union.

95 President George W. Bush Speech (June 24, 2002)

President Bush Calls for New Palestinian Leadership

The Rose Garden

THE PRESIDENT: For too long, the citizens of the Middle East have lived in the midst of death and fear. The hatred of a few holds the hopes of many hostage. The forces of extremism and terror are attempting to kill progress and peace by killing the innocent. And this casts a dark shadow over an entire region. For the sake of all humanity, things must change in the Middle East.

It is untenable for Israeli citizens to live in terror. It is untenable for Palestinians to live in squalor and occupation. And the current situation offers no prospect that life will improve. Israeli citizens will continue to be victimized by terrorists, and so Israel will continue to defend herself.

In the situation the Palestinian people will grow more and more miserable. My vision is two states, living side by side in peace and security. There is simply no way to achieve that peace until all parties fight terror. . . . Peace requires a new and different Palestinian leadership, so that a Palestinian state can be born.

I call on the Palestinian people to elect new leaders, leaders not compromised by terror. I call upon them to build a practicing democracy, based on tolerance and liberty. . . . If the Palestinian people meet these goals, they will be able to reach agreement with Israel and Egypt and Jordan on security and other arrangements for independence.

And when the Palestinian people have new leaders, new institutions and new security arrangements with their neighbors, the United States of America will support the creation of a Palestinian state whose borders and certain aspects of its sovereignty will be provisional until resolved as part of a final settlement in the Middle East.

. . .

Today, the elected Palestinian legislature has no authority, and power is concentrated in the hands of an unaccountable few. A Palestinian state can only serve its citizens with a new constitution which separates the powers of government. The Palestinian parliament should have the full authority of a

DOI: 10.4324/9781003348948-101

legislative body. Local officials and government ministers need authority of their own and the independence to govern effectively.

The United States, along with the European Union and Arab states, will work with Palestinian leaders to create a new constitutional framework, and a working democracy for the Palestinian people. . . .

Today, the Palestinian people live in economic stagnation, made worse by official corruption. A Palestinian state will require a vibrant economy, where honest enterprise is encouraged by honest government. . . .

And the United States, along with our partners in the developed world, will increase our humanitarian assistance to relieve Palestinian suffering. Today, the Palestinian people lack effective courts of law and have no means to defend and vindicate their rights. A Palestinian state will require a system of reliable justice to punish those who prey on the innocent. . . .

Today, Palestinian authorities are encouraging, not opposing, terrorism. This is unacceptable. And the United States will not support the establishment of a Palestinian state until its leaders engage in a sustained fight against the terrorists and dismantle their infrastructure. This will require an externally supervised effort to rebuild and reform the Palestinian security services. The security system must have clear lines of authority and accountability and a unified chain of command.

. . .

With a dedicated effort, this state could rise rapidly, as it comes to terms with Israel, Egypt and Jordan on practical issues, such as security. The final borders, the capital and other aspects of this state's sovereignty will be negotiated between the parties, as part of a final settlement. Arab states have offered their help in this process, and their help is needed.

I've said in the past that nations are either with us or against us in the war on terror. To be counted on the side of peace, nations must act. Every leader actually committed to peace will end incitement to violence in official media, and publicly denounce homicide bombings. Every nation actually committed to peace will stop the flow of money, equipment and recruits to terrorist groups seeking the destruction of Israel – including Hamas, Islamic Jihad, and Hezbollah. Every nation actually committed to peace must block the shipment of Iranian supplies to these groups, and oppose regimes that promote terror, like Iraq. And Syria must choose the right side in the war on terror by closing terrorist camps and expelling terrorist organizations.

. . .

Israel also has a large stake in the success of a democratic Palestine. Permanent occupation threatens Israel's identity and democracy. A stable, peaceful Palestinian state is necessary to achieve the security that Israel longs for. So I challenge Israel to take concrete steps to support the emergence of a viable, credible Palestinian state.

As we make progress towards security, Israel forces need to withdraw fully to positions they held prior to September 28, 2000. And consistent with the recommendations of the Mitchell Committee, Israeli settlement activity in the occupied territories must stop.

The Palestinian economy must be allowed to develop. As violence subsides, freedom of movement should be restored, permitting innocent Palestinians to resume work and normal life. Palestinian legislators and officials, humanitarian and international workers, must be allowed to go about the business of building a better future. And Israel should release frozen Palestinian revenues into honest, accountable hands.

. . .

Ultimately, Israelis and Palestinians must address the core issues that divide them if there is to be a real peace, resolving all claims and ending the conflict between them. This means that the Israeli occupation that began in 1967 will be ended through a settlement negotiated between the parties, based on U.N. Resolutions 242 and 338, with Israeli withdrawal to secure and recognize borders.

We must also resolve questions concerning Jerusalem, the plight and future of Palestinian refugees, and a final peace between Israel and Lebanon, and Israel and a Syria that supports peace and fights terror.

. . .

I can understand the deep anger and anguish of the Israeli people. You've lived too long with fear and funerals, having to avoid markets and public transportation, and forced to put armed guards in kindergarten classrooms. The Palestinian Authority has rejected your offer at hand, and trafficked with terrorists. You have a right to a normal life; you have a right to security; and I deeply believe that you need a reformed, responsible Palestinian partner to achieve that security.

I can understand the deep anger and despair of the Palestinian people. For decades you've been treated as pawns in the Middle East conflict. Your interests have been held hostage to a comprehensive peace agreement that never seems to come, as your lives get worse year by year. You deserve democracy and the rule of law. You deserve an open society and a thriving economy. You deserve a life of hope for your children. An end to occupation and a peaceful democratic Palestinian state may seem distant, but America and our partners throughout the world stand ready to help, help you make them possible as soon as possible.

If liberty can blossom in the rocky soil of the West Bank and Gaza, it will inspire millions of men and women around the globe who are equally weary of poverty and oppression, equally entitled to the benefits of democratic government.

I have a hope for the people of Muslim countries. Your commitments to morality, and learning, and tolerance led to great historical achievements. And those values are alive in the Islamic world today. You have a rich culture, and you share the aspirations of men and women in every culture. Prosperity and freedom and dignity are not just American hopes, or Western hopes. They are universal, human hopes. And even in the violence and turmoil of the Middle East, America believes those hopes have the power to transform lives and nations.

This moment is both an opportunity and a test for all parties in the Middle East: an opportunity to lay the foundations for future peace; a test to show who is serious about peace and who is not. The choice here is stark and simple. The Bible says, "I have set before you life and death; therefore, choose life." The time has arrived for everyone in this conflict to choose peace, and hope, and life.

Thank you very much.

96 The Nusseibeh-Ayalon Agreement (July 27, 2002)

The Palestinian people and the Jewish people each recognize the other's historic rights with respect to the same land.

The Jewish people has for generations wanted to establish the Jewish State in all the Land of Israel, while the Palestinian people has similarly wanted to establish a state in all of Palestine.

The two sides hereby agree to accept a historic compromise based on the principle of two sovereign and viable states existing side by side. The following Statement of Intentions is an expression of the will of the majority of the people. Both sides believe that through this initiative they can influence their leaders and thereby open a new chapter in the region's history. This new chapter will be realized by calling on the international community to guarantee security in the region and to help in rehabilitating and developing the region's economy.

The People Vote – Statement of Intentions

1. Two states for two peoples: Both sides will declare that Palestine is the only state of the Palestinian people and Israel is the only state of the Jewish people.
2. Borders: Permanent borders between the two states will be agreed on the basis of the June 4, 1967 lines, UN resolutions and the Arab peace initiative (known as the Saudi initiative).

   - Border modifications will be based on an equal territorial exchange (1:1) in accordance with the vital needs of both sides, including security, territorial contiguity, and demographic considerations.
   - The Palestinian State will have a connection between its two geographic areas, the West Bank and the Gaza Strip.
   - After establishment of the agreed borders, no settlers will remain in the Palestinian state.

3. Jerusalem: Jerusalem will be an open city, the capital of two states. Freedom of religion and full access to holy sites will be guaranteed to all.

DOI: 10.4324/9781003348948-102

- Arab neighborhoods in Jerusalem will come under Palestinian sovereignty; Jewish neighborhoods under Israeli sovereignty.
- Neither side will exercise sovereignty over the holy places. The State of Palestine will be designated Guardian of the Temple Mount for the benefit of Muslims. Israel will be the Guardian of the Western Wall for the benefit of the Jewish people. The status quo on Christian holy sites will be maintained. No excavation will take place in or underneath the holy sites.

4. Right of return: Recognizing the suffering and the plight of the Palestinian refugees, the international community, Israel, and the Palestinian State will initiate and contribute to an international fund to compensate them.

   - Palestinian refugees will return only to the State of Palestine; Jews will return only to the State of Israel.

5. The Palestinian State will be demilitarized and the international community will guarantee its security and independence.
6. End of conflict: Upon the full implementation of these principles, all claims on both sides and the Israeli-Palestinian conflict will end.

97 Roadmap to a Solution of the Israeli-Palestinian Conflict (April 30, 2003)

U.S. DEPARTMENT OF STATE
Office of the Spokesman
April 30, 2003

A Performance-Based Roadmap to a Permanent Two-State Solution to the Israeli-Palestinian Conflict

The following is a performance-based and goal-driven roadmap, with clear phases, timelines, target dates, and benchmarks aiming at progress through reciprocal steps by the two parties in the political, security, economic, humanitarian, and institution-building fields, under the auspices of the Quartet [the United States, European Union, United Nations, and Russia]. The destination is a final and comprehensive settlement of the Israel-Palestinian conflict by 2005, as presented in President Bush's speech of 24 June, and welcomed by the EU, Russia, and the UN in the 16 July and 17 September Quartet Ministerial statements.

A two-state solution to the Israeli-Palestinian conflict will only be achieved through an end to violence and terrorism, when the Palestinian people have a leadership acting decisively against terror and willing and able to build a practicing democracy based on tolerance and liberty, and through Israel's readiness to do what is necessary for a democratic Palestinian state to be established, and a clear, unambiguous acceptance by both parties of the goal of a negotiated settlement as described below. The Quartet will assist and facilitate implementation of the plan, starting in Phase I, including direct discussions between the parties as required. The plan establishes a realistic timeline for implementation. However, as a performance-based plan, progress will require and depend upon the good faith efforts of the parties, and their compliance with each of the obligations outlined below. Should the parties perform their obligations rapidly, progress within and through the phases may come sooner than indicated in the plan. Non-compliance with obligations will impede progress.

DOI: 10.4324/9781003348948-103

A settlement, negotiated between the parties, will result in the emergence of an independent, democratic, and viable Palestinian state living side by side in peace and security with Israel and its other neighbors. The settlement will resolve the Israel-Palestinian conflict and end the occupation that began in 1967, based on the foundations of the Madrid Conference, the principle of land for peace, UNSCRs 242, 338, and 1397, agreements previously reached by the parties, and the initiative of Saudi Crown Prince Abdullah – endorsed by the Beirut Arab League Summit – calling for acceptance of Israel as a neighbor living in peace and security, in the context of a comprehensive settlement. This initiative is a vital element of international efforts to promote a comprehensive peace on all tracks, including the Syrian-Israeli and Lebanese-Israeli tracks.

The Quartet will meet regularly at senior levels to evaluate the parties' performance on implementation of the plan. In each phase, the parties are expected to perform their obligations in parallel, unless otherwise indicated.

Phase I: Ending Terror and Violence, Normalizing Palestinian Life, and Building Palestinian Institutions – Present to May 2003

In Phase I, the Palestinians immediately undertake an unconditional cessation of violence according to the steps outlined below; such action should be accompanied by supportive measures undertaken by Israel. Palestinians and Israelis resume security cooperation based on the Tenet work plan to end violence, terrorism, and incitement through restructured and effective Palestinian security services. Palestinians undertake comprehensive political reform in preparation for statehood, including drafting a Palestinian constitution, and free, fair, and open elections upon the basis of those measures. Israel takes all necessary steps to help normalize Palestinian life. Israel withdraws from Palestinian areas occupied from September 28, 2000 and the two sides restore the *status quo* that existed at that time, as security performance and cooperation progress. Israel also freezes all settlement activity, consistent with the Mitchell report.

At the outset of Phase I:

- Palestinian leadership issues unequivocal statement reiterating Israel's right to exist in peace and security and calling for an immediate and unconditional cease-fire to end armed activity and all acts of violence against Israelis anywhere. All official Palestinian institutions end incitement against Israel.
- Israeli leadership issues unequivocal statement affirming its commitment to the two-state vision of an independent, viable, sovereign Palestinian state living in peace and security alongside Israel, as expressed

by President Bush, and calling for an immediate end to violence against Palestinians everywhere. All official Israeli institutions end incitement against Palestinians.

SECURITY

- Palestinians declare an unequivocal end to violence and terrorism and undertake visible efforts on the ground to arrest, disrupt, and restrain individuals and groups conducting and planning violent attacks on Israelis anywhere.
- Rebuilt and refocused Palestinian Authority security apparatus begins sustained, targeted, and effective operations aimed at confronting all those engaged in terror and dismantlement of terrorist capabilities and infrastructure. This includes commencing confiscation of illegal weapons and consolidation of security authority, free of association with terror and corruption.
- GOI takes no actions undermining trust, including deportations, attacks on civilians; confiscation and/or demolition of Palestinian homes and property, as a punitive measure or to facilitate Israeli construction; destruction of Palestinian institutions and infrastructure; and other measures specified in the Tenet work plan.
- Relying on existing mechanisms and on-the-ground resources, Quartet representatives begin informal monitoring and consult with the parties on establishment of a formal monitoring mechanism and its implementation.
- Implementation, as previously agreed, of U.S. rebuilding, training and resumed security cooperation plan in collaboration with outside oversight board (U.S.-Egypt-Jordan). Quartet support for efforts to achieve a lasting, comprehensive cease-fire.

    * All Palestinian security organizations are consolidated into three services reporting to an empowered Interior Minister.
    * Restructured/retrained Palestinian security forces and IDF counterparts progressively resume security cooperation and other undertakings in implementation of the Tenet work plan, including regular senior-level meetings, with the participation of U.S. security officials.

- Arab states cut off public and private funding and all other forms of support for groups supporting and engaging in violence and terror.
- All donors providing budgetary support for the Palestinians channel these funds through the Palestinian Ministry of Finance's Single Treasury Account.
- As comprehensive security performance moves forward, IDF withdraws progressively from areas occupied since September 28, 2000 and the two sides restore the *status quo* that existed prior to September 28, 2000. Palestinian security forces redeploy to areas vacated by IDF.

PALESTINIAN INSTITUTION-BUILDING

- Immediate action on credible process to produce draft constitution for Palestinian statehood. As rapidly as possible, constitutional committee circulates draft Palestinian constitution, based on strong parliamentary democracy and cabinet with empowered prime minister, for public comment/debate. Constitutional committee proposes draft document for submission after elections for approval by appropriate Palestinian institutions.
- Appointment of interim prime minister or cabinet with empowered executive authority/decision-making body.
- GOI fully facilitates travel of Palestinian officials for PLC and Cabinet sessions, internationally supervised security retraining, electoral and other reform activity, and other supportive measures related to the reform efforts.
- Continued appointment of Palestinian ministers empowered to undertake fundamental reform. Completion of further steps to achieve genuine separation of powers, including any necessary Palestinian legal reforms for this purpose.
- Establishment of independent Palestinian election commission. PLC reviews and revises election law.
- Palestinian performance on judicial, administrative, and economic benchmarks, as established by the International Task Force on Palestinian Reform.
- As early as possible, and based upon the above measures and in the context of open debate and transparent candidate selection/electoral campaign based on a free, multi-party process, Palestinians hold free, open, and fair elections.
- GOI facilitates Task Force election assistance, registration of voters, movement of candidates and voting officials. Support for NGOs involved in the election process.
- GOI reopens Palestinian Chamber of Commerce and other closed Palestinian institutions in East Jerusalem based on a commitment that these institutions operate strictly in accordance with prior agreements between the parties.

HUMANITARIAN RESPONSE

- Israel takes measures to improve the humanitarian situation. Israel and Palestinians implement in full all recommendations of the Bertini report to improve humanitarian conditions, lifting curfews and easing restrictions on movement of persons and goods, and allowing full, safe, and unfettered access of international and humanitarian personnel.

. . .

CIVIL SOCIETY

- Continued donor support, including increased funding through PVOs/ NGOs, for people to people programs, private sector development, and civil society initiatives.

SETTLEMENTS

- GOI immediately dismantles settlement outposts erected since March 2001.
- Consistent with the Mitchell Report, GOI freezes all settlement activity (including natural growth of settlements).

Phase II: Transition – June 2003–December 2003

In the second phase, efforts are focused on the option of creating an independent Palestinian state with provisional borders and attributes of sovereignty, based on the new constitution, as a way station to a permanent status settlement. As has been noted, this goal can be achieved when the Palestinian people have a leadership acting decisively against terror, willing and able to build a practicing democracy based on tolerance and liberty. With such a leadership, reformed civil institutions and security structures, the Palestinians will have the active support of the Quartet and the broader international community in establishing an independent, viable state.

Progress into Phase II will be based upon the consensus judgment of the Quartet of whether conditions are appropriate to proceed, taking into account performance of both parties. Furthering and sustaining efforts to normalize Palestinian lives and build Palestinian institutions, Phase II starts after Palestinian elections and ends with possible creation of an independent Palestinian state with provisional borders in 2003. Its primary goals are continued comprehensive security performance and effective security cooperation, continued normalization of Palestinian life and institution-building, further building on and sustaining of the goals outlined in Phase I, ratification of a democratic Palestinian constitution, formal establishment of office of prime minister, consolidation of political reform, and the creation of a Palestinian state with provisional borders.

- INTERNATIONAL CONFERENCE: Convened by the Quartet, in consultation with the parties, immediately after the successful conclusion of Palestinian elections, to support Palestinian economic recovery and launch a process, leading to establishment of an independent Palestinian state with provisional borders.

  - * Such a meeting would be inclusive, based on the goal of a comprehensive Middle East peace (including between Israel and Syria, and

Israel and Lebanon), and based on the principles described in the preamble to this document.
* Arab states restore pre-intifada links to Israel (trade offices, etc.).
* Revival of multilateral engagement on issues including regional water resources, environment, economic development, refugees, and arms control issues.

* New constitution for democratic, independent Palestinian state is finalized and approved by appropriate Palestinian institutions. Further elections, if required, should follow approval of the new constitution.
* Empowered reform cabinet with office of prime minister formally established, consistent with draft constitution.
* Continued comprehensive security performance, including effective security cooperation on the bases laid out in Phase I.
* Creation of an independent Palestinian state with provisional borders through a process of Israeli-Palestinian engagement, launched by the international conference. As part of this process, implementation of prior agreements, to enhance maximum territorial contiguity, including further action on settlements in conjunction with establishment of a Palestinian state with provisional borders.
* Enhanced international role in monitoring transition, with the active, sustained, and operational support of the Quartet.
* Quartet members promote international recognition of Palestinian state, including possible UN membership.

Phase III: Permanent Status Agreement and End of the Israeli-Palestinian Conflict – 2004–2005

Progress into Phase III, based on consensus judgment of Quartet, and taking into account actions of both parties and Quartet monitoring. Phase III objectives are consolidation of reform and stabilization of Palestinian institutions, sustained, effective Palestinian security performance, and Israeli-Palestinian negotiations aimed at a permanent status agreement in 2005.

* SECOND INTERNATIONAL CONFERENCE: Convened by Quartet, in consultation with the parties, at beginning of 2004 to endorse agreement reached on an independent Palestinian state with provisional borders and formally to launch a process with the active, sustained, and operational support of the Quartet, leading to a final, permanent status resolution in 2005, including on borders, Jerusalem, refugees, settlements; and, to support progress toward a comprehensive Middle East settlement between Israel and Lebanon and Israel and Syria, to be achieved as soon as possible.
* Continued comprehensive, effective progress on the reform agenda laid out by the Task Force in preparation for final status agreement.

- Continued sustained and effective security performance, and sustained, effective security cooperation on the bases laid out in Phase I.
- International efforts to facilitate reform and stabilize Palestinian institutions and the Palestinian economy, in preparation for final status agreement.
- Parties reach final and comprehensive permanent status agreement that ends the Israel-Palestinian conflict in 2005, through a settlement negotiated between the parties based on UNSCR 242, 338, and 1397, that ends the occupation that began in 1967, and includes an agreed, just, fair, and realistic solution to the refugee issue, and a negotiated resolution on the status of Jerusalem that takes into account the political and religious concerns of both sides, and protects the religious interests of Jews, Christians, and Muslims worldwide, and fulfills the vision of two states, Israel and sovereign, independent, democratic and viable Palestine, living side-by-side in peace and security.
- Arab state acceptance of full normal relations with Israel and security for all the states of the region in the context of a comprehensive Arab-Israeli peace.

98 The Geneva Accord

A Model Israeli-Palestinian Peace Agreement (December 1, 2003)

Draft Permanent Status Agreement

Preamble

The State of Israel (hereinafter "Israel") and the Palestine Liberation Organization (hereinafter "PLO"), the representative of the Palestinian people (hereinafter the "Parties"):

Reaffirming their determination to put an end to decades of confrontation and conflict, and to live in peaceful coexistence, mutual dignity and security based on a just, lasting, and comprehensive peace and achieving historic reconciliation;

Recognizing that peace requires the transition from the logic of war and confrontation to the logic of peace and cooperation, and that acts and words characteristic of the state of war are neither appropriate nor acceptable in the era of peace;

Affirming their deep belief that the logic of peace requires compromise, and that the only viable solution is a two-state solution based on UNSC Resolution 242 and 338;

. . .

Confirming that this Agreement is concluded within the framework of the Middle East peace process initiated in Madrid in October 1991, the Declaration of Principles of September 13, 1993, the subsequent agreements including the Interim Agreement of September 1995, the Wye River Memorandum of October 1998 and the Sharm El-Sheikh Memorandum of September 4, 1999, and the permanent status negotiations including the Camp David Summit of July 2000, the Clinton Ideas of December 2000, and the Taba Negotiations of January 2001;

Reiterating their commitment to United Nations Security Council Resolutions 242, 338 and 1397 and confirming their understanding that this Agreement is based on, will lead to, and —by its fulfillment— will constitute the full implementation of these resolutions and to the settlement of the Israeli-Palestinian conflict in all its aspects;

Declaring that this Agreement constitutes the realization of the permanent status peace component envisaged in President Bush's speech of June 24, 2002 and in the Quartet Roadmap process.

DOI: 10.4324/9781003348948-104

. . . and

Resolved to pursue the goal of attaining a comprehensive regional peace, thus contributing to stability, security, development and prosperity throughout the region;

Have agreed on the following

Article 1 – Purpose of the Permanent Status Agreement

1. The Permanent Status Agreement (hereinafter "this Agreement") ends the era of conflict and ushers in a new era based on peace, cooperation, and good neighborly relations between the Parties.
2. . . .

Article 2 – Relations between the Parties

1. The state of Israel shall recognize the state of Palestine (hereinafter "Palestine") upon its establishment. The state of Palestine shall immediately recognize the state of Israel.
2. The state of Palestine shall be the successor to the PLO with all its rights and obligations.
3. Israel and Palestine shall immediately establish full diplomatic and consular relations with each other and will exchange resident Ambassadors, within one month of their mutual recognition.
4. The Parties recognize Palestine and Israel as the homelands of their respective peoples. The Parties are committed not to interfere in each other's internal affairs.
5. . . .
6. . . .
7. With a view to the advancement of the relations between the two States and peoples, Palestine and Israel shall cooperate in areas of common interest. . . .
8. The Parties shall cooperate in areas of joint economic interest, to best realize the human potential of their respective peoples. . . . Relevant standing bodies shall be established by the Parties to this effect.
9. The Parties shall establish robust modalities for security cooperation, and engage in a comprehensive and uninterrupted effort to end terrorism and violence directed against each others persons, property, institutions or territory. . . .
10. Israel and Palestine shall work together and separately with other parties in the region to enhance and promote regional cooperation and coordination in spheres of common interest.
11. The Parties shall establish a ministerial-level Palestinian-Israeli High Steering Committee to guide, monitor, and facilitate the process of implementation of this Agreement, . . .

Article 3 – Implementation and Verification Group

1. Establishment and Composition

    i. An Implementation and Verification Group (IVG) shall hereby be established to facilitate . . . disputes relating to the implementation of this Agreement.
    ii. The IVG shall include the US, the Russian Federation, the EU, the UN, and other parties, both regional and international, to be agreed on by the Parties.
    iii. . . .
    iv. . . .

2. Structure

    i. A senior political-level contact group (Contact Group), composed of all the IVG members, shall be the highest authority in the IVG.
    ii. . . .
    iii. The IVG permanent headquarters and secretariat shall be based in an agreed upon location in Jerusalem.
    iv. . . .
    v. The Multinational Force (MF) established under Article 5 shall be an integral part of the IVG. . . .
    vi. The IVG shall establish a dispute settlement mechanism, in accordance with Article 16.

3. Coordination with the Parties . . .
4. Functions . . .
5. Termination . . .

Article 4 – Territory

1. The International Borders between the States of Palestine and Israel

    i. In accordance with UNSC Resolution 242 and 338, the border between the states of Palestine and Israel shall be based on the June 4th 1967 lines with reciprocal modifications on a 1:1 basis as set forth in attached Map 1 . . .

2. Sovereignty and Inviolability

    i. The Parties recognize and respect each other's sovereignty, territorial integrity, and political independence, as well as the inviolability of each other's territory, including territorial waters, and airspace. . . .
    ii. The Parties recognize each other's rights in their exclusive economic zones in accordance with international law.

3. Israeli Withdrawal

    i.   Israel shall withdraw in accordance with Article 5.
    ii. Palestine shall assume responsibility for the areas from which Israel withdraws.
    iii. . . .
    iv. . . .

4. Demarcation

    . . .

5. Settlements

    i.   The state of Israel shall be responsible for resettling the Israelis residing in Palestinian sovereign territory outside this territory.
    ii. . . .
    iii. Existing arrangements in the West Bank and Gaza Strip regarding Israeli settlers and settlements, including security, shall remain in force in each of the settlements until the date prescribed in the timetable . . .
    iv   . . .
    v.   Israel shall keep intact the immovable property, infrastructure and facilities in Israeli settlements to be transferred to Palestinian sovereignty. . . .
    vi. The state of Palestine shall have exclusive title to all land and any buildings, facilities, infrastructure or other property remaining in any of the settlements on the date prescribed in the timetable for the completion of the evacuation of this settlement.

6. Corridor

    i.   The states of Palestine and Israel shall establish a corridor linking the West Bank and Gaza Strip. This corridor shall:

        a. Be under Israeli sovereignty.
        b. Be permanently open.
        c. Be under Palestinian administration in accordance with Annex X of this Agreement. . . .
        d. Not disrupt Israeli transportation and other infrastructural networks, or endanger the environment, public safety or public health. . . .
        e. Allow for the establishment of the necessary infrastructural facilities linking the West Bank and the Gaza Strip. Infrastructural facilities shall be understood to include, inter alia, pipelines, electrical and communications cables, and associated equipment . . .
        f. Not be used in contravention of this Agreement.

ii. Defensive barriers shall be established along the corridor and Palestinians shall not enter Israel from this corridor, nor shall Israelis enter Palestine from the corridor.

iii. The Parties shall seek the assistance of the international community in securing the financing for the corridor.

iv. . . .

v. . . .

vi. The arrangements set forth in this clause may only be terminated or revised by agreement of both Parties.

Article 5 – Security

General Security Provisions

The Parties acknowledge that mutual understanding and co-operation in security-related matters will form a significant part of their bilateral relations and will further enhance regional security. . . .

Palestine and Israel each shall:

a. Recognize and respect the other's right to live in peace within secure and recognized boundaries free from the threat or acts of war, terrorism and violence;

b. refrain from the threat or use of force against the territorial integrity or political independence of the other . . . ;

c. refrain from joining, assisting, promoting or co-operating with any coalition, organization or alliance of a military or security character, the objectives or activities of which include launching aggression or other acts of hostility against the other;

d. refrain from organizing, encouraging, or allowing the formation of irregular forces or armed bands, including mercenaries and militias within their respective territory and prevent their establishment . . .

e. refrain from organizing, assisting, allowing, or participating in acts of violence in or against the other . . .

To further security cooperation, the Parties shall establish a high level Joint Security Committee that shall meet on at least a monthly basis. . . .

Regional Security

Israel and Palestine shall work together with their neighbors and the international community to build a secure and stable Middle East, free from weapons of mass destruction, both conventional and non-conventional, in the context of a comprehensive, lasting, and stable peace, characterized by reconciliation, goodwill, and the renunciation of the use of force.

. . .

Defense Characteristics of the Palestinian State

No armed forces, other than as specified in this Agreement, will be deployed or stationed in Palestine.

Palestine shall be a non-militarized state, with a strong security force. Accordingly, the limitations on the weapons that may be purchased, owned, or used by the Palestinian Security Force (PSF) or manufactured in Palestine shall be specified in Annex X. . . .

a. No individuals or organizations in Palestine other than the PSF and the organs of the IVG, including the MF, may purchase, possess, carry or use weapons except as provided by law.

The PSF shall:

a. Maintain border control;
b. Maintain law-and-order and perform police functions;
c. Perform intelligence and security functions;
d. Prevent terrorism;
e. Conduct rescue and emergency missions; and
f. Supplement essential community services when necessary.

The MF shall monitor and verify compliance with this clause.
Terrorism
The Parties reject and condemn terrorism and violence in all its forms. . . . In addition, the parties shall refrain from actions and policies that are liable to nurture extremism and create conditions conducive to terrorism on either side.

. . .

Incitement
Without prejudice to freedom of expression and other internationally recognized human rights, Israel and Palestine shall promulgate laws to prevent incitement to irredentism, racism, terrorism and violence and vigorously enforce them.

. . .

Multinational Force
A Multinational Force (MF) shall be established to provide security guarantees to the Parties, act as a deterrent, and oversee the implementation of the relevant provisions of this Agreement.

. . .

. . .

Evacuation
Israel shall withdraw all its military and security personnel and equipment, including landmines, and all persons employed to support them, and all military installations from the territory of the state of Palestine, . . . in stages.

The staged withdrawals shall commence immediately upon entry into force of this Agreement . . .

iii.   The stages shall be designed subject to the following principles:

    a.   The need to create immediate clear contiguity and facilitate the early implementation of Palestinian development plans.

    b.   Israel's capacity to relocate, house and absorb settlers. . . .

    c.   The need to construct and operationalize the border between the two states.

    d.   . . .

iv.   Accordingly, the withdrawal shall be implemented in the following stages:

    a.   The first stage shall include the areas of the state of Palestine, . . . and shall be completed within 9 months.

    b.   The second and third stages shall include the remainder of the territory of the state of Palestine and shall be completed within 21 months of the end of the first stage.

Israel shall complete its withdrawal from the territory of the state of Palestine within 30 months of the entry into force of this Agreement, and in accordance with this Agreement.

. . .

Early Warning Stations

Israel may maintain two EWS in the northern, and central West Bank . . .

The EWS shall be staffed by the minimal required number of Israeli personnel and shall occupy the minimal amount of land necessary for their operation . . .

Internal security of the EWS shall be the responsibility of Israel. The perimeter security of the EWS shall be the responsibility of the MF.

The MF and the PSF shall maintain a liaison presence in the EWS. The MF shall monitor and verify that the EWS is being used for purposes recognized by this Agreement . . .

. . .

Airspace

Civil Aviation

. . .

Training

a.   The Israeli Air Force shall be entitled to use the Palestinian sovereign airspace for training purposes . . .

11.   Law Enforcement

The Israeli and Palestinian law enforcement agencies shall cooperate in combating illicit drug trafficking, illegal trafficking in archaeological artifacts and objects of arts, cross-border crime, including theft and fraud, organized crime, trafficking in women and minors, counterfeiting, pirate TV and radio stations, and other illegal activity.

12. International Border Crossings

. . . All border crossings shall be monitored by joint teams composed of members of the PSF and the MF. These teams shall prevent the entry into Palestine of any weapons, materials or equipment that are in contravention of the provisions of this Agreement.

The MF representatives and the PSF will have, jointly and separately, the authority to block the entry into Palestine of any such items. . . .

In passenger terminals, for thirty months, Israel may maintain an unseen presence in a designated on-site facility, to be staffed by members of the MF and Israelis, utilizing appropriate technology. . . .

For the following two years, these arrangements will continue in a specially designated facility in Israel, utilizing appropriate technology. . . .

In cargo terminals, for thirty months, Israel may maintain an unseen presence in a designated on-site facility, to be staffed by members of the MF and Israelis, utilizing appropriate technology. . . .

viii. For the following three years, these arrangements will continue from a specially designated facility in Israel, utilizing appropriate technology. This shall not cause delays beyond the timelines outlined in this clause.

A high level trilateral committee composed of representatives of Palestine, Israel, and the IVG shall meet regularly to monitor the application of these procedures and correct any irregularities, and may be convened on request.

Border Control

The PSF shall maintain border control . . .

Article 6 – Jerusalem

1. Religious and Cultural Significance:

    i.   The Parties recognize the universal historic, religious, spiritual, and cultural significance of Jerusalem and its holiness enshrined in Judaism, Christianity, and Islam. In recognition of this status, the Parties reaffirm their commitment to safeguard the character, holiness, and freedom of worship in the city . . .

    ii. The Parties shall establish an inter-faith body consisting of representatives of the three monotheistic faiths, to act as a consultative body to the Parties on matters related to the city's religious significance . . .

2. Capital of Two States
    The Parties shall have their mutually recognized capitals in the areas of Jerusalem under their respective sovereignty.

3. Sovereignty
    Sovereignty in Jerusalem shall be in accordance with attached Map . . .

4. Border Regime:

The border regime shall . . . taking into account the specific needs of Jerusalem (e.g., movement of tourists and intensity of border crossing use including provisions for Jerusalemites) and the provisions of this Article.

5. al-Haram al-Sharif/Temple Mount (Compound)

   i. International Group

      a. An International Group, composed of the IVG and other parties to be agreed upon by the Parties, . . . shall hereby be established to monitor, verify, and assist in the implementation of this clause.

      b. For this purpose, the International Group shall establish a Multinational Presence on the Compound, . . .

      c. The Multinational Presence shall have specialized detachments dealing with security and conservation. . . .

      d. The Multinational Presence shall strive to immediately resolve any problems arising . . .

      e. The Parties may at any time request clarifications or submit complaints to the International Group . . .

      f. The International Group shall draw up rules and regulations to maintain security on . . . the Compound. . . .

   ii. Regulations Regarding the Compound

      a. In view of the sanctity of the Compound, and in light of the unique religious and cultural significance of the site to the Jewish people, there shall be no digging, excavation, or construction on the Compound, unless approved by the two Parties. . . .

      b. The state of Palestine shall be responsible for maintaining the security of the Compound and for ensuring that it will not be used for any hostile acts against Israelis or Israeli areas. . . .

      c. In light of the universal significance of the Compound, . . . visitors shall be allowed access to the site. . . .

   iii. Transfer of Authority

      a. At the end of the withdrawal period stipulated in Article 5/7, the state of Palestine shall assert sovereignty over the Compound.

      b. The International Group and its subsidiary organs shall continue to exist and fulfill all the functions stipulated in this Article unless otherwise agreed by the two Parties.

6. The Wailing Wall

The Wailing Wall shall be under Israeli sovereignty.

7. The Old City:

   i. Significance of the Old City

     a.   The Parties view the Old City as one whole enjoying a unique character. . . .

     b.   The Parties shall act in accordance with the UNESCO World Cultural Heritage List regulations, in which the Old City is a registered site.

ii. ...

     c. ...

iii. Free Movement within the Old City

    Movement within the Old City shall be free and unimpeded subject to the provisions of this article and rules and regulations pertaining to the various holy sites.

iv. Entry into and Exit from the Old City

    ...

v. Suspension, Termination, and Expansion

     a.   Either Party may suspend the arrangements set forth in Article 6.7.iii in cases of emergency for one week. . . .

     b.   This clause shall not apply to the arrangements set forth in Article 6/7/vi.

     c.   Three years after the transfer of authority over the Old City, the Parties shall review these arrangements. . . .

vi. Special Arrangements

vii. Color-Coding of the Old City

    A visible color-coding scheme shall be used in the Old City to denote the sovereign areas of the respective Parties.

viii. Policing

     a.   An agreed number of Israeli police shall constitute the Israeli Old City police detachment and shall exercise responsibility for maintaining order and day-to-day policing functions in the area under Israeli sovereignty.

     b.   An agreed number of Palestinian police shall constitute the Palestinian Old City police detachment and shall exercise responsibility for maintaining order and day-to-day policing functions in the area under Palestinian sovereignty.

     c.   All members of the respective Israeli and Palestinian Old City police detachments shall undergo special training, including joint training exercises, to be administered by the PU . . .

ix. Arms

    No person shall be allowed to carry or possess arms in the Old City, with the exception of the Police Forces provided for in this agreement. In addition, each Party may grant special written permission to carry or possess arms in areas under its sovereignty.

x.   Intelligence and Security

   a.   The Parties shall establish intensive intelligence cooperation regarding the Old City, including the immediate sharing of threat information.

   b.   . . .

8.   Mount of Olives Cemetery:

   i.   The area outlined in [the attached map of] (the Jewish Cemetery on the Mount of Olives) shall be under Israeli administration; . . .

     a.   There shall be a designated road to provide free, unlimited, and unimpeded access to the Cemetery. . . .

9.   Special Cemetery Arrangements
   Arrangements shall be established in the two cemeteries designated in [the attached map of] (Mount Zion Cemetery and the German Colony Cemetery), to facilitate and ensure the continuation of the current burial and visitation practices, including the facilitation of access.

10.   The Western Wall Tunnel

   i.   The Western Wall Tunnel . . . shall be under Israeli administration, including:

     a.   Unrestricted Israeli access and right to worship and conduct religious practices.

     b.   Responsibility for the preservation and maintenance of the site in accordance with this Agreement . . .

     c.   Israeli policing.

     d.   IVG monitoring

     e.   The Northern Exit of the Tunnel shall only be used for exit and may only be closed in case of emergency . . .

11.   Municipal Coordination

   i.   The two Jerusalem municipalities shall form a Jerusalem Co-ordination and Development Committee ("JCDC"). . . . The JCDC and its sub-committees shall be composed of an equal number of representatives from Palestine and Israel. . . .

   ii.   The JCDC shall ensure that the coordination of infrastructure and services best serves the residents of Jerusalem, and shall promote the economic development of the city to the benefit of all. . . .

   iii.   The JCDC shall have the following subcommittees . . .

12.   Israeli Residency of Palestinian Jerusalemites
   Palestinian Jerusalemites who currently are permanent residents of Israel shall lose this status upon the transfer of authority to Palestine of those areas in which they reside.

13.   Transfer of authority

The Parties will apply in certain socio-economic spheres interim measures to ensure the agreed, expeditious, and orderly transfer of powers and obligations from Israel to Palestine. . . .

Article 7 – Refugees

1. Significance of the Refugee Problem

    i. The Parties recognize that, in the context of two independent states, Palestine and Israel, living side by side in peace, an agreed resolution of the refugee problem is necessary . . .
2. UNGAR 194, UNSC Resolution 242, and the Arab Peace Initiative

    i. The Parties recognize that UNGAR 194, UNSC Resolution 242, and the Arab Peace Initiative (Article 2.ii.) concerning the rights of the Palestinian refugees represent the basis for resolving the refugee issue, . . .
3. Compensation

    i. Refugees shall be entitled to compensation for their refugeehood and for loss of property. This shall not prejudice or be prejudiced by the refugee's permanent place of residence.
    ii. The Parties recognize the right of states that have hosted Palestinian refugees to remuneration.
4. Choice of Permanent Place of Residence (PPR)

    . . . PPR options from which the refugees may choose shall be as follows;
    i. The state of Palestine, in accordance with clause a below.
    ii. Areas in Israel being transferred to Palestine in the land swap, . . .
    iii. Third Countries . . .
    iv. The state of Israel, in accordance with clause c below.
    v. Present Host countries, in accordance with clause d below.

    a. PPR options i and ii shall be the right of all Palestinian refugees and shall be in accordance with the laws of the State of Palestine.
    b. Option iii shall be at the sovereign discretion of third countries and shall be in accordance with numbers that each third country will submit to the International Commission. . . .
    c. Option iv shall be at the sovereign discretion of Israel . . . This number shall represent the total number of Palestinian refugees that Israel shall accept. . . .
    d. . . .
    Priority in all the above shall be accorded to the Palestinian refugee population in Lebanon.

5. Free and Informed Choice
    The process by which Palestinian refugees shall express their PPR choice shall be on the basis of a free and informed decision. . . .
6. End of Refugee Status
    Palestinian refugee status shall be terminated upon the realization of an individual refugee's permanent place of residence (PPR) . . .
7. End of Claims
    This agreement provides for the permanent and complete resolution of the Palestinian refugee problem. No claims may be raised except for those related to the implementation of this agreement.
8. International Role
    The Parties call upon the international community to participate fully in the comprehensive resolution of the refugee problem in accordance with this Agreement . . .
9. Property Compensation

    i.   Refugees shall be compensated for the loss of property resulting from their displacement.
    ii. The aggregate sum of property compensation shall be calculated as follows:
         . . .
    iii. The aggregate value agreed to by the Parties shall constitute the Israeli "lump sum" contribution to the International Fund. . . .
    iv. Israel's contribution shall be made in installments . . .
    v.   The value of the Israeli fixed assets that shall remain intact in former settlements and transferred to the state of Palestine will be deducted from Israel's contribution to the International Fund. . . .

10. Compensation for Refugeehood

    i.   A "Refugeehood Fund" shall be established in recognition of each individual's refugeehood. . . .
    ii. . . .

11. The International Commission (Commission)

    i. Mandate and Composition . . .
    ii. Structure . . .
    iii. Specific Committees . . .
    iv. Status-determination Committee . . .
    v. Compensation Committee . . .
    vi. Host State Remuneration Committee . . .
    vii. Permanent Place of Residence Committee (PPR Committee) . . .
    viii. Refugeehood Fund Committee . . .
    ix. Rehabilitation and Development Committee . . .

12. The International Fund

    i.   An International Fund (the Fund) shall be established to receive contributions outlined in this Article and additional contributions from the international community. The Fund shall disburse monies to the Commission to enable it to carry out its functions. . . .

13. UNRWA

    i.   UNRWA should be phased out in each country in which it operates, based on the end of refugee status in that country . . .

14. Reconciliation Programs

    i.   The Parties will encourage and promote the development of cooperation between their relevant institutions and civil societies in creating forums for exchanging historical narratives and enhancing mutual understanding regarding the past.

    ii. The Parties shall encourage and facilitate exchanges in order to disseminate a richer appreciation of these respective narratives, in the fields of formal and informal education, by providing conditions for direct contacts between schools, educational institutions and civil society . . .

Article 8 – Israeli-Palestinian Cooperation Committee (IPCC)

1. The Parties shall establish an Israeli-Palestinian Cooperation Committee immediately . . .
2. The IPCC shall develop and assist in the implementation of policies for cooperation in areas of common interest . . .

Article 9 – Designated Road Use Arrangements:

  . . .

Article 10 – Sites of Religious Significance:

1. The Parties shall establish special arrangements to guarantee access to agreed sites of religious significance, . . . These arrangements will apply, inter alia, to the Tomb of the Patriarchs in Hebron and Rachel's Tomb in Bethlehem, and Nabi Samuel.

. . .

10. In the event of any incidents involving Israeli citizens and requiring criminal or legal proceedings, there will be full cooperation between the Israeli and Palestinian authorities according to arrangements to be agreed upon. The Parties may call on the IVG to assist in this respect.

. . .

Article 11 – Border Regime

1. There shall be a border regime between the two states, . . .
2. Movement across the border shall only be through designated border crossings.
3. Procedures in border crossings shall be designed to facilitate strong trade and economic ties, including labor movement between the Parties.
4. . . .
5. . . .

Article 12 – Water

Article 13 – Economic Relations

Article 14 – Legal Cooperation

. . .

Article 15 – Palestinian Prisoners and Detainees

1. In the context of this Permanent Status Agreement between Israel and Palestine, . . . all the Palestinian and Arab prisoners detained in the framework of the Israeli-Palestinian conflict prior to the date of signature of this Agreement, DD/MM/2003, shall be released in accordance with the categories set forth below . . .

Article 16 – Dispute Settlement Mechanism

1. Disputes related to the interpretation or application of this Agreement shall be resolved by negotiations within a bilateral framework to be convened by the High Steering Committee.

. . .

Article 17 – Final Clauses

Including a final clause providing for a UNSCR/UNGAR resolution endorsing the agreement and superseding the previous UN resolutions.

The English version of this text will be considered authoritative.

99 Exchange of Letters Between Israeli Prime Minister Ariel Sharon and U.S. President George W. Bush (April 14, 2004)

Letter From Prime Minister Ariel Sharon to US President George W. Bush

The Honorable George W. Bush
President of the United States of America
The White House
Washington, D.C.

Dear Mr. President,

The vision that you articulated in your 24 June 2002 address constitutes one of the most significant contributions toward ensuring a bright future for the Middle East. Accordingly, the State of Israel has accepted the Roadmap, as adopted by our government. For the first time, a practical and just formula was presented for the achievement of peace, opening a genuine window of opportunity for progress toward a settlement between Israel and the Palestinians, involving two states living side-by-side in peace and security.

This formula sets forth the correct sequence and principles for the attainment of peace. . . . As you have stated, a Palestinian state will never be created by terror, and Palestinians must engage in a sustained fight against the terrorists and dismantle their infrastructure. Moreover, there must be serious efforts to institute true reform and real democracy and liberty, including new leaders not compromised by terror. . . . We believe that this formula is the only viable one.

The Palestinian Authority under its current leadership has taken no action to meet its responsibilities under the Roadmap. . . . Israel must preserve its capability to protect itself and deter its enemies, and we thus retain our right to defend ourselves against terrorism and to take actions against terrorist organizations.

Having reached the conclusion that, for the time being, there exists no Palestinian partner with whom to advance peacefully toward a settlement . . . I have decided to initiate a process of gradual disengagement with the hope of reducing friction between Israelis and Palestinians. The Disengagement

DOI: 10.4324/9781003348948-105

Plan is designed to improve security for Israel and stabilize our political and economic situation. . . .

I attach, for your review, the main principles of the Disengagement Plan. This initiative, . . . represents an independent Israeli plan, yet is not inconsistent with the roadmap. According to this plan, the State of Israel intends to relocate military installations and all Israeli villages and towns in the Gaza Strip, as well as other military installations and a small number of villages in Samaria.

In this context, we also plan to accelerate construction of the Security Fence, whose completion is essential in order to ensure the security of the citizens of Israel. The fence is a security rather than political barrier, temporary rather than permanent, and therefore will not prejudice any final status issues including final borders. The route of the Fence, as approved by our Government's decisions, will take into account, consistent with security needs, its impact on Palestinians not engaged in terrorist activities.

Upon my return from Washington, I expect to submit this Plan for the approval of the Cabinet and the Knesset, and I firmly believe that it will win such approval.

. . . Additionally, the Plan will entail a series of measures with the inherent potential to improve the lot of the Palestinian Authority, providing that it demonstrates the wisdom to take advantage of this opportunity. The execution of the Disengagement Plan holds the prospect of stimulating positive changes within the Palestinian Authority that might create the necessary conditions for the resumption of direct negotiations.

We view the achievement of a settlement between Israel and the Palestinians as our central focus and are committed to realizing this objective. Progress toward this goal must be anchored exclusively in the Roadmap and we will oppose any other plan.

In this regard, we are fully aware of the responsibilities facing the State of Israel. These include limitations on the growth of settlements; removal of unauthorized outposts; and steps to increase, to the extent permitted by security needs, freedom of movement for Palestinians not engaged in terrorism. Under separate cover we are sending to you a full description of the steps the State of Israel is taking to meet all its responsibilities.

The government of Israel supports the United States efforts to reform the Palestinian security services to meet their roadmap obligations to fight terror. Israel also supports the American's efforts, working with the International Community, to promote the reform process, build institutions and improve the economy of the Palestinian Authority and to enhance the welfare of its people, in the hope that a new Palestinian leadership will prove able to fulfill its obligations under the roadmap.

I want to again express my appreciation for your courageous leadership in the war against global terror, your important initiative to revitalize the Middle East as a more fitting home for its people and, primarily, your personal friendship and profound support for the State of Israel.

Sincerely,

Ariel Sharon

Letter from US President George W. Bush to Prime Minister Ariel Sharon

His Excellency
Ariel Sharon
Prime Minister of Israel

Dear Mr. Prime Minister,

Thank you for your letter setting out your disengagement plan.

The United States remains hopeful and determined to find a way forward toward a resolution of the Israeli-Palestinian dispute. I remain committed to my June 24, 2002 vision of two states living side by side in peace and security as the key to peace, and to the roadmap as the route to get there.

We welcome the disengagement plan you have prepared, . . . These steps described in the plan will mark real progress toward realizing my June 24, 2002 vision, and make a real contribution towards peace. We also understand that, in this context, Israel believes it is important to bring new opportunities to the Negev and the Galilee. . . .

The United States appreciates the risks such an undertaking represents. I therefore want to reassure you on several points.

First, the United States remains committed to my vision and to its implementation as described in the roadmap. . . . Under the roadmap, Palestinians must undertake an immediate cessation of armed activity and all acts of violence against Israelis anywhere, and all official Palestinian institutions must end incitement against Israel. . . . Palestinians must undertake a comprehensive and fundamental political reform that includes a strong parliamentary democracy and an empowered prime minister.

Second, there will be no security for Israelis or Palestinians until they and all states, in the region and beyond, join together to fight terrorism and dismantle terrorist organizations. The United States reiterates its steadfast commitment to Israel's security, including secure, defensible borders, and to preserve and strengthen Israel's capability to deter and defend itself, by itself, against any threat or possible combination of threats.

Third, Israel will retain its right to defend itself against terrorism, including to take actions against terrorist organizations. . . . The United States understands that after Israel withdraws from Gaza and/or parts of the West Bank, and pending agreements on other arrangements, existing arrangements regarding control of airspace, territorial waters, and land passages of the West Bank and Gaza will continue.

The United States is strongly committed to Israel's security and well-being as a Jewish state. It seems clear that an agreed, just, fair and realistic framework for a solution to the Palestinian refugee issue as part of any final status agreement will need to be found through the establishment of a Palestinian state, and the settling of Palestinian refugees there, rather than in Israel.

As part of a final peace settlement, Israel must have secure and recognized borders, which should emerge from negotiations between the parties in accordance with UNSC Resolutions 242 and 338. In light of new realities on the ground, including already existing major Israeli populations centers, it is unrealistic to expect that the outcome of final status negotiations will be a full and complete return to the armistice lines of 1949, and all previous efforts to negotiate a two-state solution have reached the same conclusion. It is realistic to expect that any final status agreement will only be achieved on the basis of mutually agreed changes that reflect these realities.

I know that, as you state in your letter, you are aware that certain responsibilities face the State of Israel. Among these, your government has stated that the barrier being erected by Israel should be a security rather than political barrier, should be temporary rather than permanent, and therefore not prejudice any final status issues including final borders, and its route should take into account, consistent with security needs, its impact on Palestinians not engaged in terrorist activities.

As you know, the United States supports the establishment of a Palestinian state that is viable, contiguous, sovereign, and independent, . . . The United States will join with others in the international community to foster the development of democratic political institutions and new leadership committed to those institutions, the reconstruction of civic institutions, the growth of a free and prosperous economy, and the building of capable security institutions dedicated to maintaining law and order and dismantling terrorist organizations.

A peace settlement negotiated between Israelis and Palestinians would be a great boon not only to those peoples but to the peoples of the entire region. Accordingly, the United States believes that all states in the region have special responsibilities: to support the building of the institutions of a Palestinian state; to fight terrorism, and cut off all forms of assistance to individuals and groups engaged in terrorism; and to begin now to move toward more normal relations with the State of Israel. These actions would be true contributions to building peace in the region.

Mr. Prime Minister, you have described a bold and historic initiative that can make an important contribution to peace. I commend your efforts and your courageous decision which I support. As a close friend and ally, the United States intends to work closely with you to help make it a success.

Sincerely,

George W. Bush

100 The Disengagement Plan From the Gaza Strip and Northern Samaria (April 18, 2004)

(Communicated by the Prime Minister's Office)

1. General

Israel is committed to the peace process and aspires to reach an agreed resolution of the conflict on the basis of the principle of two states for two peoples, the State of Israel as the state of the Jewish people and a Palestinian state for the Palestinian people, as part of the implementation of President Bush's vision.

Israel is concerned to advance and improve the current situation. Israel has come to the conclusion that there is currently no reliable Palestinian partner with which it can make progress in a bilateral peace process. Accordingly, it has developed a plan of unilateral disengagement, based on the following considerations:

  i. The stalemate dictated by the current situation is harmful. In order to break out of this stalemate, Israel is required to initiate moves not dependent on Palestinian cooperation.
 ii. The plan will lead to a better security situation, at least in the long term.
iii. The assumption that, in any future permanent status arrangement, there will be no Israeli towns and villages in the Gaza Strip. On the other hand, it is clear that in the West Bank, there are areas which will be part of the State of Israel, including cities, towns and villages, security areas and installations, and other places of special interest to Israel.
 iv. The relocation from the Gaza Strip and from Northern Samaria (as delineated on Map) will reduce friction with the Palestinian population and carries with it the potential for improvement in the Palestinian economy and living conditions.
  v. The hope is that the Palestinians will take advantage of the opportunity created by the disengagement in order to break out of the cycle of violence and to reengage in a process of dialogue.
 vi. The process of disengagement will serve to dispel claims regarding Israel's responsibility for the Palestinians in the Gaza Strip.

DOI: 10.4324/9781003348948-106

vii. The process of disengagement is without prejudice to the Israeli-Palestinian agreements. Relevant arrangements shall continue to apply.

When there is evidence from the Palestinian side of its willingness, capability, and implementation in practice of the fight against terrorism and the institution of reform as required by the Road Map, it will be possible to return to the track of negotiation and dialogue.

2. Main Elements

i.   Gaza Strip:

1. Israel will evacuate the Gaza Strip, including all existing Israeli towns and villages, and will redeploy outside the Strip. This will not include military deployment in the area of the border between the Gaza Strip and Egypt ("the Philadelphi Route") as detailed below.
2. Upon completion of this process, there shall no longer be any permanent presence of Israeli security forces or Israeli civilians in the areas of Gaza Strip territory which have been evacuated.
3. As a result, there will be no basis for claiming that the Gaza Strip is occupied territory.

ii. West Bank:

1. Israel will evacuate an Area in the Northern Samaria Area . . . , including four villages and all military installations, and will redeploy outside the vacated area.
2. Upon completion of this process, there shall no longer be any permanent presence of Israeli security forces or Israeli civilians in the Northern Samaria Area.
3. The move will enable territorial contiguity for Palestinians in the Northern Samaria Area.
4. . . .
5. . . .
6. The Security fence: Israel will continue to build the security fence, in accordance with the relevant decisions of the government. The route will take into account humanitarian considerations.

3. Security Situation Following the Disengagement

i.   The Gaza Strip:

1. Israel will guard and monitor the external land perimeter of the Gaza Strip, will continue to maintain exclusive authority in Gaza air space, and will continue to exercise security activity in the sea off the coast of the Gaza Strip.

2. The Gaza Strip shall be demilitarized and shall be devoid of weaponry, the presence of which does not accord with the Israeli-Palestinian agreements.
3. Israel reserves its inherent right of self-defense, both preventive and reactive, including where necessary the use of force, in respect of threats emanating from the Gaza Strip.

ii. The West Bank:

1. Upon completion of the evacuation of the Northern Samaria Area, no permanent Israeli military presence will remain in this area.
2. Israel reserves its inherent right of self-defense, both preventive and reactive, including where necessary the use of force, in respect of threats emanating from the Northern Samaria Area.
3. In other areas of the West Bank, current security activity will continue. However, as circumstances permit, Israel will consider reducing such activity in Palestinian cities.
4. Israel will work to reduce the number of internal checkpoints throughout the West Bank.

4. Military Installations and Infrastructure in the Gaza Strip and Northern Samaria

In general, these will be dismantled and removed, with the exception of those which Israel decides to leave and transfer to another party.

5. Security Assistance to the Palestinians

Israel agrees that by coordination with it, advice, assistance, and training will be provided to the Palestinian security forces for the implementation of their obligations to combat terrorism and maintain public order, by American, British, Egyptian, Jordanian, or other experts, as agreed with Israel. No foreign security presence may enter the Gaza Strip or the West Bank without being coordinated with and approved by Israel.

6. The Border Area Between the Gaza Strip and Egypt . . .

Initially, Israel will continue to maintain a military presence along the border between the Gaza Strip and Egypt. . . . This presence is an essential security requirement. At certain locations security considerations may require some widening of the area in which the military activity is conducted.

Subsequently, the evacuation of this area will be considered. Evacuation of the area will be dependent, *inter alia*, on the security situation and the extent of cooperation with Egypt in establishing a reliable alternative arrangement.

If and when conditions permit the evacuation of this area, Israel will be willing to consider the possibility of the establishment of a seaport and airport in the Gaza Strip, in accordance with arrangements to be agreed with Israel.

7. Israeli Towns and Villages

Israel will strive to leave the immovable property relating to Israeli towns and villages intact. The transfer of Israeli economic activity to Palestinians carries with it the potential for a significant improvement in the Palestinian economy . . .

Israel reserves the right to request that the economic value of the assets left in the evacuated areas be taken into consideration.

8. Civil Infrastructure and Arrangements

Infrastructure relating to water, electricity, sewage, and telecommunications serving the Palestinians will remain in place. Israel will strive to leave in place the infrastructure relating to water, electricity, and sewage currently serving the Israeli towns and villages. In general, Israel will enable the continued supply of electricity, water, gas, and petrol to the Palestinians, in accordance with current arrangements. Other existing arrangements, such as those relating to water and the electro-magnetic sphere shall remain in force.

9. Activity of International Organizations

Israel recognizes the great importance of the continued activity of international humanitarian organizations assisting the Palestinian population. Israel will coordinate with these organizations' arrangements to facilitate this activity.

10. Economic Arrangements

In general, the economic arrangements currently in operation between Israel and the Palestinians shall, in the meantime, remain in force. These arrangements include, *inter alia*:

  i. the entry of workers into Israel in accordance with the existing criteria.
 ii. the entry and exit of goods between the Gaza Strip, the West Bank, Israel, and abroad.
iii. the monetary regime.
 iv. tax and customs envelope arrangements.
  v. postal and telecommunications arrangements.

In the longer term, and in line with Israel's interest in encouraging greater Palestinian economic independence, Israel expects to reduce the number of Palestinian workers entering Israel. Israel supports the development of sources of employment in the Gaza Strip and in Palestinian areas of the West Bank.

11. Erez Industrial Zone

The Erez industrial zone, situated in the Gaza Strip, employs some 4,000 Palestinian workers. The continued operation of the zone is primarily a clear Palestinian interest. Israel will consider the continued operation of the zone on the current basis, on two conditions:

i.   The existence of appropriate security arrangements.
ii. The express recognition of the international community that the continued operation of the zone on the current basis shall not be considered continued Israel control of the area.

Alternatively, the industrial zone shall be transferred to the responsibility of an agreed Palestinian or international entity.

Israel will seek to examine, together with Egypt, the possibility of establishing a joint industrial area in the area between the Gaza Strip, Egypt, and Israel.

12. International Passages

i.   The international passage between the Gaza Strip and Egypt

1.   The existing arrangements shall continue.
2.   Israel is interested in moving the passage to the "three borders" area, approximately two kilometers south of its current location. This would need to be effected in coordination with Egypt. This move would enable the hours of operation of the passage to be extended.

ii. The international passages between the West Bank and Jordan:

The existing arrangements shall continue.

13. Erez Crossing Point

The Israeli part of Erez crossing point will be moved to a location within Israel in a time frame to be determined separately.

14. Timetable

The process of evacuation is planned to be completed by the end of 2005. The stages of evacuation and the detailed timetable will be notified to the United States.

15. Conclusion

Israel looks to the international community for widespread support for the disengagement plan. This support is essential in order to bring the Palestinians to implement in practice their obligations to combat terrorism and effect reforms, thus enabling the parties to return to the path of negotiation.

   . . .

101 International Court of Justice Advisory Opinion Finds Israel's Construction of Wall "Contrary to International Law" (July 9, 2004)

THE HAGUE, 9 July (ICJ) – The International Court of Justice (ICJ), principal judicial organ of the United Nations, has today rendered its Advisory Opinion in the case concerning the Legal Consequences of the Construction of a Wall in the Occupied Palestinian Territory (request for advisory opinion).

In its Opinion, the Court finds unanimously that it has jurisdiction to give the advisory opinion requested by the United Nations General Assembly and decides by 14 votes to 1 to comply with that request.

The Court responds to the question as follows:

"A. By 14 votes to 1,

The construction of the wall being built by Israel, the occupying Power, in the occupied Palestinian territory, including in and around East Jerusalem . . . are contrary to international law";

"B. By 14 votes to 1,

Israel is under an obligation to terminate its breaches of international law; it is under an obligation to cease forthwith the works of construction of the wall being built in the occupied Palestinian territory, including in and around East Jerusalem, to dismantle forthwith the structure therein situated, and to repeal or render ineffective forthwith all legislative and regulatory acts relating thereto, in accordance with paragraph 151 of this Opinion";

"C. By 14 votes to 1,

Israel is under an obligation to make reparation for all damage caused by the construction of the wall in the occupied Palestinian territory, including in and around East Jerusalem";

"D. By 13 votes to 2,

All States are under an obligation not to recognize the illegal situation resulting from the construction of the wall and not to render aid or assistance in maintaining the situation created by such construction . . .";

"E. By 14 votes to 1,

The United Nations, and especially the General Assembly and the Security Council, should consider what further action is required to bring

DOI: 10.4324/9781003348948-107

to an end the illegal situation resulting from the construction of the wall and the associated regime, taking due account of the present Advisory Opinion."

Reasoning of Court

The Advisory Opinion is divided into three parts: jurisdiction and judicial propriety; legality of the construction by Israel of a wall in the occupied Palestinian territory; legal consequences of the breaches found.

Jurisdiction of Court and Judicial Propriety

The Court states that, when it is seized of a request for an advisory opinion, it must first consider whether it has jurisdiction to give that opinion. It finds that the General Assembly, which requested the opinion by resolution ES-10/14 of 8 December 2003, is authorized to do so by Article 96, paragraph 1, of the Charter.

. . . It finds that the General Assembly, in requesting an advisory opinion from the Court, did not exceed its competence . . . which provides that, while the Security Council is exercising its functions in respect of any dispute or situation, the Assembly must not make any recommendation with regard thereto unless the Security Council so requests.

The Court further refers to the fact that the General Assembly adopted resolution ES-10/14 during its Tenth Emergency Special Session, . . . The Court finds that the conditions laid down by that resolution were met when the Tenth Emergency Special Session was convened; that was particularly true when the General Assembly decided to request an opinion, as the Security Council was at that time unable to adopt a resolution concerning the construction of the wall as a result of the negative vote of a permanent member.

The Court then rejects the argument that an opinion could not be given in the present case on the ground that the question posed in the request is not a legal one.

Having established its jurisdiction, the Court considers the propriety of giving the requested opinion. . . . The Court concludes . . . that there is no compelling reason precluding it from giving the requested opinion.

Legality of Construction by Israel of Wall

Before addressing the legal consequences of the construction of the wall (the term which the General Assembly has chosen to use and which is also used in the Opinion, since the other expressions sometimes employed are no more accurate if understood in the physical sense), the Court considers whether or not the construction of the wall is contrary to international law.

... The Court begins by citing, with reference to Article 2, paragraph 4, of the United Nations Charter and to General Assembly resolution 2625 (XXV), the principles of the prohibition of the threat or use of force and the illegality of any territorial acquisition by such means, as reflected in customary international law. It further cites the principle of self-determination of peoples, as enshrined in the Charter. . . . As regards international humanitarian law, the Court refers to the provisions of the Hague Regulation of 1907 . . . , as well as the Fourth Geneva Convention relative to the Protection of Civilian Persons in Time of War of 1949, applicable in those Palestinian territories which before the armed conflict of 1967 lay to the east of the 1949 Armistice demarcation line (or "Green Line") and were occupied by Israel during that conflict. The Court further notes that certain human rights instruments (International Covenant on Civil and Political Rights, International Covenant on Economic, Social and Cultural Rights and the United Nations Convention on the Rights of the Child) are applicable in the occupied Palestinian territory.

The Court ascertains whether the construction of the wall has violated the above-mentioned rules and principles. It first observes that the route of the wall as fixed by the Israeli Government includes within the "Closed Area" (between the wall and the "Green Line") some 80 percent of the settlers living in the occupied Palestinian territory. Recalling that the Security Council described Israel's policy of establishing settlements in that territory as a "flagrant violation" of the Fourth Geneva Convention, the Court finds that those settlements have been established in breach of international law. It further considers certain fears expressed to it that the route of the wall will prejudge the future frontier between Israel and Palestine; it considers that the construction of the wall and its associated regime "create a '*fait accompli*' on the ground that could well become permanent, in which case, . . . [the construction of the wall] would be tantamount to *de facto* annexation." The Court notes that the route chosen for the wall gives expression *in loco* to the illegal measures taken by Israel, and deplored by the Security Council, with regard to Jerusalem and the settlements, and that it entails further alterations to the demographic composition of the Occupied Palestinian Territory. It finds that the "construction [of the wall], along with measures taken previously . . . severely impedes the exercise by the Palestinian people of its right to self-determination, and is, therefore, a breach of Israel's obligation to respect that right."

The Court then considers the information furnished to it regarding the impact of the construction of the wall on the daily life of the inhabitants of the occupied Palestinian territory (destruction or requisition of private property, restrictions on freedom of movement, confiscation of agricultural land, cutting-off of access to primary water sources, etc.). It finds that the construction of the wall and its associated regime are contrary to the relevant provisions of the Hague Regulations of 1907 and of the Fourth Geneva Convention; that they impede the liberty of movement of the inhabitants of the territory as guaranteed by the International Covenant on Civil and Political Rights; and that they also impede the exercise by the persons concerned of the right to work, to health, to education, and to an adequate standard of living as proclaimed in the International Covenant on Economic, Social and Cultural Rights and in the Convention on the Rights of the Child. Lastly, the Court finds that this construction and its associated regime, coupled with the establishment of settlements, are tending to alter the demographic composition of the occupied Palestinian territory and thereby contravene the Fourth Geneva Convention and the relevant Security Council resolutions.

. . .

In conclusion, the Court considers that Israel cannot rely on a right of self-defence or on a state of necessity in order to preclude the wrongfulness of the construction of the wall. The Court accordingly finds that the construction of the wall and its associated regime are contrary to international law.

Legal Consequences of Violations Found

The Court draws a distinction between the legal consequences of these violations for Israel and those for other States.

In regard to the former, the Court finds that Israel must respect the right of the Palestinian people to self-determination and its obligations under humanitarian law and human rights law. Israel must also put an end to the violation of its international obligations flowing from the construction of the wall in the occupied Palestinian territory and must accordingly cease forthwith the works of construction of the wall, dismantle forthwith those parts of that structure situated within the occupied Palestinian territory, and forthwith repeal or render ineffective all legislative and regulatory acts adopted with a view to construction of the wall and establishment of its associated regime, except insofar as such acts may continue to be relevant for compliance by Israel with its obligations in regard to reparation. Israel must further make reparation for all damage suffered by all natural or legal persons affected by the wall's construction.

As regards the legal consequences for other States, the Court finds that all States are under an obligation not to recognize the illegal situation resulting from the construction of the wall and not to render aid or assistance in maintaining the situation created by such construction. The Court further finds that it is for all States, while respecting the United Nations Charter and international law, to see to it that any impediment, resulting from the construction of the wall, in the exercise by the Palestinian people of its right to self-determination is brought to an end. In addition, all States parties to the Fourth Geneva Convention are under an obligation, while respecting the Charter and international law, to ensure compliance by Israel with international humanitarian law as embodied in that Convention.

Finally, the Court is of the view that the United Nations, and especially the General Assembly and the Security Council, should consider what further action is required to bring to an end the illegal situation resulting from the construction of the wall and its associated regime, taking due account of the present Advisory Opinion.

The Court concludes by stating that the construction of the wall must be placed in a more general context. In this regard, the Court notes that Israel and Palestine are "under an obligation scrupulously to observe the rules of international humanitarian law." In the Court's view, the tragic situation in the region can be brought to an end only through implementation in good faith of all relevant Security Council resolutions. The Court further draws the attention of the General Assembly to the

> need for . . . efforts to be encouraged with a view to achieving as soon as possible, on the basis of international law, a negotiated solution to the outstanding problems and the establishment of a Palestinian State, existing side by side with Israel and its other neighbours, with peace and security for all in the region.

. . .

A summary of the Advisory Opinion is published in the document entitled "Summary No. 2004/2," to which summaries of the declaration and separate opinions appended to the Advisory Opinion are attached. This Press Communiqué, the summary of the Advisory Opinion, and the latter's full text can also be accessed on the Court's Web site by clicking on "Docket" and "Decisions" (www.icj-cij.org).

102 Prime Minister Ariel Sharon's Address to the Knesset Prior to the Vote on the Disengagement Plan (October 25, 2004)

Mr. Speaker, Members of Knesset,

This is a fateful hour for Israel. We are on threshold of a difficult decision, the likes of which we have seldom faced, the significance of which for the future of our country in this region is consistent with the difficulty, pain, and dispute it arouses within us. You know that I do not say these things with a light heart to the representatives of the nation and to the entire nation watching and listening to every word uttered here in the Knesset today. This is a people who has courageously faced, and still faces the burden and terror of the ongoing war, which has continued from generation to generation; in which, as in a relay race, fathers pass the guns to their sons; in which the boundary between the frontline and the home front has long been erased; in which schools and hotels, restaurants and marketplaces, cafes and buses have also become targets for cruel terror and premeditated murder.

Today, this nation wants to know what decision this house will make at the end of this stormy discussion. What will we say to them, and what message will we convey to them? For me, this decision is unbearably difficult. During my years as a fighter and commander, as a politician, Member of Knesset, as a minister in Israel's governments and as Prime Minister, I have never faced so difficult a decision.

I know the implications and impact of the Knesset's decision on the lives of thousands of Israelis who have lived in the Gaza Strip for many years, who were sent there on behalf of the Governments of Israel, and who built homes there, planted trees and grew flowers, and who gave birth to sons and daughters, who have not known any other home. I am well aware of the fact that I sent them and took part in this enterprise, and many of these people are my personal friends. I am well aware of their pain, rage, and despair. However, as much as I understand everything they are going through during these days and everything they will face as a result of the necessary decision to be made in the Knesset today, I also believe in the necessity of taking the step of disengagement in these areas, with all the pain it entails, and I am determined to complete this mission. I am firmly convinced and truly believe that this disengagement will strengthen Israel's hold over territory which is essential to our existence, and will be welcomed and appreciated by those near and far,

DOI: 10.4324/9781003348948-108

reduce animosity, break through boycotts and sieges, and advance us along the path of peace with the Palestinians and our other neighbors.

I am accused of deceiving the people and the voters because I am taking steps which are in total opposition to past things I have said and deeds I have done. This is a false accusation. Both during the elections and as Prime Minister, I have repeatedly and publicly said that I support the establishment of a Palestinian state alongside the State of Israel. I have repeatedly and openly said that I am willing to make painful compromises in order to put an end to this ongoing and malignant conflict between those who struggle over this land, and that I would do my utmost in order to bring peace.

And I wish, Mr. Chairman, to say that many years before, in 1988, in a meeting with Prime Minister Yitzchak Shamir and with the Ministers of the Likud, I said there that I believe that if we do not want to be pushed back to the 1967 lines, the territory should be divided.

As one who fought in all of Israel's wars, and learned from personal experience that without proper force, we do not have a chance of surviving in this region, which does not show mercy towards the weak, I have also have learned from experience that the sword alone cannot decide this bitter dispute in this land.

I have been told that the disengagement will be interpreted as a shameful withdrawal under pressure, and will increase the terror campaign, present Israel as weak, and will show our people as a nation unwilling to fight and to stand up for itself. I reject that statement outright. We have the strength to defend this country and to strike at the enemy which seeks to destroy us.

And there are those who tell me that, in exchange for a genuine signed peace agreement, they too would be willing to make these painful compromises. However, regrettably, we do not have a partner on the other side with whom to conduct genuine dialogue, in order to achieve a peace agreement. Even prime ministers of Israel who declared their willingness to relinquish the maximum territory of our homeland were answered with fire and hostility. Recently, the chairman of the Palestinian Authority declared that "a million shaheeds will break through to Jerusalem." In the choice between a responsible and wise action in history, which may lead to painful compromise and a "holy war" to destroy Israel, Yasser Arafat chose the latter – the path of blood, fire, and shaheeds. He seeks to turn a national conflict which can be terminated through mutual understanding into a religious war between Islam and Jews, and even to spill the blood of Jews who live far away.

. . .

And I ask you: what are we doing and what are we struggling over in the face of these terrible dangers? Are we not capable of uniting to meet this threat? This is the true question.

The Disengagement Plan does not replace negotiations and is not meant to permanently freeze the situation which will be created. It is an essential and necessary step in a situation which currently does not enable genuine negotiations for peace. However, everything remains open for a future agreement, which will hopefully be achieved when this murderous terror ends, and our neighbors will realize that they cannot triumph over us in this land.

Mr. Chairman, with your permission, I will read several lines from a famous essay which was published in the midst of the Arab Revolt of 1936 – and we must bear in mind that the Jewish community in Israel numbered less than 400,000. This essay by Moshe Beilinson was published in "Davar," as I mentioned, during the murderous Arab Revolt of 1936 (and I quote):

> How much longer? People ask. How much longer? Until the strength of Israel in its land will condemn and defeat in advance any enemy attack; until the most enthusiastic and bold in any enemy camp will know; there are no means to break the strength of Israel in its land, because the necessity of life is with it, and the truth of life is with it, and there is no other way but to accept it. This is the essence of this campaign.

I am convinced that everything we have done since then confirms these emphatic words.

We have no desire to permanently rule over millions of Palestinians, who double their numbers every generation. Israel, which wishes to be an exemplary democracy, will not be able to bear such a reality over time. The Disengagement Plan presents the possibility of opening a gate to a different reality.

Today, I wish to address our Arab neighbors. Already in our Declaration of Independence, in the midst of a cruel war, Israel, which was born in blood, extended its hand in peace to those who fought against it and sought to destroy it by force (and I quote):

> We appeal – in the very midst of the onslaught launched against us now for months – to the Arab inhabitants of the State of Israel to preserve peace and participate in the upbuilding of the State on the basis of full and equal citizenship and due representation in all its provisional and permanent institutions.

A long time has passed since then. This land and this region have known more wars, and have known all the wars between the wars, terror and the difficult counter-actions undertaken by Israel, with the sole purpose of defending the lives of its citizens. In this ongoing war, many among the civilian population, among the innocent, were killed. And tears met tears. I would like you to know that we did not seek to build our lives in this homeland on your ruins. Many years ago, Zeev Jabotinsky wrote in a poem his vision for partnership and peace among the peoples of this land (and I quote): "There he will be saturated with plenty and joy, the son of the Arab, the son of Nazareth and my son."

. . .

Forty-eight years ago, on the eve of our Independence Day in 1956, against the background of the return of the bodies of 10 terrorists who committed crimes in Israel, murderous acts in Israel, and who were delivered in wooden coffins to the Egyptians at a border crossing in the Gaza Strip. On this, the Hebrew poet, Natan Alterman wrote the following:

> Arabia, enemy unknown to you, you will awake when you rise against me, My life serves as witness with my back against the wall and to my history and my G-d, Enemy, the power of whose rage in the face of those who rise to destroy him until the day Will be similar only to the force of his brotherhood in a fraternal covenant between one nation and another.

This was during the time of the terrorist killings and our retaliatory raids.

Members of Knesset,

With your permission, I wish to end with a quotation from Prime Minister Menahem Begin, who at the end of December 1977, said on this podium (and I quote):

> Where does this irresponsible language come from, in addition to other things which were said? I once said, during an argument with people from Gush Emunim, that I love them today, and will continue to like them tomorrow. I told them: you are wonderful pioneers, builders of the land, settlers on barren soil, in rain and through winter, through all difficulties. However, you have one weakness – you have developed among yourselves a messianic complex.
>
> You must remember that there were days, before you were born or were only small children, when other people risked their lives day and night, worked and toiled, made sacrifices and performed their tasks without a hint of a messianic complex. And I call on you today, my good friends from Gush Emunim, to perform your tasks with no less modesty than your predecessors, on other days and nights.
>
> We do not require anyone to supervise the Kashrut of our commitment to the Land of Israel! We have dedicated our lives to the land of Israel and to the struggle for its liberation, and will continue to do so.

I call on the people of Israel to unite at this decisive hour. We must find a common denominator for some form of "necessary unity" which will enable us to cope with these fateful days with understanding, and through our common destiny, and which will allow us to construct a dam against brotherly hatred which pushes many over the edge. We have already paid an unbearably high price for murderous fanaticism. We must find the root which brings us all together and must carry out our actions with the wisdom and responsibility which allow us to lead our lives here as a mature and experienced nation. I call on you to support me at this decisive time.

Thank you.

103 U.N. Security Council

Resolution 1701 (August 11, 2006)

The Security Council,

Recalling all its previous resolutions on Lebanon, in particular resolutions 425 (1978), 426 (1978), 520 (1982), 1559 (2004), 1655 (2006), 1680 (2006), and 1697 (2006), as well as the statements of its President on the situation in Lebanon, in particular the statements of 18 June 2000 (S/PRST/2000/21), of 19 October 2004 (S/PRST/2004/36), of 4 May 2005 (S/PRST/2005/17), of 23 January 2006 (S/PRST/2006/3), and of 30 July 2006 (S/PRST/2006/35),

Expressing its utmost concern at the continuing escalation of hostilities in Lebanon and in Israel since Hizbollah's attack on Israel on 12 July 2006, which has already caused hundreds of deaths and injuries on both sides, extensive damage to civilian infrastructure, and hundreds of thousands of internally displaced persons,

Emphasizing the need for an end of violence, but at the same time emphasizing the need to address urgently the causes that have given rise to the current crisis, including by the unconditional release of the abducted Israeli soldiers,

Mindful of the sensitivity of the issue of prisoners and encouraging the efforts aimed at urgently settling the issue of the Lebanese prisoners detained in Israel,

Welcoming the efforts of the Lebanese Prime Minister and the commitment of the Government of Lebanon, in its seven-point plan, to extend its authority over its territory, through its own legitimate armed forces, such that there will be no weapons without the consent of the Government of Lebanon and no authority other than that of the Government of Lebanon, welcoming also its commitment to a United Nations force that is supplemented and enhanced in numbers, equipment, mandate, and scope of operation, and bearing in mind its request in this plan for an immediate withdrawal of the Israeli forces from southern Lebanon,

Determined to act for this withdrawal to happen at the earliest,

Taking due note of the proposals made in the seven-point plan regarding the Shebaa farms area,

DOI: 10.4324/9781003348948-109

Welcoming the unanimous decision by the Government of Lebanon on 7 August 2006 to deploy a Lebanese armed force of 15,000 troops in South Lebanon as the Israeli army withdraws behind the Blue Line and to request the assistance of additional forces from UNIFIL as needed, to facilitate the entry of the Lebanese armed forces into the region, and to restate its intention to strengthen the Lebanese armed forces with material as needed to enable it to perform its duties,

Aware of its responsibilities to help secure a permanent ceasefire and a long-term solution to the conflict,

Determining that the situation in Lebanon constitutes a threat to international peace and security,

1. Calls for a full cessation of hostilities based upon, in particular, the immediate cessation by Hizbollah of all attacks and the immediate cessation by Israel of all offensive military operations;
2. . . .
3. . . .
4. Reiterates its strong support for full respect for the Blue Line;
5. Also reiterates its strong support, as recalled in all its previous relevant resolutions, for the territorial integrity, sovereignty, and political independence of Lebanon within its internationally recognized borders, as contemplated by the Israeli-Lebanese General Armistice Agreement of 23 March 1949;
6. Calls on the international community to take immediate steps to extend its financial and humanitarian assistance to the Lebanese people . . .
7. Affirms that all parties are responsible for ensuring that no action is taken contrary to paragraph 1 that might adversely affect the search for a long-term solution, humanitarian access to civilian populations, including safe passage for humanitarian convoys, or the voluntary and safe return of displaced persons, and calls on all parties to comply with this responsibility and to cooperate with the Security Council;
8. Calls for Israel and Lebanon to support a permanent ceasefire and a long-term solution based on the following principles and elements:

    • full respect for the Blue Line by both parties;
    • security arrangements to prevent the resumption of hostilities, including the establishment between the Blue Line and the Litani river of an area free of any armed personnel, assets, and weapons other than those of the Government of Lebanon and of UNIFIL as authorized in paragraph 11, deployed in this area;
        . . .
    • provision to the United Nations of all remaining maps of land mines in Lebanon in Israel's possession;

9. ...
10. ...
11. ...
12. ...
13. ...
14. Calls upon the Government of Lebanon to secure its borders and other entry points to prevent the entry in Lebanon without its consent of arms or related materiel and requests UNIFIL as authorized in paragraph 11 to assist the Government of Lebanon at its request;
15. Decides further that all States shall take the necessary measures to prevent, by their nationals or from their territories or using their flag vessels or aircraft:

   (a) The sale or supply to any entity or individual in Lebanon of arms and related materiel of all types, including weapons and ammunition, military vehicles and equipment, paramilitary equipment, and spare parts for the aforementioned, whether or not originating in their territories; and

   (b) The provision to any entity or individual in Lebanon of any technical training or assistance related to the provision, manufacture, maintenance, or use of the items listed in subparagraph (a) above; except that these prohibitions shall not apply to arms, related material, training, or assistance authorized by the Government of Lebanon or by UNIFIL as authorized in paragraph 11;

16. ...
17. Requests the Secretary-General to report to the Council within one week on the implementation of this resolution and subsequently on a regular basis;
18. Stresses the importance of, and the need to achieve, a comprehensive, just, and lasting peace in the Middle East, based on all its relevant resolutions including its resolutions 242 (1967) of 22 November 1967, 338 (1973) of 22 October 1973, and 1515 (2003) of 18 November 2003;
19. Decides to remain actively seized of the matter.

104 Announcement of Annapolis Conference (November 20, 2007)

On November 27, the United States will host Israeli Prime Minister Olmert, Palestinian Authority President Abbas, along with the Members of the Quartet, the Members of the Arab League Follow-on Committee, the G-8, the permanent members of the UN Security Council, and other key international actors for a conference at the U.S. Naval Academy in Annapolis, Maryland. Secretary Rice will host a dinner the preceding evening here in Washington, where President Bush will deliver remarks. President Bush and the Israeli and Palestinian leaders will deliver speeches to open the formal conference in Annapolis.

The Annapolis Conference will signal broad international support for the Israeli and Palestinian leaders' courageous efforts and will be a launching point for negotiations leading to the establishment of a Palestinian state and the realization of Israeli-Palestinian peace.

Those invited to attend the conference are:

United States	India
Israel	Indonesia
Palestinian Authority	Iraq
Algeria	Italy
Arab League Secretary General	Japan
Bahrain	Jordan
Brazil	Lebanon
Canada	Malaysia
China	Mauritania
Denmark	Morocco
Egypt	Norway
EU Commission	Oman
EU High Rep	Pakistan
EU Pres Portugal	Poland
France	Qatar
Germany	Russia
Greece	Saudi Arabia

DOI: 10.4324/9781003348948-110

Senegal
Slovenia
South Africa
Spain
Sudan
Sweden
Syria
Quartet Special Envoy Tony Blair
Tunisia

Turkey
United Arab Emirates
United Kingdom
UNSYG
Yemen
Observers:
    IMF
    World Bank

105 Joint Understanding on Negotiations (November 27, 2007)

The representatives of the Government of the State of Israel and the Palestine Liberation Organization (PLO), represented respectively by Prime Minister Ehud Olmert and President Mahmoud Abbas . . . , have convened in Annapolis, Maryland, under the auspices of President George W. Bush of the United States of America, and with the support of the participants of this international conference, having concluded the following Joint Understanding:

We express our determination to bring an end to bloodshed, suffering, and decades of conflict between our peoples, to usher in a new era of peace, based on freedom, security, justice, dignity, respect, and mutual recognition, to propagate a culture of peace and non-violence, and to confront terrorism and incitement, whether committed by Palestinians or Israelis.

In furtherance of the goal of two states, Israel and Palestine, living side by side in peace and security:

- We agree to immediately launch good faith bilateral negotiations in order to conclude a peace treaty resolving all outstanding issues, including all core issues, without exception, as specified in previous agreements.
- We agree to engage in vigorous, ongoing, and continuous negotiations, and shall make every effort to conclude an agreement before the end of 2008.
- For this purpose, a steering committee, led jointly by the head of the delegation of each party, will meet continuously, as agreed.
- The steering committee will develop a joint work plan and establish and oversee the work of negotiations teams to address all issues, to be headed by one lead representative from each party.
- The first session of the steering committee will be held on 12 December 2007.
- President Abbas and Prime Minister Olmert will continue to meet on a bi-weekly basis to follow up the negotiations in order to offer all necessary assistance for their advancement.

The parties also commit to immediately implement their respective obligations under the Performance-Based Road Map to a Permanent Two-State

DOI: 10.4324/9781003348948-111

Solution to the Israel-Palestinian Conflict, issued by the Quartet on 30 April 2003 (hereinafter, "the Roadmap") and agree to form an American, Palestinian, and Israeli mechanism, led by the United States, to follow up on the implementation of the Roadmap. The parties further commit to continue the implementation of the ongoing obligations of the Roadmap until they reach a peace treaty. The United States will monitor and judge the fulfillment of the commitments of both sides of the Roadmap.

Unless otherwise agreed by the parties, implementation of the future peace treaty will be subject to the implementation of the Roadmap, as judged by the United States.

In conclusion, we express our profound appreciation to the President of the United States and his Administration, and to the participants of this international conference, for their support for our bilateral peace process.

106 Confidential Summary of Israeli Prime Minister Olmert's "Package" Offer to Palestine President Abu Mazen (August 31, 2008)[1]

General

- The preamble will state that the agreement represents the implementation of UNSC Res. 242 and 338, as well as fulfillment of the API (no mention of UNGA Res. 194).

Territory[2]

- Israel would annex 6.8% of the West Bank,[3] including the four main settlement "blocs" of Gush 'Etzion (with Efrata), Ma'ale Adumim, Giv'at Ze'ev and Ariel), as well as all of the settlements in East Jerusalem (with Har Homa), in exchange for the equivalent of 5.5% from Israeli territory.
- The "safe passage" (i.e., territorial link) between Gaza and the West Bank would be under Israeli sovereignty with Palestinian control, and is not included in the above percentages.
- There will be a special road connecting Bethlehem with Ramallah, thus by-passing East Jerusalem (most likely the same road currently planned around Adumim).
- East Jerusalem would be divided territorially along the lines of the Clinton Parameters, with the exception of the "Holy Basin", whose sovereignty would be delayed to a later stage (see Jerusalem below).
- There was no mention of the Jordan Valley.

Jerusalem

- Sovereignty over the "Holy Basin", which Olmert said comprises 0.04% of the West Bank (approximately 2.2 km^2), would be delayed to a later stage.
- The issue would continue to be negotiated bilaterally between Israel and Palestine with the involvement of the United States, Saudi Arabia, Jordan and Egypt, but without the ability of these third parties to force an agreement on the parties.

DOI: 10.4324/9781003348948-112

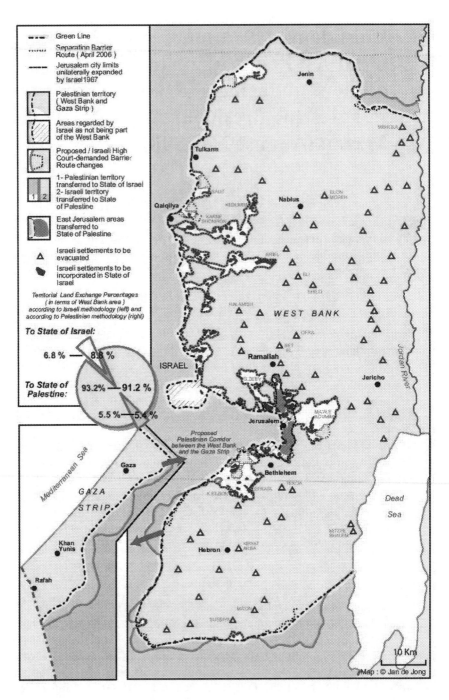

Map 18 The Olmert Maps, 2008

Source: Permission granted by the Palestinian Academic Society for the Study of International Affairs to reprint their map from the 2008 "Olmert Maps" in this book. The original can be found at: www.passia.org/maps/view/78.

Refugees

- Israel would acknowledge the suffering of – but not responsibility for – Palestinian refugees (language is in the preamble). In parallel, there must also be a mention of Israeli (or Jewish) suffering.
- Israel would take in 1,000 refugees per year for a period of 5 years on "humanitarian" grounds. In addition, programs of "family reunification" would continue.
- Israel would contribute to the compensation of the refugees through the mechanism and based on suffering.
- Not clear what the heads of damage for compensation would be, just that there would be no acknowledgement of responsibility for the refugees, and that compensation, and not restitution or return (apart from the 5,000), would be the only remedy.

Security

- The "package" apparently made no mention of security.

Notes

1. Summary is based on information provided by Dr. Erakat on 9 September 2008.
2. A map was presented to Abu Mazen, but he was not allowed to keep it. See revised NSU map projections (jersep08P.pdf and wbgazasep08P.pdf).
3. Percentages are based on Israeli calculations for the West Bank (i.e., excluding the NML and East Jerusalem).

107 Israeli Prime Minister Ehud Olmert Declares Unilateral Ceasefire in Gaza (January 17, 2009)

Citizens of Israel,

Exactly three weeks ago as the Sabbath ended, we sat here before you – my friend Ehud Barak, the Vice Prime Minister Tzipi Livni, and myself – and detailed the considerations and goals which guided us in launching a military operation in the Gaza Strip. Today, we face you again and can say that the conditions have been created so that our targets, as defined when we launched the operation, have been fully achieved, and more so:

Hamas was badly stricken, both in terms of its military capabilities and in the infrastructure of its regime. . . . The Hamas's capabilities for conveying weapons within the Gaza Strip have been damaged. The scope of missile fire directed at the State of Israel has been reduced. The areas from which most of the missiles were launched are under the control of IDF forces . . .

During all the days of fighting, the Israeli home front demonstrated its strength, despite hundreds of rockets and mortar shells indiscriminately fired at a population which numbers one million residents. . . . Two years of preparation on the home front proved that we learned our lessons and were properly organized . . .

Alongside the successes, we must also remember the fallen and those who sacrificed their lives to achieve a better reality in the South. The campaign claimed the lives of three residents of the South and 10 of our soldiers. . . . We send our wishes for a speedy recovery to the residents of the South and to the IDF soldiers injured during the operation.

Today, . . . the entire international community is ready to mobilize in order to achieve maximum stability, and knows that, for this to occur, the process of Hamas's strengthening must stop. To this end, we reached a number of understandings . . . which will ensure that the strengthening of Hamas will decrease. We formulated understandings with the Egyptian government with regard to a number of central issues, the realization of which will bring about a significant reduction in weapons smuggling from Iran and Syria to the Gaza Strip.

DOI: 10.4324/9781003348948-113

On Friday we signed a memorandum of understanding with the American government, in the framework of which the United States will mobilize to take the necessary steps, together with the other members of the international community, to prevent weapons smuggling by terrorists in Gaza. . . .

Today I received a letter from the Prime Minister of Great Britain, Gordon Brown, the Prime Minister of Italy, Silvio Berlusconi, the Chancellor of Germany, Angela Merkel and the President of France, Nicolas Sarkozy, in which all four expressed their profound commitment to assisting in any way in order to ensure that weapons will not succeed in reaching the murderous terrorist organizations in Gaza . . .

Citizens of Israel,

The Government decided to launch the operation in Gaza only after long thought and great consideration, and only after all attempts through other means to stop the firing and other acts of terror by Hamas failed. . . . Hamas's methods are incomprehensible. It placed its military system in crowded residential neighborhoods, operated among a civilian population which served as a human shield, and operated under the aegis of mosques, schools, and hospitals, while making the Palestinian population a hostage to its terrorist activities, with the understanding that Israel – as a country with supreme values – would not act . . .

Hamas in Gaza was built by Iran as a foundation for power and is backed through funding, through training, and through the provision of advanced weapons. Iran, which strives for regional hegemony, tried to replicate the methods used by Hizbullah in Lebanon in the Gaza Strip as well. Iran and Hamas mistook the restraint Israel exercised as weakness. They were mistaken. They were surprised . . .

During the operation, the State of Israel demonstrated great sensitivity in exercising its force in order to avoid, as much as possible, harming the civilian population not involved in terror. In cases where there was any doubt that striking at terrorists would lead to harming an innocent civilian population – we abstained from acting. There are not many countries which would act thusly.

We have no disagreement with the residents of Gaza. We consider the Gaza Strip a part of the future Palestinian state with which we hope to live a life of good neighborliness, and we wish for the day when the vision of two states is realized.

. . .

Citizens of Israel,

Today, before the Government meeting, I spoke with the President of Egypt, Hosni Mubarak, who presented Egypt's initiative to me, along with his request for a ceasefire. I thanked the President for Egypt's commitment to finding a solution to this crisis and for the important role it plays in the Middle East. I presented the President's statement to the Cabinet, along with the totality of our achievements in the operation, as well as the completion of the goals. The Cabinet decided to accept my proposal to declare a ceasefire.

Beginning at 2:00 a.m., Israel will cease its actions against the terrorist organizations in the Gaza Strip and will remain deployed in the Gaza Strip and its environs.

It must be remembered that Hamas is not part of the arrangements we came to. These are agreements involving many countries, and a terrorist organization like Hamas is not and need not be a part of them. If our enemies decide that the blows they have already suffered are not enough and they wish to continue fighting, Israel will be ready for that scenario and will feel free to continue responding with force.

. . .

Hamas still does not fully appreciate the difficult blow it received. If Hamas decides to continue its wild terrorist attacks, it may find itself surprised again by the State of Israel's determination. I do not suggest that it or any other terrorist organization test us.

. . .

On a personal note:

. . .

Dear families, the things you said, the pain you expressed, the fierce spirit you demonstrated – these are the foundation for the people of Israel's strength. On behalf of the entire nation, on behalf of the Government of Israel, I share your profound pain and thank you for the encouragement, the strength, and the inspiration your strong stance has granted the entire nation.

I also wish to say something to the people of Gaza: even before the military operation began, and during it, I appealed to you. We do not hate you; we did not want and do not want to harm you. We wanted to defend our children, their parents, their families. We feel the pain of every Palestinian child and family member who fell victim to the cruel reality created by Hamas which transformed you into victims.

Your suffering is terrible. Your cries of pain touch each of our hearts. On behalf of the Government of Israel, I wish to convey my regret for the harming of uninvolved civilians, for the pain we caused them, for the suffering they and their families suffered as a result of the intolerable situation created by Hamas.

The understandings we reached with Egypt, the international backing of the United States, and the European countries – all these do not ensure that the firing by Hamas will stop. If it completely stops – the IDF will consider withdrawing from Gaza at a time which it deems right. If not, the IDF will continue to act in defense of our residents.

. . .

I wish to express my hope that tonight the first step towards a different reality, one of security and quiet for the residents of Israel, will be taken. From the bottom of my heart, I thank the people of Israel, its fighters, and their commanders for the fierceness of spirit and the social solidarity they demonstrated over these past weeks.

This is the secret of our strength – it is the foundation for our power and it is the hope of our future.

Thank you.

108 Remarks by President Barack Obama at Cairo University, "On a New Beginning" (June 4, 2009)

PRESIDENT OBAMA: Thank you very much. Good afternoon. I am honored to be in the timeless city of Cairo, and to be hosted by two remarkable institutions. For over a 1,000 years, Al-Azhar has stood as a beacon of Islamic learning; and for over a century, Cairo University has been a source of Egypt's advancement. . . .We meet at a time of great tension between the United States and Muslims around the world – tension rooted in historical forces that go beyond any current policy debate. The relationship between Islam and the West includes centuries of coexistence and cooperation, but also conflict and religious wars. More recently, tension has been fed by colonialism that denied rights and opportunities to many Muslims, and a Cold War in which Muslim-majority countries were too often treated as proxies without regard to their own aspirations. Moreover, the sweeping change brought by modernity and globalization led many Muslims to view the West as hostile to the traditions of Islam.

. . .

So long as our relationship is defined by our differences, we will empower those who sow hatred rather than peace, those who promote conflict rather than the cooperation that can help all of our people achieve justice and prosperity. And this cycle of suspicion and discord must end.

I've come here to Cairo to seek a new beginning between the United States and Muslims around the world, one based on mutual interest and mutual respect, and one based upon the truth that America and Islam are not exclusive and need not be in competition. Instead, they overlap, and share common principles – principles of justice and progress; tolerance and the dignity of all human beings.

. . .

Now part of this conviction is rooted in my own experience. I'm a Christian, but my father came from a Kenyan family that includes generations of Muslims. As a boy, I spent several years in Indonesia and heard the call of the azaan at the break of dawn and at the fall of dusk. As a young man, I worked in Chicago communities where many found dignity and peace in their Muslim faith.

DOI: 10.4324/9781003348948-114

As a student of history, I also know civilization's debt to Islam. . . . And throughout history, Islam has demonstrated through words and deeds the possibilities of religious tolerance and racial equality. (Applause.)

I also know that Islam has always been a part of America's story. The first nation to recognize my country was Morocco. In signing the Treaty of Tripoli in 1796, our second President, John Adams, wrote, "The United States has in itself no character of enmity against the laws, religion or tranquility of Muslims." And since our founding, American Muslims have enriched the United States. They have fought in our wars, they have served in our government, they have stood for civil rights, they have started businesses, they have taught at our universities, they've excelled in our sports arenas, they've won Nobel Prizes, built our tallest building, and lit the Olympic Torch. And when the first Muslim American was recently elected to Congress, he took the oath to defend our Constitution using the same Holy Koran that one of our Founding Fathers – Thomas Jefferson – kept in his personal library. (Applause.)

So I have known Islam on three continents before coming to the region where it was first revealed. That experience guides my conviction that partnership between America and Islam must be based on what Islam is, not what it isn't. And I consider it part of my responsibility as President of the United States to fight against negative stereotypes of Islam wherever they appear. (Applause.)

But that same principle must apply to Muslim perceptions of America. (Applause.) Just as Muslims do not fit a crude stereotype, America is not the crude stereotype of a self-interested empire. The United States has been one of the greatest sources of progress that the world has ever known. We were born out of revolution against an empire. We were founded upon the ideal that all are created equal, and we have shed blood and struggled for centuries to give meaning to those words – within our borders, and around the world. We are shaped by every culture, drawn from every end of the Earth, and dedicated to a simple concept: *E pluribus unum* – "Out of many, one."

Now, much has been made of the fact that an African American with the name Barack Hussein Obama could be elected President. (Applause.) But my personal story is not so unique. . . .

Moreover, freedom in America is indivisible from the freedom to practice one's religion. That is why there is a mosque in every state in our union, and over 1,200 mosques within our borders. That's why the United States government has gone to court to protect the right of women and girls to wear the hijab and to punish those who would deny it. (Applause.)

So let there be no doubt: Islam is a part of America. And I believe that America holds within her the truth that regardless of race, religion, or station in life, all of us share common aspirations – to live in peace and security; to get an education and to work with dignity; to love our families, our communities, and our God. These things we share. This is the hope of all humanity.

. . .

Now, that does not mean we should ignore sources of tension. Indeed, it suggests the opposite: We must face these tensions squarely. And so in that spirit, let me speak as clearly and as plainly as I can about some specific issues that I believe we must finally confront together.

The first issue that we have to confront is violent extremism in all of its forms.

In Ankara, I made clear that America is not – and never will be – at war with Islam. (Applause.) We will, however, relentlessly confront violent extremists who pose a grave threat to our security – because we reject the same thing that people of all faiths reject: the killing of innocent men, women, and children. And it is my first duty as President to protect the American people.

. . .

Today, America has a dual responsibility: to help Iraq forge a better future – and to leave Iraq to Iraqis . . .

The second major source of tension that we need to discuss is the situation between Israelis, Palestinians, and the Arab world.

America's strong bonds with Israel are well known. This bond is unbreakable. It is based upon cultural and historical ties, and the recognition that the aspiration for a Jewish homeland is rooted in a tragic history that cannot be denied.

. . .

On the other hand, it is also undeniable that the Palestinian people – Muslims and Christians – have suffered in pursuit of a homeland. For more than 60 years they've endured the pain of dislocation. . . . They endure the daily humiliations – large and small – that come with occupation. So let there be no doubt: The situation for the Palestinian people is intolerable. And America will not turn our backs on the legitimate Palestinian aspiration for dignity, opportunity, and a state of their own. (Applause.)

For decades then, there has been a stalemate: two peoples with legitimate aspirations, each with a painful history that makes compromise elusive. It's easy to point fingers – for Palestinians to point to the displacement brought about by Israel's founding, and for Israelis to point to the constant hostility and attacks throughout its history from within its borders as well as beyond. . . . The only resolution is for the aspirations of both sides to be met through two states, where Israelis and Palestinians each live in peace and security. (Applause.)

. . .

Now is the time for Palestinians to focus on what they can build. The Palestinian Authority must develop its capacity to govern, with institutions that serve the needs of its people. Hamas does have support among some Palestinians, but they also have to recognize they have responsibilities. To play a role in fulfilling Palestinian aspirations, to unify the Palestinian people, Hamas must put an end to violence, recognize past agreements, recognize Israel's right to exist.

At the same time, Israelis must acknowledge that just as Israel's right to exist cannot be denied, neither can Palestine's. The United States does not accept the legitimacy of continued Israeli settlements. (Applause.) This construction violates previous agreements and undermines efforts to achieve peace. It is time for these settlements to stop. (Applause.)

And Israel must also live up to its obligation to ensure that Palestinians can live and work and develop their society. Just as it devastates Palestinian families, the continuing humanitarian crisis in Gaza does not serve Israel's security; neither does the continuing lack of opportunity in the West Bank. Progress in the daily lives of the Palestinian people must be a critical part of a road to peace, and Israel must take concrete steps to enable such progress.

And finally, the Arab states must recognize that the Arab Peace Initiative was an important beginning, but not the end of their responsibilities. The Arab-Israeli conflict should no longer be used to distract the people of Arab nations from other problems. Instead, it must be a cause for action to help the Palestinian people develop the institutions that will sustain their state, to recognize Israel's legitimacy, and to choose progress over a self-defeating focus on the past.

. . .

The third source of tension is our shared interest in the rights and responsibilities of nations on nuclear weapons.

This issue has been a source of tension between the United States and the Islamic Republic of Iran. For many years, Iran has defined itself in part by its opposition to my country, and there is in fact a tumultuous history between us. . . . The question now is not what Iran is against, but rather what future it wants to build.

. . .

The fourth issue that I will address is democracy. (Applause.)

I know – I know there has been controversy about the promotion of democracy in recent years, and much of this controversy is connected to the war in Iraq. So let me be clear: No system of government can or should be imposed by one nation by any other.

That does not lessen my commitment, however, to governments that reflect the will of the people. Each nation gives life to this principle in its own way, grounded in the traditions of its own people. America does not presume to know what is best for everyone, just as we would not presume to pick the outcome of a peaceful election. . . .

Now, there is no straight line to realize this promise. But this much is clear: Governments that protect these rights are ultimately more stable, successful, and secure. Suppressing ideas never succeeds in making them go away. America respects the right of all peaceful and law-abiding voices to be heard around the world, even if we disagree with them. And we will welcome all elected, peaceful governments – provided they govern with respect for all their people.

This last point is important because there are some who advocate for democracy only when they're out of power; once in power, they are ruthless in suppressing the rights of others. (Applause.) . . . You must maintain your power through consent, not coercion; you must respect the rights of minorities and participate with a spirit of tolerance and compromise; you must place the interests of your people and the legitimate workings of the political process above your party. Without these ingredients, elections alone do not make true democracy.

AUDIENCE MEMBER: Barack Obama, we love you!

PRESIDENT OBAMA: Thank you. (Applause.) The fifth issue that we must address together is religious freedom.

Islam has a proud tradition of tolerance. We see it in the history of Andalusia and Cordoba during the Inquisition. I saw it firsthand as a child in Indonesia, where devout Christians worshiped freely in an overwhelmingly Muslim country. That is the spirit we need today. People in every country should be free to choose and live their faith based upon the persuasion of the mind and the heart and the soul. This tolerance is essential for religion to thrive, but it's being challenged in many different ways.

. . .

Freedom of religion is central to the ability of peoples to live together. We must always examine the ways in which we protect it. For instance, in the United States, rules on charitable giving have made it harder for Muslims to fulfill their religious obligation. That's why I'm committed to working with American Muslims to ensure that they can fulfill zakat.

Likewise, it is important for Western countries to avoid impeding Muslim citizens from practicing religion as they see fit – for instance, by dictating what clothes a Muslim woman should wear. We can't disguise hostility towards any religion behind the pretense of liberalism.

. . .

The sixth issue – the sixth issue that I want to address is women's rights. (Applause.) I know – I know – and you can tell from this audience, that there is a healthy debate about this issue. I reject the view of some in the West that a woman who chooses to cover her hair is somehow less equal, but I do believe that a woman who is denied an education is denied equality. (Applause.) And it is no coincidence that countries where women are well educated are far more likely to be prosperous.

. . .

I am convinced that our daughters can contribute just as much to society as our sons. . . . And that is why the United States will partner with any Muslim-majority country to support expanded literacy for girls, and to help young women pursue employment through micro-financing that helps people live their dreams. (Applause.)

Finally, I want to discuss economic development and opportunity.

. . .

On education, we will expand exchange programs, and increase scholarships, like the one that brought my father to America. (Applause.) At the same time, we will encourage more Americans to study in Muslim communities.

And we will match promising Muslim students with internships in America; invest in online learning for teachers and children around the world; and create a new online network, so a young person in Kansas can communicate instantly with a young person in Cairo.

On economic development, we will create a new corps of business volunteers to partner with counterparts in Muslim-majority countries . . .

On science and technology, we will launch a new fund to support technological development in Muslim-majority countries, and to help transfer ideas to the marketplace so they can create more jobs. We'll open centers of scientific excellence in Africa, the Middle East, and Southeast Asia, and appoint new science envoys to collaborate on programs that develop new sources of energy, create green jobs, digitize records, clean water, grow new crops . . .

I know there are many – Muslim and non-Muslim – who question whether we can forge this new beginning. Some are eager to stoke the flames of division. . . . Many more are simply skeptical that real change can occur. There's so much fear, so much mistrust that has built up over the years. But if we choose to be bound by the past, we will never move forward. And I want to particularly say this to young people of every faith, in every country – you, more than anyone, have the ability to reimagine the world, to remake this world.

. . .

It's easier to start wars than to end them. It's easier to blame others than to look inward. It's easier to see what is different about someone than to find the things we share. But we should choose the right path, not just the easy path. There's one rule that lies at the heart of every religion – that we do unto others as we would have them do unto us. (Applause.) This truth transcends nations and peoples – a belief that isn't new; that isn't black or white or brown; that isn't Christian or Muslim or Jew. It's a belief that pulsed in the cradle of civilization, and that still beats in the hearts of billions around the world. It's a faith in other people, and it's what brought me here today.

We have the power to make the world we seek, but only if we have the courage to make a new beginning, keeping in mind what has been written.

The Holy Koran tells us: "O mankind! We have created you male and a female; and we have made you into nations and tribes so that you may know one another."

The Talmud tells us: "The whole of the Torah is for the purpose of promoting peace."

The Holy Bible tells us: "Blessed are the peacemakers, for they shall be called sons of God." (Applause.)

The people of the world can live together in peace. We know that is God's vision. Now that must be our work here on Earth.

Thank you. And may God's peace be upon you. Thank you very much. Thank you. (Applause.)

109 United Nations: Human Rights in Palestine and Other Occupied Arab Territories (September 25, 2009)

Report of the United Nations Fact-Finding Mission on the [2009] Gaza Conflict [Goldstone Report]

. . .

Executive Summary

A. INTRODUCTION

1. On 3 April 2009, the President of the Human Rights Council established the United Nations Fact Finding Mission on the Gaza Conflict with the mandate to investigate all violations of international human rights law and international humanitarian law that might have been committed at any time in the context of the military operations that were conducted in Gaza during the period from 27 December 2008 and 18 January 2009, whether before, during or after.

2. The President appointed Justice Richard Goldstone, former judge of the Constitutional Court of South Africa and former Prosecutor of the International Criminal Tribunals for the former Yugoslavia and Rwanda, to head the Mission. . . .

3. . . .

4. . . .

5. Public hearings were held in Gaza on 28 and 29 June and in Geneva on 6 and 7 July 2009.

6. The Mission repeatedly sought to obtain the cooperation of the Government of Israel. After numerous attempts had failed, the Mission sought and obtained the assistance of the Government of Egypt to enable it to enter the Gaza Strip through the Rafah crossing.

7. The Mission has enjoyed the support and cooperation of the Palestinian Authority and of the Permanent Observer Mission of Palestine to the United Nations. Due to the lack of cooperation from the Israeli Government, the Mission was unable to meet members of the Palestinian Authority in the West Bank . . .

. . .

DOI: 10.4324/9781003348948-115

XXV. Conclusions

A. CONCLUDING OBSERVATIONS

1874. . . .

1875. The international community as well as Israel and, to the extent determined by their authority and means, Palestinian authorities have the responsibility to protect victims of violations and ensure that they do not continue to suffer the scourge of war or the oppression and humiliations of occupation or indiscriminate rocket attacks. . . .

. . .

B. THE ISRAELI MILITARY OPERATIONS IN GAZA: RELEVANCE TO AND LINKS WITH ISRAEL'S POLICIES VIS-À-VIS THE OCCUPIED PALESTINIAN TERRITORY

1877. The Mission is of the view that Israel's military operation in Gaza between 27 December 2008 and 18 January 2009 and its impact cannot be understood or assessed in isolation from developments prior and subsequent to it. The operation fits into a continuum of policies aimed at pursuing Israel's political objectives with regard to Gaza and the Occupied Palestinian Territory as a whole. Many such policies are based on or result in violations of international human rights and humanitarian law. Military objectives as stated by the Government of Israel do not explain the facts ascertained by the Mission, nor are they congruous with the patterns identified by the Mission during the investigation.

1878. The continuum is evident most immediately with the policy of blockade that preceded the operations and that in the Mission's view amounts to collective punishment intentionally inflicted by the Government of Israel on the people of the Gaza Strip. . . . The result, in a very short time, was unprecedented long-term damage both to the people and to their development and recovery prospects.

1879. . . .

C. NATURE, OBJECTIVES, AND TARGETS OF THE ISRAELI MILITARY OPERATIONS IN GAZA

1880. Both Palestinians and Israelis whom the Mission met repeatedly stressed that the military operations carried out by Israel in Gaza from 27 December 2008 until 18 January 2009 were qualitatively different from any previous military action by Israel in the Occupied Palestinian Territory . . .

1881. When the Mission conducted its first visit to the Gaza Strip in early June 2009, almost five months had passed since the end of the Israeli military operations. The devastating effects of the operations on the population were, however, unequivocally manifest. . . .

1882. Women were affected in significant ways . . .

1883. The Gaza military operations were, according to the Israeli Government, thoroughly and extensively planned. While the Israeli Government has sought to portray its operations as essentially a response to rocket attacks in the exercise of its right to self-defence, the Mission considers the plan to have been directed, at least in part, at a different target: the people of Gaza as a whole.

1884. In this respect, the operations were in furtherance of an overall policy aimed at punishing the Gaza population for its resilience and for its apparent support for Hamas, . . .

1885. The Mission recognizes that the principal focus in the aftermath of military operations will often be on the people who have been killed – more than 1,400 in just three weeks. . . .

1886. In this respect, the Mission recognizes that not all deaths constitute violations of international humanitarian law. . . .

. . .

1887. The timing of the first Israeli attack, at 11:30 a.m. on a weekday, when children were returning from school and the streets of Gaza were crowded with people going about their daily business, appears to have been calculated to create the greatest disruption and widespread panic among the civilian population . . .

1888 . . .

1889. The repeated failure to distinguish between combatants and civilians appears to the Mission to have been the result of deliberate guidance issued to soldiers, as described by some of them, and not the result of occasional lapses.

1890. The Mission recognizes that some of those killed were combatants directly engaged in hostilities against Israel, but many were not . . .

1891. It is clear . . . that the destruction of food supply installations, water sanitation systems, concrete factories, and residential houses was the result of a deliberate and systematic policy by the Israeli armed forces. It was not carried out because those objects presented a military threat or opportunity, but to make the daily process of living, and dignified living, more difficult for the civilian population.

1892 . . .

1893. The operations were carefully planned in all their phases. Legal opinions and advice were given throughout the planning stages and at certain operational levels during the campaign.

1894. The Mission has noted with concern public statements by Israeli officials, including senior military officials, to the effect that the use of disproportionate force, attacks on civilian population, and the destruction of civilian property are legitimate means to achieve Israel's military and political objectives. The Mission believes that such statements not only undermine the entire regime of international law, they are inconsistent with the spirit of the Charter of the United Nations and, therefore, deserve to be categorically denounced.

1895. Whatever violations of international humanitarian and human rights law may have been committed, the systematic and deliberate nature of the activities described in this report leave the Mission in no doubt that responsibility lies in the first place with those who designed, planned, ordered, and oversaw the operations.

D. OCCUPATION, RESILIENCE, AND CIVIL SOCIETY

1896 . . .

1897. . . . Israel's continuing occupation of the Gaza Strip and the West Bank emerged as the fundamental factor underlying violations of international humanitarian and human rights law against the protected population and undermining prospects for development and peace. . . .

1898. . . .

1899. . . .

E. ROCKET AND MORTAR ATTACKS IN ISRAEL

1900. Palestinian armed groups have launched thousands of rockets and mortars into Israel since April 2001. These have succeeded in causing terror within Israel's civilian population, as evidenced by the high rates of psychological trauma within the affected communities . . .

1901. Between 27 December 2008 and 18 January 2009, these attacks left four people dead and hundreds injured. That there have not been more casualties is due to a combination of luck and measures taken by the Israeli Government, including the fortification of public buildings, the construction of shelters and, in times of escalated hostilities, the closure of schools.

1902. The Mission notes, with concern, that Israel has not provided the same level of protection from rockets and mortars to affected Palestinian citizens as it has to Jewish citizens . . .

F. DISSENTING VOICES IN ISRAEL

1903. . . .

1904. . . .

G. THE IMPACT OF DEHUMANIZATION

1905. As in many conflicts, one of the features of the Palestinian-Israeli conflict is the dehumanization of the other, and of victims in particular.

1906. . . .

1907. . . .

1908. Both the Palestinians and the Israelis are legitimately angered at the lives that they are forced to lead. . . .

1909. . . .

1910. . . .

H. THE INTRA-PALESTINIAN SITUATION

1911. The division and violence between Fatah and Hamas, which culminated in the establishment of parallel governance entities and structures in the Gaza Strip and the West Bank, is having adverse consequences for the human rights of the Palestinian population in both areas, as well as contributing to erode the rule of law in the Occupied Palestinian Territory in addition to the threats already linked to foreign occupation . . .

I. THE NEED FOR PROTECTION AND THE ROLE OF THE INTERNATIONAL COMMUNITY

1912. International law sets obligations on States not only to respect but also to ensure respect for international humanitarian law. . . .

1913. . . .

1914. After decades of sustained conflict, the level of threat to which both Palestinians and Israelis are subjected has not abated, but if anything increased with continued escalations of violence, death, and suffering for the civilian population, of which the December-January military operations in Gaza are only the most recent occurrence. . . .

1915 . . .

1916 . . .

1917 . . .

J. SUMMARY OF LEGAL FINDINGS

1918. . . .

1. ACTIONS BY ISRAEL IN GAZA IN THE CONTEXT OF THE MILITARY OPERATIONS OF 27 DECEMBER 2008 TO 18 JANUARY 2009

(a) Precautions in Launching Attacks

1919. The Mission finds that in a number of cases Israel failed to take feasible precautions required by customary law . . . to avoid or minimize incidental loss of civilian life, injury to civilians, and damage to civilian objects. The firing of white phosphorus shells over the UNRWA compound in Gaza City is one of such cases in which precautions were not taken in the choice of weapons and methods in the attack . . .

1920. The Mission finds that the different kinds of warnings issued by Israel in Gaza cannot be considered as sufficiently effective in the circumstances to comply with customary law. . . . While some of the leaflet warnings were specific in nature, the Mission does not consider that general messages telling people to leave wherever they were and go to city centres, in the particular circumstances of the military campaign, meet the threshold of effectiveness. Firing missiles into or on top of buildings as a "warning" is essentially a dangerous practice and a form of attack rather than a warning.

(b) Incidents Involving the Killing of Civilians

1921. The Mission found numerous instances of deliberate attacks on civilians and civilian objects . . . in violation of the fundamental international humanitarian law principle of distinction, resulting in deaths and serious injuries . . .

1922. . . . .

1923. The Mission also concludes that Israel, by deliberately attacking police stations and killing large numbers of policemen (99 in the incidents investigated by the Mission) during the first minutes of the military operations, failed to respect the principle of proportionality between the military advantage anticipated by killing some policemen who might have been members of Palestinian armed groups and the loss of civilian life. . . . Therefore, these were disproportionate attacks in violation of customary international law.

(c) Certain Weapons Used by the Israeli Armed Forces

1924. . . . the Mission accepts that white phosphorous, flechettes, and heavy metal (such as tungsten) are not currently proscribed under international law. Their use is, however, restricted or even prohibited in certain circumstances by virtue of the principles of proportionality and precautions necessary in the attack. Flechettes, as an area weapon, are particularly unsuitable for use in urban settings, while, in the Mission's view, the use of white phosphorous as an obscurant at least should be banned because of the number and variety of hazards that attach to the use of such a pyrophoric chemical.

(d) Treatment of Palestinians in the Hands of the Israeli Armed Forces

(i) Use of Human Shields

1925. The Mission investigated several incidents in which the Israeli armed forces used local Palestinian residents to enter houses which might be booby-trapped or harbour enemy combatants. . . . The Mission found that the practice constitutes the use of human shields prohibited by international humanitarian law . . .

1926. The questioning of Palestinian civilians under threat of death or injury to extract information about Hamas and Palestinian combatants and tunnels constitutes a violation of article 31 of the Fourth Geneva Convention, which prohibits physical or moral coercion against protected persons.

(ii) Detention

1927. The Mission found that the Israeli armed forces in Gaza rounded up and detained large groups of persons protected under the Fourth Geneva Convention. The Mission finds that their detention cannot be justified either as detention of "unlawful combatants" or as internment of civilians for imperative reasons of security. . . . Such treatment amounts to measures of intimidation or terror prohibited by article 33 of the Fourth Geneva Convention.

(e) Destruction of Property

1928. The Mission finds that the attacks against the Palestinian Legislative Council building and the main prison in Gaza constituted deliberate attacks on civilian objects in violation of the rule of customary international humanitarian law whereby attacks must be strictly limited to military objectives.

1929. The Mission also finds that the Israeli armed forces unlawfully and wantonly attacked and destroyed without military necessity a number of food production or food-processing objects and facilities . . . drinking-water installations, farms, and animals in violation of the principle of distinction . . .

1930 . . .

(f) Impact of the Blockade and the Military Operations on the Gaza Population

1931. The Mission concludes that the blockade policies implemented by Israel against the Gaza Strip, in particular the closure of or restrictions imposed on border crossings in the immediate period before the military operations, subjected the local population to extreme hardship and deprivations that amounted to a violation of Israel's obligations as an occupying Power under the Fourth Geneva Convention. . . .

1932. The Mission finds that, despite the information circulated by Israel about the humanitarian relief schemes in place during the military operations, Israel has essentially violated its obligation to allow free passage of all consignments of medical and hospital objects, food and clothing that were needed to meet the urgent humanitarian needs of the civilian population in the context of the military operations, which is in violation of article 23 of the Fourth Geneva Convention.

1933. In addition to the above general findings, the Mission also considers that Israel has violated its specific obligations under the Convention on the Rights of the Child and the Convention on the Elimination of All Forms of Discrimination against Women, including the rights to peace and security, free movement, livelihood, and health.

1934. The Mission concludes that the conditions resulting from deliberate actions of the Israeli armed forces and the declared policies of the Government with regard to the Gaza Strip before, during, and after the military operation cumulatively indicate the intention to inflict collective punishment on the people of the Gaza Strip . . .

(g) Grave Breaches of the Geneva Conventions and Acts Raising Individual Criminal Responsibility Under International Criminal Law

1935. From the facts gathered, the Mission found that the following grave breaches of the Fourth Geneva Convention were committed by the Israeli armed forces in Gaza: willful killing, torture, or inhuman treatment, willfully causing great suffering or serious injury to body or health, and extensive destruction of property, not justified by military necessity and carried out unlawfully and wantonly . . .

1936. The Mission further considers that the series of acts that deprive Palestinians in the Gaza Strip of their means of subsistence, employment, housing, and water, that deny their freedom of movement and their right to leave and enter their own country, and that limit their rights to access a court of law and an effective remedy could lead a competent court to find that the crime of persecution, a crime against humanity, has been committed.

2. ACTIONS BY ISRAEL IN THE WEST BANK IN THE CONTEXT OF THE MILITARY OPERATIONS IN GAZA FROM 27 DECEMBER 2008 TO 18 JANUARY 2009

(a) Treatment of Palestinians in the West Bank by Israeli Security Forces, Including Use of Excessive or Lethal Force During Demonstrations

1937. . . .

1938. Israel also violated a series of human rights by unlawfully repressing peaceful public demonstrations and using excessive force against demonstrators . . .

1939. . . .

1940. The Mission finds that Israel failed to investigate, and when appropriate prosecute, acts by its agents or by third parties involving serious violations of international humanitarian law and human rights law.

1941. The Mission was alarmed at the reported increase in settler violence in the past year and the failure of the Israeli security forces to prevent settlers' attacks against Palestinian civilians and their property. . . .

(b) Detention of Palestinians by Israel

1942. . . .

1943. The Mission finds that the detention of members of the Palestinian Legislative Council by Israel violates the right not to be arbitrarily detained, as protected by article 9 of ICCPR . . .

(c) Violations of the Right to Free Movement and Access

1944. The Mission finds that the extensive restrictions imposed by Israel on the movement and access of Palestinians in the West Bank are disproportionate to any legitimate objective served.

1945. . . .

1946. The continued construction of settlements in occupied territory constitutes a violation of article 49 of the Fourth Geneva Convention. The extensive destruction and appropriation of property, including land confiscation and house demolitions in the West Bank, including East Jerusalem, not justified by military necessity and carried out unlawfully and wantonly, amounts to a grave breach under article 147 of the Fourth Geneva Convention.

1947. Insofar as movement and access restrictions, the settlements and their infrastructure, demographic policies vis-à-vis Jerusalem and "Area C" of the West Bank, as well as the separation of Gaza from the West Bank, prevent a viable, contiguous, and sovereign Palestinian State from arising, they are in violation of the *jus cogens* right to self-determination.

3. ACTIONS BY ISRAEL IN ISRAEL

1948. In relation to alleged violations within Israel, the Mission concludes that, although there does not appear to be a policy in this respect, there were occasions when reportedly the authorities placed obstacles in the way of protesters seeking to exercise their right to peaceful assembly and freedom of speech to criticize Israel's military actions in the Gaza Strip . . .

1949. The Mission finds that the imposition of a near blanket exclusion of the media and human rights monitors from Gaza since 5 November 2008 and throughout the operations is inconsistent with Israel's obligations with regard to the right to access to information.

4. ACTIONS BY PALESTINIAN ARMED GROUPS

1950. In relation to the firing of rockets and mortars into southern Israel by Palestinian armed groups operating in the Gaza Strip, the Mission finds that the Palestinian armed groups fail to distinguish between military targets and the civilian population and civilian objects in southern Israel. The launching of rockets and mortars which cannot be aimed with sufficient precisions at military targets breaches the fundamental principle of distinction. Where there is no intended military target and the rockets and mortars are launched into civilian areas, they constitute a deliberate attack against the civilian population . . .

1951. The Mission concludes that the rocket and mortars attacks, launched by Palestinian armed groups operating from Gaza, have caused terror in the affected communities of southern Israel. The attacks have caused loss of life and physical and mental injury to civilians as well as damaging private houses, religious buildings and property, and eroded the economic and cultural life of the affected communities and severely affected economic and social rights of the population.

1952. . . .

1953. The Mission also examined whether the Palestinian armed groups complied with their obligations under international humanitarian law to take constant care to minimize the risk of harm to the civilian population in Gaza among whom the hostilities were being conducted . . . However, launching attacks – whether of rockets and mortars at the population of southern Israel or at the Israeli armed forces inside Gaza – close to civilian or protected buildings constitutes a failure to take all feasible precautions . . .

5. ACTIONS BY RESPONSIBLE PALESTINIAN AUTHORITIES

1954. Although the Gaza authorities deny any control over armed groups and responsibility for their acts, in the Mission's view, if they failed to take the necessary measures to prevent the Palestinian armed groups from endangering the civilian population, the Gaza authorities would bear responsibility for the damage arising to the civilians living in Gaza.

1955. The Mission finds that security services under the control of the Gaza authorities carried out extrajudicial executions, arbitrary arrests, detentions, and ill-treatment of people, in particular political opponents, which constitute serious violations of the human rights to life, to liberty and security of the person, to freedom from torture or cruel, inhuman, or degrading treatment or punishment, to be protected against arbitrary arrest and detention, to a fair and impartial legal proceeding, and to freedom of opinion and expression, including freedom to hold opinions without interference.

1956. The Mission also concludes that the Palestinian Authority's actions against political opponents in the West Bank, which started in January 2006 and intensified during the period between 27 December 2008 and 18 January 2009, constitute violations of human rights and of the Palestinians' own Basic Law. Detentions on political grounds violate the rights to liberty and security of person, to a fair trial and the right not to be discriminated against on the basis of one's political opinion, which are all part of customary international law. Reports of torture and other forms of ill-treatment during arrest and detention and of death in detention require prompt investigation and accountability.

K. THE NEED FOR ACCOUNTABILITY

1957. . . .

1958. . . .

1959. After reviewing Israel's system of investigation and prosecution of serious violations of human rights and humanitarian law, in particular of suspected war crimes and crimes against humanity, the Mission found major structural flaws that, in its view, make the system inconsistent with international standards . . .

1960. The Mission noted the pattern of delays, inaction, or otherwise unsatisfactory handling by Israeli authorities of investigations, prosecutions, and convictions of military personnel and settlers for violence and offences against Palestinians, including in the West Bank, as well as their discriminatory outcome . . .

1961. In the light of the information it reviewed and its analysis, the Mission concludes that there are serious doubts about the willingness of Israel to carry out genuine investigations in an impartial, independent, prompt, and effective way as required by international law.

110 Secretary of State Hillary Rodham Clinton's Remarks to the American Task Force on Palestine (October 20, 2010)

Ritz Carlton Hotel, Washington, DC, October 20, 2010.
SECRETARY CLINTON: . . .

. . .

I have spoken frequently over the last year about why a two-state solution is critical to Israel's long-term future. America's commitment to Israel is rock-solid and unwavering, and we will continue making this case openly and often because we see that as the best way for Israel to safeguard her future.

But tonight I want to focus on why a two-state solution is essential to the future of the Palestinian people. Ziad referenced my time as First Lady. And as First Lady, I may have been the first person ever associated with an American administration to call for a Palestinian state and the two-state solution. (Applause.) This goal is now the official policy of the United States.

And for Palestinians, a two-state solution would mean an independent, viable, and sovereign state of their and your own; the freedom to travel, to do business, and govern themselves. Palestinians would have the right to chart their own destinies at last. The indignity of occupation would end and a new era of opportunity, promise, and justice would begin.

It is difficult to think of anyone who has worked harder or longer to realize the dreams of the Palestinian people than President Mahmoud Abbas. Decades ago, it was Abu Mazen who saw that only through negotiation and nonviolence would – could – these aspirations become real. . . . He is a champion for the people and he is a champion for peace. Because President Abbas understands that the path that must be trod toward that state proceeds down two simultaneous tracks: negotiations between the parties and institution building that prepares Palestinians to govern themselves as we move toward, and after, an agreement is reached.

Negotiations are not easy, but they too are absolutely necessary. It is always easier to defer decisions than it is to make them. . . . only the parties themselves can take the difficult steps that will lead to peace. That is why the Obama Administration is working so hard to support direct talks. . . . There

DOI: 10.4324/9781003348948-116

is no substitute for face-to-face discussion and, ultimately, for an agreement that leads to a just and lasting peace. . . .

But before I go further, I'd like to say a few words about the state-building track. Now, it may receive fewer headlines, but I believe, and many of you do as well, it is critically important.

Today, although Palestinians still have many obstacles to overcome, it is easier than ever to envision an independent Palestine able to govern itself, uphold its responsibilities to provide for its own people, and ensure security. . . .

Under President Abbas and Prime Minister Fayyad's leadership, and under Prime Minister Fayyad's two-year plan, the Palestinian Authority is going beyond rhetoric and actually building a new reality. . . . The pace of reform accelerated this year. The streets are safer, courts are handling more cases, taxes are being collected more efficiently. In the first half of this year, revenues were 50 percent higher than in the same period in 2009.

This has fueled continued economic growth. New businesses are opening. . . . As a result, more and more Palestinians are finding jobs. Tourists and business travelers are arriving every day to take advantage of the improved security and economic climate. In fact, a new five star hotel is due to open in Ramallah this month.

Of course, considerable work remains. On the security front, the improvements have been impressive, but Palestinians could do more to discourage and denounce incitement that inflames tensions. . . . On the economic front, many smaller communities have yet to see the benefits of greater prosperity. Unemployment remains high – above 15 percent in the West Bank and nearly 40 percent in Gaza during the second quarter of this year. . . .

The Palestinian people have many partners who are working and investing every day to improve life in the West Bank and Gaza and to help lay the foundations of a future state. Private companies, philanthropies and foundations, universities – all of them are contributing expertise, energy, and effort.

And there are many more who are looking to make a difference. The United States has launched a new initiative called Partners for a New Beginning, a regional initiative that is one of several efforts to bring together key players to focus on solving specific challenges. And our government remains fully committed.

For example, last year we invested nearly $2 million to upgrade and reopen the Jalameh crossing between Israel and the northern West Bank, adding new lanes and inspection sites. As a result, the number of vehicles able to cross has steadily increased from zero to slightly – to roughly around 7,500 cars and buses per week. . . .

We have also worked with the Palestinian Authority, Israel, and our international partners to ease the situation in Gaza and increase the flow of needed commercial goods and construction supplies, while taking appropriate measures to ensure they don't fall into the wrong hands. . . .

Now, we still need many more steps from Israel to enable more economic activity in Gaza, . . . (Applause.) Our goal is to support sustainable economic growth in Gaza, and it's a little-known fact that the Palestinian Authority is the principal financial supporter of Gaza. The people in Gaza are dependent upon the Palestinian Authority, which is another reason why the increase in economic activity in the West Bank is not only good for those who live in the West Bank, but those who live in Gaza as well.

To help spur private investment through the Palestinian territories, this summer the United States helped sponsor the Palestine Investment Conference in Bethlehem, which generated $655 million in pledges targeted at high-growth sectors.

. . .

Last month I visited Ramallah. . . . After we crossed the Beituniya checkpoint, well-equipped Palestinian security officers lined the road. They are more professional and capable than ever thanks to strong leadership and increased training that the United States has helped to assist. (Applause.) Thank you. (Applause.) We drove into the city and I could see new apartment buildings and office towers rising from the hills. The streets pulsed with commerce and activity.

. . .

Economic and institutional progress are definitely important, indeed necessary, but not sufficient. The legitimate aspirations of the Palestinian people will never be satisfied until there is a two-state solution, a two-state solution ensuring dignity, justice, and security for all. (Applause.)

. . .

We have no illusions about the difficulty of resolving the final status issues of borders and security, settlements and refugees, of Jerusalem and water.

And it's no secret that we are in a difficult period. When President Abbas and Prime Minister Netanyahu came to Washington last month to re-launch direct negotiations, we knew there would be setbacks and struggles.

Our position on settlements is well-known and has not changed. (Applause.) And our determination to encourage the parties to continue talking has not wavered.

. . .

We remain convinced that if they persevere with negotiations, the parties can agree on an outcome that ends the conflict; reconciles the Palestinian goal of an independent and viable state based on the 1967 lines, with agreed swaps – (applause) – and Israel's goal of a Jewish state with secure and recognized borders that reflect subsequent developments and meet Israel's security requirements. (Applause.) This will resolve all the core issues and, as President Abbas said the other day, end all historical claims.

Now, in any tough negotiation, it is natural to focus on what we are being asked to give up. But it is important to keep in mind what you, the Palestinians and Israelis, stand to gain. In this case, the benefits are undeniable. You can't put a price or a value on dignity, but it's a very precious commodity. (Applause.) Justice and security. For both Israeli and Palestinian children alike, they deserve to grow up free from fear and to live up to their own full God-given potential. As long as this conflict continues, that will never be possible.

Bold leaders are called to rise above obstacles and seize opportunities to make history and put their people on a path to a better future. . . . I am convinced they want to the leaders who finally end this conflict.

But they cannot do that without support from their people, and not only their people living in the region, but their people living here and elsewhere around the world. . . . You who are Palestinian Americans are here tonight because you understand that. And this organization has stood for that over so many years.

The Arab states and the people of the region have a strong interest in resolving this conflict and they too have an important role to play. I deeply appreciate the support that Arab leaders and nations have provided for direct talks and for the vision embodied in the Arab Peace Initiative. I hope they will all continue to support the Palestinians in their diplomatic efforts and the state-building work on the ground.

The Palestinian Authority needs a larger, steadier, and more predictable source of financial support. The United States is proud to be the Palestinian Authority's largest donor. (Applause.) The European Union has stepped up as well. But the broader international community, including many Arab states, can and should provide more financial support. (Applause.) . . . And in fact, as the Palestinian economy has increased, the need for future assistance has decreased, but there is still a gap and that gap has to be filled.

So as we press ahead with diplomacy, I hope that Arab states will also consider how to begin implementing the Arab Peace Initiative in concrete terms to turn that proposal into a reality as well. (Applause.)

. . .

I spend much of my time now as Secretary of State traveling around the world, speaking with people who find it so hard to move beyond the past. It is not just in the Middle East that that remains a challenge.

. . .

The American Task Force for Palestine has been a consistent advocate for this path, and I thank you for your efforts. But I know that some in this room, like many across the region and the world, have your doubts about the prospects for peace. So let me appeal to you tonight: Please don't give up in the face of difficulty.

Through your charitable work, you already make important contributions to the progress that is happening on the ground that is literally changing Palestinian lives. You have funded thousands of cataract operations that helped Palestinians see again. Students in the West Bank are learning on laptops because of your generous support. But there is so much more to be done. The Palestinian American community has so much talent and expertise. So please continue putting it to work helping build the future Palestinian state. Offer legal advice or medical training. Invest in the economy, help build the infrastructure. The Palestinian people, as you yourselves know so much better than I, are hardworking, resilient people. They're ready to work. They're ready to govern themselves. But they can't do it on their own.

There is another way you can contribute as well. Many of you are leaders in your own communities. . . . So when you leave tonight, I hope you will be champions for this cause. . . . In the end, peace is not made just at the negotiating table; it's made around the kitchen table. It grows from the quiet determination of people, men and women, who are willing to stand up and declare themselves advocates for peace. . . .

This is not easy. If it were, anybody could have done it already. We've had leaders who have given their lives to this work, and now we have a moment in time that we must seize. I urge you to help lead the way.

And I promise you this: The Obama administration will not turn our backs on either the people of Palestine or Israel. (Applause.) We will continue working for and, God willing, achieving the just, lasting, and comprehensive peace that has been a cornerstone of U.S. policy for years.

I thank you for what you have already done. I thank you for your commitment. I congratulate the honorees. And I challenge you to be part of the most important work there is, the work of peace. God bless you. (Applause.)

111 Understanding Regarding Ceasefire in Gaza Strip (November 21, 2012)

1. Ceasefire:

   a. Israel shall stop all hostilities on the Gaza Strip land, sea, and air including incursions and targeting of individuals.
   b. All Palestinian factions shall stop all hostilities from the Gaza Strip against Israel, including rocket attacks, and attacks along the border.
   c. Opening the crossings and facilitating the movement of people and transfer of goods, and refraining from restricting residents' free movement, and targeting residents in border areas and procedures of implementation shall be dealt with after 24 hours from the start of the ceasefire.
   d. Other matters as maybe requested shall be addressed.

2. Implementation Mechanism:

   a. Setting up of the zero hour for the Ceasefire Understanding to enter into effect.
   b. Egypt shall receive assurances from each party that the party commit to what was agreed upon.
   c. Each party shall commit itself not to perform any acts that would breach this understanding. In case of any observations, Egypt – as the sponsor of this understanding – shall be informed to follow up.

DOI: 10.4324/9781003348948-117

112 The 2014 Gaza Conflict

Factual and Legal Aspects: Executive Summary (May 2015)

Introduction (Chapter I)

1. The following Report . . . presents detailed factual and legal information regarding the intensive hostilities that took place from July 7 to August 26, 2014 between the State of Israel and Hamas and other terrorist organisations operating in the Gaza Strip ("the 2014 Gaza Conflict," also known as Operation "Protective Edge").
2. This Report . . . constitutes an unprecedented effort to present factual and legal aspects concerning the Conflict.
3. The Report includes an assessment of the events leading up to the 2014 Gaza Conflict, describing the overall objectives for Israel and the rationale behind Israel's strategic decisions. . . . The Report also discusses Israel's justice system, and its procedures for examining and investigating possible violations of the Law of Armed Conflict.
4. The 2014 Gaza Conflict was another peak of hostilities in the ongoing armed conflict that has been waged against Israel for well over a decade by terrorist organisations operating from the Gaza Strip . . .
5. First, the conflict occurred primarily in an urban environment. . . . Hamas's strategy was to deliberately draw the hostilities into the urban terrain, and to use built-up areas and the presence of the civilian population for tactical advantage and political gain. . . .
6. Second, the conflict involved non-state actors who defy international law, including the Law of Armed Conflict applicable to the hostilities within the Gaza Strip. More than just drawing the fighting into the urban terrain, these organisations often unlawfully intertwined their military operations with the civilian environment. IDF airborne and ground forces faced militants disguised as civilians and as IDF soldiers, residential homes converted to military command centres, multi-story buildings used as pre-prepared surveillance positions, mosque minarets employed as sniping posts, schools utilized as weapons caches, civilian structures extensively booby-trapped, and tunnel openings and infrastructure hidden in and under civilian areas.

DOI: 10.4324/9781003348948-118

7. This exploitation of civilian surroundings – which often constituted war crimes and crimes against humanity – posed significant operational, legal, and ethical challenges for the IDF. The IDF is committed to conducting all its operations in accordance with international law . . .

8. It is against this background that the harm to civilians and civilian objects in the Gaza Strip that resulted from the 2014 Gaza Conflict should be assessed. . . . The 2014 Gaza Conflict in particular involved high-intensity, protracted hostilities, including close-quarter combat and intensive urban warfare, exacerbating the risk of harm to civilians within the combat arena. Such harm was also the direct result of rockets and mortars that were launched towards Israel from within the Gaza Strip but that fell short. Furthermore, much of what may have appeared to external parties to be indiscriminate harm to civilians or purely civilian objects was in fact legitimate attacks against military targets that merely appear civilian but were actually part of the military operations of these terrorist organisations . . .

9. As stated repeatedly by the IDF and the Government of Israel's highest representatives, Israel did not intend, and deeply regrets, the harm caused to the Palestinian civilian population and surroundings during the 2014 Gaza Conflict.

Background to the 2014 Gaza Conflict (Chapter II)

10. Since its inception, Hamas has launched thousands of attacks designed to kill, injure, and terrorise the Israeli population . . . Since 2000, terrorist attacks by Hamas and other terrorist organisations have killed at least 1,265 Israelis, wounded thousands more, and terrorised millions. In recent years, Hamas has expanded its terrorist arsenal with increasingly deadly weapons and a vast network of cross-border assault tunnels with concealed exits in Israeli territory.

11. . . .

12. Hamas's ongoing armed conflict against Israel has been augmented by the actions of additional terrorist organisations operating from the Gaza Strip, including the Palestinian Islamic Jihad and the Al-Aqsa Martyrs Brigade. . . .

13. The threat to Israel reached such a critical point in the summer of 2014 when Hamas and other terrorist organisations intensified their rocket and mortar launches towards Israel, firing on an almost daily basis. In June and July 2014, Israel uncovered additional cross-border assault tunnels constructed by Hamas for the purpose of perpetrating terrorist attacks on Israeli soil.

14. . . .

15. In response to Hamas's attacks from the Gaza Strip, Israel engaged in extensive diplomatic efforts and also sought international intervention in an effort to prevent escalation, while limiting its military actions to pinpoint strikes in the Gaza Strip. . . .

16. When Hamas and other terrorist organisations fired over 60 rockets at Israel from the Gaza Strip on July 7, the Government of Israel was left with no choice but to launch an aerial campaign, termed Operation "Protective Edge," . . . , in order to protect its civilian population.

17. Under these circumstances, Israel was justified under international law in resorting to a broader military operation against Hamas and other terrorist organisations in the Gaza Strip, as part of the ongoing armed conflict being waged by these organisations.

Objectives and Phases of the 2014 Gaza Conflict (Chapter III)

18. The Operation began as a measured aerial campaign to disrupt and disable the launching of projectiles into Israel, during which Israel continued to make efforts to de-escalate the conflict, including by accepting numerous ceasefire initiatives put forward by international actors.

19. Despite these efforts, Hamas continued to intensify its attacks, rejected all ceasefire initiatives and, on July 17, conducted a major infiltration into Israeli territory through a cross-border assault tunnel . . .

20. The subterranean element of the 2014 Gaza Conflict was one of the conflict's defining features. Beginning in 2001, Hamas and other terrorist organisations in the Gaza Strip began to dig tunnels for purposes of direct military activity against Israel . . .

21. . . .

22. Hamas and other terrorist organisations prolonged the hostilities, and repeatedly rejected ceasefires or . . . violated them. Had Hamas accepted the initial Egyptian-brokered ceasefire that the Arab League endorsed and Israel accepted on July 15 – which featured the same terms as the ceasefire offer to which Hamas ultimately adhered to on August 26 – approximately 90 percent of the casualties incurred during the 2014 Gaza Conflict could have been avoided.

23. In total, six civilians in Israel (five Israeli citizens and one Thai national) and 67 IDF soldiers lost their lives during the 2014 Gaza Conflict. In the Gaza Strip, approximately 2,125 Palestinians were killed. An analysis by IDF experts found that as of April 2015, at least 44 percent of the total Palestinian fatalities have been positively identified as Hamas militants or militants of other terrorist organisations in the Gaza Strip; this figure may ultimately prove to be even higher.

Violations of the Law of Armed Conflict, War Crimes, and Crimes Against Humanity Committed by Hamas and Other Terrorist Organisations During the 2014 Gaza Conflict (Chapter IV)

24. . . .

25. Hamas and other terrorist organisations launched more than 4,500 rockets and mortars during the 2014 Gaza Conflict, approximately 4,000 of which were deliberately directed at Israel's civilian population. . . . The

range of these rockets covered more than 70 percent of Israel's civilian population, . . . Those in residential communities near the Gaza Strip had a mere 15 seconds or less to seek shelter. By deliberately targeting Israeli cities and the civilian population, as part of a widespread and systematic policy, Hamas and other terrorist organisations in the Gaza Strip violated customary norms of the Law of Armed Conflict and committed war crimes and crimes against humanity.

26. As noted above, Hamas and other terrorist organisations complemented their rocket and mortar barrage with ground infiltrations into Israel through cross-border assault tunnels designed to facilitate attacks and kidnapping of Israeli civilians and soldiers. On four different occasions in July, armed Hamas militants, in some cases disguised as IDF soldiers, emerged from cross-border assault tunnels into Israeli territory, leaving nearby residents in constant fear of sudden attack. A Hamas-run newspaper boasted that the tunnels *"terrorised millions of Israelis."*

27. Hamas and other terrorist organisations embedded their military assets and operations within densely populated areas and civilian structures in the Gaza Strip as a matter of military strategy. By conducting hostilities from within civilian surroundings, Hamas and other terrorist organisations frequently turned civilian structures into military objectives, exposing them and surrounding civilians to risk of harm, in a manner which violated the Law of Armed Conflict and often constituted war crimes and crimes against humanity. . . .

28. . . .

29. The militants of Hamas and other terrorist organisations frequently disguised themselves as civilians when carrying out attacks, a tactic that often directly violated customary international law. . . .

30. Hamas and other terrorist organisations also rigged civilian property and residential areas with booby traps and improvised explosive devices. This was a systematic and deliberate Hamas combat strategy, as confirmed by a Hamas combat manual on explosives which was recovered by IDF forces operating in the Gaza Strip. This tactic, too, substantially increased damage to civilian life and property and, in some cases, violated norms of customary international law.

The Threat to Israel's Civilian Population and Israel's Civil Defence Measures (Chapter V)

31. Between 2001 and the outset of the 2014 Gaza Conflict, rocket and mortar attacks from the Gaza Strip killed dozens of Israeli civilians and injured thousands. During the same time period, Hamas and other terrorist organisations fired more than 15,200 rockets and mortars at Israel, more than 11,600 of which came after Israel's full withdrawal from the Gaza Strip in 2005. During the 2014 Gaza Conflict, six civilians in Israel were killed directly by mortars and rockets from the Gaza Strip, and over

1,600 civilians were harmed. Seventeen percent of those evacuated to hospitals during the 2014 Gaza Conflict were children under the age of 18. The 2014 Gaza Conflict and the period immediately preceding it represented the most intense period of rocket and mortar fire against Israel's civilian population in the nation's history.

32. ...
33. ...
34. Apart from the deaths and injuries caused to Israel's civilian population as a result of rocket and mortar attacks, both the short- and long-term psychological effects of the rocket and mortar attacks from the last 14 years have been devastating, ...
35. ...
36. The intense rocket and mortar attacks against Israel's civilian population also caused significant damage to Israel's economy. Many businesses, shops, and restaurants around the country, especially in the south, closed, as persons remained home with their families near shelters. The Bank of Israel estimates that the loss of GDP deriving from the 2014 Gaza Conflict is around 3.5 billion NIS ...

IDF Conduct of Operations During the 2014 Gaza Conflict (Chapter VI)

37. ...
38. ...
39. On top of the distinct dangers inherent in urban warfare is the natural fog of war. Inevitable uncertainties exist in combat. Despite the best efforts of military forces, there is always the possibility that as events unfold in real-time forces may not be fully aware of the operational picture, technology may suffer malfunctions, and the employment of force may result in unintended consequences.
40. When combat is confined to an urban environment – and particularly, in a densely populated area – harm to civilians and civilian structures may be unavoidable. Yet no matter the context in which Israel conducts its military operations, the IDF respects its obligations under international law, including the Law of Armed Conflict ...
41. Israel has developed strict procedures and oversight for compliance with the Law of Armed Conflict. . . . The IDF's primary operational order for the Operation required compliance with the Law of Armed Conflict at all times, including an explicit statement that all attacks shall be *"strictly limited to military objectives . . . with strict adherence to the rules of distinction and proportionality."* ...
42. IDF lawyers are available at different command levels to provide advice before, during, and after operations ...
43. Despite the serious challenges posed by the conduct of Hamas and other terrorist organisations in the Gaza Strip, and despite the complex nature

of urban warfare, the IDF remains committed to the Law of Armed Conflict . . .

44. Unfortunately, some of these attacks resulted in damage to residential buildings, schools, mosques, and even medical and U.N. facilities. Damage occurred mostly when these sites became lawful military targets due to Hamas's and other terrorist organisation's use of such sites for military purposes; . . . Israel *did not* intentionally target civilians or civilian objects.

45. . . .

46. The IDF's attacks were mandated to accord with the principle of proportionality, which prohibits attacks that may be expected to cause incidental loss of civilian life, injury to civilians, damage to civilian objects, or a combination thereof, which would be excessive in relation to the concrete and direct military advantage anticipated. When assessing the expected collateral damage in this context, the adherence of civilians to prior general or specific warnings provided by the IDF was not presumed, and any lack of adherence to such warnings did not on its own alter the proportionality assessment required.

47. The IDF also aborted or suspended attacks whenever it became apparent – for example, due to real-time intelligence – that the target was not a military objective, that the target was subject to special protection, or that the expected damage to civilians and civilian property was excessive in relation to the anticipated military advantage . . .

48. In addition, Israel requires that any means of warfare used during its military operations accord with Israel's obligations under international law. Thus, for example, high-explosive artillery was required by IDF directives to be used in accordance with the rules of the Law of Armed Conflict . . .

49. Despite the IDF's efforts to mitigate the risk of incidental harm, civilian casualties and damage to civilian objects regrettably resulted from Israeli attacks against military objectives.

    . . .

50. During the 2014 Gaza Conflict, the IDF also captured individuals on the battlefield, such as those suspected of being involved in terror activity. The vast majority of such persons were released shortly after capture. All captured persons were detained pursuant to – and in conditions often exceeding – Israel's legal obligations under Israeli law and the Law of Armed Conflict.

51. Before, during, and after the 2014 Gaza Conflict, the IDF made extensive efforts to facilitate humanitarian aid to the civilian population in the Gaza Strip. The IDF did so even though Israel's obligation towards the Gaza Strip under the Law of Armed Conflict was limited generally to allowing – or at most facilitating – humanitarian aid to persons in need where hostilities are taking place. These efforts included providing medical treatment to wounded persons (including militants); facilitating the transfer of food, clothing, medicine, and additional supplies into the Gaza Strip; facilitating the repair of power lines, water supply, and other

infrastructure (oftentimes, while under fire); coordinating evacuations of wounded and sick persons within the Gaza Strip and also into Israel, the West Bank, and overseas; and unilaterally suspending military operations on multiple occasions to facilitate humanitarian assistance.

52. Hamas and other terrorist organisations frequently impeded Israel's humanitarian efforts by attacking crossings and restricting the movement of persons and supplies . . .

Israel's Investigation of Alleged Violations of the Law of Armed Conflict (Chapter VII)

53. Israel is aware of allegations that certain IDF actions during the 2014 Gaza Conflict violated international law . . .

54. Israel maintains a multi-layered investigations system, with numerous checks and balances to ensure impartiality before investigative, administrative, and judicial authorities . . .

55. In 2010, the Government of Israel created an independent public commission of inquiry headed by a former Justice of Israel's Supreme Court and that included distinguished international legal observers (the "Turkel Commission"). Following a comprehensive review, the Turkel Commission concluded in 2013 that Israel's mechanisms for examining and investigating complaints and claims of violations of the Law of Armed Conflict generally comply with its obligations under international law and made a number of recommendations to improve these mechanisms further . . .

56. . . .

57. . . .

58. . . .

59. . . .

60. As of the date of this Report, the IDF is reviewing hundreds of complaints from different sources (such as the U.N., NGOs, and private Palestinian complainants) regarding its conduct of operations during the 2014 Gaza Conflict . . .

Conclusion

61. The following Report, "The 2014 Gaza Conflict (July 7–August 26, 2014): Factual and Legal Aspects," provides detailed information about the conflict, including illustrative examples and previously unreleased information that was declassified for the purposes of this Report. Israel intends to continue to publish updated information regarding the 2014 Gaza Conflict as additional information is obtained or released and as the examination and investigation process continues. . . .

113 Israeli Foreign Ministry

The Nuclear Deal With Iran: Questions and Answers (July 27, 2015)

- Doesn't the deal make it less likely that Iran will get a nuclear weapon?

On the contrary, this deal gives Iran two paths to the bomb. The first path is by Iran violating the deal. The assumption underlying the deal is that inspections . . . will keep Iran from cheating. However, both have failed repeatedly in Iran and North Korea. For example, the United States, the United Kingdom, and Israel all failed for years to detect Iran's massive underground nuclear factories in Natanz and Qom.

The second path is by Iran complying with the deal. In about a decade, the major restrictions on Iran's nuclear program will be automatically removed, allowing Iran to have an unlimited number of centrifuges for carrying out unlimited enrichment of uranium with full international legitimacy. Iran's centrifuges will enrich uranium much faster than those it operates today because the deal allows Iran to continue research and development of advanced centrifuges. Iran's breakout time at that point will be close to zero, as the US President himself has said . . .

- What are the realistic alternatives to this deal other than war?

Israel repeatedly presented two different alternatives to this bad deal. First, Israel supported the policy of "dismantle for dismantle," whereby the sanctions regime would be dismantled only when Iran's military nuclear program is dismantled. This policy was based on successive UN Security Council resolutions and was US policy until 2013. Its implementation would have genuinely closed the Iranian nuclear file.

Second, Israel proposed a significant . . . roll-back of Iran's nuclear infrastructure combined with severe restrictions on that infrastructure that would be lifted only when Iran ceased its regional aggression, support of terrorism around the world, and efforts to destroy Israel. . . . In a decade or so, Iran will pose a formidable threat to the peace of the world and the expectation today that Iran will become a nuclear power tomorrow is enough in itself to spark a nuclear arms race in the Middle East, the most volatile region on earth.

DOI: 10.4324/9781003348948-119

In addition, the many hundreds of billions of dollars that will flow into Iran's coffers over the next decade will fund its war-making and terror machine.

All this doesn't make war less likely. It makes war – even nuclear war – more likely.

- If the deal guarantees "unprecedented" inspections of Iran's nuclear program, why is Israel so worried about Iran cheating?

While the deal provides for 24/7 surveillance of Iran's declared nuclear facilities, the inspection mechanism is sorely lacking when it comes to possible covert nuclear weapons activity. . . . The deal gives Iran 24 days before they have to allow inspectors into suspicious sites before there is even a violation. Twenty-four days gives Iran plenty of time to conceal illicit behavior because not all nuclear weapons activities leave detectable traces.

The weaknesses of the inspection and verification provisions of the deal stand out when considering that Iran, like North Korea, has a long history of successfully deceiving the international community as part of its efforts to hide its nuclear weapons program. This is far from the "anytime, anywhere" inspections promised during the negotiations.

- In the absence of this deal, wouldn't the international sanctions have fallen apart?

The crippling sanctions imposed on Iran in 2012 are what convinced the regime that it had . . . to negotiate. The most important of these sanctions were those that passed in the United States with strong bipartisan support. Faced with the choice of doing business with Iran or with the United States (whose economy is more than 40 times larger than Iran's), countries and companies around the world did the right thing – both economically and ethically. . . .

The deal itself threatens to make it impossible to re-impose meaningful sanctions following Iranian violations because of the incentives it provides for rapid, massive, and long-term investment in Iran.

- Isn't it true that this deal will make Israel and the region safer? Isn't it preferable to confront a non-nuclear Iran about its terrorism and aggression?

This deal will not prevent Iran from getting nuclear weapons. It will enable Iran to get many nuclear bombs in a decade or so and could spark a regional nuclear arms race.

In addition, the deal will provide Iran with hundreds of billions of dollars in sanctions relief, direct investment, and oil sales. . . .

The deal does not condition the removal of restrictions on Iran's nuclear program on Iran ceasing its terrorism and destabilizing activities in Lebanon, Syria, Yemen, Libya, Iraq, and elsewhere. Thus, this deal makes the problem of Iran's terrorism worse.

- Now that the deal has been adopted by the UN Security Council and the EU, what will Israel do next?

The deal poses a grave threat to the region and the world, but especially to Israel. Even during the nuclear negotiations, Iran continued to call for the annihilation of Israel while streaming offensive weapons to Iranian proxies on Israel's borders and sponsoring terrorism targeting Israelis and Jews around the world. Israelis across the political spectrum are united in opposition to this dangerous deal, which is much worse than having no deal at all. This is not a partisan issue in Israel, and it shouldn't be a partisan issue anywhere.

Israel was not a party to the negotiations and is not bound by this deal. Israel will always reserve the right to defend itself by itself against any threat.

114 Remarks by President Barack Obama on the Iran Nuclear Deal (August 5, 2015)

Thank you. . . .

Fifty-two years ago, President Kennedy, at the height of the Cold War, addressed this same university on the subject of peace. The Berlin Wall had just been built. The Soviet Union had tested the most powerful weapons ever developed. China was on the verge of acquiring a nuclear bomb. Less than 20 years after the end of World War II, the prospect of nuclear war was all too real. With all of the threats that we face today, it's hard to appreciate how much more dangerous the world was at that time.

. . .

The agreement now reached between the international community and the Islamic Republic of Iran builds on this tradition of strong, principled diplomacy. After two years of negotiations, we have achieved a detailed arrangement that permanently prohibits Iran from obtaining a nuclear weapon. It cuts off all of Iran's pathways to a bomb. It contains the most comprehensive inspection and verification regime ever negotiated to monitor a nuclear program. As was true in previous treaties, it does not resolve all problems; it certainly doesn't resolve all our problems with Iran. It does not ensure a warming between our two countries. But it achieves one of our most critical security objectives. As such, it is a very good deal. . . .

Now, when I ran for President eight years ago as a candidate who had opposed the decision to go to war in Iraq, I said that America didn't just have to end that war – we had to end the mindset that got us there in the first place. . . .

That program has been around for decades, dating back to the Shah's efforts – with U.S. support – in the 1960s and '70s to develop nuclear power. The theocracy that overthrew the Shah accelerated the program after the Iran-Iraq War in the 1980s, a war in which Saddam Hussein used chemical weapons to brutal effect, and Iran's nuclear program advanced steadily through the 1990s, despite unilateral U.S. sanctions. When the Bush administration took office, Iran had no centrifuges – the machines necessary to produce material for a bomb – that were spinning to enrich uranium. But despite repeated warnings from the United States government, by the time

DOI: 10.4324/9781003348948-120

I took office, Iran had installed several thousand centrifuges and showed no inclination to slow – much less halt – its program.

. . .

The question, then, is not whether to prevent Iran from obtaining a nuclear weapon, but how. Even before taking office, I made clear that Iran would not be allowed to acquire a nuclear weapon on my watch, and it's been my policy throughout my presidency to keep all options – including possible military options – on the table to achieve that objective . . .

What made our new approach more effective was our ability to draw upon new U.N. Security Council resolutions, combining strong enforcement with voluntary agreements from nations like China and India, Japan and South Korea to reduce their purchases of Iranian oil, as well as the imposition by our European allies of a total oil embargo.

. . .

With the world now unified beside us, Iran's economy contracted severely and remains about 20 percent smaller today than it would have otherwise been. No doubt this hardship played a role in Iran's 2013 elections, when the Iranian people elected a new government that promised to improve the economy through engagement with the world. A window had cracked open. Iran came back to the nuclear talks. And after a series of negotiations, Iran agreed with the international community to an interim deal – a deal that rolled back Iran's stockpile of near 20 percent enriched uranium, and froze the progress of its program so that the P5 + 1 – the United States, China, Russia, the United Kingdom, Germany, France, and the European Union – could negotiate a comprehensive deal without the fear that Iran might be stalling for time.

Now, let me pause here just to remind everybody that when the interim deal was announced, critics – the same critics we're hearing from now – called it "a historic mistake." They insisted Iran would ignore its obligations. They warned that sanctions would unravel. They warned that Iran would receive a windfall to support terrorism.

The critics were wrong. The progress of Iran's nuclear program was halted for the first time in a decade. Its stockpile of dangerous materials was reduced. The deployment of its advanced centrifuges was stopped. Inspections did increase. There was no flood of money into Iran, and the architecture of the international sanctions remained in place . . .

Despite the criticism, we moved ahead to negotiate a more lasting, comprehensive deal. Our diplomats, led by Secretary of State John Kerry, kept our coalition united. . . . And while Iran, like any party to the Nuclear Non-Proliferation Treaty, is allowed to access peaceful nuclear energy, the agreement strictly defines the manner in which its nuclear program can proceed, ensuring that all pathways to a bomb are cut off.

. . .

And, in fact, this deal shuts off the type of covert path Iran pursued in the past. There will be 24/7 monitoring of Iran's key nuclear facilities. For decades, inspectors will have access to Iran's entire nuclear supply chain – from the uranium mines and mills where they get raw materials, to the centrifuge production facilities where they make machines to enrich it. . . .

. . .

So this deal is not just the best choice among alternatives – this is the strongest non-proliferation agreement ever negotiated. And because this is such a strong deal, every nation in the world that has commented publicly, with the exception of the Israeli government, has expressed support. The United Nations Security Council has unanimously supported it. The majority of arms control and non-proliferation experts support it. Over 100 former ambassadors – who served under Republican and Democratic Presidents – support it. I've had to make a lot of tough calls as President, but whether or not this deal is good for American security is not one of those calls. It's not even close.

Unfortunately, we're living through a time in American politics where every foreign policy decision is viewed through a partisan prism, evaluated by headline-grabbing sound bites. . . . But if you repeat these arguments long enough, they can get some traction. So let me address just a few of the arguments that have been made so far in opposition to this deal.

First, there are those who say the inspections are not strong enough because inspectors can't go anywhere in Iran at any time with no notice.

Well, here's the truth: Inspectors will be allowed daily access to Iran's key nuclear sites. If there is a reason for inspecting a suspicious, undeclared site anywhere in Iran, inspectors will get that access, even if Iran objects . . .

Second, there are those who argue that the deal isn't strong enough because some of the limitations on Iran's civilian nuclear program expire in 15 years. Let me repeat: The prohibition on Iran having a nuclear weapon is permanent. The ban on weapons-related research is permanent. Inspections are permanent . . .

Third, a number of critics say the deal isn't worth it because Iran will get billions of dollars in sanctions relief. Now, let's be clear: The international sanctions were put in place precisely to get Iran to agree to constraints on its program. That's the point of sanctions. Any negotiated agreement with Iran would involve sanctions relief. So an argument against sanctions relief is effectively an argument against any diplomatic resolution of this issue.

. . .

Now, the final criticism – this sort of a catch-all that you may hear – is the notion that there's a better deal to be had. "We should get a better deal" – that's repeated over and over again. "It's a bad deal, need a better deal" . . . one that relies on vague promises of toughness, and, more recently, the argument that we can apply a broader and indefinite set of sanctions to squeeze the Iranian regime harder.

Those making this argument are either ignorant of Iranian society, or they're just not being straight with the American people. Sanctions alone are not going to force Iran to completely dismantle all vestiges of its nuclear infrastructure – even those aspects that are consistent with peaceful programs. That oftentimes is what the critics are calling "a better deal." Neither the Iranian government, or the Iranian opposition, or the Iranian people would agree to what they would view as a total surrender of their sovereignty. . . .

. . .

Now, because more sanctions won't produce the results that the critics want, we have to be honest. Congressional rejection of this deal leaves any U.S. administration that is absolutely committed to preventing Iran from getting a nuclear weapon with one option – another war in the Middle East.

. . .

And as someone who does firmly believes that Iran must not get a nuclear weapon, and who has wrestled with this issue since the beginning of my presidency, I can tell you that alternatives to military action will have been exhausted once we reject a hard-won diplomatic solution that the world almost unanimously supports.

So let's not mince words. The choice we face is ultimately between diplomacy or some form of war – maybe not tomorrow, maybe not three months from now, but soon . . .

Now, there are some opponents – I have to give them credit; there are opponents of this deal who accept the choice of war. In fact, they argue that surgical strikes against Iran's facilities will be quick and painless. But if we've learned anything from the last decade, it's that wars in general and wars in the Middle East in particular are anything but simple . . .

. . .

So let me sum up here. When we carefully examine the arguments against this deal, none of them stand up to scrutiny. That may be why the rhetoric on the other side is so strident. I suppose some of it can be ascribed to knee-jerk partisanship that has become all too familiar; rhetoric that renders every decision that's made a disaster, a surrender – "you're aiding terrorists; you're endangering freedom."

On the other hand, I do think it's important to acknowledge another, more understandable motivation behind the opposition to this deal, or at least skepticism to this deal, and that is a sincere affinity for our friend and ally, Israel – an affinity that, as someone who has been a stalwart friend to Israel throughout my career, I deeply share.

When the Israeli government is opposed to something, people in the United States take notice. And they should. No one can blame Israelis for having a deep skepticism about any dealings with a government like Iran's – which includes leaders who have denied the Holocaust, embrace an ideology of anti-Semitism, facilitate the flow of rockets that are arrayed on Israel's borders, are pointed at Tel Aviv. . . .

But the fact is, partly due to American military and intelligence assistance, which my administration has provided at unprecedented levels, Israel can defend itself against any conventional danger – whether from Iran directly or from its proxies. On the other hand, a nuclear-armed Iran changes that equation.

And that's why this deal ultimately must be judged by what it achieves on the central goal of preventing Iran from obtaining a nuclear weapon. This deal does exactly that. I say this as someone who has done more than any other President to strengthen Israel's security. And I have made clear to the Israeli government that we are prepared to discuss how we can deepen that cooperation even further. Already we've held talks with Israel on concluding another 10-year plan for U.S. security assistance to Israel. . . .

But I have also listened to the Israeli security establishment, which warned of the danger posed by a nuclear-armed Iran for decades. In fact, they helped develop many of the ideas that ultimately led to this deal.

So to friends of Israel, and to the Israeli people, I say this: A nuclear-armed Iran is far more dangerous to Israel, to America, and to the world than an Iran that benefits from sanctions relief.

I recognize that Prime Minister Netanyahu disagrees – disagrees strongly. I do not doubt his sincerity. But I believe he is wrong. I believe the facts support this deal. I believe they are in America's interest and Israel's interest. And as President of the United States, it would be an abrogation of my constitutional duty to act against my best judgment simply because it causes temporary friction with a dear friend and ally. . . .

"Peace is not the absence of conflict," President Reagan once said. It is "the ability to cope with conflict by peaceful means." President Kennedy warned Americans, "not to see conflict as inevitable, accommodation as impossible, and communication as nothing more than the exchange of threats." It is time to apply such wisdom. The deal before us doesn't bet on Iran changing, it doesn't require trust; it verifies and requires Iran to forsake a nuclear weapon, just as we struck agreements with the Soviet Union at a time when they were threatening our allies, arming proxies against us, proclaiming their commitment to destroy our way of life, and had nuclear weapons pointed at all of our major cities – a genuine existential threat.

. . .

We now have the opportunity to build on that progress. We built a coalition and held it together through sanctions and negotiations, and now we have before us a solution that prevents Iran from obtaining a nuclear weapon, without resorting to war. As Americans, we should be proud of this achievement. And as members of Congress reflect on their pending decision, I urge them to set aside political concerns, shut out the noise, consider the stakes involved with the vote that you will cast.

If Congress kills this deal, we will lose more than just constraints on Iran's nuclear program, or the sanctions we have painstakingly built. We will have lost something more precious: America's credibility as a leader of diplomacy; America's credibility as the anchor of the international system.

John F. Kennedy cautioned here, more than 50 years ago, at this university, that "the pursuit of peace is not as dramatic as the pursuit of war." But it's so very important. It is surely the pursuit of peace that is most needed in this world so full of strife.

My fellow Americans, contact your representatives in Congress. Remind them of who we are. Remind them of what is best in us and what we stand for, so that we can leave behind a world that is more secure and more peaceful for our children . . .

115 Report of the Middle East Quartet (July 1, 2016)

At its meeting in Munich on 12 February 2016, the Middle East Quartet reiterated its concern that current trends are imperiling the viability of the two-state solution. Underlining its commitment to supporting a comprehensive, just, and lasting resolution to the Palestinian – Israeli conflict, the Quartet agreed to prepare a report on the situation on the ground.

. . .

Summary

The Quartet reiterates that a negotiated two-state outcome is the only way to achieve an enduring peace that meets Israeli security needs and Palestinian aspirations for statehood and sovereignty, ends the occupation that began in 1967, and resolves all permanent status issues.

The Quartet recalls its previous statements and relevant United Nations Security Council resolutions and pledges its active support for ending the Israeli-Palestinian conflict on the basis of Security Council resolutions 242 (1967) and 338 (1973) . . .

. . . the Quartet remains seriously concerned that continuing on the current course will make this prospect increasingly remote. In particular, each of the following trends is severely undermining hopes for peace:

Continuing violence, terrorist attacks against civilians, and incitement to violence are greatly exacerbating mistrust and are fundamentally incompatible with a peaceful resolution;

The continuing policy of settlement construction and expansion, designation of land for exclusive Israeli use, and denial of Palestinian development is steadily eroding the viability of the two-state solution; and

The illicit arms build-up and militant activity, continuing absence of Palestinian unity, and dire humanitarian situation in Gaza feed instability and ultimately impede efforts to achieve a negotiated solution.

The Quartet stresses the urgent need for affirmative steps to reverse each of these trends in order to prevent entrenching a one-state reality of perpetual occupation and . . .

DOI: 10.4324/9781003348948-121

The Quartet calls on each side to independently demonstrate, through policies and actions, a genuine commitment to the two-state solution.

To that end, the Quartet emphasizes the importance of both parties complying with their basic commitments under existing agreements in order to promote this two-state reality and lay the groundwork for successful negotiations.

I. Violence and Incitement

Continuing violence, recent acts of terrorism against Israelis, and incitement to violence are fundamentally incompatible with advancing a peaceful two-state solution . . .

Violence. In the recent wave of violence that began in October 2015, there have been over 250 attacks and attempted attacks by Palestinians against Israelis . . .

The frequency of attacks and clashes declined significantly in 2016. This slowdown is due in large part to the effective efforts of the Palestinian Authority Security Forces, . . .

During this period, Israel has responded by expanding the use of administrative detention, resuming punitive house demolitions, and enforcing closures of whole districts, which can further exacerbate tensions. . . .

Settler violence against Palestinians, including assaults, vandalism, and the destruction of property, remains a serious concern. . . . Such attacks, which senior Israeli officials have called terrorist acts, contribute to a continuing sense of vulnerability among Palestinians.

Israel has increased efforts to curb settler violence by establishing a special police unit and enhancing preventive and punitive measures applied against extremist groups. . . .

Incitement to Violence. Palestinians who commit terrorist attacks are often glorified publicly as "heroic martyrs." . . .

Hamas and other radical factions are responsible for the most explicit and widespread forms of incitement. These groups use media outlets to glorify terrorism and openly call for violence against Jews, including instructing viewers on how to carry out stabbings. . . .

The Palestinian Authority leadership has repeatedly made statements expressing opposition to violence against civilians, . . . Regrettably, however, Palestinian leaders have not consistently and clearly condemned specific terrorist attacks. And streets, squares, and schools have been named after Palestinians who have committed acts of terrorism.

. . .

II. Settlement Expansion, Land Designations, and Denial of Palestinian Development

The continuing policy of settlement construction and expansion in the West Bank and East Jerusalem . . . is steadily eroding the viability of the two-state solution. . . . In fact, the transfer of greater powers and responsibilities to Palestinian civil authority in Area C contemplated by commitments in prior agreements has effectively been stopped . . . and should be resumed to advance the two-state solution and prevent a one-state reality from taking hold.

Designating Land for Exclusive Israeli Use. Area C comprises 60 percent of the West Bank and includes the majority of agricultural lands, natural resources, and land reserves. Some 70 percent of Area C has been unilaterally taken for exclusive Israeli use, . . . Nearly all of the remaining 30 percent of Area C, much of which is private Palestinian property, is effectively off limits for Palestinian development because it requires permits from the Israeli military authorities that are almost never granted.

. . .

Settlement Construction and Expansion. Since the beginning of the Oslo process in 1993, the population of settlements has more than doubled, with a threefold increase in Area C alone. There are currently at least 370,000 Israelis living in some 130 settlements in Area C, including at least 85,000 deep in the West Bank. Combined with some 200,000 in East Jerusalem, this brings the total settler population to at least 570,000.

The policy of steadily constructing and expanding settlements and related infrastructure continues . . .

Denying Palestinian Development. The Israel military retains full authority over development in Area C, . . . While settlements have continued to grow, there has been a near complete cessation of issuance of approvals for private Palestinian development or construction in Area C . . .

There was a significant increase in the number of Palestinian structures demolished across the West Bank in the first four months of this year, with some 500 demolitions of Palestinian structures by the Israeli authorities and nearly 800 Palestinians displaced, more than in all of 2015 . . . Although many of these were not dwellings, the loss of structures such as water wells, solar panels, and animal shelters has impacted the livelihoods of over 2,500 people since the beginning of the year.

. . .

III. The Gaza Strip and Palestinian Governance

The illicit arms buildup and militant activity by Hamas, the lack of control of Gaza by the Palestinian Authority, and the dire humanitarian situation, exacerbated by the closures of the crossings, feed instability and ultimately impede efforts to achieve a negotiated solution. . . .

Continuing Militant Build-Up. The illicit arms buildup in Gaza by Hamas and other Palestinian groups is continuing, including the building of tunnels, the smuggling of weapons, and the production and launching of rockets towards Israel. . . .

While the 2014 ceasefire is otherwise holding, it remains fragile, with at least 160 rockets and mortars fired at Israel, keeping thousands of people on both sides under constant threat of attacks. In the course of the 2014 conflict, Israel discovered 14 tunnels penetrating its territory . . .

Lack of Palestinian Unity. Reuniting Palestinians under a single, democratic, and legitimate Palestinian authority on the basis of the PLO platform and Quartet principles remains a priority. . . . The constraints of the occupation, the absence of elections, and budgetary pressures contribute to growing public discontent and undermine the popular legitimacy of Palestinian institutions and leadership. The division also damages Gaza's economic development, hinders basic service delivery, and impedes the reconstruction process.

Dire Humanitarian Situation. Severe poverty, a crippling unemployment rate, and the chronic underdevelopment of Gaza further feed instability and frustration that could create the conditions for renewed conflict. 1.3 million Gazans are in need of sustained humanitarian assistance, including temporary shelter and food. Most people have electricity less than half of the time, while only five percent of the water is safe for human consumption.

Reconstruction also remains inadequate, despite notable easing measures implemented by the Israeli government and some visible signs of progress . . .

Recommendations

The Quartet calls on each side to independently demonstrate, through policies and actions, a genuine commitment to the two-state solution and refrain from unilateral steps that prejudge the outcome of final status negotiations. The Quartet emphasizes the importance of both parties complying with their basic commitments in order to advance a peaceful two-state reality on the ground and create the conditions for successful final status negotiations. The Quartet has the following specific recommendations:

1. Both sides should work to de-escalate tensions by exercising restraint and refraining from provocative actions and rhetoric.
2. Both sides should take all necessary steps to prevent violence and protect the lives and property of all civilians, including through continuing security coordination and strengthening the capacity, capability, and authority of the Palestinian Authority Security Forces.
3. The Palestinian Authority should act decisively and take all steps within its capacity to cease incitement to violence and strengthen ongoing efforts to combat terrorism, including by clearly condemning all acts of terrorism.
4. Israel should cease the policy of settlement construction and expansion, designating land for exclusive Israeli use, and denying Palestinian development.
5. Israel should implement positive and significant policy shifts, including transferring powers and responsibilities in Area C, consistent with the transition to greater Palestinian civil authority contemplated by prior agreements. . . .

6. The Palestinian leadership should continue their efforts to strengthen institutions, improve governance, and develop a sustainable economy. Israel should take all necessary steps to enable this process, in line with the Ad Hoc Liaison Committee recommendations.

7. All sides must continue to respect the ceasefire in Gaza, and the illicit arms buildup and militant activities must be terminated.

8. Israel should accelerate the lifting of movement and access restrictions to and from Gaza, with due consideration of its need to protect its citizens from terrorist attacks.

9. Gaza and the West Bank should be reunified under a single, legitimate, and democratic Palestinian authority on the basis of the PLO platform and Quartet principles and the rule of law, including control over all armed personnel and weapons in accordance with existing agreements.

10. Both parties should foster a climate of tolerance, including through increasing interaction and cooperation in a variety of fields – economic, professional, educational, cultural – that strengthen the foundations for peace and countering extremism.

The Quartet stresses the urgent need for such affirmative steps to reverse current trends and advance the two-state solution on the ground.

The Quartet stresses the significance of the Arab Peace Initiative (API), with its vision for comprehensive settlement of the Arab-Israeli conflict and, in that context, the opportunity for building a regional security framework, and encourages further dialogue on that basis. In this regard, the Quartet welcomes the call by the Egyptian President to Israeli, Palestinian, and Arab leaders to follow the historic path towards peace taken by Israel and Egypt 37 years ago.

The Quartet also welcomes the Joint Communique issued in Paris on June 3 and its support for a negotiated two-state solution . . .

The Quartet invites the parties to engage with it on implementing the recommendations of this report and creating the conditions for the resumption of meaningful negotiations that resolve all final status issues.

116 Paris Conference Joint Communique (January 15, 2017)

(I) Following the Ministerial meeting held in Paris on 3 June 2016, the Participants met in Paris on 15 January 2017 to reaffirm their support for a just, lasting, and comprehensive resolution of the Israeli-Palestinian conflict. They reaffirmed that a negotiated solution with two states, Israel and Palestine, living side by side in peace and security, is the only way to achieve enduring peace.

They emphasized the importance for the parties to restate their commitment to this solution, to take urgent steps in order to reverse the current negative trends on the ground . . . and to start meaningful direct negotiations.

They reiterated that a negotiated two-state solution should meet the legitimate aspirations of both sides, including the Palestinians' right to statehood and sovereignty, fully end the occupation that began in 1967, satisfy Israel's security needs and resolve all permanent status issues on the basis of United Nations Security Council resolutions 242 (1967) and 338 (1973), and also recalled relevant Security Council resolutions.

They underscored the importance of the Arab Peace Initiative of 2002 as a comprehensive framework for the resolution of the Arab-Israeli conflict, thus contributing to regional peace and security.

They welcomed international efforts to advance Middle East peace, including the adoption of United Nations Security Council resolution 2334 on 23 December 2016 which clearly condemned settlement activity, incitement and all acts of violence and terror, and called on both sides to take steps to advance the two-state solution on the ground; the recommendations of the Quartet on 1 July 2016; and the United States Secretary of State's principles on the two-state solution on 28 December 2016.

They noted the importance of addressing the dire humanitarian and security situation in the Gaza Strip and called for swift steps to improve the situation.

They emphasized the importance for Israelis and Palestinians to comply with international law, including international humanitarian law and human rights law.

DOI: 10.4324/9781003348948-122

(II) The Participants highlighted the potential for security, stability, and prosperity for both parties that could result from a peace agreement. They expressed their readiness to exert necessary efforts toward the achievement of the two-state solution and to contribute substantially to arrangements for ensuring the sustainability of a negotiated peace agreement, in particular in the areas of political and economic incentives, the consolidation of Palestinian state capacities, and civil society dialogue. Those could include, *inter alia*:

- a European special privileged partnership; other political and economic incentives and increased private sector involvement; support to further efforts by the parties to improve economic cooperation; continued financial support to the Palestinian authority in building the infrastructure for a viable Palestinian economy;
- supporting and strengthening Palestinian steps to exercise their responsibilities of statehood through consolidating their institutions and institutional capacities, including for service delivery;
- convening Israeli and Palestinian civil society fora, in order to enhance dialogue between the parties, rekindle the public debate, and strengthen the role of civil society on both sides.

(III) Looking ahead, the Participants:

- call upon both sides to officially restate their commitment to the two-state solution, thus disassociating themselves from voices that reject this solution;
- call on each side to independently demonstrate, through policies and actions, a genuine commitment to the two-state solution and refrain from unilateral steps that prejudge the outcome of negotiations on final status issues, including, inter alia, on Jerusalem, borders, security, refugees and which they will not recognize;
- welcome the prospect of closer cooperation between the Quartet and Arab League members and other relevant actors to further the objectives of this Declaration.

As follow-up to the Conference, interested Participants, expressing their readiness to review progress, resolved to meet again before the end of the year in order to support both sides in advancing the two-state solution through negotiations.

France will inform the parties about the international community's collective support and concrete contribution to the two-state solution contained in this joint declaration.

117 Trump Administration Recognition of Jerusalem as the Capital of Israel (December 6, 2017)

Thank you. When I came into office, I promised to look at the world's challenges with open eyes and very fresh thinking. We cannot solve our problems by making the same failed assumptions and repeating the same failed strategies of the past. Old challenges demand new approaches.

My announcement today marks the beginning of a new approach to conflict between Israel and the Palestinians.

In 1995, Congress adopted the Jerusalem Embassy Act, urging the federal government to relocate the American embassy to Jerusalem and to recognize that that city – and so importantly – is Israel's capital. This act passed Congress by an overwhelming bipartisan majority and was reaffirmed by a unanimous vote of the Senate only six months ago.

Yet, for over 20 years, every previous American president has exercised the law's waiver, refusing to move the U.S. embassy to Jerusalem or to recognize Jerusalem as Israel's capital city.

Presidents issued these waivers under the belief that delaying the recognition of Jerusalem would advance the cause of peace. . . . After more than two decades of waivers, we are no closer to a lasting peace agreement between Israel and the Palestinians. It would be folly to assume that repeating the exact same formula would now produce a different or better result.

Therefore, I have determined that it is time to officially recognize Jerusalem as the capital of Israel.

While previous presidents have made this a major campaign promise, they failed to deliver. Today, I am delivering.

I've judged this course of action to be in the best interests of the United States of America and the pursuit of peace between Israel and the Palestinians. This is a long-overdue step to advance the peace process and to work towards a lasting agreement.

Israel is a sovereign nation with the right like every other sovereign nation to determine its own capital. Acknowledging this as a fact is a necessary condition for achieving peace.

It was 70 years ago that the United States, under President Truman, recognized the State of Israel. Ever since then, Israel has made its capital in the

DOI: 10.4324/9781003348948-123

city of Jerusalem – the capital the Jewish people established in ancient times. Today, Jerusalem is the seat of the modern Israeli government. It is the home of the Israeli parliament, the Knesset, as well as the Israeli Supreme Court. It is the location of the official residence of the Prime Minister and the President. It is the headquarters of many government ministries.

. . .

Jerusalem is not just the heart of three great religions, but it is now also the heart of one of the most successful democracies in the world. Over the past seven decades, the Israeli people have built a country where Jews, Muslims, and Christians, and people of all faiths are free to live and worship according to their conscience and according to their beliefs.

Jerusalem is today, and must remain, a place where Jews pray at the Western Wall, where Christians walk the Stations of the Cross, and where Muslims worship at Al-Aqsa Mosque.

However, through all of these years, presidents representing the United States have declined to officially recognize Jerusalem as Israel's capital. In fact, we have declined to acknowledge any Israeli capital at all.

But today, we finally acknowledge the obvious: that Jerusalem is Israel's capital. This is nothing more, or less, than a recognition of reality. It is also the right thing to do. It's something that has to be done.

That is why, consistent with the Jerusalem Embassy Act, I am also directing the State Department to begin preparation to move the American embassy from Tel Aviv to Jerusalem. This will immediately begin the process of hiring architects, engineers, and planners, so that a new embassy, when completed, will be a magnificent tribute to peace.

In making these announcements, I also want to make one point very clear: This decision is not intended, in any way, to reflect a departure from our strong commitment to facilitate a lasting peace agreement. We want an agreement that is a great deal for the Israelis and a great deal for the Palestinians. . . .

The United States remains deeply committed to helping facilitate a peace agreement that is acceptable to both sides. . . . Without question, Jerusalem is one of the most sensitive issues in those talks. The United States would support a two-state solution if agreed to by both sides.

In the meantime, I call on all parties to maintain the status quo at Jerusalem's holy sites, including the Temple Mount, also known as Haram al-Sharif.

Above all, our greatest hope is for peace, the universal yearning in every human soul. With today's action, I reaffirm my administration's longstanding commitment to a future of peace and security for the region.

There will, of course, be disagreement and dissent regarding this announcement. But we are confident that ultimately, as we work through these disagreements, we will arrive at a peace and a place far greater in understanding and cooperation.

This sacred city should call forth the best in humanity, lifting our sights to what it is possible; not pulling us back and down to the old fights that have become so totally predictable. Peace is never beyond the grasp of those willing to reach.

. . .

It is time for the many who desire peace to expel the extremists from their midst. It is time for all civilized nations, and people, to respond to disagreement with reasoned debate – not violence.

And it is time for young and moderate voices all across the Middle East to claim for themselves a bright and beautiful future.

So today, let us rededicate ourselves to a path of mutual understanding and respect. Let us rethink old assumptions and open our hearts and minds to possible and possibilities. And finally, I ask the leaders of the region – political and religious; Israeli and Palestinian; Jewish and Christian and Muslim – to join us in the noble quest for lasting peace.

Thank you. God bless you. God bless Israel. God bless the Palestinians. And God bless the United States. Thank you very much. Thank you.

118 "Peace To Prosperity" ["Trump Peace Plan"] Overview (January 2020)

Political Framework

Palestinians and Israelis alike deserve a future of peace and prosperity. A realistic two-state solution will protect Israel's security, fulfill the aspirations of self-determination for the Palestinian people, and ensure universal and respectful access to the holy sites of Jerusalem.

This Vision would achieve mutual recognition of Israel as the nation-state of the Jewish people and the future state of Palestine as the nation-state of the Palestinian people – each with equal civil rights for all its citizens. The plan designates defensible borders for the State of Israel and does not ask Israel to compromise on the safety of its people, affording them overriding security responsibility for land west of the Jordan River. For Palestinians, the Vision delivers significant territorial expansion, allocating land roughly comparable in size to the West Bank and Gaza for establishing a Palestinian State. Transportation links would allow efficient movement between Gaza and the West Bank, as well as throughout a future Palestine. The plan does not call for uprooting any Israelis or Palestinians from their homes.

Economic Framework

Generations of Palestinians have lived without knowing peace, and the West Bank and Gaza have fallen into a protracted crisis.

Yet the Palestinian story will not end here. The Palestinian people continue their historic endeavor to realize their aspirations and build a better future for their children.

With the potential to facilitate more than $50 billion in new investment over ten years, *Peace to Prosperity* represents the most ambitious and comprehensive international effort for the Palestinian people to date. It has the ability to fundamentally transform the West Bank and Gaza and to open a new chapter in Palestinian history – one defined, not by adversity and loss, but by freedom and dignity.

These three initiatives are more than just a vision of a promising future for the Palestinian people – they are also the foundation for an achievable plan.

DOI: 10.4324/9781003348948-124

If implemented, *Peace to Prosperity* will empower the Palestinian people to build the society that they have aspired to establish for generations. With the support of the international community, this vision is within reach. Ultimately, however, the power to unlock it lies in the hands of the Palestinian people. Only through peace can the Palestinians achieve prosperity.

Unleashing Economic Potential

Peace to Prosperity will establish a new foundation for the Palestinian economy, generating rapid economic growth and job creation.

This part of the plan will create a business environment that provides investors with confidence that their assets will be secure by improving property rights, the rule of law, fiscal sustainability, capital markets, and anti-corruption policies.

Opening the West Bank and Gaza

The plan will reduce constraints on Palestinian economic growth by **Opening the West Bank and Gaza** to regional and global markets. Major investments in transportation and infrastructure will help the West Bank and Gaza integrate with neighboring economies, increasing the competitiveness of Palestinian exports and reducing the complications of transport and travel. To complement these investments, this plan will also support steps to improve Palestinian cooperation with Egypt, Israel, and Jordan, with the goal of reducing regulatory barriers to the movement of Palestinian goods and people.

Constructing Essential Infrastructure

Essential infrastructure is needed for the Palestinian people and their businesses to flourish. This plan will facilitate billions of dollars of investment in the electricity, water, and telecommunications sectors, increasing generation capacity while creating efficient transmission and distribution networks. The applicable authorities will receive training and assistance to manage this infrastructure and to increase competition to keep costs low for consumers.

Promoting Private-Sector Growth

Following the adoption of key policy reforms and the construction of essential infrastructure, *Peace to Prosperity* envisions extraordinary private-sector investment in entrepreneurship, small businesses, tourism, agriculture, housing, manufacturing, and natural resources. The goal of early-stage investment will be to remove constraints to growth and to target key projects that build momentum, generate jobs, and increase gross domestic product (GDP). From the father working in his shop to support his family, to the young college graduate building her first company, Palestinians working throughout the private sector will benefit from this plan.

A lasting peace agreement will ensure a future of economic opportunity for all Palestinians.

Strengthening Regional Development and Integration

Peace to Prosperity encourages **Strengthening Regional Development and Integration**, creates new opportunities for Palestinian businesses, and increases commerce with neighboring countries. This vision will boost the economies of Egypt, Israel, Jordan, and Lebanon and reduce trade barriers across the region. Increased cooperation between trading partners will support companies in these countries, which are seeking to develop international business, particularly in the West Bank and Gaza. The plan will help the Palestinian private sector capitalize on growth opportunities by improving access to strong, neighboring economies.

Empowering the Palestinian People

Peace to Prosperity will unlock the vast potential of the Palestinian people by empowering them to pursue their goals and ambitions. This part of the vision will support the Palestinian people through education, workforce development, and an improved quality of life.

Enhance the Quality of the Education System

Enhancing the Quality of the Education System in the West Bank and Gaza will ensure no Palestinian is disadvantaged by inadequate educational opportunity. This vision supports the development and training of Palestinian educators while expanding access to educational opportunities to underserved communities and demographics. Other projects will help encourage educational reforms and innovation. By providing financial incentives to support the development of improved academic standards and curricula, this plan will help turn the West Bank and Gaza into a center of educational excellence.

Strengthen Workforce Development Programs

Peace to Prosperity will **Strengthen Workforce Development Programs**, reducing unemployment rates and increasing the occupational mobility of the Palestinian workforce. By supporting apprenticeships, career counseling, and job placement services, this vision will help ensure Palestinian youth are fully prepared to enter the job market and achieve their professional goals. Additional projects will help employed workers receive the training they need to enhance their skills or change careers. Ultimately, this plan will ensure that all Palestinians have access to the tools they need to compete in the global economy and take full advantage of the opportunities offered by this vision.

Transform the Palestinian Healthcare Sector

Peace to Prosperity will provide new resources and incentives to **Transform the Palestinian Healthcare Sector** and ensure the Palestinian people have access to the care they need within the West Bank and Gaza. This vision will rapidly increase the capacity of Palestinian hospitals by ensuring that they have the supplies, medicines, vaccines, and equipment to provide top-quality care and protect against health emergencies. Other funds will help improve services and standards in Palestinian healthcare facilities. Through targeted investments in new facilities, educational opportunities for medical staff and aspiring healthcare professionals, and public awareness campaigns to improve preventative care, the plan will significantly improve health outcomes throughout the West Bank and Gaza.

Improve the Quality of Life

Peace to Prosperity will support projects that **Improve the Quality of Life** for the Palestinian people. From investments in new cultural institutions to financial support for Palestinian artists and musicians, the plan will help the next generation of Palestinians explore their creativity and hone their talents. It will also support improved municipal services and the development of new public spaces across the West Bank and Gaza. These developments will help turn the West Bank and Gaza into a cultural and recreational center to the benefit of all Palestinians.

Enhancing Palestinian Governance

While implementing *Peace to Prosperity* will require significant international support, no vision for the Palestinians can be realized without the full support of the Palestinian people and their leadership.

Peace to Prosperity encourages the Palestinian public sector to provide the services and administration necessary for the Palestinian people to have a better future. If the government realizes its potential by investing in its people and adopting the foundational elements identified in this plan, job growth will ensue and the Palestinian people and their economy will thrive.

This vision establishes a path that, in partnership with the Palestinian public sector, will enable prosperity.

Transform the Business Environment

The strategy for reform will help the Palestinian public sector **Transform the Business Environment** by improving private property rights; safeguards against corruption; access to credit; functioning capital markets along with pro-growth policies and regulations; and certainty and predictability for investors that result in economic growth, private-sector job creation, and increased exports and foreign direct investment. Just as the Japanese, South Korean, and Singaporean governments rose to meet the daunting challenges their societies faced at critical times in their respective histories, so too can the Palestinian leadership chart a new course for its people. The plan identifies and addresses the requirements for developing human capital, igniting innovation, creating and growing small and medium businesses, and attracting international companies that will invest in the future of the West Bank and Gaza.

Build the Institutions

Building the Institutions of the Palestinian public sector and enhancing government responsiveness to the people is critical. Through this plan, government attention will be directed to increase judicial independence and grow civil society organizations. A stronger court system will better protect and secure the rights and property of the citizens. More government transparency will help foster trust from Palestinians – and outside investors – that court decisions are made fairly, contracts are awarded and enforced honestly, and business investments are safe.

Improve Government Operations

Peace to Prosperity will **Improve Government Operations** and the provision of services to the Palestinian people. In line with successful private-sector models, the Palestinian public sector must strive to be fiscally stable, financially independent, caring to its workers, and efficient in providing services to its citizens. The vision will work to eliminate public-sector arrears and implement a budgeting and tax plan that promotes long-term fiscal sustainability, without the need for budget support or donor funds. It will also assist with the adoption of new technologies that can provide Palestinian citizens the ability to directly request and access government support and services. The plan will offer new training and opportunities for civil servants to improve their productivity, help prepare them to meet governance challenges, and make it easier for them to perform their jobs. And, finally, this vision aims to provide government services at low cost and high-efficiency, which will facilitate private-sector growth.

119 Joint Statement of the United States, the State of Israel, and the United Arab Emirates (August 13, 2020)

Former President Donald J. Trump, Prime Minister Benjamin Netanyahu of Israel, and Sheikh Mohammed Bin Zayed, Crown Prince of Abu Dhabi and Deputy Supreme Commander of the United Arab Emirates spoke today and agreed to the full normalization of relations between Israel and the United Arab Emirates.

This historic diplomatic breakthrough will advance peace in the Middle East region and is a testament to the bold diplomacy and vision of the three leaders and the courage of the United Arab Emirates and Israel to chart a new path that will unlock the great potential in the region. All three countries face many common challenges and will mutually benefit from today's historic achievement.

Delegations from Israel and the United Arab Emirates will meet in the coming weeks to sign bilateral agreements regarding investment, tourism, direct flights, security, telecommunications, technology, energy, healthcare, culture, the environment, the establishment of reciprocal embassies, and other areas of mutual benefit. Opening direct ties between two of the Middle East's most dynamic societies and advanced economies will transform the region by spurring economic growth, enhancing technological innovation, and forging closer people-to-people relations.

As a result of this diplomatic breakthrough and at the request of President Trump with the support of the United Arab Emirates, Israel will suspend declaring sovereignty over areas outlined in the President's Vision for Peace and focus its efforts now on expanding ties with other countries in the Arab and Muslim world. The United States, Israel and the United Arab Emirates are confident that additional diplomatic breakthroughs with other nations are possible, and will work together to achieve this goal.

The United Arab Emirates and Israel will immediately expand and accelerate cooperation regarding the treatment of and the development of a vaccine for the coronavirus. Working together, these efforts will help save Muslim, Jewish, and Christian lives throughout the region.

This normalization of relations and peaceful diplomacy will bring together two of America's most reliable and capable regional partners. Israel and the United Arab Emirates will join with the United States to launch a

DOI: 10.4324/9781003348948-125

Strategic Agenda for the Middle East to expand diplomatic, trade, and security cooperation. Along with the United States, Israel and the United Arab Emirates share a similar outlook regarding the threats and opportunities in the region, as well as a shared commitment to promoting stability through diplomatic engagement, increased economic integration, and closer security coordination. Today's agreement will lead to better lives for the peoples of the United Arab Emirates, Israel, and the region.

The United States and Israel recall with gratitude the appearance of the United Arab Emirates at the White House reception held on January 28, 2020, at which President Trump presented his Vision for Peace, and express their appreciation for United Arab Emirates' related supportive statements. The parties will continue their efforts in this regard to achieve a just, comprehensive and enduring resolution to the Israeli-Palestinian conflict. As set forth in the Vision for Peace, all Muslims who come in peace may visit and pray at the Al Aqsa Mosque, and Jerusalem's other holy sites should remain open for peaceful worshippers of all faiths.

Prime Minister Netanyahu and Crown Prince Sheikh Mohammed bin Zayed Al Nahyan express their deep appreciation to President Trump for his dedication to peace in the region and to the pragmatic and unique approach he has taken to achieve it.

120 The Abraham Accords Declaration (September 15, 2020)

We, the undersigned, recognize the importance of maintaining and strengthening peace in the Middle East and around the world based on mutual understanding and coexistence, as well as respect for human dignity and freedom, including religious freedom.

We encourage efforts to promote interfaith and intercultural dialogue to advance a culture of peace among the three Abrahamic religions and all humanity.

We believe that the best way to address challenges is through cooperation and dialogue and that developing friendly relations among States advances the interests of lasting peace in the Middle East and around the world.

We seek tolerance and respect for every person in order to make this world a place where all can enjoy a life of dignity and hope, no matter their race, faith or ethnicity.

We support science, art, medicine, and commerce to inspire humankind, maximize human potential and bring nations closer together.

We seek to end radicalization and conflict to provide all children a better future.

We pursue a vision of peace, security, and prosperity in the Middle East and around the world.

In this spirit, we warmly welcome and are encouraged by the progress already made in establishing diplomatic relations between Israel and its neighbors in the region under the principles of the Abraham Accords. We are encouraged by the ongoing efforts to consolidate and expand such friendly relations based on shared interests and a shared commitment to a better future.

Israel-Bahrain Agreement

ABRAHAM ACCORDS: DECLARATION OF PEACE, COOPERATION, AND CONSTRUCTIVE DIPLOMATIC AND FRIENDLY RELATIONS

Announced by the State of Israel and the Kingdom of Bahrain on 15 September 2020

His Majesty King Hamad bin Isa bin Salman al-Khalifa and Prime Minister Benjamin Netanyahu have agreed to open an era of friendship and

DOI: 10.4324/9781003348948-126

cooperation in pursuit of a Middle East region that is stable, secure and prosperous for the benefit of all States and peoples in the region. In this spirit Prime Minister Netanyahu of Israel and Foreign Minister Mr. Abdullatif Al Zayani met in Washington today, at the invitation of President Donald J. Trump of the United States of America, to endorse the principles of the Abraham Accords and to commence a new chapter of peace. This diplomatic breakthrough was facilitated by the Abraham Accords initiative of President Donald J. Trump. It reflects the successful perseverance of the United States' efforts to promote peace and stability in the Middle East. The Kingdom of Bahrain and the State of Israel trust that this development will help lead to a future in which all peoples and all faiths can live together in the spirit of cooperation and enjoy peace and prosperity where states focus on shared interests and building a better future.

The parties discussed their shared commitment to advancing peace and security in the Middle East stressing the importance of embracing the vision of the Abraham Accords, widening the circle of peace; recognizing each State's right to sovereignty and to live in peace and security, and continuing the efforts to achieve a just, comprehensive, and enduring resolution of the Israeli-Palestinian conflict.

In their meeting, Prime Minister Benjamin Netanyahu and Foreign Minister Abdullatif Al Zayani agreed to establish full diplomatic relations, to promote lasting security, to eschew threats and the use of force, as well as advance coexistence and a culture of peace. In this spirit, they have today approved a series of steps initiating this new chapter in their relations. The Kingdom of Bahrain and the State of Israel have agreed to seek agreements in the coming weeks regarding investment, tourism, direct flights, security, telecommunications, technology, energy, healthcare, culture, the environment, and other areas of mutual benefit, as well as reaching agreement on the reciprocal opening of embassies.

The Kingdom of Bahrain and the State of Israel view this moment as a historic opportunity and recognize their responsibility to pursue a more secure and prosperous future for generations to come in their respective countries and in the region.

The two countries jointly express their profound thanks and appreciation to President Donald J. Trump for his untiring efforts and unique and pragmatic approach to further the cause of peace, justice and prosperity for all the peoples of the region. In recognition of this appreciation, the two countries have asked President Donald J. Trump to sign this document as a witness to their shared resolve and as the host of their historic meeting.

Israel-Morocco Agreement

JOINT DECLARATION,

The Kingdom of Morocco, the United States of America and the State of Israel,

Referring to the telephone conversation held between His Majesty King Mohammed VI and His Excellency President Donald Trump, on 10 December 2020, and to the historic statements issued on the same day by them, and by His Excellency Prime Minister Benjamin Netanyahu of the State of Israel, announcing the opening of a new era in the relations between the Kingdom of Morocco and the State of Israel;

Welcoming the opportunity created through the extraordinary efforts and leadership of the United States;

Highlighting the proclamation by the United States of America on "Recognizing the Sovereignty of the Kingdom of Morocco over the Western Sahara", according to which:

- "The United States recognizes Moroccan sovereignty over the entire Western Sahara territory and reaffirms its support for Morocco's serious, credible, and realistic autonomy proposal as the only basis for a just and lasting solution to the dispute over the Western Sahara territory".
- "To facilitate progress toward this aim, the United States will encourage economic and social development with Morocco, including in the Western Sahara territory, and to that end will open a consulate in the Western Sahara territory, in Dakhla, to promote economic and business opportunities for the region".

Recalling the exchanged views, during the same conversation between His Majesty King Mohammed VI and His Excellency Donald Trump, on the current situation in the Middle East region in which His Majesty the King reiterated the coherent, constant and unchanged position of the Kingdom of Morocco on the Palestinian question, as well as the position expressed on the importance of preserving the special status of the sacred city of Jerusalem for the three monotheistic religions in His Majesty the King's capacity as Chairman of the Al-Quds Committee;

Recognizing the historic role that Morocco has always played in bringing the people of the region closer together and promoting peace and stability in the Middle East, and given the special ties that His Majesty maintains with the Moroccan Jewish community living in Morocco and throughout the world including in Israel;

Mindful that the establishment of full diplomatic, peaceful and friendly relations is in the common interest of both countries and will advance the cause of peace in the region, improve regional security, and unlock new opportunities for the whole region;

Recalling the conversation between His Majesty King Mohammed VI and His Excellency Donald Trump His Majesty the King affirmed that the Kingdom of Morocco and the State of Israel intend to:

- Grant authorizations for direct flights between Morocco and Israel, including by Israeli and Moroccan airline companies, as well as grant rights of overflight;

- Immediately resume full official contacts between Israeli and Moroccan counterparts and establish full diplomatic, peaceful and friendly relations;
- Promote a dynamic and innovative economic bilateral cooperation;
- Pursue cooperation on trade; finance and investment; innovation and technology; civil aviation; visas and consular services; tourism; water, agriculture, and food security; development; energy and telecommunications; and other sectors as may be agreed;
- Reopen the liaison offices in Rabat and Tel Aviv.

Based on the above, the Kingdom of Morocco, the United States of America and the State of Israel agree to:

1. Commit to fully respect the elements contained in the present Declaration, promote it and defend it;
2. Decide that each party will fully implement its commitments and identify further actions, before the end of January;
3. Act accordingly at the bilateral, regional and multilateral levels.

Done at Rabat, 22 December 2020

Israel-UAE Agreement

ABRAHAM ACCORDS PEACE AGREEMENT: TREATY OF PEACE, DIPLOMATIC RELATIONS AND FULL NORMALIZATION BETWEEN THE UNITED ARAB EMIRATES AND THE STATE OF ISRAEL

The Government of the United Arab Emirates and the Government of the State of Israel (hereinafter, the "Parties")

Aspiring to realize the vision of a Middle East region that is stable, peaceful and prosperous, for the benefit of all States and peoples in the region;

Desiring to establish peace, diplomatic and friendly relations, co-operation and full normalization of ties between them and their peoples, in accordance with this Treaty, and to chart together a new path to unlock the vast potential of their countries and of the region;

Reaffirming the "Joint Statement of the United States, the State of Israel, and the United Arab Emirates" (the "Abraham Accords"), dated 13 August 2020;

Believing that the further development of friendly relations meets the interests of lasting peace in the Middle East and that challenges can only be effectively addressed by cooperation and not by conflict;

Determined to ensure lasting peace, stability, security and prosperity for both their States and to develop and enhance their dynamic and innovative economies;

Reaffirming their shared commitment to normalize relations and promote stability through diplomatic engagement, increased economic cooperation and other close coordination;

Reaffirming also their shared belief that the establishment of peace and full normalization between them can help transform the Middle East by spurring economic growth, enhancing technological innovation and forging closer people-to-people relations;

Recognizing that the Arab and Jewish peoples are descendants of a common ancestor, Abraham, and inspired, in that spirit, to foster in the Middle East a reality in which Muslims, Jews, Christians and peoples of all faiths, denominations, beliefs and nationalities live in, and are committed to, a spirit of coexistence, mutual understanding and mutual respect;

Recalling the reception held on January 28, 2020, at which President Trump presented his Vision for Peace, and committing to continuing their efforts to achieve a just, comprehensive, realistic and enduring solution to the Israeli-Palestinian conflict;

Recalling the Treaties of Peace between the State of Israel and the Arab Republic of Egypt and between the State of Israel and the Hashemite Kingdom of Jordan, and committed to working together to realize a negotiated solution to the Israeli-Palestinian conflict that meets the legitimate needs and aspirations of both peoples, and to advance comprehensive Middle East peace, stability and prosperity;

Emphasizing the belief that the normalization of Israeli and Emirati relations is in the interest of both peoples and contributes to the cause of peace in the Middle East and the world;

Expressing deep appreciation to the United States for its profound contribution to this historic achievement;

Have agreed as follows:

1. **Establishment of Peace, Diplomatic Relations and Normalization**: Peace, diplomatic relations and full normalization of bilateral ties are hereby established between the United Arab Emirates and the State of Israel.
2. **General Principles**: The Parties shall be guided in their relations by the provisions of the Charter of the United Nations and the principles of international law governing relations among States. In particular, they shall recognize and respect each other's sovereignty and right to live in peace and security, develop friendly relations of cooperation between them and their peoples, and settle all disputes between them by peaceful means.
3. **Establishment of Embassies**: The Parties shall exchange resident ambassadors as soon as practicable after the signing of this Treaty, and shall conduct diplomatic and consular relations in accordance with the applicable rules of international law.

4. **Peace and Stability**: The Parties shall attach profound importance to mutual understanding, cooperation and coordination between them in the spheres of peace and stability, as a fundamental pillar of their relations and as a means for enhancing those spheres in the Middle East as a whole. They undertake to take the necessary steps to prevent any terrorist or hostile activities against each other on or from their respective territories, as well as deny any support for such activities abroad or allowing such support on or from their respective territories. Recognizing the new era of peace and friendly relations between them, as well as the centrality of stability to the well-being of their respective peoples and of the region, the Parties undertake to consider and discuss these matters regularly, and to conclude detailed agreements and arrangements on coordination and cooperation.

5. **Cooperation and Agreements in Other Spheres**: As an integral part of their commitment to peace, prosperity, diplomatic and friendly relations, cooperation and full normalization, the Parties shall work to advance the cause of peace, stability and prosperity throughout the Middle East, and to unlock the great potential of their countries and of the region. For such purposes, the Parties shall conclude bilateral agreements in the following spheres at the earliest practicable date, as well as in other spheres of mutual interest as may be agreed:

   - Finance and Investment
   - Civil Aviation
   - Visas and Consular Services
   - Innovation, Trade and Economic Relations
   - Healthcare
   - Science, Technology and Peaceful Uses of Outer-Space
   - Tourism, Culture and Sport
   - Energy
   - Environment
   - Education
   - Maritime Arrangements
   - Telecommunications and Post
   - Agriculture and Food Security
   - Water
   - Legal Cooperation

   Any such agreements concluded before the entry into force of this Treaty shall enter into effect with the entry into force of this Treaty unless otherwise stipulated therein. Agreed principles for cooperation in specific spheres are annexed to this Treaty and form an integral part thereof.

6. **Mutual Understanding and Co-existence**: The Parties undertake to foster mutual understanding, respect, co-existence and a culture of peace between their societies in the spirit of their common ancestor, Abraham, and the new era of peace and friendly relations ushered in by this Treaty,

including by cultivating people-to-people programs, interfaith dialogue and cultural, academic, youth, scientific, and other exchanges between their peoples. They shall conclude and implement the necessary visa and consular services agreements and arrangements so as to facilitate efficient and secure travel for their respective nationals to the territory of each other. The Parties shall work together to counter extremism, which promotes hatred and division, and terrorism and its justifications, including by preventing radicalization and recruitment and by combating incitement and discrimination. They shall work towards establishing a High-Level Joint Forum for Peace and Co-Existence dedicated to advancing these goals.

7. **Strategic Agenda for the Middle East**: Further to the Abraham Accords, the Parties stand ready to join with the United States to develop and launch a "Strategic Agenda for the Middle East" in order to expand regional diplomatic, trade, stability and other cooperation. They are committed to work together, and with the United States and others, as appropriate, in order to advance the cause of peace, stability and prosperity in the relations between them and for the Middle East as a whole, including by seeking to advance regional security and stability; pursue regional economic opportunities; promote a culture of peace across the region; and consider joint aid and development programs.

8. **Other Rights and Obligations**: This Treaty does not affect and shall not be interpreted as affecting, in any way, the rights and obligations of the Parties under the Charter of the United Nations. The Parties shall take all necessary measures for the application in their bilateral relations of the provisions of the multilateral conventions of which they are both parties, including the submission of appropriate notification to the depositaries of such conventions.

9. **Respect for Obligations**: The Parties undertake to fulfill in good faith their obligations under this Treaty, without regard to action or inaction of any other party and independently of any instrument inconsistent with this Treaty. For the purposes of this paragraph each Party represents to the other that in its opinion and interpretation there is no inconsistency between their existing treaty obligations and this Treaty. The Parties undertake not to enter into any obligation in conflict with this Treaty. Subject to Article 103 of the Charter of the United Nations, in the event of a conflict between the obligations of the Parties under the present Treaty and any of their other obligations, the obligations under this Treaty shall be binding and implemented. The Parties further undertake to adopt any legislation or other internal legal procedure necessary in order to implement this Treaty, and to repeal any national legislation or official publications inconsistent with this Treaty.

10. **Ratification and Entry into Force**: This Treaty shall be ratified by both Parties as soon as practicable in conformity with their respective national

procedures and will enter into force following the exchange of instruments of ratification.

11. **Settlement of Disputes**: Disputes arising out of the application or interpretation of this Treaty shall be resolved by negotiation. Any such dispute which cannot be settled by negotiation may be referred to conciliation or arbitration subject to the agreement of the Parties.

12. **Registration**: This Treaty shall be transmitted to the Secretary-General of the United Nations for registration in accordance with the provisions of Article 102 of the Charter of the United Nations.

Done at Washington, DC, this day Elul 26th, 5780, Muharram 27th, 1442, which corresponds to 15 September 2020, in the Hebrew, Arabic and English languages, all texts being equally authentic. In case of divergence of interpretation, the English text shall prevail.

[Annexes were attached dealing with Finance and Investment; Civil Aviation; Tourism; Innovation, Trade and Economic Relations; Science, Technology and Peaceful Use of Outer-Space; Environment; Telecommunications and Post; Healthcare; Agriculture and Food Security; Water; Energy; Maritime Arrangements; and Legal Cooperation]

Sources

The documents included in this volume are all in the public domain. Most are available from either the U.S. Government Department of State website or the Government of Israel Ministry of Foreign Affairs website; others can be found online at the *Jewish Virtual Library* or one of the scholarly resource sites listed. I have listed here the sites where each of the documents included in this volume can be found at the time of publication of this book, although it is necessary for the reader to recognize that web addresses of organizations and documents can change over time as institutions reorganize their web presences. The addresses included here were correct at the time these documents were edited.

1. Herzl
   www.mideastweb.org/thejewishstate.htm

2. Ahad Ha'am
   www.gutenberg.org/cache/epub/67667/pg67667-images.html

3. Basle Program
   www.mideastweb.org/basleprogram.htm

4. Theodor Herzl letter
   Walid Khalidi, *From Haven to Conquest: Readings in Zionism and the Palestine Problem Until 1948* (Washington: The Institute for Palestine Studies, 1987), pp. 91–93

5. Uganda proposal
   www.jewishvirtuallibrary.org/the-uganda-proposal-1903

6. McMahon
   www.mideastweb.org/mcmahon.htm

7. Sykes-Picot
   www.mideastweb.org/mesykespicot.htm

8. Balfour Declaration
   www.mideastweb.org/mebalfour.htm

9. Weizmann-Feisal
www.mideastweb.org/feisweiz.htm

10. Balfour interview, 1919
Walid Khalidi, *From Haven to Conquest: Readings in Zionism and the Palestine Problem Until 1948* (Washington: The Institute for Palestine Studies, 1987), pp. 195–200.

11. White Paper 1922
www.mideastweb.org/1922wp.htm

12. Mandate
www.mideastweb.org/mandate.htm

13. Passfield White Paper
www.mideastweb.org/passfieldwp.htm

14. MacDonald Letter
www.mideastweb.org/macdonald1930.htm

15. Peel Report
www.mideastweb.org/peelmaps.htm

16. White Paper against
www.mideastweb.org/1938peeldecision.htm

17. MacDonald White Paper
www.mideastweb.org/1939.htm

18. Zionist Reaction
www.jewishvirtuallibrary.org/zionist-reaction-to-the-white-paper-of-1939

19. Biltmore Program
www.mideastweb.org/biltmore_program.htm

20. Arab Office Report
www.mideastweb.org/araboffice.htm

21. Anglo-American Committee of Inquiry
www.mideastweb.org/angloamerican.htm

22. Resolution 181
www.mideastweb.org/181.htm

23. Golda Meir Speech
www.tamilnation.org/ideology/golda.htm.

24. Plan Dalet
www.mideastweb.org/pland.htm

25. Declaration of State
www.mideastweb.org/israeldeclaration.htm

26. Resolution 194
    www.mideastweb.org/194.htm

27. Admission to UN
    www.jewishvirtuallibrary.org/un-general-assembly-resolution-273-iii-may-1949

28. Resolution 303
    www.mideastweb.org/ga303.htm

29. Law of Return
    www.jewishvirtuallibrary.org/israel-s-law-of-return

30. Resolution 95
    http://mideastweb.org/sc95.htm

31. Palestine Nat'l Charter
    https://web.archive.org/web/20101130144018/www.un.int/wcm/content/site/palestine/pid/12363

32. Eban speech to UN
    www.jewishvirtuallibrary.org/six-day-war-statement-to-general-assembly-by-foreign-minister-eban

33. The Allon Plan
    PASSIA, www.passia.org/maps/view/21

34. Johnson, Five Principles
    www.jewishvirtuallibrary.org/president-johnson-speech-on-five-principles-for-peace-in-the-middle-east-june-1967

35. Holy Places Law
    www.jewishvirtuallibrary.org/israel-protection-of-holy-places-law-1967

36. Khartoum Resolutions
    www.mideastweb.org/khartoum.htm

37. Resolution 242
    www.mideastweb.org/242.htm

38. PNC Resolutions
    www.jewishvirtuallibrary.org/the-palestine-national-charter-july-1968

39. Seven Points of Fatah
    www.jewishvirtuallibrary.org/the-seven-points-of-fatah-january-1969

40. William Rogers Plan
    www.gov.il/en/Departments/General/9-statement-by-secretary-of-state-rogers-9-december-1969

41. King Hussein's Federation Plan
    www.jewishvirtuallibrary.org/king-hussein-s-federal-plan

42. Resolution 338
www.mideastweb.org/338.htm

43. 12th PNC
www.mideastweb.org/plo1974.htm

44. Seventh Arab League Summit Resolutions
www.jewishvirtuallibrary.org/plo-recognized-as-sole-legitimate-repre
sentative-of-the-palestinians

45. Sinai II
https://peacemaker.un.org/sites/peacemaker.un.org/files/EG%20IL_
750904_Interim%20Agreement%20between%20Israel%20and%20
Egypt.pdf

46. Memorandum Israel and the United States
www.jewishvirtuallibrary.org/israel-united-states-memorandum-of-under
standing-1975

47. Sadat Speech
www.jewishvirtuallibrary.org/address-by-egyptian-president-anwar-sadat-
to-the-knesset

48. Begin Speech
www.jewishvirtuallibrary.org/prime-minister-begin-speech-to-knesset-
following-historic-speech-by-anwar-sadat-novemer-1977

49. 6 point program of PLO
https://zionism-israel.com/hdoc/PLO-Six-Point-Program-1977.htm

50. Camp David I
www.mideastweb.org/campdavid.htm

51. Camp David II
www.mideastweb.org/campdavid.htm

52. Israel-Egypt treaty
www.mideastweb.org/egyptisraeltreaty.htm

53. Arab League Summit
https://naip-documents.blogspot.com/2009/09/document-40.html

54. Basic Law: Jerusalem
https://zionism-israel.com/hdoc/Basic_Law_Jerusalem.htm

55. Fahd Plan
www.mideastweb.org/fahd_fez_plan.htm

56. Golan Heights Law
www.jewishvirtuallibrary.org/the-golan-heights-law

57. Begin Speech
www.gov.il/en/Departments/General/55-address-by-pm-begin-at-the-na
tional-defense-college-8-august-1982

58. The Reagan Plan
www.mideastweb.org/reagan_peace_plan_1982.htm

59. Report of the [Kahan] Commission
www.mideastweb.org/Kahan_report.htm

60. Israel-Lebanon agreement
www.mideastweb.org/lebanonpeace.htm

61. Jordan-PLO Agreement
www.jewishvirtuallibrary.org/the-hussein-arafat-accord

62. The Shultz Initiative
https://ecf.org.il/media_items/975

63. King Hussein, Address to the Nation
www.kinghussein.gov.jo/88_july31.html

64. PNC Declaration of Independence
www.mideastweb.org/plc1988.htm

65. Israel Peace Initiative
www.mideastweb.org/israelipeaceplan.htm

66. Baker plan
www.jewishvirtuallibrary.org/five-point-election-plan-of-secretary-of-state-baker

67. Invitation to Madrid
www.jewishvirtuallibrary.org/letter-of-invitation-to-madrid-peace-conference

68. Presentation of the New Government by Rabin
www.gov.il/en/Departments/General/1-address-to-the-knesset-by-pm-rabin-presenting-his-government-13-july-1992

69. Israel-PLO recognition
www.mideastweb.org/osloletters.htm

70. Oslo Agreement
www.mideastweb.org/meoslodop.htm

71. Israel-Jordan Agenda
www.jewishvirtuallibrary.org/israel-jordan-common-agenda

72. Gaza Strip and Jericho
www.jewishvirtuallibrary.org/agreement-on-the-gaza-strip-and-the-jericho-area

73. Washington Declaration
www.jewishvirtuallibrary.org/the-washington-declaration

74. Jordan-Israel Peace
www.mideastweb.org/israjordan.htm

75. Agreement on West Bank and Gaza
    www.mideastweb.org/meosint.htm

76. Area C
    www.btselem.org/planning_and_building

77. Rabin speech to Knesset
    www.jewishvirtuallibrary.org/pm-rabin-speech-to-knesset-on-ratifica
    tion-of-oslo-peace-accords

78. Framework Between Israel and the PLO
    www.mideastweb.org/beilinabumazen1.htm

79. Rabin speech to rally
    www.mideastweb.org/rabin1995.htm

80. Israel-Lebanon understanding
    www.mideastweb.org/megrapes.htm

81. Hussein-Netanyahu Exchange of Letters
    https://naip-documents.blogspot.com/2009/10/document-88.html

82. Madeleine Albright speech
    https://1997-2001.state.gov/www/statements/970806.html

83. Wye Memorandum
    www.mideastweb.org/mewye.htm

84. Barak speech to Knesset
    www.gov.il/en/Departments/General/1-address-in-the-knesset-by-pm-
    elect-ehud-barak-upon-presentation-of-his-government-7-july-1999

85. Sharm el-Sheikh
    www.jewishvirtuallibrary.org/the-sharm-el-sheikh-memorandum

86. Safe passage memo
    www.jewishvirtuallibrary.org/protocol-concerning-safe-passage-between-
    the-west-bank-and-the-gaza-strip

87. Israel-Syria Draft Peace Agreement
    www.jewishvirtuallibrary.org/israel-syria-draft-peace-agreement

88. Camp David 2000
    www.mideastweb.org/sum2000.htm

89. Clinton, on Middle East Peace Talks
    https://1997-2001.state.gov/regions/nea/000725_clinton_stmt.html

90. Taba
    www.jewishvirtuallibrary.org/taba-peace-talks

91. Sharm el-Sheikh final report
www.jewishvirtuallibrary.org/the-mitchell-report-may-2001

92. Israeli-Palestinian Ceasefire proposal by George Tenet
www.mideastweb.org/tenet.htm

93. UN Security Council Resolution 1397
www.mideastweb.org/1397.htm

94. Arab peace initiative
www.mideastweb.org/saudipeace.htm

95. George W. Bush Speech
http://georgewbush-whitehouse.archives.gov/news/releases/2002/06/
20020624-3.html

96. Nusseibeh-Ayalon Peace Plan July 2002
www.usip.org/sites/default/files/file/resources/collections/peace_agree
ments/nusseibeh_ayalon.pdf

97. Roadmap 2003
www.mideastweb.org/quartetrm3.htm

98. Beilin – Abed Rabbo Geneva Accord
www.mideastweb.org/geneval.htm

99. Exchange of Letters between Ariel Sharon and George W. Bush,
http://mideastweb.org/disengagement.htm

100. Disengagement from Gaza 2004
http://mideastweb.org/disengagement.htm

101. ICJ advisory Opinion
https://zionism-israel.com/hdoc/ICJ_fence.htm

102. Sharon speech
www.jewishvirtuallibrary.org/prime-minister-sharon-address-to-the-knesset-
on-the-disengagement-plan-october-2004

103. Resolution 1701
www.mideastweb.org/1701.htm

104. Annapolis
www.jewishvirtuallibrary.org/announcement-of-annapolis-conference-
november-2007

105. Joint understanding
https://peacemaker.un.org/sites/peacemaker.un.org/files/IsraelOPt_Joint
UnderstandingOnNegotiations2007.pdf

106. Abbas rejection of Olmert proposals
http://transparency.aljazeera.net/en/projects/thepalestinepapers/2012182
1046718794.html

107. Olmert Gaza withdrawal
www.jewishvirtuallibrary.org/israeli-pm-olmert-declares-unilateral-cease
fire-in-gaza-january-2009

108. Obama speech in Cairo
http://mideastweb.org/obama_cairo_speech.htm

109. UN – Human Rights [Goldstone report]
www.jewishvirtuallibrary.org/jsource/UN/goldstonereport.pdf

110. Hillary Clinton Speech
www.americantaskforce.org/secretary_hilllary_rodham_clintons_remarks_
american_task_force_palestine

111. Ceasefire in Gaza
www.jewishvirtuallibrary.org/israel-hamas-ceasefire-agreement-to-
operation-pillar-of-defense

112. Gaza Conflict report
www.jewishvirtuallibrary.org/jsource/images/mfagazaconflict.pdf

113. Nuclear deal with Iran
www.gov.il/en/Departments/General/questions-and-answers-about-the-
nuclear-deal-with-iran

114. Obama on Nuclear deal
https://obamawhitehouse.archives.gov/the-press-office/2015/08/05/remarks-
president-iran-nuclear-deal

115. Report of Quartet
www.jewishvirtuallibrary.org/jsource/images/quartet716.pdf

116. Paris Communique 2017
www.jewishvirtuallibrary.org/2017-paris-conference-joint-communique

117. Trump recognition of Jerusalem
https://il.usembassy.gov/statement-by-president-trump-on-jerusalem/

118. Peace to Prosperity: ("Trump Peace Plan")
https://trumpwhitehouse.archives.gov/wp-content/uploads/2020/01/
Peace-to-Prosperity-0120.pdf

119. Statement of the United States, Israel, and the United Arab Emirates
https://il.usembassy.gov/joint-statement-of-the-united-states-the-state-
of-israel-and-the-united-arab-emirates/

120. The Abraham Accords
www.state.gov/the-abraham-accords/

Index

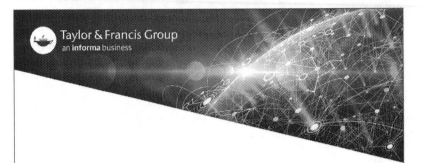

Printed in the United States
by Baker & Taylor Publisher Services